NATIONAL GEOGRAPHIC

ULTIMATE GUIDE
TO THE NATIONAL PARKS

Swiftcurrent Pass Trail, Glacier National Park (page 386)

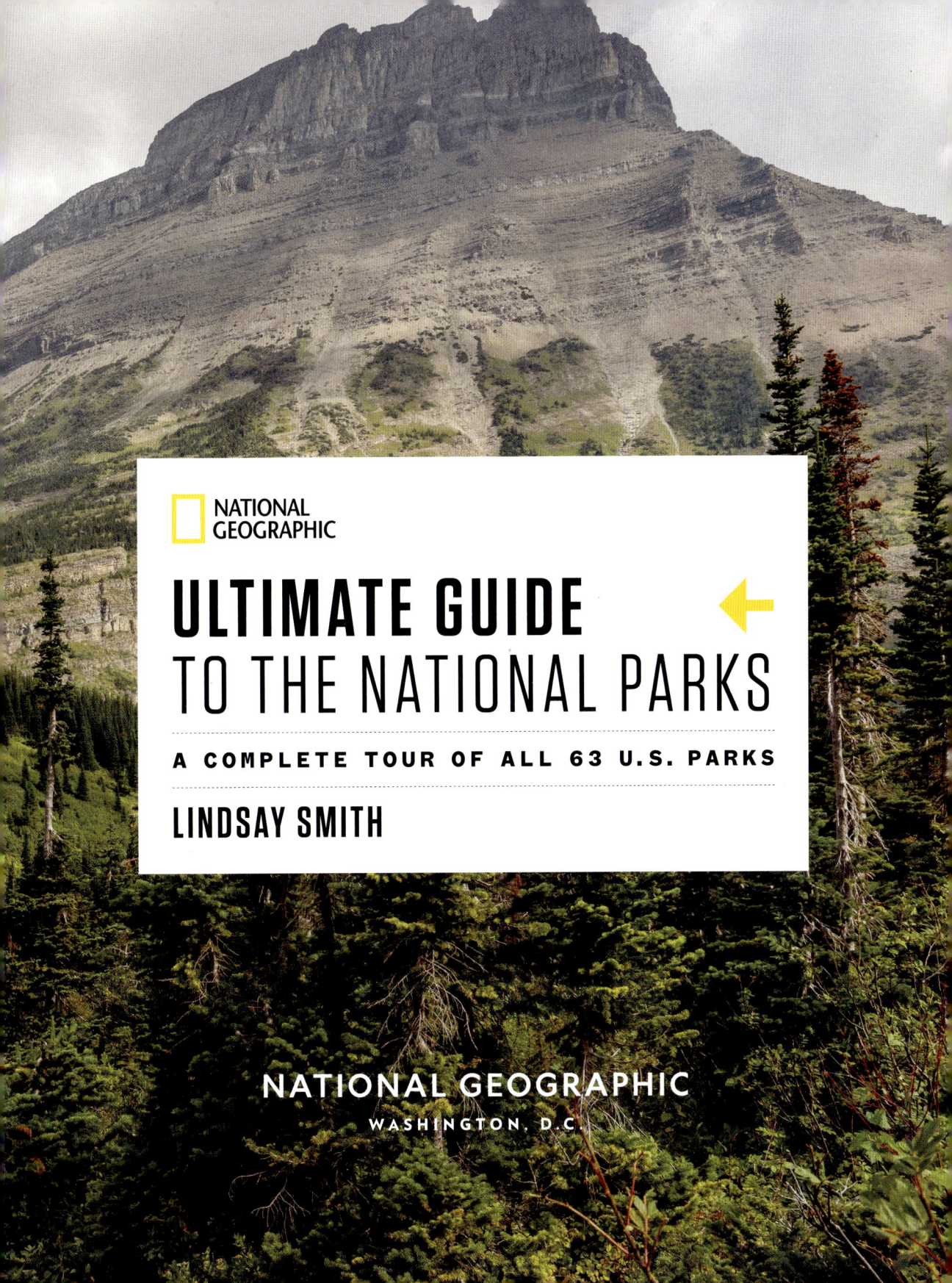

NATIONAL
GEOGRAPHIC

ULTIMATE GUIDE
TO THE NATIONAL PARKS

A COMPLETE TOUR OF ALL 63 U.S. PARKS

LINDSAY SMITH

NATIONAL GEOGRAPHIC
WASHINGTON, D.C.

CONTENTS

OPPOSITE: Sequoia & Kings Canyon National Parks (page 520)

FOREWORD ←

Welcome to National Geographic's all-new guide to exploring the 63 designated national parks around the United States. So, what makes this guide so different?

For starters, we wanted to really highlight the beauty of these parks. To do that, we sent a dozen of National Geographic's acclaimed photographers into the field to capture all-new images of the parks. What they came back with was breathtaking. Sofía Jaramillo's coverage of Badlands National Park (page 140) celebrates this treasure in South Dakota, including a captivating image of the sun rising over the park's distinctive yellow mounds. Meanwhile, Chris Burkard ventured into the heart of Sequoia & Kings Canyon National Parks (page 520), providing a sense of place with his beautiful images of the mist-shrouded forest and wildlife. In Arches National Park (page 262), Tara Kerzhner shot the breathtaking sandstone structures that put this park on the map, including magnificent Navajo Arch. And these are just a few examples of the remarkable images that highlight exactly why these parks are worth protecting—and will serve as inspiration for your next visit.

Badlands National Park (page 140)

Arches National Park (page 262)

Speaking of your next visit, let's get into the details of how to use this book. Our 63 national parks are large, with lots and lots to do and see within each. But where to start? Rather than provide travelers with an exhaustive list, which can make planning hard and confusing, this guidebook curates the top-tier experiences in every park, all National Geographic–approved.

We've divided these recommendations into categories so that you can easily find what you're looking for in the parks. They include Sleep (campgrounds, lodges, and hotels in and near the parks); Hike (trails for walking, hiking, and backcountry adventures fit for all levels of experience); Spot (wildlife and where to find it); Float (paddling, boating, swimming, and snorkeling or diving excursions); Drive (scenic road-trip routes); Look (top sights to see and overlooks); Spelunk (cave explorations); Summit (notable peaks); and Explore (unique in-park adventures, from spotting the aurora borealis to visiting fascinating historical exhibits).

In addition to these well-vetted suggestions, with each park we also feature a "Ranger Recommendation." These are tips directly from National Park Service rangers for the best experiences, hikes, and scenic spots—including many hidden gems you'd have to spend years in the parks to discover. And for every park, we provide need-to-know travel information on visitors centers, transportation options offered by the parks, and when to go, along with a map highlighting points of interest, elevation, and waterways.

Our aim is to make visiting the national parks easier than ever. There's a reason our parks have been called "America's best idea"—now it's up to you to see why for yourself.

—ALLYSON JOHNSON
Executive Editor, National Geographic Books

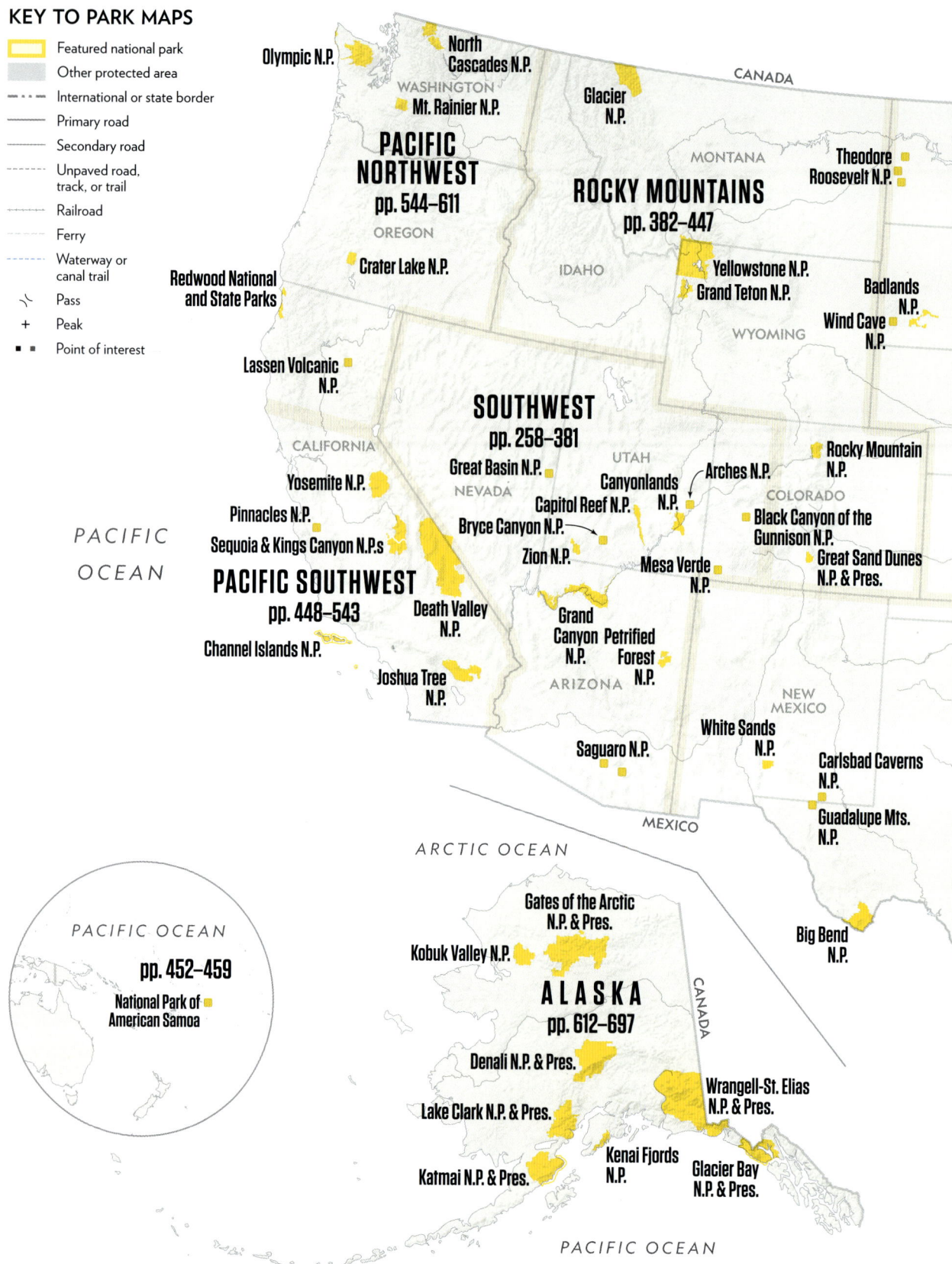

KEY TO PARK MAPS

- Featured national park
- Other protected area
- International or state border
- Primary road
- Secondary road
- Unpaved road, track, or trail
- Railroad
- Ferry
- Waterway or canal trail
- ⅄ Pass
- + Peak
- ■ ■ Point of interest

PACIFIC
OCEAN

CANADA

Olympic N.P.

North
Cascades N.P.

WASHINGTON

Mt. Rainier N.P.

Glacier
N.P.

**PACIFIC
NORTHWEST**
pp. 544–611

OREGON

MONTANA

ROCKY MOUNTAINS
pp. 382–447

Theodore
Roosevelt N.P.

Crater Lake N.P.

IDAHO

Yellowstone N.P.

Grand Teton N.P.

Badlands
N.P.

Redwood National
and State Parks

Wind Cave
N.P.

WYOMING

Lassen Volcanic
N.P.

SOUTHWEST
pp. 258–381

CALIFORNIA

Great Basin N.P.

UTAH

Canyonlands
N.P.

Arches N.P.

Rocky Mountain
N.P.

Yosemite N.P.

NEVADA

Capitol Reef N.P.

COLORADO

Black Canyon of the
Gunnison N.P.

Pinnacles N.P.

Bryce Canyon N.P.

Sequoia & Kings Canyon N.P.s

Zion N.P.

Great Sand Dunes
N.P. & Pres.

PACIFIC SOUTHWEST
pp. 448–543

Mesa Verde
N.P.

Death Valley
N.P.

Grand
Canyon
N.P.

Petrified
Forest
N.P.

Channel Islands N.P.

ARIZONA

NEW
MEXICO

Joshua Tree
N.P.

White Sands
N.P.

Saguaro N.P.

Carlsbad Caverns
N.P.

MEXICO

Guadalupe Mts.
N.P.

ARCTIC OCEAN

Big Bend
N.P.

PACIFIC OCEAN

pp. 452–459

National Park of
American Samoa

Gates of the Arctic
N.P. & Pres.

Kobuk Valley N.P.

CANADA

A L A S K A
pp. 612–697

Denali N.P. & Pres.

Wrangell-St. Elias
N.P. & Pres.

Lake Clark N.P. & Pres.

Kenai Fjords
N.P.

Glacier Bay
N.P. & Pres.

Katmai N.P. & Pres.

PACIFIC OCEAN

Voyageurs N.P.

Isle Royale N.P.

Acadia N.P.

MAINE

CANADA

NORTH DAKOTA

MINNESOTA

WISCONSIN

MICHIGAN

VT.

N.H.

NEW YORK

MASS.

CONN.

R.I.

SOUTH DAKOTA

MIDWEST
pp. 136–215

IOWA

NEBRASKA

ILLINOIS

INDIANA

Indiana Dunes N.P.

Cuyahoga Valley N.P.

OHIO

PENNSYLVANIA

NEW JERSEY

MD.

DELAWARE

D.C.

Shenandoah N.P.

KANSAS

MISSOURI

Gateway Arch N.P.

KENTUCKY

New River Gorge N.P. & Pres.

W. VA.

VIRGINIA

Mammoth Cave N.P.

EAST
pp. 30–135

NORTH CAROLINA

TENNESSEE

Great Smoky Mts. N.P.

OKLAHOMA

ARKANSAS

SOUTH CAROLINA

Congaree N.P.

SOUTH CENTRAL
pp. 216–257

Hot Springs N.P.

MISSISSIPPI

ALABAMA

GEORGIA

ATLANTIC OCEAN

TEXAS

LOUISIANA

FLORIDA

Biscayne N.P.

Everglades N.P.

Dry Tortugas N.P.

ATLANTIC OCEAN

HAWAI'I

PACIFIC OCEAN

Haleakalā N.P.

pp. 478–501

Hawai'i Volcanoes N.P.

PUERTO RICO

Virgin Islands N.P.

U.S. VIRGIN ISLANDS

pp. 126–135

HISTORY OF THE
NATIONAL PARK SERVICE

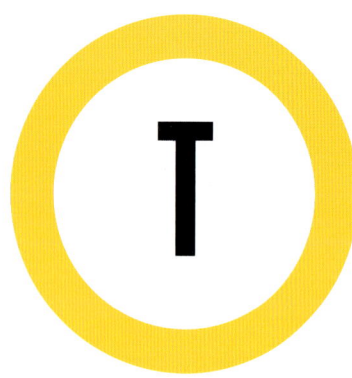

The diversity of the sites within the National Park System is reflected in the variety of titles given to them. In its official index, the National Park Service identifies more than 420 properties under Park Service protection. Within the system—which protects everything from national seashores to national trails to national monuments—lie 63 national parks. These parks generally contain a wide variety of natural resources and encompass large land or water areas to help provide adequate protection of those resources. Sometimes they also protect significant historical assets.

But how did the country come to protect these treasures? In March 1872, Congress established the first national park, Yellowstone (page 434), as a "public park or pleasuring-ground for the benefit and enjoyment of the people." Controlled and maintained by the secretary of the Department of the Interior, it paved the way for a movement that has led to the 63 parks we know today. The most recently named national park is New River Gorge National Park & Preserve (page 106) in West Virginia, designated in December 2020.

The National Park Service itself was created by President Woodrow Wilson in 1916. At that time, the new federal bureau was established to protect 35 national parks and monuments. The scope of what the National Park Service protects has expanded over the years. It now safeguards more than 84 million acres of the United States, including in the 50 states, the District of Columbia, American Samoa, Guam, Puerto Rico, Saipan, and the U.S. Virgin Islands.

Additions to the National Park System—and the creation of a new national park—are made through acts of Congress. The president of the United States can also proclaim national monuments on lands already under federal jurisdiction.

The National Park Service continues to serve its original goals: to protect the country's diverse cultural and recreational treasures and to safeguard our environment and America's open spaces. The establishment of our Park Service sparked a movement, not just in the U.S. but abroad, setting an example for other countries to follow in putting their own natural spaces under protection.

Today, the National Park Service and its devoted employees care for these special places, working with communities to preserve their unique cultural histories, natural wonders, and recreational opportunities.

Wading in Great Fountain Geyser, Yellowstone National Park, circa 1908 (page 434)

Lower Falls, Yellowstone National Park, 1871 (page 434)

Bullfrog Lake, seen from the Rae Lakes Loop, Sequoia & Kings Canyon National Parks (page 520)

Great Sand Dunes National Park & Preserve (page 412)

Redwood National and State Parks (page 600)

Thunder Hole, Acadia National Park (page 34)

Steep Cone Geyser, Yellowstone National Park (page 434)

North Cascades National Park (page 576)

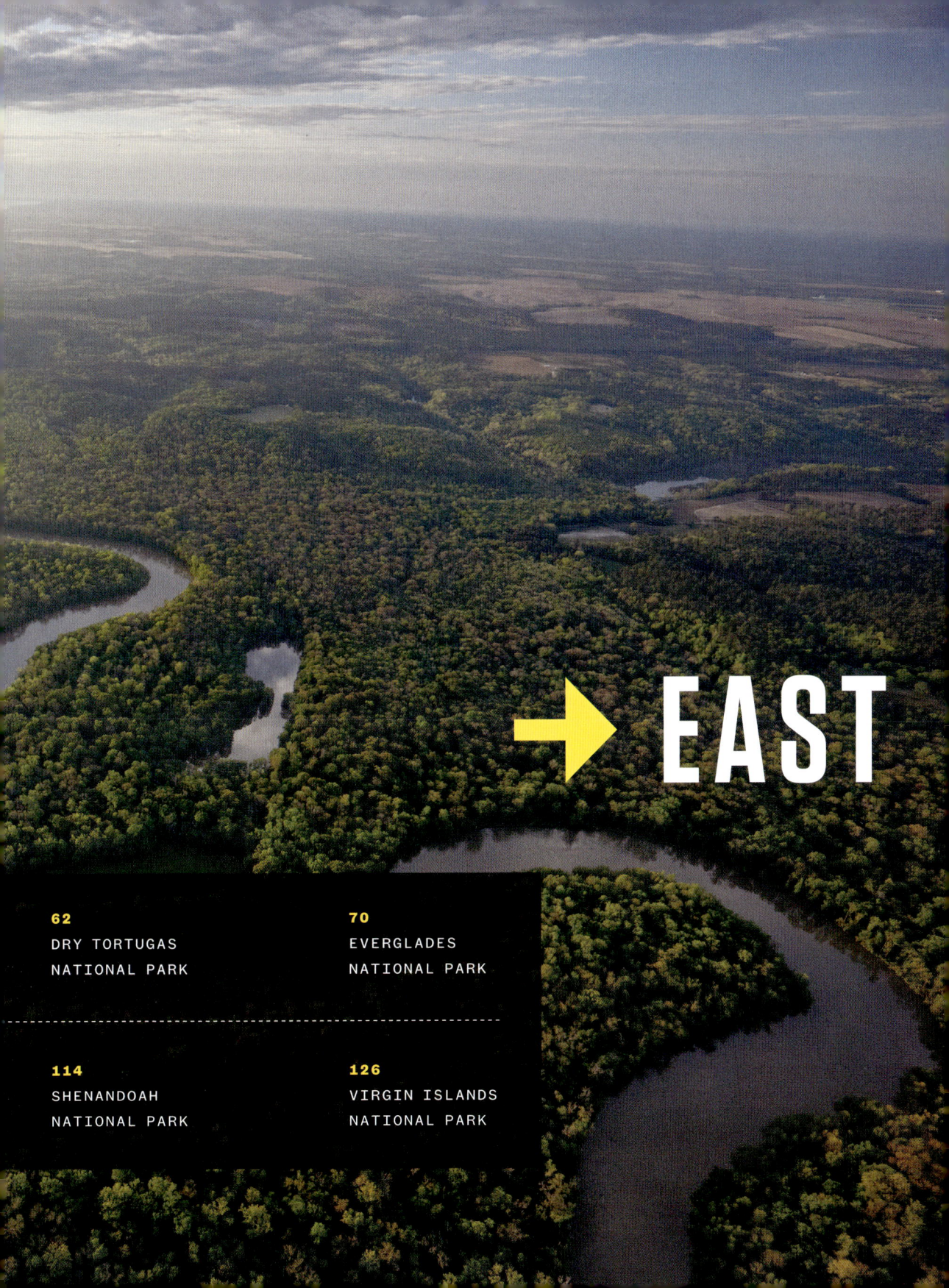

→ EAST

Lake Superior

MINN.

WISCONSIN

CANADA

Lake Michigan

MICHIGAN

Lake Huron

MAINE

Lake Ontario

Acadia
National Park

VT.

N.H.

IOWA

ILLINOIS

INDIANA

OHIO

NEW YORK

MASS.

CONN.

R.I.

PENNSYLVANIA

NEW
JERSEY

Lake Erie

MISSOURI

KENTUCKY

W. VA.

MD.

D.C.

DELAWARE

Shenandoah
National Park

New River Gorge
National Park & Preserve

VIRGINIA

ATLANTIC

Mammoth Cave
National Park

OCEAN

TENNESSEE

Great Smoky Mts.
National Park

NORTH
CAROLINA

ARKANSAS

SOUTH
CAROLINA

MISSISSIPPI

ALABAMA

GEORGIA

Congaree
National Park

LA.

ATLANTIC OCEAN

Virgin Islands
National Park

PUERTO
RICO

U.S. VIRGIN
ISLANDS

50 mi

50 km

FLORIDA

200 mi

200 km

Everglades
National Park

Biscayne
National Park

Dry Tortugas National Park

Between 1919 and 1926, Congress authorized the first three eastern parks, today's Acadia (page 34), Great Smoky Mountains (page 82), and Shenandoah (page 114)—now among the most visited national parks. Six other parks round out the roster. In Kentucky, Mammoth Cave (page 96) awes with 426 miles of mapped passages. South Carolina's Congaree (page 56) protects 11,000 acres of old-growth forest. In Florida, an underwater wilderness awaits in Biscayne (page 48), while Everglades (page 70) safeguards an enormous variety of wildlife and Dry Tortugas (page 62) offers a fortress to wander. Farther afield, Virgin Islands (page 126) is known for its beaches. One thing's for sure: These parks deliver in spades.

LEFT: Big Meadows, Shenandoah National Park (page 114) **PREVIOUS PAGES:** Congaree River, Congaree National Park (page 56)

The aurora borealis over a frozen pond

ACADIA NATIONAL PARK

MAINE

ESTABLISHED: February 26, 1919

SIZE: 50,000 acres

VISITORS CENTERS: The Hulls Cove Visitor Center (open May–October) in the park has resource trip planning, passes and permits, and a store. The Sieur de Monts Nature Center (open May–October) has family-friendly science exhibits. The Rockefeller Welcome Center (summer only) has exhibits, trip planning resources, and a store. The Bar Harbor Chamber of Commerce downtown serves as the park's visitors center in the winter and spring. The Islesford Historical Museum (June–September) on Little Cranberry Island has permanent exhibits about island life.

TRANSPORTATION: Island Explorer, a free shuttle system with eight bus routes (summer and early fall only)

DOGS ALLOWED: Only in certain areas

WHEN TO GO: April–December (June–September is busy season)

CONTACT: 207-288-3338; nps.gov/acad
25 Visitor Center Road
Bar Harbor, ME 04609

People have connected with the high rocky headlands of Acadia National Park for 10,000 years, starting with the Wabanaki people and continuing with its four million current annual visitors. Though that seems like a lot of people traversing the park's 50,000 acres, there's still plenty of space for peace, solitude, and personal discovery to be found on the more than 150 miles of hiking trails and plenty of driving routes. Whether you stick with the crowds during busy season or find solitude in the offseason, you'll see why Acadia is so beloved.

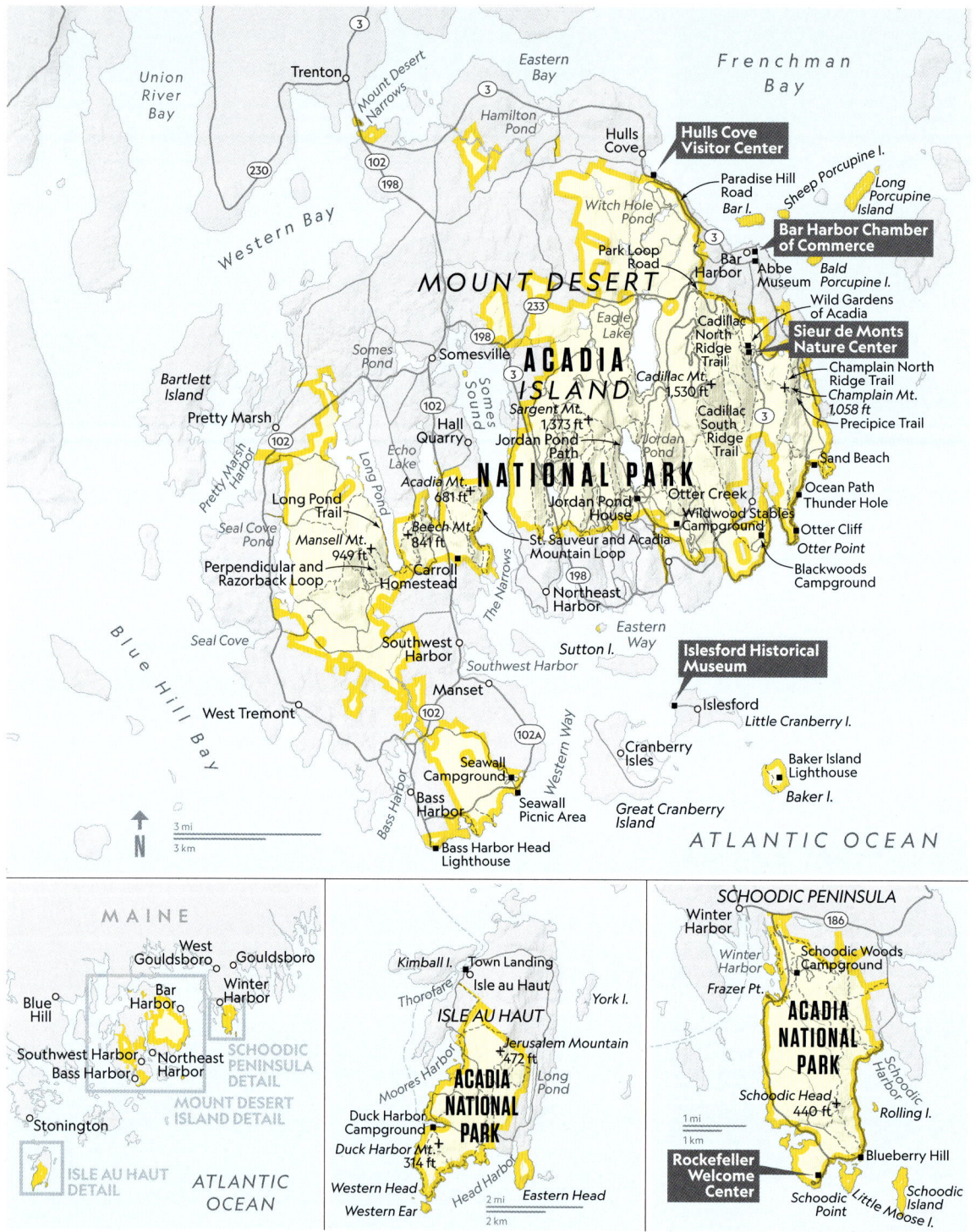

Union River Bay

Trenton

Mount Desert Narrows

Eastern Bay

Hamilton Pond

Frenchman Bay

Hulls Cove

Hulls Cove Visitor Center

Paradise Hill Road
Bar I.

Sheep Porcupine I.

Long Porcupine Island

Witch Hole Pond

Park Loop Road

Bar Harbor

Abbe Museum

Bar Harbor Chamber of Commerce

Bald Porcupine I.

Wild Gardens of Acadia

Sieur de Monts Nature Center

Western Bay

(230)

(102)

(198)

MOUNT DESERT

(233)

(198)

Eagle Lake

Somesville

Somes Pond

ACADIA ISLAND

Bartlett Island

Pretty Marsh

Somes Sound

Echo Lake

Hall Quarry

Cadillac Mt. 1,530 ft

Cadillac North Ridge Trail

Champlain North Ridge Trail
Champlain Mt. 1,058 ft
Precipice Trail

Sargent Mt. 1,373 ft

Cadillac South Ridge Trail

(3)

Jordan Pond

Jordan Pond Path

NATIONAL PARK

Acadia Mt. 681 ft

Long Pond Trail

Long Pond

Seal Cove Pond

Mansell Mt. 949 ft

Beech Mt. 841 ft

Perpendicular and Razorback Loop

Carroll Homestead

Jordan Pond House

St. Sauveur and Acadia Mountain Loop

Otter Creek

Wildwood Stables

Campground

Pretty Marsh Harbor

Seal Cove Pond

Sand Beach

Ocean Path
Thunder Hole

Otter Cliff

Otter Point

Blackwoods Campground

The Narrows

Northeast Harbor

Eastern Way

Southwest Harbor

Manset

West Tremont

Seal Cove

Blue Hill Bay

(102)

(198)

(102)

Sutton I.

Islesford Historical Museum

Islesford

Little Cranberry I.

Cranberry Isles

Southwest Harbor

Western Way

(102A)

Seawall Campground

Bass Harbor

Seawall Picnic Area

Great Cranberry Island

Baker Island Lighthouse

Baker I.

ATLANTIC OCEAN

3 mi
3 km
N

Bass Harbor

Bass Harbor Head Lighthouse

MAINE

West Gouldsboro

Gouldsboro

Bar Harbor

Winter Harbor

Blue Hill

Southwest Harbor
Bass Harbor

Northeast Harbor

SCHOODIC PENINSULA DETAIL

MOUNT DESERT ISLAND DETAIL

Stonington

ISLE AU HAUT DETAIL

ATLANTIC OCEAN

Kimball I.

Town Landing

Isle au Haut

Thorofare

York I.

ISLE AU HAUT

Jerusalem Mountain
472 ft

Moores Harbor

Long Pond

Duck Harbor Campground

ACADIA NATIONAL PARK

Duck Harbor Mt. 314 ft

Western Head

Head Harbor

Eastern Head

Western Ear

2 mi
2 km

SCHOODIC PENINSULA

Winter Harbor

Winter Harbor

(186)

Schoodic Woods Campground

Frazer Pt.

ACADIA NATIONAL PARK

Schoodic Harbor

Schoodic Head 440 ft

Rolling I.

1 mi
1 km

Rockefeller Welcome Center

Schoodic Point

Blueberry Hill

Little Moose I.

Schoodic Island

A campsite on the shore of Mount Desert Island

Agamont Park and Bar Harbor Inn

S Staying as close to the park as possible will give you early access to popular hikes and overlooks and a chance to beat the crowds. There are really just two options: to camp within park bounds or to stay outside them in Bar Harbor.

→ *On the east side of Mount Desert Island, the wooded sites at* **Blackwoods Campground** *are less than a 10-minute walk to the ocean and close to the park's most popular locations. There are flush toilets and potable water for the 281 tent and RV sites.*

→ *The 202 tent and RV sites at* **Seawall Campground** *on the west side of Mount Desert Island are less crowded than Blackwoods, but you'll still find modern amenities and seasonal staff.*

→ *Out on the Schoodic Peninsula,* **Schoodic Woods Campground** *is the newest in the park. It's just 1.5 miles from Winter Harbor and is open between Memorial Day weekend and Indigenous Peoples' Day.*

→ **Duck Harbor Campground** *on Isle au Haut is rustic and remote. Once you arrive—by ferry from Stonington—you'll find five lean-to shelters with floors, composting toilets, and fire rings. It's a great launching point for paddling excursions.*

→ *Horseback riders can sleep with their steeds at* **Wildwood Stables Campground**. *Carriage tours are available for those without a horse, but you won't be able to spend the night.*

→ *If you prefer four walls, try the luxurious* **Bar Harbor Inn**, *with its ocean views and spa services, or the family-friendly* **Salt Cottages**, *with its swimming pool and game shed. The* **Harborside Hotel, Spa & Marina** *provides an upscale experience and access to the elegant Bar Harbor Club.*

S
L
E
E
P

Cadillac Mountain

Must-Do
Activity

HIKE

It's best to plan your hikes along Acadia's 158 miles of trails by first determining which side of the park you'll visit that day. Many visitors stick to the eastern side, and there's plenty to fill an entire trip there, but adding the western side to your itinerary will pay off with peace, solitude, and opportunities to test your grit.

Consider these hikes on the eastern side:

→ The rugged **Precipice Trail**, for experienced hikers, rises more than 1,000 feet in under a mile and traverses open cliff faces and iron-rung ladders. Avoid this one if you're afraid of heights. Don't take the same trail back as the descent is dangerous—the safer path down is on the **Champlain North Ridge Trail** of Champlain Mountain.

→ Find the flatter and more moderate 4.4-mile round-trip **Ocean Path** along the Maine coast from Sand Beach to Otter Point. On the way, you'll pass Thunder Hole, Monument Cove, and Otter Cliff.

→ The approachable 3.3-mile **Jordan Pond Path** loops along the shores of the glacier-carved pond, providing views of one of the park's most awe-inspiring landscapes. The peak-rimmed shores are also great for spotting wildlife, including loons, beavers, and peregrine falcons. Prepare for uneven boardwalks, rocks, and footbridges—and don't swim in this public water supply.

→ There are two ways to hike to Acadia's gem peak: Cadillac Mountain. Take the 4.4-mile **Cadillac North Ridge Trail**, a popular sunrise or sunset hike, or trek the more scenic 7.1-mile **Cadillac South Ridge Trail**. The first is more moderate, while the second will push you across a granite ridgeline and up one iron-rung ladder.

Consider these hikes on the western side:

→ The strenuous 2.7-mile **Perpendicular and Razorback Loop**, starting on the **Long Pond Trail**, takes you up Mansell Mountain through a wooded trail completed by the Civilian Conservation Corps in 1934. Add the spur trail to look over Beech Mountain, Long Pond, and the nearby islands—and be careful as you traverse the wet granite staircase.

→ Take the challenging **St. Sauveur and Acadia Mountain Loop** up two mountain peaks, with views of Somes Sound, green islands, and the Atlantic Ocean. You'll move through multiple exposed granite slopes during the 3.7-mile round-trip climb.

Pausing to take in Maine's fall foliage

Acadia's rugged coastline views

Park Loop Road

DRIVE

H Hiking is the name of the game in Acadia, but many of the park's most iconic and well-loved spots are accessible by vehicle—either your own or the free summer shuttle. Especially on the east side, there are plenty of sites to be seen as you drive. Try these routes:

→ Take your time as you drive the classic 27-mile **Park Loop Road** around the east side of Mount Desert Island. Start at the Hulls Cove Visitor Center and take Paradise Hill Road south to the loop. Once you're on it, stop at the Sieur de Monts Nature Center, play at Sand Beach, watch the tides at Thunder Hole, look out over Otter Point, and skip stones at Little Hunters Beach. Don't forget to check out the Jordan Pond House (known for its popovers) and Dam Bridge. Take a short hike to Bubble Pond. This road is also the only one with sections open to vehicles in the winter.

→ If you'd rather not trek to the top of Cadillac Mountain, add **Cadillac Summit Road** to your drive. You need a reservation to drive to the summit, so book ahead. The three-mile drive will take you past several overlooks on the way to a scenic and striking view from the peak. You'll also find restrooms, a gift shop, and parking once you arrive.

→ Ditch your car while you're in the park and get around on the free **Island Explorer**, which runs from late June through mid-October. Travel between overlooks, campgrounds, trailheads, and surrounding villages—nearly everywhere in the park except the Cadillac Mountain summit.

SPOT

It's hard to know what wildlife you'll find in Acadia because the species are so vast and varied. Talking with rangers will help you narrow down where certain creatures have been spending their time. That said, there are a few tried-and-true locations for spotting the animals who call the park home:

➜ *More than 300 bird species* have been seen in and around the park, making it a fantastic bird-watching destination. Join park rangers on their daily Cadillac Mountain Hawkwatch to get a unique look at the park's winged friends. Look for songbirds all over Acadia's carriage roads, including at Eagle Lake and Aunt Betty Pond, and listen for seabirds as you travel the coastline of Otter Point.

➜ Walk the boardwalk of the Jesup Path at Sieur de Monts to see **white-tailed deer**, **barred owls**, and **songbirds**. If you look closely, you might spot **mink** and **otters** playing at the edge of the water.

➜ It's rare to see **moose**, Maine's official state animal, in Acadia, but many people try. Be patient on the Schoodic Peninsula; since it's relatively remote, you might get lucky—and if you do, keep your distance.

➜ Look for **painted and snapping turtles** sunning themselves along the Witch Hole Pond Loop—and turn your gaze up toward the sky while you're here to find a soaring **bald eagle**.

➜ If marine life is more your speed, head to the coastline at Bar Island, Ocean Path, Schoodic Point, and Seawall, where **harbor porpoises**, **seals**, and **shorebirds** spend time. For **whales** or **puffins**, take a boat tour.

➜ Search for smaller creatures, like **snails** and **crabs**, in the tide pools along the Wonder Trail 90 minutes before or after low tide. Keep yourself and the tide pools safe by stepping carefully, minimizing any chemicals on your body, and leaving everything where you find it.

A breaching North Atlantic right whale

A barred owl clings to a tree trunk.

A sea star moves across the seabed.

An American bullfrog perches on a lily pad.

A double-crested cormorant stands at attention.

The Milky Way as seen from the park

→ EXPLORE

There's more to do in Acadia than hiking and driving its peaks. Sprinkle in some extra adventure and discovery with some of these add-ons:

→ You could walk the park's 45 miles of **carriage roads**, designed by John D. Rockefeller, Jr., but there are more thrilling ways to traverse these paths. Cars are banned here, so find a bicycle, horse, or carriage for a little more speed. The **Witch Hole Pond Loop** is a good place to start. In the winter, explore the roads by cross-country ski or snowshoe.

→ Take the kids to the **Carroll Homestead** drop-in program to learn about life on an 1800s farm, or get close to tide pool creatures at a **touch-tank talk** on the Schoodic Peninsula. In the evening, join a **family campfire talk** at the campground amphitheaters, whether you're staying there or not.

→ Book a spot on a **boat cruise** either with the park rangers or an authorized outfitter. See puffins or whales, the Somes Sound fjord, and the lighthouses as you putter along the clear, cold water.

→ Tour more than 400 native plants at the **Wild Gardens of Acadia** in the Sieur de Monts region. Each one of the plants featured here is found somewhere in Acadia's 13 different habitats.

→ The **Abbe Museum** began as a small trailside exhibit in Acadia but has since grown into a larger Smithsonian-affiliated space in downtown Bar Harbor. Despite being outside park bounds, it is worth a trip to better understand and show respect to the region's Indigenous people, including Maine's Wabanaki community.

→ Stargaze at **Ocean Path**, with its unobstructed views of the night sky. Or pack a snack and watch the stars at the **Seawall Picnic Area**, with its northeastern and southern views over the ocean. Be sure to bring layers for the cold evening weather.

→ In the summer, swim at the quiet, freshwater **Echo Lake** to get a bit more space to yourself. If sand and ocean are a must, head to **Sand Beach**, where the crowds are bigger and the water is colder.

→ Stop to eat **wild blueberries** along the trails and on the mountain slopes. They ripen in July or August, and the park has given its stamp of approval for picking the fruit.

→ **Rock climb at Otter Cliff**, one of the park's four commonly accessed climbing areas. You'll get to tackle crack and face climbing on the 60-foot sea cliffs, and there's also rappel access. If you have a group of six or more, you'll need to get a permit ahead of time. (Note: Groups are limited to 12 people.)

Family Friendly

→ RANGER RECOMMENDATION ←

Snowmobile, ski, walk, or snowshoe the scenic **Park Loop Road** *during the winter. This popular road is much less so when the weather turns, so you'll get the benefit of fewer people on the route. Be thoughtful about the weather and darkness so that you don't get stuck along the way. If you don't have your own equipment, rent some in Bar Harbor.*

A mangrove in shallow water at sunrise

BISCAYNE NATIONAL PARK

FLORIDA

ESTABLISHED: June 28, 1980

SIZE: 172,971 acres

VISITORS CENTER: The Dante Fascell Visitor Center is open year-round and offers trip resources, a museum, and a starting point for ranger-led activities.

TRANSPORTATION: Homestead National Parks Trolley (seasonal), boat rentals, and guided tours

DOGS ALLOWED: Only at Convoy Point, and a leash is required.

WHEN TO GO: November–April for drier weather and visiting the park's island; summer for snorkeling

CONTACT: 305-230-1144; nps.gov/bisc
9700 SW 328th Street, Sir Lancelot Jones Way
Homestead, FL 33033

B Biscayne is a peaceful respite now, but its birth is a story of conflict. A swell of visitors and home buyers arrived in the 1950s. Then in 1961, a group attempted to turn the region into a major industrial seaport. Thankfully, another group saw what it could become instead: a distinct and important national park. As tensions grew, some landowners brought bulldozers and cleared "Spite Highway." In the end, the conservationists won out. In 1968, Congress designated Biscayne National Monument, protecting its clear waters, green islands, teeming coral reefs, and deep mangroves. Today, Spite Highway is a canopied hiking route through a tropical forest.

Elliott Key Harbor

SLEEP

If you want to stay in Biscayne, you're going to have to camp— and you're going to have to get to your site by boat. You have two choices: The campground at **Elliott Key**, the park's largest island, has restrooms, showers, and drinking water, though it's wise to bring your own. **Boca Chita Key** is easy to find by its iconic 1930s lighthouse. Its campsites have waterfront views, grassy lots, and toilets, but no water. Whatever your choice, don't forget the bug spray.

If you don't want to camp, stay at any of the hotels in nearby **Homestead** or **Florida City**. If you choose Homestead, take advantage of the free city trolley to the park.

FLORIDA KEYS NATI

S.S. *Arratoon Apcar* wreck

LEGARE

KEY BISCAYNE

Soldier Key
(closed area)

Boca Chita Key

Sands Key

Biscayne Channel

Stiltsville

SAFETY VALVE

Ragged Keys
(private)

campground
lighthouse

Lewis Cut

Sands Cut

Sands Key

INTRACOASTAL WATERWAY

BISCAYNE NATIO

Featherbed
Bank

BISCAYNE

To
Cocount Grove

To
Miami

1

Old Cutler Rd.

Black Point

Black Point
Jetty Trail

Fender
Point

821

Coconut Palm Dr.
(SW 248th St.)

SW 107th Ave.

Florida's
Turnpike
(toll)

Map

ATLANTIC OCEAN

← N

3 mi
3 km

NATIONAL MARINE SANCTUARY

Lugano wreck ■
Mandalay wreck ■
Erl King wreck ■
Alicia wreck ■

ANCHORAGE

HAWK CHANNEL

Sea Grape Point
Point Adelle
campground ■
ELLIOTT KEY
Elliott Key Harbor
Spite Highway Trail
Petrel Point
Ott Point
Billys Point

NAL PARK

Christmas Point
Caesar Creek
Adams Key
Hurricane Creek
Rubicon Keys
Totten Key
Jones Lagoon
Old Rhodes Key
Swan Key
Broad Creek

BAY

KEY LARGO

Cutter Bank Shallows

Arsenicker Key
Midnight Pass
West Arsenicker
(closed area)
Long Arsenicker Key

CARD SOUND

INTRACOASTAL WATERWAY

Dante Fascell Visitor Center
Turkey Point

Convoy Point Jetty Trail

SW 328th St.

FLORIDA

To Homestead
↓
To Florida City
↓

Must-Do Activity

T Though land is rare in Biscayne, there are a few hikes worth taking:

→ Follow the 0.8-mile round-trip **Convoy Point Jetty Trail** from the Dante Fascell Visitor Center out along the Jetty Walk Bridge and to eastern views at the end of the point.

→ The mile-long loop around **Elliott Key** campground is a great way to stretch your legs and explore the landscapes of the island.

→ Initially created to intentionally ruin the land, **Spite Highway** on Elliott Key is now a recreational treasure. It's a six-mile walk beneath a canopy of trees.

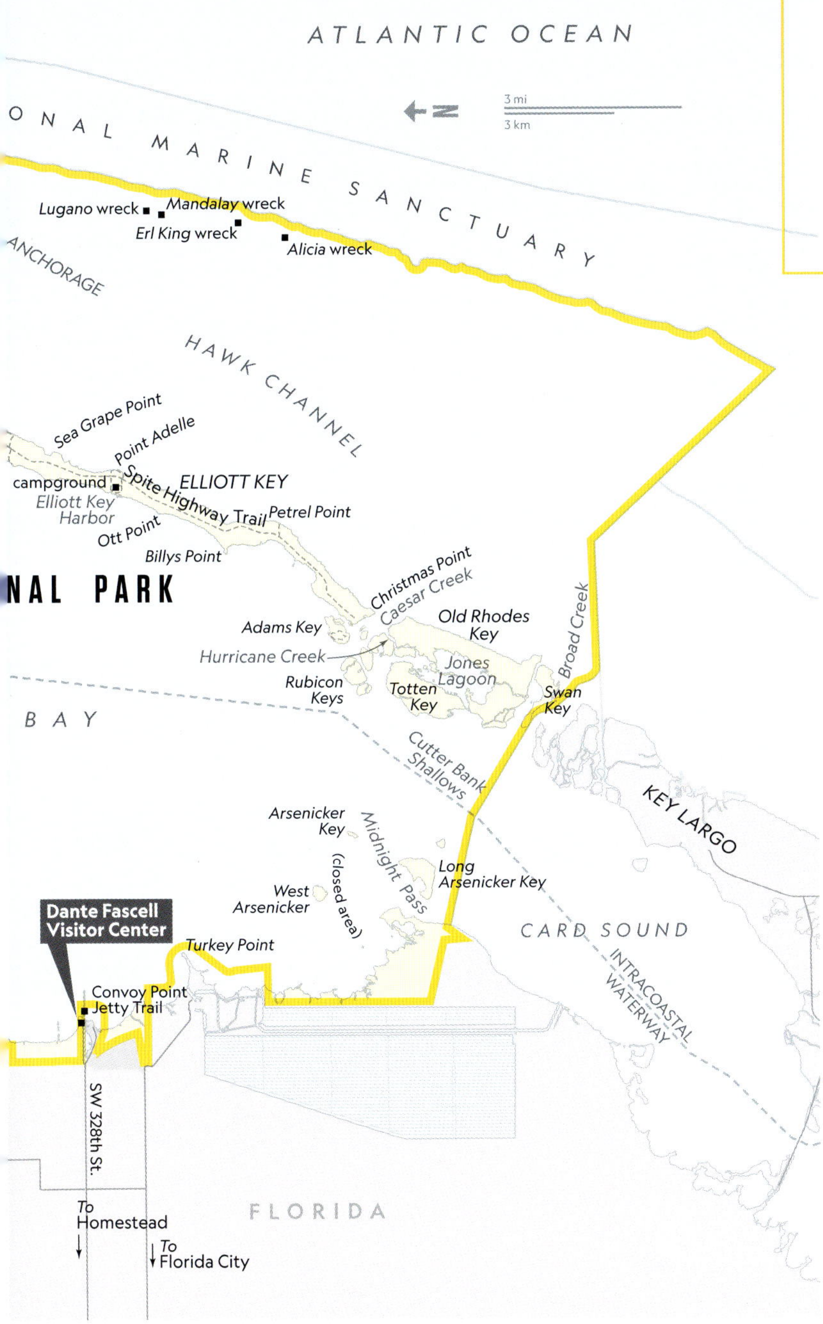

↑

HIKE

A paved walking path

The protected waters of Biscayne provide respite for wildlife, including the 500 species of fish in its coral ecosystems, birds above its clear waters, and animals roaming its mangrove forests. You're guaranteed to see wildlife, but here are a few specific spots:

→ *To search for a manatee, paddle the harbor just north of the visitors center. They're more likely to be around in the winter, when they migrate to the area in search of warmer water. Remember to mind your distance if you spot one.*
→ *Follow the Biscayne Birding Trail to Convoy Point, Black Point, and Jones Lagoon, where loons, petrels, gulls, pelicans, herons, egrets, raptors, and sandpipers soar. Hint: Rely on your ears, not just your eyes.*
→ *Snorkel with an outfitter like Ace Diving, Nice Aquatic, or Diver's Paradise to see the park's many threatened, endangered, or protected underwater species. Move slowly and look out for sea turtles, sharks, parrotfish, barracudas, rays, and sea stars.*

Brown pelicans rush the sea beak-first.

LOOK

Even though the park is known for its water, there is plenty to see on land too. From the mainland, walk out into the water along the **Black Point Jetty Trail** or along the shore near the **Dante Fascell Visitor Center**. From the Keys, stop at the **Boca Chita Key Lighthouse**, **Sea Grape Point**, **Ott Point**, **Billys Point**, and **Christmas Point**.

A manatee peeks above the water's surface.

SPOT

Canoe the waterways of Biscayne Bay.

FLOAT

W With 95 percent of the park aquatic, Biscayne is meant to be discovered by water. Pick your vessel and start exploring.

→ In the past, **Hurricane Creek** served as a respite for boaters when storms arrived. Paddle along the creek and snorkel around the mangrove roots to see sea squirts, crabs, and anemones.

→ Launch your kayak from **Adams Key** to check out the lagoons, creeks, and channels south of Caesar Creek. These spots are too shallow for boats with motors, so you won't be disturbed.

→ Paddle, sail, or cruise across the water with the **Biscayne National Park Institute**. Explore Jones Lagoon on an eco-adventure, paddle the mangroves, kayak the seagrasses of Stiltsville, or cruise from Coconut Grove to Boca Chita Key with experienced guides sharing their knowledge along the way.

→ Kayak along the shorelines of the park's **mangroves**, where you'll see young fish, rare plants, local birds, tree crabs, and snakes.

→ **Kiteboard** with outfitters like South Florida Kiteboarding or Wind Addict in Miami, both of which will help you find the best spots and conditions, as well as show newbies the ropes.

T Though explorations on the water take priority, adding something extra to a trip to Biscayne will only boost your experience. Try one of these:

→ Do your part and book a **marine-debris cleanup tour** with the Biscayne National Park Institute. Paddle through these delicate environments with a guide, learn about the space, and pick up harmful trash.

→ Join the twice-monthly **Nature Journaling Club**, which provides supplies for you to sketch, paint, or write about the park's wonders. Meetings are held at the Dante Fascell Visitor Center.

→ **Snorkel** or **scuba dive** around the coral reefs with Diver's Paradise, the only outfitter allowed to access the park's northern quadrant. The PADI-certified dive center provides resources for research and restoration to the University of Miami.

→ Explore shipwrecks along the **Maritime Heritage Trail**, the only underwater archaeological trail in the National Park System. Visit S.S. Arratoon Apcar, an iron-hulled sail and merchant ship that sank in 1878; Erl King, a 306-foot steam-powered ship that ran aground in 1891; Alicia, a three-masted steamship that sank in 1905; Lugano, a British steamer that sank in 1913 and lies 25 feet underwater; and Mandalay, a schooner that ran aground on Long Reef in 1966.

→ Check out one-of-a-kind **Stiltsville**. The first shack on stilts was built in the 1930s, and more followed over the decades. Storms and fires have since taken most of them down, and only seven remain.

Stiltsville

EXPLORE

*Snorkel the massive reef at **Jones Lagoon**. There is lots of space in the shallow waters to explore away from other visitors. Even if you've been here before, you're bound to find something new. Navigate with the mooring buoys and look out for rays, upside-down jellyfish, fish, and birds. Give the bird rookery plenty of space.*

Fireflies illuminate the night at Congaree.

CONGAREE
NATIONAL PARK

SOUTH CAROLINA

ESTABLISHED: November 10, 2003

SIZE: 27,000 acres

VISITORS CENTER: The Harry Hampton Visitor Center is open year-round and serves as an excellent starting point for aquatic or land-based adventures.

TRANSPORTATION: No in-park transportation

DOGS ALLOWED: Yes; must be leashed

WHEN TO GO: Spring and fall; autumn foliage peaks from late October to early November

CONTACT: 803-776-4396; nps.gov/cong
100 National Park Road
Hopkins, SC 29061

C Congaree National Park has romance at its core. The river, the moss, the fallen trees. The sun shining through the deep greenery. The wistful reflections off dark waters. It's all a lesson in lushness. The park's incredible biodiversity is supported by the region's shifting waters and expanse of old-growth bottomland hardwood forest. These floodplains are constantly nourishing the landscape and its residents. A quiet, intimate trip through its abundance is sure to be just as nurturing for you.

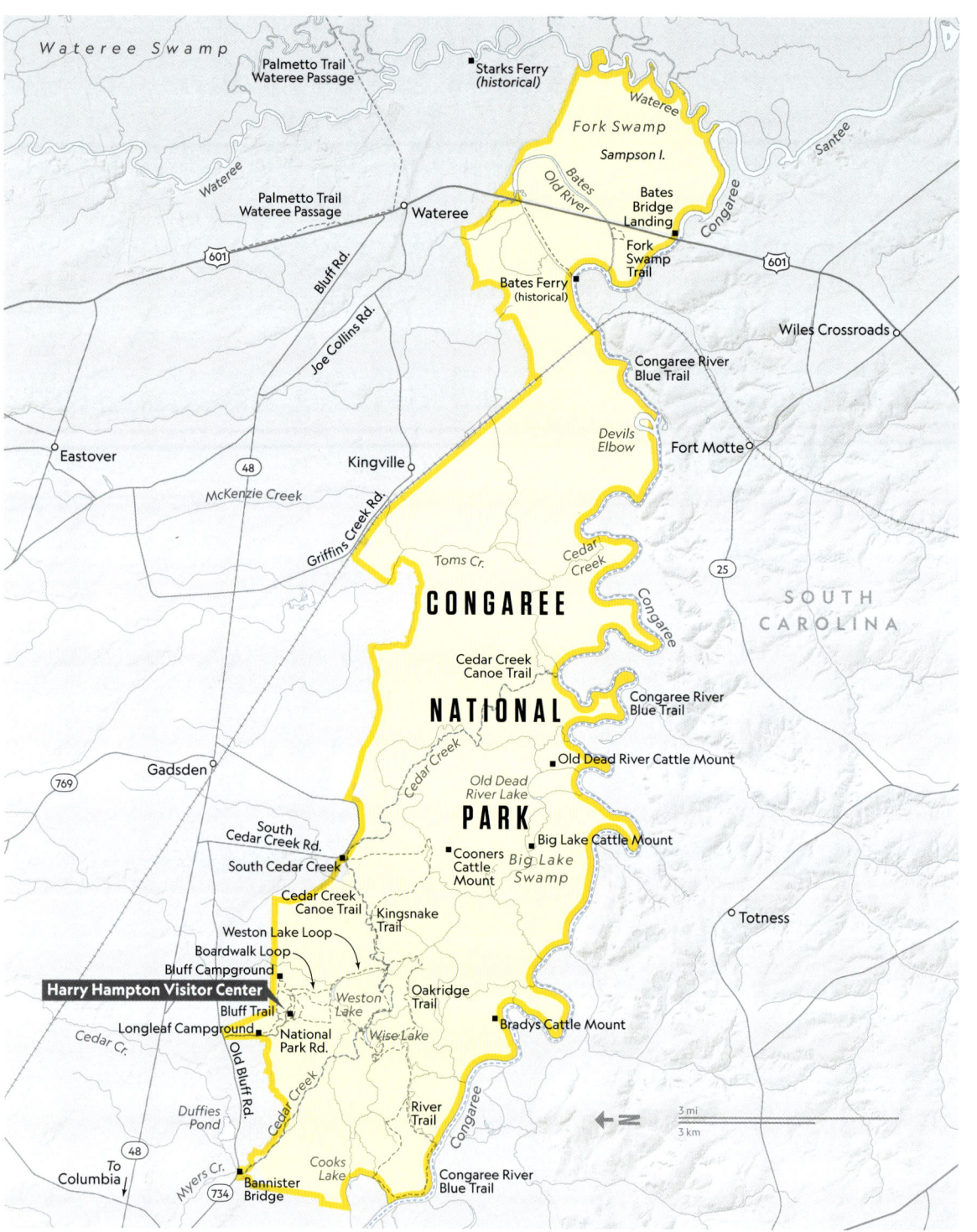

Wateree Swamp

Palmetto Trail
Wateree Passage

Starks Ferry
(historical)

Wateree

Fork Swamp

Sampson I.

Santee

Palmetto Trail
Wateree Passage

Bates
Old River

Wateree
Wateree
601
Bluff Rd.

Bates
Bridge
Landing

601

Fork
Swamp
Trail

Joe Collins Rd.

Bates Ferry
(historical)

Wiles Crossroads

Congaree River
Blue Trail

Congaree

Eastover

48

Kingville

McKenzie Creek

Griffins Creek Rd.

Devils
Elbow

Fort Motte

Toms Cr.

Cedar
Creek

Congaree

25

SOUTH
CAROLINA

CONGAREE

Cedar Creek
Canoe Trail

NATIONAL

Congaree River
Blue Trail

769

Gadsden

Cedar Creek

Old Dead River Cattle Mount

Old Dead
River Lake

PARK

Big Lake Cattle Mount

Cooners
Cattle
Mount

Big Lake
Swamp

Totness

South
Cedar Creek Rd.

South Cedar Creek

Cedar Creek
Canoe Trail

Kingsnake
Trail

Weston Lake Loop

Boardwalk Loop

Bluff Campground

Harry Hampton Visitor Center

Bluff Trail

Longleaf Campground

Old Bluff Rd.

National
Park Rd.

Weston
Lake

Oakridge
Trail

Wise Lake

Bradys Cattle Mount

Cedar Cr.

Cedar Creek

River
Trail

Congaree

Duffies
Pond

48

To
Columbia

Myers Cr.

734

Bannister
Bridge

Cooks
Lake

Congaree River
Blue Trail

3 mi
3 km

A hammock makes for a lightweight camp when hiking in and out.

SLEEP

T There are only two overnight options in the park, and they're both primitive campgrounds. The first, **Longleaf**, is near the park entrance road and has vault toilets, access to the water at the visitors center, fire rings, and picnic tables. The second, **Bluff**, is a mile off the Bluff Trail, so you'll have to hike in all your supplies; there are also fire rings and picnic tables here, but no toilets or water. Both sites require a permit (free) and registration. If you'd prefer not to camp, find lodging in nearby **Columbia**, the South Carolina capital.

W While water is key to the Congaree's existence, the landscape is also crucial to the ecosystem. Explore by foot through these winding forests that protect this disappearing terrain.

→ Take the easy 2.6-mile round-trip **Boardwalk Loop** from the Harry Hampton Visitor Center into an old-growth forest with bald cypress and tupelo trees and past an oxbow lake that is slowly filling with clay and dirt. Get more out of your walk by grabbing the self-guided brochure at the visitors center; it covers the natural and cultural history of the park. The 1.8-mile round-trip **Bluff Trail** cuts between two portions of the Boardwalk Loop. On it, you'll get a closer look at the thriving ecosystems behind the Harry Hampton Visitor Center.

→ Look for otters and wading birds while you hike the 4.5-mile **Weston Lake Loop**, along which you'll also find the knees (woody, cone-shaped outgrowths from shallow roots) of cypress trees sticking up out of the dried riverbed. The trail starts on an elevated boardwalk and takes you through old-growth forest. Follow it until it ends and continue on past toward Weston Lake and Cedar Creek. Look for wildlife and take a break on one of the many benches to enjoy the scenery and a snack.

→ The challenging 7.1-mile round-trip **Oakridge Trail** travels along a subtle ridge covered in oak trees and then opens up into great lookouts for deer and wild turkey.

→ Take the 11.1-mile round-trip **River Trail** to Congaree's namesake rolling waters. Congaree River is the heart of the park. Along the trail you'll see how the river sometimes overflows its banks and shifts into the forest; when this happens, you might see a sandbar in its place.

→ Birders love the 12-mile **Kingsnake Trail**, which is a difficult round-trip route through diverse habitats and sloughs that are sometimes filled with water. You'll get gorgeous views for your troubles, and you might also spot the red, black, yellow, and white snake that gave this trail its name.

HIKE

Accessible Option

Paddling Congaree's shaded waters

SPOT

T Thanks to the park's unique ecosystem, there's tremendous diversity in the wildlife that lives here. Congaree is a dynamic place, constantly shifting based on the water levels and the weather. As the old-growth bottomland forests of the park are flooded with water from the Congaree and Wateree Rivers, the soil is reinvigorated and rejuvenated, boosting its benefits for the creatures who call it home.

Wildlife is hiding in plain sight all over the park. Here are some ways to see it:

→ *Get out your paddles to see* **crocodiles**, **turtles**, *and* **river otters** *lazing their way along the water, or look to the shores to see* **snakes** *and* **frogs** *winding through the wetlands.*

→ *Designated as an Important Bird Area by the National Audubon Society, Congaree is home to* **red-tailed hawks**, **barred owls**, **red-bellied woodpeckers**, **red-cockaded woodpeckers**, **wrens**, *and* **warblers**. *In the spring and fall,* **migratory birds** *come to visit the park.*

→ *Look out for, and stay away from, the* **wild boars** *that wander through Congaree. The invasive species are likely the descendants of escaped farmed boars. They have caused significant and negative impacts on the habitat.*

→ *Stay into the evening to watch several different species of* **fireflies**, *including the synchronous* Photuris frontalis *(two weeks between mid-May and mid-July), float through the night sky.*

Must-Do Activity

FLOAT

Y You'd be remiss to leave the park without getting out on its waters, the lifeblood of the entire space. Take a short day trip or plan a backcountry overnight adventure—there's plenty of water to explore during either one. For a quintessential experience, try one of these routes:

→ *The 15-mile* **Cedar Creek Canoe Trail** *runs through the heart of the park, with its cypress trees and shallow waters. Book a guided trip with River Runner Outdoor Center, Palmetto Outdoors, J.K. Adventure Guides, or Carolina Outdoor Adventures. To paddle it on your own, navigate using the creek's hidden markers, and make sure to check the water levels ahead of time and pack supplies.*

→ *Take your canoe or kayak to the 50-mile* **Congaree River Blue Trail**, *which runs from Columbia into Congaree National Park, moving from an urban landscape into a wide, green riverscape. The route is a joint effort between local, state, and federal agencies, connecting the public to the wonders of the park. Continue on past the official trail if you want, or stop along the park's shores and hike its miles of established trails. For a longer trip, secure a backcountry permit in advance so you can camp within the park.*

Bird-watcher's Paradise

EXPLORE

C Congaree is really about paddling or hiking its unique waterscape, but a few extra activities will elevate your trip. Try these:

→ **Fish** *in any region of the park to find bass, perch, crappie, mudfish, and sturgeon. You'll need to secure a state fishing license, follow local regulations, and stay 25 feet from any human-constructed structure.*

→ *Check the park calendar to join a* **ranger-led experience**, *which change through the seasons. Join a nature discovery walk, a forest journaling session, yoga in the park, or an evening search for owls.*

→ RANGER RECOMMENDATION ←

Hike back into the old groves along the 7.1-mile **Oakridge Trail**, where you'll find a number of big old-growth trees and plenty of solitude. You'll also have a chance to see wildlife that hide away from the boardwalks, like deer, bobcats, river otters, and wild turkeys. This backcountry wilderness will give you a better sense of the true nature and purpose of the park.

Fort Jefferson

DRY TORTUGAS
NATIONAL PARK

ESTABLISHED: October 26, 1992

SIZE: 64,700 acres

VISITORS CENTERS: The Garden Key Visitor Center, inside Fort Jefferson, has artifacts, park information, and a store. You can also find trip information at the Florida Keys Eco-Discovery Center in Key West.

TRANSPORTATION: A ferry and seaplane drop visitors at Garden Key, but no in-park transportation is provided.

DOGS ALLOWED: Only on Garden Key, and with leash restrictions

----

WHEN TO GO: Spring for bird migration; winter for mild weather; summer for snorkeling

----

CONTACT: 305-242-7700; nps.gov/drto
40001 SR-9336
Homestead, FL 33034

T The Dry Tortugas were a boating magnet for decades, with shipping routes running frequently through the channel. Though commercial activity is now barred, the park's seven small islands are still impacted by the waters that surround them. The park's most notable on-land feature, Fort Jefferson, was protected as a national monument by President Franklin D. Roosevelt in 1935. Congress redesignated (and expanded) the monument as a national park in 1992 to protect the islands and its marine ecosystems.

Just 70 miles west of Key West, Florida, the park feels worlds away, especially because it's accessed only by boat or plane. Once you arrive, most of your adventures will be by water.

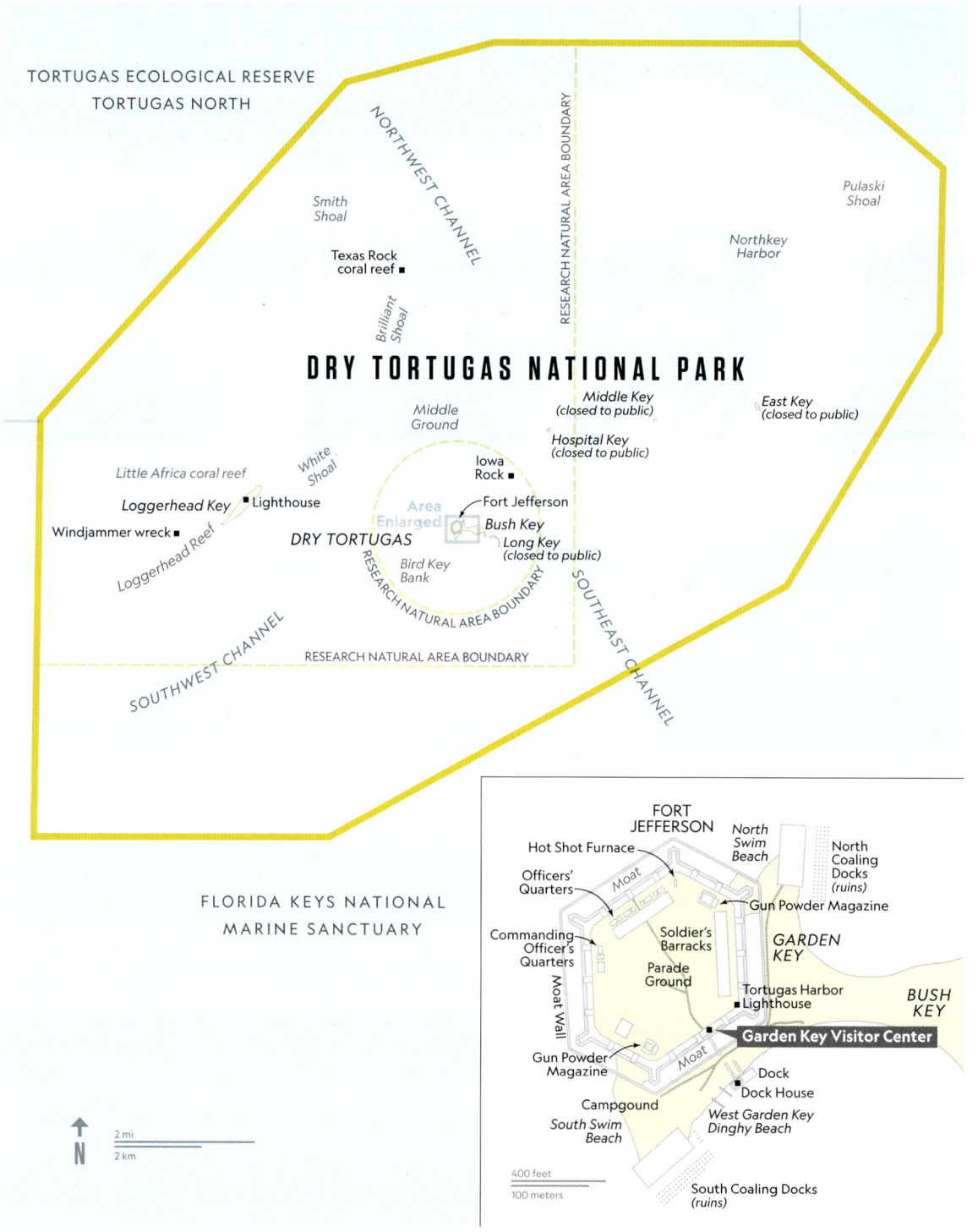

TORTUGAS ECOLOGICAL RESERVE
TORTUGAS NORTH

NORTHWEST CHANNEL

RESEARCH NATURAL AREA BOUNDARY

Smith Shoal

Pulaski Shoal

Texas Rock
coral reef ■

Northkey Harbor

Brilliant Shoal

DRY TORTUGAS NATIONAL PARK

Middle Key
(closed to public)

East Key
(closed to public)

Middle Ground

Hospital Key
(closed to public)

Iowa
Rock ■

Little Africa coral reef

White Shoal

← Fort Jefferson

Loggerhead Key ■ Lighthouse

Area
Enlarged

Bush Key

Windjammer wreck ■

Long Key
(closed to public)

DRY TORTUGAS

Loggerhead Reef

*Bird Key
Bank*

RESEARCH NATURAL AREA BOUNDARY

SOUTHEAST CHANNEL

SOUTHWEST CHANNEL

RESEARCH NATURAL AREA BOUNDARY

FLORIDA KEYS NATIONAL
MARINE SANCTUARY

FORT
JEFFERSON

*North
Swim
Beach*

Hot Shot Furnace

North
Coaling
Docks
(ruins)

Officers'
Quarters

Moat

Gun Powder Magazine

Commanding
Officer's
Quarters

Soldier's
Barracks

*GARDEN
KEY*

*BUSH
KEY*

Moat Wall

Parade
Ground

Tortugas Harbor
■ Lighthouse

Garden Key Visitor Center

Moat

Gun Powder
Magazine

■ Dock
■ Dock House

*West Garden Key
Dinghy Beach*

Campground
*South Swim
Beach*

400 feet
100 meters

South Coaling Docks
(ruins)

↑ N
2 mi
2 km

A campground and picnic area in Dry Tortugas

T The only option in Dry Tortugas is camping, which is a plus for the outstanding and private late-night stargazing, evening sunsets, and early-morning snorkeling. Campsites are available on **Garden Key**, and you'll have to bring everything you need with you. While the campsites are first come, first served, no one will be left without a place to stay. If the sites are full, share the grassy overflow area.

S

L

E

E

P

HIKE

E Explore **Fort Jefferson**, which the U.S. began building in 1846 as a fortifying measure in the region. Designed to hold 1,500 soldiers and withstand a siege of up to a year, it's massive. Though it took 16 million bricks and 30 years to construct the walls, the fort was never technically finished. It served as a prison for Union deserters during the Civil War, but its military service didn't last long. It was abandoned in 1874, became a wildlife refuge to protect the sooty tern rookery in 1908, and then became the world's first marine protected area in 1935. Walk along the grounds on a self-guided tour, or board the ferry *Yankee Freedom* at the Key West Terminal for a guided tour. While you're there, take the time to wander around the 70-foot-wide moat walls as well and listen as the water laps against them.

The moat at Fort Jefferson

Pulling away from Dry Tortugas

FLOAT

ⓘ If you don't have a plane, a boat is the only way to get to Dry Tortugas, and a trip on the water affords a different view of the park. Try one of these boating adventures:

→ The ferryboat **Yankee Freedom** runs a well-oiled trip to the park every day from the Key West Terminal. You'll get breakfast, lunch, a narrated tour, complimentary snorkeling gear, and a ticket to the fort. Take the ferry to the island for your camping trip or bring a kayak onboard. Check packing limits and book an accessible trip ahead of time if needed.

→ Paddle to and around **Loggerhead**

Key, the largest island in the park and home of the Loggerhead Lighthouse. Once you're there, swim, snorkel the Little Africa coral reef (shallow and calm, it's great for families looking to spot barracuda, lobsters, and tropical fish), or check out the popular Windjammer wreck, the site of a three-masted ship that sank in 1907. No overnight stays are allowed, so be sure to plan your trip back.

→ You can **bring your own boat** into the park's waters, but you'll have to get a permit ahead of time. To anchor overnight, find a sandy spot within a mile of the Tortugas Harbor Lighthouse (formerly the Garden Key Lighthouse), first lit in 1826.

Accessible Option

A seaplane on shore at Dry Tortugas

Must-Do Activity

SPOT

D Dry Tortugas' protected waters safeguard an abundance of wildlife. Take care when you search for the park's fragile creatures.

→ Paddle to Bush and Long Keys, near Garden Key, in the spring to see thousands of nesting birds. From March until September, 100,000 **sooty terns** nest on Bush Key—and you'll also definitely see plenty of seabirds.

→ Book an outfitter like Finz Dive Center or Key West Charter Boat for a wildlife-packed scuba diving trip. If you're lucky, you'll see **dolphins** and **turtles** while you're quietly moving above the colorful hard and soft corals. You'll also see colorful **tropical reef fish**, **goliath groupers**, **squid**, and **octopus**. Keep an eye out for the unique conch. Snorkeling is also a great way to see what lies below the surface in Dry Tortugas' extensive reef system if you aren't scuba certified.

A moon jellyfish bobs just below the surface.

W While the park is small—just over 100 square miles—it has plenty to offer, both above and below the surface.

→ Snorkel or scuba through the park's protected underwater habitats and cultural sites. Visit the historic **South Coaling Docks**, built by the U.S. Navy in the late 1800s to refuel ships and now an artificial reef. The **Texas Rock coral reef**, a large coral mound that emerges out of the water, is known for its schools of fish, sea fans, and black coral (a rarity).

→ Snorkel the **moat wall** at night, when you'll see docile fish, octopus, and sea stars more easily than during the day. Be sure to pack a dive light and check for any closures ahead of time.

→ Fishing is prohibited in half the park, but **casting a line** from the seaplane dock on Garden Key or the main ferry dock is allowed. Get a license before you do and follow regulations.

→ Book a **seaplane excursion** with Key West Seaplane Adventures, which offers half-day and full-day tours of the park. Take a flightseeing tour or make a special request to focus on bird and wildlife spotting.

→ Splash at one of the two designated swim areas in the park. The beaches at **Garden Key** slope gently into the water and are great for beginner swimmers and snorkelers. The **Loggerhead Key** swimming area is shallow and calm, with coral formations nearby for exploring.

→ Check out the calendar of **ranger-led events** in the park, which include options such as a Fort Jefferson history tour, a living history demonstration, and a guided night-sky and stargazing program.

EXPLORE

→ RANGER RECOMMENDATION ←

Plan an **overnight snorkeling trip** to experience what feels like an entirely different park than the one you see during the day. Either camp on land or bring your own boat. You'll snorkel to see calm nocturnal creatures, watch the sunset, and get a clear view of the night sky.

Roseate spoonbills are among the park's 360 species of birds

EVERGLADES
NATIONAL PARK

FLORIDA

ESTABLISHED: December 6, 1947

SIZE: 1,500,000 acres

VISITORS CENTERS: There are four visitors centers in the park, each set at a different corner: the Ernest F. Coe Visitor Center, Guy Bradley Visitor Center (Flamingo), Shark Valley Visitor Center, and Gulf Coast Visitor Center.

TRANSPORTATION: Tram tours (available from the Shark Valley Visitor Center) or booked boat and airboat tours

DOGS ALLOWED: Only in restricted areas; not allowed on trails, unpaved roads, or the Shark Valley Tram Trail

WHEN TO GO: December–April for the dry season; November–December or April–May to avoid the crowds. Summer months are busy, so visit in the morning to avoid the rush and the heat.

CONTACT: 305-242-7700; nps.gov/ever
40001 State Road 9336
Homestead, FL 33034

E Everglades National Park—a UNESCO World Heritage site and International Biosphere Reserve—is recognized around the world as an extraordinary and distinctive wonder. It was the first large area of wilderness protected not for mountains, canyons, or scenic features but for its amazing ecological diversity. Once you arrive, you'll understand why. There's truly no place like it. The massive wetlands are the largest subtropical wilderness in the United States and famous for their American crocodiles, as well as manatees and Florida panthers. There's no way to tackle it all in one trip, so take your time exploring and know you'll be back.

Everglades City
Turner River Paddling Trail
Monroe Station
Tamiami Trail
41
Sandfly Island
Gulf Coast Visitor Center
Chokoloskee
BIG CYPRESS NATIONAL PRESERVE
Shark Valley Visitor Center
Ten Thousand Islands
Sunday Bay
Oyster Bay
Huston
Loop Rd.
Miccosukee Cultural Center
Otter Cave Hammock Trail
Tram Road
Chevelier Bay
Chatham
Shark Valley Loop Road
Alligator Bay
Everglades Wilderness Waterway
Shark Valley Observation Tower
Lostmans
Big Lostmans Bay
SHARK RIVER SLOUGH
Key Mclaughlin
Broad
EVERGLADES NATIONAL
Pa-hay-Okee Overlook
Harney
Tarpon Bay
Pine Glades Lake
Long Pine Key Trail
Shark
Sisal Pond
Watson
Main Park Road
Oyster Bay
Mahogany Hammock Trail
Whitewater Bay
Paurotis Pond
Nine Mile Pond Canoe Trail
CAPE SABLE
Everglades Wilderness Waterway
Hells Bay Canoe Trail
Noble Hammock Canoe Trail
Joe
Roberts
Northwest Cape
West Lake Trail
West Lake
Cuthbert L.
Mud Lake Canoe Trail
Coot Bay
Snake Bight Trail
Mud L.
Rowdy Bend Trail
Middle Cape
Bear Lake Canoe Trail
Bear L.
Snake Bight
Lake Ingraham
Flamingo
East Cape
Clubhouse Beach
Flamingo Campground
Christian Pt. Trail
Coastal Prairie Trail
Guy Bradley Visitor Center
F L O R I D A

10 mi
N
10 km

FLORIDA KEYS NATIONAL MARINE SANCTUARY

Camp right on the beach for a memorable experience.

SLEEP

C Camping is the only way to stay within the bounds of Everglades, either at one of its two drive-in campgrounds or a backcountry site. **Long Pine Key Campground** is open to tent campers and RVs from November through May with 108 sites on a first-come-first-serve basis. Meanwhile, **Flamingo Campground**, with 274 tent and 65 RV sites, is open year-round. Both offer hot showers, toilets, and potable water, but only Flamingo has electrical hookups. Flamingo also has a camp store, year-round staffing, and a wide array of trailheads branching from the campground.

To **backcountry camp**, you'll need a permit, which is issued the day before or day of your trip online or at the Guy Bradley Visitor Center in Flamingo. Most wilderness sites are accessible only by water. Plan ahead, pack everything you need, and steer clear of the wildlife you'll likely encounter.

If you prefer a hotel, try one in nearby **Homestead** and take advantage of the city's free trolley to the Ernest F. Coe Visitor Center.

Map labels:

FLORIDA
997
821
27
95
Hialeah
Florida's Turnpike
Tamiami Trail 41
836
Miami
41
826
1
874
Coral Gables
94
South Miami
Kendall
L-67 Extension Trail
997
Krome Ave.
1
821
BISCAYNE NATIONAL PARK
PARK
Homestead
Florida City
Pinelands Trail
Long Pine Key Campground
9336
Ernest F. Coe Visitor Center
HM69 Nike Missile Base
Anhinga Trail
1
Card Sound
CROCODILE LAKE NATIONAL WILDLIFE REFUGE
TAYLOR SLOUGH
Joe Bay
Barnes Sound
KEY LARGO
Blackwater Sound
1
FLORIDA KEYS NATIONAL MARINE SANCTUARY
B A Y
Key Largo
Tavernier
Plantation
1
Islamorada
ATLANTIC OCEAN

**H
I
K
E**

(T) The most popular way to
explore Everglades is by
boat, but add a few of these hikes to
your trip to get another perspective of
the park:

→ *To protect the Cape Sable through-
wort growing in the area, the 7.5-mile one-
way* **Coastal Prairie Trail** *is not currently
being maintained, but it's still open to
careful hikers. Camp at* **Clubhouse Beach**
at the end of the trail (permit required).
→ *Take the full 15-mile round-trip adventure on the* **Tram Road** *to the Shark Valley
Observation Tower. The flat, paved route
is a good jaunt for spotting alligators, herons, egrets, deer, and turtles.*
→ *The unmaintained 1.8-mile out-and-
back* **Christian Point Trail** *begins in the
mangroves and opens up to a coastal prairie. You'll end up along the shore of Snake
Bight, which is best seen near high tide
and is a great spot for bird-watchers. Walk
carefully to avoid damaging the vegetation
that grows here—it's a critical habitat for
the Cape Sable thoroughwort.*
→ *Wander through the dense hardwood
hammock on the half-mile round-trip*
Mahogany Hammock Trail *boardwalk.
Try to spot the gumbo-limbo trees and the
largest living mahogany tree along the way.*
→ *Travel the boardwalk along the* **West
Lake Trail** *through a white, black, and red
mangrove forest. You can access the half-
mile round-trip trail just north of the Guy
Bradley Visitor Center in Flamingo.*
→ *Head into a wildflower-filled pine and
palmetto forest on the nearly half-mile*
Pinelands Trail. *Catch the trailhead off
Main Park Road.*
→ *Walk the half-mile one-way* **Otter
Cave Hammock Trail** *through a tropical
hardwood forest, across footbridges, and
over streams.*

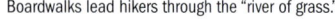

Boardwalks lead hikers through the "river of grass."

FLOAT

In most parks, trails are paths traveled by foot. Not in the Everglades. Follow paddling trails into places you could never reach by land. Kayak rentals are available from Everglades Florida Adventures on the Gulf Coast and Flamingo Adventures in the Flamingo area. Either outfitter, and others, will provide you with everything you need to explore the water for a day or more.

Here are some fantastic routes you can take:

→ Follow the five-mile **Sandfly Island Loop** from the Gulf Coast Visitor Center through intercoastal mangrove tree islands, oyster banks, and brackish marine environments. At Sandfly Island, stretch your legs on its one-mile hiking trail.

→ The **Turner River Paddling Trail** travels nearly 10 miles and takes up to seven hours to complete. Access it west of Turner River Road. On the daylong adventure, you'll paddle through the freshwater cypress swamp of Big Cypress National Preserve, filled with—what else—giant cypress trees, as well as sawgrass prairie and mangrove trees.

→ Take the two-mile **Noble Hammock Canoe Trail** through mangrove-lined creeks, shady ponds, and narrow waterways. Find access off the park's main road, and be sure to check water levels before you push out, as things can get low during dry season.

→ **Hells Bay** was given its name because the old-timers used to say the route was

Paddling at sunset with man's best friend

"hell to get into, hell to get out of." Challenge yourself on the marked canoe trail through mangrove creeks and ponds out into the small bay.

→ Look for flamingos and other water-loving birds along the **Mud Lake Canoe Trail**. The seven-mile round-trip route leaves from Coot Bay Pond and takes you through mangroves that connect the Buttonwood Canal, Coot Bay, Mud Lake, and Bear Lake.

Off-the-trail aquatic adventures can be had in the park too. Here are some exceptional ones:

→ The most popular way to see the Everglades is of course by **airboat**. Book through a reliable outfitter like Everglades Safari Park, Gator Park, or Coopertown for a thrilling ride gliding on the water. For the best wildlife spotting, book for the morning in the summer and midday in the winter.

→ The mazes of mangrove-lined creeks and bays through the **Everglades Wil-**derness Waterway are a challenge to navigate, and completing the trip requires serious planning and advice from a ranger. If you finish this trip, which culminates between Flamingo and Everglades City, however, you'll be one of the few.

→ Even visitors who don't feel confident paddling through the water can explore the park by booking a **boat trip** with an outfitter like Everglades Adventures Tours, Everglades Florida Adventures, or Wootens. You'll get the benefit of both a guide and a more experienced boater.

→ Book a **houseboat** from an outfitter like Flamingo Adventures to spend as much time as possible on the water. You'll pick up your home away from land, which sleeps up to four adults, from the backcountry marina at Flamingo.

→ Take Everglades' **free boater education course** online if you're new to the activity or region—or if you plan to use a powerboat. You'll learn how to keep yourself and the ecosystem safe as you explore.

Experts Only

A turquoise-eyed cormorant

An American alligator

S
P
O
T

(T) The vast ecosystems protected in the park lend themselves to a varied world of wildlife. Your best bets to see these creatures will be either from the water or along the park's established boardwalks.

→ Rangers and boat outfitters will be able to give good advice on where creatures are currently swimming. Shallow inland waters—like those visible from the Anhinga Trail and Shark Valley in the spring—are home to **river otters**, while **dolphins** swim around the Florida Bay.

→ If you're looking for **manatees**, you might find them in the waters around Flamingo or inside the tidal creeks. Ask rangers about recent sightings.

→ Bird-watching is excellent in Everglades and will depend on the season and your chosen entrance. From the main entrance near Homestead, check out the Anhinga Trail for **wading birds** and nesting **anhingas** in the winter or Eco Pond to see **ospreys**, **warblers**, **red-shouldered hawks**, and **rails** in the morning. Look for **bald eagles**, **pelicans**, and **shorebirds** near the Gulf Coast Visitor Center, and search out **wood storks**, **snail kites**, and other wading birds from the Shark Valley Tram Road.

→ **American alligators** live throughout Everglades' freshwater swamps and marshes, though you also might spot them in rivers and lakes. In the winter, they'll dig down into alligator holes and are more difficult to see. The best way to spot these prehistoric-looking creatures is on an airboat tour, along the Anhinga Trail, or on a drive through Big Cypress National Preserve.

Shark Valley Loop Road

DRIVE

There's only one road that's open to cars in Everglades: **Main Park Road**. The out-and-back route goes from the Ernest F. Coe Visitor Center to the Guy Bradley Visitor Center in Flamingo and has tons of pullouts for hikes and overlooks. Stop to hike the Anhinga Trail, get views of the "river of grass" from the Pa-hay-Okee platform, check out Sisal and Paurotis Ponds, hike the Snake Bight Trail to a shoreline overlook, and trek the Christian Point Trail.

An entrance to Everglades National Park

P Paddling adventures take the lead in Everglades, but there's more to be done in the park. Bring a bike, a fishing rod, or an inquisitive mind and try one of these activities:

→ Fish for **freshwater** or **saltwater fish** in Everglades with the right license. Bring your own gear or book a trip with one of the many local outfitters. Follow guidelines and warnings, like those about the high levels of mercury in bass and other species.

→ Take the two-hour **Shark Valley Tram Tour** to learn about the history of the park from an expert wildlife guide. Run by a concessionaire from the Shark Valley Visitor Center, it will take you to see alligators, birds, and various observation points, including the 70-foot-tall Shark Valley Observation Tower, with views stretching up to 20 miles on clear days.

→ Hit one of the park's **five cycling trails**. The Shark Valley Tram Road goes past the same observation tower. The Rowdy Bend Trail, an overgrown former road, is a great route for bird-watchers. The Long Pine Key Trail is a 14-mile dirt path that ends at Pine Glades Lake, a great spot for a picnic and to see alligators. The six-mile L-67 Extension Trail is great for bird-spotting in the winter, while the three-mile Snake Bight Trail explores the park's variety of trees.

→ Join a **ranger-led bike program** in the winter, which takes you to a perfect spot to see the full moon or meteor showers.

→ Visit the **HM69 Nike Missile Base**, a Cold War relic shuttered in 1979. Catch a seasonal visitor program to learn more about its history and explore the virtually unchanged base.

Kayaking turquoise waters ahead of a storm

E
X
P
L
O
R
E

Take an off-trail *slough slog* with a park ranger to get an up-close-and-personal look at the Everglades. Reservations are required and can be made at the Ernest F. Coe Visitor Center. The wet hike through the swamplike shallow water takes about two hours and ends in the cypress dome.

A sunset view of Great Smoky Mountains National Park

GREAT SMOKY MOUNTAINS NATIONAL PARK

NORTH CAROLINA & TENNESSEE

ESTABLISHED: June 15, 1934

SIZE: 522,000 acres

VISITORS CENTERS: Sugarlands in the North District, Oconaluftee in the South District, and Cades Cove all have exhibits, seasonal ranger-led programming, and stores. Kuwohi—formerly Clingmans Dome—offers sweeping views on the park's tallest peak, as well as a small bookstore and shop (closed in winter).

TRANSPORTATION: Shuttles (March–October)

DOGS ALLOWED: Only on the Gatlinburg and Oconaluftee River Trails

WHEN TO GO: Spring for shoulder-season crowds; fall for foliage (peaks mid-October to early November) and elk; winter for frozen waterfalls and solitude. Summer is busiest.

CONTACT: 865-436-1200; nps.gov/grsm
107 Park Headquarters Road
Gatlinburg, TN 37738

G Great Smoky Mountains National Park is steeped in human history, from the prehistoric Paleo-Indians who called it home to the early European settlers of the 1800s to the Southern Appalachian community whose culture has permeated its every corner. Its historic structures—found throughout the ridges of forest bordering North Carolina and Tennessee—all tell stories of the people who have traversed its lands and slept in its valleys. The marvels of the park are embedded in its miles and miles of gorgeous trails and its flowing waters. Try not to get overwhelmed by your options. There's no way to lose when it comes to exploring the most popular park in the U.S.

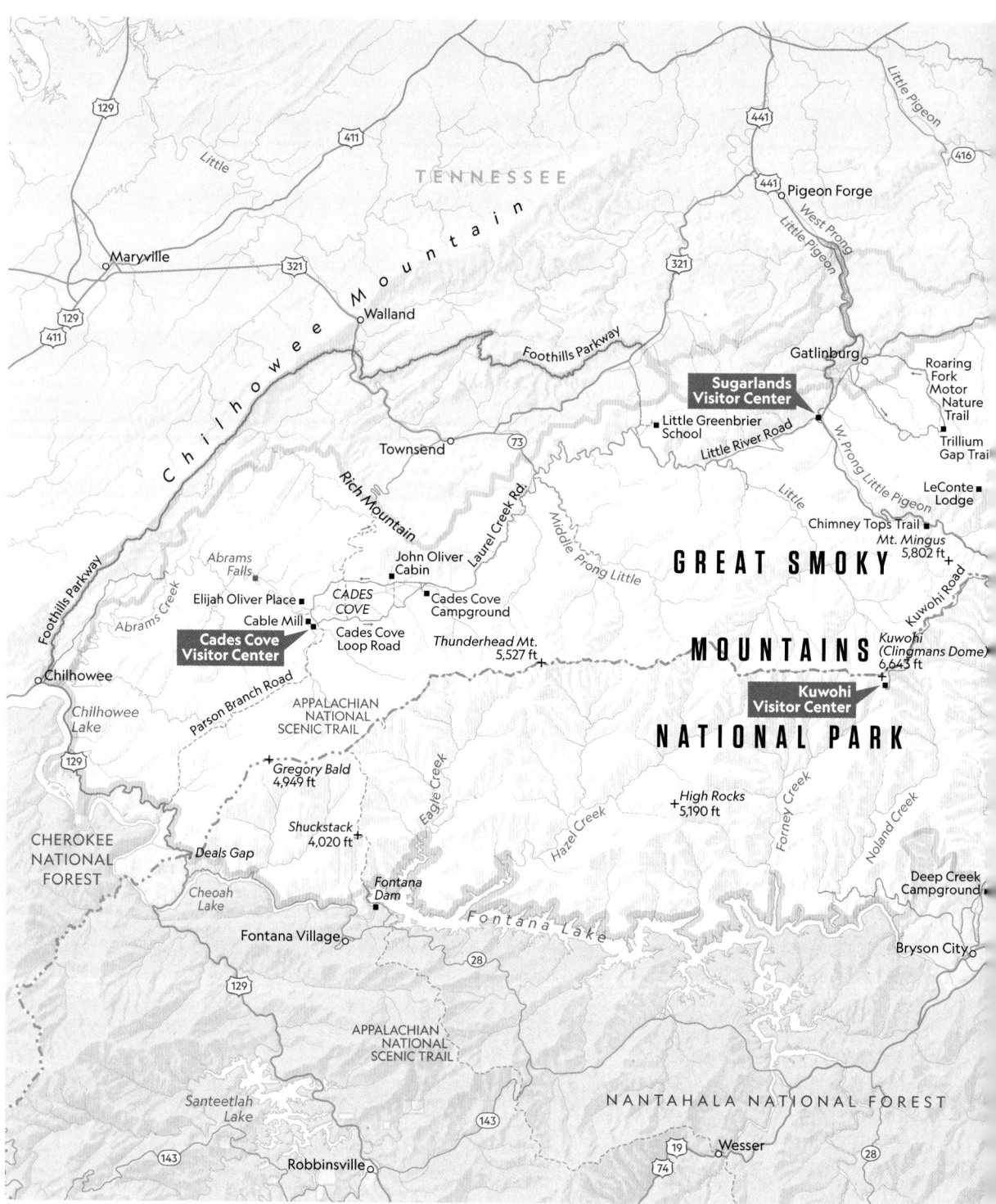

Maryville

TENNESSEE

Little Pigeon

Pigeon Forge

West Prong Little Pigeon

Walland

Foothills Parkway

Gatlinburg

Roaring Fork Motor Nature Trail

Sugarlands Visitor Center

Little Greenbrier School

Little River Road

Trillium Gap Trail

Townsend

Chilhowee Mountain

Rich Mountain

Laurel Creek Rd.

Middle Prong Little

Little

Chimney Tops Trail

Mt. Mingus 5,802 ft

LeConte Lodge

GREAT SMOKY

Abrams Falls

John Oliver Cabin

CADES COVE

Cades Cove Campground

Elijah Oliver Place

Cable Mill

Kuwohi Road

Abrams Creek

Cades Cove Visitor Center

Cades Cove Loop Road

Thunderhead Mt. 5,527 ft

MOUNTAINS

Kuwohi (Clingmans Dome) 6,643 ft

Foothills Parkway

Chilhowee

Parson Branch Road

APPALACHIAN NATIONAL SCENIC TRAIL

Kuwohi Visitor Center

NATIONAL PARK

Chilhowee Lake

Gregory Bald 4,949 ft

Eagle Creek

High Rocks 5,190 ft

Forney Creek

Noland Creek

Shuckstack 4,020 ft

Hazel Creek

CHEROKEE NATIONAL FOREST

Deals Gap

Cheoah Lake

Fontana Dam

Fontana Village

Fontana Lake

Deep Creek Campground

Bryson City

APPALACHIAN NATIONAL SCENIC TRAIL

Santeetlah Lake

NANTAHALA NATIONAL FOREST

Wesser

Robbinsville

The map shows Great Smoky Mountains area with various labels:

CHEROKEE NATIONAL FOREST

Cosby
Foothills Parkway
Pigeon
321
339
Pittman Center
321
Cosby Cr.
32
40
Big Creek Trail
Big Creek
Mouse Creek Falls
PISGAH NATIONAL FOREST

APPALACHIAN NATIONAL SCENIC TRAIL

Ramsey Cascades
Mt. Guyot 6,621 ft
Balsam Mountain

Porters Creek Trail

Cataloochee Creek

Cataloochee Campground
Cove Creek Rd.

Newfound Gap 5,046 ft
Laura Spelman Rockefeller Memorial
Swinging Bridge
Quiet Walkway
Kephart Prong Trail
Newfound Gap Road
Oconaluftee
Raven Fork
Balsam Mt. Rd.
Cataloochee Valley

Heintooga Ridge Road

Bradley Fork Trail
Big Cove Rd.
Blue Ridge Parkway
Black Camp Gap
Maggie Valley

Mingus Mill
19

Oconaluftee Visitor Center
Mountain Farm Museum
CHEROKEE INDIAN RESERVATION (QUALLA BOUNDARY)
441
Cherokee
Soco Creek
Indian Creek Falls
19

NORTH CAROLINA
Blue Ridge Parkway

74
441
Tuckasegee
23 74
Alarka Mountains
Sylva
23
441

5 mi
5 km
N

SLEEP

(S) Staying inside the park at a campsite or hike-in cabin will give you early access to its trails and activities, plus you'll get the benefit of a night (or two) under the stars. If roughing it isn't your style, find a hotel in Gatlinburg, Tennessee, or Cherokee, North Carolina. There are tons of options, from family-friendly hotels to luxurious lodges with spas.

→ Book a cabin ahead of time at **LeConte Lodge**, the highest guest lodge in the eastern U.S., at about 6,400 feet. You'll have to hike one of five trails to the hand-built cabins, where you'll enjoy propane heat, kerosene lanterns, cozy beds, and hearty meals.

→ The park has 10 developed campgrounds. Though none of the sites have showers or hookups, you'll find cold running water, flush toilets, picnic tables, and fire grates. Try **Cades Cove Campground** (year-round, 161 sites) for nearby amenities, **Deep Creek** (open March–October, 92 sites) for access to trails, or **Cataloochee** (open March–October, 27 sites) for quiet. Reservations are required for all three and can be made up to six months in advance.

→ Book a permit through the park's website to **backcountry camp** and then hike along the 800 miles of park trails to find a spot that's safe for you and the environment. Park trail maps show backcountry shelters, but be sure to check in with the rangers before you start your trip.

Hiking in fall with an incredible view

HIKE

H Hiking in Great Smoky Mountains National Park is a treat any time of year, and each season brings a different experience. The dense forests clear in the winter, providing glorious views of peaks and valleys. In the spring, wildflowers cover the rolling fields, and the waterfalls cascade with even more power than usual. Summer hikers find respite in cool streams and under shady spruce-fir canopies, while fall visitors enjoy the changing colors of the trees.

→ Hop on to a portion of the **Appalachian Trail** just past the Rockefeller Memorial. It passes over Newfound Gap Road and follows the state line between Tennessee and North Carolina for most of this length. A little more than 70 miles of the Appalachian Trail cut through the park, offering a great way to experience the trail even if you can't commit to hiking through 14 states.

→ Take the one-mile round-trip **Kuwohi Trail** to the Kuwohi Overlook and the Kuwohi Observation Tower, constructed in 1959. From 45 feet up, you'll be at the highest point in the park as you look out over the Smokies.

→ The **Chimney Tops Trail** gains 1,400 feet of elevation in just two miles, so the steep climb isn't for everyone. The summit isn't open to hikers, but the 3.5-mile hike still brings you up to gorgeous views of Mount Le Conte.

→ Parking is a challenge at the **Roaring Fork Motor Nature Trail**, since the region is popular with both history and waterfall lovers. Get there early to see the fast-flowing stream without the stress of the crowds. After you're done, head over to the **Noah "Bud" Ogle Nature Trail** to see a 19th-century farmstead, including a cabin, tub mill, wooden plumbing system, and barn.

→ A one-mile walk along a portion of the **Porters Creek Trail**, beginning at its trailhead, showcases both the lush forests of the park and its human history. See remnants of old homesteads, stone fences, stairs, a cemetery, a barn, and a cabin from the region's first European settlers. Turn back after a mile, or continue on the 7.2-mile round-trip trail for more.

→ Get a good look at **Ramsey Cascades**, the tallest waterfall in the park, on an eight-mile round-trip hike, which gains almost 2,000 feet in elevation. You'll pass through old-growth forests with silverbells and yellow birches before reaching the towering waterfall.

→ While **Abrams Falls** isn't the park's tallest waterfall, its massive rush of water makes it just as impressive. The lovely five-mile round-trip hike travels through pine-oak and hemlock forests.

→ Hike the **Trillium Gap Trail** through the hemlock forest to eventually wind behind the 25-foot Grotto Falls. The trail begins in the Cherokee Orchard and runs 3.4 miles to the cascade, a moderate hike that ends up in the perfect respite for summer hikers and salamander seekers. Safety tip: Don't try to climb the waterfall or any of its rocky surfaces. Turn back here or continue hiking the full 9.1 miles to Mount Le Conte and its lodge.

→ Walk through history on the four-mile round-trip **Kephart Prong Trail**, which showcases the impact of people on the park from the logging era through the days of the Civilian Conservation Corps. Forests have reclaimed this section, which was heavily logged before the park's establishment.

Must-Do Activity

A buck rests in the grass.

A coyote at Cades Cove

SPOT

(T) The dense forests of Great Smoky Mountains make it easy for wildlife to hide and difficult for you to spot. Still, the region is packed with creatures that thrive in the various ecosystems, so you're bound to see some animals you wouldn't spot at home. Tip: Bring your binoculars.

→ The **American black bear** is the symbol of the Smokies, and many visitors hope to spot one from afar while they are here. It's a possibility, since 1,900 of them live in the park, the largest protected bear habitat in the eastern United States—and they roam at all elevations.

While it's thrilling to see one, keep your distance if you do.

→ Look for **white-tailed deer**, **elk**, **black bears**, **raccoons**, **woodchucks**, and **wild turkeys** in open areas like Cataloochee Valley and Cades Cove. In the winter, you'll have better luck because the barer trees offer less coverage.

→ **Llamas** travel up the Trillium Gap Trail to supply LeConte Lodge a few days a week. Ask the rangers when you might be able to watch them work.

→ The park has been called the "salamander capital of the world," which might seem surprising for a mountain region. Thirty species of **salamanders** live in the park's wet regions, mostly around its cascades and waterfalls.

→ Birders will be full of joy searching for the more than 240 species that call the park home. Keep an eye out for vulnerable ones like the **yellow-bellied sapsucker**, **golden-winged warbler**, **chimney swift**, **belted kingfisher**, **red-headed woodpecker**, and **scarlet tanager**.

T To cover more ground, take a drive through Great Smoky Mountains along the 384 miles of road through the park. The well-traveled and popular stretch offers numerous ways to see the natural landscapes. Two routes in particular will take you to the best vehicle-accessible overlooks and trailheads in the park:

→ *Newfound Gap Road cuts through the middle of the park, from the north entrance near Gatlinburg to the south entrance near Cherokee. Travel the classic mountain route and stop at the Sugarlands Visitor Center, Bullhead View Quiet Walkway (a 1.1-mile out-and-back loop), and overlooks at West Prong Little Pigeon River Bridge (a popular trout stream in the park), Mount Mingus (for picnic areas and views over the plateau), Newfound Gap (at 5,046 feet, the lowest drivable gap in the park), Swinging Bridges (cascading mountain views and nearby access to the Swinging Bridge Quiet Walkway trailhead), and Beech Flats (a great spot for watching the sunset or walking the moderately challenging 1.3-mile out-and-back trail). End at the Oconaluftee Visitor Center.*

→ *Rich Mountain Road will lead you down to the 11-mile* **Cades Cove Loop Road** *to explore the human and natural history of the park. Wednesdays from late spring to early fall are car-free days on the road, allowing for exploration by foot or bicycle. Stop at Whistling Branch (a great spot to see wildlife, including deer and birds of prey, while getting uninterrupted views), Tipton Place (an early 1900s barn once part of a 640-acre homestead within the park), John Oliver Cabin (the oldest log cabin in Cades Cove, dating to 1818), Hyatt Lane (a scenic cut-through), multiple trailheads, and Cades Cove Campground.*

D R I V E

Winding through autumn color

Vibrant displays of color across the mountainside

Horseback riders can use the Bradley Fork Trail.

In a park so steeped with history and natural beauty, there's plenty to add to your trip. Consider these experiences:

→ Visit the **Mountain Farm Museum** to see the historic log buildings once used to support the region's homesteaders. Wander around the log farmhouse, barn, apple house, springhouse, and blacksmith shop—most built in the late 19th century.

→ Stop at the **John Oliver Cabin**, the oldest log house in Cades Cove. It belonged to a family who started homesteading in 1818; the matriarch later said that they survived that first winter only because of the generosity of the Cherokee community. See the home of the family's son at **Elijah Oliver Place**, which includes a corncrib, smokehouse, and barn.

→ Walk across the massive **Fontana Dam**. At 480 feet, it's the tallest concrete dam east of the Rocky Mountains. Impounding the Little Tennessee River, the dam's reserve is massive, at 11,700 acres, with a 240-mile shoreline. This is not your average dam, and it won't be an average trip across it.

→ **Fish** for headwater trout, smallmouth bass, and more in the park's 2,100 miles of streams. With a proper license you can cast a line all year long. Just be sure not to spread "rock snot," the park's gross nickname for the invasive and destructive didymo algae.

→ Bring your camera to capture the fall colors as you drive along **Kuwohi Road**, the **Blue Ridge Parkway**, or the **Foothills Parkway**. Visit in mid-October though early November for the most striking landscapes.

→ Participate in a course on park wildlife, a day hike, or a family activity with the **Smoky Mountain Field School**. The school is part of the educational outreach program at the University of Tennessee, and sessions are run by expert instructors.

→ Join one of the **ranger-led festivals** held at the park, from the Wildflower Pilgrimage (professionally guided walks, exhibits, and learning activities) to the Music of the Mountains (two days of traditional Appalachian music) to the Smokies Harvest Celebrations (interactive farm and homestead demonstrations). Check the park's calendar for schedules.

→ Book a **horseback riding trip** from Cades Cove Riding Stables, Smokemont Riding Stables, or Sugarlands Riding Stables for a one-to-three-hour guided trail ride. If you'd like the experience of a horse-led trip, but don't want to be on horseback, take a two-hour hayride or a 30-minute carriage ride from Cades Cove.

Family Friendly

EXPLORE

Hike **Big Creek Trail** along old railroad grades built to carry lumber out of the forest. First, you'll pass Midnight Hole, a deep pool below small waterfalls, then you'll come upon 45-foot Mouse Creek Falls— the highlight of the hike. Safety tip: Don't climb on the rocks along this four-mile round-trip hike; scrambling along the slick surfaces is dangerous.

Part of the Frozen Niagara section of the cave

MAMMOTH CAVE
NATIONAL PARK

KENTUCKY

ESTABLISHED: July 1, 1941

SIZE: 52,830 acres

VISITORS CENTER: The Mammoth Cave Visitor Center has educational exhibits and is the departure point for many cave tours and a trailhead for forest hikes.

TRANSPORTATION: Green River Ferry (free) and buses (to and from cave entrances and exits)

DOGS ALLOWED: Only on surface trails; dogs are not permitted in the cave.

WHEN TO GO: Summer is busiest but best for stargazing; spring for wildflowers; fall for ranger-led surface programs.

CONTACT: 270-758-2180; nps.gov/maca
1 Visitor Center Parkway
Mammoth Cave, KY 42259

B Buried deep under the surface in Kentucky, Mammoth Cave has 426 miles of mapped passageways, making it the longest cave in the world. This "solution cave" formed when acidic water created passageways in the rocks more than 10 million years ago. Today, Mammoth Cave is a UNESCO World Heritage site and International Biosphere Reserve, with 12 miles of the cave open to the public, as well as a diverse array of aboveground experiences, including hiking through lush forests teeming with wildlife and exploring 72 miles of the Green River, one of North America's most diverse waterways.

SLEEP

If you want to stay inside the park, you have a few choices:

→ **The Lodge at Mammoth Cave** is the park's only non-camping option. Its terrace rooms, historic hotel cottages, and woodland cottages are all close to the visitors center and serve as a great starting point for cave tours and park trails.

→ One of three campgrounds in the park, **Mammoth Cave Campground** is a quarter mile from the visitors center and is staffed by helpful rangers. It offers 111 primitive sites (tent and RV), and reservations are available March 1 to November 30.

→ On the north side of the park, **Maple Springs Group Campground** is more remote and great for large groups, horseback riders, and backcountry hikers looking to hit the park's 70 miles of backcountry trails. There are only seven sites here (all with electric hookups for RVs). Reservations are available March 1 to November 30.

→ Tent campers can stay on the banks of the Green River at **Houchin Ferry Campground**. The rustic site has 12 tent-only sites and portable toilets, but not much else. Reservations are required.

→ If you prefer a less developed camping experience, get a permit for one of the 13 hiking-accessible designated **backcountry sites** or along the Green and Nolin Rivers at boat-accessible **riverside campsites**. Permits are available in advance or through same-day reservations on recreation.gov or at the Mammoth Cave Campground information kiosk.

728

1827

Dennison
Ferry Road

Cub Run

private
land

Green

Lincoln

1827

Double J Stables
and Campground

private land

Ugly Creek

Big
Woods

White Oak

1352

Green River Ferry Rd.

Collie Ridge Trail

Raymer
Hollow
Trail

Ugly Creek Rd.

Goblin Knob
744 ft

White Oak
Trail

Green

Great Onyx
Cave

White Oak

Good Spring
Church

Big Hollow Trail
North Loop

Crystal Cave

Dennison
Ferry Road

CAVE NATIONAL PARK

Great Onyx
Cave Road

Crystal Cave
Road

Maple Springs Group
Campground

Big Hollow Trail
South Loop

Flint Ridge

Mammoth Cave
Baptist Church

Flint Ridge Rd.

Sal Hollow Trail

Green River
Bluffs Trail

Green River Bluffs Overlook
River Styx Spring Trail
Sunset Point

**Mammoth Cave
Visitor Center**

The Lodge at Mammoth Cave

Heritage Trail

Turnhole
Bend Trail

Echo River Spring Trail

Green River
Ferry

Mammoth Cave
Campground

JOPPA RIDGE

Park Ridge Rd.

private land

Turnhole
Bend
Overlook

Turnhole
Spring

Joppa
Church

Doyel Valley
Overlook

Cave City Road

Brownsville Rd.

Mammoth Cave Ridge

Sand Cave
Sand Cave Trail

Turnhole Bend
Nature Trail

Cedar Sink Trail

Cedar Sink

Sloan's Crossing
Pond Walk

Mammoth Cave
Railroad Bike
and Hike Trail

255

Woolsey Valley

Mammoth Cave Parkway

Cedar Sink Road

Pig

70

255

70

Cedar
Spring

private land

Chaumont Road

Cedar Hill Church Rd.

Park City Road

65

259

Chaumont Road

31w

Park City

R Rangers offer a variety of cave tours, depending on season and interest. You can also take a self-guided tour (ticket required), but that option is not always available, so call in advance to see if it's being offered the day of your visit. Remember to avoid flash photography to help protect the cave formations as you explore.

Inside Mammoth Cave

Family Friendly

→ Learn more about the anatomy and science of the cave on the **Domes & Dripstones Tour**. Move through a sinkhole, massive domes, and a dripstone section and see striking stalactites and stalagmites.
→ Use the elevator entrance to emerge near the Snowball Room on the **Mammoth Cave Accessible Tour**. Follow your guide through portions of the cave that avoid any staircases or narrow pass-throughs.
→ Go back in time on the three-hour **Violet City Lantern Tour**. Wind through the cave's broad tunnels by lantern as you walk the steep dirt trails the original cave explorers followed.
→ **Mammoth Passage** is a good choice for small children or anyone who doesn't like tight spaces. See artifacts from historic and prehistoric communities from the walkways in the entrance and large rooms of the cave.
→ The lantern-lit **Star Chamber Tour** runs only in the evening and takes visitors into the historic Star Chamber, once a respite for tuberculosis patients searching for a cure, as well as on a stroll through Gothic Avenue. You'll emerge from the cave at night to see the brilliant stars above.
→ History buffs will enjoy the **Grand Historic Tour**, which takes four hours and covers a number of the cave's must-see points, including the Giant's Coffin (a 1,000-ton boulder) and River Styx (one of two underground rivers).

→ For the most adventurous, the **Introduction to Caving** tour crawls and climbs through some of the cave's more difficult-to-access spots. The journey takes 3.5 hours and requires being comfortable in tight spaces. (Note: No alternative routes are available, so once you start, you're committed.)

S P E L U N K

HIKE

W While many visitors save their walks for inside the cave, plenty of first-rate hikes can be had on the surface.

→ Take the one-mile **Cedar Sink Trail** to a huge collapsed sinkhole. In the spring and summer, see wildflowers bloom along a bit of underground river that has risen to the surface.

→ On the short **Echo River Spring Trail**, you'll make your way to an overlook with a view of the Green River and a large bubbling spring.

→ The 0.4-mile out-and-back **River Styx Spring Trail** brings you from the visitors center to where an underground river springs from Mammoth Cave and into the Green River. If you catch the hike during a high-water moment, the river will flow in the other direction.

→ You have to share the 9.1-mile **Big Hollow Trail** with mountain bikers, but it's a great loop to hike through the woodlands and rocky outcroppings from the Maple Springs Group Campground trailhead.

→ Hike the 8.6-mile **Sal Hollow Trail** through the forest for incredible solitude. Add the 4.4-mile **Buffalo Creek Trail** to your trip for a longer loop. You'll mostly stay under the welcome shade of tree cover. It's also one route where dogs are welcome.

→ See Old Guides Cemetery (the final resting place of Mammoth's earliest cave guides) and Sunset Point on the short **Heritage Trail** loop just south of the visitors center. Time the walk right, and you'll see why that end point got its name.

Venture beyond the cave

A snapping turtle clings to a rock.

T There are three major regions for wildlife spotting in the park: the forest, cave, and water.

→ On the surface, you might see **foxes**, **raccoons**, **mink**, **opossums**, and **quail** as you hike—or perhaps a **copperhead** or **rattlesnake**. From the visitors center, keep an eye out for **white-tailed deer** and **wild turkeys** during the day and **bats** in the evening.

→ Take the raised path of Sloan's Crossing Pond Walk and look for **marsh birds**. There's parking, a picnic area, and an easy loop around a wetland ecosystem that birds love. Definitely bring bug spray.

→ More than 130 life-forms have been found inside the cave at different times, but not all of them call it home. **Eyeless fish** and **crayfish**, however, are full-time residents, along with **cave crickets** that sometimes creep out visitors. Fourteen of the species discovered in the cave are endemic.

→ Get in a kayak or canoe and look for **turtles**, **blue herons**, **river otters**, and any of the 50 species of **mussels** in the park's rivers.

SPOT

Accessible Option

DRIVE

W While there are roads through the park, they're mostly a means of getting from place to place. You'll get your best views on hikes. Still, one drive is worth adding to your list: the **Sand Cave Almanac tour**. You'll join a caravan of other visitors in your own car and drive 5.2 miles from the Sand Cave Trailhead to Mammoth Cave Baptist Church. A ranger will lead you through the various stopping points along the way and share the story of Floyd Collins, who was trapped in the cave in 1925.

A tree-lined view through the park

T The underground cave isn't the only place for spectacular views in the park. Head to one of these four overlooks, accessible by foot or car, to get sweeping views of the landscape.

➜ *Only one overlook in the park is accessible by car. The **Doyel Valley Overlook**, off the Mammoth Cave Parkway, has information panels, a picnic table, and access to the Mammoth Cave Railroad Bike and Hike Trail.*

➜ *At sunset, watch the sky change colors over the valley of the Green River at aptly named **Sunset Point**, off the half-mile-long Heritage Trail.*

➜ ***Turnhole Bend Overlook** is in the middle of a loop trail of the same name and provides great views of the north side of the park—a region accessible only by riding the Green River Ferry.*

➜ *See how the Green River weaves through the park from the **Green River Bluffs Overlook** on the Green River Bluffs Trail. The stop is not just beautiful but a nice break from the hike.*

Green River Ferry

LOOK

T The park is filled with opportunities to connect with nature outside of the cave, whether that's on horseback, at a special ranger-led program, or along its rivers.

→ *Bike the nine-mile **Mammoth Cave Railroad Bike and Hike Trail** from Park City to the Mammoth Cave Parkway and the visitors center. The trail follows a portion of the Mammoth Cave Railroad, which brought visitors to the cave from 1886 to 1931, and stops at historic and natural sites.*

→ *Paddle down the **Green River** and get great views of the wildlife within it, on its shores, and on the bluffs above. The Green River Ferry will also take you across the river if the water is high enough.*

→ *Take part in one of the **park's special programs**, like Wildflower Day or Bat Night, with guided tours, educational talks, children's activities, and evening programs. On Wildflower Day, kids craft their own flowers, and on Bat Night visitors help with data collection.*

→ ***Fishing** is allowed without a license inside Mammoth Cave National Park, as long as you follow Kentucky's fishing guidelines. Green River is a great place to start.*

→ *Bring your own horse to the backcountry trails—try the White Oak Trail for a good one—or book a **horseback riding trip** with Double J Stables and Campground. Your horse can spend the night with you under the stars at Maple Springs Group Campground.*

→ *Bring the family for the **Nature Tracks for Kids program** at the visitors center. Kids will join a ranger to learn about the park's wildlife, cave, and ecosystem.*

Canoeing the Green River

Family Friendly

*Join a six-hour **Wild Cave Tour**, where you'll get to crawl and climb your way through a route chosen by your guide based on interests and abilities. Navigate features like the Bear Hole and the Birth Canal, named for their difficulty. Be sure to adhere to specific clothing and body measurement requirements to participate in this strenuous trek—and book in advance.*

A hiker appreciates the vastness of the gorge.

NEW RIVER GORGE
NATIONAL PARK & PRESERVE
WEST VIRGINIA

ESTABLISHED: December 27, 2020

SIZE: 70,000 acres

VISITORS CENTERS: Canyon Rim Visitor Center, Sandstone Visitor Center, Grandview Visitor Center, and Thurmond Depot Visitor Center

TRANSPORTATION: No in-park transportation

DOGS ALLOWED: Yes, on all trails. Look into the B.A.R.K. Ranger Program.

WHEN TO GO: Late summer through mid-fall for cooler weather and fall foliage

CONTACT: 304-465-0508; nps.gov/neri
104 Main Street
Glen Jean, WV 25846

N New River Gorge National Park & Preserve is named after its most iconic features: the river and the space it has carved into the landscape. The river is one of the oldest on the planet (estimated to be at least 65 million years old) and has drawn deep lines into the mountains and hills around it. It's served as a place for nature-centric adventures, pioneer homesteading, and coal mining—and a visit to the park will inevitably combine its human and natural history.

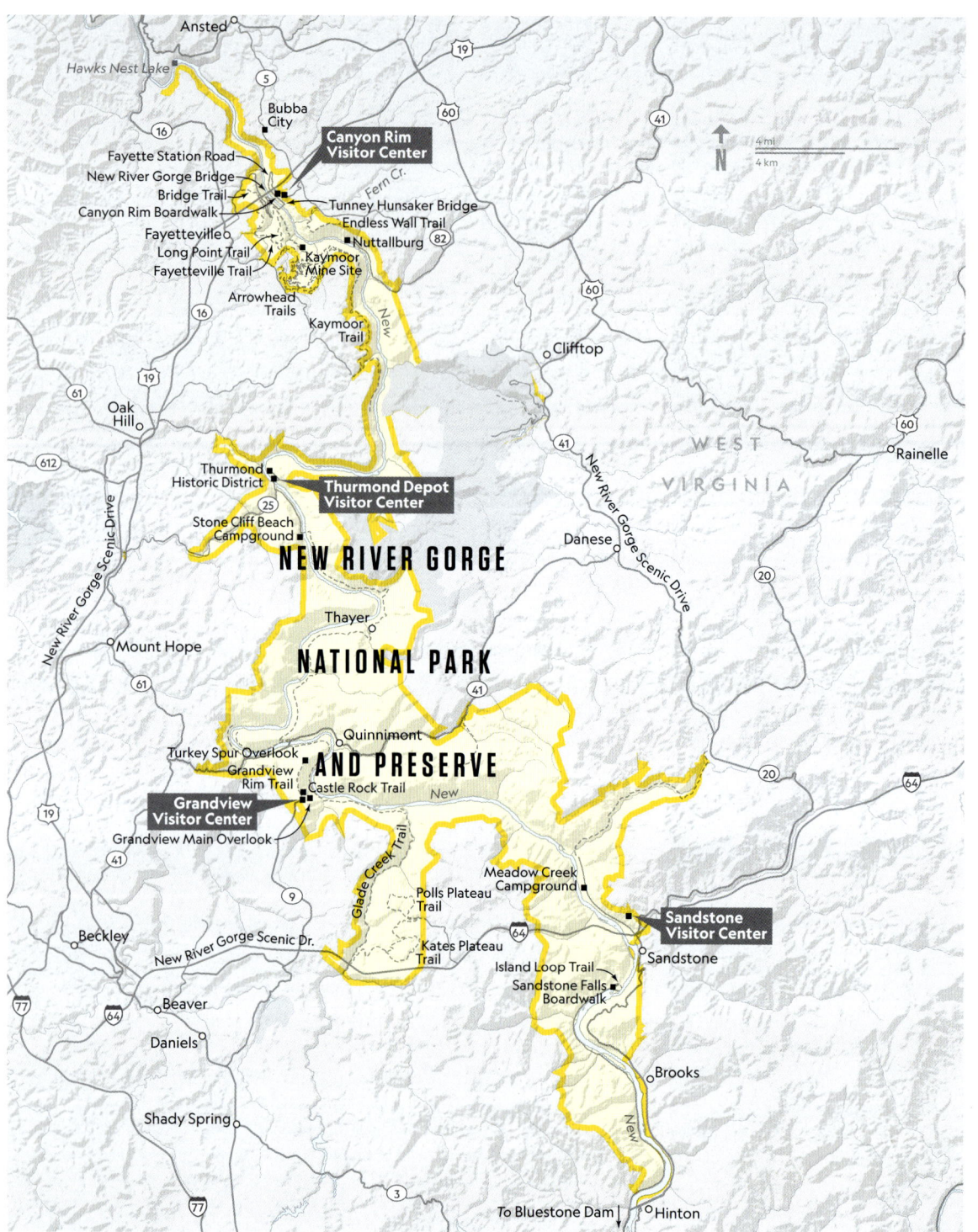

Ansted

Hawks Nest Lake

19

5

16

Bubba City

60

41

N

4 mi
4 km

Fayette Station Road
New River Gorge Bridge
Bridge Trail
Canyon Rim Boardwalk
Fayetteville
Long Point Trail
Fayetteville Trail

Canyon Rim Visitor Center

Fern Cr.

Tunney Hunsaker Bridge
Endless Wall Trail
Nuttallburg

82

Arrowhead Trails

Kaymoor Mine Site

Kaymoor Trail

New

60

Clifftop

61

19

Oak Hill

612

Thurmond Historic District

25

Thurmond Depot Visitor Center

Stone Cliff Beach Campground

NEW RIVER GORGE

41

New River Gorge Scenic Drive

60

Rainelle

WEST
VIRGINIA

Danese

20

New River Gorge Scenic Drive

Mount Hope

61

Thayer

NATIONAL PARK

41

Quinnimont

Turkey Spur Overlook
Grandview Rim Trail
Castle Rock Trail

AND PRESERVE

Grandview Visitor Center

Grandview Main Overlook

19

41

9

Beckley

New River Gorge Scenic Dr.

Glade Creek Trail

Polls Plateau Trail

Kates Plateau Trail

New

20

64

Meadow Creek Campground

64

Sandstone Visitor Center

Island Loop Trail
Sandstone Falls Boardwalk

Sandstone

77

64

Beaver

Daniels

Brooks

Shady Spring

New

77

3

To Bluestone Dam

Hinton

SLEEP

C Camping is the only option if you want to stay within park bounds. Of the eight primitive campgrounds, all but one sit next to the river—and they're all first come, first served. **Meadow Creek Campground** (26 sites, tent only) is just a mile from the Sandstone Visitor Center, while **Stone Cliff Beach Campground** (7 sites, tent only) is just south of the Thurmond Historic District. Find the best backcountry sites along the **Glade Creek**, **Kates Plateau**, and **Polls Plateau Trails**. Reservations and permits are not required for backcountry camping, but be mindful of restricted areas.

If you'd rather not sleep under the stars, find lodging in **Fayetteville**, **Oak Hill**, **Mount Hope**, or **Beckley**.

After a night under the stars, find a kid-perfect hike with a waterfall view.

Must-Do Activity

M Most people head to New River Gorge for the views, the waterfalls, and the trails. There are miles of paths that serve as excellent day hikes:

→ The **Canyon Rim Boardwalk** is a short route to one of the park's most popular overlooks. The first viewpoint is accessible, while a staircase leads down to a lower overlook.

→ The 1.6-mile **Long Point Trail** provides panoramic views of the gorge and the bridge, but first you'll have to navigate a steep hike and unprotected cliffs.

→ Wander through forests, cross Fern Creek, then travel along the edge of a cliff on the 2.4-mile **Endless Wall Trail**. Walk a half mile back along the road or turn around at the Diamond Point overlook and return on the trail.

→ The tough 0.6-mile **Castle Rock Trail** will get you right up against the park's towering rock walls and coal seams. Add the **Grandview Rim Trail** to turn it into a one-mile loop.

→ Follow an abandoned railroad route along the 5.6-mile **Glade Creek Trail**, popular with visitors searching for swimming holes and small waterfalls.

→ The easy **Island Loop Trail**, which starts at the accessible quarter-mile Sandstone Falls Boardwalk, will take you on a half-mile walk around an island just below the falls. Once used for agriculture, the island is now turning back to forest.

HIKE

Family Friendly

A hooded warbler

New River Gorge is all about the river—and for paddlers, it's a true whitewater experience. There are 53 miles of **New River** that flow through the park, beginning just north of the Bluestone Dam and ending at Hawks Nest Lake. The upper portion, which is the southern section, is home to easier rapids, longer pools, and year-long runs. The lower portion, which is the northern section, is packed with massive and difficult rapids. Often called the Lower Gorge, this section has a powerful current, large boulders, and dangerous undercut rocks. Only paddle here with a guide or if you're an experienced kayaker or rafter.

It's possible to paddle the river on your own, but you'd better be well prepared. Intermediate paddlers can tackle the section between Hinton and Thurmond, with its Class I, II, and III rapids. Only expert paddlers should continue downstream from there.

It's best to book a trip with an outfitter, all of which offer one-day or multiday trips. Try Adventures on the Gorge, New & Gauley River Adventures, River Expeditions, or West Virginia Adventures.

SPOT

New River Gorge has long been used as a migration corridor for wildlife, so you're likely to see both creatures on the move and ones endemic to the land.

➜ Look for **warblers**, **vireos**, and **thrushes** with your binoculars, as well as the **peregrine falcon** population that the park has been working to restore.

➜ Abandoned mines provide a safe space for 10 species of **bats**, including two endangered ones: Virginia big-eared and Indiana bats. Just don't enter the mines.

➜ Find **groundhogs**, **raccoons**, **squirrels**, and **white-tailed deer** as you hike—and maybe **beavers**, **mink**, or **river otters** as you paddle. Though **black bears** and **bobcats** live in the park, they're difficult to spot.

Peaceful moments abound on the New River.

FLOAT

Tunney Hunsaker Bridge

Must-Do Activity

DRIVE

T The New River Gorge is a well-connected park, with multiple access points and roads that cut through to various pull-offs, trailheads, and river access points.

→ Steer along the **New River Gorge Scenic Drive**, which goes past many essential park sites, including the Kaymoor Mine Site (closed in 1962), the Grandview Main Overlook (the highest in the park), and Sandstone Falls. The biggest loop connects sites inside and outside park bounds, with offshoot roads into deeper regions. Don't miss the iconic New River Gorge Bridge and the Grandview Road offshoot to the Grandview Main and Turkey Spur Overlooks.

→ Take **Fayette Station Road** from the Canyon Rim Visitor Center for eight miles until you reach U.S. 19. The narrow, hairpin-filled route travels past views of the river, gorge, and New River Gorge Bridge, along with the trailheads for Kaymoor, Fayetteville, and Bridge Trails. Listen to an audio tour of the route by downloading it ahead of time on the National Park Service's mobile app.

→ Drive the **African American Heritage Tour** following the auto tour on the park's app—or get a free CD from a visitors center—to listen to stories of Black coal miners, railroad workers, and community members. You'll make stops at sites in Summers, Raleigh, Fayette, and Nicholas.

G Get a deeper perspective on the natural and human history of the park with these adventures:

→ Tackle some of the park's more than 1,400 established **rock-climbing routes**. Many of these are best for experienced climbers, with most sports routes coming in at 5.10 to 5.12. Popular spots include the Endless Wall, Kaymoor, South Nuttall Wall, and Bubba City.

→ Explore the **Thurmond Historic District**, a mostly untouched town that flourished in the early 1900s with the mines. The train depot saw as many as 75,000 passengers a year before the mines started to close. Follow the walking tour to see the best of the town.

→ Bike the 12.8-mile loops of the **Arrowhead Trails**, built by the Boy Scouts of America. These four loops—the Clovis, Adena, Dalton, and LeCroy Trails—vary in difficulty and width, but all offer exceptional views.

→ Participate in a festival at the park. The **Spring Nature Fling** celebrates the start of the season with free art exhibits, trail walks, naturalist courses, and full-moon hikes. **Hidden History Happenings** in the fall honors Appalachian heritage with living history demonstrations, nature hikes, hands-on activities, and night-sky story times.

→ Get a **fishing license** and send out a line for bass, walleye, crappie, bluegill, carp, and more. Just be familiar with catch-and-release rules before you start.

→ Learn some history at **Nuttallburg**, a restored coal mining complex. It was leased by Henry Ford for his steel mills, became the workplace of historian Carter Godwin Woodson, and was the advocacy location of Mother Jones.

→ Celebrate **Bridge Day** on the third Saturday of October. Visitors walk the New River Gorge Bridge to honor its 1977 completion as the longest single-span arch bridge in the Western Hemisphere. No bikes, carts, strollers, or pets are allowed. You might also spot BASE jumpers or rappellers while you're there.

EXPLORE

Family Friendly

Spend a **backcountry overnight trip** in the park by starting at the Bridge Trail and then linking up with other trails in the loop system as you hike. Eventually either head down to the river or into Fayetteville.

A break in the clouds illuminates a Shenandoah hillside.

SHENANDOAH
 NATIONAL PARK

VIRGINIA

ESTABLISHED: December 26, 1935

SIZE: 199,000 acres

VISITORS CENTERS: The Harry F. Byrd Sr. Visitor Center (south end, year-round) provides ranger programs, park information, ranger advice, and maps. The Dickey Ridge Visitor Center (north end, seasonal) provides trip advice, a bookstore, and maps.

TRANSPORTATION: No in-park transportation

DOGS ALLOWED: Check individual trail regulations.

WHEN TO GO: Fall for foliage (peak is typically third week of October); spring for wildflowers; summer is busiest, so book early.

CONTACT: 540-999-3500; nps.gov/shen
21073 Skyline Drive
Front Royal, VA 22630

Once you step foot in Shenandoah National Park, you'd never believe you're just 75 miles from bustling Washington, D.C. You'll be met with dense forests, flowing waterfalls, towering mountaintops with rocky slopes and sheer walls, and vast meadows packed with colorful wildflowers.

The land has been occupied by people for at least 9,000 years, starting with Native American communities who hunted and gathered on Shenandoah's slopes and continuing with European settlers who moved to the foothills in the 1750s. Eventually, people were pushed out for mining and mill operations, and others started to build resorts in the space. Keen on creating a national park, Virginia state officials acquired 1,088 privately owned stretches of land and resettled around 465 families. The park was designated in December 1935 and received its dedication from President Franklin Roosevelt on July 3, 1936.

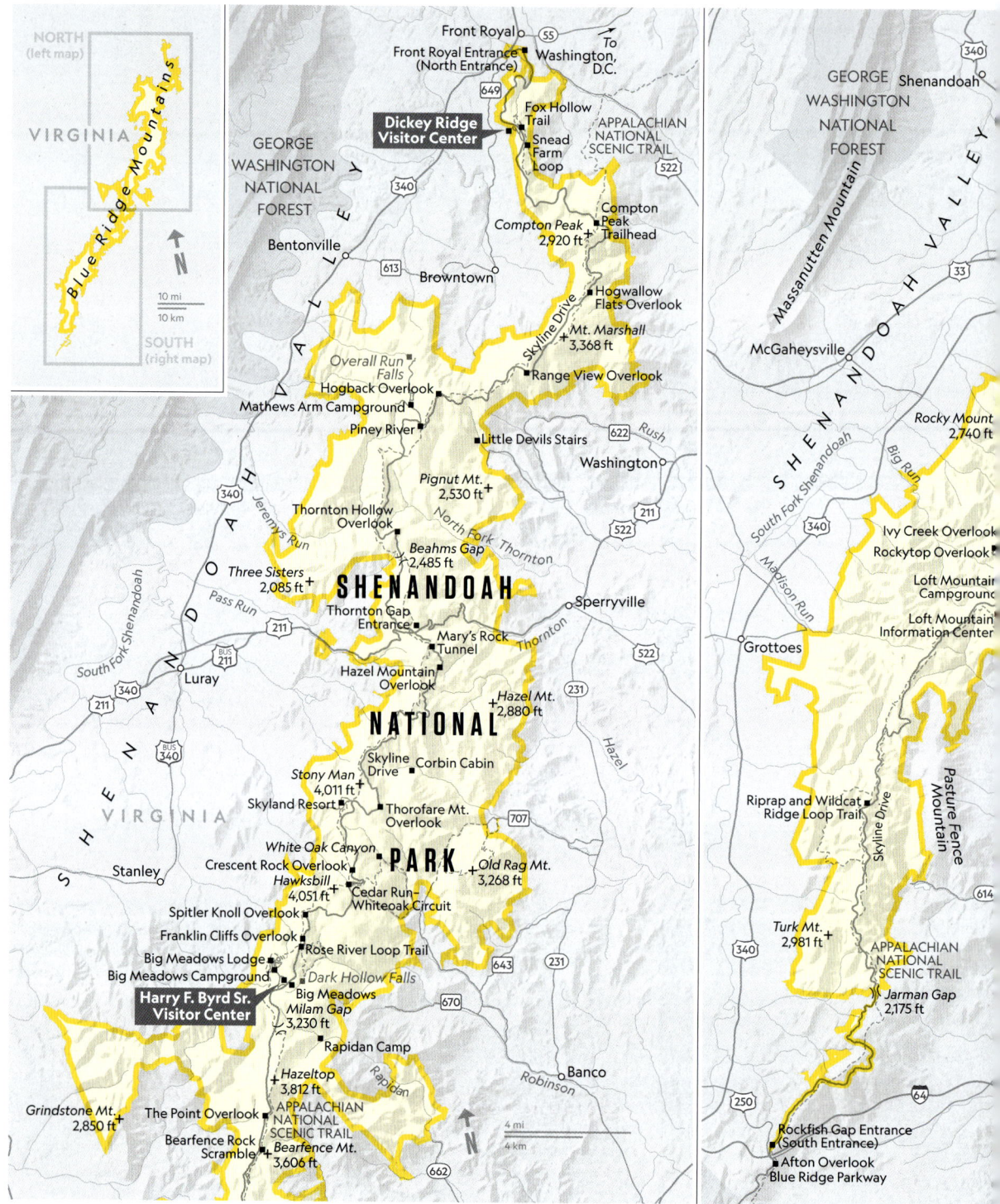

NORTH
(left map)

VIRGINIA

Blue Ridge Mountains

10 mi
10 km

SOUTH
(right map)

N

Front Royal

55

To
Washington,
D.C.

Front Royal Entrance
(North Entrance)

649

Fox Hollow
Trail

Dickey Ridge
Visitor Center

Snead
Farm
Loop

522

APPALACHIAN
NATIONAL
SCENIC TRAIL

GEORGE
WASHINGTON
NATIONAL
FOREST

340

Compton
Peak
Trailhead

Compton Peak
2,920 ft

Bentonville

613

Browntown

340

Hogwallow
Flats Overlook

Mt. Marshall
3,368 ft

Skyline Drive

Range View Overlook

Overall Run
Falls

Hogback Overlook

Mathews Arm Campground

Piney River

Little Devils Stairs

622

Rush

Washington

Pignut Mt.
2,530 ft

211

340

Jeremys Run

Thornton Hollow
Overlook

North Fork Thornton

Beahms Gap
2,485 ft

522

Three Sisters
2,085 ft

SHENANDOAH

Thornton Gap
Entrance

Sperryville

522

Pass Run

211

Mary's Rock
Tunnel

Thornton

South Fork Shenandoah

340

BUS
211

Luray

Hazel Mountain
Overlook

Hazel Mt.
2,880 ft

231

NATIONAL

BUS
340

Skyline
Drive

Corbin Cabin

Hazel

VIRGINIA

Stony Man
4,011 ft

Skyland Resort

Thorofare Mt.
Overlook

707

Stanley

White Oak Canyon

Crescent Rock Overlook

Hawksbill
4,051 ft

Cedar Run–
Whiteoak Circuit

PARK

Old Rag Mt.
3,268 ft

Spitler Knoll Overlook

Franklin Cliffs Overlook

Rose River Loop Trail

Big Meadows Lodge

Big Meadows Campground

Dark Hollow Falls

Harry F. Byrd Sr.
Visitor Center

Big Meadows

Milam Gap
3,230 ft

643

670

231

Rapidan Camp

Banco

Hazeltop
3,812 ft

Rapidan

Robinson

Grindstone Mt.
2,850 ft

The Point Overlook

APPALACHIAN
NATIONAL
SCENIC TRAIL

Bearfence Rock
Scramble

Bearfence Mt.
3,606 ft

4 mi
4 km

N

662

GEORGE
WASHINGTON
NATIONAL
FOREST

Shenandoah

340

Massanutten Mountain

SHENANDOAH VALLEY

McGaheysville

33

Rocky Mount
2,740 ft

South Fork Shenandoah

Big Run

Ivy Creek Overlook

Rockytop Overlook

340

Madison Run

Loft Mountain
Campground

Loft Mountain
Information Center

Grottoes

Pasture Fence Mountain

Skyline Drive

Riprap and Wildcat
Ridge Loop Trail

614

Turk Mt.
2,981 ft

340

APPALACHIAN
NATIONAL
SCENIC TRAIL

Jarman Gap
2,175 ft

250

64

Rockfish Gap Entrance
(South Entrance)

Afton Overlook

Blue Ridge Parkway

A tent perched on a granite formation on Old Rag Mountain

SLEEP

T There are plenty of places to stay within the bounds of Shenandoah, from modern, luxurious lodges to comfortable, cozy cabins to wildflower-covered campsites. Here are a few in-park choices:

→ Book a site at one of the park's campgrounds. **Mathews Arm** (165 sites, reservations and first come, first served available) is closest to its northern entrance, and there's a camp shop just two miles away. **Big Meadows** (221 sites, reservations only) provides easy access to many of the most popular spots, while **Lewis Mountain** (30 sites, first come, first served)—which once served as a segregated site for African American visitors—provides more solitude, despite its convenient location. **Loft Mountain** (207 sites, reservations and first come, first served available) rests atop Big Flat Mountain and provides excellent views

and nearby waterfalls. All four close in the winter; dates vary by year so check the park's website.

→ Stay at a lodge room or a cabin at **Skyland Resort**, where 28 buildings sit along Skyline Drive's highest elevation at miles 41.7 and 42.5. There's also a tap-room, restaurant, and store on-site. Bonus: Some of the rooms are pet friendly.

→ Just a mile from the grassy meadows along Skyline Drive, the rooms and cabins at **Big Meadows Lodge** are perfect for stargazing. Stop at mile 51 to find the site, and enjoy the restaurant, taproom, and craft shop while you're there.

→ **Lewis Mountain Cabins** are a modern way to experience the park without many frills. There are comfortable beds and a shop, but there's no Wi-Fi or restaurant. Entertainment consists of the views of the Blue Ridge Mountains and a firepit.

→ Rent one of the primitive cabins around the park run by the **Potomac Appalachian Trail Club**. They have beds, blankets, and cookware, along with pit toilets. Book ahead to be sure you get a spot.

→ Plan a **backcountry camping trip** among the thousands of acres of wilderness. The park has published lists of suggested itineraries, though you're welcome to build your own. Permits must be purchased in advance online via recreation.gov.

Hikers pause amid the splendor.

Sunrise from Old Rag Mountain

T There are more than 500 miles of trails throughout the park. Whatever your preference, from an easy stroll through wildflower meadows to a strenuous hike up rocky peaks, you'll find something that either pushes or rejuvenates you.

→ The 1.2-mile **Fox Hollow Trail** provides an opportunity for a leisurely walk through a bit of the park's human history. Pass historic rock walls, a cemetery, and periwinkles that were planted by former residents. Catch the trailhead at mile 4.6, near the Dickey Ridge Visitor Center.

→ About 100 miles of the **Appalachian Trail** weave through Shenandoah; hop on and off along the Blue Ridge Mountains. Much of the trail follows Skyline Drive, so it has relatively easy access points.

HIKE

→ Hike the four-mile **Rose River Loop Trail** at mile 49.4 to stunning views of the 67-foot-tall Dark Hollow Falls. When you get there, walk the Dark Hollow Falls Trail down its base and back.

→ Find outstanding views of the Shenandoah Valley at the end of the **Bearfence Rock Scramble** at mile 56.4. The adventurous 1.4-mile round-trip hike takes you up 311 feet of a steep, rocky route before returning back along the Appalachian Trail.

→ Hiking the 9.8-mile **Riprap and Wildcat Ridge Loop Trail** at mile 90 is an incredible feat. On it, you'll gain 2,365 feet of elevation as you move through forests, over stream crossings, and up to panoramic views of the valleys.

→ Getting to the summit of **Old Rag Mountain** is a must-do for many park visitors and locals alike. Take the difficult Old Rag Circuit, with its rock scrambles, or head up the summit via Berry Hollow, which avoids the more challenging boulders. Try it on a weekday morning to avoid the crowds.

→ Challenge yourself to hike the 8.1-mile **Cedar Run–Whiteoak Circuit**. It takes you up 2,794 feet of elevation from mile 45.6 and past six stunning waterfalls.

Experts Only

T Though early explorers reported a vast array of wildlife in what is now Shenandoah, most populations have steadily diminished over time. American bison were eliminated by hunting around 1798; the same with elk in 1855. There were once large groups of eastern timber wolves, eastern cougars, and turkeys too. Don't lose hope—today the space is still a refuge for wildlife, just of a different ilk. Patience will bring them to your sight line.

An endangered Shenandoah salamander

→ *Bird-watchers should stop at Beahms Gap, where the Appalachian Trail crosses Skyline Drive, to look for* **indigo buntings** *and* **rose-breasted grosbeaks** *in the summer, then* **eastern towhees**, **sparrows**, *and* **warblers** *in the fall.*
→ *See wildlife wandering the park as you do, including* **white-tailed deer**, **spotted skunks**, *and* **black bears**. *Though you're more likely to see a gray squirrel than a bobcat, it's possible that with a little luck and patience, you'll come across creatures you won't find at home.*
→ **Big Meadows** *is a gathering place for park wildlife and visitors. The colorful field provides respite for insects and birds just as it does for travelers. It's also a great spot for night-sky viewing, and you never know what creatures will arrive once the sun goes down.*

SPOT

Black bears near the Pinnacles area of Skyline Drive

DRIVE

(S) **Skyline Drive**, which was first constructed by the Civilian Conservation Corps in the 1930s, runs about 100 miles north to south through the park. It's a popular route for both hikers headed to a trailhead and for drivers, motorcyclists, and cyclists who want to take in gorgeous views on a long, uninterrupted route.

Along Skyline Drive, there are frequent overlooks and trailheads—too many to list. A few to note: The Compton Peak Trailhead will take you to some interesting columnar jointing, while hiking up to the Stony Man summit will provide panoramas over Shenandoah Valley. Imagine what it would be like to ranch on this land at Spitler Knoll Overlook. Meanwhile, the Rockytop Overlook provides views of endless rolling peaks. Bring the camera to Hogwallow Flats, Range View, Hogback, Thornton Hollow, Hazel Mountain, Thorofare Mountain, Crescent Rock, Franklin Cliffs, The Point, and Ivy Creek.

Fall delivers peak golden color on a section of Skyline Drive.

Climbers attempt Old Rag Mountain.

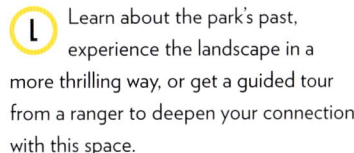
Learn about the park's past, experience the landscape in a more thrilling way, or get a guided tour from a ranger to deepen your connection with this space.

→ Get a history lesson at **Rapidan Camp**, a rustic complex built by President Herbert Hoover and First Lady Lou Henry Hoover while they were serving in the White House. Now a national historic landmark, it provides the same respite they sought, especially when fall colors are changing.

→ Drive through **Mary's Rock Tunnel**, a 670-foot rugged throughway carved into the rock to allow for the path of Skyline Drive.

→ Explore the farming history of this landscape as you wander through a former apple orchard on the 3.7-mile **Snead Farm Loop**. Take the loop off the Dickey Ridge Trail.

→ **Rock climbing** is popular in Shenandoah, and there are routes to fit nearly every skill level. Just review and follow the rock-climbing guidelines set by the park. Try Bearfence Rock Scramble, White Oak Canyon, or Old Rag.

→ Rangers at Shenandoah run a full schedule of **programming**, especially in the spring and summer months. Catch educational wildlife talks, guided hikes, porch talks, meadow walks, evening programs, and star parties. Check the seasonal posting or calendar.

→ Bring your own horse or book a **horseback riding tour** from Skyland Resort with the official park concessionaire. There are 180 miles of trails open to horses, and these guided tours take you past the Limberlost area through an old apple orchard.

Skyline Drive at mile marker 32

E
X
P
L
O
R
E

Experience Shenandoah's night sky at
Big Meadows *in the center of the park. A lot of the*
park is forest, so this is one spot to get fantastic
views of the stars without leaves in the way.
Attend the annual Night Sky Festival in August
to look through telescopes with park rangers, who
will educate visitors on constellations and other
night-sky trivia.

Sunrise at Trunk Bay

VIRGIN ISLANDS
NATIONAL PARK

U.S. VIRGIN ISLANDS

ESTABLISHED: August 2, 1956

SIZE: 15,000 acres

VISITORS CENTERS: The Cruz Bay Visitor Center is open year-round during weekday mornings and offers educational exhibits, trip advice, and tour planning. There are also facilities at Trunk Bay.

TRANSPORTATION: Ferry or the VITRAN bus system will get you in and out of the park.

DOGS ALLOWED: Leashed dogs allowed on certain trails; dogs are not allowed on beaches.

WHEN TO GO: Winter through spring for less rainfall and milder temperatures

CONTACT: 340-776-6201; nps.gov/viis
1300 Cruz Bay Creek
St. John, VI 00830

T There's more to the Virgin Islands than white, sandy beaches—though you shouldn't deny yourself the enjoyment of that particular wonder while you're there. Go deeper by learning about the human history of the park, the hidden world of a coral reef beneath its waves, and the patterns of the migratory birds visiting the islands. A trip to the park brings a powerful combination of exhilaration and relaxation.

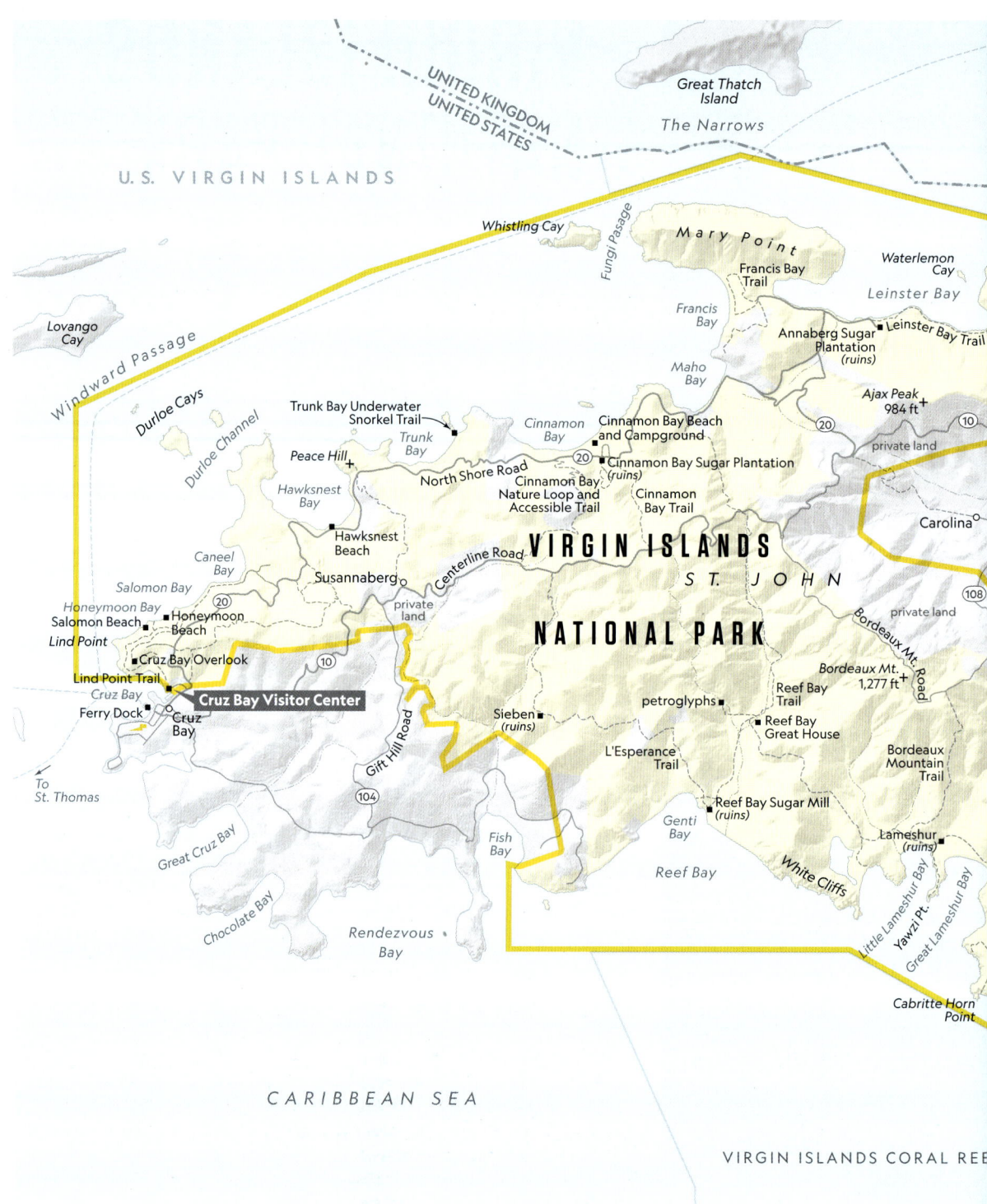

UNITED KINGDOM
UNITED STATES

Great Thatch
Island

The Narrows

U.S. VIRGIN ISLANDS

Whistling Cay

Mary Point

Fungi Passage

Francis Bay
Trail

Waterlemon
Cay

Leinster Bay

Francis
Bay

Annaberg Sugar
Plantation
(ruins)

Leinster Bay Trail

Lovango
Cay

Windward Passage

Durloe Cays

Durloe Channel

Trunk Bay Underwater
Snorkel Trail

Peace Hill +

Hawksnest
Bay

Caneel
Bay

Salomon Bay

Honeymoon Bay

Salomon Beach

Lind Point

Cruz Bay Overlook

Lind Point Trail

Cruz Bay

Ferry Dock

Cruz
Bay

To
St. Thomas

Maho
Bay

Cinnamon
Bay

Trunk
Bay

North Shore Road

Cinnamon Bay
Nature Loop and
Accessible Trail

Hawksnest
Beach

Susannaberg

private
land

Honeymoon
Beach

Centerline Road

Cruz Bay Visitor Center

Gift Hill Road

104

Great Cruz Bay

Chocolate Bay

Rendezvous
Bay

Cinnamon Bay Beach
and Campground

Cinnamon Bay Sugar Plantation
(ruins)

Cinnamon
Bay Trail

Ajax Peak
984 ft +

20

private land

Carolina

10

108

VIRGIN ISLANDS

ST. JOHN

NATIONAL PARK

Bordeaux Mt. Road

private land

petroglyphs

Sieben
(ruins)

L'Esperance
Trail

Fish
Bay

Genti
Bay

Reef Bay

Reef Bay
Trail

Bordeaux Mt. +
1,277 ft

Reef Bay
Great House

Reef Bay Sugar Mill
(ruins)

White Cliffs

Bordeaux
Mountain
Trail

Lameshur
(ruins)

Little Lameshur Bay

Yawzi Pt.

Great Lameshur Bay

Cabritte Horn
Point

CARIBBEAN SEA

VIRGIN ISLANDS CORAL REE

Map Labels

Frenchman
Cay

Little Thatch
Island

BRITISH VIRGIN ISLANDS

SIR FRANCIS DRAKE CHANNEL

VIRGIN ISLANDS CORAL REEF
NATIONAL MONUMENT

U.K.
U.S.

Johnny Horn
Trail

Brown
Bay

Brownsbay ■
(ruins)

Brown Bay Trail

Hermitage

private
land

Princess Bay

Gowed Point

10

Coral
Bay

Palestina

Hurricane
Hole

Fortsberg
+ 426 ft

Round Bay

East End

Coral Bay

VIRGIN ISLANDS
CORAL REEF
NAT. MON.

107

Calabash Boom

Sabbat Channel

Leduck Island

Minna Hill
+ 989 ft

Johns Folly

1 mi

N

1 km

Salt Pond
Bay Trail

Salt Pond Beach

Saltpond Bay

Salt
Pond

Eagle Shoal

Ram Head
Trail

Flanagan Passage

Ram Head

NATIONAL MONUMENT

Cinnamon Bay ruins

SLEEP

R Reserve a site ahead of time to stay at **Cinnamon Bay Beach and Campground**, which reopened in 2022 after a post-hurricane rebuild. Rent a cottage or a family-size eco-tent, a tented platform, or a bare platform for your own tent. The campground hosts a restaurant and has water sport equipment rentals. You'll also have easy access to the Cinnamon Bay Nature Loop and Accessible Trail, which will take you through the ruins of the Cinnamon Bay Sugar Plantation and the white beaches of the bay. Reservations are recommended, and there is a two-night minimum.

Outside the park, you'll find lots of lodging options, from budget hotels to luxury resorts. Take your pick of places on **St. John** or **St. Thomas**.

(H) Hiking is a great way to get from beach to beach, experience the history of the island, and wander through its natural wonders.

→ Take the **Lind Point Trail** from the back of the visitors center to Honeymoon Beach. Travel the lower loop to get to Salomon Beach first, then take the upper loop to stop at the Cruz Bay Overlook.

→ Hiking the **Reef Bay Trail** is not an easy task, with its steep, uneven, and slippery pathways. Still, it's worth the effort to explore the Danish sugar plantation ruins, waterfalls and pools, stone walls from cattle grazing, and ancient petroglyphs of Taino Indians. Take a ranger-led tour to get even more details.

→ While the 1.9-mile out-and-back **Leinster Bay Trail** is popular, hiking it early in the day will provide some solitude and peace. The coastline trail is rocky but flat.

→ Bring your dogs on the 2.8-mile out-and-back **Ram Head Trail**, which is a moderate route across the sandy and rocky coastline. Access the trail from the Salt Pond Bay Trail and hike up 200 feet to get gorgeous ocean views from the cliffs. Don't forget a hat and sunscreen.

→ Weave through the historic Cinnamon Bay Sugar Plantation on the **Cinnamon Bay Nature Loop and Accessible Trail** and the **Cinnamon Bay Trail**, both of which are accessed across from the campground. The loop is easier—and a great spot to look for birds—while the trail is a more challenging route. Both take you past the plantation ruins.

H
I
K
E

A ranger-led hike on St. John

The Ram Head Trail at Salt Pond Beach

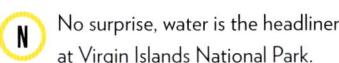

Snorkeling Trunk Bay

→ FLOAT

N No surprise, water is the headliner at Virgin Islands National Park.

→ Swim off any of the soft sandy beaches in the park, like the ones in **Salomon** and **Honeymoon Bays** with their several species of coral just steps from the shore.

→ Take a swimming and snorkeling trip to the calm waters of **Saltpond Bay**. After enjoying the beach and looking for green sea turtles and stingrays, walk the short trail to the salt pond and listen for the local birds.

→ Travel the **Trunk Bay Underwater Snorkel Trail** and read the underwater signs about the wildlife in the coral that you're seeing and lessons on protecting the reef.

→ **Waterlemon Cay** is packed with blue chromis fish, sea turtles, and gorgonian coral. Grab your snorkel and move seamlessly between the coral and seagrass to see different marine creatures. Stick to the south side for the best experience.

→ Take your four-wheel-drive vehicle out to **Great Lameshur Bay** and **Little Lameshur Bay**. The little bay is sandy, and Yawzi Point, which separates the two, is a perfect snorkeling spot. Find fish and other creatures hanging out along the rocky coral shore.

→ **Cinnamon Bay**, the longest beach on St. John, is great for swimming and snorkeling. You'll have plenty of sandy spots to yourself, and when you decide to jump in to find wildlife, you'll have good

luck at the small cay with lobsters, snappers, and other fish.

→ If you're set on swimming with sea turtles, bring your snorkel to **Maho Bay**, where they often float through the grass. Give the turtles their space, and remember: Do not touch.

→ Snorkeling at **Francis Bay** is an experience in excess—and great for beginners. You'll likely see sea turtles, pelicans, and large fish chasing smaller ones. There are also gorgonians, tube sponges, and colonial anemones.

→ A few **scuba diving** moorings are in the park. Eagle Shoal is a nice location for beginner divers, with its tunnels, caves, and arches, or dive at Lind Point, Whistling Cay, or Cabritte Horn Point.

*Family
Friendly*

DRIVE

Only one drive is truly worth a day trip in the park. Travel **North Shore Road** between the Cruz Bay Visitor Center and the split between the Annaberg Sugar Plantation and Francis Bay. Stop at the overlooks on the Lind Point Trail, at Caneel Bay and Trunk Bay, up the trail at Peace Hill, and along Maho Bay Beach.

The windmill tower ruins at Annaberg Sugar Plantation historic site

Sea kayaking Cinnamon Bay

E X P L O R E

H Hiking, swimming, and snorkeling are the main attractions in the park, but other activities will add more depth to your discovery.

→ *Take some time to understand the history of St. John. Walk the* **Annaberg Sugar Plantation***, where 600 enslaved people once lived and worked. It's now part of the National Underground Railroad Network to Freedom, since many people used the bay to escape captivity.*

→ *Hike with a ranger along the* **Reef Bay Trail***. The experience takes all day, and you'll get intimate insights into the cultural and natural history of the region. At the end, you'll take a 40-minute boat ride back to the Cruz Bay Visitor Center.*

→ *Rent a kayak and set off at* **Princess Bay***. Paddle through the mangroves that serve as fish nurseries and jump out to snorkel at certain spots along the way.*

→ *Book a* **fishing trip** *with a local outfitter, of which there are many. Fish offshore for yellowfin and skipjack tuna, mahi-mahi, white marlin, and more—or inshore for barracuda, rainbow runner, yellowtail snapper, and more.*

→ ***Gaze at the stars*** *with an experienced ranger at Cinnamon Bay Beach and Campground. Get educated on the constellations, celestial bodies, and the impact of light pollution on these views.*

Snorkel at **Hawksnest Bay** to avoid crowds and get an intimate look at fragile and federally protected elkhorn coral. There's easy parking if you get there in the morning, since it's not quite as popular as other spots. There's also a sandy beach with good shade and amenities for visitors, like bathrooms and picnic tables.

→ MIDWEST

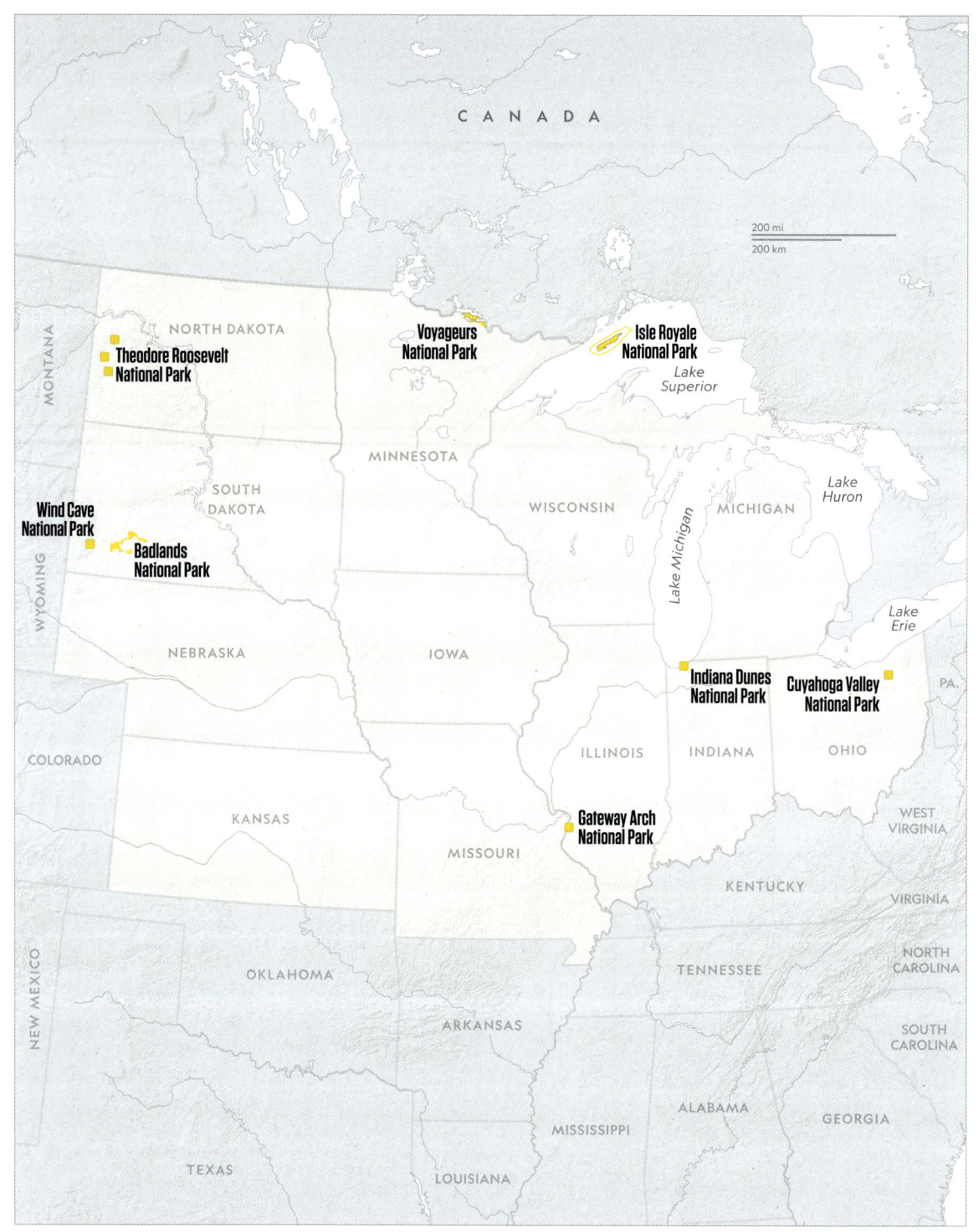

CANADA

200 mi
200 km

MONTANA

NORTH DAKOTA

Theodore Roosevelt
National Park

Voyageurs
National Park

Isle Royale
National Park

Lake
Superior

MINNESOTA

WISCONSIN

MICHIGAN

Lake
Huron

Wind Cave
National Park

SOUTH
DAKOTA

Badlands
National Park

WYOMING

Lake Michigan

Lake
Erie

NEBRASKA

IOWA

Indiana Dunes
National Park

Cuyahoga Valley
National Park

PA.

COLORADO

ILLINOIS

INDIANA

OHIO

WEST
VIRGINIA

KANSAS

MISSOURI

Gateway Arch
National Park

KENTUCKY

VIRGINIA

NEW MEXICO

OKLAHOMA

TENNESSEE

NORTH
CAROLINA

ARKANSAS

SOUTH
CAROLINA

TEXAS

MISSISSIPPI

ALABAMA

GEORGIA

LOUISIANA

The eight parks of the Midwest offer a variety of experiences, some urban, like Gateway Arch in St. Louis (page 158), and others more rugged and otherworldly. Ohio's Cuyahoga Valley (page 150) provides easy access to the natural world right in Cleveland's backyard. Meanwhile, the seashell-hued buffs of South Dakota's Badlands (page 140) reveal layers of sedimentary history. These wilds so inspired President Theodore Roosevelt, he decided to dedicate himself to conservation, and his legacy endures in the North Dakota park that bears his name (page 186). At Wind Cave (page 208), bison roam and graze more than 30,000 acres of pine forest and prairie land. Meanwhile, scores of streams and lakes lace through Voyageurs (page 198).

LEFT: White River Valley Overlook, Badlands National Park (page 140) **PREVIOUS PAGES:** Little Missouri River, Theodore Roosevelt National Park (page 186)

Big Badlands Overlook at sunrise

BADLANDS NATIONAL PARK

SOUTH DAKOTA

ESTABLISHED: November 10, 1978

SIZE: 244,300 acres

VISITORS CENTERS: The Ben Reifel Visitor Center, open year-round, provides educational exhibits, ranger advice, and a theater. The White River Visitor Center, on the Pine Ridge Reservation, is staffed in the summer.

TRANSPORTATION: No in-park transportation

DOGS ALLOWED: Only in developed areas (no hiking trails or backcountry) and on leash

WHEN TO GO: April–May or September to avoid the hottest and busiest months; in winter, while it's magical to see the park dusted with snow, prepare for extreme cold and road closures.

CONTACT: 605-433-5361; nps.gov/badl
25216 Ben Reifel Road
Interior, SD 57750

T The geology and archaeology of Badlands National Park link past and present in a way that's rare to find. You'll be hiking the same trails that ancient horses and rhinos once traveled, and you just may be part of the continual discovery happening in one of the globe's richest fossil beds. This is a fantastic landscape of pyramids, pillars, bluffs, knife-edge ridges, and narrow cannons. The star in these formations: water. It's been carving away the cliffs for the past half million years or so. This park is a place of great theatricality—colorful, dramatic, and not quite real. Go explore on foot, on horseback, or by car.

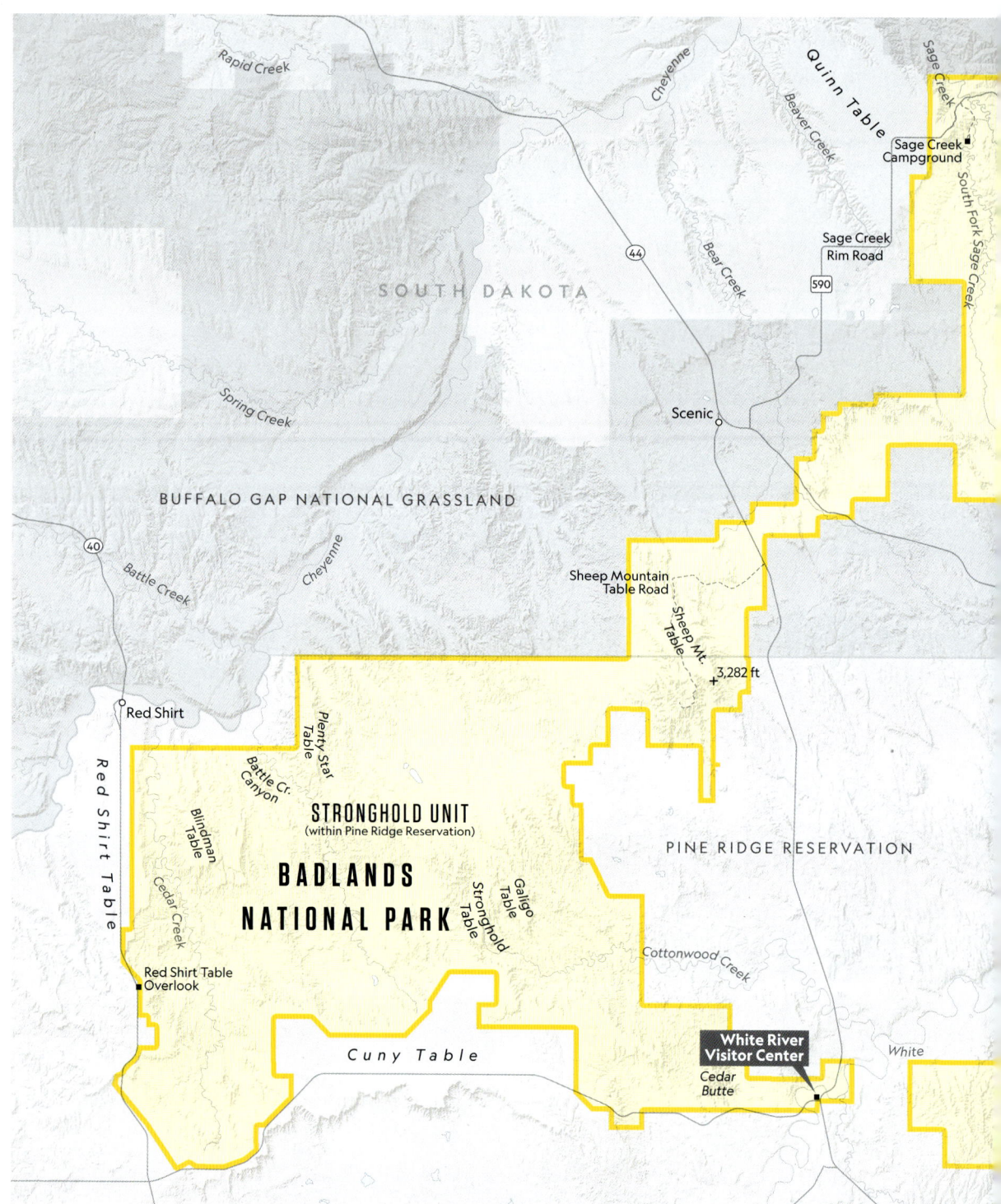

Rapid Creek

Cheyenne

Quinn Table

Sage Creek

Beaver Creek

Sage Creek
Campground

South Fork Sage Creek

44

Sage Creek
Rim Road

590

SOUTH DAKOTA

Bear Creek

Spring Creek

Scenic

BUFFALO GAP NATIONAL GRASSLAND

40

Battle Creek

Cheyenne

Sheep Mountain
Table Road

Sheep Mt. Table

+ 3,282 ft

Red Shirt

Plenty Star Table

Battle Cr. Canyon

Red Shirt Table

Blindman Table

Cedar Creek

STRONGHOLD UNIT
(within Pine Ridge Reservation)

BADLANDS
NATIONAL PARK

Galigo Table

Stronghold Table

PINE RIDGE RESERVATION

Cottonwood Creek

Red Shirt Table
Overlook

Cuny Table

White River
Visitor Center

White

Cedar
Butte

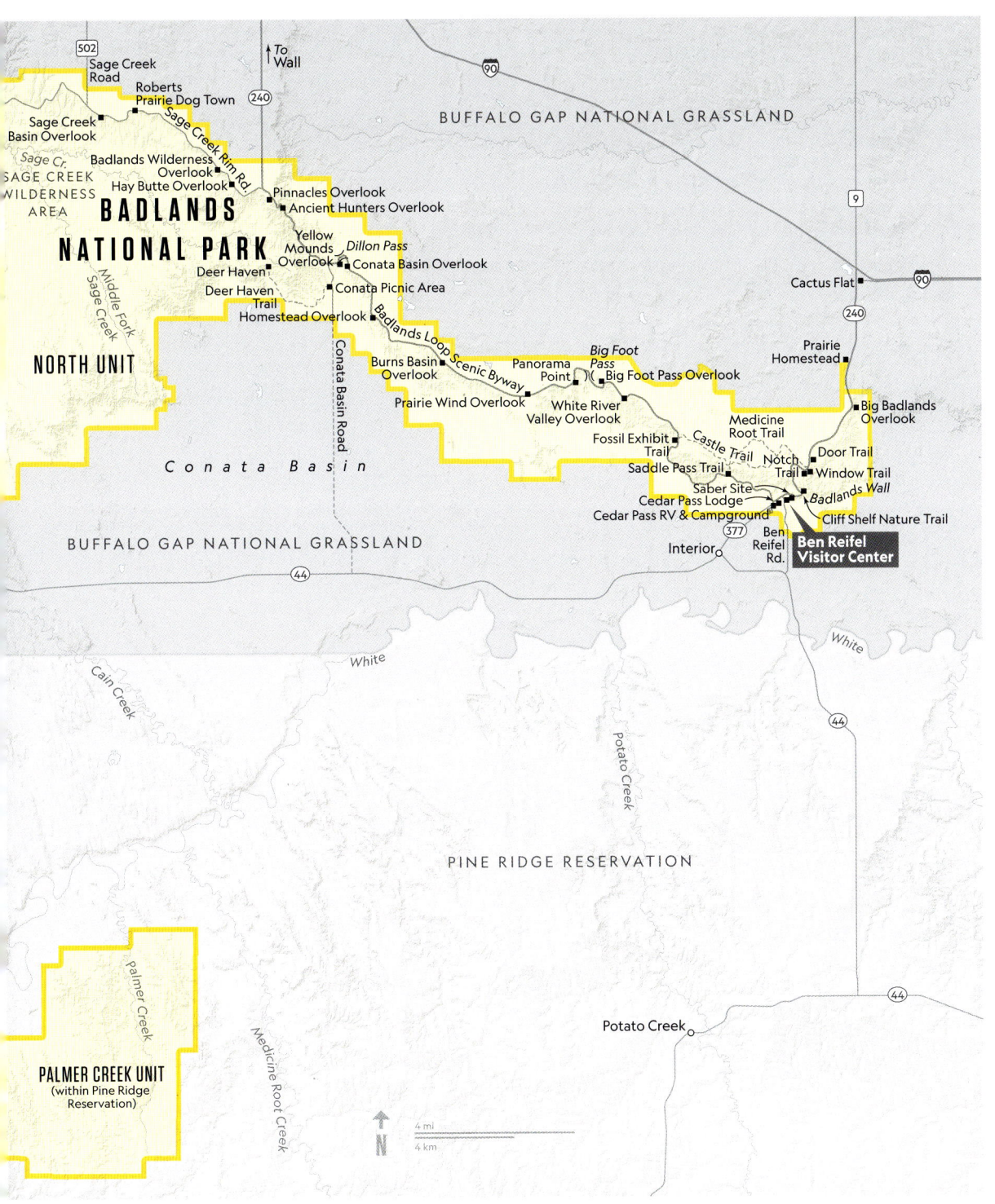

502
Sage Creek
Road
Roberts
Prairie Dog Town
To Wall
240
90
BUFFALO GAP NATIONAL GRASSLAND
9
Sage Creek
Basin Overlook
Badlands Wilderness
Overlook
Hay Butte Overlook
Sage Cr.
SAGE CREEK
WILDERNESS
AREA
BADLANDS
NATIONAL PARK
Pinnacles Overlook
Ancient Hunters Overlook
Yellow
Mounds
Overlook
Dillon Pass
Conata Basin Overlook
Cactus Flat
90
240
Deer Haven
Deer Haven
Trail
Conata Picnic Area
Homestead Overlook
Prairie
Homestead
*Middle Fork
Sage Creek*
NORTH UNIT
Badlands Loop Scenic Byway
*Big Foot
Pass*
Burns Basin
Overlook
Panorama
Point
Big Foot Pass Overlook
Big Badlands
Overlook
Conata Basin Road
Prairie Wind Overlook
White River
Valley Overlook
Medicine
Root Trail
C o n a t a   B a s i n
Fossil Exhibit
Trail
Castle Trail
Door Trail
Notch
Trail
Window Trail
Saddle Pass Trail
Badlands Wall
Saber Site
Cedar Pass Lodge
Cedar Pass RV & Campground
Cliff Shelf Nature Trail
BUFFALO GAP NATIONAL GRASSLAND
377
Ben
Reifel
Rd.
**Ben Reifel
Visitor Center**
Interior
44
White
White
Cain Creek
Potato Creek
44
PINE RIDGE RESERVATION
Palmer Creek
Medicine Root Creek
44
Potato Creek
PALMER CREEK UNIT
(within Pine Ridge
Reservation)
N
4 mi
4 km

A cabin at Cedar Pass Lodge

Y You have a few options for staying in and around the park, from cabins to campsites. If you prefer a hotel, look for one in nearby **Wall**.

→ Stay within park bounds at the **Cedar Pass Lodge**. The modern, eco-friendly cabins were created to mimic those originally built in 1928 and are available April through October. Cabins have air-conditioning and heat, TVs, mini-fridges with freezers, and access to on-site dining, plus there's a convenience and souvenir shop. There are ADA-accessible cabins too.

→ The lodge also manages **Cedar Pass RV and Campground**, which boasts 96 sites with scenic views. Open year-round (spots are limited in winter), it features electric sites, picnic tables, and access to nearby bathrooms—but no campfires (charcoal grills and camp stoves are permitted).

→ Stay at the free **Sage Creek Campground**, run by the park on a first-come-first-serve basis year-round. Along with 22 tent sites, it allows trailers and motor homes under 18 feet and has pit toilets and picnic tables.

→ Plan a backcountry camping trip in the park; just chat with a ranger before you head out on your adventure. Permits are not currently required. **Deer Haven** and **Sage Creek Wilderness Area** are both popular spots to set out on your own.

SLEEP

A sign points the way to Cedar Pass Lodge

A ladder on the Notch Trail

Use the boardwalk of the Window Trail to see the unique formations.

→ HIKE

T The badlands can be a treacherous place to travel, but the park makes an effort to ensure that the space is incredibly accommodating for hikers of all levels.

→ Explore a juniper forest along the edge of the badlands when you walk the short and easy **Cliff Shelf Nature Trail**. This loop is a mix of trail, boardwalk, and stairs, and you may pass a small pond, depending on the weather and time of year.

→ Hike the **prairie wash** just across the road from the Ben Reifel Visitor Center. This natural and unmarked trail can be difficult to find, so get some help from a ranger. Look for animal tracks, interesting rocks, and blooming flowers—and kids can complete the scavenger hunt in their Junior Ranger booklets.

→ The popular quarter-mile **Door Trail** is known for its panoramic view of the badlands. For more, go beyond the accessible boardwalk into the park's bedrock.

→ The **Fossil Exhibit Trail** is one of the easiest in the park, but that doesn't mean it isn't worth your time. Touch and feel each of the fossil replicas and learn about the extinct creatures that once lived in the region through exhibits (which incorporate braille) along the fully accessible boardwalk.

→ Follow the park's open-hike policy (you're allowed to **go off-trail** in specific areas) via the unmaintained network of trails, or so-called social trails. One option: Leave from behind the Conata Picnic Area and hike the three-mile round-trip trail through Deer Haven.

→ Hike the **Window Trail** and check out the Badlands Wall that showcases views of an eroded canyon, including the natural window for which the trail gets its name.

→ The 1.5-mile **Notch Trail** is a well-traveled one, popular for its views over the White River Valley. You'll have to climb a log ladder and follow a ledge toward the lookout; avoid it if you're afraid of heights.

→ Climb the steep Badlands Wall on the **Saddle Pass Trail**, which will take you up about 300 feet of elevation and provide lovely views of the White River Valley. End at the Castle and Medicine Root Trails.

Family Friendly

SPOT ←

A bighorn sheep wanders through dried grasses.

V Visitors are often on the lookout for large mammals when they trek through Badlands, and they're likely to have good luck, with a little patience.

→ Badlands is home to one of the largest federal **American bison** herds in North America. The animals, which can weigh up to 2,000 pounds, often roam along Sage Creek Rim Road, and there's also a herd of nearly 800 bison in the wilderness area behind the campground. April is the best time to come for calves.

→ **Bighorn sheep** were brought to the park in 1964 and now wander up on the rocky edges, visible from the Pinnacles and Big Badlands Overlooks and the Castle Trail.

→ See **prairie dog towns** all over the park, especially near the Burns Basin Overlook and Sage Creek Campground. Don't miss Roberts Prairie Dog Town, the largest in the accessible part of the park, if you're set on spotting the creatures.

→ Eastern and western birds cross paths in the park, and the diverse habitat supports 206 different species. Look for **cliff swallows**, **golden eagles**, **prairie falcons**, **rock pigeons**, **cedar waxwings**, **black-capped chickadees**, and **black-billed magpies**.

A A trip to Badlands requires a lot of driving. It's how you'll get to see the most wildlife, visit the most overlooks, and cross the most trailheads. These three roads will cover your bases:

→ The **Badlands Loop Scenic Byway** is a key avenue for the park, with tons of overlooks off the route. Don't miss Big Badlands, Yellow Mounds, Conata Basin, and Pinnacles.

→ Drive along the dirt and gravel **Sage Creek Rim Road** to spot wildlife. Watch for bison, which often cross the road; look for wildlife at the Hay Butte, Badlands Wilderness, and Sage Creek Basin Overlooks; and visit the Roberts Prairie Dog Town.

→ Take **Sheep Mountain Table Road** up to the striking overlook sitting at 3,275 feet. You should have a four-wheel-drive vehicle for the dirt road; avoid the route during or right after storms. Park at the top of the table and hike the 2.5 miles up past the overlook. Be respectful of its sacred nature to the Oglala Lakota while you're there. Horses and cattle may be seen roaming the area, thanks to the park's agreement with the Oglala Lakota Nation.

Sunrise hits the park's distinct yellow mounds, which are composed of fossilized soils.

DRIVE

The Badlands Wall, seen here at night, is the primary formation in the park's North Unit.

A saber-toothed cat fossil skull at the Saber Site

B Broaden your experience by looking up and down—into the past that's buried in the earth and up into the night sky.

→ The **Saber Site** is a newer dig area near the Ben Reifel Visitor Center started by a seven-year-old girl who was looking for fossils on her own and found the skull of a saber-toothed cat. Let the site inspire you to look for your own fossil discoveries while you hike, but don't collect or disturb anything. Instead, tell a ranger if you think you've found something.

→ Stay for an evening in the park to experience a vast swath of stars and the cosmos with little to no light pollution. The park offers ranger-led **Night Sky Viewings** every night in the summer that highlight constellations, planets, and other objects. You'll also get a chance to use the park's 11-inch Celestron telescope.

Family Friendly

*Most visitors are focused on the scenery when they visit Badlands, but if you want to see wildlife, drive along the 25-mile **Sage Creek Rim Road**. It starts on the Badlands Loop Scenic Byway, then heads into the western part of the park. You have a good chance of seeing bison, bighorn sheep, prairie dogs, and plenty of birds. You'll also pass lots of overlooks as you navigate through the Sage Creek Wilderness Area. From there, camp, hike, and search for wildlife.*

Brandywine Falls

CUYAHOGA VALLEY
NATIONAL PARK

OHIO

ESTABLISHED: October 11, 2000

SIZE: 33,000 acres

VISITORS CENTERS: The Boston Mill Visitor Center is open year-round. The Canal Exploration Center and Hunt House are open seasonally and serve mainly as educational touchpoints.

TRANSPORTATION: Cuyahoga Valley Scenic Railroad

DOGS ALLOWED: Yes, except on mountain bike trails and sledding hills in winter

WHEN TO GO: Spring for bird-watching and hiking; fall for foliage (colors peak in mid-October); winter for cross-country skiing. Summer is busy, hot, and humid, but lively with music, programming, and farmers markets.

CONTACT: 440-717-3890; nps.gov/cuva
6947 Riverview Road
Peninsula, OH 44264

C Cuyahoga Valley National Park is nestled between Akron and Cleveland, Ohio. The river that runs through it has been many things: a source of sustenance, a means of transportation, a respite for wildlife, and, unfortunately, a landscape abused by industry and development. Now, however, it's a rebuilt refuge for local animals, nature lovers, and native plants. A visit to the park places you at the center of this story of natural redemption, with its array of options, from riding the scenic railroad to visiting roadside farms to jogging along the 19th-century canal.

SLEEP

There's no camping inside the park, but you'll find plenty of places outside its borders. Look for nearby campsites in Peninsula, Stow, and Streetsboro. Lots of hotels are close to the park, in those towns as well as in Akron and Cleveland. If you want to stay inside Cuyahoga, there are two options:

→ The **Stanford House** is a remodeled home just north of the village of Boston that offers rentals for daytime activities or overnights in its nine bedrooms. You'll also find gorgeous views of the Cuyahoga River and the Ohio & Erie Canal.

→ The **Inn at Brandywine Falls** overlooks its namesake and was built in 1848. Placed on the National Register of Historic Places, it has been brought into the 21st century. Stay in one of its six remodeled rooms and enjoy candlelit breakfasts, luxurious community spaces, and easy access to nearby waterfalls and trails.

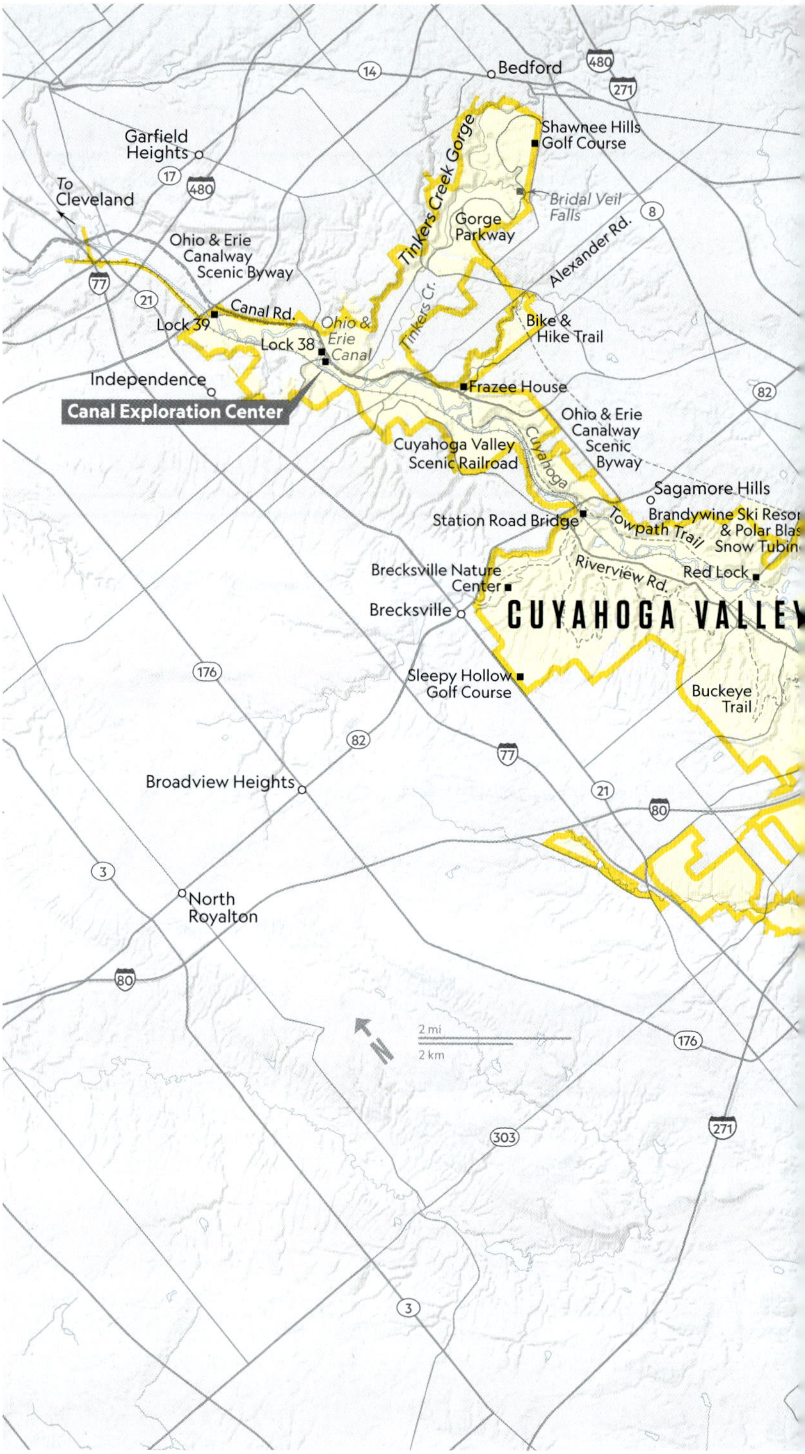

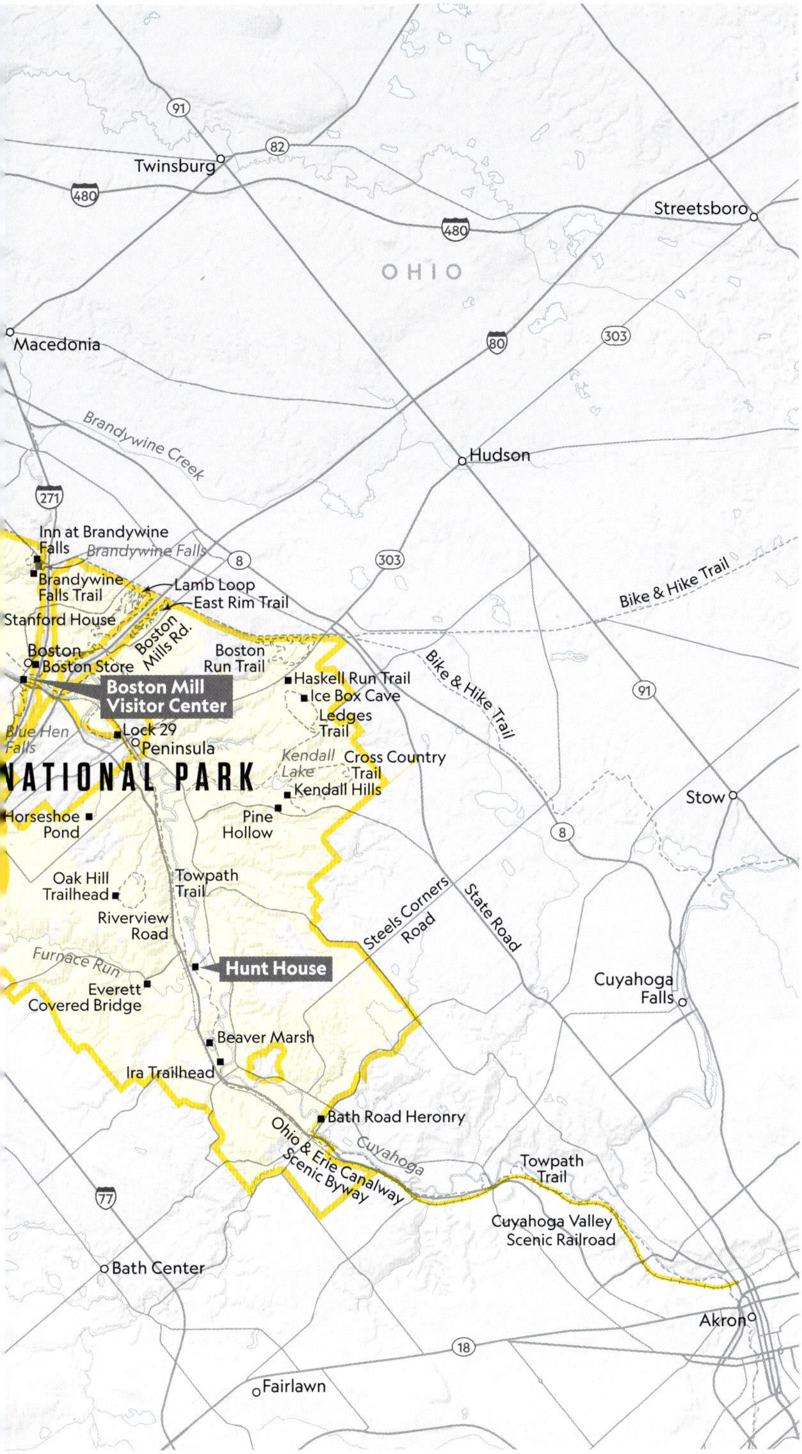

91
82
Twinsburg
480
Streetsboro
480
OHIO
Macedonia
80
303
Brandywine Creek
Hudson
271
Inn at Brandywine Falls
Brandywine Falls
8
303
Brandywine Falls Trail
Lamb Loop
East Rim Trail
Bike & Hike Trail
Stanford House
Boston Mills Rd.
Boston
Boston Store
Boston Run Trail
Boston Mill Visitor Center
Haskell Run Trail
Ice Box Cave
Bike & Hike Trail
91
Blue Hen Falls
Lock 29
Peninsula
Ledges Trail
Kendall Lake
Cross Country Trail
NATIONAL PARK
Kendall Hills
Stow
Horseshoe Pond
Pine Hollow
8
Oak Hill Trailhead
Towpath Trail
Riverview Road
Steels Corners Road
State Road
Furnace Run
Hunt House
Everett Covered Bridge
Cuyahoga Falls
Beaver Marsh
Ira Trailhead
Bath Road Heronry
Ohio & Erie Canalway Scenic Byway
Cuyahoga
Towpath Trail
77
Cuyahoga Valley Scenic Railroad
Bath Center
Akron
18
Fairlawn

Cuyahoga Valley is a maze of trails, roads, and rivers. Some routes will challenge you, some are easy strolls with pretty views, and some are moderate trails that bring a bit of both.

→ *The* ***Ledges Trail*** *takes you on a rocky route around a series of striking formations. Access Ledge Overlook, a great spot to see the sunset, changing fall colors, or magical winter icicles, from this 1.8-mile loop.*

→ *Walk the half-mile loop of the* ***Haskell Run Trail*** *to reach a healthy stream surrounded by wildflowers in the spring and birds in the summer.*

→ *Hike the popular* ***Brandywine Falls Trail*** *early in the day or later in the afternoon to avoid the crowds. The 1.5-mile trail leads to the popular 60-foot waterfall.*

→ *Trek the steep portion of the* ***Buckeye Trail*** *to the 15-foot Blue Hen Falls. The hike is three miles round-trip from the Boston Mill Visitor Center.*

→ *The* ***Towpath Trail*** *is well used by walkers, runners, hikers, bikers, and cross-country skiers. Twenty of the route's 100 miles go through the park, and those miles are easily split into short walks. Try the half-mile one-way bit from Station Road Bridge to Mudcatcher or the three-quarter-mile one-way path from Lock 29 to Peninsula Feeder. Take the train back.*

→ *Check out the* ***Ice Box Cave*** *from the Ritchie Ledges. To protect the resident bats, you can no longer enter the cave, but you can admire where it's carved into the massive sandstone formations.*

HIKE

FLOAT

P Paddle the **Cuyahoga River**, now cleaned of its polluted past, by bringing your own equipment and expertise. Activities on the water are not maintained by the park, but traversing the risky river is possible if you have the skill. Access points are at Locks 29 and 39, along with the Boston Store, Red Lock, and Station Road Bridge Trailheads.

Beaver Marsh on the Ohio & Erie Canal Towpath Trail

W Wildlife has been flourishing in the park since restoration began in the late 1960s. Birders and animal lovers will have great luck if they're quiet and slow as they travel.

→ More than **200 bird species** are often seen in the park. Beaver Marsh, the Ledges, Horseshoe Pond, and Bath Road Heronry are all good options for spotting winged creatures like wood ducks, swamp sparrows, winter wrens, barred owls, and herons.
→ Follow the Towpath Trail from the Ira Trailhead to Beaver Marsh, home to **beavers** and **wetland birds**. Along the way, boardwalk exhibits educate about the land and its wildlife.
→ Insects are vital to the complex ecological cycles in Cuyahoga Valley, just as they are everywhere. With the water's rebirth, **butterflies**, **dragonflies**, **bees**, **ants**, and **spiders** are now buzzing and climbing around the park again. Look carefully to spot these tiny creatures.

SPOT

Cuyahoga River

DRIVE

Lots of roads weave through Cuyahoga Valley to different trailheads, overlooks, and historic sites. One of note is the **Ohio & Erie Canalway Scenic Byway**, which follows the route of the Ohio & Erie Towpath Trail. The carefully planned 110-mile route is not one road but a group of them that connect the same path and chronicle the transportation of the region.

Boston Mills Road during snowfall

Cuyahoga is not your typical national park. Here are a few activities that set it apart:

→ Ride the **Cuyahoga Valley Scenic Railroad**, a nonprofit excursion railroad, for a unique look at the park's beauty. Book your tickets online ahead of time for round-trip travel, or use the train to return from your trip along the Towpath Trail or river. Just wave it down at a boarding station when you need it. Kids will love the two-hour Family Fun Loop. Dining excursions are also available.

→ Peddle along the **Ohio & Erie Towpath**, the **East Rim Trail** and **Lamb Loop**, or the Summit County **Bike & Hike Trail** with your own bicycle. If you choose the first route, load your bike on the train for the trip back.

→ Break out the golf clubs at nearby **Shawnee Hills** and **Sleepy Hollow golf courses**. Though the courses are near the park, they're not owned or managed by the Park Service.

→ Enjoy the park in the winter by **snowshoeing** or **cross-country skiing** along its many trails, **ice fishing** on its lakes and ponds, and **sledding** at Kendall Hills. Try the flat Bike & Hike Trail or the more advanced **Boston Run Trail** when they're snow-covered; rent snowshoes at the Boston Mill Visitor Center.

→ Get a history lesson at the **Canal Exploration Center**. Learn about the impacts the now destroyed canals had on the communities in the region and continue your education at the once luxurious Frazee House, a two-story federal-style building that overlooks the canal.

→ **Stargaze** at the park when you stay overnight. You might see Mercury from Beaver Marsh or the aurora borealis from the Pine Hollow parking lot. The Oak Hill Trailhead is a great place to catch a meteor shower.

→ Participate in the park's **Canalway Questing**, which turns the exploration of Cuyahoga's natural wonders into a game. On this treasure hunt, find hidden boxes using clues and a map of the Ohio & Erie Canalway—and collect stamps at each location. The annual game runs from spring until fall.

EXPLORE

Family Friendly

St. Louis's towering
Gateway Arch

GATEWAY ARCH
NATIONAL PARK

MISSOURI

ESTABLISHED: February 22, 2018

SIZE: 91 acres

VISITORS CENTER: The Gateway Arch Visitor Center is
open year-round and houses a museum, theater, store, and
café. It's also the starting point for your tram trip and for
ranger-led programs.

TRANSPORTATION: Tram rides to the top

DOGS ALLOWED: Yes, on leash in outdoor areas

WHEN TO GO: Year-round; summer and November–December
are busiest

CONTACT: 314-655-1600; nps.gov/jeff
11 North Fourth Street
St. Louis, MO 63102

A A visit to Gateway Arch National Park is a glimpse into American history, from the push for westward expansion to the African American fight for freedom. President Franklin D. Roosevelt designated the property as the Jefferson National Expansion Memorial in 1935, and a nationwide design competition for the memorial kicked off in 1948. Construction began in 1963 and was completed two years later. The arch is an engineering marvel: To build the massive 630-foot monument, double-walled, triangular sections were placed on top of one another and welded together, all covered in stainless and carbon steel to create a seamless arch.

From a guided walk around its grounds to a music-filled river cruise to a trip up to the top of the arch itself, the country's smallest national park allows you to soak in what the city of St. Louis meant for the growth of the country.

Washington Ave.

North 8th St.

North 6th St.

Locust St.

North 4th St.

Pine St.

Eads Bridge

Explorer's Garden

Hilton Pennywell St. Louis at the Arch

St. Louis

Kiener Plaza Park

Market St.

North Pond

Hyatt Regency St. Louis at the Arch

North Leonor K. Sullivan Blvd.

Old Courthouse

Luther Ely Smith Square

GATEWAY ARCH

Gateway Arch Visitor Center

Dred and Harriet Scott statue

Drury Plaza Hotel St. Louis at the Arch

Old Cathedral

Gateway Arch

Grand Staircase

MISSISSIPPI RIVER

Clark Ave.

NATIONAL PARK

Gateway Arch Riverboats

South Pond

South 4th St.

N

200 ft
200 m

South Leonor K. Sullivan Blvd.

MISSOURI

ILLINOIS

South 4th St.

Congressman William L. Clay Sr. Bridge

Rooms at the Hyatt Regency St. Louis offer views of the arch

The Pennywell hotel's snack bar is inside an old bank vault.

SLEEP

There are plenty of hotels in downtown St. Louis, and you'll find something with whatever amenities you are looking for. The **Hilton Pennywell St. Louis at the Arch** and the **Hyatt Regency St. Louis at the Arch** are within a couple of blocks of the park and have rooms with memorable views.

The entrance to the Gateway Arch Visitor Center

SPOT

S Since Gateway Arch is sandwiched between the Mississippi River and the busy city of St. Louis, wildlife finds some refuge in the park's green spaces. **Squirrels, opossums, coyotes, raccoons, woodchucks,** and **rabbits** have all been spotted at Gateway Arch.

As far as bird-watching goes, spot **Canada geese, mallards, peregrine falcons, mourning doves, robins, northern mockingbirds, blue jays, house finches,** and **northern cardinals** any time of year. In the summer, get a glimpse of traveling **chimney swifts, barn swallows, eastern wood pewees,** and **warbling vireos**. By the river, look for **brown thrashers** and **red-winged blackbirds**. Walk through the trees, along the water, and in quieter spaces for the best luck.

HIKE

S Several paved pathways and trails wind through the park, giving you the option to explore the 62 acres of park grounds however you'd like. None of the paths are marked, so for a bit more guidance, **join a ranger** on a daily walk. You'll meet at the visitors center and hear about the history of the city and the park.

I If you want a new perspective on the Gateway Arch take the tram up to its top. Get **panoramic views** of the region from atop the 630-foot-tall structure (the tallest monument in the United States), and learn about how the unique tram system was developed and built in the 1960s. Once you reach the top, you'll get eight to 10 minutes inside your tram to gaze out at the views below from 32 windows—half looking east over the Mississippi and half looking west over St. Louis. On clear days you'll see as far as 30 miles in each direction.

LOOK

The museum's New Frontiers gallery

A statue of Dred Scott and his wife, Harriet Robinson Scott, by Harry Weber

The Old Courthouse's Circuit Court 13, restored to its 1910 appearance

W While getting to the top of the Gateway Arch is the park's main attraction, there's plenty more to add to your day. Dig into the city's history, get out on the water, and learn about the park's construction with one of these activities.

→ *Gain a deeper understanding of St. Louis and its place in American history at the **free underground museum**. The 140,000-square-foot museum sits under the arch and contains exhibits on colonial St. Louis, Thomas Jefferson, western settlers and expansion, the steamboat, and the arch itself.*

→ *Check out the park's calendar ahead of time for **ranger-led programs**. Join a museum tour that covers America's westward expansion, the city's French origins, and the construction of the arch—or bring kids to the education classroom on the weekends for a puppet show about the park.*

→ *The **Old Courthouse** (completed in 1839) offers ranger-led tours of the historic space, with exhibits on Dred Scott's fight for freedom, African American life in St. Louis, and more.*

→ *Book a seat on one of the many **riverboat cruises** offered by the official outfitter of the park. Take the classic one-hour St. Louis Riverfront Cruise with a view of the arch and downtown, enjoy music and a meal on the two-hour Skyline Dinner Cruise, or plan your visit for one of the seasonal offerings—from a Halloween costume cruise to PJ's and Pancakes With Santa.*

→ *Watch "**Monument to the Dream**," a film about the construction of the massive Gateway Arch. The 35-minute documentary (tickets required) runs about every hour at the visitors center's Tucker Theater.*

→ *Attend one of the **events** held throughout the year. The park hosts sunrise yoga sessions, art displays, an ice-skating rink, pet-friendly activities, and more. Along with the various fee-free tours, they're a great way to get a new perspective on the space.*

→ *Explore history through technology with the park's award-winning virtual reality experience "**Cobblestones & Courage.**" A headset transports you into a 360-degree version of the bustling St. Louis riverfront in the 1850s.*

EXPLORE

Family Friendly

Enjoy a picnic at the **north or south reflection ponds**. While the rest of the Gateway Arch experience can feel busy—even the trip up the arch—there's plenty of space on the grounds to enjoy the natural scenery if you head toward the water and throw down a blanket.

INDIANA DUNES NATIONAL PARK

INDIANA

ESTABLISHED: February 15, 2019

SIZE: 15,177 acres

VISITORS CENTERS: The Indiana Dunes Visitor Center is open year-round and has educational displays and a bookstore. The Paul H. Douglas Center for Environmental Education has similar hours and provides hands-on exhibits, ranger-led hikes, a nature play zone, and educational programming.

TRANSPORTATION: Shuttle bus and the South Shore Line

DOGS ALLOWED: Yes; must be leashed

WHEN TO GO: Spring for wildflowers; summer for beach time (May–September is best for swimming); fall for foliage; winter for cross-country skiing

CONTACT: 219-395-1882; nps.gov/indu
1215 IN-49
Porter, IN 46304

Indiana Dunes' shoreline at dusk

The 15 miles of coastline along Lake Michigan in Indiana Dunes National Park have been shaped by wind and waves for millennia, creating a special lakeshore long sought after by conservationists and industrialists. In 1899, a group attempted to officially protect the land, but it wasn't until 2019 that it was named a national park.

A trip here can be as bustling or as quiet as you'd like it. Visit the beaches in the summer. Walk the marshes in the spring with fellow wildflower and bird lovers. Strap on cross-country skis and cover miles without seeing another soul come winter. The park is truly what you make of it, and there are plenty of choices to build a trip you'll love.

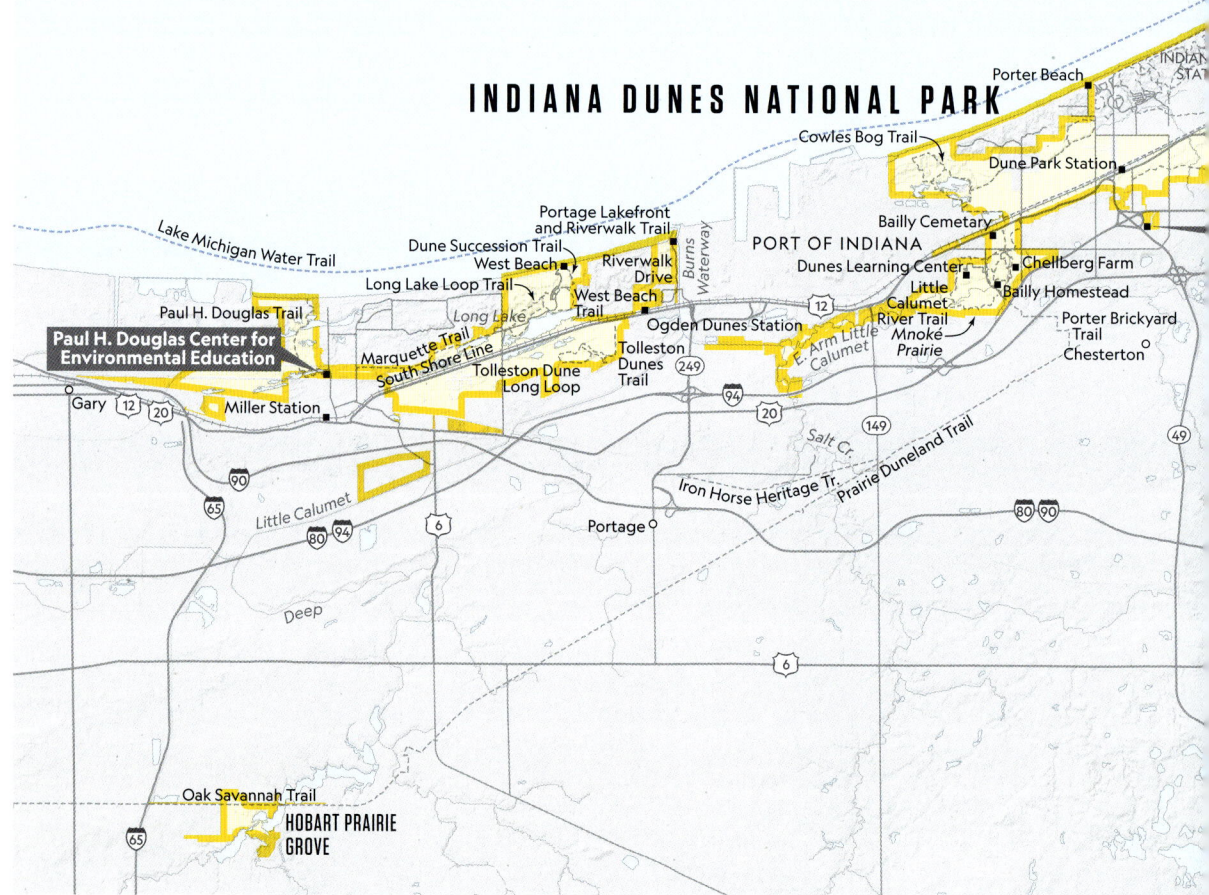

LAKE MICHIGAN

INDIANA DUNES NATIONAL PARK

Porter Beach

Cowles Bog Trail

Dune Park Station

Bailly Cemetary

PORT OF INDIANA

Dunes Learning Center

Chellberg Farm

Bailly Homestead

Little Calumet River Trail

Mnoké Prairie

Porter Brickyard Trail

Chesterton

Portage Lakefront and Riverwalk Trail

Dune Succession Trail

West Beach

Riverwalk Drive

Burns Waterway

Lake Michigan Water Trail

Long Lake Loop Trail

West Beach Trail

Paul H. Douglas Trail

Long Lake

12

Marquette Trail

South Shore Line

Ogden Dunes Station

Paul H. Douglas Center for Environmental Education

Tolleston Dune Long Loop

Tolleston Dunes Trail

249

E. Arm Little Calumet

149

Gary

12 20

Miller Station

94

20

Salt Cr.

49

90

65

Little Calumet

80 94

6

Portage

Iron Horse Heritage Tr.

Prairie Duneland Trail

80 90

Deep

6

Oak Savannah Trail

65

HOBART PRAIRIE GROVE

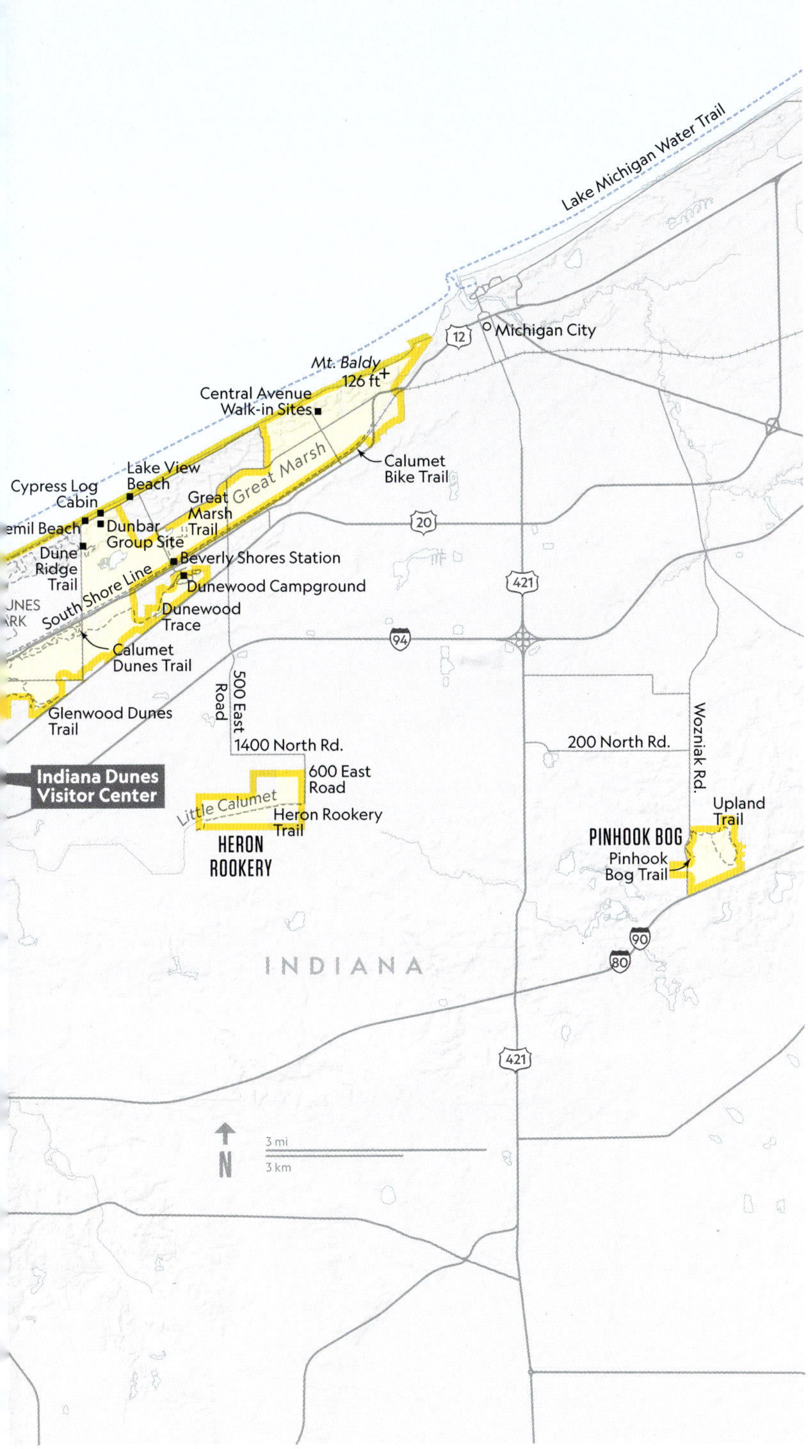

An Indiana Dunes campground

SLEEP

There are three campgrounds within the park and a cabin option. Outside the park, there's plenty of lodging in nearby **Portage** and **Chesterton**.

→ *Dunewood Campground*, 1.5 miles from Lake View Beach, has 66 sites (tent and RV, open April–October), including four accessible ones, and modern bathrooms and showers. Book the sites up to six months in advance.

→ The **Dunbar Group Site** (open April–October) overlooks the Great Marsh and Lake Michigan and is less than 500 feet from the beach. Reservations can be made online up to six months in advance.

→ The primitive **Central Avenue Walk-in Sites** (open May–October) near the beach have five tent-only spaces, a primitive toilet, and no drinkable water.

→ *Cypress Log Cabin*, originally constructed for the 1933 Chicago World's Fair, offers Lake Michigan views, TVs, air-conditioning, a firepit, a gourmet kitchen, and cozy living space. The cabin sleeps up to 12 guests, and there is a four-night minimum in the summer (two nights in the off-season). Book far in advance.

Map labels

Lake Michigan Water Trail

Michigan City

Mt. Baldy 126 ft

Central Avenue Walk-in Sites

Calumet Bike Trail

Cypress Log Cabin

Lake View Beach

Great Marsh

Great Marsh Trail

Dunbar Group Site

Emil Beach

Dune Ridge Trail

Beverly Shores Station

Dunewood Campground

South Shore Line

Dunewood Trace

DUNES PARK

Calumet Dunes Trail

Glenwood Dunes Trail

Indiana Dunes Visitor Center

500 East Road

1400 North Rd.

600 East Road

Little Calumet

Heron Rookery Trail

HERON ROOKERY

200 North Rd.

Wozniak Rd.

Upland Trail

PINHOOK BOG

Pinhook Bog Trail

INDIANA

N

3 mi
3 km

(T) There are 15 trail systems within the park, winding through more than 50 miles of distinct and varied habitats. Grab a trail map from a visitors center and ask a ranger which ones would work best for you—or plan one of these excellent options:

➔ Move through multiple ecosystems on the 3.4-mile **Paul H. Douglas Trail**. Check out the wetlands, black oak savanna, open dunes, and beach—and plan on photo-worthy views of the lake. There's also a shorter loop around the educational center.

➔ For plant diversity, head to the **Cowles Bog Trail**. The 4.7-mile route covers ponds, marshes, savannas, and beaches, each with different flora. Pack lunch for a shoreline picnic.

➔ Trek through the **Bailly Homestead and Cemetery**, **Little Calumet River**, **Mnoké Prairie**, and **Chellberg Farm** in the fall to see how people lived on this land in decades past and take in the colors of the changing leaves. The 3.4-mile outer loop will give you the most comprehensive experience.

➔ The **Long Lake Loop Trail** is part of the West Beach trail system, and it follows Long Lake into the dunes. Get a good view of the lake right away, then follow a steep descent at the end—or tackle it as part of the larger three-loop trail, which includes the **Dune Succession** and **West Beach Trails**.

➔ The **Tolleston Dunes** are the youngest of the three in the park, though they're still thousands of years old. The trail is a good one for spotting blue lupine flowers and eastern prickly pear cactus.

H

I

K

E

Along the Cowles Bog Trail

An eastern bluebird

SPOT

W Wildlife has managed to survive in the dunes over hundreds of years through adaptation. Look for **shrews, moles, bats, chipmunks, woodchucks, squirrels, muskrats, foxes, raccoons, beavers,** and **deer** roaming the landscape. The park is also a great spot for bird-watchers, who should try one of these two walks:

→ *The Heron Rookery Trail follows a section of the Little Calumet River. It used to be a nesting ground for the great blue heron; while that's no longer the case, it is still a haven for many other birds. Look for* **kingfishers, woodpeckers,** *and* **nesting warblers**. *In the spring, it's filled with wildflowers, like spring beauties and Dutchman's-breeches.*

→ *The Great Marsh Trail has wide views of the largest wetland complex in the Lake Michigan watershed. Spot* **coots, mallards, wood ducks, green herons, egrets, warblers,** *and* **red-winged blackbirds**. *During migratory periods, look for* **kingfishers, tree swallows,** *and* **rusty blackbirds**. *If you're lucky, you might also see a beaver.*

Sunrise over Cowles Bog

→ DRIVE

Y You can't drive yourself through the park, but that doesn't mean there isn't a transportation option. The **South Shore Line** stops at four stations within the park (Beverly Shores, Dune Park, Portage/Ogden Dunes, and Miller). There are plenty of worthwhile sites to visit within two miles of each station.

A great blue heron wades through shallow water.

A wintry view of shelf ice formed atop Lake Michigan

Mount Baldy

A Any hike you take will include gorgeous views, but a few off-trail spots are worth visiting as well:

→ *Get panoramic vistas from atop* **Mount Baldy***, a 126-foot-tall dune on the southern tip of Lake Michigan. The hike up the Summit Trail is only available with an authorized staff member, as restoration and preservation efforts are under way. Catch daytime and sunset hikes with rangers on summer weekends. You can also see the dune from lower ground on Mount Baldy Beach if the dune itself is closed.*

→ *Have a picnic at* **Lake View Beach***—even better if it's dinner with a sunset. There's a great view of Lake Michigan from the accessible, covered picnic shelters.*

→ **Portage Lakefront and Riverwalk Trail** *is a wonderful location for observing Lake Michigan during any season. The trail is paved, with some sections of boardwalk and stairs. Watch for migratory birds in spring and summer, ice shelves in winter, and rolling storms in fall. There's a small lighthouse and pavilion with restrooms, a seasonal snack bar, and meeting space.*

LOOK

Maple Sugar Time Festival at Chellberg Farm

H Hiking the dunes is the cornerstone of most Indiana Dunes trips. Add to it by getting out into the water, exploring tucked-away ecosystems, or finding a different means of travel.

→ Explore the Pinhook Bog trail system on either the Upland or Pinhook Bog Trail during a **ranger-led hike**. The fragile habitat is a remnant of the landscape's glacial past; it became so acidic that only certain plants, like sphagnum moss and pitcher plants, could survive.

→ In the evening, head to **Kemil Beach**, with its 24-hour parking lot, to take in the night sky. There's no camping at the beach, but staying late to stargaze is allowed—and excellent on dark nights.

→ Multiple beaches are within park bounds, but **West Beach** is the only one staffed with lifeguards. It also has bathrooms, water, showers, and lockers available. Add one of the nearby hikes to your swim for a boosted experience.

→ Attend the **Maple Sugar Time Festival** every March in the park. Take self-guided tours through the maple forest, purchase bottled syrup, and enjoy a pancake breakfast.

→ The **Glenwood Dunes Trail** is the park's only one open to equestrians. Ride horseback along these 15 miles when the weather allows or cross-country ski it in the winter.

→ Snowshoe or cross-country ski the 2.9-mile **Tolleston Dunes Trail** (though be aware that a few of the hills can be difficult to navigate in the snow). It's best left to more experienced winter trekkers.

→ **Bike the trail system** that connects 37 miles across the length of the park. The trails vary from easy rides to all-day challenges; check with a ranger to see what might be best for you when you get a trail map at a visitors center.

Experts Only

EXPLORE

Take the **Dune Succession Trail** around the West Beach area. No matter the season, there will be unique biodiversity, and the hike is beautiful and peaceful. If it's too crowded, switch to the **Long Lake Loop Trail**, which covers similar biodiversity and has a lovely beach for spotting beavers.

The rocky shoreline of Isle Royale

ISLE ROYALE ← NATIONAL PARK

MICHIGAN

ESTABLISHED: April 3, 1940

SIZE: 571,790 acres

VISITORS CENTERS: The Rock Harbor Visitor Center in the north and the Windigo Visitor Center in the south are open from spring until early fall. The main park headquarters is in Houghton, on the other side of Lake Superior, and open from late spring to late fall.

TRANSPORTATION: Four ferry options

DOGS ALLOWED: No

WHEN TO GO: Summer for hiking, camping, and wildlife; September for thinner crowds. The park is closed November 1 through April 15 due to winter conditions.

CONTACT: 906-482-0984; nps.gov/isro
800 East Lakeshore Drive
Houghton, MI 49931

Ⓐ A fog-shrouded archipelago of glacier-scoured rock and dark coniferous forest, Isle Royale National Park comprises a main island known for its wolves and moose and some 400 small isles dotting the clear chilly waters of Lake Superior. Isolation brings beauty to this park, one of the least visited in the U.S. An adventure here during its limited visitor season is packed with peace, play, and inspiration. This is a wild space without roads, and to access most places, you must travel by foot or boat. The park is the perfect canvas for finding a bit of solitude and exploration—as long as you plan ahead.

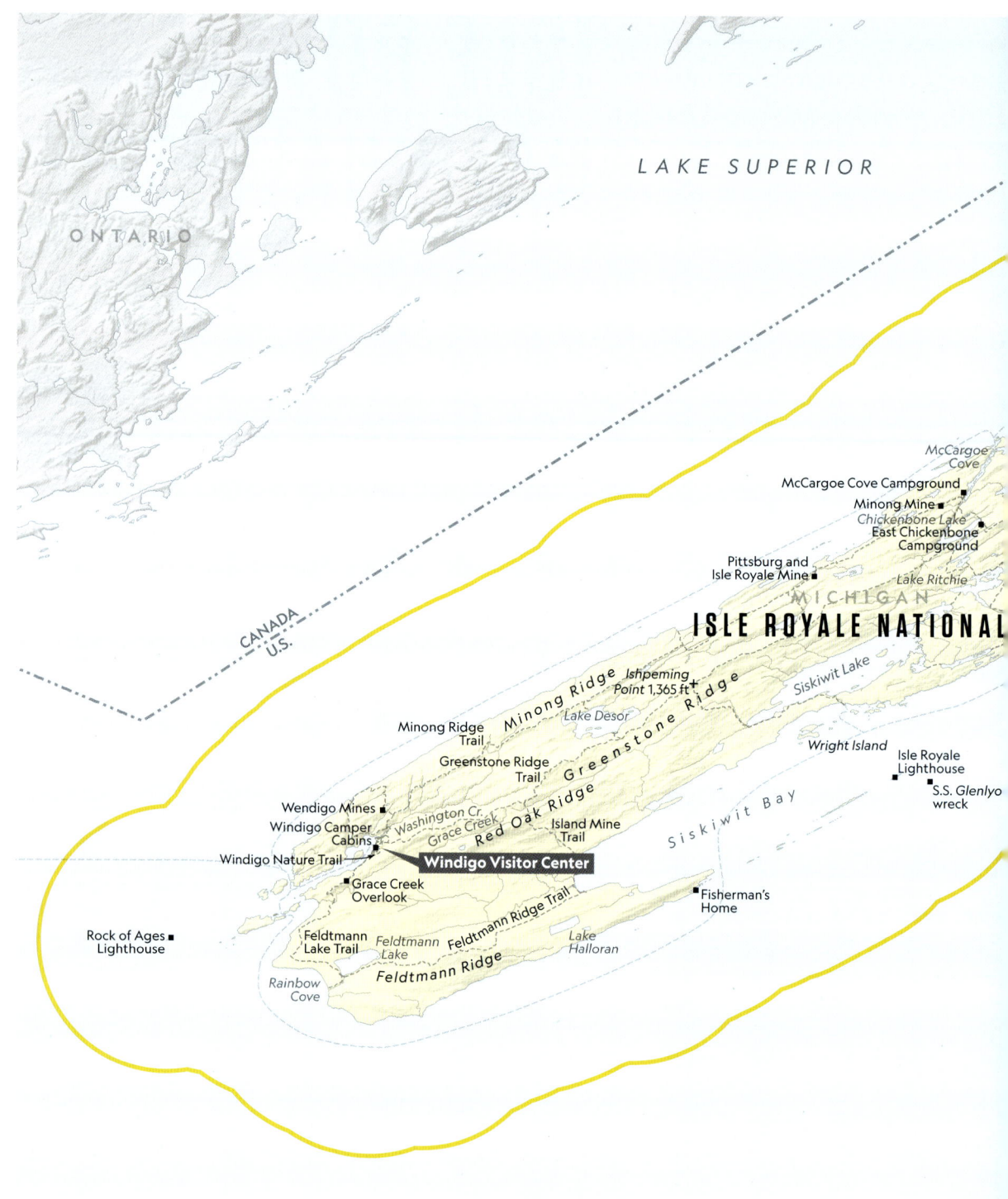

LAKE SUPERIOR

ONTARIO

CANADA
U.S.

McCargoe
Cove

McCargoe Cove Campground

Minong Mine

Chickenbone Lake
East Chickenbone
Campground

Pittsburg and
Isle Royale Mine

Lake Ritchie

MICHIGAN

ISLE ROYALE NATIONAL

Minong Ridge

Ishpeming
Point 1,365 ft

Minong Ridge
Trail

Lake Desor

Greenstone Ridge

Siskiwit Lake

Greenstone Ridge
Trail

Wright Island

Isle Royale
Lighthouse

Wendigo Mines

Washington Cr.

Grace Creek

Red Oak Ridge

Island Mine
Trail

S.S. Glenlyo
wreck

Windigo Camper
Cabins

Siskiwit Bay

Windigo Nature Trail

Windigo Visitor Center

Grace Creek
Overlook

Fisherman's
Home

Rock of Ages
Lighthouse

Feldtmann
Lake Trail

Feldtmann
Lake

Feldtmann Ridge Trail

Lake
Halloran

Rainbow
Cove

Feldtmann Ridge

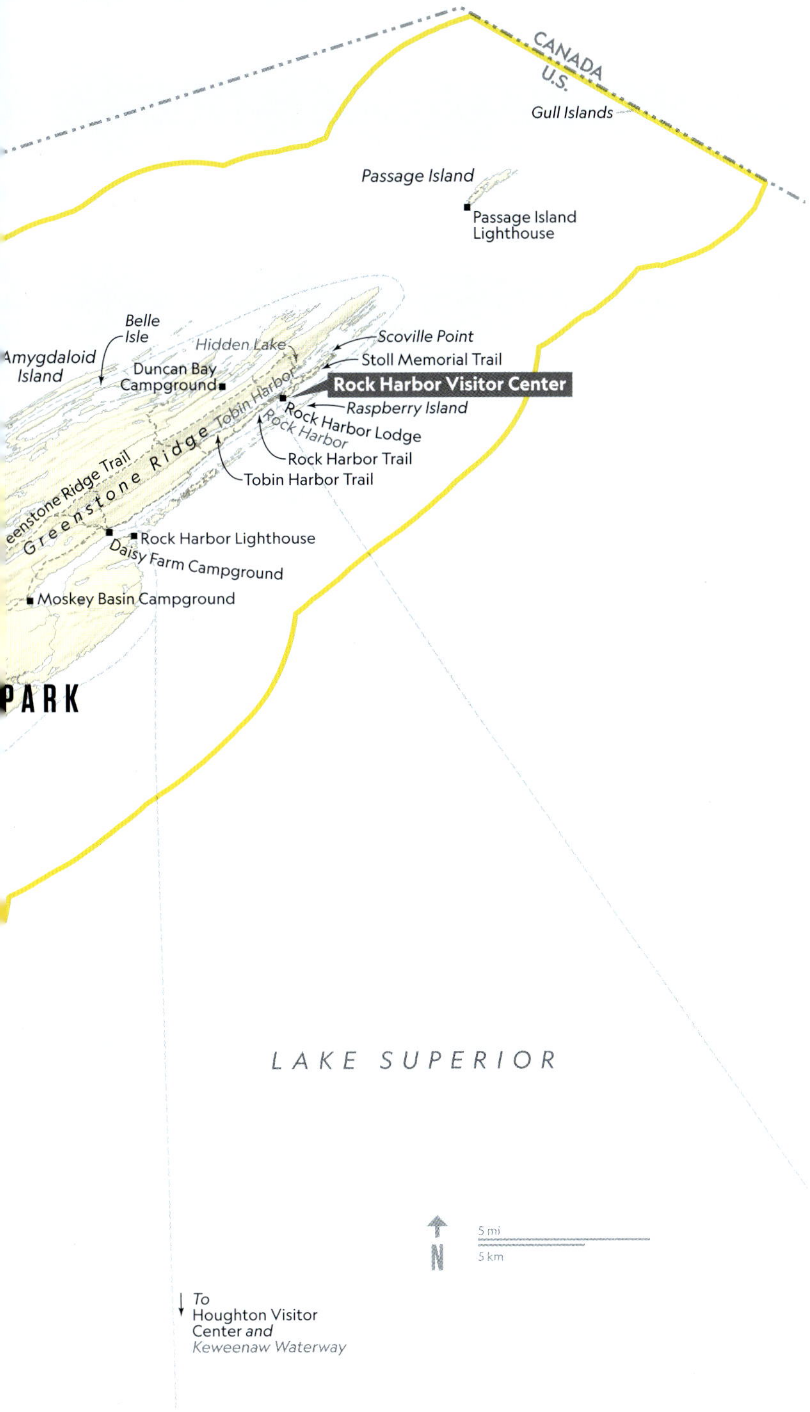

Map labels:

CANADA
U.S.

Gull Islands

Passage Island

Passage Island Lighthouse

Belle Isle
Amygdaloid Island
Hidden Lake
Duncan Bay Campground
Scoville Point
Stoll Memorial Trail
Rock Harbor Visitor Center
Raspberry Island
Rock Harbor Lodge
Rock Harbor
Rock Harbor Trail
Tobin Harbor Trail
Tobin Harbor
Greenstone Ridge Trail
eenstone Ridge Trail
Rock Harbor Lighthouse
Daisy Farm Campground
Moskey Basin Campground

PARK

LAKE SUPERIOR

5 mi
5 km
N

To Houghton Visitor Center and Keweenaw Waterway

SLEEP

Y You have lots of options when it comes to overnights on Isle Royale, though there's only one lodge. Permits are required for all campers but are free to groups of six or fewer. Note: Several campgrounds on the Lake Superior shoreline have docks for powerboats and sailboats, while others are only accessible by canoe or kayak. The park website has a list of boat-in campsites.

→ The north end's **Rock Harbor Lodge** makes for a perfect base camp. Reserve a lakeside lodge room or housekeeping cabin. The lodge also offers sightseeing and fishing tours, paddling equipment rentals, a restaurant, and a shop.

→ Reserve one of the two **Windigo Camper Cabins**. The six-person west-end cabins each have a futon and bunk beds, propane grills, and electricity, along with access to water spigots and toilets.

→ Pitch a tent at one of the 36 free **campgrounds** accessible by boat and trail along the inland paddling routes, off hiking trails, and near shoreline docks. Sites are first come, first served. Daisy Farm, the island's largest campground, is accessible by boat off Lake Superior. Catch the perfect sunrise at Moskey Basin Campground or hike the Lane Cove Trail to Lane Cove Campground on the north shore for a peaceful evening.

→ Plan a **cross-country camping trip**, which is what the park calls its backcountry camping. One particular rule to note: No campfires.

→ HIKE

Experts Only

H Hiking is the name of the game on Isle Royale, and there are routes that will take you all over the park. Here are some great choices:

→ The narrow boardwalk on the 1.2-mile **Windigo Nature Trail** starts just past the Windigo Visitor Center and winds through cedar lowlands and boreal forest. Keep an eye out for wildlife during the easy stroll.

→ Hike the trails that make up the 30-mile **Feldtmann Loop**. The **Feldtmann Lake Trail**, which starts in Windigo, is a good day hike option, at about 8.5 miles. You'll pass the Grace Creek Overlook, then travel an old shoreline as you weave toward the lake. Turn back here if you don't want to tackle the whole loop, or continue on the **Feldtmann Ridge Trail** (10.3 miles) to Siskiwit Bay and the 4.4-mile **Island Mine Trail**, and finish at Washington Creek via the 6.6-mile **Greenstone Ridge Trail**.

→ The 30-mile **Minong Ridge Trail** is only for hikers who have strong navigation skills and can manage with little or no trail maintenance. Catch it off McCargoe Cove, the Windigo Nature Trail, or the Greenstone Ridge Trail. The effort affords ridgetop views of Lake Superior, Canada, beaver dams, and interior lakes, but it involves strenuous climbs and five days of hiking.

→ Have fun tracking your hike on the **Stoll Memorial Trail**. The figure-eight trek totals 4.2 miles but can be broken into smaller sections. It's wooded on one side and rocky on the other, and you'll eventually head up to Scoville Point.

→ The three-mile-long **Tobin Harbor Trail** is both a connection point and lovely walk. Hike from Rock Harbor along the gentle slopes of Tobin Harbor to the Mount Franklin Trail, which will lead you to Suzy's Cave (a sea arch formed 4,000 years ago), Three Mile Campground, and the Greenstone Ridge Trail.

→ On the other side of the same peninsula, the more challenging **Rock Harbor Trail** travels the same route but along the Lake Superior shoreline.

→ The **Greenstone Ridge Trail**, the longest on the island, at 42 miles, can fill your entire trip. Build your own adventure or follow a ranger-created itinerary from one of its three starting points.

→ Boat over to **Raspberry Island** from Rock Harbor and hike the trail there for half a day. See a boreal forest, a bog, and the island's rocky shoreline—and keep an eye out for insect-eating plants.

The Greenstone Ridge Trail from East Chickenbone Campground

An open shaft at the Minong Mine west of McCargoe Cove Campground

W Water is everywhere in Isle Royale, from Lake Superior to the park's inland lakes and rivers. That means one of the best ways to explore the park is by boat.

→ Paddle the **Chain of Lakes**, the connected waterways of inland lakes around the island, and stay at one of the many campgrounds along the route. There are nightly limits at these small sites, so check out the portages ahead of time and talk with a ranger about conditions before you set off.

→ Book a three-hour cruise down the **Keweenaw Waterway** on the decades-old Ranger III ferry. Reserve your spot early, as it runs only on select Thursdays in the summer. Look for a free family event. Don't forget a jacket.

→ Enjoy one of the ranger-led trips from **Rock Harbor**. Take a boat ride to the Hidden Lake Trailhead and then go on a guided hike to Lookout Louise, or ride the same boat to a hike to the Passage Island Lighthouse.

→ For a **guided paddle trip**, book a tour with an outfitter, like Keweenaw Adventure Company or Uncommon Adventures. They help with navigation and camp setup and share the history of the park's landscape and wildlife.

→ **Sail** around the island either with your own vessel or on a guided trip from an outfitter. Try Northern Breezes Sailing or Superior Charters.

Ranger III parked at the Rock Harbor dock

Family Friendly

FLOAT

A butterfly on a thistle flower at Daisy Farm Campground

S

P

O

T

(T) The remote island is a wildlife haven, making it easier to see animals you might have trouble spotting elsewhere. Check out these locations for a chance to scope out moose, beavers, loons, and more:

→ *Moose have long called Isle Royale home, and the population shifts with the number of gray wolves at any given time. Spy moose around the inland lakes and ponds, where they cool off and chow down on plants. Your best bets might be Hidden Lake, Feldtmann Lake, and Washington Creek.*

→ *The best way to find a bird in Isle Royale is to listen. Keep your ears alert for the calls of* **pileated woodpeckers**, **common loons**, *and* **sharp-tailed grouse**.

→ *The island's wetlands support a breadth of amphibian life, including* **wood frogs**, **spring peepers**, **mink frogs**, **green frogs**, **salamanders**, *and* **newts**. *Look for them in the flooded meadows, peat bogs, marshes, and inland lakes.*

→ *Search for water-loving mammals, like* **otters** *and* **beavers**, *along the shorelines of the inland lakes and Lake Superior. You might even see an otter lounging on a dock if you're lucky.*

A female moose traversing the Isle Royale waters

A female coaster brook trout

EXPLORE

There are other ways to explore Isle Royale, including a guided trip, a seaplane adventure, a sailing trip, and scuba diving.

→ *To see any of the 10 major shipwrecks at Isle Royale, take a **scuba diving trip** with Isle Royale Charters (bring your own equipment). Make sure you're comfortable in cold, dark, and deep conditions and have the proper gear for the temps.*

→ ***Fish** for freshwater coaster brook trout, a colorful species found only in Lake Superior. Isle Royale is one of the few locations to catch them, and catch-and-release is required.*

→ *Book a **guided backpacking trip** with one of the many outfitters identified by the Park Service, like Backpack the Trail, Iconic Adventures, or True North Expeditions. They help with navigation, camp setup, and park history along the way.*

→ *Fly into the park on an **Isle Royale Seaplane**, the park's sole concessionaire for this stellar park entrance. You'll get a bird's-eye view of the park before an exhilarating water landing at one of its docks.*

Exploring the wreckage of the S.S. *Glenlyon*, a popular diving site

The view from Mount Franklin

*Paddle around **Tobin Harbor**, near Rock Harbor and its lodge. When conditions are good, observe wildlife and listen for loons from your canoe or kayak. Even though the harbor is close to the busiest region in the park, its kayak rentals ensure you can find some peaceful solitude on the water away from everyone else.*

Theodore Roosevelt National Park and the Little Missouri River

THEODORE ROOSEVELT NATIONAL PARK

NORTH DAKOTA

ESTABLISHED: November 10, 1978

SIZE: 70,467 acres

VISITORS CENTERS: South Unit, North Unit, and Painted Canyon all offer trip information, ranger services, and exhibits on the park. Only the South Unit Visitor Center is open year-round, and it also has a theater and gift shop.

TRANSPORTATION: No in-park transportation

DOGS ALLOWED: Yes, but not on trails

WHEN TO GO: May–June and September–October are less crowded and cooler; fall offers foliage; winter offers snowshoeing and cross-country skiing (but roads may be closed).

CONTACT: 701-623-4466; nps.gov/thro
315 Second Avenue
Medora, ND 58645

The badlands have been called Mako Sica, or "land of no good," by the Dakota people, and *mauvais terres à traverser*, or "bad lands to travel through," by French explorers. Both of those names aptly describe the rugged and tough landscape you'll find in this North Dakota park. Theodore Roosevelt formed a deep connection to the land when he arrived to hunt bison in 1883, and it shaped his conservation policy once he became president. His attachment led to his naming of five national parks and 18 national monuments. It's only fitting that he should have a park named in his honor—the only national park named for a person.

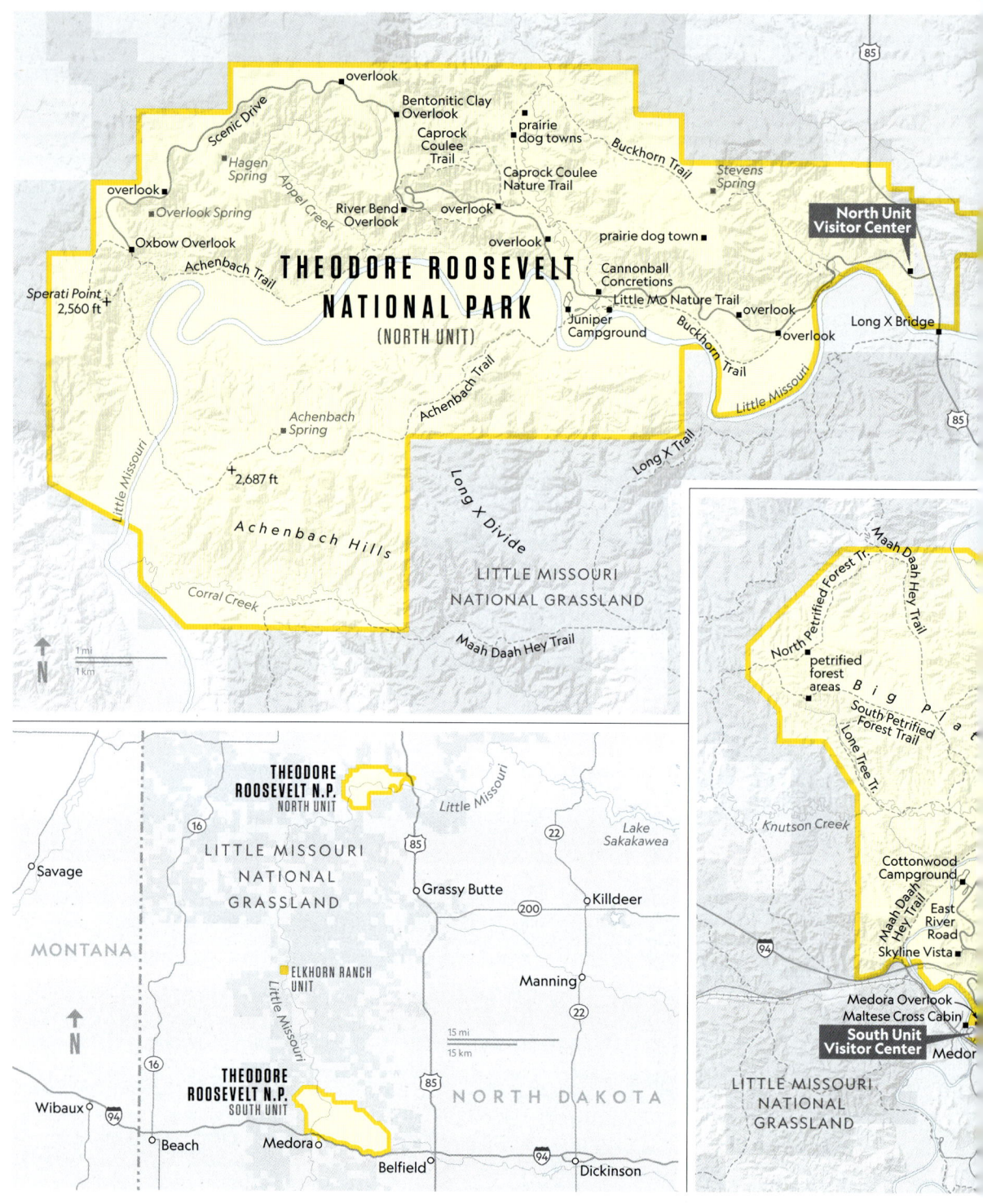

THEODORE ROOSEVELT
NATIONAL PARK
(NORTH UNIT)

North Unit
Visitor Center

Sperati Point
2,560 ft

overlook
Bentonitic Clay
Overlook
Caprock
Coulee
Trail

prairie
dog towns

Buckhorn Trail

Stevens
Spring

Hagen
Spring

Caprock Coulee
Nature Trail

overlook

Overlook Spring

Appel Creek

River Bend
Overlook

overlook

prairie dog town

Oxbow Overlook

Achenbach Trail

Cannonball
Concretions

Little Mo Nature Trail

overlook

Long X Bridge

Juniper
Campground

Buckhorn
Trail

overlook

Achenbach
Spring

Achenbach Trail

Little Missouri

Long X Trail

2,687 ft

Long X Divide

LITTLE MISSOURI
NATIONAL GRASSLAND

Achenbach Hills

Little Missouri

Corral Creek

Maah Daah Hey Trail

1 mi
1 km

N

North Petrified Forest Tr.

Maah Daah Hey Trail

petrified
forest
areas

Big Plat

South Petrified
Forest Trail

Lone Tree Tr.

Knutson Creek

Cottonwood
Campground

Maah Daah
Hey Trail

East
River
Road

Skyline Vista

Medora Overlook
Maltese Cross Cabin

South Unit
Visitor Center

Medor

LITTLE MISSOURI
NATIONAL
GRASSLAND

THEODORE
ROOSEVELT N.P.
NORTH UNIT

Little Missouri

LITTLE MISSOURI
NATIONAL
GRASSLAND

Savage

MONTANA

16

85

Grassy Butte

22

Lake
Sakakawea

Killdeer

200

ELKHORN RANCH
UNIT

Little Missouri

Manning

22

N

16

THEODORE
ROOSEVELT N.P.
SOUTH UNIT

15 mi
15 km

Wibaux

94

85

NORTH DAKOTA

Beach

Medora

Belfield

94

Dickinson

The South Unit's Cottonwood Campground

SLEEP

K Keeping in line with the park's goal of ultimate preservation, the only places to stay in Theodore Roosevelt are primitive campgrounds. If you need something with more amenities, head to nearby **Medora** or **Dickinson** for a hotel. Inside the park, you have three choices:

→ *Year-round **Cottonwood Campground** in the South Unit of the park has some reservable sites from May through September; all campsites are first come, first served the rest of the year. There are 76 spaces for tents and RVs, though no hookups are available.*

→ *All 50 of the regular year-round sites for tents and RVs at **Juniper Campground** in the North Unit are first come, first served, though group sites (only available May–September) can be booked in advance. There's staff on-site and potable water available seasonally.*

→ *Campers arriving by horseback can stay at **Roundup Group Horse Campground** in the South Unit of the park. It can be reserved by only one group at a time and is open only May through October.*

P Plan to visit both the North and South Units of the park. In each, you'll find hikes that share impactful representations of the power and strength of the badlands. The third unit, Elkhorn Ranch, has a pathway to the spot of Teddy Roosevelt's ranch home (see page 197) but no other marked trails.

Try these South Unit hikes:

→ Get the best view of the Little Missouri River by hiking the **Wind Canyon Trail**. This 0.4-mile trip takes you up a wind-sculpted canyon. It's also a great location to stop for the sunset.

→ See examples of the flora that thrives in these dry, tough badlands as you hike the 0.6-mile **Ridgeline Nature Trail**. Look for native silver sagebrush, chokecherry, prairie wild rose, and purple coneflowers.

→ Take the inner or outer loop of the **Coal Vein Trail** to experience how the region has developed over the past 60 million years. See an ever changing landscape that includes ancient swamps; a depression formed by a coal vein fire that burned for 26 years beginning in 1956; and bentonitic clay, the remnants of a volcanic explosion 55 million years ago.

→ The 96-mile **Maah Daah Hey Trail** stretches across the national grassland of all three park units, including the more remote Elkhorn Ranch Unit. Jump into the portion in the South Unit and travel just 7.1 miles along the path—or use the route to go between the South and North Units.

Plan for these North Unit hikes:

→ Take the **Caprock Coulee Nature Trail** for 1.6 miles round-trip through the various ecosystems in the badlands. Continue after reaching the end of the trail to the Caprock Coulee Trail to make it a 4.1-mile trek. You'll see the narrow valleys of the coulees, rivulet erosion on the hillsides, and the differences between northern- and southern-facing slopes.

→ The 18-mile **Achenbach Trail** is not an easy one to tackle, with its steep climbs, tough descents, and two river crossings. But it takes you deep into the park. Time your hike right and you'll cross the Missouri River at daybreak, then get to the buttes for sunrise.

→ For a greener experience, hike the paved 0.7-mile **Little Mo Nature Trail**. Weave through the wetter and more verdant landscape along the river on a raised boardwalk—and grab a trail brochure ahead of time to learn more as you trek.

Experts Only

HIKE

A petrified tree stump in the South Unit

There are 19 marked trail options within Theodore Roosevelt's petrified forest.

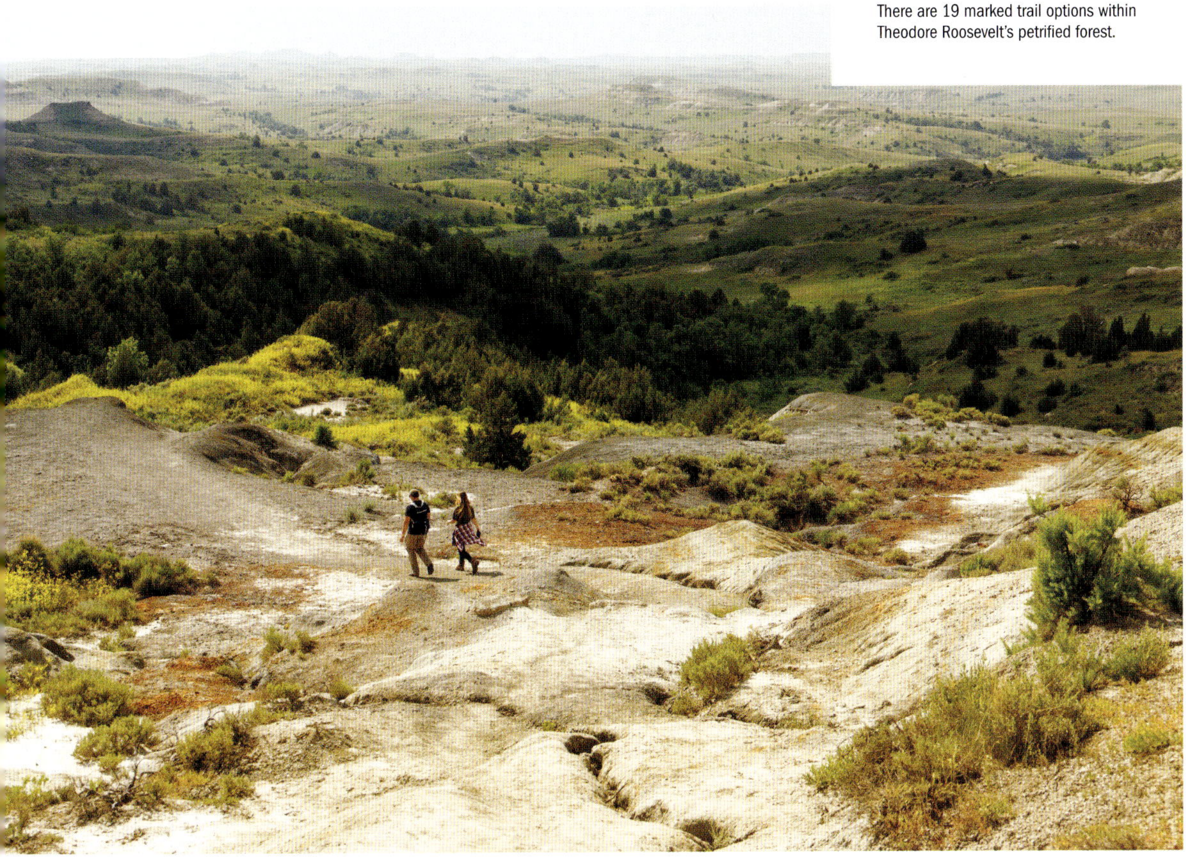

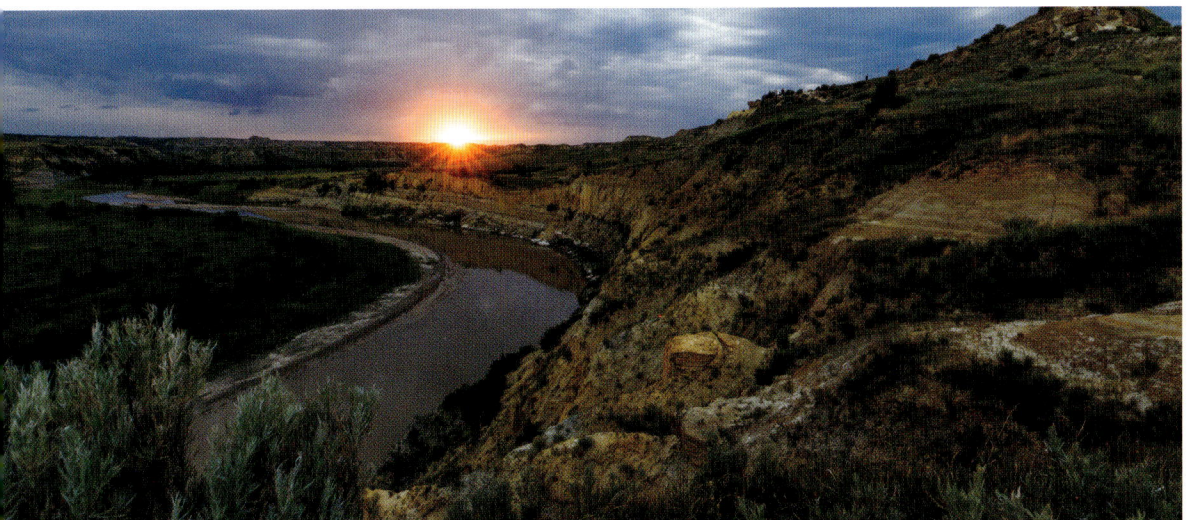

The Wind Canyon Trail at sunset

A wild turkey checks for predators.

(Y) You might think a place with as tough a reputation as the badlands would be lacking in wildlife, but that's not the case in Theodore Roosevelt. Birds, snakes, and mammals occupy nearly every corner of the park.

→ Look for **longhorn cattle** as you enter the North Unit. A small herd is kept nearby to honor the history of ranching in the area. You'll see them as you drive the scenic route.

→ **Bison** are all over the park, and they're usually visible from the roads. There are two herds, one in the South Unit that numbers as high as 500, and one in the North Unit, with about 300 bison. Ask the rangers at a visitors center where bison have been seen recently. As you search for these main characters, also keep an eye out for **elk**, **sheep**, and **mule deer**.

→ Check out a prairie dog town to see the famous **black-tailed prairie dogs** of the Great Plains. Take the Buckhorn Trail off the Caprock Coulee Trailhead, where you'll find a colony, with its network of tunnels and large social units. Just don't feed them.

Two herds of bison call the park home.

Rocky Mountain elk cross the river.

There's only one paddling trip to take in Theodore Roosevelt, and it's a good one. Spend five days traveling the **107.5 miles of the Missouri River** from Medora to the Long X Bridge on U.S. Highway 85. The route connects the South Unit to the North. On the way, you'll have to navigate different water levels and a varying number of portages, depending on the season and the weather.

Carry the water you need and plan for your own first aid as you travel. Also be sure to map out campsites ahead of time, avoiding private land.

FLOAT

The Little Missouri River near Medora

DRIVE

(T) Travel the park on two drives, one in the North Unit and one in the South. Both are packed with overlooks, trailheads, and wildlife. The roads, which are also open to bicycles, serve as a great starting point for any adventure.

→ *The 48-mile loop along the **South Unit Scenic Drive** begins at the South Unit Visitor Center. Go past the Skyline Vista, Peaceful Valley Ranch, Wind Canyon, and Buck Hill viewpoints, as well as the Boicourt and Boicourt East Overlooks. Stretch your legs on a short trail to the Old East Entrance, Badlands Overlook, and Ridgeline Nature Trail Overlook. Add a short detour onto Coal Vein Road for the easy Coal Vein Trail loop.*

→ *The **North Unit Scenic Drive** is a 28-mile round-trip route along the bottom of the badlands to the cannonball concretions. Take the short hike to the River Bend Overlook before driving on and upward to the Bentonitic Clay Overlook, then down to the Oxbow Overlook at the end of the road. Take a short detour to the Little Missouri River Overlook by pulling off onto the Juniper Campground road.*

Cannonball concretions

Keep a respectful distance as you observe bison near the road.

E X P L O R E

If you have an itch to get off the park's trails, dig more deeply into its history, explore it in the offseason, or stay late under the stars, try one of these activities:

→ Visit the **Maltese Cross Cabin** and **Elkhorn Ranch Unit** to get a personal look at how Theodore Roosevelt lived in this area in the 1880s. The Maltese Cross Cabin has been rebuilt with original ponderosa pine, while the Elkhorn Ranch (see page 197) buildings are no more.

→ Guided trail rides are no longer offered, but you can go **horseback riding** on your own steed on the park's backcountry trails. Follow guidelines, including keeping horses off nature trails and leaving no trace behind.

→ Don't be put off by winter weather. While the park doesn't groom trails for **cross-country skiing**, the sport is permitted and you can make your own tracks. Another option is to **traverse the frozen Little Missouri River** once the weather turns; just be sure the ice is strong.

→ **Fish** for chubs, minnows, bluegills, carpsuckers, and catfish in the muddy Little Missouri River. Get a license ahead of time, and hope for luck in the cloudy water. Follow catch-and-release restrictions.

→ Enjoy clear night skies at the park for stargazing almost any time of year, or join the annual **Dakota Nights Astronomy Festival** with telescope viewing sessions, expert talks, and ranger hikes.

→ Any of the roads in Theodore Roosevelt are open to **cyclists**, who should be cautious, as they share the narrow paths with trucks and RVs.

Maltese Cross Cabin

Family Friendly

*Visit **Elkhorn Ranch**, where Theodore Roosevelt found refuge in this spot on the Little Missouri River after his wife and mother died. Today, the ranch and building he constructed are gone, and there are no facilities, but the beautiful cottonwood grove and bluffs provide a landscape of serene vistas.*

VOYAGEURS
NATIONAL PARK

ESTABLISHED: April 8, 1975

SIZE: 218,045 acres

VISITORS CENTERS: The Rainy Lake Visitor Center on Black Bay is open year-round, but hours vary seasonally. In the summer, rely on the Kabetogama Lake and Ash River Visitor Centers.

TRANSPORTATION: No in-park transportation

DOGS ALLOWED: Only in developed sites like campgrounds, picnic areas, boat launch ramps, and visitors centers

WHEN TO GO: July through mid-August for warmer lake temperatures; fall for foliage (peak colors in mid-September to early October); winter for cross-country skiing, snowshoeing, ice fishing, and snowmobiling

CONTACT: 218-283-6600; nps.gov/voya
360 Highway 11 East
International Falls, MN 56649

Evergreens at lakeside

Named for the backcountry travelers who started exploring this seemingly endless landscape of lakes and streams, dense forests, and granite cliffs more than 250 years ago, Voyageurs National Park was shaped by a legacy of exploration. While people have lived on the land and in its waters for the last 10,000 years, it still feels like a wonderland of new discovery. The park is 40 percent water, and relatively little of it is accessible without a boat. Imagine having a private campground on one of its 500 islands or along its 655 miles of shoreline. Come here for the beauty of the remote landscape, the breadth of wildlife, and the complexity of human history in one singular experience.

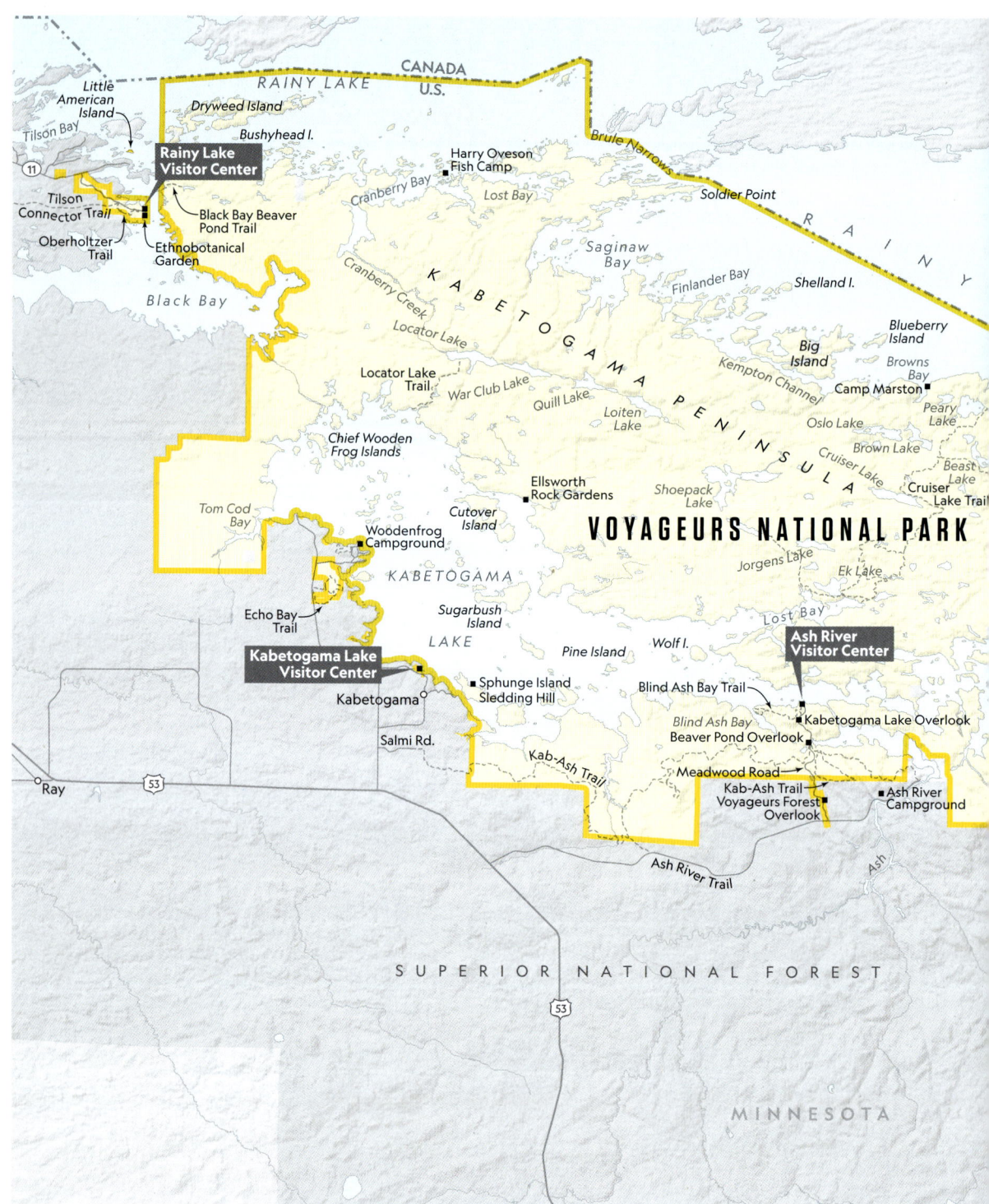

CANADA
U.S.

RAINY LAKE

Little
American
Island
Dryweed Island
Tilson Bay
Bushyhead I.
Brule Narrows
Rainy Lake
Visitor Center
Harry Oveson
Fish Camp
Soldier Point
Tilson
Connector Trail
Black Bay Beaver
Pond Trail
Cranberry Bay
Lost Bay
R A I N Y
Oberholtzer
Trail
Ethnobotanical
Garden
Black Bay
Cranberry Creek
Saginaw
Bay
Finlander Bay
Shelland I.
Locator Lake
K A B E T O G A M A
Blueberry
Island
Locator Lake
Trail
War Club Lake
Quill Lake
Loiten
Lake
Kempton Channel
Big
Island
Browns
Bay
Camp Marston
Chief Wooden
Frog Islands
Oslo Lake
Brown Lake
Peary
Lake
Beast
Lake
Cruiser Lake
Cruiser
Lake Trail
Tom Cod
Bay
Cutover
Island
Ellsworth
Rock Gardens
Shoepack
Lake
P E N I N S U L A
VOYAGEURS NATIONAL PARK
Woodenfrog
Campground
K A B E T O G A M A
Jorgens Lake
Ek Lake
Echo Bay
Trail
Sugarbush
Island
L A K E
Pine Island
Wolf I.
Lost Bay
Ash River
Visitor Center
Kabetogama Lake
Visitor Center
Kabetogama
Sphunge Island
Sledding Hill
Blind Ash Bay Trail
Kabetogama Lake Overlook
Salmi Rd.
Blind Ash Bay
Beaver Pond Overlook
Ray
53
Kab-Ash Trail
Meadwood Road
Kab-Ash Trail
Voyageurs Forest
Overlook
Ash River
Campground
Ash River Trail
Ash
S U P E R I O R   N A T I O N A L   F O R E S T
53
M I N N E S O T A
11

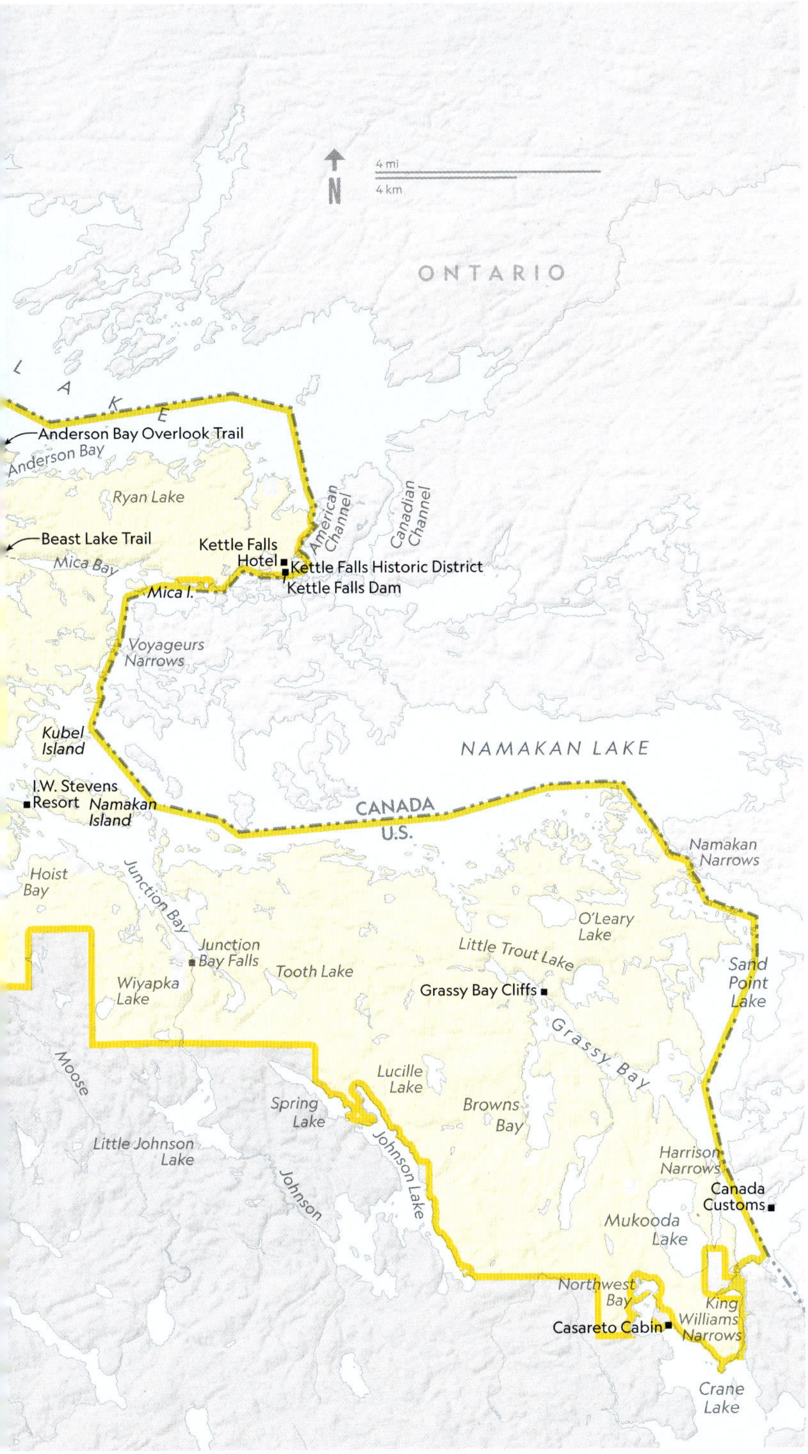

Map labels

ONTARIO

L A K E

Anderson Bay Overlook Trail
Anderson Bay

Ryan Lake

Beast Lake Trail
Mica Bay

Kettle Falls Hotel
Mica I.

American Channel
Canadian Channel

Kettle Falls Historic District
Kettle Falls Dam

Voyageurs Narrows

Kubel Island

NAMAKAN LAKE

I.W. Stevens Resort
Namakan Island

CANADA
U.S.

Namakan Narrows

Hoist Bay

Junction Bay

Junction Bay Falls
Tooth Lake

Wiyapka Lake

O'Leary Lake

Little Trout Lake

Grassy Bay Cliffs

Sand Point Lake

Grassy Bay

Moose

Lucille Lake

Spring Lake
Browns Bay

Little Johnson Lake

Johnson Lake

Johnson

Harrison Narrows

Canada Customs

Mukooda Lake

Northwest Bay

King Williams Narrows

Casareto Cabin

Crane Lake

N
4 mi
4 km

SLEEP

(W) Whether you take a paddle camping trip or rent a houseboat, your adventure will be guided by the flow of the lakes and streams.

→ *Choose a* **backcountry site on an inland lake** *or a* **front-country site along the shore** *of a larger lake. Reserve your permit in advance to make sure your campground is available. Print your permit within five days of your trip.*

→ *Two park* **campsites** *are accessible by foot, and both are off the mainland's Kab-Ash Trail—one at the trailhead along the Ash River Trail and one at the trailhead along Meadwood Road. Both require hiking to reach. Pack a GPS and hike some or all of the 28-mile Kab-Ash Trail through the forests and wetlands during your stay.*

→ *Nearby state parks offer* **drive-up campgrounds***. There are public and private ones at Kabetogama Lake, Ash River, Rainy Lake, and Crane Lake.*

→ **Kettle Falls Hotel** *makes for a comfortable base camp, with its trading post, bar, restaurant, boat portage, canoe and kayak rentals, swimming pool, and Wi-Fi. Travel between the hotel and park by water shuttle, your own boat, or plane.*

→ **Rent a houseboat** *from an outfitter like Voyagaire Lodge & Houseboats or Ebel's Voyageur Houseboats to explore the shorelines from the comfort of your vacation home. Permits are issued for the boat, not the sites, so feel free to move to any of the designated or undesignated mooring spots as they're available.*

W While almost half the park is water, there's still plenty to discover by land at Voyageurs. These trails promise gorgeous views, plenty of wildlife, and peaceful forests.

→ Hop on to the narrow, rocky **Blind Ash Bay Trail** from the Ash River Visitor Center parking lot. From there, trek to the Kabetogama Lake Overlook and then the overlook at the edge of Blind Ash Bay.

→ From the Rainy Lake Visitor Center, explore the edges of the park's wetlands on the **Oberholtzer Trail**. The full trail is 1.6 miles round-trip, but the first quarter mile is an accessible, wide, gravel trail. Follow it through the forest, around the wetlands, and past rocks deposited by glaciers.

→ The 27.9-mile one-way **Kab-Ash Trail** is a difficult but rewarding route between the Kabetogama and Ash River regions. Make sure your navigation skills are up to par.

→ Hike the rugged, backcountry **Cruiser Lake Trail** off Anderson or Lost Bay. The hike is accessible only by boat, meaning you'll experience lands most people never see.

→ The short but challenging four-mile round-trip **Locator Lake Trail** will take you over ridges and through forests to the southern shore of its namesake.

→ The 0.4-mile round-trip **Kabetogama Lake Overlook Trail** goes from the Ash River Visitor Center through a pine forest and up to the viewpoint over the lake.

→ The trailhead for **Black Bay Beaver Pond Trail** is just a mile-long boat trip from the Rainy Lake Visitor Center. It's a short and direct route to an active beaver pond.

→ Hike the short uphill **Beaver Pond Overlook Trail** off Meadwood Road. It's a great spot for bird-watchers and wildlife seekers, and even better if you go in the morning or evening.

H I K E

Black Bay Beaver Pond Trail

A tree gnawed by beavers beside Kabetogama Lake

A great blue heron

Park wildlife is abundant, as Voyageurs' remote location gives animals plenty of space and freedom. You're bound to see creatures you won't find at home, and here are some good ways to ensure that happens.

→ Hundreds of bird species live at Voyageurs. Look for **bald eagle** nests along the water, 12 species of **breeding warblers** and **black-backed woodpeckers** in Anderson Bay, **turkey vultures** around the Rainy Lake Visitor Center, and **hooded mergansers** at Dryweed Island.

→ Black bears, porcupines, deer, coyotes, beavers, and wolves are spread throughout the park, but **moose** take first billing on many visitors' wish lists. Most live on the Kabetogama Peninsula, so you'll have the best luck along the Cruiser Lake Trail or at a quiet beaver pond.

SPOT

FLOAT

B Boating and paddling are the best ways to discover the park—and often the *only* ways. Bring your own vessel, rent one nearby, or take a guided tour. (Visitors can rent canoes from the park through *recreation.gov* or use nearby outfitters.)

→ Join the **North Canoe Voyage** and paddle a 26-foot-long reproduction of the canoe that historic voyageurs used to transport trade goods.

→ Book a **ranger-led boat tour**. Try the wildlife-finding Discovery Cruise, the evening Starwatch Cruise from Rainy Lake, or the boat-hike hybrid tour of Ellsworth Rock Gardens from the Kabetogama Lake or Ash River Visitor Centers.

→ Take a self-guided trip paddling the **Chain of Lakes**. A canoe rental is included with the purchase of your backcountry camping permit for this network of waterways linking the park's four main lakes and dozens of smaller waterways. Be sure to get a map from a visitors center, have a GPS device, and pack everything you need for camping and first aid.

One worthwhile kayaking spot: Junction Bay Falls on Namakan Lake

Take a wildlife-spotting cruise aboard one of Voyageurs' tour boats.

The aurora borealis over Voyageurs

→ EXPLORE

E Expand your park experience by digging into its history, staying up late, or learning about its plant life. These extra adventures are worth adding to your itinerary:

→ Visit the **Ethnobotanical Garden** near the Rainy Lake Visitor Center. Come in the spring for cherry blossoms, summer for berries and ferns, autumn for vibrant fall colors, and winter for snow-covered evergreens.

→ Gold miners in the late 1800s saw promise in the region, but their efforts were fruitless. See the remnants of their futile labor on a self-guided quarter-mile tour across **Little American Island**, with its mining shafts and machinery, or visit **Bushyhead Island**, where a mineshaft was carved into the rock.

→ See the **aurora borealis** on a dark, clear night at the park. While longer nights in the winter help, it's possible to see the phenomenon any time of year. Try the Rainy Lake Visitor Center parking lot or join one of the park's Star Party events.

→ Don't sell the park, or yourself, short by skipping it in the winter. Rent **cross-country skis** or **snowshoes** in adult and children's sizes at the Rainy Lake Visitor Center, then head out on a winter trail. Try the groomed Tilson Connector Trail or the Echo Bay Trail.

→ For more thrills, **snowmobile** any of the 110 miles of groomed trails on frozen lake surfaces. Just avoid pressure ridges, slush, and open water.

→ Sled down the **Sphunge Island Sledding Hill**, on the banks of Kabetogama Lake, off Kab-Ash Ice Road to enjoy the snow and the speed.

→ Literally walk on water—OK, drive—on one of the two ice roads. **Rainy Lake Ice Road** leaves from that visitors center's boat launch, and **Kabetogama Lake Ice Road** takes you between the Ash River and Kabetogama Lake Visitor Centers. Follow the rules and check the conditions ahead of time.

→ Brave the solitude to **ice fish** in the winter. Put out your own icehouse, so long as you follow the regulations, or book a guided trip with an outfitter like Voyageur Park Lodge.

Family Friendly

→ **RANGER RECOMMENDATION** ←

*Hike the less traversed **Cruiser Lake Trail** to try to spot a moose. The eight-mile route is accessible only by boat and leads down a path most visitors never take. Start at either Anderson Bay or Lost Bay; reserve a campsite to turn it into a longer backcountry trip. The trail crosses the peninsula and goes up rocky cliffs and down into the wetlands.*

A prairie at Wind Cave National Park

WIND CAVE NATIONAL PARK

SOUTH DAKOTA

ESTABLISHED: January 9, 1903

SIZE: 33,851 acres

VISITORS CENTER: The Wind Cave Visitor Center is open year-round and houses educational exhibits and a bookstore. Stop in for ranger advice on your trip, or start your tours and treks from the location.

TRANSPORTATION: No in-park transportation

DOGS ALLOWED: Only on grassy areas at the visitors center, at Elk Mountain Campground, and on both the Prairie Vista and Elk Mountain Nature Trails. All other areas are restricted, including cave tours and backcountry.

WHEN TO GO: Late spring to early fall for outdoor activities; cave tours are available year-round.

CONTACT: 605-745-4600; nps.gov/wica
26611 U.S. Highway 385
Hot Springs, SD 57747

The two ecosystems of Wind Cave National Park might feel completely distinct, one below the surface and one above it. In actuality, they coexist in a unique and compelling way. Underground lies one of the world's most complex and unusual caves; above is a globally significant expanse of mixed-grass prairie, home to wildlife—from massive bison to playful prairie dogs to mountain bluebirds. Plan a trip to explore both—it will be worth the while.

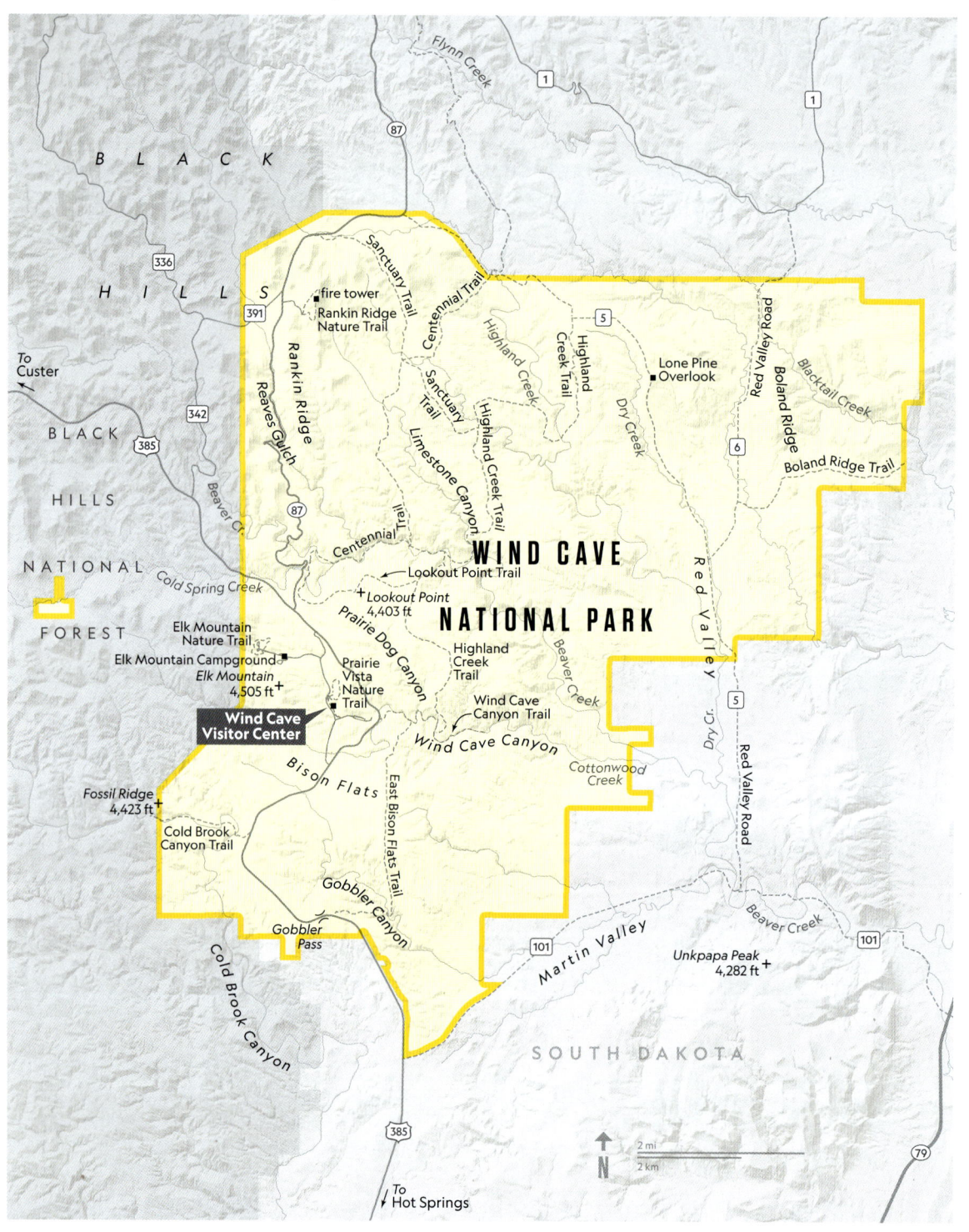

BLACK

HILLS

BLACK

HILLS

NATIONAL

FOREST

To
Custer

Flynn Creek

1

1

87

336

391

342

385

5

Reaves Gulch

Rankin Ridge

Beaver Cr.

Cold Spring Creek

87

fire tower
Rankin Ridge
Nature Trail

Sanctuary Trail

Centennial Trail

Highland Creek

Highland
Creek Trail

Highland Creek Trail

Sanctuary
Trail

Limestone Canyon

Centennial Trail

Lookout Point Trail

Lookout Point
4,403 ft

Prairie Dog Canyon

Elk Mountain
Nature Trail

Elk Mountain Campground
Elk Mountain
4,505 ft

Prairie
Vista
Nature
Trail

**Wind Cave
Visitor Center**

Bison Flats

Fossil Ridge
4,423 ft

Cold Brook
Canyon Trail

East Bison Flats Trail

Gobbler Canyon

Gobbler
Pass

Cold Brook Canyon

5

Lone Pine
Overlook

Dry Creek

Red Valley Road

Boland Ridge

Blacktail Creek

6

Boland Ridge Trail

Red Valley

Dry Cr.

Red Valley Road

5

WIND CAVE

NATIONAL PARK

Highland
Creek
Trail

Wind Cave
Canyon Trail

Wind Cave Canyon

Beaver Creek

Cottonwood
Creek

Beaver Creek

101

101

Martin Valley

Unkpapa Peak
4,282 ft

79

385

To
Hot Springs

SOUTH DAKOTA

2 mi

2 km

N

→ SLEEP

W Wind Cave has only one in-park option: **Elk Mountain Campground**. The 64-site tent and RV campground sits between a ponderosa pine forest and an open prairie, so you might wake up to find wildlife wandering around its edges. There are two accessible sites and two group sites available, along with flush toilets and drinking water. Reservations are required. Check the calendar before arrival, as ranger-led programs are often offered in the campground's amphitheater, including elk bugling and cultural and historical programming.

Backcountry camping is also an option. The park has an open-hike policy, so you're welcome to set up camp anywhere that's safe for you and the ecosystem. Free permits are required for all backcountry camping and can be obtained at the visitors center. If you prefer a less rugged night's rest, look for hotels and lodging in **Custer** or **Hot Springs**.

Elk Mountain Campground

HIKE

The park might seem like it's all about the caves, but there's plenty to discover on its surface. Add one of these hikes to your itinerary:

→ The one-mile **Rankin Ridge Nature Trail** winds through the trees up to the highest point in the park. From there, see faraway Badlands National Park and Buffalo Gap National Grassland, along with the nearby historic fire tower.

→ The **Wind Cave Canyon Trail** is an easy 3.6-mile round-trip path down an old road into a canyon of the same name. Keep an eye on the limestone cliffs while you hike and you might see cliff swallows, canyon wrens, and great horned owls.

→ The peaceful one-mile round-trip **Elk Mountain Nature Trail** takes you around the campground and through the nearby forests. It's an easy walk and showcases just how calm the environment can be in the park. It's also one of the few hikes where dogs are welcome.

→ For a more difficult hike, take the **Boland Ridge Trail** up a tough 5.2-mile trek from the parking lot on NPS 6. The route offers sweeping views of the Black Hills and Red Valley. Watch for elk as you go.

→ The **Lookout Point Trail** runs 2.2 miles to Beaver Creek. For a longer loop, adding the Highland Creek and Centennial Trails will get you more scenic views and a total of 4.5 miles.

→ Check out the cave's natural entrance during a walk along the **Prairie Vista Nature Trail** from behind the visitors center. Learn about the grasslands through educational signs on the trail.

→ Find the trailhead for the **East Bison Flats Trail** just north of the park's southern boundary. Take the 3.7-mile route up a steep climb toward panoramic views of the prairie, Buffalo Gap, and Black Hills.

Family Friendly

Prairie dogs

The wildlife in the park is diverse and plentiful, but it's not always easy to find. You'll probably have better luck from the roads and overlooks.

→ You're likely to see **bison** wandering through the Bison Flats, or you might get stuck in a bison jam as they cross U.S. Highway 385 or NPS 5 and 6. The animals were reintroduced along with **elk** and **pronghorns** in 1912 after the land was designated as Wind Cave National Game Preserve.

→ Wind Cave Canyon Trail will take you past bluffs that make for great bird-watching. Look for **western meadowlarks**, **eastern** and **mountain bluebirds**, **burrowing** and **great horned owls**, **golden eagles**, **black-backed woodpeckers**, **yellow warblers**, and **orioles**.

→ Slow down along U.S. Highway 385 or South Dakota Highway 87 to spot **prairie dogs** popping in and out of the landscape.

SPOT

DRIVE

B Both **U.S. Highway 385** and **South Dakota Highway 87**, the two main paved roads in the park, offer scenic views, pullouts for trailheads and exhibits, and parking to watch the wildlife. You'll likely be traveling along these roads to get from place to place in the park no matter what—though you could do some of it by bicycle too. **NPS 5** (dirt road) and **NPS 6** (gravel road) are great for spotting wildlife.

E Exploring the caves is the priority for most visitors. Take a tour to get the most from that adventure. Offerings change with the seasons, so check the schedule ahead of time. The **Natural Entrance Tour** highlights examples of boxwork, the **Fairgrounds Tour** explores upper and middle levels of the cave, the quick **Garden of Eden Tour** is the least strenuous of the bunch, and the tough **Wild Cave Tour** (summer only) will get you crawling through tight spaces.

Exploring during a Wild Cave Tour, an experience-required, summer-only guided route

NPS 6

SPELUNK

*Drive along **NPS 5**, a dirt road that goes through the park's backcountry, to a small pull-off called Lone Pine, named for the one pine tree on its ridge. Visit during a supermoon and bring a chair. Watch the sunset to the west and then turn your chair to see the gigantic, blood-red moon rising. You're likely to be there alone—unless you happen to see a park ranger.*

→ SOUTH CENTRAL

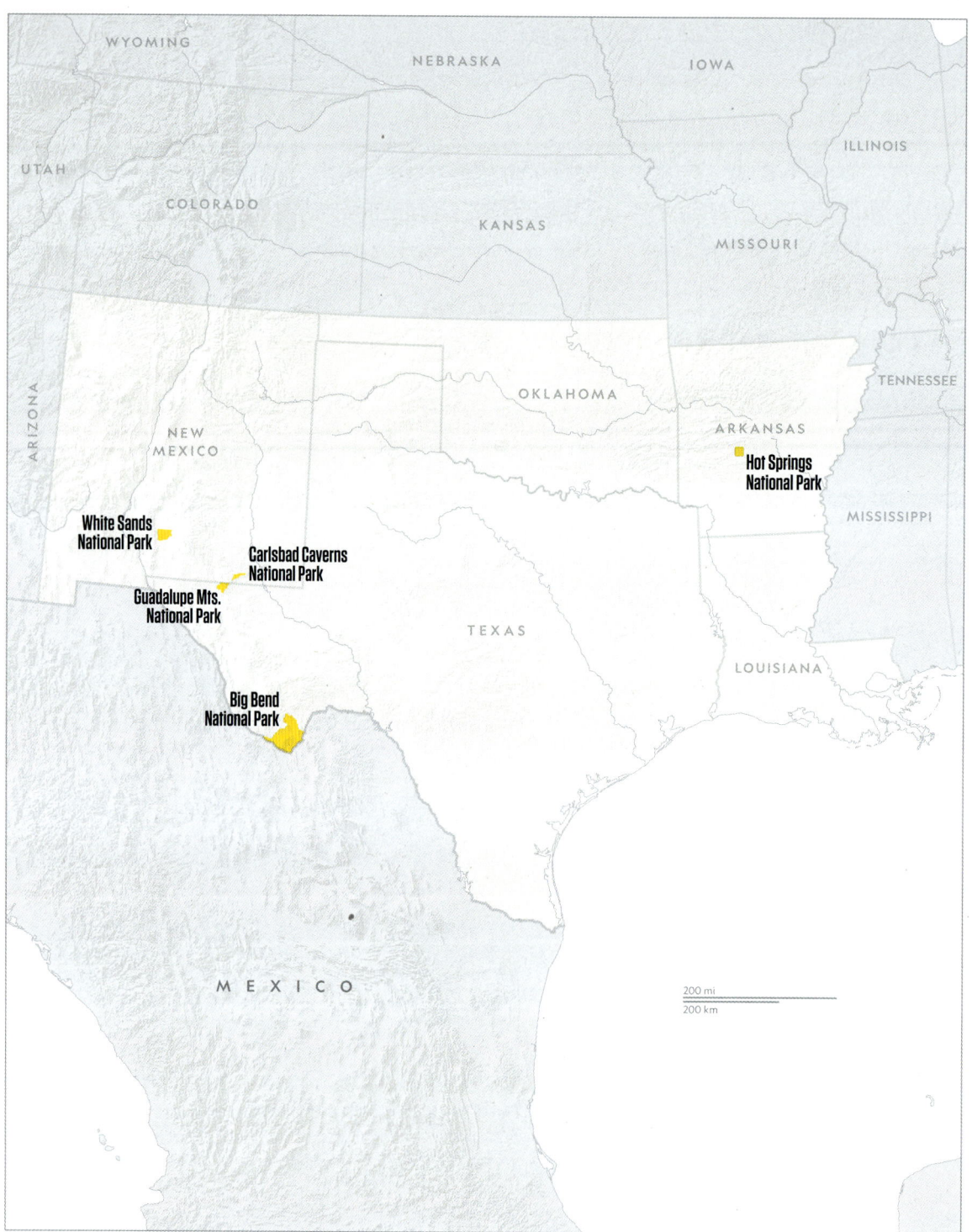

WYOMING

NEBRASKA

IOWA

ILLINOIS

UTAH

COLORADO

KANSAS

MISSOURI

ARIZONA

NEW
MEXICO

OKLAHOMA

ARKANSAS

TENNESSEE

**Hot Springs
National Park**

MISSISSIPPI

**White Sands
National Park**

**Carlsbad Caverns
National Park**

**Guadalupe Mts.
National Park**

TEXAS

LOUISIANA

**Big Bend
National Park**

MEXICO

200 mi
200 km

The five national parks of the South Central region offer scenery ranging from historical and underground to high and rugged. Hikers can climb into pine-fir forests in the peaks of Texas's Guadalupe Mountains (page 236). In New Mexico's Carlsbad Caverns (page 230), discover the underworld along 30 miles of mapped passageways and the thrilling drama of nightly bat flights. Aboveground, White Sands (page 250) offers otherworldly landscapes. Rivers etched the dramatic Texas canyons of Big Bend (page 220), where paleontologists have unearthed fossils, including the Big Bend pterosaur, the largest animal ever to fly. Meanwhile, Arkansas's Hot Springs (page 244) offers a different experience with its bubbling, heated waters—once the grand dame of healing culture in the U.S.

LEFT: Lake of the Clouds, Carlsbad Caverns National Park (page 230) **PREVIOUS PAGES:** Salt Basin Dunes, Guadalupe Mountains National Park (page 236)

Boquillas Canyon on the Rio Grande

BIG BEND
NATIONAL PARK

TEXAS

ESTABLISHED: June 12, 1944

SIZE: 801,163 acres

VISITORS CENTERS: Most visitors start their trip at the year-round Panther Junction Visitor Center, with its exhibits, advice, theater, and amenities. The Chisos Basin Visitor Center is also open all year, while the Rio Grande Village Visitor Center, Castolon Visitor Center, and Persimmon Gap Visitor Center are open seasonally.

TRANSPORTATION: No in-park transportation

DOGS ALLOWED: Only where vehicles can go

WHEN TO GO: Late fall through early spring for the best weather (but most crowds); summer for warmer water; winter for starry nights

CONTACT: 432-477-2251; nps.gov/bibe
1 Panther Junction
Big Bend National Park, TX 79834

S Sea fossils. Dinosaur bones. Volcanic dikes. The history of Big Bend National Park spans millennia, and when you wander its foothills, hike its peaks, and paddle its waters, you'll see evidence of it all. It's home to 500-million-year-old rocks at Persimmon Gap, windblown dunes at Boquillas Canyon, historic rancher homes, and evidence of the Comanche Indians and Spanish gold miners. The land has shifted again and again, geologically and culturally, and a visit to this wide-open park is like an intimate conversation with its past.

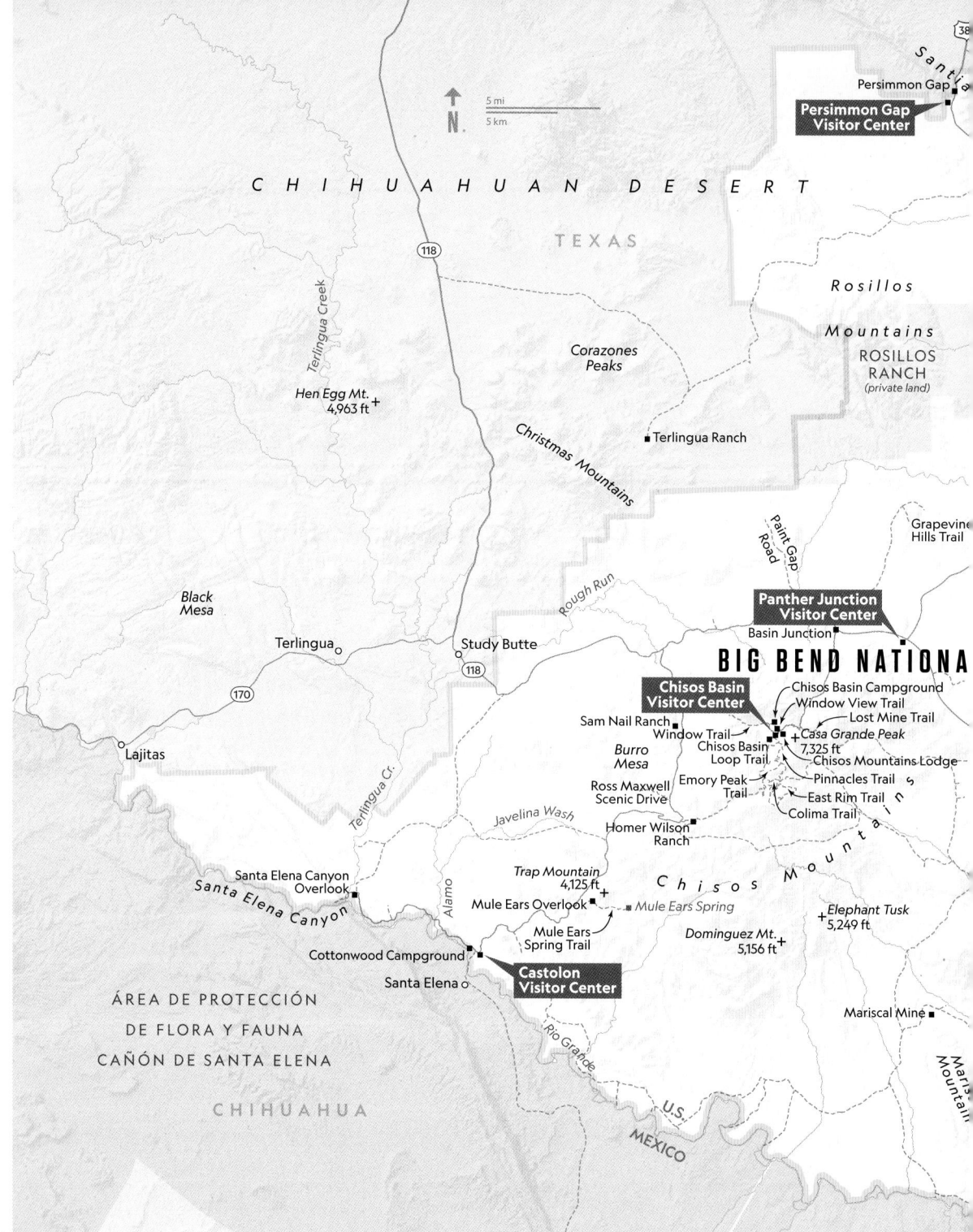

N

5 mi
5 km

CHIHUAHUAN DESERT

TEXAS

Rosillos

Mountains
ROSILLOS
RANCH
(private land)

Corazones
Peaks

Hen Egg Mt.
4,963 ft

Christmas Mountains

■ Terlingua Ranch

Grapevine
Hills Trail

Paint Gap
Road

Rough Run

Panther Junction
Visitor Center

Basin Junction ■ ■

BIG BEND NATIONA

Black
Mesa

Terlingua

Study Butte

118

170

Chisos Basin
Visitor Center

Chisos Basin Campground
Window View Trail
Lost Mine Trail

Sam Nail Ranch ■

Window Trail
Casa Grande Peak
7,325 ft

Lajitas

Burro
Mesa

Ross Maxwell
Scenic Drive

Chisos Basin
Loop Trail

Chisos Mountains Lodge

Pinnacles Trail

Emory Peak
Trail

East Rim Trail

Colima Trail

Terlingua Cr.

Homer Wilson
Ranch

Chisos Mountains

Santa Elena Canyon
Overlook

Trap Mountain
4,125 ft

Alamo

Javelina Wash

Mule Ears Overlook

Santa Elena Canyon

Mule Ears Spring

Elephant Tusk
5,249 ft

Mule Ears
Spring Trail

Dominguez Mt.
5,156 ft

Cottonwood Campground ■

Castolon
Visitor Center

Mariscal Mine ■

Santa Elena

ÁREA DE PROTECCIÓN

DE FLORA Y FAUNA

Rio Grande

CAÑÓN DE SANTA ELENA

U.S.

MEXICO

CHIHUAHUA

Maris
Mountain

Persimmon Gap ■

**Persimmon Gap
Visitor Center**

38

Santia

118

Dagger Flat Auto Trail

Dagger Flat

2627

S I E R R A   D E L   C A R M E N

Sierra Larga

Sierra del Caballo Muerto

Roys Peak
3,945 ft

ARK

Rio Grande

Tornillo Creek

Park Route 12

Ernst Basin

MADERAS
DEL CARMEN
BIOSPHERE
RESERVE

Boquillas
Canyon

**Rio Grande Village
Visitor Center**

Boquillas Overlook

Rio Grande Village RV Park

Langford Hot Springs

Rio Grande Village Campground

Rio Grande Village
Nature Trail

U.S.

MEXICO

San Vicente

Rio Grande

Sierra San Vicente

Cerro El Veinte

C O A H U I L A

ÁREA DE PROTECCIÓN DE
FLORA Y FAUNA OCAMPO

➡ SLEEP

T To stay inside the park borders, book a room at the lodge, reserve a site at one of the park's four campgrounds, or hike to a backcountry campsite. One rule: no campfires anywhere. Outside of those options, search for a hotel in nearby Study Butte, Terlingua, or Lajitas. Here are your in-park choices:

➡ *Chisos Mountains Lodge* offers modern amenities, mountain views, and easy access to hiking trails. It also has a restaurant, two stores, and a visitors center on-site.

➡ The east-side *Rio Grande Village RV Park* is run by Chisos Mountains Lodge and hosts 25 RV sites with full hookups, public showers, a laundry, and a village store. All sites are back-in only and reservations are required. It's also the access point for the Rio Grande Village Nature Trail.

➡ *Chisos Basin Campground* sits at the base of a mountain in an open woodland, with views of Casa Grande and Emory Peaks. It features 56 sites for tents and RVs, a camp store, and on-site staff year-round. Reservations are required. The popular seven group sites are a quarter mile away from the main campground. Both are sandwiched between many of the park's most beloved trails.

➡ Reserve one of 93 tent, RV, or group campsites at *Rio Grande Village Campground*. The roads in the campground are paved, and it has flush toilets, running water, picnic tables, and grills. Reservations are required.

➡ *Cottonwood Campground*, open from November through April, is a more rustic option. Reservations are required and can be booked up to 14 days in advance. It's less popular, meaning you might find yourself some solitude nestled between the Castolon Historic District and Santa Elena Canyon.

➡ Overnight in the wild with a backcountry permit at one of the 42 *backpacking campsites* along the park's trails, including Colima, Pinnacles, and East Rim, or one of the 64 *primitive sites* along its backcountry roads, accessible with high-clearance, four-wheel-drive vehicles. Composting vault toilets protect the environment. Permits are required, and most designated backcountry campsites are available online in advance through recreation.gov. Permits for desert backpacking and primitive roadside sites are only available in person at park visitors centers.

Overlooks along trails offer sweeping park views.

HIKE

There are three types of hikes in Big Bend: through the desert, up the mountains, or along the river. Some trails cover all three. Read on for your best options for exploring the park by foot:

→ Take the 3.8-mile round-trip **Mule Ears Spring Trail** from the Mule Ears Overlook parking area through the base of the Chisos Mountains, around Trap Mountain, and across several arroyos (dry riverbeds that fill seasonally). The shady area by the spring may provide some respite from the heat, but don't jump in and swim—waterborne microorganisms can be hazardous.

→ Getting to the 2.2-mile **Grape-vine Hills Trail** is a feat; you'll need a high-clearance vehicle to reach the trail-head. From there, hike up to the balanced rocks at the heart of the hills. It's a steep, fun climb, but coming down is difficult.

→ Beautiful vistas await on the two-mile round-trip **Chisos Basin Loop Trail**. The water along the way attracts bears, mountain lions, and Mexican jays, so be prepared for great wildlife spotting.

→ Even if you can't tackle the entire 4.8-mile round-trip **Lost Mine Trail**, the first mile and back offers a great peek into the mountain's wildlife and Casa Grande Peak and Juniper Canyon.

→ Descend along the 5.6-mile round-trip **Window Trail** until you reach the "window of the mountains," which frames stunning panoramic vistas of the desert. When it's been raining, you might have to cross Oak Creek multiple times.

→ From the same trailhead, travel the 0.3-mile **Window View Trail**. Circle a low hill on a paved trail to see mountain peaks and the natural windows created by them.

→ Take the **Pinnacles Trail** up 3.5 miles from the Chisos Basin parking lot to the **Emory Peak Trail**, which runs another 1.5 miles to the peak. The last bit is a steep scramble up an exposed rock face.

→ The **Rio Grande Village Nature Trail** is a three-quarter-mile loop with a great payoff for reasonable effort. At the top of a limestone hill, find sweeping views of the river framed by the Chisos Mountains and Sierra del Carmen.

Experts Only

T Take a **canoe** or **raft trip** down the Rio Grande with an outfitter like Wild Adventure Outfitters, Big Bend River Tours, Far Flung Outdoor Center, Desert Sports, or Big Bend Boating and Hiking Company. While you're floating, keep your eyes and ears out for beavers, turtles, great blue herons, and green kingfishers. You'll cross the border to Mexico and back to the States multiple times as you paddle through tranquil waters (and the occasional rapid); just don't make landfall on Mexican soil unless it's an emergency, as it's considered an illegal crossing.

Kayaking the Rio Grande below Santa Elena Canyon

FLOAT

SPOT

B Big Bend is home to more types of birds, bats, butterflies, ants, scorpions, and cacti than any other national park. Here are two ways to get a view of its creatures:

→ *More than **450 species of birds** have been spotted at Big Bend. See many of them at Rio Grande Village, where 305 of the species have been spotted. Keep an eye out for golden-fronted woodpeckers, common black hawks, and green kingfishers.*
→ *If you're searching for mammals, the Chisos Basin is a good place to start. Look afar to spot **bears**, **mountain lions**, **bobcats**, **elk**, **coyotes**, **rabbits**, and **squirrels**.*

A Mexican jay

Park Route 12 with the Sierra del Carmen in the distance

→ EXPLORE

W When you've finished with your hikes, soothe your weary muscles at the hot springs or learn more about the history of this complex land.

→ Find rest and relaxation at the **Langford Hot Springs** at the end of the Hot Springs dirt road. The bathhouse of the past has been destroyed, but you can take a dip in the spring waters that remain. Just be aware of the heat and enter cautiously—some temperatures can reach scalding levels.

→ Stop at two historic ranches along the Ross Maxwell Scenic Drive to see how past homesteaders lived on this land. Explore what's left of the family home, orchard, and garden at the **Sam Nail Ranch**, dating back to 1916, accessible from a pullout with parking. Farther down the road, the ruins of the **Homer Wilson Ranch**, dating back to 1928, are accessible from the overlook off the road. You'll find a dipping vat for farm animals and what remains of a ranch house with a porch.

→ Cyclists can **bike** along any of the paved or unpaved roads in the park. If you have someone to shuttle you back and forth, take the 35-mile route from Panther Junction to Castolon on the **Ross Maxwell Scenic Drive**. If you don't, try the rocky **Paint Gap Road** or the gentle seven-mile **Dagger Flat Auto Trail**.

→ Join a free, ranger-led **night-sky program**. Check the schedule on the park's website to see if there will be star parties, moonlight walks, or night-sky talks when you visit.

Homer Wilson Ranch

*Spend a **night with the birds** of Big Bend by booking a campsite at Cottonwood Campground. Drink your morning coffee with wild turkeys, Lucy's warblers, gray hawks, or Mississippi kites, then stroll the campground's diverse habitats, ranging from mesquite thicket to cottonwood trees.*

The Giant Dome formation within Carlsbad's Big Room

CARLSBAD CAVERNS NATIONAL PARK

NEW MEXICO

ESTABLISHED: May 14, 1930

SIZE: 46,766 acres

VISITORS CENTER: The visitors center, with its restaurant and shop, is open year-round and is the starting point for most of your adventures.

TRANSPORTATION: No in-park transportation

DOGS ALLOWED: No

WHEN TO GO: April–May or September–October for fewer crowds and mild temperatures; bat-flight programs run late May–October.

CONTACT: 575-785-2232; nps.gov/cave
727 Carlsbad Caverns Highway
Carlsbad, NM 88220

W While Carlsbad Caverns National Park's landscapes are stunning, what draws most visitors here lies beneath the surface. Underground, you'll find 119 impressive caves, with massive stalactites hanging from the ceilings and huge blocks of gypsum lining the floors.

While most limestone caves in the world were carved out by water, those in this park are different. Hydrogen sulfide, area microbes, and oxygen came together to create sulfuric acid, which then dissolved the rocks and earth, creating passageways. As the Guadalupe Mountains rose, the water table dropped, draining away that "acid bath" and leaving behind the caves. One wild consequence of this unique process: Not all the caves have an opening to the world above.

Floods have damaged some of the park's infrastructure, but the caves are open year-round, the bats are flying, and the desert is thriving.

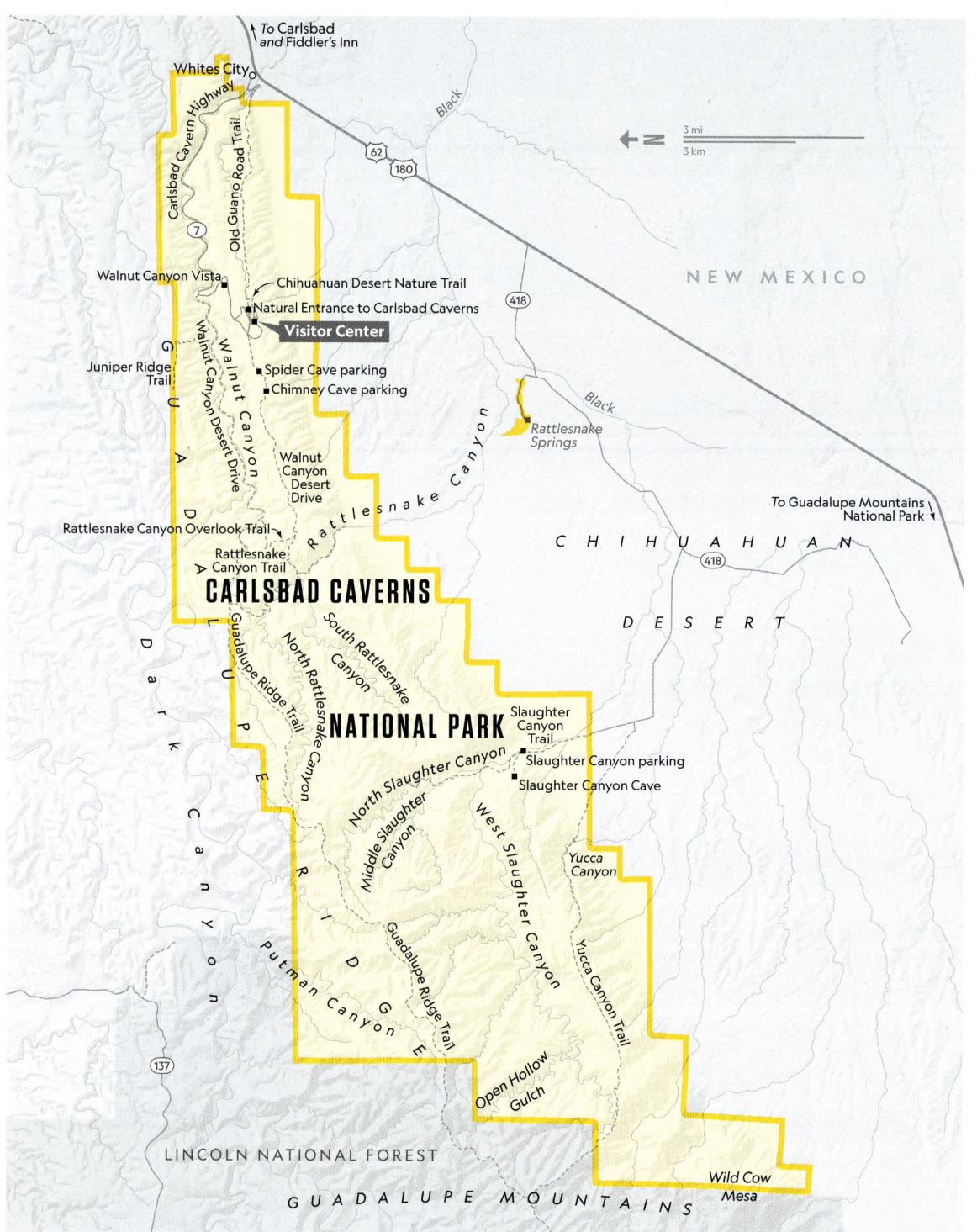

To Carlsbad
and Fiddler's Inn

Whites City

Black

NEW MEXICO

62
180

3 mi
3 km

Carlsbad Cavern Highway

Old Guano Road Trail

7

418

Walnut Canyon Vista

Chihuahuan Desert Nature Trail

Natural Entrance to Carlsbad Caverns

Visitor Center

Juniper Ridge Trail

Spider Cave parking

Chimney Cave parking

Black

Rattlesnake
Springs

Walnut Canyon Desert Drive

Walnut
Canyon
Desert
Drive

Rattlesnake Canyon

CHIHUAHUAN

418

Rattlesnake Canyon Overlook Trail

Rattlesnake
Canyon Trail

DESERT

CARLSBAD CAVERNS

To Guadalupe Mountains
National Park

Walnut Canyon

GUADALUPE

South Rattlesnake
Canyon

North Rattlesnake Canyon

NATIONAL PARK

Slaughter
Canyon
Trail

Slaughter Canyon parking

Dark Canyon

Guadalupe Ridge Trail

North Slaughter Canyon

Middle Slaughter Canyon

West Slaughter Canyon

Slaughter Canyon Cave

RIDGE

Guadalupe Ridge Trail

Yucca
Canyon

137

Putman Canyon

Yucca Canyon Trail

Open Hollow
Gulch

LINCOLN NATIONAL FOREST

Wild Cow
Mesa

GUADALUPE MOUNTAINS

Opt for a stay at the Fiddler's Inn, in Carlsbad, 30 minutes from the park.

SLEEP

T There aren't any lodges or established campgrounds in Carlsbad Caverns, but a same-day permit (available at the visitors center) provides access to **backcountry camping**. If you're looking for a more established campground, find one in nearby **Whites City** or **Carlsbad**. Carlsbad also has plenty of hotels.

Combine a trip to the park with a stay at Guadalupe Mountains National Park (page 236), which is only 40 minutes away and home to an established campground.

A Above- and belowground hikes are available in the park, though you'd be remiss not to get into the caverns. There are two options for discovering the wonder of the Carlsbad caves: self-guided treks and ranger-guided tours.

A Above- and belowground hikes are available in the park, though you'd be remiss not to get into the caverns. There are two options for discovering the wonder of the Carlsbad caves: self-guided treks and ranger-guided tours.

→ The **Big Room Trail** *(1.25 miles), which goes through the largest chamber, is the most popular of two self-guided trails. It is also the only wheelchair-accessible route in the cavern and has elevator access. Make a reservation before you arrive.*
→ *Travel the routes of early explorers past Devil's Spring, the Whale's Mouth, and Iceberg Rock on the steep, self-guided* **Natural Entrance Trail** *(1.25 miles). Make a reservation in advance.*
→ *On the ranger-led* **King's Palace Tour***, you'll walk through four chambers and the deepest section of the cave visitors are allowed to enter. The 90-minute tour ends 830 feet below the surface—be prepared for rangers to turn out their lights.*

There's plenty to see on the surface of the park, so take a few desert hikes while you're there.

→ *Hop off the road leading to the visitors center for the 180-yard walk to the* **Walnut Canyon Vista***. It takes only five minutes to get to this broad, sweeping view of the desert.*
→ *The 7.7-mile* **Yucca Canyon Trail** *isn't an easy one. Find its trailhead at the end of a dirt route past the Slaughter Canyon parking lot. Travel up a side canyon, along a ridge, and across a plateau until you get to a sheer drop with canyon views. You'll need to overnight to get there and back, so make sure you get a backcountry permit and pack the supplies you need.*
→ *The* **Chihuahuan Desert Nature Trail** *is a half-mile paved route that takes just 30 minutes and is packed with educational markers about native plants and wildlife.*
→ *If you're in it for a long haul, trek the 100-mile* **Guadalupe Ridge Trail** *through Carlsbad Caverns, Lincoln National Forest, Bureau of Land Management land, and Guadalupe Mountains National Park. Twenty miles run through Carlsbad Caverns, and the trail will take you about a week to traverse in total.*

HIKE

Family Friendly

SPOT

C Carlsbad Caverns is home to plenty of wildlife, from bats to birds to reptiles. Practice some patience, and try to find some of these creatures while you're there:

→ *Join rangers for the free Bat Flight Program (late May–October) at the amphitheater near the Natural Entrance of the cavern. Up to 500,000 **Brazilian free-tailed bats** reside permanently in the caves; during migration season that number may be more than a million. Learn about the bats from rangers, and then watch the winged creatures swoop out from the entrance to feed as dusk settles in. The events are free and open on a first-come-first-serve basis, so arrive early.*

→ *Come to the park on the third Saturday of July for the annual **Dawn of the Bats**, when rangers and visitors gather at dawn to watch the bats return from their evening of feeding and flying.*

→ *More than **300 species of birds** call this park home, either year-round or seasonally. Look for ladder-backed woodpeckers, cactus wrens, and northern mockingbirds any time of year, and try to spot the protected Bell's vireo or gray vireo during migration season.*

→ *Keep an eye out for reptiles while you hike, especially lizards. You're most likely to see **whiptail**, **spiny**, and **horned lizards**, but you also might spot a **skink**, **gecko**, or **Chihuahuan hook-nosed snake**.*

Walnut Canyon Desert Drive

DRIVE ←

T The 9.5-mile **Walnut Canyon Desert Drive** loops through the park and provides a unique look at the Chihuahuan Desert. Start near the visitors center, then stop at the educational Walnut Canyon Vista Trail, the short Rattlesnake Canyon Overlook Trail, the longer Rattlesnake Canyon Trail, and parking lots for Chimney Cave and Spider Cave. (Though damaged by floods in 2022, this unpaved route is being repaired and is expected to reopen to visitors. Check ahead to plan for route closures.)

→ EXPLORE

I If you stay into the evening, you'll be treated to a brilliant night sky, albeit one dotted by bats *and* stars. Attend a **Star Party** with the park rangers, during which you can use powerful telescopes, participate in activities and lectures, and take stargazing hikes to discover the beauty of the stars and planets above the park. Guided **night hikes** are also available throughout the year outside of Star Parties; check the calendar for dates.

→ **RANGER RECOMMENDATION** ←

*Pack a picnic and stop at **Rattlesnake Springs**, a green haven amid the desert. You'll find picnic tables and grills under tall cottonwood trees that make it a great place to relax, eat, and bird-watch. Just don't try to swim in the off-limits spring.*

El Capitan rock formation

GUADALUPE MOUNTAINS
NATIONAL PARK

TEXAS

ESTABLISHED: September 30, 1972

SIZE: 86,376 acres

VISITORS CENTERS: The Pine Springs Visitor Center, open year-round, offers trip advice, camping permits, a museum, and a store. The Dog Canyon Ranger Station and McKittrick Canyon Visitor Center are also useful resources; check ahead for hours, as they are staffed intermittently.

TRANSPORTATION: No in-park transportation

DOGS ALLOWED: Only in campground and picnic areas or on the Pine Springs Campground connector trail and the Pinery Trail from Pine Springs Visitor Center to Butterfield Stage Station. Must be leashed.

WHEN TO GO: Spring and fall offer the best weather but are busiest, so plan for crowded parking lots and consider visiting during the week rather than on weekends; November–March is the windy season, but far less crowded; June–August can be extremely hot.

CONTACT: 915-828-3251; nps.gov/gumo
400 Pine Canyon
Salt Flat, TX 79847

A Amid Guadalupe Mountains National Park's basins and mountains, you'll find riverbeds teaming with life, high-elevation forests filled with the songs of birds, and the world's most extensive Permian fossil reef. The story of the landscape is much like the story of the region—one of struggle, survival, and strength. Over its 10,000 years of human history, the park has seen tragic conflicts between the Mescalero Apache and buffalo soldiers, the pressures felt by ranchers and settlers, and, eventually, the struggle, started by one landowner, to protect this special space.

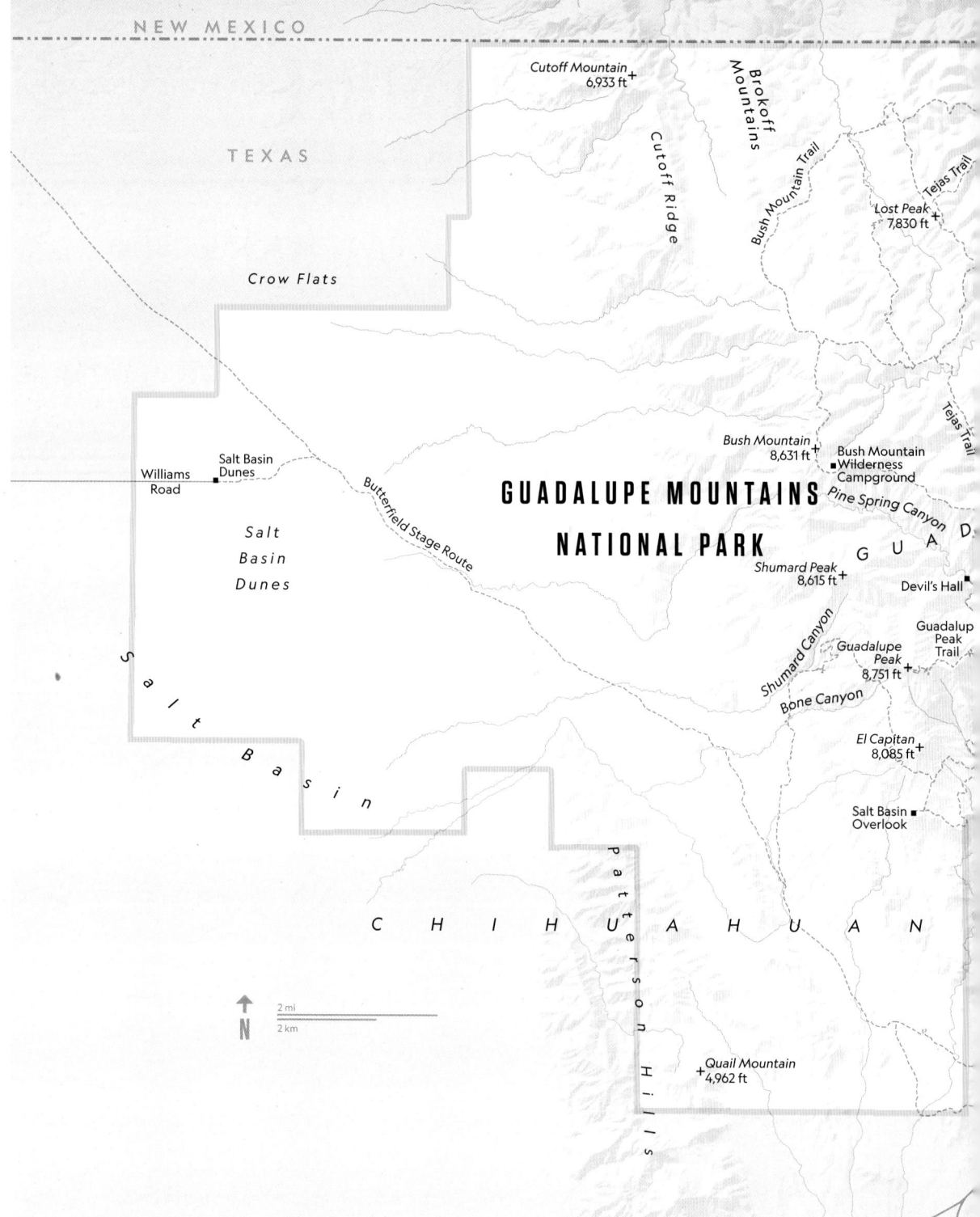

NEW MEXICO

TEXAS

Crow Flats

Cutoff Mountain
6,933 ft

Cutoff Ridge

Brokoff
Mountains

Bush Mountain Trail

Tejas Trail

Lost Peak
7,830 ft

Williams
Road

Salt Basin
Dunes

Butterfield Stage Route

GUADALUPE MOUNTAINS

NATIONAL PARK

Bush Mountain
8,631 ft

Bush Mountain
Wilderness
Campground

Pine Spring Canyon

D

G U A

Salt
Basin
Dunes

Shumard Peak
8,615 ft

Devil's Hall

Salt Basin

Shumard Canyon

Guadalupe
Peak
8,751 ft

Bone Canyon

Guadalup
Peak
Trail

El Capitan
8,085 ft

Salt Basin
Overlook

Patterson Hills

C H I H U A H U A N

↑
N

2 mi
2 km

Quail Mountain
4,962 ft

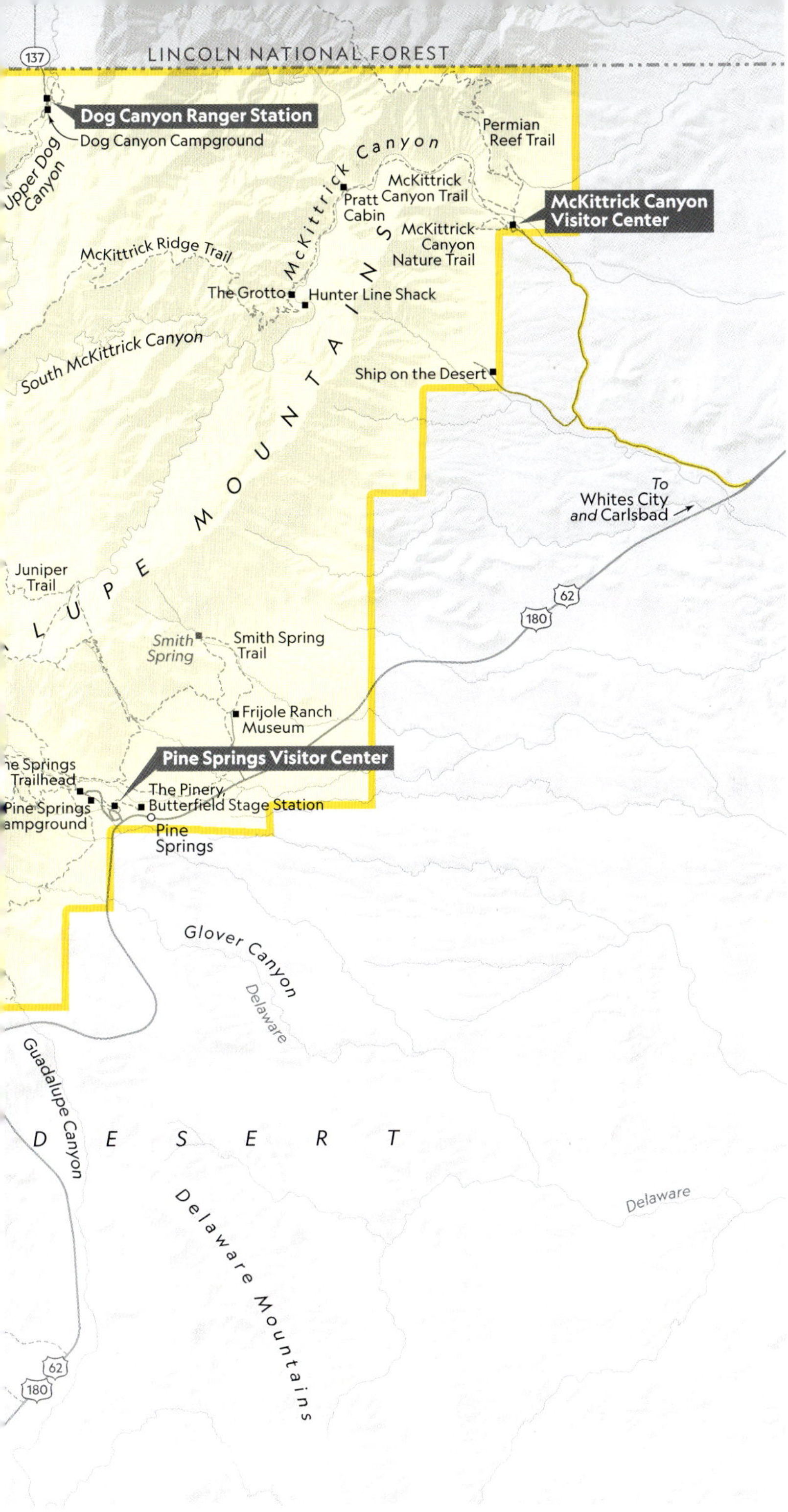

Sunrise from a campsite

SLEEP

C Camping is the only way to stay inside the park:

→ **Dog Canyon Campground** is a two-hour drive from Pine Springs and sits at 6,300 feet in elevation. It has nine tent and four RV sites, drinking water, and flush toilets. Campfires are not permitted. Reservations are recommended.

→ **Pine Springs Campground** is larger, with 20 tent, 13 RV, and two group sites. There's seasonal staff on-site, as well as an amphitheater, drinking water, and flush toilets. Reservations are recommended. Wood and charcoal fires are prohibited.

→ For a more remote experience, pitch a tent at one of the park's 60 **backcountry sites**. Just get a permit the same day from the visitors center and bring all the water you need.

Map labels

LINCOLN NATIONAL FOREST

137

Dog Canyon Ranger Station
Dog Canyon Campground

Upper Dog Canyon

Permian Reef Trail

McKittrick Canyon

McKittrick Canyon Trail
Pratt Cabin

McKittrick Canyon Visitor Center

McKittrick Canyon Nature Trail

McKittrick Ridge Trail

The Grotto   Hunter Line Shack

South McKittrick Canyon

GUADALUPE MOUNTAINS

Ship on the Desert

To Whites City and Carlsbad

62

180

Juniper Trail

Smith Spring   Smith Spring Trail

Frijole Ranch Museum

Pine Springs Visitor Center

Pine Springs Trailhead
The Pinery
Pine Springs Campground   Butterfield Stage Station
Pine Springs

Glover Canyon

Delaware

Guadalupe Canyon

DESERT

Delaware Mountains

Delaware

62
180

A cairn at Guadalupe Peak

HIKE ⬅

D Driving isn't an option through the mostly roadless Guadalupe Mountains, so you'll have to rely on your own two feet to explore the park. Try one of these hikes:

➜ The entire **McKittrick Canyon Trail and Ridge Trail hike** runs 10.9 miles and requires a steep climb to its 7,916-foot high point, where you'll be treated to amazing views into the canyon and along the ridges. You descend into the Tejas Trail junction. This is a long and challenging hike, so plan to spend the night in the backcountry.

Pro tip: Don't rush past the beauty of the canyon floor.

➜ Hike the 8.4-mile round-trip **Guadalupe Peak Trail** to the mountain's summit, taking in tremendous views at every switchback. It's a steep climb, then an easier walk through the forest before you eventually reach a false summit. Spend the night backcountry camping if you're committed, then cross a wooden bridge toward a slight descent until rising again to reach the true summit.

➜ The 2.3-mile loop of **Smith Spring Trail** begins at the Frijole Ranch Trailhead and goes past two springs before reaching the main attraction: a lush, forested oasis.

➜ The **Permian Reef Trail** showcases the geologic and fossil features preserved by the park. It's a favorite for both budding and experienced geologists, who can explore the past under the sweeping views of the canyon. Get a detailed book from a visitors center before your trek.

➜ Hike 4.2 miles round-trip from the **Pine Springs Trailhead** to reach Devil's Hall. A rocky wash leads to a natural rock staircase and a narrow walk between towering canyon walls decorated by unique geological formations.

➜ Get an easy summit win on the short **Lost Peak** route off the **Tejas Trail**. You'll be 7,830 feet above sea level, but you won't have to hike a steep route to get there.

➜ The strenuous 13.2-mile out-and-back **Bush Mountain Trail** goes to the top of the park's second highest peak. The less traveled trek isn't short, so consider staying at Bush Mountain Wilderness Campground just below the southeastern side of the summit.

The unique landscape of the Guadalupe Mountains has a variety of ecosystems. There are harsh deserts, rushing streams, dense woodlands, and rugged mountaintop forests—each home to distinct creatures and plants. Wherever you are, look for wildlife when the sun sets and rises, or stick to shaded areas with water. You might spot **black-tailed rattlesnakes**, **rainbow trout**, **scorpions**, or **skunks**.

Bird-watchers should grab a field guide from a visitors center and head out to the Frijole Ranch Museum, Smith Spring, and McKittrick Canyon. See **northern flickers**, **red-naped sapsuckers**, and **Lewis's woodpeckers** at the first two locations and **rock wrens**, **greater roadrunners**, and **white-winged doves** at the third.

Salt Basin Dunes

EXPLORE

Add to your trail-trekking experience by exploring the park's history, seeing some of its more unique locations, and participating in ranger-designed programming. Here are a few choices:

→ *Once you're inside McKittrick Canyon, search for the* **cabin owned by oil geologist Wallace Pratt** *in the 1930s. He and his family used the stone building as a summer respite; do the same on the still-standing shady porch.*

→ *Find a stark peace in the* **Salt Basin Dunes**. *Ancient streams in the region started to evaporate, leaving gypsum and salt deposits in the basin, which have been rearranged by the wind. It's become a striking landscape beneath the high points of the rest of the park. Remember to stay on established routes to protect the dunes.*

→ *Find some solitude in* **Dog Canyon**, *a remote section offering a quiet spot for camping and hiking. Take easy day hikes around the canyon and through the park's high country.*

→ *Guadalupe Mountains is a great spot for kids to start, or continue, their foray into the National Park Service's* **Junior Paleontologist Program**. *Get information and resources at a visitors center. Activities include in-park scavenger hunts and multiday ranger-led explorations of the park.*

A striped bark scorpion

SPOT

*Spend a day exploring **McKittrick Canyon** in the heart of the park. The journey to the floor of the canyon has been called one of the toughest in the park—but the difficulty comes with incredible rewards. See the tremendous diversity of plants and animals, watch the water run through this massive geological wonder, and visit the historic Pratt Cabin, the Grotto (an open face of a small cave where stone tables and benches await), and Hunter Line Shack.*

Hot Water Cascade

HOT SPRINGS
NATIONAL PARK
ARKANSAS

ESTABLISHED: March 4, 1921

SIZE: 5,500 acres

VISITORS CENTER: The Fordyce Bathhouse Visitor Center and Museum (open year-round) was once the largest bathhouse on Bathhouse Row. It now offers accessible exhibits, trip planning, and a theater.

TRANSPORTATION: Hot Springs Trolley (guided tours) and the Intracity Transit public bus system

DOGS ALLOWED: On trails and inside the Superior Bathhouse. Not allowed in other buildings.

WHEN TO GO: April–May for flowers and cherry blossoms; September–October for fall colors; December for holiday festivities

CONTACT: 501-620-6715; nps.gov/hosp
369 Central Avenue
Hot Springs, AR 71901

H   Hot Springs National Park, set in a valley of the rugged Ouachita Mountains, is unlike any other in the park system. First protected by Congress in 1832, its thermal springs, which flow from the earth at 143°F on average, have long attracted visitors for their supposed therapeutic properties, including Native Americans who came to the springs well before European settlers. Between 1892 and 1923, and into today, many of the natural springs were diverted to pipes that serve bathhouses and hotels built for guests seeking health benefits along what became known as Bathhouse Row. Though it's no longer a destination spa town, you can still experience the water's benefits, and the accompanying mountain views, during your trip to the park.

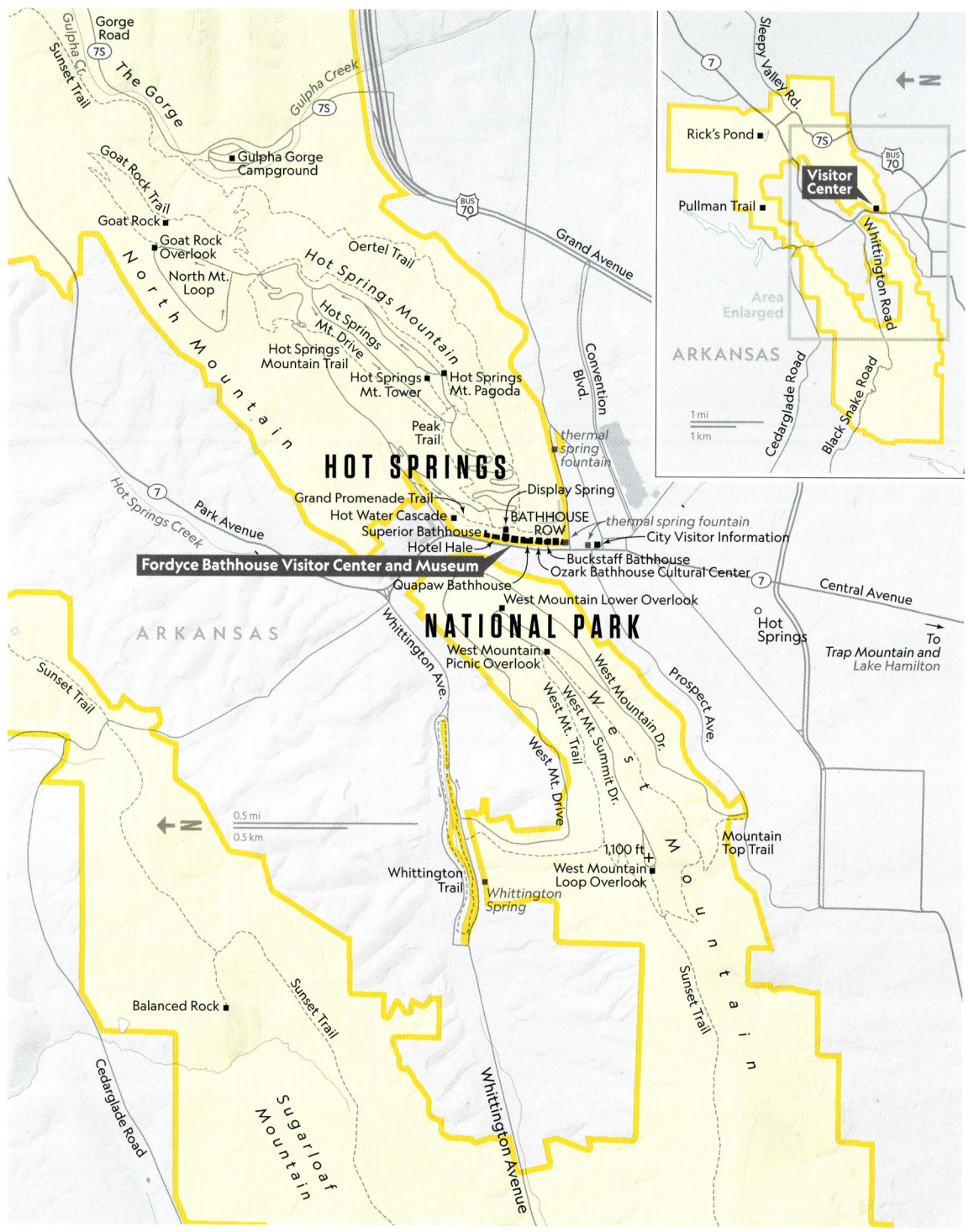

Gorge Road

Gulpha Cr.

Sunset Trail

7S

The Gorge

Gulpha Creek

7S

Gulpha Gorge Campground

Goat Rock Trail

Goat Rock

Goat Rock Overlook

North Mt. Loop

Oertel Trail

Hot Springs Mountain Trail

Hot Springs Mt. Drive

Hot Springs Mt. Tower

Hot Springs Mt. Pagoda

Peak Trail

Hot Springs Mountain

Grand Avenue

BUS 70

Convention Blvd.

North Mountain

thermal spring fountain

HOT SPRINGS

Grand Promenade Trail

Display Spring

Hot Water Cascade

BATHHOUSE ROW

Superior Bathhouse

thermal spring fountain

City Visitor Information

Hotel Hale

Buckstaff Bathhouse

Fordyce Bathhouse Visitor Center and Museum

Ozark Bathhouse Cultural Center

Quapaw Bathhouse

7

7

Park Avenue

Hot Springs Creek

Central Avenue

West Mountain Lower Overlook

ARKANSAS

NATIONAL PARK

Hot Springs

West Mountain Picnic Overlook

Whittington Ave.

West Mt. Trail

West Mt. Summit Dr.

West Mountain Dr.

Prospect Ave.

West Mountain

To Trap Mountain and Lake Hamilton

Sunset Trail

0.5 mi
0.5 km

West Mt. Drive

1,100 ft

West Mountain Loop Overlook

Mountain Top Trail

Whittington Trail

Whittington Spring

Sunset Trail

Balanced Rock

Sunset Trail

Cedarglade Road

Sugarloaf Mountain

Whittington Avenue

Inset map:

7

Sleepy Valley Rd.

Rick's Pond

7S

BUS 70

Visitor Center

Pullman Trail

Whittington Road

Area Enlarged

ARKANSAS

Cedarglade Road

Black Snake Road

1 mi
1 km

Sunset Trail

SLEEP

P Plenty of large hotels are outside the park, but you'll get a more intimate experience within its bounds. There are two ways to do that:

→ Once the Hale Bathhouse, **Hotel Hale** is now a luxury boutique accommodation on Bathhouse Row. The historic site boasts original interior features, suites with large mineral-water soaking tubs, and a garden restaurant.
→ Both tent and RV campers can set up at **Gulpha Gorge Campground**, which offers 40 sites (all with full hookups), picnic tables, and flush toilets. Reservations are required—if you book early enough, grab a site on Gulpha Creek.

Hale Bathhouse, now known as Hotel Hale

M Many of the hikes in Hot Springs loop around the mountains—or climb up their switchbacks—stopping at various overlooks or spots where the springs emerge.

→ The one-mile out-and-back **Grand Promenade Trail** is paved with bricks and serves as the park's entry point for many visitors. It's also a trailhead for the **Oertel Trail**, which starts at the grand staircase behind the visitors center, and the **Peak Trail**, which leads to the Hot Springs Mountain Tower.
→ **Sunset Trail** is the longest and most remote in the park. The trail is 10 miles one way, but combine it with the **Hot Springs Mountain Trail**, **North Mountain Loop**, and **West Mountain Trail** to piece together a 15- to 17-mile loop. The trail itself is well maintained, with plenty of shaded areas and stops to take in views.
→ Take the north or south portion of the **West Mountain Trail**, or walk them both along with a portion of the **Mountain Top Trail**, to create a loop that starts and stops with an overlook and shelter on West Mountain Summit Drive.
→ Get to the parking lot at the North Mountain Loop early to avoid the crowds, then head out on the **Goat Rock Trail** for spectacular views of the Ouachita Mountains. Gulpha Gorge Campground also provides easy access.
→ At the top of the mountain, the 1.7-mile one-way **Hot Springs Mountain Trail** is an easy stroll with plenty of lovely overlooks.
→ Take the spur from the **Sunset Trail** that leads to Balanced Rock, a striking outcrop of novaculite (hard rock made of almost pure silica).

HIKE

Family Friendly

DRIVE

(T) There are two main drives through the park: West Mountain Summit Drive and Hot Springs Mountain Drive.

→ *West Mountain Summit Drive will lead you up to the Summit Loop and its three overlooks. Stop at the West Mountain Lower Overlook for a glimpse of downtown Hot Springs. Have lunch at the West Mountain Picnic Overlook and then continue to the West Mountain Loop Overlook, with views of Trap Mountain and Lake Hamilton.*

→ *On the other side of the park, Hot Springs Mountain Drive was originally a carriage road. Travel its switchbacks up the mountain and stop at the Hot Springs Mountain Lookout Point, Hot Springs Mountain Pagoda, and Goat Rock Overlook for a peek at Zigzag and Indian Mountains. Finally, visit Hot Springs Mountain Tower for views from 1,256 feet above sea level. Built first in 1877, and entirely rebuilt for the public in 1983, it has a 216-foot observation deck accessible by elevator.*

SPOT

(F) Finding wildlife in the park isn't easy, because its spaces are either well occupied by people or covered in dense forest. Still, with binoculars and quiet walks, you might be able to spot **wild-tailed deer**, **groundhogs**, and **chipmunks**.

Patient bird-watchers will be treated to more than **100 bird species** in the park, 23 of which are migratory. Hot Springs also has plenty of **snakes**, **turtles**, and **lizards**—hikers should beware of the five venomous snakes that call it home, including copperheads.

EXPLORE

(T) The beauty of Hot Springs National Park is that it has something for everyone, from wilderness lovers to luxury vacationers. Try one of these off-trail activities:

→ *Visit **Bathhouse Row** to take a dip in the thermal waters (there are no outdoor options in the park). Check out spas of the past, relax in a traditional bath, and book a treatment at a modern-day spa. Two spots pipe their water directly from the springs: **Buckstaff Bathhouse**, which has been operating since 1912, and the renovated **Quapaw Bathhouse**, which opened in 1922. (Keep in mind that kids nine and under won't be allowed to enter the springs at Buckstaff; the age restriction is 13 and under at Quapaw.)*

→ *Drink water from one of the **thermal spring fountains** around the park—and take a jug of spring water home to enjoy after your trip.*

→ *You can't submerge in the scalding natural springs, but you can reach out and touch the water in the cooled pools of the **Display Spring** behind Maurice Bathhouse and **Hot Water Cascade** at Arlington Lawn.*

→ *Drink a beer at **Superior Bathhouse**, a bathhouse turned brewery that uses local spring water for its libations.*

→ *Stop in the art gallery at the **Ozark Bathhouse Cultural Center**, where the work of the artist-in-residence is displayed on the walls of the 1922 Art Deco building.*

→ *Bike the **Pullman Trail** connecting downtown Hot Springs to more than 31 miles of mountain biking at Northwoods Trails. The short trail was completed in 2020 and provides access to the single-track, multitrack, flow trails, jump lines, and skills park at Northwoods.*

Discover pieces of the Fordyce-Ricks estate, including a bathhouse, at **Rick's Pond** *off the Sunset Trail. Samuel W. Fordyce, a prominent railway executive who contributed to the building of more than 24,000 miles of American railroad, bought the land in 1878 and had the log house completed in 1909. He dammed the creek below the house to form a lake for his wife, naming it Lake Lillian in her honor.*

The variegated dunes at sunset

WHITE SANDS
NATIONAL PARK

NEW MEXICO

ESTABLISHED: December 20, 2019

SIZE: 145,762 acres

VISITORS CENTER: The White Sands Visitor Center is open year-round with rangers to answer questions, museum exhibits, a theater, and a gift shop. The historic location is worth a stop for its architecture and artisanship.

TRANSPORTATION: No public transportation is currently offered in the park.

DOGS ALLOWED: Only on leash. Remember to bring plenty of water for them.

WHEN TO GO: Year-round. Spring offers mild weather; summer has unique programming; fall and winter have fewer crowds.

CONTACT: 575-479-6124; nps.gov/whsa
19955 Highway 70 West
Alamogordo, NM 88310

T   The giant waves of gypsum sand that make up White Sands National Park were created from deposits of a seafloor more than 200 million years ago. Today, the park protects the world's largest collection of this type of sandy phenomena. The landscape provides thrilling (dune sledding), peaceful (backcountry camping), or discovery-filled (hiking explorations) experiences—so do whatever feels right, or plan for all three.

WHITE SANDS MISSILE RANGE
(no public access)

HOLLOMAN
AIR FORCE
BASE

Alkali Flat

ZONE OF
COOPERATIVE USE
(restricted area, permits required)

Alkali Flat
Trail

amphitheater

Yucca Picnic Area
Backcountry Trail

Roadrunner Picnic Area
Primrose Picnic Area

Sunset Stroll meeting area

Interdune
Boardwalk

Playa Trail

Dune Life Nature Trail

Dunes Drive

To
Alamogordo, Oliver Lee
Memorial State Park,
and Lincoln
National Forest

White Sands
Visitor Center

White Sands
Trading Company

70

WHITE SANDS NATIONAL PARK

Lake Lucero

NEW MEXICO

WHITE SANDS MISSILE RANGE
(no public access)

3 mi

3 km

N

70

To Las Cruces and Aguirre Springs
Recreation Area and Campground

Backcountry camp for solitude with a view.

SLEEP

S Spend the night inside the bounds of the park by **backcountry camping**. Permits are issued in person at the park on the day of camping only. Pick up sandwiches, drinks, and snacks at the White Sands Trading Company gift shop before heading out.

Public campgrounds are available at nearby Oliver Lee Memorial State Park, Aguirre Springs Recreation Area and Campground, and Lincoln National Forest. If four walls are more your thing, there are plenty of **hotels** in Alamogordo and Las Cruces, 13 and 50 miles from the park, respectively.

HIKE

H Hike anywhere that's safe for you and the environment in the dunes, but only if you have navigation skills and a plan. If you aren't comfortable navigating, follow one of the established trails off the main road. Either way, pack enough water for your group and be aware of high temperatures, which can quickly turn deadly.

→ The **Dune Life Nature Trail** is an easy one-mile loop with interpretive signs about the native plants and wildlife that call the park home. Look for animal tracks.

→ Walk the **Playa Trail** in as little as 15 minutes. This area is usually a dry lake bed, but it sometimes fills with water during monsoons, creating new ecosystems as it shifts from dry to wet to dry again.

→ The **Interdune Boardwalk** is elevated over the fragile inter-dune ecosystem. Along the 0.4-mile round-trip walkway you'll get views of the dunefield and the Sacramento Mountains as you learn about the park's wildlife and geology.

→ Don't let the name of the **Alkali Flat Trail** confuse you: This hike is anything but flat. Follow rolling sandy hills away from the road and toward the dry bed of what was once Lake Otero. The five-mile loop is strenuous, and you'll need sun protection and water.

→ The **Backcountry Trail**, a two-mile loop, showcases the San Andres Mountains and the lives of the bleached earless lizards and white moths that occupy the landscape. Follow the markers, and time your trip for the sunset.

→ Go on a monthly ranger-led **Lake Lucero Tour** to learn about the geology and creation of the park. Check out the thousands of selenite crystals on the surface of the lake bed after you hike down a steep trail.

→ Join a ranger for a daily **Sunset Stroll**, which will leisurely take you along a path to a panoramic viewpoint.

O Only one road goes through the park, **Dunes Drive**. The eight-mile scenic stretch travels from the visitors center into the heart of the dunes. Stop at the Dune Life Nature Trail, Playa Trail, and Interdune Boardwalk on the way to stretch your legs and explore. Motorcycles and bicycles are also welcome on the route, but you'll need to be aware of blind curves and large vehicles.

Sometimes the road is closed for a few hours because of active military testing at the nearby White Sands Missile Range, so check ahead of time.

Navigate the road into the heart of the gypsum dunefield.

DRIVE

A lizard blends into the sand.

SPOT

Y You might be surprised at the number of creatures that call this desert home, from **owls** to **frogs** to **turtles**. Different animals and insects occupy different ecosystems—and do so at different times of day—so careful planning will give you better odds of spotting them.

→ *Keep an eye out for tracks. Because of the heat, many of the desert's creatures come out only at night, so finding their tracks can show you what's been traveling the paths after dark. You'll likely find evidence of* **caterpillars**, **darkling beetles**, **roadrunners**, *and* **pocket mice** *in the sand, and maybe even the pawprints of* **coyotes**, **foxes**, *and* **badgers***.*
→ *The park's white sands have pushed some of its residents to evolve to blend in. Look closely to see* **Apache pocket mice**, **bleached earless lizards**, **sand-treader camel crickets**, *and* **white moths**—*all of which have developed camouflage to match the sand.*
→ *Birdwatchers should bring out their binoculars around the visitors center and entrance station, where plant life draws in* **barn swallows**, **black-chinned hummingbirds**, *and* **burrowing owls***.*

B Boost your experience with a wildly one-of-a-kind picnic setting, a walk under a full moon, or a family-friendly event in the park.

→ *Stop for a picnic at the* **Yucca Picnic Area**, **Roadrunner Picnic Area**, *or* **Primrose Picnic Area**, *all with uniquely designed, modern shaded picnic tables available.*
→ *If you've only ever gone sledding on white snow, try out* **sandboarding** *on white sand. Buy or rent a waxed saucer from the gift shop, or rent a sandboard from an outfitter, and head to either the tall dunes at the Alkali Flat Trailhead or the family-friendly hills at the Roadrunner Picnic Area.*
→ *Attend one of the free* **Full Moon Nights** *at the park's amphitheater. The park stays open late for musicians, rangers, artists, and performers to come together to celebrate the occasion and honor the region's deep cultural legacy.*
→ *Attend* **MothaPalooza**, *an annual event celebrating the more than 60 endemic moth species of the park. Be part of the continual discoveries that scientists are making about the entomology of the land. The event's date shifts, so check calendars to plan to attend.*

The sand is soft enough for sledding with a waxed sled.

EXPLORE

Take part in a ranger-guided **Full Moon Hike**, which provides a chance for visitors to hike the dunes when they're illuminated by a full moon. The park usually closes at sunset, so this hike and its views are a rare opportunity for a peaceful, dark experience in this protected area. During Full Moon Nights, when the park is open late, you can explore on your own if you can't get a ticket for a Full Moon Hike.

→ SOUTHWEST

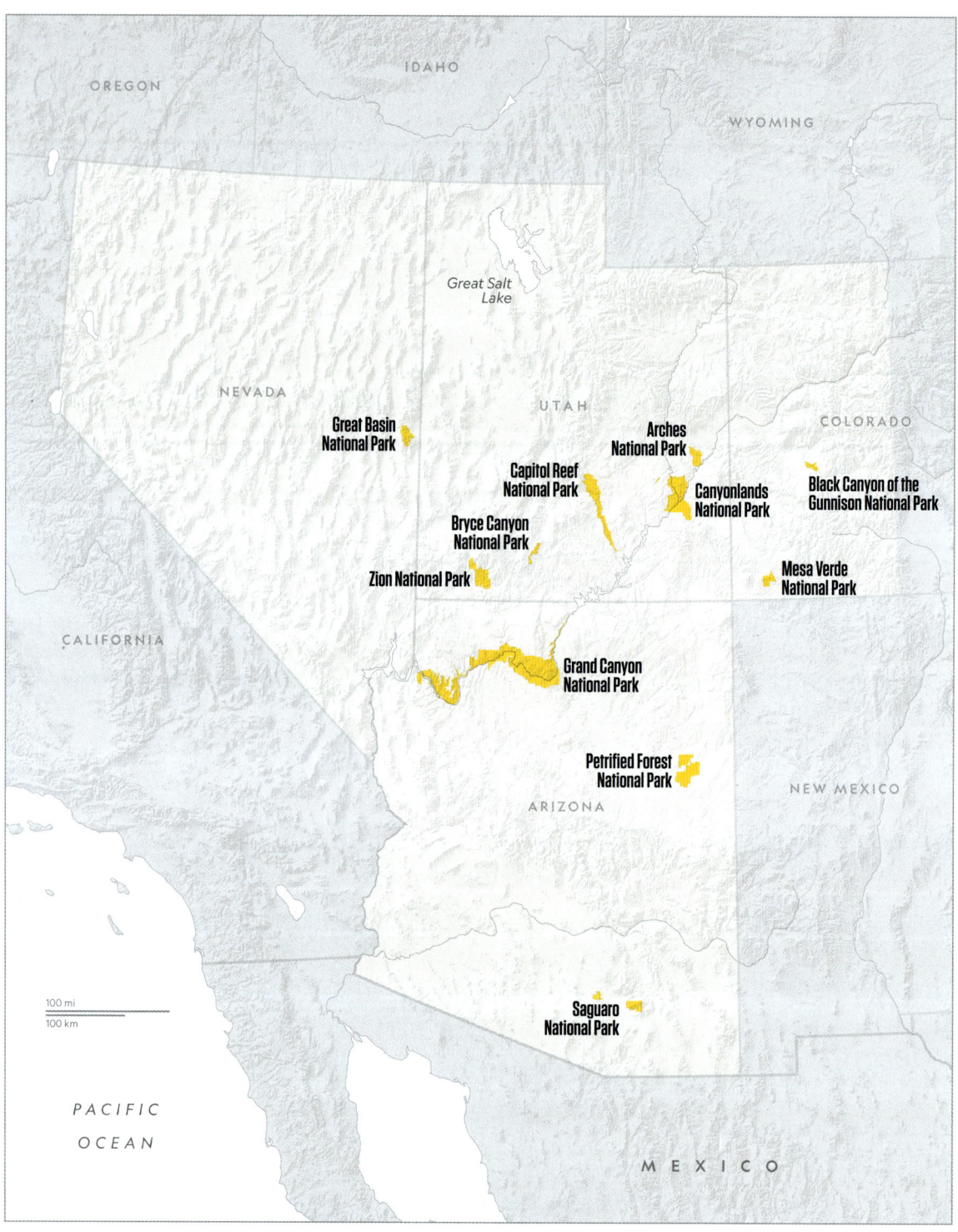

OREGON

IDAHO

WYOMING

Great Salt Lake

NEVADA

UTAH

COLORADO

Great Basin
National Park

Arches
National Park

Capitol Reef
National Park

Canyonlands
National Park

Black Canyon of the
Gunnison National Park

Bryce Canyon
National Park

Zion National Park

Mesa Verde
National Park

CALIFORNIA

Grand Canyon
National Park

Petrified Forest
National Park

NEW MEXICO

ARIZONA

100 mi
100 km

Saguaro
National Park

PACIFIC

OCEAN

MEXICO

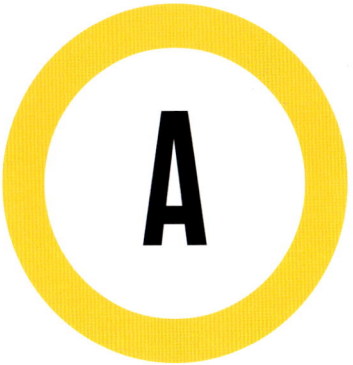

Amerimericans have always been fascinated with the Wild West, and today many consider the Grand Canyon (page 314), one of 11 parks in this chapter, an emblem of the region's heritage. But the allure of the Southwest extends far beyond the Arizona icon. Consider the sandstone spires of Utah's Bryce Canyon (page 282). Or the swooping arches, built from eons of wind, rain, and natural elements, in nearby Arches (page 262). In Mesa Verde (page 338), cliff dwellings are a reminder of the ancestral Puebloans who inhabited the mesas for hundreds of years. With plenty more to discover, these parks are robust in natural wonders and human history.

LEFT: Courthouse Towers, Arches National Park (page 262) **PREVIOUS PAGES:** Green River Overlook, Canyonlands National Park (page 292)

Double O Arch

ARCHES
NATIONAL PARK

UTAH

ESTABLISHED: November 12, 1971

SIZE: 76,519 acres

VISITORS CENTER: The Arches Visitor Center is open year-round and offers exhibits, ranger advice, and a bookstore.

TRANSPORTATION: None in-park; bus tours are available.

DOGS ALLOWED: Only on roads, in parking lots, at campgrounds (except Devils Garden), and at pullouts along paved scenic drives

WHEN TO GO: Spring or fall for mild temperatures (but expect crowds); summer can be incredibly hot; winter is cold and quiet, and snow or ice can close roads and hiking trails.

CONTACT: 435-719-2299; nps.gov/arch
5 miles north of Moab, UT, on U.S. 191
Moab, UT 84532

First shaped more than 65 million years ago in deep seabeds and carved later by wind and weather, the arches, pinnacles, rock fins, and giant balanced rocks are why visitors flock to Arches National Park.

Native American communities hunted and gathered throughout Arches for around 10,000 years, at the end of the last Ice Age. Two thousand years ago, ancestral Puebloans settled the region and began cultivating plants. By the 1880s, European traders and trappers, ranchers, prospectors, and farmers had moved in. President Herbert Hoover established the Windows area—240 square miles of the world's most concentrated display of natural rock formations—as Arches National Monument in 1929. The larger park was established in 1971 and signed into law by President Richard Nixon.

Visit to see the more than 2,000 towering structures for yourself. Every view is a unique and powerful one, just like every experience you'll have here.

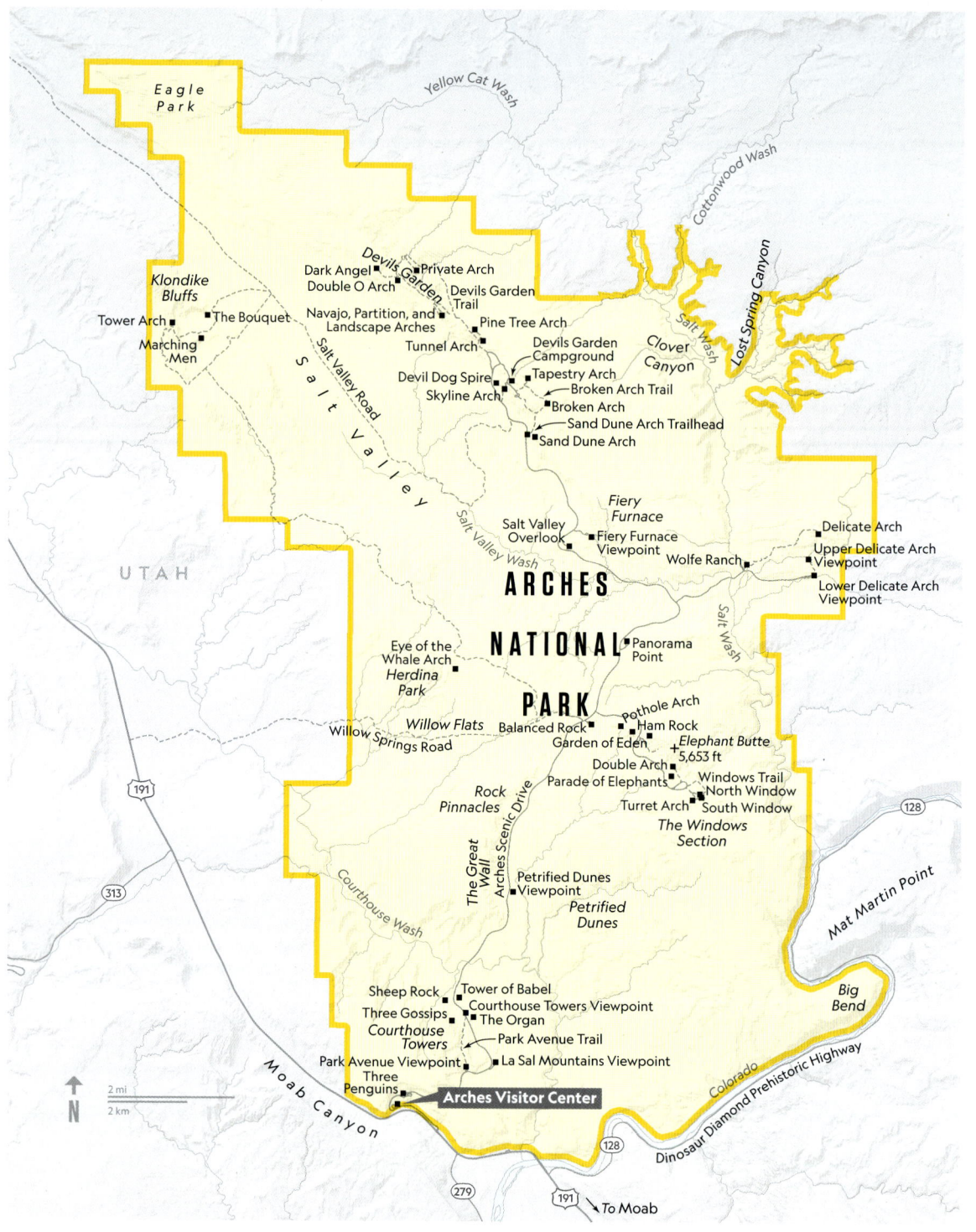

Eagle Park

Yellow Cat Wash

Cottonwood Wash

Klondike Bluffs

Tower Arch

The Bouquet

Marching Men

Dark Angel
Double O Arch

Devils Garden

Private Arch

Devils Garden Trail

Navajo, Partition, and Landscape Arches

Pine Tree Arch

Tunnel Arch

Devils Garden Campground

Clover Canyon

Lost Spring Canyon

Salt Wash

Devil Dog Spire

Tapestry Arch

Skyline Arch

Broken Arch Trail

Broken Arch

Sand Dune Arch Trailhead

Sand Dune Arch

Salt Valley Road

Salt Valley

Salt Valley Wash

Salt Valley Overlook

Fiery Furnace

Fiery Furnace Viewpoint

Wolfe Ranch

Delicate Arch

Upper Delicate Arch Viewpoint

Lower Delicate Arch Viewpoint

UTAH

ARCHES

NATIONAL

PARK

Salt Wash

Eye of the Whale Arch

Herdina Park

Panorama Point

Willow Flats

Balanced Rock

Pothole Arch

Ham Rock

Garden of Eden

Elephant Butte 5,653 ft

Willow Springs Road

Double Arch

Windows Trail
North Window

Parade of Elephants

Rock Pinnacles

Turret Arch

South Window

The Windows Section

128

191

313

The Great Wall

Arches Scenic Drive

Petrified Dunes Viewpoint

Petrified Dunes

Mat Martin Point

Courthouse Wash

Sheep Rock

Tower of Babel

Courthouse Towers Viewpoint

Three Gossips

The Organ

Big Bend

Courthouse Towers

Park Avenue Trail

Park Avenue Viewpoint

La Sal Mountains Viewpoint

Three Penguins

Arches Visitor Center

Colorado

Dinosaur Diamond Prehistoric Highway

Moab Canyon

N
2 mi
2 km

128

279

191

To Moab

SLEEP

T There's only one place to camp in the park: **Devils Garden Campground**, open year-round. Reservations are available for stays between March 1 and October 31—book early, because sites usually get reserved months in advance. Between November 1 and February 28, the 51 tent and RV sites are available on a first-come-first-serve basis. If you score a spot, you'll get the once-in-a-lifetime experience of sleeping amid the wild rock formations that make the park famous. If you can't get a reservation, you'll find plenty of campgrounds and hotels in nearby **Moab**.

Be sure to reserve your campground early.

C Cover the most ground during your trip along **Arches Scenic Drive**, stopping at its overlooks and trailheads. Along with the famous Windows Section and Delicate Arch, don't miss viewpoints for Park Avenue (a corridor of towering rock walls and spires), La Sal Mountains (rising nearly 13,000 feet), Courthouse Towers (sandstone features), Petrified Dunes (200-million-year-old dunes cemented in sediment by quart and calcite), and Fiery Furnace (a maze of sandstone canyons). Be sure to stop at the Salt Valley Overlook and Panorama Point for expansive vistas.

Salt Valley Road is a more challenging drive than the highway. Two-wheel drive is fine for this dirt road in normal conditions, but on wetter days you'll need a four-wheel-drive vehicle. This route provides access to the primitive trail around Klondike Bluffs and Tower Arch.

DRIVE

Chasing golden hour on a paved Arches road

HIKE

M Many of the park's outstanding formations are visible from overlooks, but hiking around these dynamic, massive structures offers a surreal experience. Take one of these routes for an adventure that truly can't be matched.

→ The **Park Avenue Trail** is packed with stunning sights. Start at its namesake viewpoint, then descend into the canyon and hike for a mile to the Courthouse Towers sandstone formations. Either turn back at this point for an out-and-back hike or continue on to see Queen Victoria, Sausage, and Queen Nefertiti rocks. This is an easy two-mile round-trip hike.

→ Hike the entire **Devils Garden Trail** to take in the Tunnel, Pine Tree, Landscape, Partition, Navajo, and Double O Arches, as well as the Dark Angel sandstone tower. The full route, including all trails and spurs, is 7.9 miles round-trip—and some parts are easier than others. On the more difficult stretches, you'll traverse narrow ledges, steep exposures, and rock scrambles, so skip this one if you're not up to those strenuous escapades.

→ Even the start of the **Windows Trail** is impressive. As soon as you pull up to the parking lot, the massive North Window looms into view. Take the easy one-mile out-and-back for views of Turret Arch and South Window too.

→ **Delicate Arch**—the largest freestanding arch in the park, at 46 feet high and 32 feet wide—is a top priority for most

visitors. But it takes effort to see it up close: three miles round-trip on a steady uphill climb gaining 480 feet. Starting out from Wolfe Ranch will give you a more intimate look at the formation than from the lower or upper viewpoints.

→ Learn about the native desert plants and their traditional uses on the short **Arches Visitor Center Nature Trail**. It's just behind the visitors center and offers a good overview of the plant life throughout the park.

→ To explore the famous **Fiery Furnace**, grab a sought-after ticket to join a ranger-led hike (spring–fall) or secure an individual hiking permit (permits are limited and can be booked between two and seven days in advance of your hike). Traveling these rocky mazes with an experienced guide provides a unique opportunity to learn about the past and present of these natural formations.

→ The 1.8-mile round-trip trail to **Courthouse Towers** follows a smooth canyon bottom before ascending rock-cut stairs to the Park Avenue Viewpoint.

→ Hike to Broken Arch—which isn't actually broken … yet—either straight out and back from the **Sand Dune Arch Trail**, covering 1.2 miles, or as a 2.3-mile loop. The loop passes underneath Broken Arch and requires moderate scrambling. Add a side trip to Sand Dune Arch, which requires wading through deep sand to a hidden arch tucked inside taller sandstone fins. Protect this fragile formation by staying off it.

→ Make time during your drive on Arches Scenic Drive to pull over and hike the short loop at the **Balanced Rock Trail** to get close to the base of the formation. If you time this correctly after the sun sets, you'll see the stars arrive.

Experts Only

Climb skyward for incredible views.

A rabbit on alert

A bighorn sheep navigating the rocky terrain

Arches is a calm and tranquil park, but you'll see wildlife all around if you look closely. Most animals are more active at night, so you may find only their tracks during the day. Still, at dawn and dusk it's possible to spot certain creatures, like **mule deer**, **coyotes**, **porcupines**, **desert cottontails**, and **black-tailed jackrabbits**.

Bird-watchers will have better luck than visitors searching for mammals. Nearly 200 species have been seen in the park. **Grosbeaks, yellow-breasted chats**, and **canyon wrens** fly through Courthouse Wash and along the Colorado River. Look for **piñon jays, juniper titmice**, and **black-throated warblers** up in the woodlands and for **western meadowlarks** and **black-throated sparrows** in the grasslands.

If you search carefully, you'll find creatures that most visitors miss. Look down at the soil and the sandstone to find **lichens** of all shapes, colors, and sizes. One of the most challenging to spot is the bumpy, crusty **biological soil crust**: communities of living organisms that provide nutrients and prevent erosion.

SPOT

Balanced Rock

P Partaking in one of these rock climbing or history experiences can bolster your trip:

→ *Explore history, both natural and human, at* **Courthouse Wash**. *The sandstone rock panel has a fascinating series of petroglyphs, believed to be made first by Archaic Indians, then later added to by ancestral Puebloans. Search the surrounding dense vegetation for beaver dams and animal footprints. Watch out for quicksand as you trek.*

→ *Take 10 minutes to listen to a* **patio talk from a ranger** *at the Arches Visitor Center, held twice a day and appropriate for all ages. Rangers cover different topics each day, depending on what's going on at the park or during the season.*

→ **Canyoneer** *your way through the park—with a permit. While there aren't real slot canyons, the narrow passages intersect with sandstone walls to provide a similar feel. Groups of experienced folks looking to rappel through the rock often head to Fiery Furnace and Lost Spring Canyon. Permits must be obtained in advance online.*

→ **Rock climbers** *have a lot of freedom in Arches, though guidelines must be followed to protect the formations; park staff also close some formations to protect*

the park's birds of prey, depending on the birds' whereabouts. Three Penguins, Devil Dog Spire, Ham Rock, the Bouquet, and Marching Men are popular climbing spots.

→ *Arches became an International Dark Sky Park in 2019, in honor of its unobscured night skies, thanks to its relative isolation from urban areas. Plan your own* **stargazing excursion** *at Balanced Rock Picnic Area, the Windows Section, Garden of Eden Viewpoint, or Panorama Point. Or join a ranger-led program. Either way, bring a star chart, use a red light, and give your eyes time to adjust.*

→ **Bike** *along the Salt Valley and Willow Springs dirt roads, which require mountain bikes to navigate their washboards, deep sand, and obstacles. There's also a paved path that connects the park to Moab.*

→ **Book a four-wheel driving tour** *with Adrift Adventures, NAVTEC Expeditions, or Moab Scenic Adventures to get closer to the park's wondrous formations without wearing out your hiking boots.*

→ *Prepare your kids for a visit to Arches by printing out* **family-friendly educational activities** *from the park's website. Complete a scavenger hunt, write a fill-in-the-blanks story about the park, mimic its features through yoga poses, and learn how to pack a desert hiking bag.*

For Mountain Bikers

Drive to **Klondike Bluffs** on the unpaved, unmaintained road by the same name. On arrival, you'll find stunning views of Salt Valley and other formations. Walk a trail from this less visited region with views of the seven Marching Men pillars and Tower Arch. Keep an eye on the weather before you make the trip.

Sunlight highlights the craggy folds of the canyon.

BLACK CANYON OF THE GUNNISON NATIONAL PARK

COLORADO

ESTABLISHED: October 21, 1999

SIZE: 30,750 acres

VISITORS CENTERS: The South Rim Visitor Center is open year-round and offers exhibits, trip advice, and a bookstore. On the less visited side of the park, the North Rim Ranger Station is open intermittently in summer and closed in winter.

TRANSPORTATION: No in-park transportation

DOGS ALLOWED: Only in developed areas (roads, picnic areas, and campgrounds) and on two trails: the Rim Rock Trail and the Chasm View Nature Trail

WHEN TO GO: September–October for thinner crowds and the annual astronomy festival; January–March for ranger-led snowshoeing; summer for stargazing programs

CONTACT: 970-641-2337; nps.gov/blca
South Rim Visitor Center
9800 Highway 347
Montrose, CO 81401

The landscape in Black Canyon of the Gunnison National Park has been eons in the making. To hear roaring rapids while peering down 2,000 feet into an abyss of dark rocks is to bear witness to two billion years of geological history. Today, the park protects 14 miles of a 53-mile-long gorge carved by the Gunnison River over millennia. Its scale—with narrow crevasses, steep cliffs, and towering spires—puts life into perspective.

SLEEP

(T) There are plenty of hotels around the park, but you'll have to camp to stay inside park bounds. Here are some options:

→ **South Rim Campground** (88 sites, 23 with electric hookups) takes reservations from mid-May to mid-October and is first come, first served the rest of the year. It has seasonal potable water, fire rings, and vault toilets.

→ The more remote **North Rim Campground** (13 sites) is first come, first served. It's open late April or early May through November, closing in winter when the road does the same. This primitive campground has vault toilets, seasonal potable water, and fire rings.

→ Alternatively, sleep on the canyon floor at **East Portal Campground** (15 tent sites), technically within the Curecanti National Recreation Area accessed through the park. The campground is typically open May to mid-October and is first come, first served.

→ Experienced campers can **backcountry camp** in the inner canyon wilderness with a permit. A limited number of permits are available each day in person, on a first-come-first-serve basis, from the visitors centers.

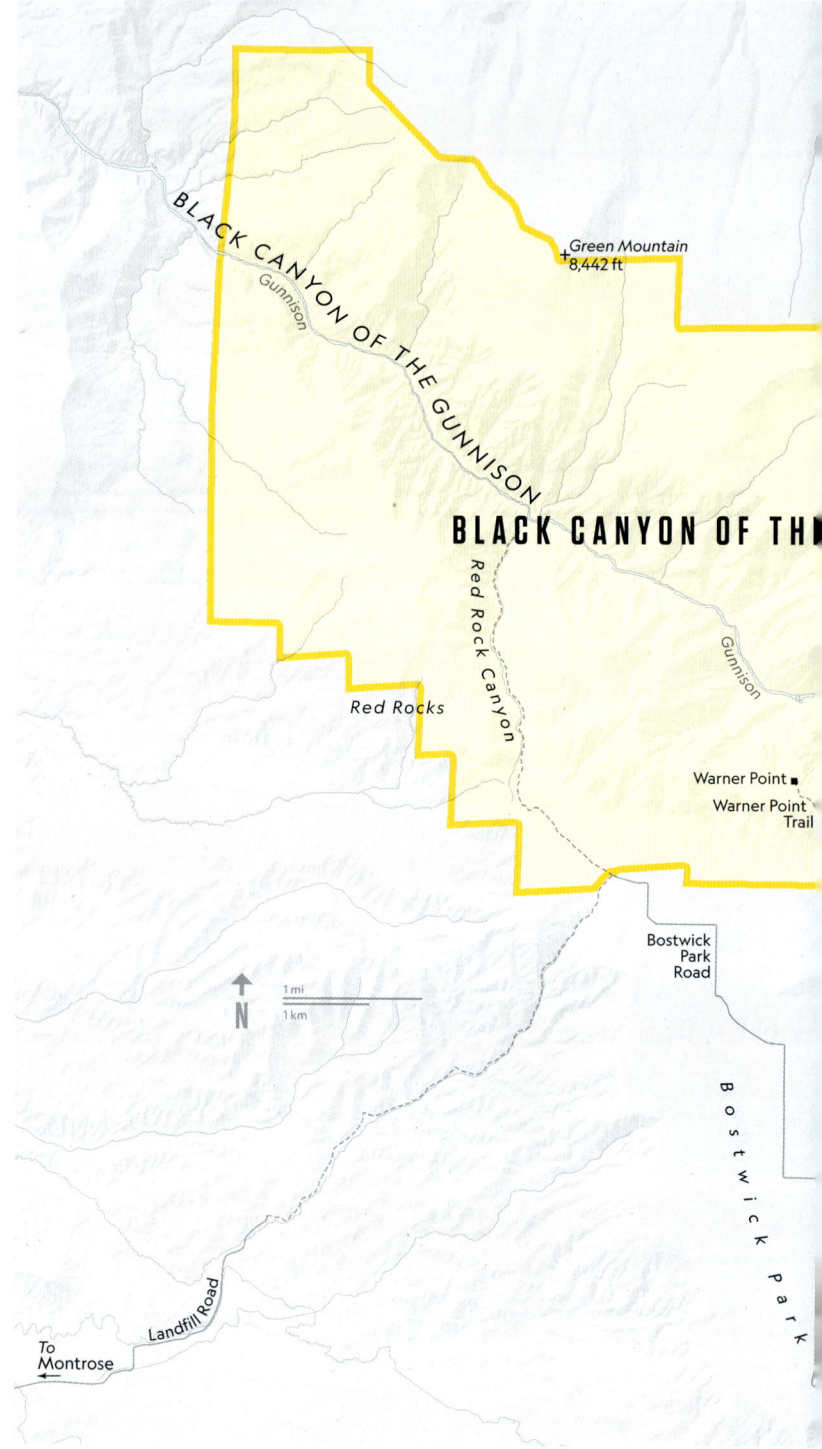

BLACK CANYON OF THE GUNNISON

Gunnison

Green Mountain
8,442 ft

BLACK CANYON OF TH

Red Rock Canyon

Gunnison

Red Rocks

Warner Point
Warner Point
Trail

Bostwick
Park
Road

1 mi
1 km

N

Bostwick park

Landfill Road

To
Montrose

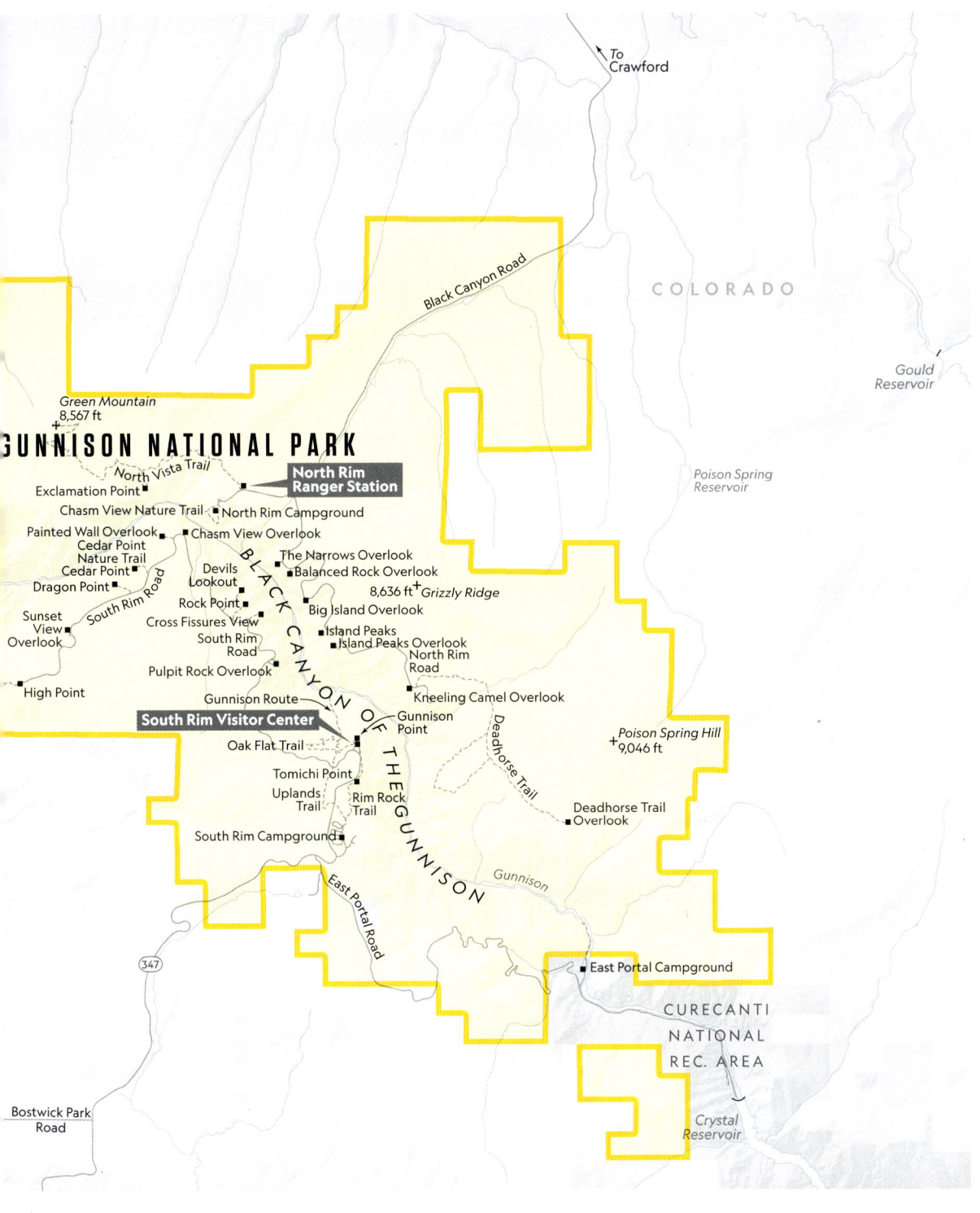

To
Crawford

COLORADO

Gould
Reservoir

Black Canyon Road

Poison Spring
Reservoir

Green Mountain
8,567 ft

GUNNISON NATIONAL PARK

North Vista Trail

**North Rim
Ranger Station**

Exclamation Point

Chasm View Nature Trail · North Rim Campground

Painted Wall Overlook · Chasm View Overlook
Cedar Point
Nature Trail
The Narrows Overlook
Cedar Point
Devils
Balanced Rock Overlook
Dragon Point
Lookout
8,636 ft Grizzly Ridge
Rock Point
Big Island Overlook
Cross Fissures View

Sunset
View
Overlook
Island Peaks
Island Peaks Overlook
South Rim
North Rim
Road
Road
Pulpit Rock Overlook

High Point
Kneeling Camel Overlook

Gunnison Route
Gunnison
Point
Poison Spring Hill
9,046 ft

South Rim Visitor Center

Oak Flat Trail

BLACK CANYON OF THE GUNNISON

Deadhorse Trail

Tomichi Point
Uplands
Trail
Rim Rock
Trail
Deadhorse Trail
Overlook

South Rim Campground

East Portal Road

Gunnison

(347)

East Portal Campground

CURECANTI

NATIONAL

REC. AREA

Bostwick Park
Road

Crystal
Reservoir

HIKE

H Hiking trails lead to stunning overlooks, down into the canyon, and around the rim. Here are some of the best:

→ The **Rim Rock Trail** connects the South Rim Visitor Center to its campground. The one-mile (one-way) stretch weaves along the canyon rim with overlooks into the river, canyon, and mountains. Stop at Tomichi Point for a break and the views.

→ Student volunteers built the challenging two-mile round-trip **Oak Flat Trail**, a loop that winds through a grove of aspens, a thicket of oaks, and a forest of firs.

→ The 1.5-mile round-trip **Warner Point Trail** isn't easy, but you'll be rewarded with views of the San Juan Mountain Range, Uncompahgre Valley, and Bostwick Park.

→ See Painted Wall—the tallest cliff in Colorado, at 2,250 feet— on the 0.2-mile **Cedar Point Nature Trail**, with its educational guideposts and two astonishing river views.

→ Hike the 0.3-mile **Chasm View Nature Trail** to take in the expanse of the river from 1,800 feet. Keep an eye out for swallows, swifts, and raptors while also looking out over Painted Wall and Serpent Point.

→ It's just over three miles round-trip on the **North Vista Trail** to Exclamation Point or a little more than seven miles round-trip to Green Mountain. Find striking views of the inner canyon at the first stop and a panoramic vista at the second.

→ The popular yet challenging **Gunnison Route** is a great first inner-canyon trek. The 1.5-mile hike drops 1,800 feet, with a chain on the route to help hikers down steeper sections. Get a wilderness permit during the summer and stay at one of the three campsites at the bottom. The descent typically takes one and a half hours, while the ascent takes two.

→ Head into **Red Rock Canyon Wilderness** after you secure one of the eight daily permits (reservation windows open in April and July). You'll get two days to traverse the 3.5-mile one-way route, which drops down 1,300 feet to the Gunnison River. Note: The route is not marked or maintained, so tackle it only if you have backpacking and navigational experience.

W Wildlife-watching in Black Canyon is a careful balance. Protect the plants and animals in the park—and protect yourself from them.

→ Bird-watchers in Black Canyon are a lucky bunch. Start at the Deadhorse Trail and look for **red-tailed hawks**, **golden eagles**, **turkey vultures**, **canyon wrens**, **blue grouse**, and **peregrine falcons**—the world's fastest bird.

→ Listen to the **coyotes** sing before dawn at either the South or North Rim Campgrounds.

→ Try to spot a **mountain lion** in the early morning or late evening, when they might be sneaking into the forests or across roads. If you do, keep your distance.

→ Smaller mammals are more common in the park. Walk along the inner canyons and roadsides to see **yellow-bellied marmots** sunbathing or **badgers** and **long-tailed weasels**.

A coyote at attention

SPOT

Multiple road options enable exploration.

DRIVE

D Driving the South and North Rim Roads is a fantastic way to experience the park's enormity and beauty.

→ On **South Rim Road**, don't miss Gunnison Point, Chasm View, Painted Wall, and Sunset View. If you have the time, also stop at Tomichi Point, Cross Fissures, Rock Point, Devils Lookout, and High Point.

→ Pull off on **North Rim Road** to hike the North Vista Trail to Exclamation Point and Green Mountain for the best inner-canyon views. Back on the road, add stops at The Narrows, Balanced Rock, Big Island, Island Peaks, and Kneeling Camel Overlooks. Note that the road is closed to vehicles in the winter and early spring.

→ **East Portal Road** is accessible to smaller vehicles. It leads down a series of switchbacks to the Gunnison River inside the Curecanti National Recreation Area. Stop to camp, picnic, and fish on the canyon floor. The road is windy and steep, with two-way traffic; it also closes in winter.

W While most people experience Black Canyon by foot or car, there's plenty more to do outside (though some, flagged accordingly, are best left to the experts). Consider these worthwhile excursions:

→ Black Canyon, an International Dark Sky Park, is the perfect spot for **stargazing**, since artificial light is limited to safety requirements. Find exceptional skies and educational programming—or plan your trip around the annual **Black Canyon AstroFest**, with its expert talks, ranger walks, and telescope viewings.

→ Drive or hike to the Gunnison River to **fish for rainbow trout**. Follow the park's catch-and-release guidelines for less stress on the trout population.

→ **Rock climbing** in Black Canyon is truly an exercise in exploration. While some guides exist, detailed information on the 145 known routes in the park is hard to come by. Talk to those who have climbed before or rangers and outfitters. Spring and fall are the best climbing seasons; most of the climbing is rated between 5.10 and 5.13.

→ Winter is just as thrilling and beautiful at Black Canyon as summer. While the roads are closed to vehicles, **cross-country ski** along South Rim Drive or join a ranger for a **snowshoe expedition** around the rim.

→ **Kayak** through the canyon, but only if you're a pro. The river's Class V rapids and unrunnable portions are dangerous, and experienced local kayakers say the hydraulics make it even more difficult to navigate than that rating indicates.

→ **Horseback riders** have access to one trail in Black Canyon. The five-mile round-trip Deadhorse Trail is open for day use without permits, but you'll have to bring your horse by trailer to the Kneeling Camel Overlook for the trailhead.

Experts Only

EXPLORE

RANGER RECOMMENDATION

*Drive to the North Rim to get away from most visitors. Though the visitors center isn't consistently staffed, it's a good starting point for the **North Vista Trail**. Bask in the splendor of the inner canyon at Exclamation Point, then continue to Green Mountain for panoramic views of the San Juan Mountains, Grand Mesa, and the canyon itself.*

Iconic hoodoo rock formations

BRYCE CANYON NATIONAL PARK

UTAH

ESTABLISHED: February 25, 1928

SIZE: 35,835 acres

VISITORS CENTER: The Bryce Canyon Visitor Center (open year-round) provides ranger advice and a museum.

TRANSPORTATION: The Bryce Canyon Shuttle, free with park admission, is available April–October.

DOGS ALLOWED: Only on paved surfaces

WHEN TO GO: Summer for warm weather and ranger-led programs, though busiest; fall and spring for thinner crowds and either foliage or wildflowers, respectively; winter for magical, snowy scenery, cross-country skiing, and snowshoeing, though some trails and accommodations are closed.

CONTACT: 435-834-5322; nps.gov/brca

Highway 63

Bryce, UT 84764

There are towering hoodoos all over the globe, but Bryce Canyon is home to the largest concentration. These wild formations are the machinations of 50 million years of geological history. To hike among the sunstruck hoodoos or gaze at them from one of the park's 14 amphitheaters is surreal. The park's high altitude (8,000–9,000 feet) and pristine air allow for views of up to 200 miles. On a moonless night, the stars shine so bright they even make their own shadows. Bryce Canyon is the definition of a slow burn, and a trip to the park should take the same pace.

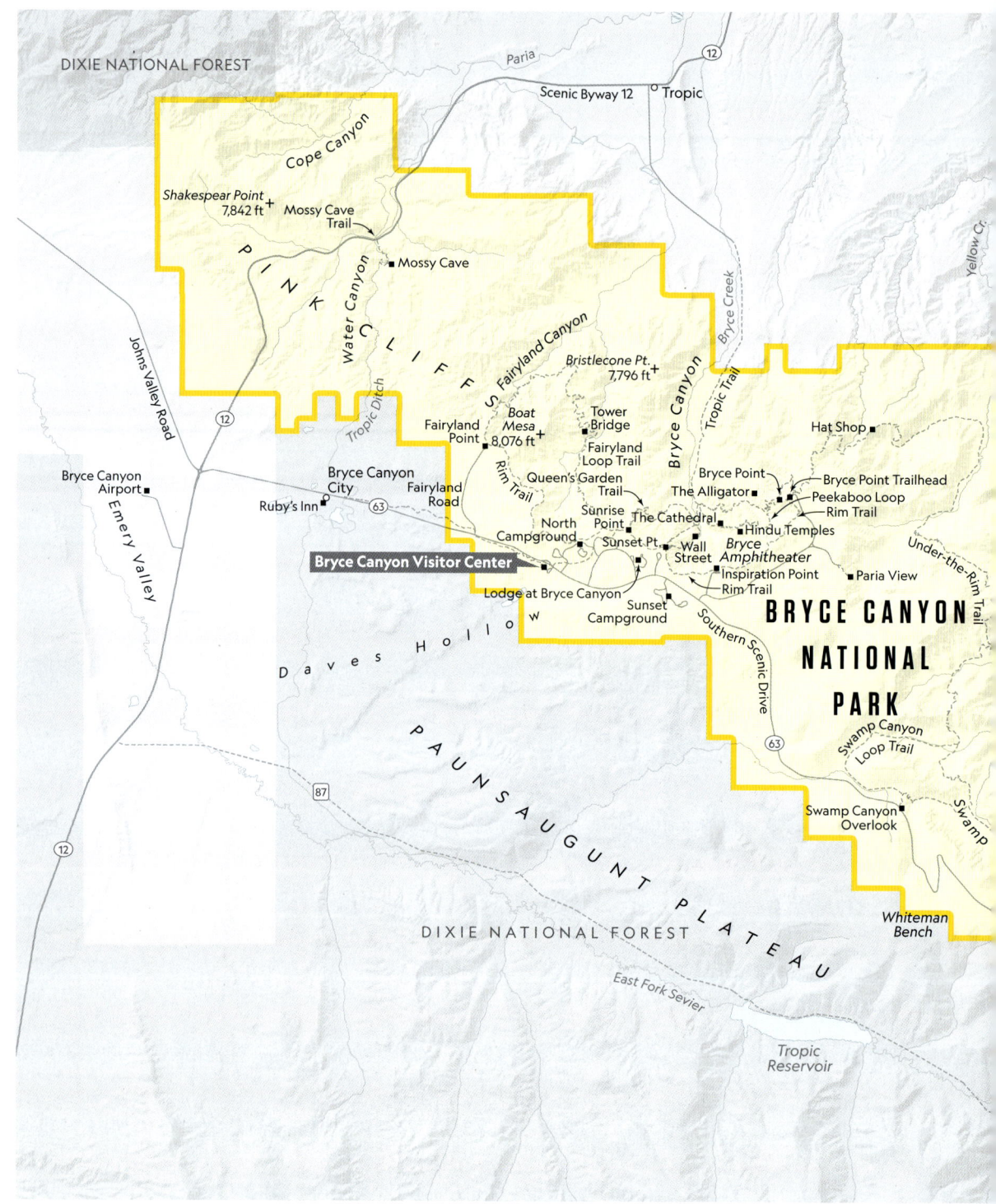

DIXIE NATIONAL FOREST

Paria

Scenic Byway 12   Tropic

PINK CLIFFS

Cope Canyon

Shakespear Point
7,842 ft

Mossy Cave
Trail

Mossy Cave

Water Canyon

Tropic Ditch

Johns Valley Road

Fairland Canyon

Bristlecone Pt.
7,796 ft

Boat
Mesa
8,076 ft

Tower
Bridge

Fairyland
Loop Trail

Queen's Garden
Trail

Fairyland
Point

Bryce Canyon
City

Bryce Canyon
Airport

Ruby's Inn

Fairyland
Road

Rim Trail

North
Campground

Sunrise
Point

Sunset Pt.

Bryce Canyon Visitor Center

Lodge at Bryce Canyon

Sunset
Campground

The Cathedral

Wall
Street

The Alligator

Bryce Point

Bryce
Amphitheater

Hindu Temples

Inspiration Point

Rim Trail

Hat Shop

Bryce Point Trailhead

Peekaboo Loop

Rim Trail

Paria View

Bryce Canyon

Tropic Trail

Bryce Creek

Yellow Cr.

Under-the-Rim Trail

BRYCE CANYON

NATIONAL

PARK

Swamp Canyon
Loop Trail

Swamp Canyon
Overlook

Swamp

Whiteman
Bench

Emery Valley

Daves Hollow

PAUNSAUGUNT PLATEAU

DIXIE NATIONAL FOREST

East Fork Sevier

Tropic
Reservoir

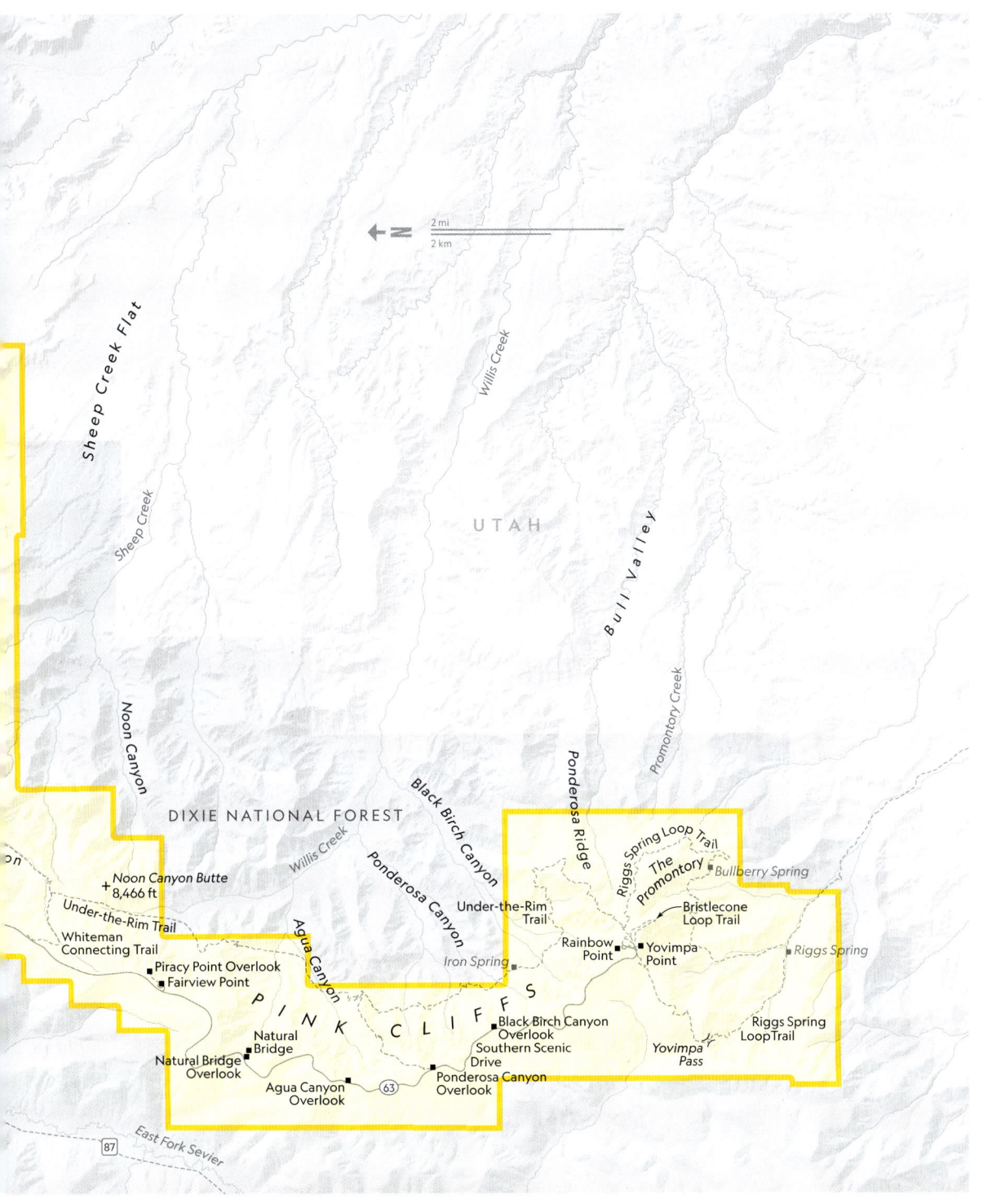

Sheep Creek Flat

Willis Creek

UTAH

Bull Valley

Sheep Creek

Noon Canyon

Promontory Creek

DIXIE NATIONAL FOREST

Black Birch Canyon

Ponderosa Ridge

Riggs Spring Loop Trail

The Promontory

Bullberry Spring

Willis Creek

Noon Canyon Butte
+ 8,466 ft

Under-the-Rim Trail

Ponderosa Canyon

Under-the-Rim Trail

Bristlecone Loop Trail

Whiteman Connecting Trail

Agua Canyon

Rainbow Point

Yovimpa Point

Riggs Spring

Piracy Point Overlook
Fairview Point

Iron Spring

PINK CLIFFS

Natural Bridge

Black Birch Canyon Overlook
Southern Scenic Drive

Riggs Spring Loop Trail

Natural Bridge Overlook

Yovimpa Pass

Agua Canyon Overlook

(63)

Ponderosa Canyon Overlook

East Fork Sevier

(87)

Cabins at the Lodge at Bryce Canyon

A At Bryce Canyon, you can stay at a campground or the park lodge, or rest outside the park. For hikers who prefer more solitude and a wilder experience, 11 backcountry camping sites are open; permits for peak season can be reserved three months in advance, while winter permits are issued up to 48 hours in advance in person at the visitors center. Here are your established options:

→ **North Campground** has 100 sites (split between RV and tent only), some of which can be reserved ahead of time—and that's recommended in peak season. There aren't any hookups, but there is potable water by the dump station. This campground is close to the visitors center and general store.

→ **Sunset Campground** has nearly as many sites (52 tent only, 46 RV only) and is just 1.5 miles from the visitors center. Again, you won't find hookups, but you will find water and nearby access to Sunset Point. Reservations are recommended; the campground closes in the winter.

→ Stay at the historic **Lodge at Bryce Canyon** (open March–November). Combined with its surrounding Sunset and Sunrise Hotels, as well as the lodge-run Western Cabins, the site offers 114 rooms to visitors, along with a restaurant and gift shop. The location and amenities make it a comfortable and convenient jumping-off point for your canyon adventures.

→ If you can't get a room at the Lodge site, book a room just outside the park at **Ruby's Inn**, which has been open since 1916. It also has an RV park and campground.

SLEEP

Family Friendly

Pause along your route to capture the views.

→ DRIVE

 There's one scenic drive through the park, the **Southern Scenic Drive**, and it starts at the visitors center. You'll see a lot of the main attractions from your vehicle, but get out of the car as much as possible for the best experience. Take the pull-off drive down Fairyland Road to see the hoodoos and spires of the Bryce Amphitheater before heading south down the main road. Then stop at Inspiration Point, Paria View, Bryce Point, Paunsaugunt Plateau, Swamp Canyon Overlook, Piracy Point Overlook, Natural Bridge Overlook, Agua Canyon Overlook, and Black Birch Canyon for various sandstone formation and hoodoo views. The route ends at the Bristlecone Loop Trail, which is an easy one-miler through the forest at the highest point in the park.

 Nothing will get you as up close and personal with the landscape as walking through it. Add one or more of these hikes to your trip:

→ Take the **Rim Trail**, which stretches 5.5 miles from Bryce Point to Fairyland Point. Along the way you'll see Inspiration, Sunset, and Sunrise Points; turn back at any time if you want a shorter hike.

→ Jump on the 5.5-mile **Peekaboo Loop** from the Bryce Point Trailhead and travel clockwise. The trail descends 670 feet before a steep ascent back. Along the way you'll see numerous hoodoos, and quite possibly some horses and mules in the summer months.

→ You may hike all of the 1.7-mile **Tropic Trail** without seeing another person. The trek starts in the forest below the rim and climbs up to the Peekaboo Loop, Navajo Loop, and Queen's Garden Trail. Take these to the rim for a steep hike, or enjoy the gentle Tropic Trail on its own.

→ The **Swamp Canyon Loop Trail** might look tame, but it's more challenging than the other trails around the Bryce Amphitheater. This sheltered hike isn't well marked, so bring a map and confident navigation skills.

→ The 22-mile **Under-the-Rim Trail** is difficult, with an ascent to 5,884 feet. This backcountry route weaves through forests and meadows, providing great views of the cliffs and hoodoos in the distance. Camp in designated spots along this trail with a permit.

→ The easy **Bristlecone Loop Trail** travels one mile through forests loved by grouse, woodpeckers, and owls. You'll start at a high elevation and won't gain much.

HIKE

↑

SPOT

C Changing climates, ecosystems, seasons, and predators in Bryce Canyon push animals from place to place—and you're likely to see migrating hummingbirds, peregrine falcons, Rocky Mountain elk, and pronghorn.

➜ Keep an eye out for vast colonies of **Utah prairie dogs** as you look over the meadows along the park's northern roads, especially in Daves Hollow. Keep your distance and don't feed them.

➜ While you're likely to see plenty of birds as you trek through the park, most of them are there for just a short time or a season. Look for **Steller's jays, ravens, Clark's nutcrackers,** and **nuthatches**.

➜ Contribute to the conservation and scientific efforts of the park by joining rangers for their annual **Christmas Bird Count**. The citizen-scientist event explores 15 miles surrounding the park (with routes from strenuous hikes to easy drives) and has recorded as many as 90 different species in the past.

Two male Utah prairie dogs scuffle for territory.

A Steller's jay

Fairyland Point

L Learn more about Bryce Canyon by experiencing it in the evening, heading to a less popular part of the park, or exploring its human history.

→ Visit the log cabin of Mormon settler and park namesake **Ebenezer Bryce**, the **Tropic Ditch** used to divert water and develop the region, and the exhibits at the visitors center on the **Southern Paiute Indians** to discover more about the land's early residents.

→ Take a **full-moon hike** with a ranger to see the shadows of the hoodoos by moonlight. Choose from a more strenuous hike through the steep trails or an easier hike along the rim's plateau.

→ **Winter hike, snowshoe, or crosscountry ski** along the maintained roads and lots near Sunset Point. The Rim Trail, Navajo Loop, and Queen's Garden Trail are all good options. Check ahead for any weather-related closures.

→ Once a less explored section of the park, **Mossy Cave** has been seeing more visitors lately. Begin with a climb on the Mossy Cave Trail—you'll reach the eponymous cave in one direction, or you can descend into Water Canyon in the other.

→ Participate in the annual summer **Bryce Canyon Geology Festival**. Listen to family-friendly geology programming, go out on evening hikes, and complete activities at the visitors center.

Family Friendly

E X P L O R E

RANGER RECOMMENDATION

Plan your trip to Bryce Canyon around the **phases of the moon**. During a new moon, stargaze beneath the canyon's dark sky at Sunrise Point, Paria View, or Whiteman Bench. At the quarter moon, hike among the hoodoos by the bright overhead moonlight. Take a guided full-moon hike for extra illumination, though don't expect much stargazing. The night before the full moon, watch it rise at Sunrise Point or Inspiration Point with the full colors of the sunset still shining on the landscape.

A view of formations from Mesa Arch

CANYONLANDS NATIONAL PARK

UTAH

ESTABLISHED: September 12, 1964

SIZE: 337,598 acres

VISITORS CENTERS: The Island in the Sky Visitor Center (open year-round) and The Needles Visitor Center (closed in winter) have ranger information, gift shops, vault toilets, and permits. The Hans Flat Ranger Station has limited daily hours, and the Canyonlands Backcountry Office in Moab is open on weekdays.

TRANSPORTATION: No in-park transportation

DOGS ALLOWED: Only in developed campgrounds, in parking lots, and on paved roads. Dogs are not permitted on trails.

WHEN TO GO: April–May or September–October for mild weather and fewer crowds; summer for stargazing, but be mindful of extreme heat in daytime

CONTACT: 435-719-2313; nps.gov/cany
2282 Resource Boulevard
Moab, UT 84532

T The desert in Canyonlands National Park is complex. After millions of years, the sedimentary rock has been eroded and shaped, first by the rising of the Colorado Plateau and then by wind, water, and the elements.

The park's history is just as elaborate. Nomadic hunter-gatherers roamed the region from 8000 to 500 B.C., then ancestral Puebloans thrived in the region. Eventually, local ranchers established the area as a winter pasture, and cowboys rode through the valleys to find water.

Today, Canyonlands National Park is split into four different districts: The Needles, Island in the Sky, The Maze, and Cataract Canyon. Explore from the road or go as deep as you can safely manage into the heart of the park. Getting out of your car, even for a short hike, will inspire a new perspective on what it means to struggle and thrive.

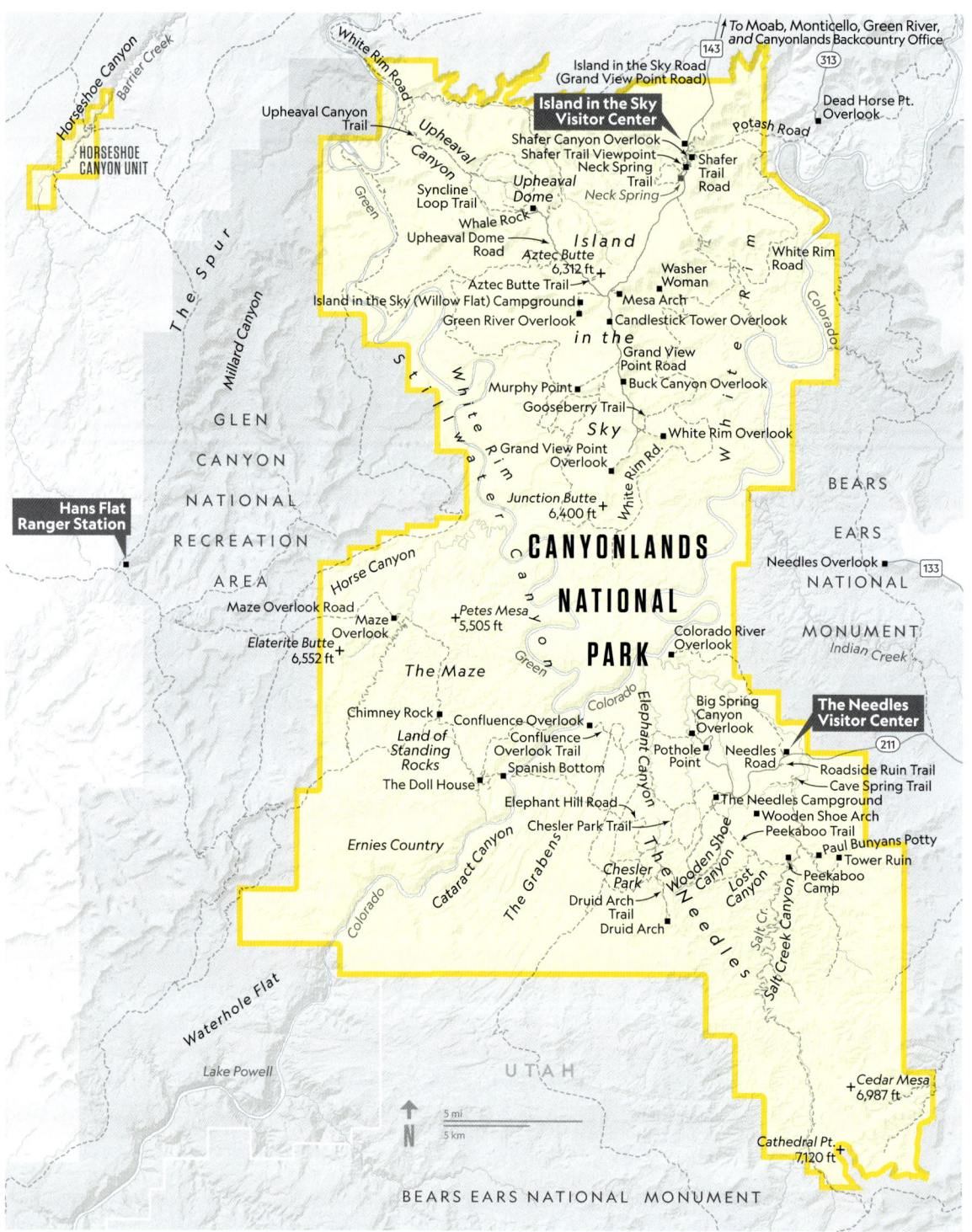

Horseshoe Canyon
Barrier Creek

HORSESHOE
CANYON UNIT

White Rim Road

To Moab, Monticello, Green River,
and Canyonlands Backcountry Office

143

Island in the Sky Road
(Grand View Point Road)

313

Dead Horse Pt.
Overlook

**Island in the Sky
Visitor Center**

Upheaval Canyon
Trail

Upheaval
Canyon

Shafer Canyon Overlook
Shafer Trail Viewpoint
Neck Spring
Trail

Potash Road

Shafer
Trail
Road

The Spur

Millard Canyon

Green

Syncline
Loop Trail

Upheaval
Dome

Neck Spring

Whale Rock

Upheaval Dome
Road

Island

White Rim
Road

Aztec Butte
6,312 ft

Stillwater Canyon

Aztec Butte Trail

Island in the Sky (Willow Flat) Campground

Green River Overlook

Washer
Woman

Mesa Arch

Candlestick Tower Overlook

in the

White
Rim

Colorado

GLEN

CANYON

Murphy Point

Gooseberry Trail

Grand View
Point Road

Buck Canyon Overlook

Sky

White Rim Overlook

NATIONAL

Grand View Point
Overlook

White Rim Rd.

White Rim

BEARS

EARS

RECREATION

Hans Flat
Ranger Station

Junction Butte
6,400 ft

CANYONLANDS

NATIONAL

MONUMENT

AREA

Horse Canyon

Maze Overlook Road

Petes Mesa
5,505 ft

PARK

Needles Overlook

133

Indian Creek

Maze
Overlook

Colorado River
Overlook

Elaterite Butte
6,552 ft

The Maze

Green

Colorado

Big Spring
Canyon
Overlook

**The Needles
Visitor Center**

Chimney Rock

Confluence Overlook

Confluence
Overlook Trail

Spanish Bottom

Elephant Canyon

Pothole
Point

Needles
Road

211

Roadside Ruin Trail
Cave Spring Trail

Land of
Standing
Rocks

The Doll House

Elephant Hill Road

Chesler Park Trail

Wooden Shoe Canyon

The Needles Campground
Wooden Shoe Arch
Peekaboo Trail
Paul Bunyans Potty
Tower Ruin

Ernies Country

Cataract Canyon

The Grabens

Chesler
Park

The Needles

Lost Canyon

Peekaboo
Camp

Druid Arch
Trail

Druid Arch

Salt Cr.

Salt Creek Canyon

Waterhole Flat

Colorado

Cedar Mesa
6,987 ft

Lake Powell

UTAH

Cathedral Pt.
7,120 ft

N

5 mi
5 km

BEARS EARS NATIONAL MONUMENT

S Stay in the park at one of the two official campgrounds, or head into the wilderness:

→ The year-round ***Island in the Sky (Willow Flat) Campground*** *offers 12 sites on a first-come-first-serve basis (the camp fills fast spring–fall) with toilets, picnic tables, and fire rings—but no water. You'll be sleeping near the Green River Overlook too.*

→ ***The Needles Campground*** *is just a short drive from The Needles Visitor Center. It has 26 sites, toilets, picnic tables, and fire rings. Reservations are available for Loop B and group sites March through November; the sites on Loop A are first come, first served.*

→ *Explore the* ***backcountry*** *of the park by four-wheel-drive vehicle, mountain bike, and foot, as long as you get a permit and protect the environment. Overnight permits are available by advance reservation—and you should try for one. Once you're out there, stay at a backcountry site that you choose. White Rim and Needles trips in particular are incredibly competitive spring through fall. Permits become available on a seasonal basis, four months before the start of the season.*

→ *If you prefer a hotel, you'll find many of them in* ***Moab***, ***Monticello***, *and* ***Green River***.

SLEEP

Camping affords unobstructed views.

Cloud cover creates a moody, memorable landscape.

Top
View

Whale Rock's 0.8-mile round-trip trail leads to this view.

HIKE

① If you're in Island in the Sky, add these well-marked hikes to your itinerary:

→ Tackle the **Syncline Loop Trail** if you're feeling strong and confident. Hike switchbacks and scrambles around the rim of Upheaval Dome for 1.8 miles, covering a 1,300-foot elevation change. This loop is the location of most park rescues, so you'll need good fitness, navigation skills, and supplies to make this hike a success.

→ The 1.4-mile round-trip **Aztec Butte Trail** is all about the views. First, climb the butte, then drop down to two ancestral Puebloan structures. Look, but don't touch.

→ Get a lesson in the human history of the park along the **Neck Spring Trail**, which will take you for a 5.6-mile loop by historic ranching features and two springs that were once popular with local cowboys.

→ Watch the sunrise at the cliff-edge **Mesa Arch** after a short and easy 0.6-mile hike. Even if you get there later in the day, you'll still be treated to striking views of the La Sal Mountains.

→ The **Gooseberry Trail** is this side of the park's steepest trail. It quickly descends 1,400 feet—along cliffs and through rough switchbacks—until you reach the White Rim sandstone bench. The route is difficult but worth it for the views. Allow at least four to six hours to tackle this route.

The Needles side of the park has a few more challenging trails. Try these treks:

→ Take the short **Cave Spring Trail** to a historic cowboy camp and prehistoric rock painting site. While just 0.6 mile, the route includes climbing two ladders.

→ The challenging 10.8-mile round-trip **Peekaboo Trail** to Salt Creek Canyon crosses two other canyons, Wooden Shoe and Lost. Traverse steep slopes and cliff edges, along with ladders, to get to Peekaboo camp and its nearby rock paintings.

→ Get one of the most striking views in The Needles by hiking the 10.8-mile round-trip **Druid Arch Trail**. Start by following the Chesler Park Trail, then branch off to get to the bottom of Elephant Canyon. Finally, end with a steep scramble.

→ Follow the cairns of the **Pothole Point Trail** along uneven slickrock. It takes 0.6 mile to get to the diverse potholes—

sandstones dimpled with pockets that sometimes fill with water—at the end of the route.

→ Trek through dry, open land for 11 miles on the **Confluence Overlook Trail**. You'll travel along the northern edge of the faults that create this unit and eventually reach a cliff that overlooks the place where the Green and Colorado Rivers meet.

If you venture to The Maze, you'll have to navigate steep, unmarked, and mostly unmaintained trails—some even require climbing skills. These routes can be dangerous; they are for experts only.

→ Take the one-mile **Maze Overlook Trail**. The trek requires climbing, scrambling, and difficult maneuvering. If you're not ready to end the trip, continue with a 15-mile backpacking adventure on an unmarked trail to **Land of Standing Rocks**. Make note: You'll need a four-wheel-drive vehicle to access the Maze Overlook Trail or two-wheel drive between the overlook and Land of Standing Rocks if you don't want to hike.

→ Join a ranger for a strenuous seven-mile hike through **Horseshoe Canyon** in the spring or fall. There, see some of the most impactful rock art on the continent, including life-size figures and drawings of beautiful flowers, dating back as early as 9000 to 7000 B.C.

Experts
Only

A pair of cougars lap from a water-filled depression.

SPOT

C Canyonlands is quiet, but that doesn't mean it's without life. Find the best wildlife by traveling along the Salt Creek corridor in The Needles district. There you might find signs of the park's mostly nocturnal creatures, such as **bobcats**, **ringtails**, and **bats**, or daytime critters such as **hawks**, **squirrels**, and **lizards**.

Spot birds like **grosbeaks**, **canyon wrens**, and **great blue herons** along the more verdant corridors of the Green and Colorado Rivers.

A stoic coyote makes eye contact.

Motorcyclists roam the edge of an overlook.

(M) Most people who visit Canyonlands barely leave the car, thanks to scenic overlooks along the Island in the Sky and Needles Roads.

→ Take **Island in the Sky Road** to the unit's most prominent and popular lookouts and trailheads. Don't miss the Shafer Trail Viewpoint, Mesa Arch Trailhead and Overlook, Candlestick Tower Overlook, Buck Canyon Overlook, and the final stop: the Grand View Point Overlook and Trailhead.

→ Turn onto **Upheaval Dome Road** from Island in the Sky Road to access the Green River Overlook, hike the Aztec Butte Trail, and reach the Upheaval Dome Overlook and Trail.

→ Drive **Needles Road** and stop at the short Roadside Ruin Trail, Pothole Point Trail, and Big Spring Canyon Trail and Overlook.

→ Get to the park's Maze unit through **Maze Overlook Road** on its west side. The road is a difficult and rugged route that requires a four-wheel-drive vehicle with high clearance. Drive up to the Maze Overlook.

DRIVE

A winding dirt road in the park

Expert Drivers Only

Star trails in a long-exposure image of the park

E

X

P

L

O

R

E

(A) Add a bit more adventure to your trip by changing up the scenery, trying a new transportation method, or joining a ranger program.

→ Head to the park in the winter to **capture beautiful photographs** of the bright snow against the intense red rocks.

→ **Float** on the Green and Colorado Rivers with one of the many outfitters to guide you through the mostly hidden waters. Take a half-day adventure or plan a week-long float through the park. Stop at Spanish Bottom to avoid the dangerous rapids of Cataract Canyon—or head out to them with an experienced guide if you feel prepared.

→ Take the kids to **climb Whale Rock**, a massive sandstone dome that is perfect for anyone who wants to do some scrambling. Just be careful of steep drop-offs.

→ Go **off-roading** in a four-wheel-drive vehicle along some of the 50 miles of backcountry routes in the park, like White Rim Road. Get a permit to take on this adventure and camp with your vehicle at a few of the backcountry sites, including many on Elephant Hill Road.

→ Get into the park at night to benefit from its dark skies. Plan your own **stargazing trip**, which will be easier if you're staying at a park campsite, or join a stargazing program with a ranger.

Experts Only

Temple of the Sun

CAPITOL REEF
NATIONAL PARK

UTAH

ESTABLISHED: December 18, 1971

SIZE: 243,921 acres

VISITORS CENTER: The Capitol Reef National Park Visitor Center (open year-round)

TRANSPORTATION: No in-park transportation; outside shuttle services offered from Wilderness Ridge Adventures and Meridian Tours.

DOGS ALLOWED: Only in restricted areas (mostly trails by the visitors center or on campgrounds); not permitted on hiking trails, in backcountry areas, or in buildings

----

WHEN TO GO: Spring for mild temps; fall for hiking and biking; winter for solitude and snow. Summer brings heat and flash floods.

CONTACT: 435-425-3791; nps.gov/care
52 West Headquarters Drive
Torrey, UT 84775

"The Reef" is defined by the nearly 100-mile-long Waterpocket Fold, a sandstone barricade that kept travelers at bay for centuries. Its intricate landscape was carved by Triassic tidal flats, Jurassic dunes, and late Cretaceous seas 35 to 75 million years ago.

The land now protected by Capitol Reef National Park has been used for thousands of years. First by the ancient Fremont, who left behind petroglyphs; then by Mormon pioneers, who arrived in the 1880s and planted thousands of fruit trees in the fertile soil; then by the advocates who sought to protect its wilderness of domes, natural bridges, spires, and slot canyons. A visit to this space provides an intimate education in the power of complexity.

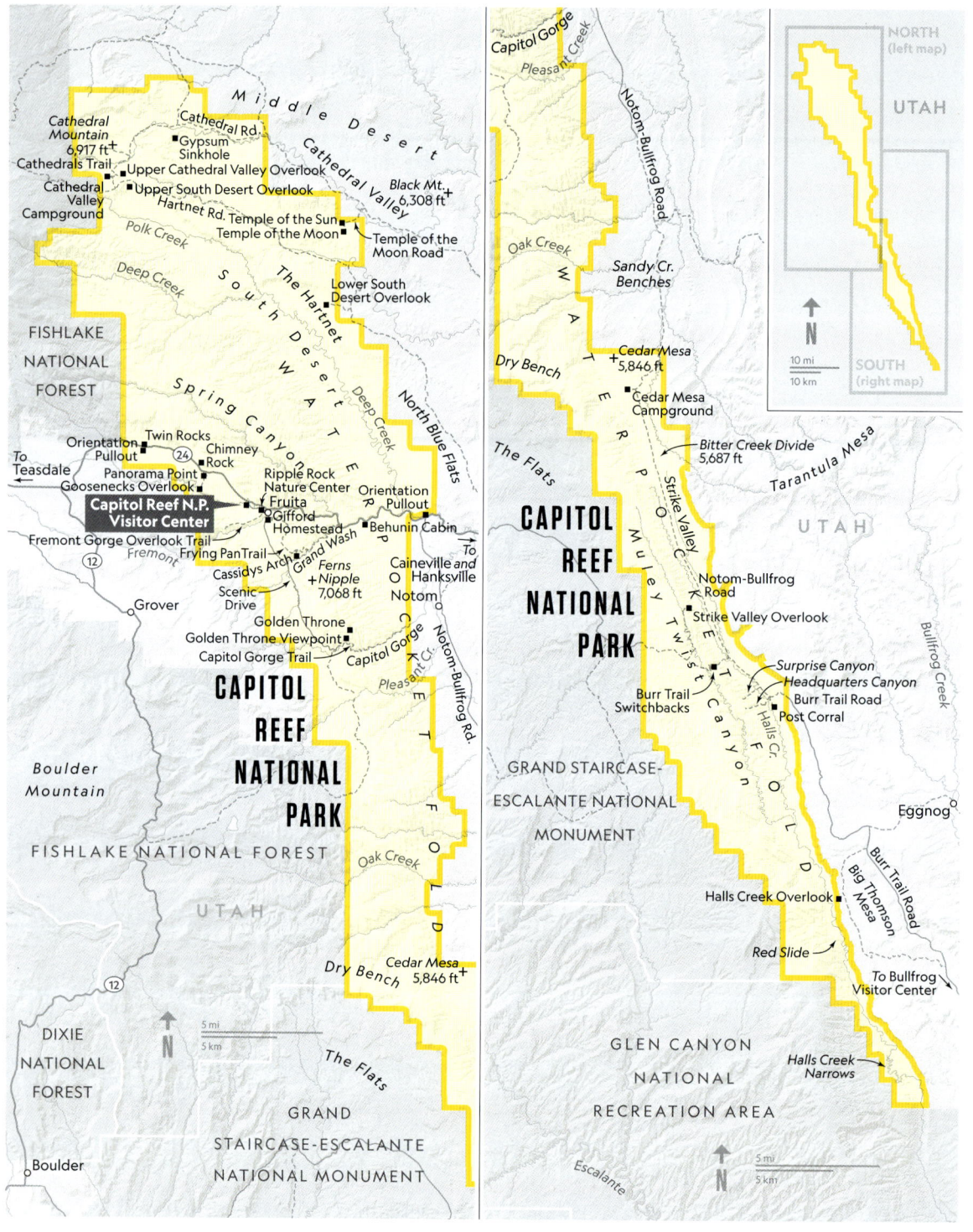

Cathedral
Mountain
6,917 ft
Cathedrals Trail
Cathedral
Valley
Campground

Gypsum
Sinkhole

Cathedral Rd.

Middle Desert

Cathedral Valley

Upper Cathedral Valley Overlook
Upper South Desert Overlook
Hartnet Rd.
Temple of the Sun
Temple of the Moon

Black Mt.
6,308 ft

Temple of the
Moon Road

Polk Creek

The Hartnet

South Desert

Lower South
Desert Overlook

FISHLAKE
NATIONAL
FOREST

Deep Creek

Spring Canyon

W A T E R

Deep Creek

North Blue Flats

To Teasdale

Orientation
Pullout

Twin Rocks
Chimney
Rock

24

Panorama Point
Goosenecks Overlook

Ripple Rock
Nature Center
Fruita
Capitol Reef N.P.
Visitor Center
Gifford
Homestead
Frying Pan Trail
Cassidys Arch
Scenic
Drive

Orientation
Pullout

Behunin Cabin

Fremont Gorge Overlook Trail

12

Fremont

Grand Wash

Ferns
Nipple
7,068 ft

Caineville and
Hanksville

Notom

Grover

Golden Throne
Golden Throne Viewpoint
Capitol Gorge Trail

Capitol Gorge

Pleasant Cr.

Notom-Bullfrog Rd.

Boulder
Mountain

CAPITOL
REEF
NATIONAL
PARK

FISHLAKE NATIONAL FOREST

UTAH

Oak Creek

W A T E R P O C K E T   F O L D

12

DIXIE
NATIONAL
FOREST

5 mi
5 km
N

Dry Bench

Cedar Mesa
5,846 ft

The Flats

Boulder

GRAND
STAIRCASE-ESCALANTE
NATIONAL MONUMENT

Capitol Gorge

Pleasant Creek

Notom-Bullfrog Road

Oak Creek

Sandy Cr.
Benches

Dry Bench

Cedar Mesa
5,846 ft
Cedar Mesa
Campground

Bitter Creek Divide
5,687 ft

The Flats

W A T E R P O C K E T

Strike Valley

Muley Twist Canyon

F O L D

Tarantula Mesa

UTAH

Bullfrog Creek

CAPITOL
REEF
NATIONAL
PARK

Notom-Bullfrog
Road
Strike Valley Overlook

Surprise Canyon
Headquarters Canyon
Burr Trail Road
Post Corral

Burr Trail
Switchbacks

Halls Cr.

GRAND STAIRCASE-ESCALANTE NATIONAL
MONUMENT

Eggnog

Burr Trail Road

Big Thomson
Mesa

Halls Creek Overlook

Red Slide

To Bullfrog
Visitor Center

GLEN CANYON
NATIONAL
RECREATION AREA

Escalante

Halls Creek
Narrows

5 mi
5 km
N

NORTH
(left map)

UTAH

SOUTH
(right map)

N

10 mi
10 km

Camping in Lower Muley Twist Canyon

Accessible
Option

SLEEP

C Camping is the only option for staying within park bounds. Outside of that, look for lodging in Torrey, Teasdale, Caineville, and Hanksville. Here are your in-park choices:

→ There's one established campground in the park: **Fruita**. Nestled between orchards, the campground offers 71 sites with picnic tables, firepits, and grills but no hookups. Find potable water near the entrance and flush toilets. Reservations are required—book early, as the campground fills fast. Reservations open six months ahead of time.

→ The park is also home to two primitive campgrounds: **Cathedral Valley** (6 sites), at 7,000 feet, is accessible along Cathedral Road, but you'll need a four-wheel-drive vehicle to reach it. **Cedar Mesa** (5 sites) is on Notom-Bullfrog Road at 5,500 feet elevation; a two-wheel-drive vehicle is usually sufficient, but that can change with the weather. Both sites have pit toilets and picnic tables but no water.

Must-Do Hike

M Most of the park is accessible only by foot. Try these trails:

→ *Hike the* ***Fremont Gorge Overlook Trail****, which offers spectacular scenery without a lot of crowds. The 4.4-mile out-and-back trail gains elevation quickly, offering views of the Fruita Rural Historic District and the Fremont River Gorge.*

→ *Walk the one-mile (one-way)* ***Capitol Gorge Trail*** *into a deep canyon to see petroglyphs and climb to the nearby water pockets. The trail ends at The Tanks, a series of sandstone potholes.*

→ *Hike either the 2-mile round-trip* ***Surprise Canyon Route*** *or the 3.2-mile round-trip* ***Headquarters Canyon Route*** *off Burr Trail Road. Both are out-and-back treks that head deep into the canyon's sheer walls, dry washes, and rocky ravines.*

→ *Take the switchbacks up* ***Burr Trail Road****, a former 1880s sheep trail, to the Top of Burr Overlook and the Muley Twist Picnic Area. Then continue to the Strike Valley Overlook for an overnight.*

→ *At the park's northern end, access the* ***Cathedrals Trail****, an easy 2.4-mile out-and-back route toward and around the bases of the Needle and Cathedral Mountains.*

→ *If you're set on some solitude,* ***back-country hike*** *through the Upper and Lower Muley Twist Canyons—named because they were thought to be so narrow they could "twist a mule." Begin your trek at Burr Trail Road; watch for flood warnings before you start.*

HIKE

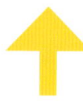

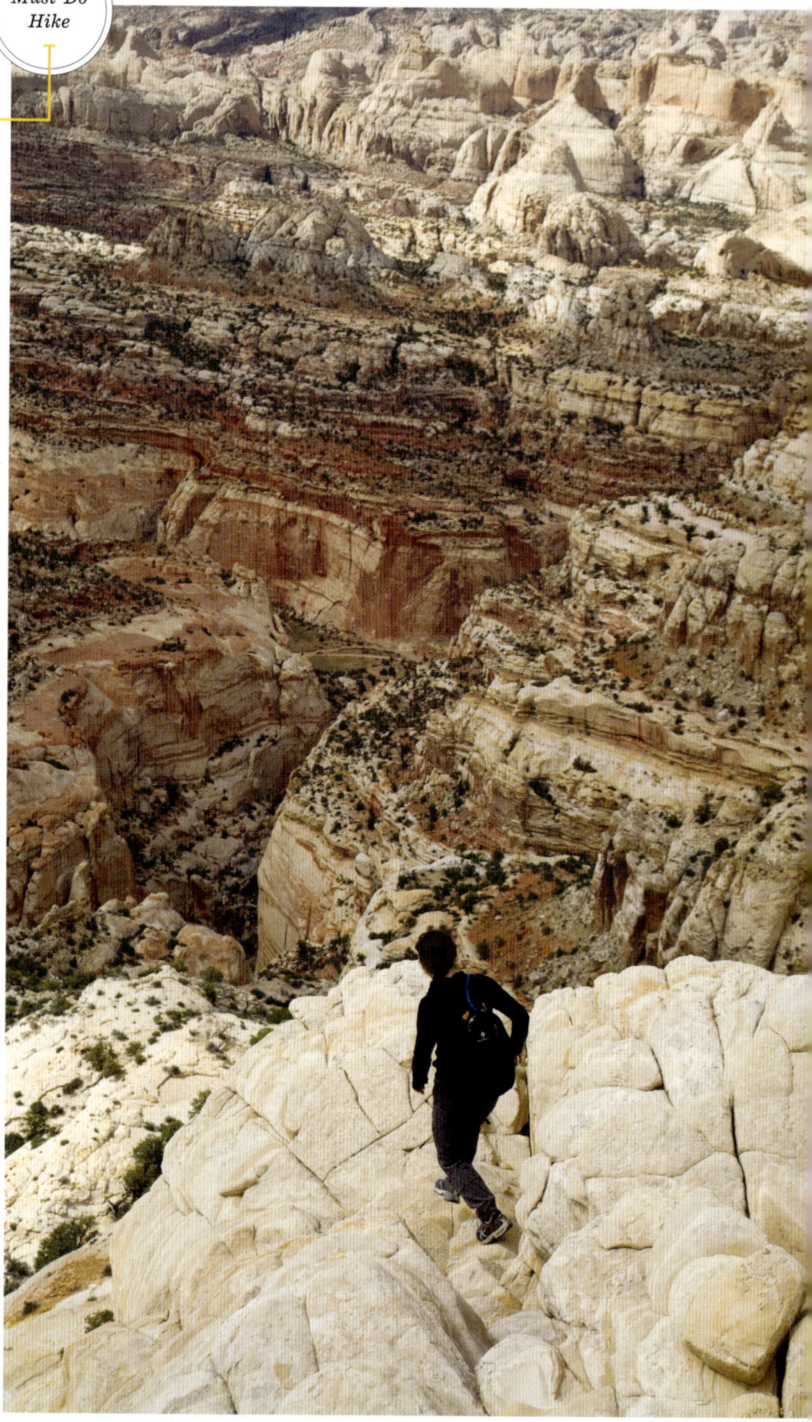

Ferns Nipple is an iconic dome in the park.

Birders can spot chukar partridges.

SPOT

Ⓣ The park's different ecosystems lend themselves to varied plant life and wildlife. Upper Muley Twist Canyon is a worthwhile visit for bird-watching. Look for **ash-throated flycatchers**, **warblers**, **western kingbirds**, and **canyon wrens**. While you're there, keep an eye out for **desert bighorn sheep**, **mule deer**, and **mountain lions**. If you look carefully, you might see the long, bushy, banded tails of the park's **ringtails** up in the trees of Fruita and Pleasant Creek.

Keep your eyes peeled for the Great Basin collared lizard.

A A few roads connect road-trippers to sights and trails.

→ Drive **Utah Highway 24**, the main road across the park, east to west or vice versa. Make a day of driving from one end to the other to access the Behunin Cabin (built in 1883), Grand Wash Trailhead, Hickman Bridge hikes, Petroglyph Panel pull-off, Fruita Campground and Historic District, Panorama Point Hike and Overlook, and Chimney Rock Loop Trailhead.

→ Pull off Utah Highway 24 into the **Fruita Rural Historic District**, known for its orchard planted by Mormon pioneers in the 1880s. Drive past the campground and onto the Scenic Drive. There are 11 stops on the route, including fruit orchards, the historic Gifford House and Pendleton Barn, and overlooks of the cliffs and bluffs. The route ends at the Golden Throne and Capitol Gorge Trailheads.

→ Drive the rough **Notom-Bullfrog Road** past the primitive campsites at Cedar Mesa and Waterpocket District viewpoints to reach the trailheads for the narrow slot canyons. You'll have to hike to get into them. Have a driver meet you at the end point: the Bullfrog Visitor Center in the adjacent Glen Canyon National Recreational Area.

→ Check out the Temple of the Sun and Temple of the Moon formations off the four-wheel-drive-vehicles-only **Lower Cathedral Valley Spur Road** in the northeastern section of the park, included in the park during its 1970s expansion.

DRIVE

Pendleton Barn, part of the Gifford Homestead

Meander past immense canyons on a leisurely drive.

Petroglyphs of horseback riders carved by Indigenous people

EXPLORE

E Expand your park experience by going deeper into its canyons, learning about its human history, discovering its geological past, and celebrating its night skies.

→ Tour the historic **Fruita Rural Historic District** near the campground of the same name. Explore an old barn, restored schoolhouse, flourishing orchards, and a blacksmith shop with an original tractor. Continue to the restored Gifford House, which now serves as a pioneer museum.

→ The layers of rock at Capitol Reef have created a rare environment for **canyoneers**. Take the popular passes through the Navajo and Wingate Sandstone formations, or find your own route through the tight canyon walls. Be sure to get a permit from the visitors center ahead of time.

→ **Rock climb** in certain zones along the rugged park. Check out the conditions at Capitol Gorge, Chimney Rock Canyon, Cohab Canyon, and Grand Wash before heading out to climb—and get a permit ahead of time from the visitors center. Note: Leave the white chalk at home.

→ Bring the kids to the **Ripple Rock Nature Center** for indoor and outdoor activities. Most of the programming happens from mid-spring to mid-summer, so keep an eye on the calendar.

→ Look for the **Fremont Culture petroglyphs** along Utah Highway 24. The Fremont Culture lived in the region for a thousand years, from A.D. 300 to 1300, and their drawings offer a special peek into their lives.

→ Learn about the park's natural history during **ranger-led archaeology, geology**, and **astronomy programs**, most of which run spring through summer.

→ Celebrate night skies during the park's annual **Heritage StarFest**. In early fall, rangers and visitors join to look at the sky, celebrate the stars, and talk about astronomy.

Family Friendly

*Hike the **Frying Pan Trail**, which connects two popular trails but is much less traveled. Find solitude as you immerse yourself in the diverse geology of the park. Another major benefit to Frying Pan is that it's easily accessible from the park's front country. Pay attention to trail markers and signs, since you're likely to be alone on the hike and there are challenging elevation changes.*

The cliffside at Desert View at the South Rim

GRAND CANYON NATIONAL PARK

ARIZONA

ESTABLISHED: February 26, 1919

SIZE: 1,218,375 acres

VISITORS CENTERS: South Rim: Grand Canyon Visitor Center, Verkamp's Visitor Center; North Rim Visitor Center (closed in winter)

TRANSPORTATION: Free shuttle bus system on the South Rim; mule rides year-round on the South Rim, May–October on the North Rim

----

DOGS ALLOWED: Only leashed. Dogs are not allowed on shuttle buses or below the canyon rim. The Grand Canyon Kennel, on the South Rim, offers overnights for pets whose humans want to explore below the rim (reservations recommended).

WHEN TO GO: Spring brings moderate temperatures, wildflowers, and active wildlife. Fall brings turning aspens. The North Rim closes October–May, while the South Rim stays busy through the less crowded winter. Summer is busiest.

CONTACT: 928-638-7888; nps.gov/grca
20 South Entrance Road
Grand Canyon, AZ 86023

G Grand Canyon National Park is a monument to the power of time. The transformation of this tremendous landscape began when tectonic plates lifted the Colorado Plateau. After millions of years of the Colorado River carving through the rocky layers, the Grand Canyon as we know it was formed—from rim to rim, the canyon is 18 miles across at its widest point, one mile deep, and 278 river miles long. It's also the second-most visited national park in the country, with about five million visitors each year. Those numbers can mean crowded experiences, but they also mean excellent amenities, fabulous lodging, and well-maintained trails. Shake the crowds by visiting the North Rim (elevation 8,000 feet); 90 percent of visitors congregate on the South Rim (elevation 7,000 feet).

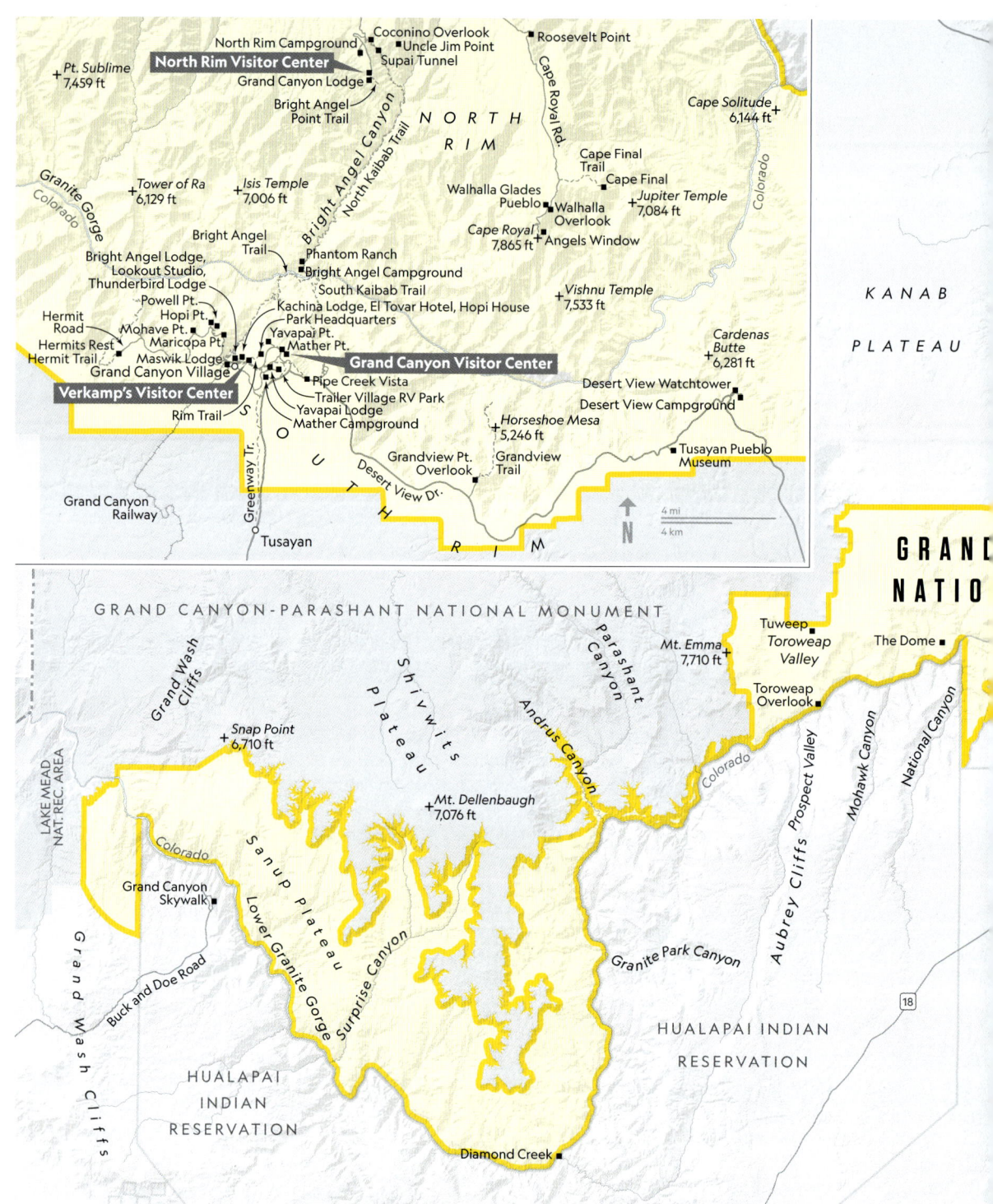

Pt. Sublime
7,459 ft

North Rim Campground
Coconino Overlook
Uncle Jim Point
North Rim Visitor Center
Supai Tunnel
Grand Canyon Lodge
Bright Angel
Point Trail

Roosevelt Point

NORTH
RIM

Cape Solitude
6,144 ft

Granite Gorge

Colorado

Cape Royal Rd.

Tower of Ra
6,129 ft

Isis Temple
7,006 ft

Bright Angel Canyon

North Kaibab Trail

Walhalla Glades
Pueblo

Cape Final
Trail
Cape Final

Jupiter Temple
7,084 ft

Walhalla
Overlook

Bright Angel
Trail

Phantom Ranch
Bright Angel Lodge,
Lookout Studio,
Thunderbird Lodge
Powell Pt.
Hopi Pt.
Hermit
Road
Mohave Pt.
Hermits Rest
Maricopa Pt.
Hermit Trail
Maswik Lodge
Grand Canyon Village
Verkamp's Visitor Center

Bright Angel Campground
South Kaibab Trail
Kachina Lodge, El Tovar Hotel, Hopi House
Park Headquarters
Yavapai Pt.
Mather Pt.

Cape Royal
7,865 ft

Angels Window

Vishnu Temple
7,533 ft

Cardenas
Butte
6,281 ft

Grand Canyon Visitor Center

Pipe Creek Vista
Trailer Village RV Park
Yavapai Lodge
Mather Campground

Rim Trail

Desert View Watchtower
Desert View Campground

Horseshoe Mesa
5,246 ft

SOUTH RIM

Greenway Tr.

Desert View Dr.

Grandview Pt.
Overlook

Grandview
Trail

Tusayan Pueblo
Museum

Grand Canyon
Railway

Tusayan

KANAB

PLATEAU

Colorado

4 mi
4 km

N

GRAND CANYON-PARASHANT NATIONAL MONUMENT

GRAND
NATIO

Grand Wash
Cliffs

Shivwits
Plateau

Parashant
Canyon

Andrus Canyon

Mt. Emma
7,710 ft

Tuweep
Toroweap
Valley

The Dome

Snap Point
6,710 ft

Toroweap
Overlook

Colorado

LAKE MEAD
NAT. REC. AREA

Mt. Dellenbaugh
7,076 ft

Colorado

Sanup Plateau

Lower Granite Gorge

Surprise Canyon

Granite Park Canyon

Aubrey Cliffs

Prospect Valley

Mohawk Canyon

National Canyon

18

Grand Canyon
Skywalk

Grand Wash Cliffs

Buck and Doe Road

HUALAPAI
INDIAN
RESERVATION

HUALAPAI INDIAN
RESERVATION

Diamond Creek

KAIBAB INDIAN RESERVATION

Lees Ferry
GLEN CANYON
NATIONAL RECREATION AREA
Marble Canyon

Paria Plateau

Vermilion Cliffs

Colorado

Echo Cliffs

ALT 89

Jacob Lake Inn

House Rock Valley

Bitter Springs

89

Marble Canyon

KAIBAB NATIONAL FOREST

K A I B A B

67

South Canyon

P A I N T E D

Kaibab Lodge
De Motte Campground

P L A T E A U

North Rim Entrance

NAVAJO
NATION
RESERVATION

CANYON
L PARK

Granite Narrows
Colorado

Great Thumb Mesa

Middle Granite Gorge

Mauv Canyon

Swamp Point
7,517 ft

Point Imperial
8,803 ft

Colorado

Mt. Sinyella
5,441 ft

Powell Plateau

Vista Encantada

D E S E R T

Havasu Canyon

Supai

Havasupai Pt.
6,635 ft

Aztec
Amphitheater

North Rim Visitor Center

Bright Angel Canyon

Walhalla
Plateau

Cape Solitude
6,144 ft

HAVASUPAI
RESERVATION

Granite
Gorge

Verkamp's Visitor Center

Phantom Ranch

Hermit Road
Hermits Rest
Grand Canyon Kennel

Grand Canyon
Village

**Grand Canyon
Visitor Center**

Desert View Watchtower

Tusayan Pueblo
Museum

Area
Enlarged

ARIZONA

Tusayan

Grand Canyon
Airport

Tusayan-Montane
Campground

C o c o n i n o   R i m

64

C O C O N I N O

Grand Canyon Railway

64

KAIBAB NATIONAL FOREST

P L A T E A U

10 mi
N
10 km

To Valle, Red Lake, Williams, *and* Flagstaff

SLEEP

(T) The closest lodges to the South Rim are in Grand Canyon Village and Market Plaza. Free shuttles run from the lodges to park headquarters, the South Rim's visitors centers, Yavapai Point, the Yavapai Geology Museum, and a few nearby trailheads.

On the South Rim, there are a number of lodges and hotels available. There's also one seasonal offering on the North Rim:

→ *Yavapai Lodge is closest to the Grand Canyon Visitor Center, provides great access to the paved Greenway Trail, and has modern rooms.*

→ *The historic and luxurious El Tovar Hotel, opened in 1905, sits directly on the canyon's rim—and a few suites have unobstructed views of the wonder.*

→ *The front porch of Bright Angel Lodge, a national historic landmark designed by Mary E. J. Colter in 1935, provides similarly striking views.*

→ *Family-friendly Maswik Lodge has big rooms and a food court; Thunderbird Lodge, with its multiple canyon-side rooms, is also a great family option.*

→ *The contemporary Kachina Lodge puts you right in the middle of the historic district, with easy access to restaurants, gift shops, Kolb Studio, and the Bright Angel Trailhead.*

→ *Book a stay at the North Rim's Grand Canyon Lodge. It's closed in the winter, but in warmer seasons you'll find gorgeous canyon views from its sunroom and veranda.*

For camping in the canyon:

→ *Get a permit for Bright Angel Campground, where you'll sleep under two-billion-year-old granite walls or beside its rolling namesake creek.*

→ *If you're feeling lucky, enter the hard-to-win lottery to stay at the nearby Phantom Ranch. The remote cabins and dorms are accessible only by foot, mule, or raft. It takes either 7.5 miles down the South Kaibab Trail or 10 miles descending the Bright Angel Trail to get to this once-in-a-lifetime experience. Phantom Ranch has a canteen offering breakfast, sack lunches, and dinners—reserve in advance.*

There are also six developed campgrounds at the canyon's rim: four in the south and two in the north.

→ *In the south, Trailer Village RV Park has 123 sites, including 80 with full hookups, and a designated shuttle stop.*

It's open all year, and reservations can be made up to 13 months in advance; book at least one year in advance for busy season (May–October).

→ *Just down the road, Mather Campground is also open year-round and has a quiet, tent-only section with 55 sites. There are 327 sites total at this massive campground, which includes flush toilets, picnic tables, drinkable water, and fire rings. There are no hookups. Reservations are recommended March through November; 15 sites are available first come, first served and go on sale at 8 a.m.*

→ *Desert View (49 sites, reservations only) and Tusayan-Montane (142 sites, reservations recommended but with 42 sites first come, first served) in the south are open seasonally and a bit farther from the main stretch.*

→ *Two campgrounds are on the northern rim, both open only May to October: North Rim Campground (87 sites, reservations only), within park bounds, and De Motte Campground (38 sites, reservations only) on national forest land.*

→ *To backcountry camp, get a permit ahead of time from the Backcountry Information Center or at recreation.gov. There are two ways to get a permit: early access via a lottery online and based on availability thereafter. Up to 750 applicants will receive a permit from the lottery.*

Outside the park, plenty of hotels are in **Valle**, **Red Lake**, **Williams**, and **Flagstaff** on the south side. Try the **Kaibab Lodge** and **Jacob Lake Inn** on the north side.

Resting alongside the Colorado River

Expansive canyon views reward a hiker's efforts.

For an alternate path, navigate the Walter Powell Route (2.4 miles one-way) to the South Rim.

The Grand Canyon is one of the country's most popular national parks and also requires some of the most rescues. Hiking in the hot desert can be tough, so be prepared. Pack enough water and food, travel light, and take breaks often.

Most people explore the park's South Rim, which has plenty of hikes for a variety of skill levels.

→ The **Rim Trail** is a must-do in the Grand Canyon. It runs approximately 13 miles from the South Kaibab Trailhead west to Hermits Rest and is perfect for anyone who wants classic canyon views with a relatively easy walk. It's also accessible from Lookout Studio to the South Kaibab Trailhead. Stop for sunset at Mohave Point, look for raptors at Pipe Creek Vista, and visit Yavapai Point and the Yavapai Geology Museum.

→ Follow one million years of Grand Canyon history as you walk the nearly three-mile-long, paved **Trail of Time**. It's designed to mirror the geologic timeline of the canyon and the magnitude of its creation. Walk into the past from the Yavapai Geology Museum or the present from Grand Canyon Village.

→ The most popular trail into the Grand Canyon travels along a huge fault and down through miles of switchbacks. It also requires foresight. For some, it's a breeze to trek down **Bright Angel Trail**, but for almost everyone, the hike back up isn't so easy. Plan for the trip to take twice as long heading up as going down, and don't expect to go all the way to the Colorado River and back in one day. Safety tip: Watch out for mules as you hike.

→ Ride the free shuttle to the **Hermit Trail**, which you can follow down to the Colorado River. The steep route traverses a series of switchbacks, once paved with large hand-fitted rock slabs. A few remain as a reminder of the trail's past. Turn back at the quiet Maria Spring rest house for a day hike.

→ Only experienced desert hikers should attempt the strenuous, seven-mile round-trip **Grandview Trail**, originally built to connect the rim to the copper mines in Horseshoe Mesa. Navigate old cobblestone, sloping ledges, and sandstone cliffs before you reach the overlook. Leave the "trash" from the past mining operations alone; it's protected as an archaeological resource.

→ The short walk to **Mather Point** takes only five minutes, but it will quickly transport you from the bustle of the Grand Canyon Visitor Center to the beauty of the canyon. Accessible walkways lead to a fantastic sunset viewpoint.

→ Take the shuttle to the **South Kaibab Trail** and prepare for a long walk without any resources. Turn around at Ooh Aah Point, Cedar Ridge, or Skeleton Point for a day hike—or head down to Phantom Ranch (if you won a spot) or Bright Angel Campground for an overnight.

The North Rim of the canyon is less popular, but that just means you'll find more solitude.

→ The flat, forested **Cape Final Trail** won't give you many views as you hike its 4.2 miles, but it will lead you to an outstanding panoramic overlook of Vishnu and Jupiter Temples, two noteworthy summits on the North Rim.

→ The **North Kaibab Trail** is the least visited and most difficult trek of the major inner-canyon routes. It's best to avoid the trail unless you're an experienced hiker, but if you can manage it, you'll be rewarded with scenic views, including sweeping expanses of Bright Angel Canyon. If you want to tackle only a portion, turn around at the stunning Coconino Overlook (which sits about 500 feet below the rim) or the distinct Supai Tunnel, which allows hikers to travel through the ancient rocks.

→ The family-friendly **Bright Angel Point Trail** is just a half-mile round-trip, moving through the Kaibab Plateau to a piñon and juniper forest. Take in canyon views as you stroll.

HIKE

North Rim Entrance signage

DRIVE

G Grand Canyon is a popular destination for all ages and abilities, and many of its main wonders are open to drivers. If you'd like to see the park from the comfort of a car or shuttle, try one of these routes:

→ The free **Hermit Road Route** shuttle bus is a fantastic way to see the South Rim; catch it at the western edge of The Village. The route takes 80 minutes without stops, but you'll definitely want to stop. Take a hike from the Hermit or Bright Angel Trailheads. Look over the canyon at Pima Point, Monument Creek Vista, Mohave Point, Hopi Point, Powell Point, and Maricopa Point.

→ Travel the South Rim's **Desert View Drive** and stop at five awe-inspiring viewpoints over the canyon, as well as at the iconic 70-foot-tall Desert View Watchtower, a stone tower designed by architect Mary E. J. Colter and built in

1932. The Desert View Inter-Tribal Welcome Center is being constructed along the route with exhibits designed by local tribes and space for cultural demonstrations. Get a history lesson at the Tusayan Pueblo Museum, and stop for a meal at one of the four picnic areas.

→ Drive through the forest on **Cape Royal Road** on the North Rim, stopping to turn off toward Point Imperial, then return to picnic at Vista Encantada. Take in the views at Roosevelt Point and Walhalla Overlook, or do a short hike toward Cape Final or Angels Window. Time your drive right to watch the sunset at one of the viewpoints.

A desert bighorn sheep

An elk on the South Rim of the park

G Grand Canyon isn't as desolate as it may seem. The park's various ecosystems are teeming with wildlife, and you can spot a lot of it with a bit of patience. Stay at least 100 feet away from large mammals and 50 feet away from small mammals, birds, and reptiles. The rock squirrels in particular are known as the most dangerous in the park, given the number of emergency room visits they've caused—you'll see signage reminding you to keep your distance.

→ *Designated as a Globally Important Bird Area, Grand Canyon has welcomed 447 known species of birds. Keep an eye out for five species of concern: the* **southwestern willow flycatcher**, **Mexican spotted owl**, **California condor**, **western yellow-billed cuckoo**, *and* **Yuma clapper rail**. *Search for riparian birds on the river, like* **American dippers** *and* **belted kingfishers**.

→ *As you hike through the desert, look for the reptiles that thrive there.* **Gila monsters** *at its western edge,* **gopher snakes** *and* **greater mountain short-horned lizards** *along the rims, and* **rattlesnakes** *and* **yellow-backed spiny lizards** *all over.*

→ *Find the* **Kaibab Plateau Bison Herd** *along the North Rim, and see the* **North American elk** *that were introduced in the early 1900s from Yellowstone National Park.* **Mule deer** *are incredibly common, whereas* **mountain lions** *and* **ringtail cats** *often hide from visitors.*

SPOT

Hold on tight while rafting the rapids.

F L O A T

Ⓡ Rafting the Colorado River—the beating heart of the Grand Canyon—is a bucket-list item for many adventurers. The river boasts Class III to V rapids in its upper two-thirds, while the lower third is milder, with Class II to III rapids that are better suited for beginners and families. Take to the Colorado River for a half-day trip, a guided trip over two to 18 days, or a self-guided trip lasting 12 to 25 days. You'll need to win a weighted lottery for the last one.

Book a trip with one of the outfitters that runs these guided trips from Lees Ferry to Diamond Creek. Western River Expeditions, Arizona Raft Adventures, Wilderness River Adventures, Grand Canyon Whitewater, and Outdoor Unlimited all run multiday rafting trips. Arizona River Runners and Hatch River Expeditions take guests over the water on both motorized and oar boats.

Awe-inspiring rock formations greet rafters.

Wildflowers along the Colorado River

→ EXPLORE

T There's truly no shortage of activities to fill your time in Grand Canyon. Add some of these to your itinerary:

→ *Spend time eating, drinking, shopping, and learning in the historic district. Walk through the glamorous* **El Tovar Hotel**, *have a meal at a* **Bright Angel Lodge restaurant**, *tour the* **Grand Canyon Railway Depot**, *and visit the* **Lookout** *and* **Kolb Studios**.

→ *Mary E. J. Colter designed the* **Hopi House** *(now a national historic landmark) in the style of an ancestral Puebloan home. You can still purchase authentic Native American crafts here—as visitors have been able to do since it opened in 1905—and learn about the traditions and cultures of the area's Indigenous communities through placards around the building.*

→ *Book a* **guided mule trip**. *From the South Rim, ride for two hours with canyon vistas or do an overnight into the canyon to Phantom Ranch. From the North Rim, take a one-hour tour of the rim or a three-hour ride to Supai Tunnel or Uncle Jim Point.*

→ *Dive into the past at archaeological sites like the* **Tusayan Pueblo Museum**, *the sacred 1,000-year-old* **Walhalla Glades Pueblo**, *and the* **Yavapai Geology Museum**.

→ *Take the* **Grand Canyon Railway** *from Williams to the Grand Canyon Depot. Sit in the budget-friendly Pullman-class car, with its big windows; relax in coach or first-class seats; or lounge in the Luxury Dome car (must be 15 or older) with its bar service.*

→ **Bike** *the Rim Trail from the Monument Creek Vista to Hermit's Rest or the paved Greenway Trail. Stop at striking Pima Point along the way. Ease the trip by biking one way and racking it on the free shuttle to get back.*

→ *Sign up for a course or trip with the* **Grand Canyon Conservancy Field Institute**. *It offers Kolb Studio tours, multiday hiking trips, journaling and painting courses, and more.*

→ *Catch a* **cultural demonstration program** *at the Desert View Watchtower, like a craft showcase or a musical performance, to connect with the people who consider the Grand Canyon sacred.*

→ *Visit the* **Havasupai Reservation**. *The village of the Supai within Havasu Canyon is accessible only by foot or horseback, and hiking and camping here is by tribal permit only. No day-trippers are allowed. Campground reservations are available February through November and lodge reservations April through November. Havasupai means "people of the blue-green waters," an homage to the spectacular waterfall in the reservation.*

Family Friendly

*Watch **winter storms** move through the canyon. Try to find a clear spot along the rim and wait for the clouds to break—this experience does take quite a bit of luck and timing. If you're lucky and are gifted with a storm, the lower angle of the sun gives the horizon a sense of depth and contrast that has no equal.*

Lehman Caves

GREAT BASIN
NATIONAL PARK

NEVADA

ESTABLISHED: October 27, 1986

SIZE: 77,180 acres

VISITORS CENTERS: The Lehman Caves Visitor Center (open year-round), the only one inside the park, has a café and gift shop, which stay open spring through early fall. The Great Basin Visitor Center (summer only) is outside the park, just north of Baker.

TRANSPORTATION: No in-park transportation

DOGS ALLOWED: Only in restricted areas. Dogs are not allowed on trails, in the backcountry, or at swimmable beaches.

WHEN TO GO: Spring for wildflowers; fall for foliage. Summer is busiest and has temperatures in the mid-80s; be prepared for thunderstorms in July and August. Parts of Wheeler Peak Scenic Drive close due to weather in winter.

CONTACT: 775-234-7331; nps.gov/grba
Lehman Caves Visitor Center
Nevada 488
Baker, NV 89311

Great Basin National Park is dominated by 13,063-foot-tall Wheeler Peak but offers plenty more to explore through its diverse landscapes, ecosystems, and wildlife. Get deep into the park's dark Lehman Caves, take gorgeous photographs of wildflowers in the foothills, or hike its high-altitude desert valleys or salt flats. See mountain lions hunting or fish for trout. Drive from overlook to overlook, or hike your way from lake to lake. Stay after dark when the night sky dazzles. Great Basin is a park that reaches across experiences.

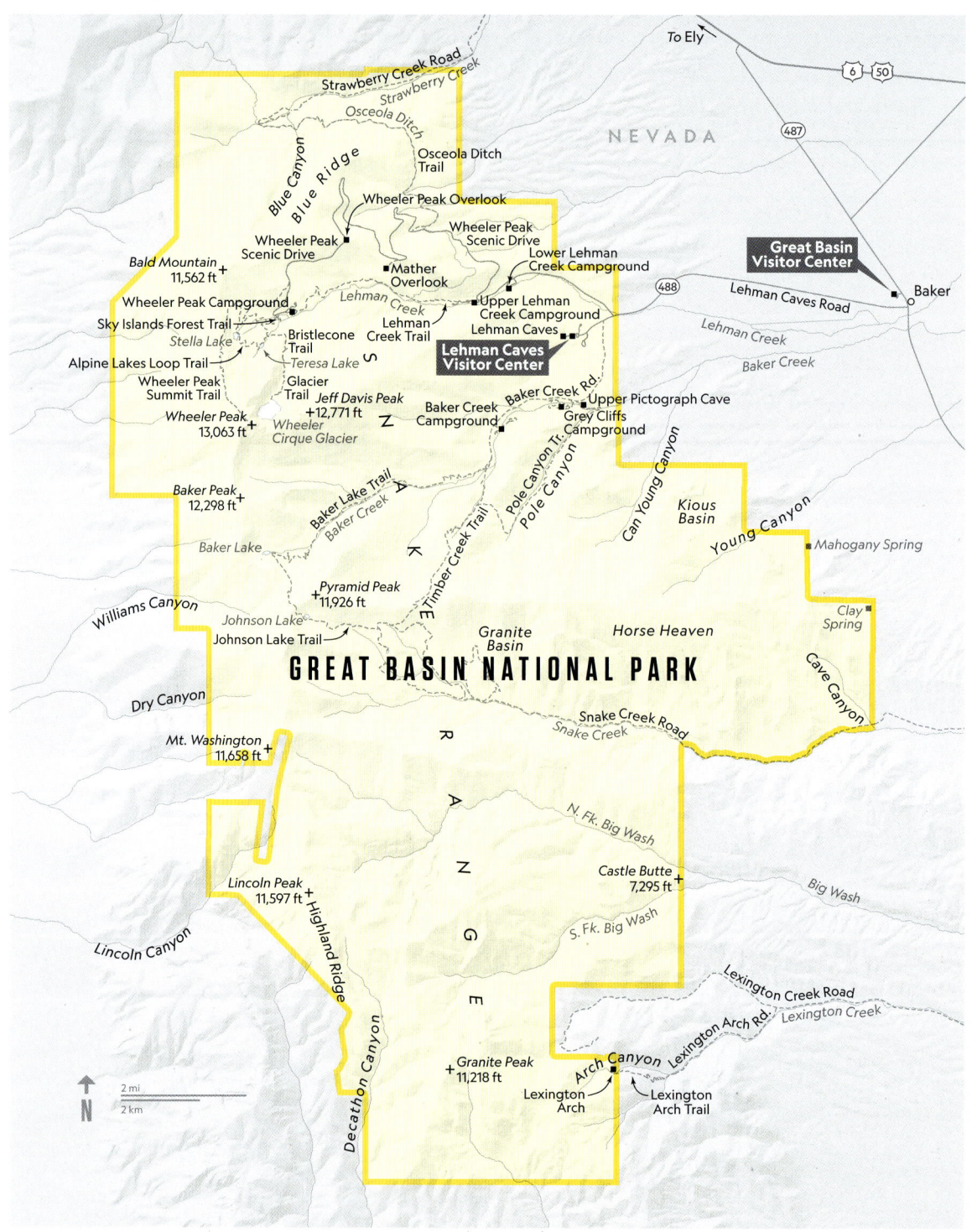

To Ely

NEVADA

Great Basin Visitor Center

Baker

Strawberry Creek Road

Strawberry Creek

Osceola Ditch

Osceola Ditch Trail

Wheeler Peak Overlook

Wheeler Peak Scenic Drive

Wheeler Peak Scenic Drive

Lower Lehman Creek Campground

Lehman Caves Road

Lehman Creek

Baker Creek

Bald Mountain 11,562 ft

Mather Overlook

Upper Lehman Creek Campground

Lehman Creek

Lehman Caves

Wheeler Peak Campground

Sky Islands Forest Trail

Stella Lake

Bristlecone Trail

Lehman Creek Trail

Lehman Caves Visitor Center

Alpine Lakes Loop Trail

Teresa Lake

Wheeler Peak Summit Trail

Glacier Trail

Jeff Davis Peak 12,771 ft

Baker Creek Campground

Baker Creek Rd.

Upper Pictograph Cave

Grey Cliffs Campground

Wheeler Peak 13,063 ft

Wheeler Cirque Glacier

S N A K E

Pole Canyon Tr.

Pole Canyon

Pole Canyon

Can Young Canyon

Kious Basin

Baker Peak 12,298 ft

Baker Lake Trail

Baker Creek

Timber Creek Trail

Young Canyon

Mahogany Spring

Baker Lake

Williams Canyon

Pyramid Peak 11,926 ft

Johnson Lake

Johnson Lake Trail

Granite Basin

Horse Heaven

Clay Spring

Cave Canyon

GREAT BASIN NATIONAL PARK

Dry Canyon

R

Snake Creek Road

Snake Creek

Mt. Washington 11,658 ft

A

N. Fk. Big Wash

N

Lincoln Peak 11,597 ft

Castle Butte 7,295 ft

Big Wash

G

Highland Ridge

S. Fk. Big Wash

Lincoln Canyon

E

Decathon Canyon

Lexington Creek Road

Lexington Arch Rd.

Lexington Creek

N

2 mi

2 km

Granite Peak 11,218 ft

Arch Canyon

Lexington Arch

Lexington Arch Trail

A camper sets up for the night.

![arrow down]

SLEEP

S Sleeping at Great Basin means camping. Book a site at one of the six established campgrounds or find a free primitive site along the creek roads. If camping isn't your jam, find hotels in nearby **Baker** and **Ely**.

→ ***Upper Lehman Creek Campground***, close to Wheeler Peak Scenic Drive, sits at 7,500 feet elevation and offers 23 sites. Stay there and fall asleep to the sounds of the stream. Typically, sites are reservable from Memorial Day through September, and first come, first served the rest of the year.

→ ***Lower Lehman Creek Campground*** is open year-round with 11 sites on a first-come-first-serve basis. Bird-watchers will love this spot, which is also just minutes from Lehman Caves.

→ *Even higher,* ***Wheeler Peak Campground*** *has 37 sites set beneath aspens at 9,500 feet. Pack all your water and for the cold, since temperatures will drop even in summer. Sites are reservable early July through September and first come, first served all other times.*

→ *First-come-first-serve* ***Baker Creek Campground*** *has water spigots and vault toilets. Its 37 sites are open Memorial Day through Labor Day.*

→ ***Grey Cliffs Campground*** *makes for a quiet, convenient base camp with great night-sky views from the desert. Some of its 16 sites are reservable, while others are first come, first served. The campground is open Memorial Day through Labor Day.*

→ *The 12 primitive sites at Snake Creek are first come, first served and free.*

**Must-Do
Hike**

Ⓗ Hikers of all levels will find something at Great Basin, whether you want to ascend to views of nearby peaks, walk under dense forests, or weave around the park's calm waters.

➜ Hop on the 2.8-mile round-trip **Bristlecone Trail**. Walk among thousand-year-old trees and through a short loop with interpretive signs about the lifespan of the trees.

➜ Take the 2.7-mile **Alpine Lakes Loop Trail** from near the Wheeler Peak Campground around Stella and Teresa Lakes to find great views.

➜ Hike the 8.6-mile round-trip **Wheeler Peak Summit Trail**, which begins from the Summit Trail parking area. Start early to avoid afternoon storms and follow the ridge of the mountain up to its 13,063-foot summit.

➜ Find the difficult 5.2-mile **Baker Lake Trail** at the end of Baker Creek Road, with its views of surrounding peaks leading to its namesake lake.

➜ Hike the **Baker and Johnson Lakes loop**, which runs along a steep ridge route between the two lakes. The 11.7-mile loop is challenging and for expert hikers only, but the rewards include stunning panoramic views over the water, Wheeler Peak, and Baker Peak.

➜ Explore the nearly half-mile **Sky Islands Forest Trail**, with a rubber-matted, relatively even route from Wheeler Peak Scenic Drive through a high alpine forest.

➜ Cross Baker Creek to find the **Pole Canyon Trail**, once an old mining road. Take the shaded route through the forest and sagebrush meadow, then join the **Timber Creek Trail** and campground connector trails to loop back to the picnic area.

➜ Hop on the easy 0.3-mile **Mountain View Nature Trail** from the Lehman Caves Visitor Center. Get a trail guide ahead of time to learn about the park's geology and ecology.

**H
I
K
E**

**Accessible
Option**

A trail curves through a forested area of the park.

A hummingbird atop her nest

Look for mule deer in the mornings or at dusk.

SPOT

K Know what creatures to look for during different seasons and times of day to have the best wildlife-spotting luck during your trip. Look for **mountain lions** when they hunt at dusk or dawn—the same time you're most likely to see their prey: **mule deer** and **elk**. Find **yellow-bellied marmots** in high-elevation rock piles or sometimes sunning on the rocks at Baker Lake during the spring and early summer. If you hear them whistle, they're scared.

Categorize your bird-watching by park region. In the sagebrush grasslands, find **red-tailed hawks**, **California quail**, and **golden eagles**. Piñon-juniper woods are home to **mountain chickadees** and **white-crowned sparrows**. Look for the **black rosy finches** that nest in the rocks above the tree line along the Bristlecone and Glacier Trails.

Wheeler Peak Scenic Drive

T Two driving routes will get you to some of the park's most significant and compelling spots, but you'll need to get out of your car to truly take in the glory.

→ **Wheeler Peak Scenic Drive** *is a popular route—and a great way to organize your trip. Start on its eastern border and either head toward the Lehman Caves Visitor Center or keep going down the road. On the way up to Wheeler Peak, stop in the juniper forests at Upper Lehman Creek Campground, the trailhead for the challenging Osceola Ditch Trail, the must-see Mather and Wheeler Peak Overlooks, and the trailheads for the Summit, Bristlecone, Alpine Lakes, and Sky Islands Forest hikes.*

→ *The shorter and unpaved **Baker Creek Road** goes to the Grey Cliffs and Baker Creek Campgrounds, along with the Pole Canyon and Baker Creek trailheads. It's closed to cars in the winter and open for snowshoers and cross-country skiers. In the fall, it's a great route to see the changing leaves (peak foliage is mid-September–October). Just watch for crossing marmots.*

DRIVE

An entrance sign to Great Basin National Park

Stalagmites and stalactites in Lehman Caves

A stargazing party at twilight

→ EXPLORE

M Much of the beauty of this park is underground or up in the clouds. Add to your experience by exploring the caves, spending an evening under the stars, or digging into the park's past.

→ Head down into **Lehman Caves** with a ranger for a guided tour of the longest cave system in Nevada. Book either the one-hour Lodge Room tour, which brings you through the main rooms, or the Grand Palace tour along the full route of the cave for a 90-minute, more strenuous trip.

→ Adventurous and experienced cave explorers can get into seven of the park's wild and undeveloped caves. You'll need a permit and expertise in cave conservation, techniques, and equipment. Crawl through **Little Muddy**, take the short route through **Catamount**, or get up high at **Broken**.

→ See **blooming wildflowers** in the spring and summer at lower elevations. Get great views across beautiful fields from Wheeler Peak Scenic Drive, the Sky Islands Forest Trail, and the Baker Creek Trail.

→ Sign up at a visitors center for a ranger-led **full-moon hike** during the summer. The routes change, but they'll generally be an easy two-mile walk.

→ See the stars at the **Astronomy Amphitheater** near the Lehman Caves Visitor Center and Mather Overlook on Wheeler Peak Scenic Drive. If you're staying in Baker, spend the evening at the Baker Archaeological Site.

→ **Fishing** is popular at Lehman Creek, Baker Creek, and Snake Creek, though you should practice only catch-and-release at that last location. The first two spots contain a decent number of trout. You will need a license wherever you fish.

→ Most national parks tell you to leave their plant life alone, but gathering **piñon pine nuts** is a beloved fall activity at Great Basin. Collect up to 25 pounds per household of the nutritious nuts from these single-leaf pines.

→ Slip into the past with a visit to the **Upper Pictograph Cave**, where the walls are covered in rock art depicting people and animals. These are thought to have been painted by the Fremont people, who lived in Snake Valley from 1000 to 1300 B.C.

Experts Only

→ **RANGER RECOMMENDATION** ←

*Take it slow when you hike the **Pole Canyon Trail**.
Start with a picnic at the trailhead, then meander
through the meadows and low mountain passes, with
their views of the aspen groves and Snake Valley.
In the winter, take the same trip in snowshoes.*

Spruce Tree House

MESA VERDE
NATIONAL PARK

COLORADO

ESTABLISHED: June 29, 1906

SIZE: 52,485 acres

VISITORS CENTER: The Mesa Verde Visitor and Research Center offers detailed exhibits, a bookstore, and planning resources.

TRANSPORTATION: Ranger-guided bus tours available

DOGS ALLOWED: Only in developed areas (paved roads, campgrounds, parking lots) and some (limited) paved trails

WHEN TO GO: Many roads, including Cliff Palace Loop Road, and archaeological sites close in winter. The road to Wetherill Mesa is open late May to early September.

CONTACT: 970-529-4465; nps.gov/meve
Mile 0.7 Headquarters Loop Road
Mesa Verde National Park, CO 81330

Open a window to the past at Mesa Verde National Park, which is the only national park to preserve not only natural wonders but also the spellbinding heritage of the ancestral Puebloans who found shelter, food, and spiritual inspiration here. From A.D. 500 to 1300, 26 tribes built their homes into the mesas and cliffs of Mesa Verde. The park protects more than 5,000 archaeological sites, including cliff dwellings that date back more than a millennium. It's the richest archaeological cache in the American Southwest. The cliff dwellings are best explored on a guided tour—the only way to get inside—but other natural wonders are open to self-discovery.

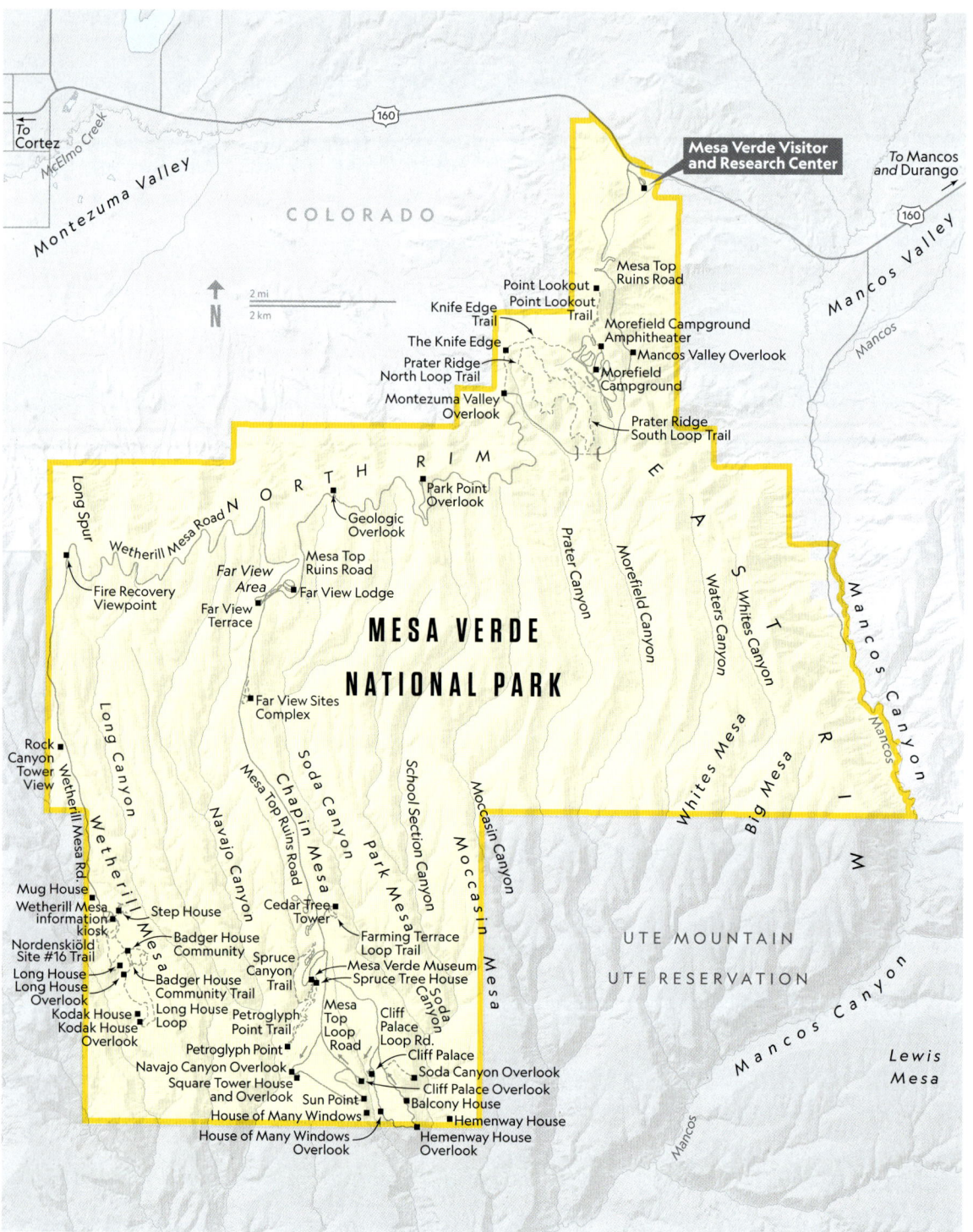

To Cortez

McElmo Creek

Montezuma Valley

COLORADO

Mesa Verde Visitor and Research Center

To Mancos and Durango

Mancos Valley

Mancos

Mesa Top Ruins Road

Point Lookout
Point Lookout Trail

Knife Edge Trail
The Knife Edge
Prater Ridge North Loop Trail
Montezuma Valley Overlook

Morefield Campground Amphitheater
Mancos Valley Overlook
Morefield Campground

Prater Ridge South Loop Trail

NORTH RIM

Long Spur

Wetherill Mesa Road

Geologic Overlook

Park Point Overlook

Prater Canyon

Morefield Canyon

Waters Canyon

Whites Canyon

Mancos Canyon

Mancos

Fire Recovery Viewpoint

Far View Area
Mesa Top Ruins Road
Far View Lodge
Far View Terrace

MESA VERDE NATIONAL PARK

Far View Sites Complex

Whites Mesa

Big Mesa

Rock Canyon Tower View

Long Canyon

Wetherill Mesa Road

Navajo Canyon

Mesa Top Ruins Road

Chapin Mesa

Soda Canyon

School Section Canyon

Park Mesa

Moccasin Canyon

Moccasin Mesa

UTE MOUNTAIN

UTE RESERVATION

Mancos Canyon

Lewis Mesa

Mug House
Wetherill Mesa information kiosk
Nordenskiöld Site #16 Trail
Long House
Long House Overlook
Kodak House
Kodak House Overlook

Step House

Badger House Community

Spruce Canyon Trail

Cedar Tree Tower

Farming Terrace Loop Trail
Mesa Verde Museum
Spruce Tree House

Soda Canyon

Badger House Community Trail

Long House Loop
Petroglyph Point Trail

Mesa Top Loop Road

Cliff Palace Loop Rd.

Petroglyph Point
Navajo Canyon Overlook
Square Tower House and Overlook
House of Many Windows
House of Many Windows Overlook

Sun Point

Cliff Palace
Soda Canyon Overlook
Cliff Palace Overlook
Balcony House

Hemenway House
Hemenway House Overlook

N
2 mi
2 km

A wilderness campground in the mountains of the park

Stargaze from the Far View Lodge

W While there are plenty of places to stay outside in the park, you will get the most out of your visit by staying at its campground or lodge. Both options are family-friendly, accessible, and packed with amenities.

→ *Book one of 267 sites (15 with electrical hookups) at **Morefield Campground**, with its wildflower fields, camp store, coin-operated laundromat, and internet connectivity. Fuel your day with an all-you-can-eat pancake breakfast at the café, browse souvenirs at the gift shop, and plan excursions with the help of campground staff. The campground is closed November through April, with limited off-season camping April 11–25.*

→ *Rooms at the **Far View Lodge** offer incredible views over Mesa Verde, balconies from which to enjoy them, and free Wi-Fi. The lodge also has a restaurant and a lounge.*

SLEEP

Petroglyph Point Trail

Dog
Friendly

H Hiking off-trail in Mesa Verde is strictly prohibited to protect the fragile archaeology, but luckily there is an extensive system of maintained trails for visitors. These are some of the best:

→ Walk the 2.25-mile round-trip **Badger House Community Trail** and move through 600 years of history on the gravel and paved path.

HIKE

→ Three landscape-centric trails start at Morefield Campground. The easy two-mile round-trip **Knife Edge Trail** is the perfect route for a sunset view. The steep switchbacks out of Morefield Canyon make the **Point Lookout Trail** (2.2 miles round-trip) a doable challenge, with views of the San Juan and La Plata Mountains. Finally, the tougher **Prater Ridge Trail** (7.8 miles round-trip) takes you up to the North and South Loops, looking over the Montezuma Valley, Prater Canyon, and Morefield Canyon.

→ The **Petroglyph Point Trail**, a 2.4-mile loop, combines history with adventure. From the Mesa Verde Museum, head down Spruce Canyon, between boulders and through narrow stone staircases, to reach a massive petroglyph panel—then scramble up a rocky slope before reaching a piñon-juniper forest.

→ The 2.4-mile **Spruce Canyon Trail** travels mostly through scenic, shady switchbacks. Explore the ecosystem, then stop for a picnic after climbing out of the canyon.

→ The one-mile round-trip **Step House** route takes you up and down a winding path on a self-guided tour of pit structures and a masonry pueblo. It's open only when a ranger is on duty. Start at the Wetherill Mesa information kiosk.

→ Bring your dog along the paved **Long House Loop**, which traverses five miles with stops at the Badger House Community, Long House Overlook, and Kodak House Overlook.

→ Do your research before heading out on backcountry hikes to some of the park's most fragile sites: **Mug House** and **Square Tower House**.

Four main routes loop through the park.

DRIVE

The main route of the park, **Mesa Top Ruins Road**, takes you from the entrance down to its other loops. From it, take a short trail to the Mancos Valley, Montezuma Valley, Park Point, and Geologic Overlooks. If you travel to its end, enjoy one of these three additional drives:

→ *The six-mile **Mesa Top Loop Road** is an easy way to access 12 ancestral Puebloan sites. Stop along the way at short, paved trails to surface sites and overlooks of the cliff dwellings. Download the audio tour ahead of time from the National Park Service app. Make sure to stop at the Square Tower House Overlook, Sun Point View, and Sun Temple.*

→ ***Cliff Palace Loop Road** is open until sunset. Take ranger-guided tours of Cliff Palace and Balcony House, or find the trailhead for the Soda Canyon Overlook Trail and plenty of gorgeous overlooks, including Cliff Palace, Cliff Canyon, House of Many Windows, and Hemenway House.*

→ ***Wetherill Mesa Road** connects Far View to Wetherill Mesa, though the steep, narrow route is open only seasonally. If you're here while it's open, you'll get valley views, overlooks from the Nordenskiöld Site #16 Trail, and the Kodak House Overlook as you drive.*

Look for the green-tailed towhee.

M Mesa Verde is geographically isolated, providing a home to both native and migrating wildlife. Certain fish and amphibians stay in their small niches, while other animals, like coyotes and deer, move through the park. Keep an eye out for some of these creatures:

➜ *Bird-watchers should look for **wood-warblers**, **sparrows**, **wrens**, **hummingbirds**, and **woodpeckers**. You also might be able to spot **peregrine falcons**, **Mexican spotted owls**, and a variety of **hawks** flying above the skyline. The Petroglyph Point, Spruce Canyon, and Knife Edge Trails are great locations to find winged friends.*
➜ *While hiking, keep an eye out for **mule deer**, **Rocky Mountain elk**, **marmots**, **desert cottontails**, **lizards**, **snakes**, and **American black bears**.*
➜ *Overnight guests should look for the many species of **bats** that call the park home.*

SPOT

A male mule deer

A panel at Petroglyph Point

A ranger-led cultural tour with cliff dwellings in the distance

Cliff Palace

EXPLORE

M Many adventures teach you more about the ancestral Puebloan communities who lived here. Others will bring you extra peace and solitude in the popular park.

→ The only way to get up close and personal with the park's cliff dwellings is on a ranger-led or ranger-assisted tour, available in the spring, summer, and fall. On separate tours, you'll be able to explore **Cliff Palace** (a 150-room dwelling built in the 1200s, the largest cliff dwelling in North America), **Balcony House** (built around 1300; tour requires walking down a 130-step metal staircase), and **Square Tower House** (at 28 feet, the tallest standing structure in the park). Get ready to climb uneven stone steps.

→ Learn more about the land's human history at the **Mesa Verde Museum**. Built with the same sandstone that the ancestral Puebloan people used to create the nearby Spruce Tree House, the museum houses galleries of ancestral Puebloan ceramics, jewelry, and sandals—and shows a film about the communities who lived there.

→ While you can't go into **Spruce Tree House**, you can see this third largest and best-preserved cliff dwelling from several overlooks, including ones near the museum.

→ Get onto the mesa to check out the **Far View Sites Complex**, mesa-top villages, and **Cedar Tree Tower**. At its height, the mesa was filled with small family homes and farms. Walk the woodland trail between the six sites and the **Farming Terrace Loop Trail** through ancient dams and the tower.

→ Attend an evening program under the stars at **Morefield Campground Amphitheater**. The summer campfire program— a 60-minute history of the park—is a legacy of archaeologist Jesse Fewkes, who started it in 1907. Stay after to join a star party and look to the skies.

→ Though its trails and sites are closed at night, this International Dark Sky Park still provides fantastic **stargazing** opportunities. Stay at Morefield Campground or the Far View Lodge for access to the least interrupted views.

→ Though certain roads, access points, and lodges might be closed in the winter, Mesa Verde is very much open. Stop at a visitors center and talk with a ranger about your options for **snowshoeing**, **winter hiking**, or **cross-country skiing**.

→ **RANGER RECOMMENDATION** ←

*At 7.8 miles, the **Prater Ridge Trail** is the longest—and least traveled trail—in the park. The lack of crowds means you'll find solitude among the outstanding views. In the spring, the wildflowers will be blooming.*

The Blue Mesa region

PETRIFIED FOREST
NATIONAL PARK

ARIZONA

ESTABLISHED: December 9, 1962

SIZE: 138,788 acres

VISITORS CENTERS: The Painted Desert Visitor Center, Rainbow Forest Museum, and Painted Desert Inn are all open year-round. You'll find history lessons, trip resources, and staff at each.

TRANSPORTATION: No in-park transportation

DOGS ALLOWED: Only on developed trails and leashed. A fenced-in dog park is near the Painted Desert Visitor Center.

WHEN TO GO: Fall and spring for mild temperatures and wildflowers; winter for unlimited visibility. Summer is the most popular time, but be mindful of extreme heat.

CONTACT: 928-524-6228; nps.gov/pefo
Exit 311
Interstate 40
Petrified Forest, AZ 86028

P Petrified Forest National Park has one of the largest concentrations of petrified logs on Earth. The 200-million-year-old logs fell into an ancient river system and were buried under sediment and debris. Given the lack of oxygen, the decay process took centuries, and the porous wood absorbed minerals, turning the wood into stone. Today, there's a wide range of sizes to dazzle visitors, from tiny chips to entire logs—their colors glistening in the sun.

In addition to those fossils, the park is home to ancient petroglyphs, colorful wildflowers, extended mesas, and unique rock formations. Whether you have an hour to drive the park road or a few days to backcountry camp, you'll be able to dive back in time as you explore.

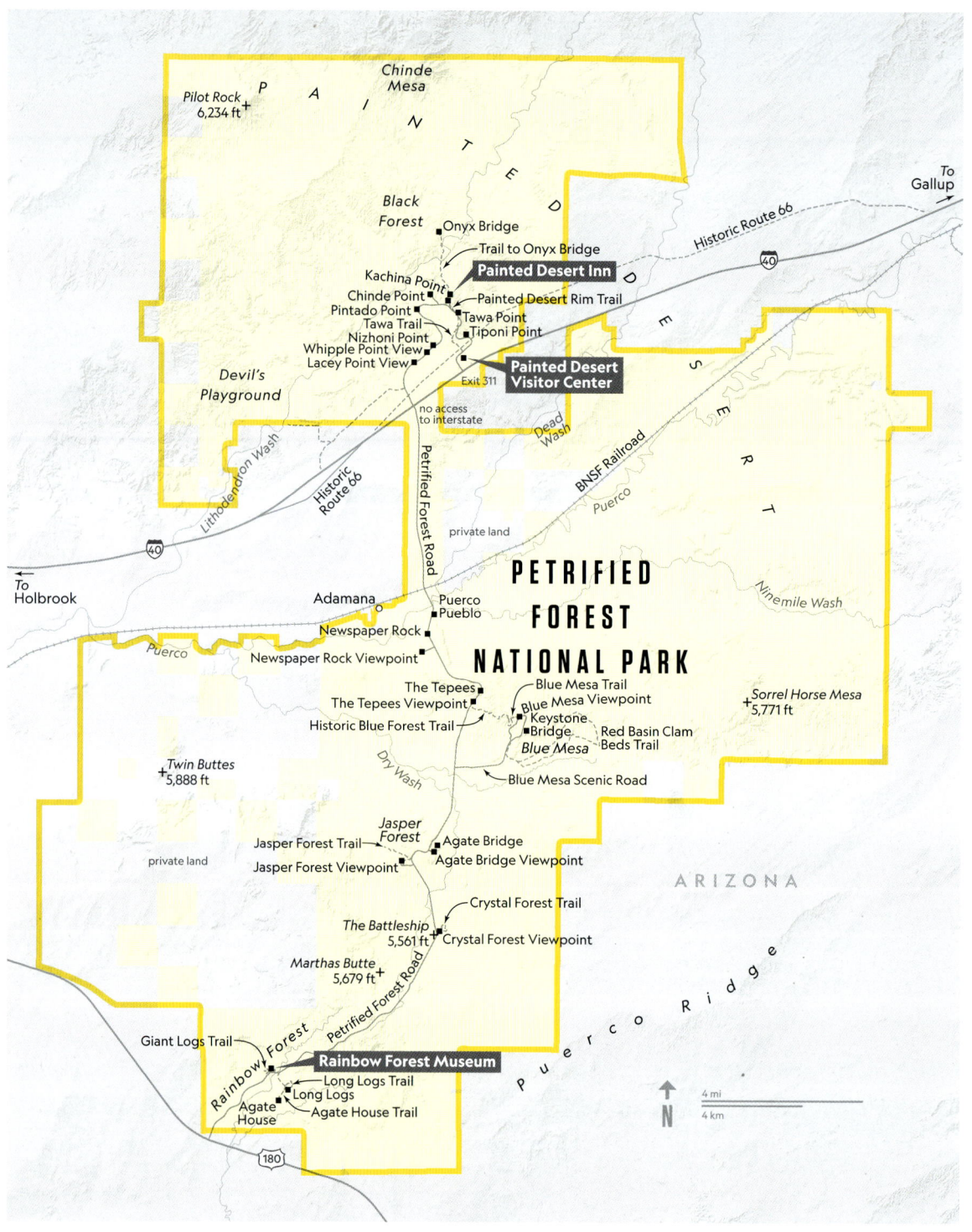

Chinde
Mesa

Pilot Rock
6,234 ft

P A I N T E D

To
Gallup

Black
Forest

Onyx Bridge
Trail to Onyx Bridge
Painted Desert Inn

Historic Route 66

40

Kachina Point
Chinde Point — Painted Desert Rim Trail
Pintado Point
Tawa Trail — Tawa Point
Nizhoni Point — Tiponi Point
Whipple Point View
Lacey Point View

Devil's
Playground

**Painted Desert
Visitor Center**

D

Exit 311

E

no access
to interstate

Dead
Wash

S

Lithodendron Wash

Historic
Route 66

Petrified Forest Road

private land

BNSF Railroad

Puerco

E

Ninemile Wash

R

40

To
Holbrook

Adamana

Puerco
Pueblo

Newspaper Rock

**PETRIFIED
FOREST
NATIONAL PARK**

T

Puerco

Newspaper Rock Viewpoint

The Tepees — Blue Mesa Trail
The Tepees Viewpoint — Blue Mesa Viewpoint
Keystone
Historic Blue Forest Trail — Bridge — Red Basin Clam
Blue Mesa — Beds Trail

Sorrel Horse Mesa
5,771 ft

Twin Buttes
5,888 ft

Dry Wash

Blue Mesa Scenic Road

*Jasper
Forest*

Jasper Forest Trail — Agate Bridge
Jasper Forest Viewpoint — Agate Bridge Viewpoint

private land

A R I Z O N A

Crystal Forest Trail

The Battleship
5,561 ft — Crystal Forest Viewpoint

Marthas Butte
5,679 ft

Petrified Forest Road

Puerco Ridge

Giant Logs Trail

Rainbow Forest

Rainbow Forest Museum

Long Logs Trail
Long Logs
Agate — Agate House Trail
House

180

4 mi
N
4 km

Tent camping in Painted Desert

SLEEP

T The only way to stay inside the park bounds is to **backcountry camp**. Permits are free and must be obtained in person from the Painted Forest Visitor Center or Rainbow Forest Museum on the day you plan to venture out into the park. Private campgrounds are available in Navajo and Apache Counties, as well as in nearby national monument, national forest, and state park sites. No lodges are inside the park, but motels are available in nearby **Holbrook** or farther away in **Gallup**, **New Mexico**.

HIKE

Must-See Fossil

M Much of the park's land is open desert, so you're welcome to backcountry hike as long as it's safe for you and the environment. For a successful backcountry trek, you'll need to be skilled at orienteering, pack enough water for the trip, and share your plan for your unmarked-trail adventure.

Still, some short, popular trails will give you a great perspective on the park:

→ Walk the 0.4-mile **Giant Logs Trail** to check out "Old Faithful," a colorful petrified log that is almost 10 feet wide at its base. The loop trail, which includes multiple sets of stairs, starts behind the Rainbow Forest Museum.

→ Descend from the mesa down into petrified wood deposits and badlands on the one-mile **Blue Mesa Trail** loop. Paleontologists have discovered plant and animal fossils in the sedimentary layers here.

→ The unmaintained **Red Basin Clam Beds Trail** splits off from Blue Mesa Scenic Road. The 8.5-mile round-trip hike will take you past petrified wood, petroglyphs, hoodoos, and badlands that are more than 215 million years old.

→ Get one of the three weekly permits (available on Wednesdays on a first-come-first-serve basis) to hike to the **Devil's Playground**. Make your way to the area from the rugged access road. There are no marked trails, so you're on your own to explore the unique and colorful landscape of hoodoos and other fascinating rock formations.

→ The **Crystal Forest Trail**, a three-quarter-mile loop, will give you an up-close view of the crystals that can grow inside petrified logs. Don't even think about grabbing any of the wood to take home.

→ The **Painted Desert Rim Trail** is true to its name, providing picturesque views of the desert rim. Catch the one-mile round-trip trail at Tawa Point or Kachina Point.

→ Discover the region's history as you hike the 0.3-mile **Puerco Pueblo** paved loop or the **Agate House Trail** (2 miles round-trip). The first brings you to a 100-room village occupied between A.D. 1250 and 1400, while the second ends at the 700-year-old Agate House, an ancestral Puebloan village of petrified wood pieces that was reconstructed in the 1930s.

DRIVE

D Drive or cycle the **Petrified Forest Road** through the park, stopping along its 28 miles for overlooks and trailheads. If you take the route from north to south, your first stop is the historic Painted Desert Inn, which dates back to 1924 and was popular with Route 66 travelers. Once you cross the highway, you'll see boulders covered in petroglyphs at Newspaper Rock and a long petrified log spanning a dry wash at Agate Bridge. Check out desert vistas at Tawa, Kachina, Chinde, and Pintado Points. You'll also pass the Blue Mesa and Crystal Forest Trailheads if you want to get out and stretch your legs. End the road trip at the Rainbow Forest Museum, with its paleontological exhibits, bookstore, gift shop, and access to the Giant Logs, Long Logs, and Agate House Trails.

Wind your way through the hills of Painted Desert.

Petrified Forest is home to an array of wildlife, and the best time to see it all is when the weather is cool. Many creatures come out of the woodwork to find food at dawn or dusk, while some are purely nocturnal; for some, like snakes and lizards, this shifts with the seasons.

Birders will find both permanent residents and migratory species in the park. See the **house finch**, **common raven**, **red-tailed hawk**, **roadrunner**, and **horned lark** anytime, while **rufous hummingbirds**, **cedar waxwings**, **ruby-crowned kinglets**, and **warblers** travel through the air in August and September.

Agate House

Search for the park's collared lizards.

SPOT

→ EXPLORE

While most people explore the park by foot or car, there is a lot to be gained by taking some extra time to learn about the history and culture of the space—or finding an alternative adventure.

→ *Catch a daily cultural demonstration at the **Painted Desert Inn** from local artisans connected to one of the many affiliated tribes in the region. Learn from weavers, beaders, potters, and others at the site, which is now a museum and visitors center.*

→ *Complete a natural treasure hunt when you **geocache** in the park. Find hidden containers using GPS-enabled devices through either a website or an app.*

→ *Bring your own horse for a **horseback riding trip** along the Painted Desert Wilderness access trail near Kachina Point—and add on a camping trip north of Lithodendron Wash to extend the adventure.*

→ *Go on a ranger-guided experience to the **Keystone Bridge** off Blue Mesa Scenic Road. The irregular natural stone arch is unique for its fractures.*

Family Friendly

A forest of saguaro cacti
in the Red Hills

SAGUARO
NATIONAL PARK

ARIZONA

ESTABLISHED: October 14, 1994

SIZE: 91,442 acres

VISITORS CENTERS: The Red Hills Visitor Center, in the west, and the Rincon Mountain Visitor Center, in the east, are both open year-round and offer trip guidance, educational exhibits, and programming.

TRANSPORTATION: No in-park transportation

DOGS ALLOWED: Only on limited trails (stay on paved options to avoid thorns), in picnic areas, and on roadways

WHEN TO GO: October–April for mild weather and hiking. Wildflowers bloom mid-March through mid-April, and the saguaro cacti typically bloom in late April. If you visit in the summer, arrive early to avoid the hottest part of the day.

CONTACT: 520-733-5153; nps.gov/sagu
3693 S. Old Spanish Trail
Tucson, AZ 85730

If any natural symbol embodies the American West, it's the giant saguaro. These massive cacti are the largest in the country. Rising tall with resilience and persistence, these towering plants grow only an inch during their first eight years but can reach up to 60 feet high—and live for as long as 200 years.

The strength and tenacity of these cacti have been reflected in the people who explored, cultivated, and survived on this unforgiving land. Though conflict arose between Native and early homesteading communities across the region, the groups had one thing in common: the determination to thrive in a space that was primed for anything but. Today, a visit to Saguaro is sure to inspire that same strength and grit.

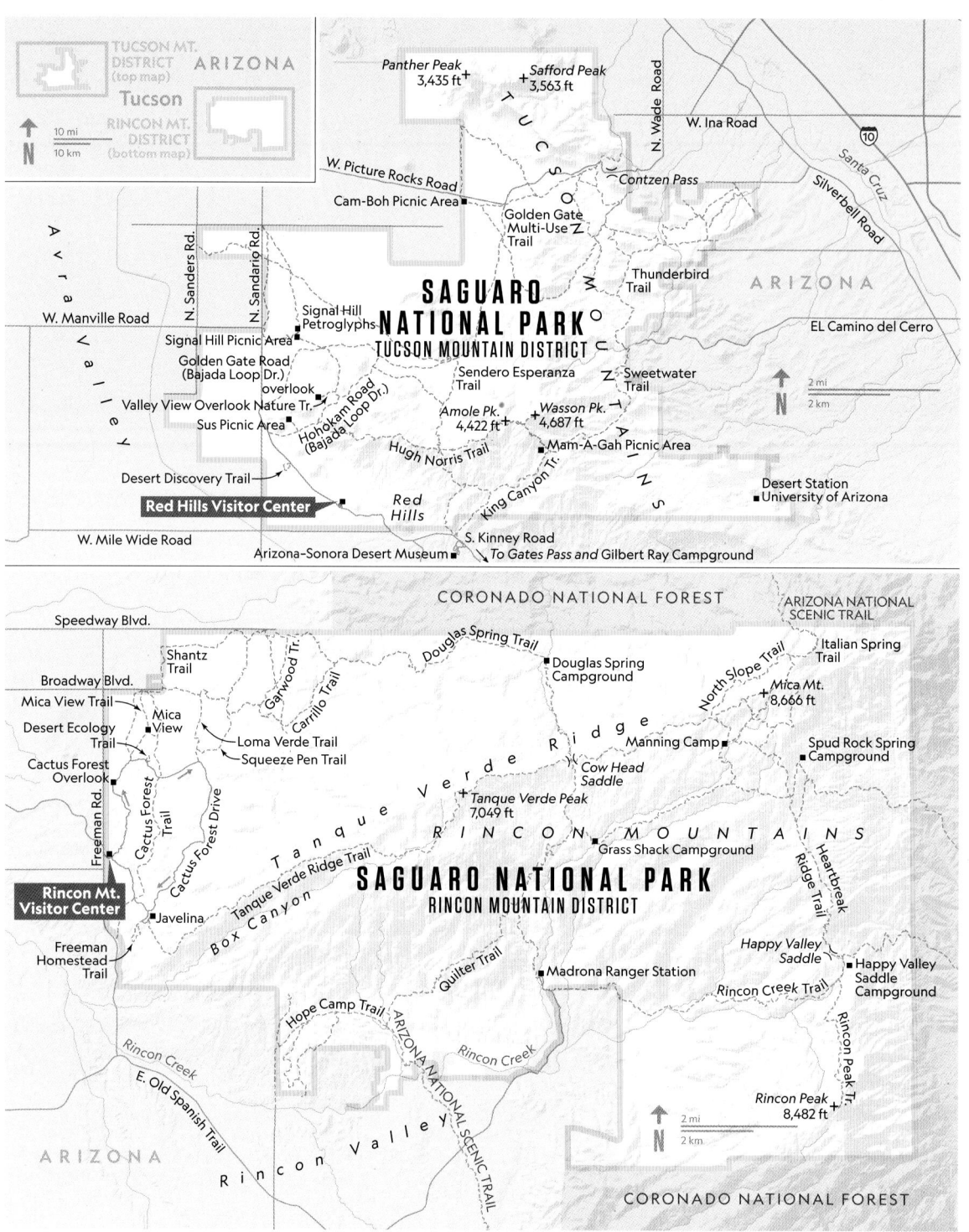

Gilbert Ray Campground in Tucson is a convenient option 3.6 miles from the park.

(T) The only option for staying within the bounds of the park is tent camping at one of the six designated **backcountry campgrounds** in the Rincon Mountain District (east). Get a spot at high-elevation **Manning Camp**, where you'll find reliable water and close trails. Otherwise, **Grass Shack Campground** has plenty of shade and great southern views. Reservations for permits are required and can be obtained at *recreation.gov*. The campsites are not accessible by vehicle and must be reached by foot. It's recommended to pack one gallon of water per day per person.

Outside the park, plenty of campgrounds and hotels are available in and around **Tucson**. You'll have your pick of amenities and locations—including camping at **Catalina State Park**.

A camper parked at Gilbert Ray Campground

S
L
E
E
P

Giant saguaros put this park on the map.

A blooming saguaro with the Milky Way in the background

HIKE

0 Organize your hikes in the park by its two districts: Rincon Mountain District (east) and Tucson Mountain District (west). A few tips from the rangers, no matter which you choose: Pack enough water, check yourself for ticks, and stay away from the protected plants.

In the Rincon Mountain District, you'll be happy if you add any of these hikes to your itinerary:

→ If your heart is set on finding tall saguaros, hike the **Loma Verde Trail**. The 3.8-mile loop crosses a variety of landscapes, including a seasonally flowing wash and a bluff to climb.

→ Hike the easy quarter-mile **Desert Ecology Trail** to see many of the common plants that have adapted to the changing climate of the park, with signage explaining the park's unique ecology. The trail is ADA-compliant and paved.

→ Trek the one-mile **Freeman Homestead Trail** to dive into the park's human history. Learn along the way with the trail's interpretive signs—which also offer kid-friendly activities—and then eventually end up at the remains of a 1933 adobe house.

→ The more challenging nine-mile **Tanque Verde Ridge Trail**, which begins near the Javelina Picnic Area, takes you to Tanque Verde Peak, but it's worthwhile even if you don't reach the end. At just 0.6 mile from the trailhead is an overlook that provides a perfect spot to catch the sunset. Backcountry campsites can be found along the multiday trail.

For a trip to the Tucson Mountain District, be sure to consider these treks:

→ Take the ADA-compliant **Desert Discovery Trail** from the Red Hills Visitor Center to learn about the ecosystem from the identifying signs on the cacti and other plants along the path.

→ Try one of the few routes that will take you up to 4,687-foot-tall **Wasson Peak**, each one combining multiple trails. Start the 8-mile round-trip at the switchback-filled Sendero Esperanza Trail to the Hugh Norris Trail junction, then walk along the ridge until the spur trail to Wasson Peak. If you do the full hike, you'll gain 1,600 feet of elevation. You can also take the King Canyon Trail, which runs 3.5 miles to the peak.

→ The **Valley View Overlook Nature Trail** was built in the 1930s by the Civilian Conservation Corps. The 0.8-mile route eventually ends at benches with wide views of the park.

→ DRIVE

S Saguaro is a great park for visitors who either can't or choose not to hike the landscape. Its two scenic drives offer plenty of overlooks showcasing the beauty of the space.

Travel the unpaved **Bajada Loop Drive** in the Tucson Mountain District through the saguaro forest. It combines two roads: Golden Gate and Hohokam. Get gorgeous views of the Tucson Mountains from the Red Hills Visitor Center, then walk the easy Valley View Overlook Nature Trail for views over the Avra Valley from the eponymous overlook. Stop at the Sus Picnic Area for a respite and meal.

Time your drive between the two districts to stop at Gates Pass for stunning sunset views over the park.

In the Rincon Mountain District, drive along the **Cactus Forest Drive**. The paved loop has two pullouts with picnic areas, plenty of overlooks, and multiple trailheads if you want to stretch your legs. Be sure to stop at the Javelina Rocks Overlook to watch the sun set behind the towering saguaros. And take the unpaved road and short trail out to the Mica View Picnic Area for views of the skyline dotted with saguaros.

An unpaved road winds between cacti at sunset.

A pair of pumas among the rocks at the Arizona–Sonora Desert Museum

The striped body of a milk snake warns off predators.

Look to the trees for a ferruginous hawk.

SPOT

(T) The ecosystem of Saguaro thrives in a careful balance, a perfect harmony of flora and fauna. Rangers ask for the same careful balance from visitors: Enjoy the unique plants and animals while maintaining enough distance to not disturb them.

Here are a few animals and unique plants you may be lucky enough to see while wandering through this delicate environment.

→ Saguaro has birds that you're unlikely to see anywhere else, including the **vermilion flycatcher** and **whiskered screech owl**. Look for **roadrunners**, **pyrrhuloxias**, **Harris's hawks**, **Gila woodpeckers**, and **Gambel's quail** as well. You might also spot **great horned owls** in the cliffs over the end of the Freeman Homestead Trail.

→ There's nothing quite like seeing a **towering**, **blossoming cactus**. Head to the park around the end of April to see the saguaros bloom. You'll need to venture out in the evening when the big white blooms open.

→ **Long-eared antelope** and **black-tailed jackrabbits** live in the park, along with the **white-nosed coati**. If you're lucky, you might spot a female-led group of **javelina**. Don't be fooled by their looks—they're not pigs.

→ The park is also a testament to the importance of wildlife connectivity. Saguaro has been working to remove barriers to wildlife movement in the region, helping develop safe corridors that will protect animals and their habitats. Learn about one effort, the **Tucson Mitigation Corridor**, while you're at the park.

Must-Do Activity

EXPLORE

C Create a personalized experience for yourself by booking a horseback tour, sightseeing by bicycle, or following a guided ranger tour.

→ *Check the calendar for a **ranger-led tour** focused on bird-watching, stargazing, geology, or ecology. Catch a **daily ranger walk** to learn about how the saguaro survives and provides—or stay late for a twilight stroll by flashlight.*

→ *If you plan to **bike the park**, get an early start on your day to avoid the midday heat. Both districts have scenic loops that are great by bicycle: the eight-mile paved Cactus Forest Drive in the Rincon Mountain District and the six-mile gravel Bajada Loop Drive in the Tucson Mountain District. Bring lots of water so that you stay hydrated in the sun.*

→ *Wander the **cactus gardens** outside both visitors centers. They are good places to see the plants of the park up close and with ranger guidance.*

→ *Bring your lunch to the Signal Hill Picnic Area and then check out the **Signal Hill Petroglyphs** along the nearby rocky hill. This prehistoric Native American rock art was carved between 550 and 1,550 years ago.*

→ *Book one of many nearby outfitters to guide you through some of the **100 miles of trails open for horses, mules, and donkeys**. Just don't wander off-trail.*

→ *Add a visit to the **Arizona–Sonora Desert Museum** to your trip. While not part of the park itself, you'll find insights on the plants, animals, and people to enhance your experience in these protected spaces. The family-friendly spot allows kids to climb through a playhouse, watch raptors fly, and get up-close views of underground animals.*

Family Friendly

Explore on horseback for a unique desert experience.

Visit the **Rincon Mountain District** of the park
to experience it with fewer crowds. Drive the Cactus
Forest Drive loop and stop at its many overlooks, then
hike the Mica View Trail to get close to the cacti that
give the park its name and find great views of the
Rincon Mountains.

ZION
NATIONAL PARK

UTAH

Winter at Zion

ESTABLISHED: November 18, 1919

SIZE: 148,732 acres

VISITORS CENTERS: The Zion Canyon Visitor Center (open year-round) offers exhibits, ranger advice, trip resources, and a bookstore and is a hub for the park shuttle, lodging, and excursions. The Kolob Canyons Visitor Center (open year-round) provides a good base for adventures on that side of the park.

TRANSPORTATION: Zion Canyon Shuttle System (hours vary by season)

DOGS ALLOWED: Only in developed areas (campgrounds, public roads, picnic areas) and on the Pa'rus Trail, which starts at the Zion Canyon Visitor Center

----

WHEN TO GO: Spring for the Virgin River in full flow and waterfalls; summer for extended hours (but lots of crowds); fall and winter for cooler temperatures, foliage, and snow

----

CONTACT: 435-772-3256; nps.gov/zion
Zion Park Boulevard
Springdale, UT 84767

People have relied on the land that's now Zion National Park for thousands of years, finding sustenance, solace, and adventure in the canyons between the tremendous sandstone cliffs. After a federal land survey in 1908 exposed the previously hidden wonders of the landscape, President William Howard Taft set aside acres of it as a national monument. In 1919, it became Zion National Park, and in 1956 it was expanded.

Walking these paths will connect you to a long history of environmental appreciation and marvel. From the Native people who tracked mammoths and Shasta ground sloths through the canyons to the European American fur trappers to the pioneers sent by Brigham Young, you'll join a long line of land stewards when you visit this awe-inspiring space.

→ SLEEP

S Staying inside Zion's borders will keep you under the spell of its landscape for your entire trip. Reserve a site at one of the established campgrounds, pop a tent at any of designated backpacking sites, or book an overnight at the historic Zion Lodge.

→ *Watchman Campground*, which is right next to the Zion Canyon Visitor Center, is open year-round and requires reservations (available six months in advance). Tent and RV sites have electric hookups, picnic tables, and fire rings. There's also potable water and flush toilets.

→ Sites at the **South Campground** (temporarily closed for rehabilitation at the time of this writing) have picnic tables, fire rings, and access to toilets and water. It's near the Zion Nature Center (open seasonally) and offers a Junior Ranger program. The campground accepts reservations two weeks before your travel.

→ *Lava Point Campground* off Kolob Terrace Road is usually open May through September. The six primitive sites sit 7,890 feet above sea level and have pit toilets and trash cans but no water access.

→ Reservations for **backpacking** sites are available in December, March, June, and September for up to three months in advance of your trip. They're popular spots—and only half can be booked in advance, so it's best to plan ahead. If sites go unbooked, you can reserve up to one day before your trip. The remaining sites are available on a first-come-first-serve, walk-in basis from the Zion Canyon Visitor Center Wilderness Desk the day of or before your trip. Try sites at the East Rim Camp Area, Hop Valley, The Narrows, and West Rim.

→ If you'd prefer more amenities, book a stay at the historically rebuilt **Zion Lodge**, the only non-camping option in the park. The site, situated in the heart of the park's towering sandstone cliffs, offers hotel rooms, suites, and cabins—all designed in the 1920s. Each has comfortable beds, and some even have fireplaces or balconies, providing a cozy spot to enjoy your morning coffee or a perfect sunset view. The lodge has two dining options: Red Rock Grill restaurant and Castle Dome Café snack bar. Zion Lodge also makes for a good starting point for hikes and ranger-led activities.

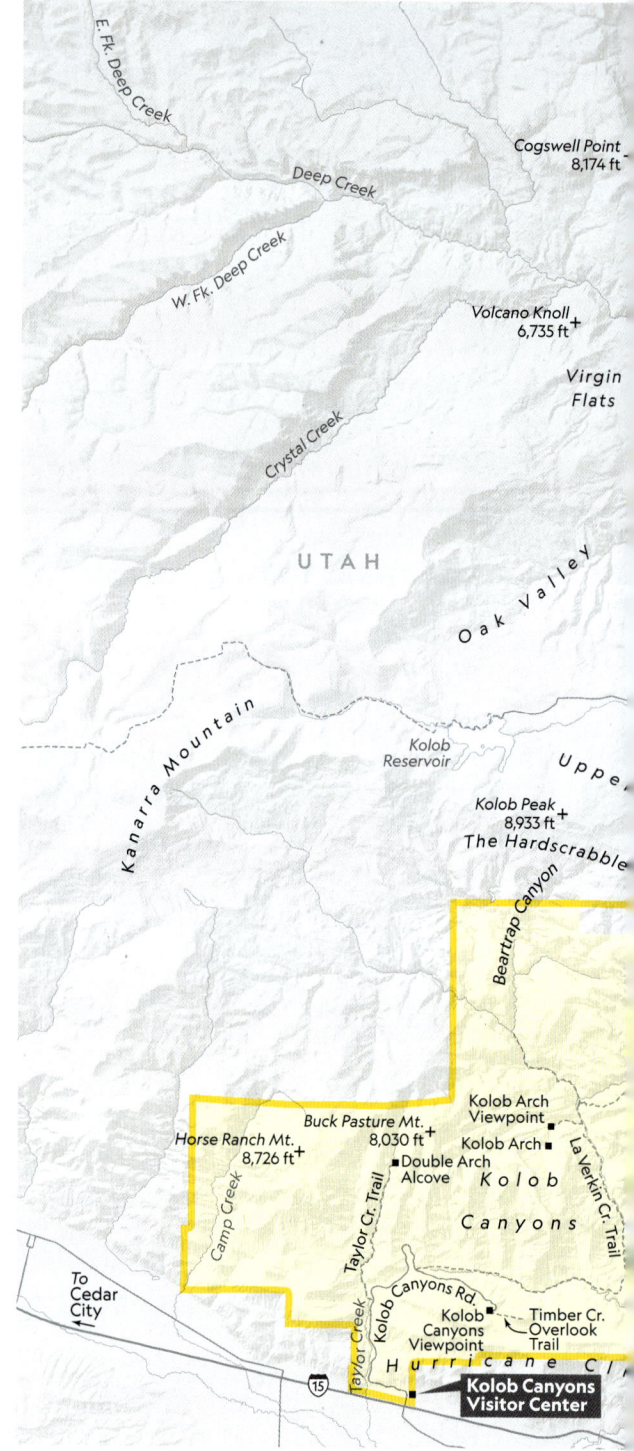

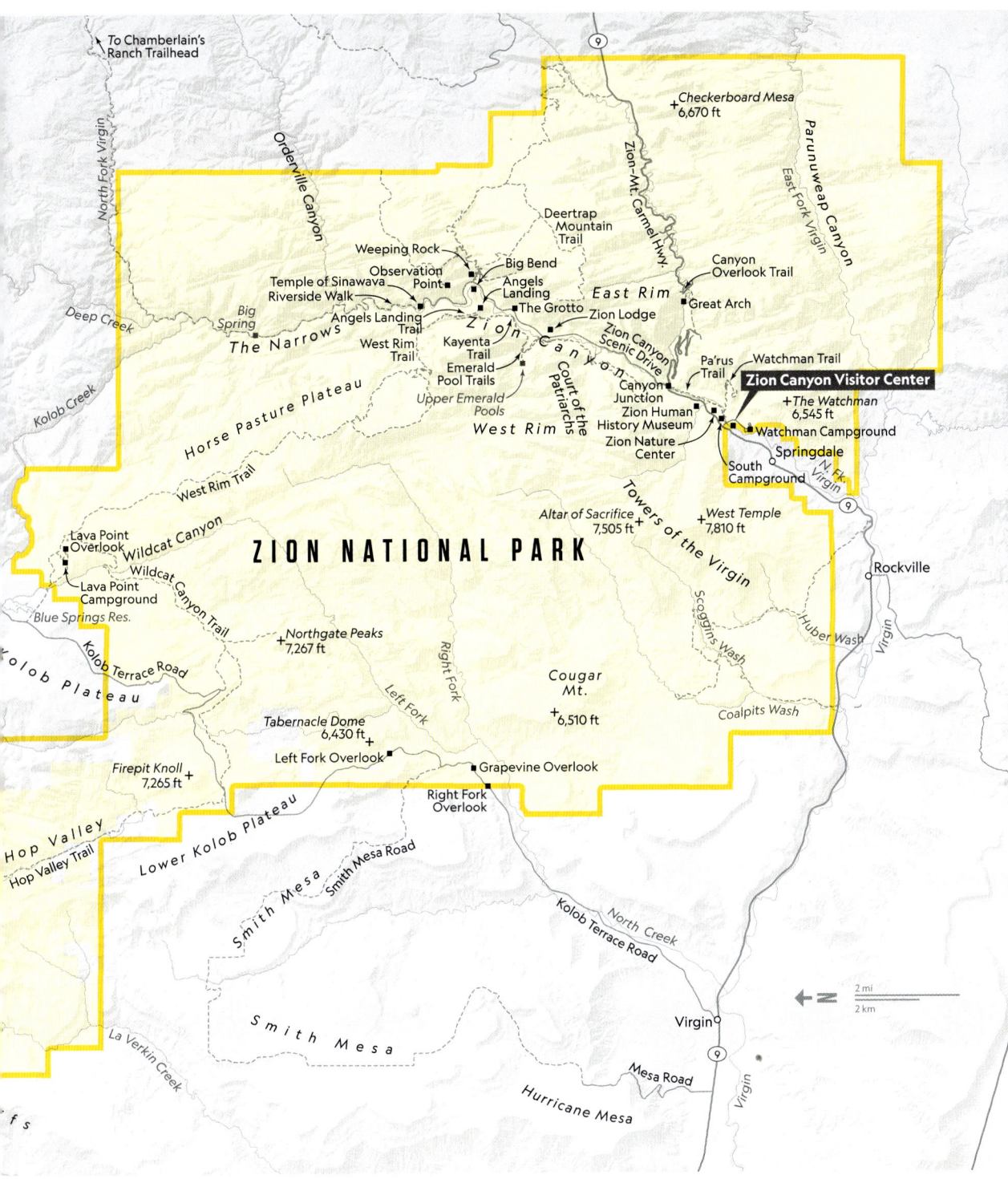

To Chamberlain's Ranch Trailhead

North Fork Virgin

9

Orderville Canyon

Checkerboard Mesa
6,670 ft

Zion-Mt. Carmel Hwy.

Parunuweap Canyon

East Fork Virgin

Deertrap Mountain Trail

Deep Creek

Big Spring

Weeping Rock

Observation Point

Temple of Sinawava

Riverside Walk

Angels Landing Trail

West Rim Trail

Big Bend

Angels Landing

The Grotto

Zion Lodge

Canyon Overlook Trail

Great Arch

East Rim

Zion Canyon Scenic Drive

Kayenta Trail

Emerald Pool Trails

Upper Emerald Pools

Court of the Patriarchs

West Rim

Pa'rus Trail

Watchman Trail

Zion Canyon Visitor Center

Canyon Junction

Zion Human History Museum

Zion Nature Center

The Watchman
6,545 ft

Watchman Campground

Springdale

South Campground

N Fk Virgin

9

The Narrows

Zion Canyon

Kolob Creek

Horse Pasture Plateau

West Rim Trail

Altar of Sacrifice
7,505 ft

Towers of the Virgin

West Temple
7,810 ft

Lava Point Overlook

Wildcat Canyon

Wildcat Canyon Trail

Lava Point Campground

Blue Springs Res.

Kolob Plateau

Kolob Terrace Road

Northgate Peaks
7,267 ft

Left Fork

Right Fork

Cougar Mt.
6,510 ft

Scoggins Wash

Huber Wash

Rockville

Virgin

ZION NATIONAL PARK

Tabernacle Dome
6,430 ft

Firepit Knoll
7,265 ft

Left Fork Overlook

Grapevine Overlook

Right Fork Overlook

Coalpits Wash

Hop Valley

Hop Valley Trail

Lower Kolob Plateau

Smith Mesa

Smith Mesa Road

Kolob Terrace Road

North Creek

Virgin

La Verkin Creek

S m i t h   M e s a

Virgin

Mesa Road

9

Hurricane Mesa

2 mi
2 km

A zigzagging trail

Check rain and flood reports before hiking in the Virgin River Narrows.

Zion boasts more than 100 trails.

Permit Required

HIKE

M Most of the popular trails in the park explore Zion Canyon, where you'll also find the largest crowds. Hikes through Kolob and Parunuweap Canyons are also worthwhile.

➜ Hiking into **The Narrows**, the narrowest part of Zion, is a bucket-list item for many visitors. You'll need a permit if you want to trek from Chamberlain's Ranch down into the Virgin River Narrows to the Temple of Sinawava, but you won't need one if you're hiking them upstream as far as Big Spring. It's safest to take this trip in the summer and early fall, when water levels are low.

➜ The 3.5-mile paved **Pa'rus Trail** is accessible from the Zion Canyon Visitor Center or Canyon Junction. It follows the Virgin River from South Campground to Canyon Junction; pets and bicycles are permitted.

➜ Get off the park's shuttle at Weeping Rock or park across the street from the trailhead to hike the **Weeping Rock Trail**. This 0.4-mile round-trip walk is steep with some small drop-offs, so be prepared. There are trailside exhibits along the way to the sandstone formation.

➜ The easy 2.2-mile round-trip **Riverside Walk** follows the Virgin River to the northern end of Zion Canyon. Take the paved route from the Temple of Sinawava up through steep slopes and into The Narrows route.

➜ Start the 3.3-mile round-trip **Watchman Trail** at the campground near the Zion Canyon Visitor Center and take this quiet route all the way to a viewpoint of the Temples and Towers, Zion Canyon, The Watchman, and Springdale. The trek may be peaceful, but it's challenging. Be sure to fill up your water bottles before you begin.

➜ The unpaved, two-mile round-trip **Kayenta Trail** takes you across the nearby bridge at The Grotto and all the way to the Emerald Pool Trails. From there, explore the shade of the forest and green waters—but don't jump in, given water contamination concerns.

➜ Hike the moderate one-mile **Canyon Overlook Trail**, which starts with rocky terrain over a slow canyon and ends at a fenced-off cliff at the edge of Zion Canyon. You'll get great views of the Towers of the Virgin when you arrive.

➜ Secure a permit to hike the **Angels Landing Trail**, accessible from the West Rim Trail. This 5.4-mile round-trip trek covers a 1,488-foot elevation change, and its narrow ridges aren't for anyone afraid of heights—the final ascent is only a few feet across and has a chain-link rail to help support you, but traffic runs two ways. Definitely leave the kids behind if you attempt this one.

Getting into the other canyons is a great way to experience similar astounding rock formations with fewer crowds.

➜ While hikes from Kolob Canyons Road can be hard to access due to partial road closures, the five-mile round-trip **Taylor Creek Trail** is worth the effort if you can reach it. This path takes you down into a narrow box canyon and to the gorgeous, colorful Double Arch Alcove.

➜ Explore Wildcat Canyon by hiking the **Wildcat Canyon Trail** off Kolob Terrace Road. Travel past views of the Northgate Peaks before the trail opens up into wide meadows and eventually reaches the edge of Wildcat Canyon.

T There are a few roads to drive on your own in Zion, including the popular and necessary Zion–Mount Carmel Highway, but the key route for your Zion Canyon experience will be Zion Canyon Scenic Drive (shuttle or bike only, no private vehicles). Those two routes, and Kolob Terrace Road, are packed with trailheads and overlooks.

→ *Drive the **Zion–Mount Carmel Highway** from the park's southern border toward the Zion Canyon Visitor Center and then east out of the park—or vice versa. You'll travel past various river access points, the Pa'rus Trailhead, Zion Human History Museum, Canyon Junction Overlook, Great Arch, Canyon Overlook Trailhead, and Checkerboard Mesa.*
→ *Catch the free shuttle that travels along **Zion Canyon Scenic Drive** at the Zion Canyon Visitor Center. It stops at nine spots, including Zion Lodge, The Grotto, Weeping Rock, Big Bend, and the Temple of Sinawava. Hop on and off to explore as you wish, but grab a shuttle schedule from a visitors center so you know when the next pick-up will arrive. Or rent an e-bike before the park gates and ride along Zion Canyon Scenic Drive to avoid the busy shuttle and experience the landscape in a whole new way.*
→ *Drive **Kolob Terrace Road** along the western edge of the park, passing trailheads for Right Fork, Grapevine, Left Fork, Hop Valley, Wildcat Canyon, and Lava Point—with overlooks to match.*

DRIVE

Zion Canyon illuminated by starlight and headlights

SPOT

7 Zion National Park is home to a multitude of mammals, birds, reptiles, amphibians, and fish.

→ *Designated as an Important Bird Area, Zion is home to nearly **291 bird species**—either permanently or temporarily. Look for **white-throated sparrows**, **American coots**, and **canyon wrens**. Bird-watchers should also keep a special eye out for the **peregrine falcons** and **condors** that have recently returned to the park.*

→ ***Kangaroo rats**, **bighorn sheep**, **mule deer**, **foxes**, **bats**, and **rock squirrels** all wander their way through Zion. Though many of the animals in the park are nocturnal, like the **coyote** and **gray fox**, they usually leave behind some evidence. Look for their scat and tracks during the day.*

→ *Elusive **Mojave desert tortoises** have adapted to survive in the dry, hot environment of Zion. They spend 95 percent of their lives in underground burrows, avoiding the heat of the summer and hibernating in the winter. They can also survive long periods of drought by holding up to 40 percent of their body weight in water. If you are lucky enough to see one of these fascinating creatures, don't touch it or get too close. Also, check under your car before driving, since tortoises sometimes hide under autos for the shade.*

A desert bighorn ewe with two lambs

Paddling The Narrows

G Get a permit to traverse the waters of Zion—either on your own or book an outfitter trip. The **Virgin River** is the lifeblood of the park, and paddling or tubing along it highlights the magnitude of the canyons. Check out the tubing excursions from Zion River's Edge Adventures or Float Zion River Tubing for an easy meander, or find a guided paddling trip that can take you farther along the water. Spring runoff season (usually mid-April–late May) is great for rafting intense rapids.

While those guided trips can be done by paddlers of different skill levels, only experts should attempt The Narrows.

FLOAT

W Weave experiences beyond hiking and paddling into your trip to enjoy a little extra relaxation, learn more about the land and its people, or boost your thrills.

→ Pack a picnic to enjoy in the shade at **The Grotto**, a serene spot among large cottonwood trees with views of the Virgin River and Angels Landing. The free shuttle will drop you off right at the spot. When you're done eating your meal, cross the river at the bridge for more gorgeous views.

→ Visit the **Zion Human History Museum** to see artifacts and archival materials that showcase the history of the park. You'll learn from exhibits on geology, plants, animals, survival, and community, and see how water has created and changed the local landscape.

→ Hire an outfitter for a **horseback ride excursion** through the park. Ride along the Hop Valley, Northgate Peaks, West Rim, East Rim, East Mesa, Deertrap Mountain, or Sand Bench Trails. Horses are also permitted off-trail at the Lower Coalpits, Scoggins, and Huber Washes. Try East Zion Adventures, Canyon Trail Rides, or Zion Ponderosa Ranch Resort.

→ Elevate your Zion adventure by planning your trip according to the sky. Get there early to watch the **sunrise over the cliffs** at the museum patio, stay later to see it set along the Pa'rus Trail, or **stargaze** at the South and Watchman Campgrounds.

→ **Rock climb** up the world-renowned big walls of the park's massive 2,000-foot sandstone cliffs. Bolted routes have little protection, and the best conditions will come from March to May and in September.

A climber tackles Zion's cliffs.

Experts
Only

EXPLORE

→ RANGER RECOMMENDATION ←

*Choose a hike in **Kolob Canyons** to avoid the crowds
in Zion Canyon. The Timber Creek Overlook Trail is only
a mile round-trip and has a picnic area. On the other
end of the spectrum, the La Verkin Creek Trail is 14 miles
round-trip and gets you into the wild areas of Zion,
where you'll be mostly alone. Halfway through, you'll
get a view of Kolob Arch.*

→ ROCKY MOUNTAINS

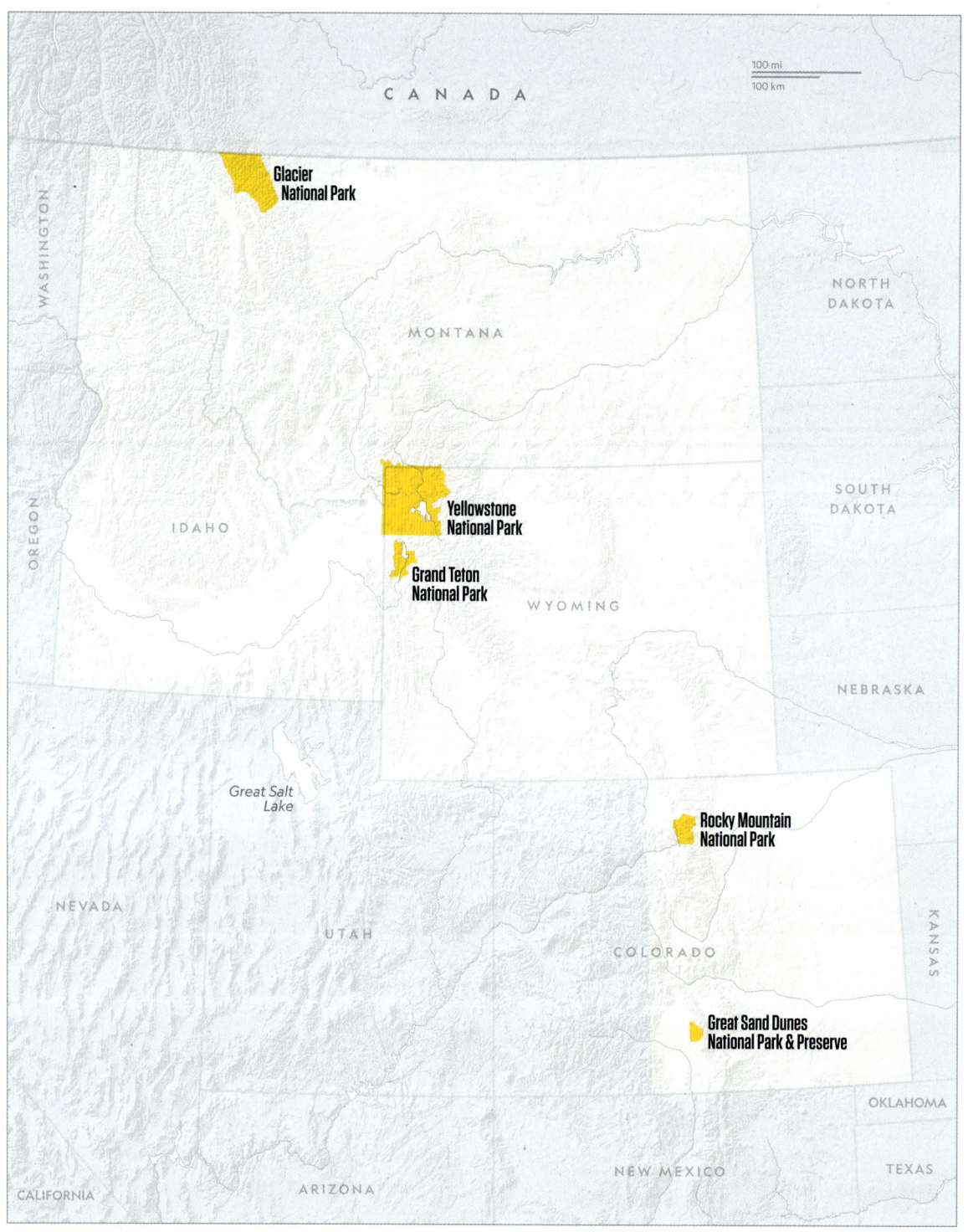

CANADA

100 mi
100 km

WASHINGTON

Glacier
National Park

MONTANA

NORTH
DAKOTA

OREGON

IDAHO

Yellowstone
National Park

Grand Teton
National Park

WYOMING

SOUTH
DAKOTA

NEBRASKA

Great Salt
Lake

Rocky Mountain
National Park

NEVADA

UTAH

COLORADO

KANSAS

Great Sand Dunes
National Park & Preserve

OKLAHOMA

CALIFORNIA

ARIZONA

NEW MEXICO

TEXAS

These five parks abound with glaciers, fields run riot with wildflowers, and bright blue lakes. In Rocky Mountain National Park (page 422), explore a 48-mile throughway among forests and alpine tundra. Marvel at Colorado's 750-foot-tall dunes at Great Sand Dunes (page 412), where the Tijeras Peak tops out at 13,604 feet. Yellowstone (page 434), the country's first national park, teems with wildlife and natural wonders. While Grand Teton (page 398) offers rugged landscapes and the spirit of America's last frontier, Glacier National Park (page 386) remains a stronghold for the grizzly bear. These parks provide a case study in how wilderness manages itself—discover their wonders for yourself.

LEFT: McDonald Creek, Glacier National Park (page 386) **PREVIOUS PAGES:** Logan Pass, Glacier National Park (page 386)

The park's Garden Wall was shaped by Ice Age glaciers.

GLACIER NATIONAL PARK

MONTANA

ESTABLISHED: May 11, 1910

SIZE: 1,013,322 acres

VISITORS CENTERS: The St. Mary Visitor Center (east side) and the Apgar Visitor Center (west side) are open late spring to early fall. The Logan Pass Visitor Center (open peak season) sits at the highest point along Going-to-the-Sun Road and offers exhibits and ranger activities.

TRANSPORTATION: A free shuttle system travels Going-to-the-Sun Road from July through Labor Day. A hiker-biker shuttle service operates weekends only May 11–June 30.

DOGS ALLOWED: Only in developed areas; not allowed on trails, along lakeshores, or in the backcountry

----

WHEN TO GO: Summer is most popular; fall has fewer crowds; spring offers more than 200 waterfalls and a chance to see the northern lights.

CONTACT: 408-888-7800; nps.gov/glac
64 Grinnell Drive
West Glacier, MT 59936

F From Indigenous tribes to European explorers, miners, and settlers, people have been on the lands that are now Glacier National Park for more than 10,000 years, benefiting from the clear waters, vast meadows, and extensive valleys. The Great Northern Railway brought homesteaders—and eventually naturalists. Now, many of the park's buildings are protected on the National Register of Historic Places, and its landscapes are returned to wilderness, protected for both wildlife and guests.

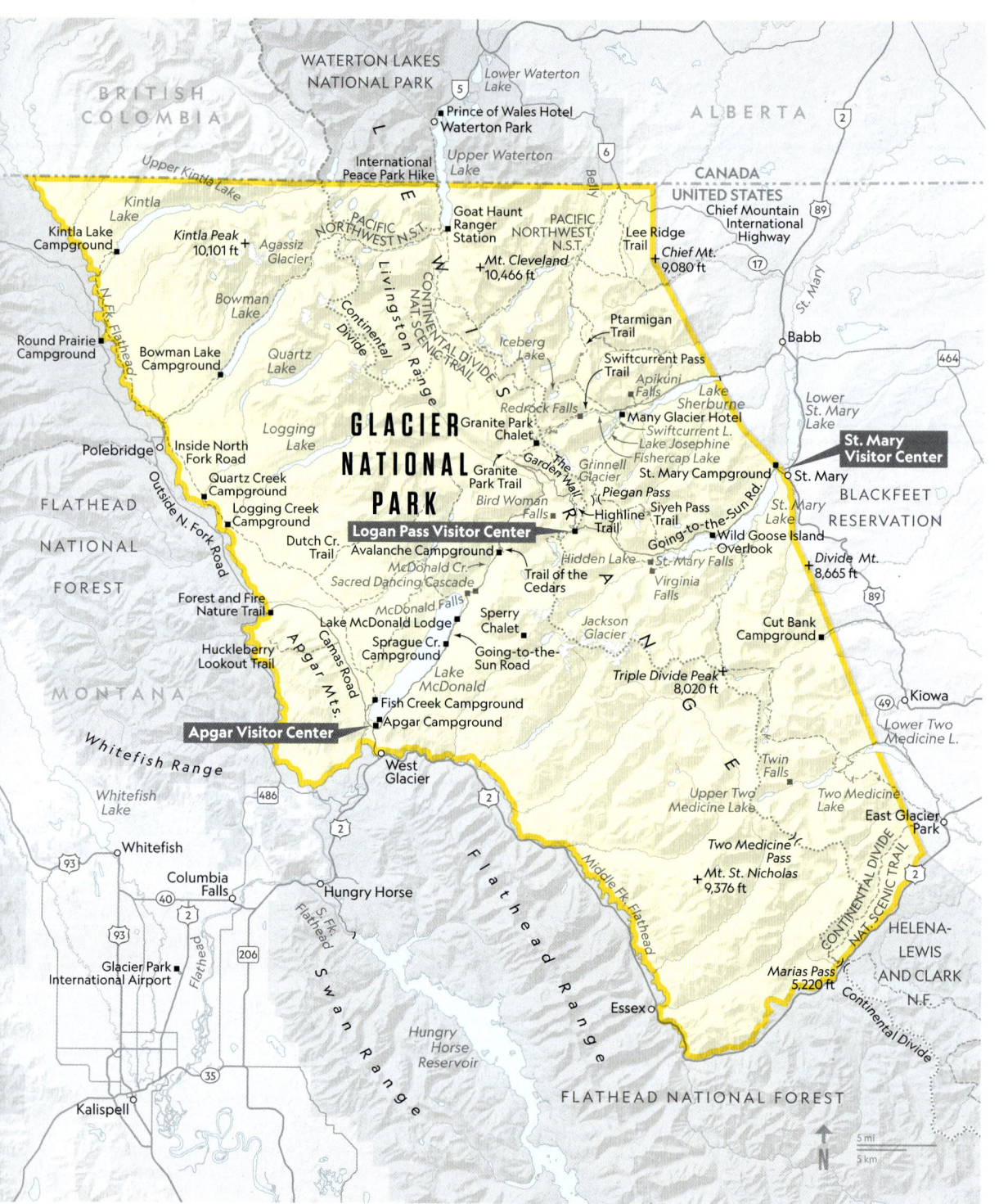

Many Glacier Hotel

→ SLEEP

It's not surprising that a park as popular as Glacier is packed with lodges and campgrounds. You'll find more than a dozen of both, from rustic to luxurious. Here are some favorite options:

→ Stay in the heart of the park at the 1913-built **Lake McDonald Lodge**, right off Going-to-the-Sun Road and on the shore of the park's iconic body of water.

→ Book your stay at **Many Glacier Hotel** on the shores of Swift-current Lake. You'll have gorgeous views, a restaurant and snack shop, and optional park excursions.

→ On the other end of the park, you can book a night in **St. Mary village**, with its 127 options, from budget motel rooms to tiny homes and cabins to upscale hotels. It also has plenty of amenities: a restaurant and café, coffee bar and candy shop, souvenir shop, outdoor-gear shop, and gas station.

→ If you want to cross over into Canada's Waterton Lakes National Park, you can book a stay at the **Prince of Wales Hotel**. You'll find panoramic views of the park and lake from both your room and the communal spaces. Be sure to pack your passport.

→ There are **13 front-country campgrounds** within the bounds of Glacier National Park, most open late spring to early fall. Along Going-to-the-Sun Road, you can stay at the modern Apgar (194 sites, reservations required) and year-round St. Mary (148 sites, reservations required) campgrounds or at the primitive Sprague Creek (25 sites, reservations required), Avalanche (87 sites, reservations required), and Rising Sun (84 sites, first come, first served) campgrounds. Find peace at Cut Bank (14 sites, first come, first served), solitude at Bowman Lake (48 sites, first come, first served), and lake views at Fish Creek (178 sites, reservations required).

→ A backcountry experience in Glacier can mean two things: lodges or campsites. At the wilderness lodges **Granite Park Chalet** and **Sperry Chalet**, you'll find both modern amenities and the quiet that comes with a location reachable only by foot.

→ Take it a step further and **camp in the wilderness**. Permits can be reserved in advance for a portion of campsites in the summer; all other sites are available via walk-up permits the day of or before your trip. You'll also need to watch a mandatory video on resource protection, safety, and guidelines. Winter wilderness camping (November–April) is free.

St. Mary Lake

G Glacier has 700 miles of hikeable trails, so there's truly something for everyone. You can take a short walk to a waterfall or trek for days into the wilderness. You can head out on your own or follow the lead of an experienced ranger. No matter what you choose, you're bound to see flora and fauna you can't find anywhere else.

→ The wheelchair-accessible *Trail of the Cedars* is a forested one-mile boardwalk loop that takes you through red cedars and lush green ferns to a beautiful viewpoint of the lower cascade of Avalanche Gorge.

→ You can choose from a few routes to take to the historic and trail-accessible *Granite Park Chalet*, built between 1914 and 1915 for backcountry hikers. You can hike 7.6 miles from the Logan Pass Visitor Center; climb four miles from the switchback on Going-to-the-Sun Road; check out the waterfalls on the 7.5-mile hike from the Swiftcurrent Store; or take the long 24.8-mile trek from the Goat Haunt Ranger Station.

→ The rugged *Highline Trail* runs for nearly 15 miles out-and-back. You'll hike over Going-to-the-Sun Road, along the edge of cliffs, and out to epic overlooks.

→ Pull off Going-to-the-Sun Road at the *St. Mary Falls Trailhead* to take the route to St. Mary Falls and Virginia Falls, then turn back the way you came. (Get there early for a parking spot.)

→ Explore the *Swiftcurrent Nature Trail* from the boat dock at Many Glacier

Hotel. Keep an eye out for grizzly bears and bighorn sheep along the mountain slopes as you walk—and be sure to stop at one of the benches for a lakeside break.

→ Head out from the *Iceberg Lake Trailhead* and onto the *Ptarmigan Trail* for a 9.7-mile round-trip trek. On the hike you're guaranteed mountain views and possible bear sightings—and take the time to stop at wildflower-filled valleys and glacial lakes along the way. (Park in front of the Swiftcurrent Motor Inn if the lot is full.)

→ Start your hike on the *Swiftcurrent Pass Trail* to reach Redrock Falls. The mostly level route follows a 3.7-mile out-and-back path to a series of cascades. Take the short offshoot trail near the beginning of the hike to get gorgeous views at Fishercap Lake.

→ Take a trek to Piegan Pass along the 9.2-mile round-trip *Siyeh Pass Trail*. Look for mountain goats as you hike and try to find the stone platform where a massive locomotive bell once stood.

→ Find the trailhead for the nearly two-mile out-and-back *Apikuni Falls hike* at the parking lot off Many Glacier Road. You'll see the snow-fed waters cascade 100 feet over the rocky cliffs.

→ You start the *International Peace Park Hike* in Canada, at Waterton Lakes National Park, and end up in Glacier National Park. This hike is led by rangers from both parks—and you'll need to go through customs before finally reaching Goat Haunt. (Book this hike in advance.)

H
I
K
E

Pack Your Passport

Hike along ridges and above the tree line.

G Glacier is a popular park, but there's enough land for wildlife to thrive alongside its visitors. As you wander through the alpine meadows, deep valleys, and glacial lakes, keep an eye out for the mammals, amphibians, reptiles, and birds that call these spaces home.

→ **Grizzly bears** reign in Glacier; in fact, the core of the largest population of grizzlies in the contiguous United States lives mostly within park bounds. In the spring and summer, you might spot them in Glacier's wildflower-laden valleys. A lot of research on the species is happening in the park, including population estimates and hair sampling. If you're set on seeing one, try the Siyeh Pass or Ptarmigan Trails. Bring bear spray just in case.

→ The **moose** in Glacier aggregate around the water, where they find most of their food. Look for them around Fishercap Lake, McDonald Creek, or Two Medicine Lake.

→ As you ascend the mountains of Glacier, look for the animals that thrive at higher elevations: **bighorn sheep**, **pikas**, and **mountain goats**. Keep your eyes along the ridgelines to spot these creatures.

→ Bring your binoculars to spot the **bald** and **golden eagles** that search for prey from the sky, the **American dippers** that bob in the cold rivers and streams, and the **Clark's nutcrackers** that feed on the pine seeds from the park's trees.

SPOT

A grizzly bear near St. Mary Lake

A herd of bighorn sheep on Logan Pass

FLOAT

G Glacier National Park is famous for its clear waters. Paddle, boat, and float your way across the park with one of these aquatic adventures:

→ Book a **Waterton Lakes tour boat** through Waterton Shoreline Cruise to Goat Haunt, the true center point of Waterton-Glacier International Peace Park. You'll float along Upper Waterton Lake for about eight miles until you reach a ranger station.

→ You can **bring your own boat** to paddle at the park, but you'll have to get it inspected for aquatic invasive species before you drop into the water. Stop by a ranger or inspection station before heading to the lakes to check for freshwater zebra and quagga mussels. Afterward, head to Swiftcurrent Lake or Lake Josephine.

→ Take a tour through Lake McDonald, St. Mary, Two Medicine, or Many Glacier on a **historic wooden boat** with Glacier Park Boat Company—or rent your own vessel in Apgar Village.

→ Book a **rafting tour** down the Middle and North Forks of the Flathead River with one of the outfitters with park permits. Though the river doesn't pass through the park, it travels along its border. (The North Fork is a bit calmer.)

Take the *Sinopah* tour boat on Two Medicine Lake.

Must-Do Activity

Wild Goose Island Overlook

→ DRIVE

W While Glacier is a well-protected and wild park, its major sights are easily accessed by road. Driving along its main pass, Going-to-the-Sun Road, will get you to nearly all of the park's best overlooks and trailheads.

→ *Going-to-the-Sun Road* is the most popular route across the park for good reason. All along the route, you'll find scenic viewpoints. Don't miss the sights along Lake McDonald, nearby Sacred Dancing Cascade, the McDonald Falls Overlook, the McDonald Creek Overlook, the western switchback at the Loop, and 492-foot-tall Bird Woman Falls. Add to the trip by driving through the 408-foot-long Eastside Tunnel, heading out at the trailheads at Siyeh Bend, and taking the short, 200-foot trail to the Sunrift Gorge Overlook, an 80-foot-deep gorge with rushing water from Baring Creek. Don't miss two must-see views at the Jackson Glacier Overlook and the Wild Goose Island Overlook, and pause for a creek-side picnic at Red Rock Point. If you want to avoid traffic, take the free park shuttle (summer only) instead of driving.

→ Drive through the northeastern corner of the park along **Chief Mountain International Highway**, which continues north into Canada (bring your passport if you plan to cross). You'll pass the Chief Mountain and Lee Ridge Trailheads, then cross over Lee and Jule Creeks.

→ Jump on the long **Inside North Fork Road** from the Fish Creek Ranger Station and take it north. You'll pass the trailheads for McDonald Lake, Howe Ridge, Howe Lake, Camas Creek, and Dutch Creek and then go by Logging Creek and Quartz Creek Campgrounds, ending at Kintla Lake.

→ *Camas Road* runs from Outside North Fork Road on the west side of the park to the Apgar Visitor Center. Stop at the Forest and Fire Nature Trail, Huckleberry Lookout Trailhead, McGee Meadow viewpoint, and Apgar Bridge.

Going-to-the-Sun Road

The historic Polebridge Mercantile storefront

A Red Bus tour on Going-to-the-Sun Road

F From shopping for locally made souvenirs to gliding through a quiet, snowy afternoon, there's a unique adventure in Glacier for you.

→ *Just outside the park, you can shop for clothing, souvenirs, jewelry, and specialty food items at the* **Polebridge Mercantile**. *This century-old general store also rents out rustic cabins on historic Bakers' Row.*

→ *Venture out onto disappearing* **Grinnell Glacier**, *a retreating spot where rangers once led visitors on tours. You can still experience the space on your own, but beware of fresh snow hiding deep crevasses and the dangers of a solo trip.*

→ *Get a ticket for a classic* **Red Bus tour**, *which Glacier National Park Lodges has been operating since the 1930s. You'll hear about both human and natural history as you travel in the snug benches of this historic fleet of vehicles.*

→ **Snowshoe** *or* **cross-country ski** *the unplowed section of Going-to-the-Sun Road in the winter. If you're quiet, you may get to see white-tailed deer and waterfowl as you trek through the snow. Book a guided tour with a permitted outfitter or the Glacier Institute for a carefully planned experience.*

→ *Attend an event by the longest running Indigenous speaker series in the National Park Service,* **Native America Speaks**. *Every summer, you can hear from members of the Blackfeet Nation and Confederated Salish and Kootenai Tribes as they share their history and culture.*

→ *Travel on* **horseback** *with Swan Mountain Outfitters, which will get you out into the park the same way people have experienced it for over a hundred years.*

→ *Going-to-the-Sun Road isn't only for drivers.* **Bicyclists** *have increasingly found the route to be a great way to see the park's sights. Just stick to the spring or fall if you aren't experienced cycling through heavy traffic.*

EXPLORE

Experts Only

→ RANGER RECOMMENDATION ←

Turn one of the most popular activities in Glacier National Park into a personal experience by putting in a little more work. Instead of heading to the big-hit lakes on a hike, do some investigating with a ranger at a station beforehand. Get ready for a hike of 15 or more miles to one of the **700 glacially carved lakes** *in the park that most people never see. The ranger can pick one that will work best for you based on your abilities and the park's current conditions.*

A view of the Snake River
and the Teton Range

GRAND TETON NATIONAL PARK

WYOMING

ESTABLISHED: February 26, 1929

SIZE: 310,000 acres

VISITORS CENTERS: Craig Thomas Discovery and Visitor Center (open March–October), Laurance S. Rockefeller Preserve Center (open June–September), Jenny Lake Visitor Center (mid-May–late October), and Colter Bay Visitor Center (open mid-May–September)

TRANSPORTATION: No in-park transportation

DOGS ALLOWED: Only where cars can go. Dogs are not allowed on hiking trails or inside facilities.

WHEN TO GO: July and August are peak season, with wildflowers and warm weather (though snow can linger in parts into June). September and October are sunny with good wildlife. Winter is beautiful and great for snowshoeing and cross-country skiing, but temperatures drop and many roads close.

CONTACT: 307-739-3399; nps.gov/grte
103 Headquarters Loop
Moose, WY 83012

T The Teton Range is more than majestic. It rises far above the forests that change color in the fall, far above the meadows that fill with wildflowers in late spring, far above the glistening lakes and rivers that weave through the valleys. The monumental region was once a destination for homesteaders, and their legacy lives on in the trails, paddling routes, and fields open for exploration today. Wander these acres and connect to the long history of environmentalists, nature lovers, and inhabitants of the park's beautiful, rugged frontier.

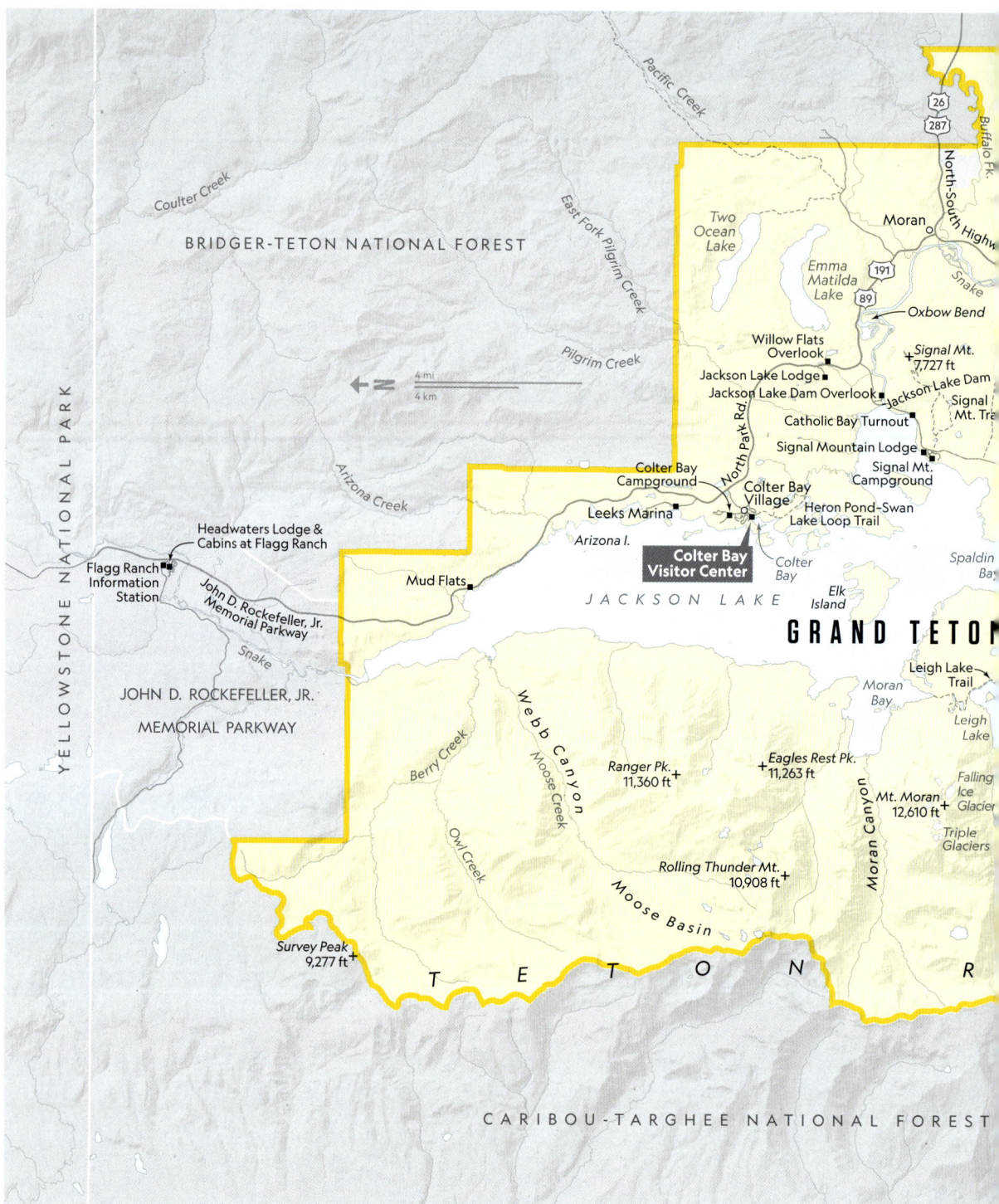

BRIDGER-TETON NATIONAL FOREST

Coulter Creek

Pacific Creek

East Fork Pilgrim Creek

Pilgrim Creek

Arizona Creek

YELLOWSTONE NATIONAL PARK

Headwaters Lodge & Cabins at Flagg Ranch

Flagg Ranch Information Station

John D. Rockefeller, Jr. Memorial Parkway

Snake

JOHN D. ROCKEFELLER, JR. MEMORIAL PARKWAY

Mud Flats

Arizona I.

Leeks Marina

Colter Bay Campground

Colter Bay Village

Colter Bay Visitor Center

Colter Bay

JACKSON LAKE

Elk Island

Two Ocean Lake

Moran

Emma Matilda Lake

Oxbow Bend

Willow Flats Overlook

Jackson Lake Lodge

Jackson Lake Dam Overlook

Catholic Bay Turnout

Signal Mountain Lodge

North Park Rd.

North-South Highway

Snake

Buffalo Fk.

26 287

191

89

Signal Mt. 7,727 ft

Jackson Lake Dam

Signal Mt. Tra

Signal Mt. Campground

Heron Pond-Swan Lake Loop Trail

Spaldin Bay

GRAND TETON

Leigh Lake Trail

Moran Bay

Leigh Lake

Falling Ice Glacier

Triple Glaciers

Webb Canyon

Moose Creek

Berry Creek

Owl Creek

Ranger Pk. 11,360 ft

Eagles Rest Pk. 11,263 ft

Mt. Moran 12,610 ft

Rolling Thunder Mt. 10,908 ft

Moran Canyon

Moose Basin

Survey Peak 9,277 ft

T E T O N

R

CARIBOU-TARGHEE NATIONAL FOREST

4 mi
4 km

BRIDGER-TETON NATIONAL FOREST

GROS VENTRE RANGE

Lower Slide Lake

Sheep Mountain

WYOMING

Elk Ranch Reservoir

Spread Creek

J. P. Cunningham Cabin

Triangle X Ranch

Gros Ventre Road

Gros Ventre

Kelly

Potholes Turnout
Mt. Moran Turnout

River Road

North-South Highway

Ditch Creek

Antelope Flats

JACKSON

Teton Park Rd.

Snake

Schwabacher Landing

Mormon Row

Gros Ventre Campground

NATIONAL ELK REFUGE

Blacktail Butte 7,688 ft

NATIONAL PARK

Jenny Lake Rd.

Jenny Lake Overlook

Jenny Lake Visitor Center

Teton Glacier Turnout

Moose

Craig Thomas Discovery and Visitor Center

HOLE

Jenny Lake Lodge

Jenny Lake

shuttle boat

Cottonwood Cr.

Grand Teton Climbers' Ranch

Murie Ranch
Sawmill Ponds Overlook

26 89 191

Jackson Hole Airport

National Elk Refuge & Greater Yellowstone Visitor Center

Jackson

String L. Trail

Hidden Falls

Bradley Lake

Taggart Lake Trail

Laurance S. Rockefeller Preserve Center

Paintbrush Canyon

Cascade Canyon

Cascade Canyon Trail

Teton Glacier

Garnet Canyon Trail

Taggart Lake

Amphitheater Lake

Valley Trail

Phelps Lake

Grand Teton 13,775 ft

Phelps Lake Overlook

Teton Village

Moose-Wilson Rd.

Snake

Middle Teton 12,809 ft

South Teton 12,519 ft

Jackson Hole Mountain Resort

390

Lake Solitude

R   A   N   G   E

Death Canyon

Open Canyon

Granite Canyon

Wilson

BRIDGER-TETON NATIONAL FOREST

Teton Crest Trail

→ SLEEP

U Unlike some national parks, Grand Teton is full of places to stay, from luxurious lodges to backcountry campsites. Take your pick, depending on whether you value modern amenities or wilderness seclusion. Here are your choices:

→ *Cabins are available for rent at the* **Grand Teton Climbers' Ranch**, *run by the American Alpine Club, and at* **Colter Bay Village**. *The Climbers' Ranch, opened in 1970, is a rustic complex with co-ed, dorm-style lodging with wooden bunks (pack your own sleeping pad and bag), but it's a great starting point for adventurers looking to connect. Ranch season runs June through mid-September, and reservations open in April. Colter Bay Village, on the other hand, is an inclusive experience with modern cabins, a general store and restaurant, and excursions. The family-friendly options are available on a 12-month rolling basis.*

→ *Book a room at one of the many modern lodges within the park's bounds, including* **Jackson Lake Lodge** *(a 385-room eco-hotel),* **Jenny Lake Lodge** *(historic, private cabins), and* **Signal Mountain Lodge** *(a 78-room lakefront resort). Or stay just outside park bounds at the* **Headwaters Lodge & Cabins at Flagg Ranch**. *The ranch is on protected land sandwiched between Grand Teton and Yellowstone National Parks.*

→ *Stay at a dude ranch inside the park when you reserve a space at the family-owned* **Triangle X Ranch**. *Take in the beauty of the park by horseback and learn about the western legacy of the region. Ranch staff will arrange river and pack trips for you through the park too. There is a six-night minimum during peak season.*

→ *Reservations are required at any of the* **eight campgrounds** *within park bounds, most of which are open May through October. Colter Bay and Signal Mountain Campgrounds are both near the water and offer lots of modern amenities, including bathrooms, shops, and gas stations. Gros Ventre Campground is the largest campsite and the closest to Jackson.*

→ *There are also* **14 campsites** *along the John D. Rockefeller, Jr. Memorial Parkway available on a first-come-first-serve basis when the road is accessible in mid-June. You'll need a permit and a bear canister.*

→ *Get a* **backcountry** *permit in advance for peak season (May–October); they become available in January. Winter permits can be obtained over the phone.*

Hunkered down for a night in the mountains

Phelps Lake with views of the
southern end of the Teton Range

Taggart Lake Trail

HIKE

M Most trails in Grand Teton are rugged, steep, and subject to extreme weather. Prepare for bears, storms, navigation issues, and gorgeous mountain views. Here are some hikes worth the challenge:

→ Enjoy the scenery on the popular and relatively easy 3.8-mile **Taggart Lake Trail** loop. Walk through an aspen forest, gaining and losing elevation until the path eventually levels out and reaches the lake, with views of the Tetons rising above.

→ Take the 3.7-mile **String Lake Trail**, which hugs the east side of the lake. The moderately challenging loop offers views of the Grand Teton range and is also great for birders.

→ Ride the boat shuttle from the Jenny Lake Visitor Center across the lake to a group of trails. Hike the short **Hidden Falls Trail** to the cascades, continue on to Inspiration Point, or trek along the **Cascade Canyon Trail**. Or forgo the shuttle and hike along the south side of the lake to get there.

→ Hike from the Lupine Meadows Trailhead to Amphitheater Lake along the **Valley Trail** and the switchbacks of the **Garnet Canyon Trail**. You'll gain 3,070 feet of elevation and trek through blooming fields of wildflowers in early summer.

→ The challenging 13.2-mile out-and-back **Valley Trail** gains 2,360 feet of elevation from the trail's start at Teton Village to the valley lakes of the park. End your hike at the Phelps Lake Overlook.

→ Get to the 1.8-mile round-trip **Leigh Lake Trail** from the String Lake Trail or Jenny Lake Trail. Either way, end up at the less visited lake and get gorgeous views of the mountain range from its shores.

→ From the trailhead near the eponymous lodge, take the 6.8-mile out-and-back **Signal Mountain Trail**, a narrow path through the forest to the summit, where you'll be rewarded with panoramic views of the Teton Range and Jackson Hole.

→ Stroll the 3.1-mile **Heron Pond–Swan Lake Loop Trail** with views of the Teton Range towering above but little elevation gain on your amble. Keep an eye out for birds and wildlife while you wind through the forests and wetlands.

Family Friendly

Gray wolves returned to Grand Teton in the late 1990s.

The land protected in Grand Teton is part of the 20 million acres of the Greater Yellowstone Ecosystem—all home to a vast array of wildlife.

→ **Elk** summer in Grand Teton, then migrate to the National Elk Refuge southeast of the park. The nearly 11,000 elk that call this area home are closely managed and monitored. Look for them in the Willow Flats area between Jackson Lake Dam and Lodge or along Moose-Wilson Road.

→ Hike around Schwabacher Landing, a mix of wetlands, reflecting ponds, meadows, and cottonwood forest, to spot **beavers** at work in the region building a giant dam.

→ See **bison**, **moose**, **bald eagles**, and **great blue herons** as you paddle along the Snake River. Take your time on the slower sections to boost the chances of a sighting.

→ Mormon Row is a great spot to find **bison** and **pronghorn sheep** in the spring, summer, and fall. It's also possible to catch sight of a **coyote**, **Northern harrier**, or **American kestrel**.

Beavers have called Grand Teton home for thousands of years.

SPOT

A bison slips into the forest in a remote area of the park.

FLOAT

String and Leigh Lakes at the foot of Mount Moran

G Getting to the top of the Teton Range is one way to experience the wonders of the park. Getting down to the bottom of its valleys, where its river and lakes sit, is another. Find your way out onto the water with one of these trips:

→ Paddle the **Snake River**, weaving through the valley floor of the park and taking in striking views of the Teton peaks. The river changes every year, depending on the flow of the snow-melt, so you'll need strong paddling and navigational skills—or book the trip with an outfitter. With normal water flow, rapids range between Class II and III, but heavier water flow can mean tougher rapids. Rangers can help identify which sections are right for your skill level.

→ Rent a canoe, kayak, or motorboat at Colter Bay Village and travel along the shore of **Jackson Lake**, visiting its different islands and bays. The outfitter will give you life jackets and a map.

→ Bring your own boat to Grand Teton and enjoy the clear mountain lakes from the **Signal Mountain**, **Colter Bay**, and **Leeks Marinas** in summer. Motors are permitted only on Jackson and Jenny Lakes.

Kayaking Colter Bay

D Drive through Grand Teton to take in many of the park's most popular sights.

→ Drive **North Park Road**, which turns into North-South Highway and traverses the length of the park. From north to south, pass many of the most popular overlooks, pullouts, and trailheads—from the Mud Flats overlook to Colter Bay Village to Teton Point.

→ **Teton Park Road** cuts toward Jackson Lake from North Park Road and North-South Highway. Stop at the Jackson Lake Dam Overlook, Catholic Bay Turnout, Potholes and Mount Moran Turnouts, Jenny Lake sights and overlooks, Teton Glacier Turn-out, and Craig Thomas Discovery and Visitor Center. You can also take a turn off the route onto Signal Mountain Road to drive to the summit for views.

→ Hop off Teton Park Road and onto **Jenny Lake Road**. Stop at the Cathedral Group Turnout, Alder Fire Overlook, Leigh Lake and String Lake Trailheads, and Jenny Lake Overlook. It's a great short drive for getting close to two of the mountain's popular lakes.

→ Take **Moose-Wilson Road** from near the Craig Thomas Discovery and Visitor Center. Stop at the Sawmill Ponds Overlook and see plenty of wildlife, including elk and moose.

DRIVE

Must-Do Activity

Fly-fishing at Oxbow Bend on the Snake River

→ EXPLORE

T   There are miles of trails, plenty of clear mountain lakes, and acres filled with wildlife in Grand Teton—and there are also history lessons to be learned, waters to swim, and mountains to climb. Add to your trip with one of these activities:

→ *Go for a swim at the* **Jackson Lake beaches** *of Colter Bay. Pack a picnic, enjoy the view, and jump into the cool water from the rocky shore.*

→ *Don't be deterred from traveling in winter, which brings plenty of snow to Grand Teton.* **Cross-country ski**, **snowshoe**, *or* **snow hike** *the 14-mile portion of Teton Park Road from the Taggart Lake Trailhead to Signal Mountain Lodge, which is groomed in the winter. Explore Moose-Wilson Road, checking out Phelps Lake along the route. Be on guard for moving water under the ice.*

→ *Visit* **J. P. Cunningham Cabin** *to get a taste of pioneer life. Though nearly 400 homestead claims were filed in the 1880s, it's one of the few that's still standing. Watch out for aggressive bison while there.*

→ *With its massive peaks,* **Grand Teton** *draws mountain climbers hoping to reach one of its multiple summits. You don't need a permit for mountaineering, but you do need one for backcountry camping. These aren't for inexperienced climbers.*

→ *Walk through* **Mormon Row**, *once the location of 27 Mormon pioneer homesteads. Unlike many other pioneers, these families settled close to one another to share labor and community. Check out the water that still flows through some of the agricultural ditches they dug.*

→ **Fishing** *is a popular draw for many visitors. Get a state fishing license inside the park to participate. Just follow the seasonal rules around closures and catch-and-release.*

→ *Explore the park by* **horseback** *with one of the three authorized outfitters: Triangle X Ranch, Headwaters Lodge & Cabins at Flagg Ranch, and Grand Teton Lodge Company. The trails are shared with hikers, and the routes can be rocky and steep.*

→ RANGER RECOMMENDATION ←

Visit the **Murie Ranch**, which has been called the "heart of American wilderness" and served as a base camp for conservation leaders for decades. Conservationists Mardy and Olaus Murie and Adolph and Louise Murie bought the former dude ranch in 1945 and took down all the fences so that wildlife could freely pass. It's now a national historic landmark comprised of cabins and a visitors center with daily tours. Drive there on the unpaved Murie Ranch Road or hike the easy out-and-back Murie Ranch Trail from the Craig Thomas Discovery and Visitor Center.

Star Dune, one of the two tallest dunes in the U.S.

GREAT SAND DUNES
NATIONAL PARK
& PRESERVE

COLORADO

ESTABLISHED: September 13, 2004

SIZE: 149,137 acres

VISITORS CENTER: The Great Sand Dunes Visitor Center is open year-round with historical exhibits, a night-sky video, 3D models, and informative park rangers for assistance.

TRANSPORTATION: Rent a sandboard from the visitors center; sand wheelchairs can be reserved in advance by calling the visitors center.

DOGS ALLOWED: Only in some areas (not in backcountry). Be mindful that the sand can blister dogs' paws.

WHEN TO GO: Spring and fall (especially September) for mild weather and fewer visitors. Summer is busiest; visit early in the morning to avoid extreme heat or come in the evening for night-sky programming (the park is open 24 hours a day). Winter is cold and relatively empty.

CONTACT: 719-378-6395; nps.gov/grsa
11999 State Highway 150
Mosca, CO 81146

T The tallest dunes in North America are found in Great Sand Dunes National Park, which also boasts wetlands, forests, and tundra. Every one of these ecosystems is home to flora and fauna that have adapted to the environment—and the diverse landscapes provide just as varied an array of experiences for visitors. Hike in the morning, swim in the afternoon, and stargaze in the evening.

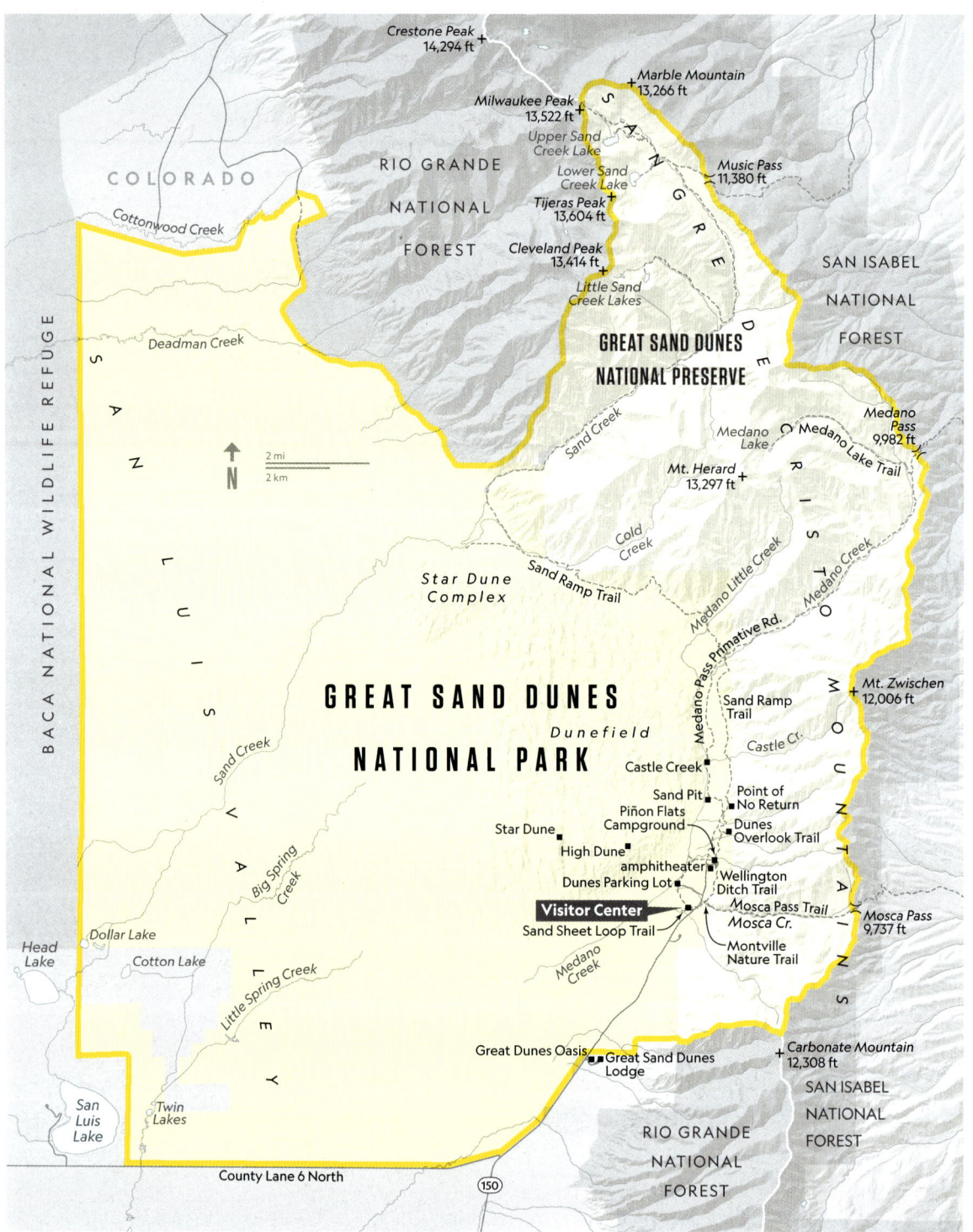

Crestone Peak
14,294 ft

Marble Mountain
13,266 ft

Milwaukee Peak
13,522 ft

SANGRE

Upper Sand
Creek Lake

Music Pass
11,380 ft

RIO GRANDE

Lower Sand
Creek Lake

NATIONAL

Tijeras Peak
13,604 ft

COLORADO

SAN ISABEL

FOREST

Cleveland Peak
13,414 ft

NATIONAL

Cottonwood Creek

Little Sand
Creek Lakes

FOREST

Deadman Creek

GREAT SAND DUNES
NATIONAL PRESERVE

DE

Medano
Pass
9,982 ft

Medano Lake Trail

Medano
Lake

2 mi
2 km

Sand Creek

CRISTO

Mt. Herard
13,297 ft

BACA NATIONAL WILDLIFE REFUGE

N

Cold
Creek

Star Dune
Complex

Sand Ramp Trail

Medano Little Creek

Medano Creek

SAN

Mt. Zwischen
12,006 ft

GREAT SAND DUNES

Dunefield

Sand Ramp
Trail

MOUNTAINS

LUIS

NATIONAL PARK

Castle Creek

Castle Cr.

Sand Pit

Point of
No Return

Star Dune

Piñon Flats
Campground

Dunes
Overlook Trail

High Dune

amphitheater

Wellington
Ditch Trail

Dunes Parking Lot

Mosca Pass Trail

VALLEY

Visitor Center

Mosca Cr.

Mosca Pass
9,737 ft

Sand Sheet Loop Trail

Montville
Nature Trail

Dollar Lake

Head
Lake

Cotton Lake

Medano
Creek

Big Spring Creek

Little Spring Creek

Sand Creek

Great Dunes Oasis

Carbonate Mountain
12,308 ft

Great Sand Dunes
Lodge

SAN ISABEL

San
Luis
Lake

Twin
Lakes

NATIONAL

FOREST

County Lane 6 North

150

RIO GRANDE

NATIONAL

FOREST

Backcountry camping on the vast dunefield

→ SLEEP

(T) To spend the night within the bounds of the park, you'll have to camp. Either stay at the campground or book a backcountry permit, but planning ahead is essential for both.

→ *Just a mile past the visitors center, **Piñon Flats Campground** (open April–October) books quickly in the summer. There aren't any hookups, but it has drive-in sites, modern toilets, and access to the Dunes Overlook Trail.*

→ ***Backcountry sites*** *are spread throughout the park. Stop along Medano Pass Primitive Road to access one of the 18 campsites, camp in designated spots along the Sand Ramp Trail, or head out into the dunes backcountry from the parking lot. Backpacking permits are available only in advance online at* recreation.gov.

If you don't want to camp, consider a night at the modern **Great Sand Dunes Lodge** (open March–October), near the park entrance. Primitive cabins and tent and RV sites are available at **Great Dunes Oasis** (open April–October), just south of the park entrance, where you'll also find a camp store, showers, and a restaurant.

H Hiking is the best way to see everything the park has to offer. Stick to maintained trails for views and dune experiences, or go off the beaten path to explore on your own.

→ Get to the Sand Creek Lakes by driving from the visitors center and then following Music Pass to the **Sand Creek Lakes** or

HIKE

Little Sand Creek Lakes Trails. Check with rangers ahead of your trip to ensure conditions are good.

→ If you have a four-wheel-drive vehicle, take Medano Pass Primitive Road up to the **Medano Lake Trail.** This long and rocky hike leads to the summit of Mount Herard and provides a broad view of the dunefield from above. Beware: There's been heavy treefall on the trails as of late.

→ While there aren't any established trails, hike through, across, and up the dunes in the park yourself. Get to **High Dune,** the tallest dune on first ridge, and **Star Dune,** the tallest dune in the park, at 741 feet, from the Dunes Parking Lot. Pro tip: Hike them in the early morning or evening.

→ The half-mile **Montville Nature Trail** is an easy and popular way to explore the

Experts Only

forest and get great views of the dunes and valley. Extend the hike on the **Mosca Pass Trail** (7 miles round-trip), which makes its way up 1,400 feet in the Sangre de Cristo Mountains.

→ Trek the unmaintained trail up to the 12,308-foot summit of **Carbonate Mountain.** It starts at the visitors center and is about eight miles round-trip.

→ The **Sand Sheet Loop Trail** is just a quarter mile long, but it shares a glimpse into the park's unique grasslands. Keep an eye out for miniature short-horned lizards.

→ Find striking overlooks by getting high in the park. The **Dunes Overlook Trail** runs 2.7 miles out and back from Piñon Flats Campground. You end at a ridge with a few benches and views over the dunes, mountain range, river, and valley.

Hike in the evening to enjoy sunset atop the dunes.

Piñon Flats Campground

Lower Sand Creek Lake

DRIVE

T There isn't much driving to be done in Great Sand Dunes. **Highway 150** runs up past the visitors center to either the Dunes Parking Lot or Piñon Flats Campground. From there, continue down **Medano Pass Primitive Road** for access to deeper trailheads and sights—but only with a four-wheel-drive vehicle.

A pika gathers grass for winter.

A At first glance, the sand dunes might not seem like a welcoming place for wildlife, but the park is full of plants and animals that thrive in this environment.

→ *More than 10,000 migratory **sandhill cranes** spend spring and fall in the region, but not in areas of the park open to the public. Join the crowds at nearby Monte Vista National Wildlife Refuge for a near-guaranteed viewing.*

→ *More than **250 bird species** have been reported in the park, and many of them come in the summer to nest. Look for **brown-capped rosy finches** in the cliffs, **white-tailed ptarmigans** walking around, and **peregrine falcons** flying above the forest. Try Mosca Pass for great views.*

→ *Up in the mountains, try to spot **American pikas**, **black bears**, **bighorn sheep**, and **yellow-bellied marmots**. Down in the dunes, search for **tiger salamanders** and **Ord's kangaroo rats**, one of the few mammals that spend their whole lives in this desert ecosystem.*

→ *Though you'd be hard-pressed to spot some of these creatures during the day, keep an eye out for tracks from **coyotes**, **mule deer**, and **bobcats** as you traverse the wet sand near the creek.*

SPOT

↑

Explore the dunes by horseback.

T The non-hiking excursions at Great Sand Dunes can change by the season, so it's best to schedule your visit around your preferred adventure.

➜ Catch **Medano Creek** at its peak flow and play in the water in late May and June. You can also surf the waves or float along in inner tubes when it's flowing strongly. Just be sure to check the water rates on the park website before your trip, since there are times when it's dry.

➜ **Ride your horse** along Medano Pass Primitive Road, where you'll also find the park's horse trailer parking. Pay attention to closed areas and pack-animal rules.

➜ Go on an interactive **ranger-led program**, during which you'll be able to touch ancient artifacts, learn about the constellations, or become a Junior Ranger Bat Explorer.

➜ **Stargaze** in the park, certified in 2019 as an International Dark Sky Park. Stare up at the stars in solitude on a camping trip or follow along with a ranger.

➜ To **sandboard** or **sand sled**, rent equipment at the visitors center or from outfitters outside the park. Stop by the Oasis Store or SpinDrift Sandboards to get boards that are specifically meant for sand. Do not try to use a snow sled or snowboard.

➜ **Fat-tire biking** is allowed along Medano Pass Primitive Road, though it can be a challenging route, with sandy sections, creek crossings, and rocks. Turn your cycling trip into an overnight adventure at backpacking sites along the route.

➜ **Fish** in the Medano and Sand Creek drainages of the park with a proper license. It's a great spot to find Rio Grande cutthroat trout. Just be sure to catch and release.

E
X
P
L
O
R
E

Night-Sky Wonders

→ RANGER RECOMMENDATION ←

Hike the **Dunes Overlook Trail** for gorgeous views of the sandy landscape. While it's a well-known hike, solitude is possible on the 2.7-mile out-and-back trail if you go early or late in the day.

A conifer forest and snow-covered alpine meadow

ROCKY MOUNTAIN NATIONAL PARK

COLORADO

ESTABLISHED: January 26, 1915

SIZE: 265,807 acres

VISITORS CENTERS: The Beaver Meadows, Fall River, and Kawuneeche Visitor Centers are open year-round, while the Alpine Visitor Center is open summer through early fall. The Moraine Park Discovery Center is open year-round, the Holzwarth Historic Site is open in summer, and the Sheep Lakes Information Station is also staffed in summer.

TRANSPORTATION: Shuttle buses on two routes: Bear Lake and Moraine Park

---

DOGS ALLOWED: Only on roads and in developed picnic areas and campgrounds

---

WHEN TO GO: June–August is peak season (and has peak crowds); spring and fall offer milder weather and wildlife spotting.

CONTACT: 970-586-1206; nps.gov/romo
1000 U.S. Highway 36
Estes Park, CO 80517

The peaks and valleys in Rocky Mountain National Park have seen the Ute people, Spanish explorers and French fur trappers, gold spectators, resilient homesteaders, and, eventually, tourists seeking some relaxation and adventure.

In the early 1900s, the lands were protected by President Woodrow Wilson. Today, more than 4.5 million people venture into the park to see its clear, glistening lakes, sweeping forests and tundras, towering summits, and deep canyons. Though the space has seen the impact of people, it remains as wild as it was hundreds of years ago.

Camping grants visitors peaceful nights amid the peaks.

SLEEP

C Camping is the name of the game for in-park stays. **Glacier Basin**, **Aspenglen**, **Longs Peak**, and **Timber Creek Campgrounds** are open from spring through early fall, while **Moraine Park Campground** is open all year. Reservations are required for most sites, especially in peak season—book ahead as they fill fast.

Outside of those spots, **backcountry camp** with a permit at one of the more than 200 sites, including temporary camps near climbing routes. Permit reservation requests can be made for trips May through October; walk-ins are available at the Wilderness Office next to the Beaver Meadows Visitor Center for trips November through April 30. All permits must be picked up in person at the Wilderness Office.

If you aren't up for camping, find hotels and resorts at **Estes Park** and **Grand Lake**.

The spectacular view from the Stanley Hotel, an accommodation option in Estes Park.

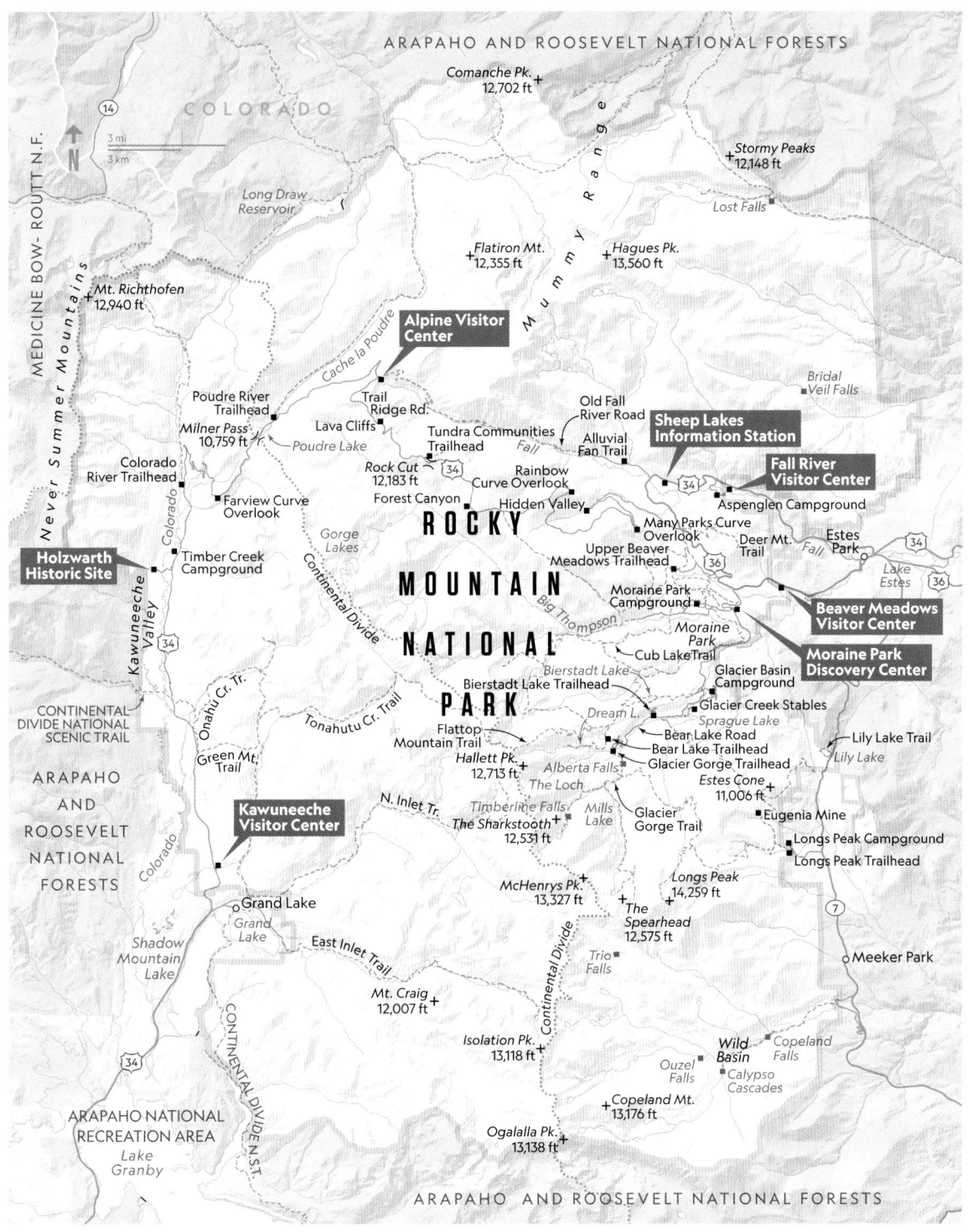

ARAPAHO AND ROOSEVELT NATIONAL FORESTS

COLORADO

14

3 mi
3 km
N

MEDICINE BOW- ROUTT N.F.

NEVER SUMMER Mountains

Long Draw
Reservoir

Comanche Pk.
12,702 ft

Stormy Peaks
12,148 ft

Lost Falls

Flatiron Mt.
12,355 ft

Hagues Pk.
13,560 ft

Mummy Range

Mt. Richthofen
12,940 ft

Bridal
Veil Falls

Cache la Poudre

**Alpine Visitor
Center**

Poudre River
Trailhead

Milner Pass
10,759 ft

Trail
Ridge Rd.

Lava Cliffs

Poudre Lake

Tundra Communities
Trailhead

Old Fall
River Road

Fall

Alluvial
Fan Trail

**Sheep Lakes
Information Station**

**Fall River
Visitor Center**

Colorado
River Trailhead

Farview Curve
Overlook

Colorado

Rock Cut
12,183 ft

34

Forest Canyon

Rainbow
Curve Overlook

Hidden Valley

Aspenglen Campground

ROCKY

Gorge
Lakes

Many Parks Curve
Overlook

Deer Mt.
Trail

Estes
Park

34

**Holzwarth
Historic Site**

Timber Creek
Campground

MOUNTAIN

Upper Beaver
Meadows Trailhead

36

Fall

Lake
Estes

36

Kawuneeche Valley

34

Continental Divide

Big Thompson

NATIONAL

Moraine Park
Campground

Moraine
Park

**Beaver Meadows
Visitor Center**

Cub Lake Trail

**Moraine Park
Discovery Center**

Onahu Cr. Tr.

Tonahutu Cr. Trail

PARK

Bierstadt Lake

Bierstadt Lake Trailhead

Dream L.

Glacier Basin
Campground

Glacier Creek Stables

Sprague Lake

Lily Lake Trail

CONTINENTAL
DIVIDE NATIONAL
SCENIC TRAIL

Green Mt.
Trail

Flattop
Mountain Trail

Hallett Pk.
12,713 ft

Alberta Falls

Bear Lake Road

Bear Lake Trailhead

Glacier Gorge Trailhead

Lily Lake

ARAPAHO

AND

ROOSEVELT

NATIONAL

FORESTS

Colorado

N. Inlet Tr.

Timberline Falls

The Sharkstooth
12,531 ft

The Loch

Mills
Lake

Glacier
Gorge Trail

Estes Cone
11,006 ft

Eugenia Mine

Longs Peak Campground

Longs Peak Trailhead

**Kawuneeche
Visitor Center**

McHenrys Pk.
13,327 ft

Longs Peak
14,259 ft

7

Grand Lake

Grand
Lake

East Inlet Trail

The
Spearhead
12,575 ft

Shadow
Mountain
Lake

Mt. Craig
12,007 ft

Continental Divide

Trio
Falls

Meeker Park

CONTINENTAL DIVIDE N.ST.

Isolation Pk.
13,118 ft

Ouzel
Falls

Wild
Basin

Calypso
Cascades

Copeland
Falls

34

ARAPAHO NATIONAL
RECREATION AREA

Lake
Granby

Copeland Mt.
13,176 ft

Ogalalla Pk.
13,138 ft

ARAPAHO AND ROOSEVELT NATIONAL FORESTS

HIKE

F Find everything from accessible routes with great lake views to challenging scrambles up towering peaks.

→ Hike to the cascading waterfall on the **Alluvial Fan Trail** in the fall to catch the drama of the changing colors in the aspen groves below. Bonus: This route was specifically designed in 2020 for full accessibility.

→ The 3.1-mile one-way **Deer Mountain Trail** has two things that might deter you: its popularity and its propensity for lightning strikes. Still, the risk and the elevation gain will be worth it when you encounter the gorgeous views of Longs Peak, Moraine Park, Upper Beavers Meadows, and Estes Park.

→ The 2.3-mile one-way **Cub Lake Trail** is a favorite of many visitors—and for good reason. It crosses meadows, the Big Thompson River, and the western edge of Moraine Park.

→ Get to the top of **Estes Cone** by following the steep switchbacks from the Longs Peak Trailhead. Pass the Eugenia mine and a historic homestead along the way. Be prepared for the altitude.

→ Start at the **Glacier Gorge Trailhead** off Bear Lake Road to see Alberta Falls, Mills Lake, and The Loch—the last two being some of the park's most striking mountain lakes.

→ The **Flattop Mountain Trail** is well maintained but also incredibly difficult. It runs nearly nine miles round-trip from the Bear Lake area, with an elevation gain of about 2,850 feet. The payoff: fantastic views of Dream Lake and Hallett Peak.

→ Walk the 1.8-mile route from the Wild Basin area to the **Calypso Cascades**, named for a rare orchid that grows here. Then continue on another mile to the impressive Ouzel Falls.

→ Follow the **Lily Lake Trail** loop around the lake and wetlands for just under a mile. The easy and level path has plenty of spots for relaxation, including picnic tables, benches, and miniature overlooks.

→ Around 30 miles of the **Continental Divide National Scenic Trail** run through Rocky Mountain National Park. Access the trail from the Bowen Gulch Trail on the north end, then hike along the Onahu Creek and Green Mountain Trails.

Dream Lake, near the snow-covered base of Hallett Peak

The rushing waters of the Fall River

A bull elk calls out for the herd.

→ SPOT

(R) Rocky Mountain is one of the most popular in the National Park System, in no small part because it's a marvelous wildlife-watching destination. Stay alert and bring your binoculars.

→ *Look for* **mule deer** *and* **elk** *along the roads in the park, and for* **bighorn sheep** *hanging out around the natural minerals of Horseshoe Park or Sheep Lakes. If you're set on spotting these animals, it's best to chat with a ranger about where they were last spotted.*

→ *Summon your patience to spot* **black bears**, **moose**, *or* **mountain lions**, *which are more evasive. Try waking up early to see them at dawn.*

→ *Smaller wildlife, including* **porcupines**, **snowshoe hares**, *and* **chipmunks**, *are more common around the park. Look for* **yellow-bellied marmots** *along Trail Ridge and Old Fall River Roads, while* **pikas** *like to spend time in rock piles.*

→ *Bird-watchers should look to the skies for some of the* **270 species** *in the park, especially along Trail Ridge Road. Look for* **magpies**, **jays**, **bluebirds**, **chickadees**, *and* **sapsuckers** *at lower elevations, while* **gray jays**, **grosbeaks**, *and* **red crossbills** *are common in higher forests. Follow the skyline to see* **eagles**, **hawks**, **ospreys**, **falcons**, **kestrels**, *and* **vultures**.

→ **Beavers** *used to be common in the park, but they are fewer and farther between today. Researchers are studying their presence and hoping to better manage the population. Try Lily Lake, Wild Basin, or Kawuneeche Valley.*

A Colorado chipmunk

One of the many scenic views from Trail Ridge Road

DRIVE

T The 48-mile trip along the park's **Trail Ridge Road** is all about sweeping views, high elevations, and perfect stops. Traveling west to east, stop at the Farview Curve Overlook (views of the Kawuneeche Valley and Never Summer Mountains), Milner Pass (on the Continental Divide, it sits at 10,759 feet with views of Poudre Lake), Lava Cliffs (a rare section of lava rock formed millions of years ago), Rock Cut (nicknamed the "Roof of the Rockies" at 12,110 feet), Forest Canyon (worth the five-minute walk down the paved trail for canyon views), the Rainbow Curve Overlook (with views of Hidden Valley and aptly named for the frequent rainbows spotted here), and Many Parks Curve, which looks out over lowland meadows. Sprinkle in a few hikes off the roadside trailheads, like the Colorado River, Poudre River, and Tundra Communities Trails.

Bear Lake Road is a shorter route that's packed with worthwhile trailheads. Stop at the Moraine Park area, Sprague Lake, the Bierstadt Lake Trailhead, and Glacier Gorge. Take this road to get to Moraine Park and Glacier Basin Campgrounds. Remember to stay flexible as you journey down the route—parking lots can fill quickly.

Hit the highway for no shortage of mountain vistas.

Beaver Meadows

EXPLORE

⬆

S Summer or winter, ranger-guided or solo-led, water or peaks—there's an adventure for everyone in Rocky Mountain National Park.

➜ People have been climbing in the region that's now Rocky Mountain National Park since the 1800s. Its different rock formations allow for alpine, big wall, and snow and ice **climbing**, along with **bouldering** and **mountaineering**. North Ridge of the Spearhead and East Gully on the Sharkstooth are good climbs for new visitors. Expert climbers with winter mountaineering experience will enjoy the Casual Route or the intense Keyhole Route up to Longs Peak.

➜ Book a trip with a park-approved outfitter and enjoy the more than 260 miles of trails open to **horseback riding**. Plenty of horse stables are outside the park, with one, Glacier Creek Stables, inside the park.

➜ **Fish** the alpine lakes and streams for brown, brook, rainbow, and cutthroat trout, along with suckers and sculpin. Just be sure to get a license and follow gear-disinfecting and catch-and-release rules.

➜ **Cycle** the Trail Ridge Road or Old Fall River Road. They're not easy routes for a bicycle, with narrow shoulders and steep drops, but it will be an epic trip.

➜ Head to Hidden Valley for **sledding** and **tubing excursions**. Hidden Valley was built as a ski destination in 1955, but it closed in the 1990s when other spots became more popular. It's not fully abandoned though and remains a great spot for family sledding adventures.

➜ **Cross-country ski** or **snowshoe** along the snow-packed trails in the park during the winter. Most paths work well for snowshoes, but those in the western portion of the park are better for skiing. For some extra guidance, reserve a spot on a ranger-led snowshoe excursion.

➜ Meet at the Upper Beaver Meadows Trailhead for an evening **stargazing program** led by a ranger, or join a family-friendly version at the Moraine Park Discovery Center. Check the calendar to make a plan.

Ranger Program

→ RANGER RECOMMENDATION ←

*Explore **Bierstadt Lake**, an alpine lake filled by melting snow and rainwater. Get there by hiking from the trailhead off Bear Lake Road. On calm days, catch views of snowcapped mountains reflecting off the lake—and at any time of year, get great views of the Continental Divide. Take the same trip in the winter with snowshoes.*

Lower Falls on the Yellowstone River

YELLOWSTONE NATIONAL PARK

WYOMING, IDAHO & MONTANA

ESTABLISHED: March 1, 1872

SIZE: 2,221,766 acres

VISITORS CENTERS: The Albright Visitor Center is open year-round, as is the Old Faithful Visitor Education Center. The Canyon Visitor Education Center is open April–October, with the exception of the winter warming hut; the Fishing Bridge Visitor Center, Grant Visitor Center, Norris Geyser Basin Museum, Madison Information Station, and West Thumb Information Station are open June–September; the Museum of the National Park Ranger is open July and August; and the West Yellowstone Visitor Information Center is open January–October.

TRANSPORTATION: No in-park transportation

DOGS ALLOWED: Only in developed areas (campgrounds, roads, and parking lots)

WHEN TO GO: Summer is peak season; spring sees fewer visitors. Fall is spectacular, with mild temperatures and foliage. Oversnow vehicles are required for winter visits.

CONTACT: 307-344-7381; nps.gov/yell
2 Officers Row
Yellowstone National Park, WY 82190

The first national park in the United States, Yellowstone is home to 67 mammal species, 290 waterfalls, 1,800 archaeological sites, and half the world's geysers. The park is an exemplary story of preservation and restoration, from protecting landscapes to reestablishing wildlife populations. Visit Yellowstone to celebrate the park's wonders, which have forever shaped the country and its wild spaces.

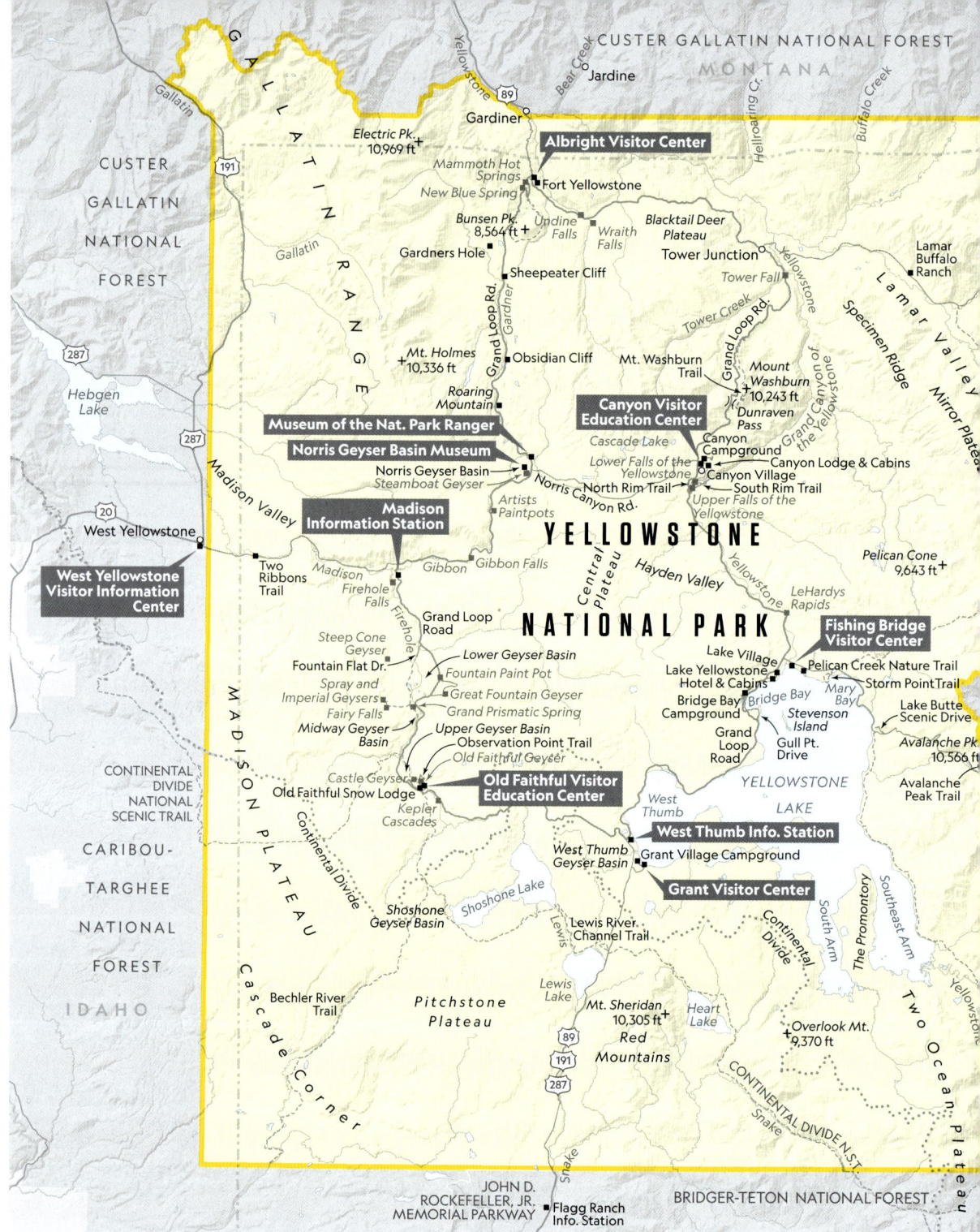

GALLATIN RANGE

CUSTER GALLATIN NATIONAL FOREST

MONTANA

Bear Creek

Jardine

Gallatin

89

Gardiner

CUSTER

GALLATIN

NATIONAL

FOREST

Electric Pk.
10,969 ft

191

Mammoth Hot
Springs
New Blue Spring

Albright Visitor Center

Fort Yellowstone

Hellroaring C.

Buffalo Creek

Bunsen Pk.
8,564 ft

Undine
Falls

Wraith
Falls

Blacktail Deer
Plateau

Lamar
Buffalo
Ranch

287

Gardners Hole

Sheepeater Cliff

Tower Junction

Yellowstone

Lamar Valley

Hebgen
Lake

Gallatin

287

Mt. Holmes
10,336 ft

Obsidian Cliff

Tower Fall

Tower Creek

Mt. Washburn
Trail

Grand Loop Rd.

Mount
Washburn
10,243 ft

Dunraven
Pass

Specimen Ridge

Mirror Plateau

Roaring
Mountain

Museum of the Nat. Park Ranger

Norris Geyser Basin Museum

Norris Geyser Basin
Steamboat Geyser

Madison Valley

**Madison
Information Station**

Gardner

Grand Loop Rd.

Cascade Lake

Lower Falls of the
Yellowstone

Norris Canyon Rd.

North Rim Trail

Artists
Paintpots

**Canyon Visitor
Education Center**

Canyon
Campground

Canyon Lodge & Cabins

Canyon Village

South Rim Trail

Upper Falls of the
Yellowstone

Grand Canyon of the Yellowstone

20

West Yellowstone

**West Yellowstone
Visitor Information
Center**

Two
Ribbons
Trail

Madison

Firehole
Falls

Gibbon

Gibbon Falls

Central Plateau

Hayden Valley

Yellowstone

Pelican Cone
9,643 ft

LeHardys
Rapids

YELLOWSTONE

NATIONAL PARK

**Fishing Bridge
Visitor Center**

Steep Cone
Geyser

Grand Loop
Road

Firehole

Lower Geyser Basin

Fountain Paint Pot

Fountain Flat Dr.

Spray and
Imperial Geysers

Great Fountain Geyser

Lake Village

Lake Yellowstone
Hotel & Cabins

Pelican Creek Nature Trail

Mary
Bay

Storm Point Trail

MADISON PLATEAU

Fairy Falls

Midway Geyser
Basin

Grand Prismatic Spring

Upper Geyser Basin

Observation Point Trail

Old Faithful Geyser

Bridge Bay
Campground

Bridge Bay

Stevenson
Island

Grand
Loop
Road

Gull Pt.
Drive

Lake Butte
Scenic Drive

Avalanche Pk.
10,566 ft

CONTINENTAL
DIVIDE
NATIONAL
SCENIC TRAIL

Continental Divide

Castle Geyser

Old Faithful Snow Lodge

Kepler
Cascades

**Old Faithful Visitor
Education Center**

West
Thumb

**YELLOWSTONE
LAKE**

Avalanche
Peak Trail

CARIBOU-

TARGHEE

NATIONAL

FOREST

IDAHO

Cascade Corner

West Thumb Info. Station

West Thumb
Geyser Basin

Grant Village Campground

Grant Visitor Center

South Arm

Continental Divide

The Promontory

Southeast Arm

Yellowstone

Two Ocean Plateau

Shoshone
Geyser Basin

Shoshone Lake

Lewis River
Channel Trail

Lewis

Bechler River
Trail

Pitchstone
Plateau

Lewis
Lake

89

191

287

Mt. Sheridan
10,305 ft

Red
Mountains

Heart
Lake

Overlook Mt.
9,370 ft

CONTINENTAL DIVIDE N.S.T.

Snake

BRIDGER-TETON NATIONAL FOREST

JOHN D.
ROCKEFELLER, JR.
MEMORIAL PARKWAY

Flagg Ranch
Info. Station

Lake Yellowstone Hotel

SLEEP

(Y) You have a range of options for spending the night in the park, from modern lodges to backcountry sites. No matter where you stay, you need to book ahead.

→ There are **293 maintained backcountry campsites** in the park. Most routes to them require river crossings, and you'll need a permit before you camp. For peak season, permits are given first to early-access lottery entrants, then to those who book in advance during the general on-sale period. Walk-ups are accepted up to two days before a trip when available. Off peak, permits can be obtained online or in person no more than two days in advance of your trip.

→ The park maintains **12 reservable campgrounds**, and all of the more than 2,000 sites get booked far in advance. Bridge Bay Campground sits at an elevation of 7,800 feet near Yellowstone Lake. Canyon Campground is just a bit higher and offers views of the canyon at Yellowstone River. Grant Village Campground is perfect for anyone who prefers more amenities, since it's close to stores, a restaurant, and a visitors center. Check for operational hours, as many are closed for the winter season.

→ **Nine lodges** are within the park. The large Canyon Lodge and Cabins has more than 400 guest rooms and 100 cabins. The suites at Lake Yellowstone Hotel & Cabins offer classic luxury. Old Faithful Snow Lodge is the only one open in winter; book a hotel-style room or a cabin.

○ **Must-Do Hike**

Ⓜ Many people drive through the massive park to get from sight to sight. If you get out of the car and start to explore, however, you'll be treated to views you can't see from the road.

➜ *Fairy Falls is such a popular sight that there are two trailheads to lead you to them—either from the Fairy Falls Parking Lot or the end of Fountain Flat Drive. Either way, you'll travel 1.6 miles to the 200-foot cascade. Continue a little more than a half mile farther to see Spray and Imperial Geysers.*

➜ *While a bit of Lower Falls is visible from the nearby parking lot in Canyon Village, hiking the steep 0.4-mile* **Brink of the Lower Falls Trail** *will bring you closer to the action. Take a short spur from the trail to see the Upper Falls.*

➜ *Head out on the one-mile* **Pelican Creek Nature Trail**, *which leads you through forest and to the shore of Yellowstone Lake, then back again. The easy hike is great for bird-watchers.*

➜ *Make your way from Dunraven Pass on the* **Mount Washburn Trail**. *The route is challenging and shouldn't be attempted in fall or winter when it's slick or snow-covered. Look for bighorn sheep as you tackle the switchbacks on the 4.5-mile trail. You may encounter bears along the route, so be prepared with bear spray.*

➜ *Travel along the Madison River, through its fields, meadows, and conifer forest, on the* **Two Ribbons Trail**. *Interpretive signs along the 1.7-mile boardwalk loop explain the ecology of the region.*

➜ *Hike through the open meadows that look over Indian Pond and Yellowstone Lake when you set out on the* **Storm Point Trail**. *At the scenic point, you may encounter a crew of yellow-bellied marmots.*

➜ *The challenging 2.1-mile* **Avalanche Peak Trail** *takes a serious amount of work but comes with unmatched views across the park's snowcapped peaks. Bring rain gear and look out for falling burned trees and grizzly bears.*

➜ *Get major rewards for a relatively easy effort on the* **South Rim Trail**, *which follows the Grand Canyon of the Yellowstone and the Yellowstone River. Pass some major viewpoints along the way: Upper Falls, Lower Falls, and Artist Point.*

➜ *Take the* **Observation Point Trail** *from the Old Faithful Visitor Education Center. Travel half a mile up a series of switchbacks to a clear view of the Upper Geyser Basin, then return back the same way.*

HIKE

Racing waters cascade from Lower Falls

A bison grazes beside Mary Bay.

→ SPOT

P People flock to Yellowstone to spot bears, bison, and other iconic wildlife. They're all there, but it's important to keep your distance, even if the animals don't.

→ After visiting the Old Faithful Geyser, drive north on Grand Loop Road and keep an eye out for wandering **bison**; the park has a population of 3,000 to 6,000, so your chances of spotting them are high.

→ Along with the bison that live year-round in Hayden Valley, find **trumpeter swans**, **white pelicans**, **Canada geese**, and **river otters** in the expansive space. You might also spot **coyotes** and **bears**.

→ The Trout Lake Trail, about 1.5 miles south of Pebble Creek Campground, is a good route to look for **fish**, **otters**, **bison**, and other critters.

→ If you're on the lookout for **wolves**, head to Lamar Valley. Keep an eye out for **bison**, **pronghorn sheep**, **badgers**, **grizzly bears**, **bald eagles**, and **coyotes**. There are pullouts along Northeast Entrance Road, which travels through the valley.

→ Bring binoculars on all your hikes to look for some of the **19 species of raptors** that breed in Yellowstone—there are even more during migration season (late August–early October).

→ Many visitors search for **bears** as they drive through Yellowstone, and you are likely to spot some in the meadows along the road. If you do, park in a pullout, stay in your car, and drive away if one approaches you.

Dawn and dusk offer the best chance for wolf sightings.

A great gray owl hunts in the snowfall.

FLOAT

G Get a new perspective on the park by seeing it from the water, whether on a guided boat tour on the biggest lake in Yellowstone or paddling the park's river system. Here are two worthwhile options:

→ *It's possible to get out on **Yellowstone Lake** in your own boat, but you'll have to follow careful guidelines around invasive species and manage dangerous conditions. A safer and simpler choice is to book a tour through one of the Yellowstone lodges, which offer scenic lake tours, boat rentals, and boat shuttles to backcountry campsites.*

→ *Paddle the **Lewis River** and explore **Shoshone Geyser Basin**. With a guide, even beginners can tackle this trip. You can turn it into an overnight excursion at one of the backcountry sites along the way. Just prepare for mosquitoes.*

You'll also find paddling options on Lewis Lake.

Visitors can fish Yellowstone Lake from motorboats.

G **Grand Loop Road** is the one most visitors use to see Yellowstone—either on their own or with a tour. Take the East Entrance Road to the Fishing Bridge Visitor Center to get started. Begin by driving south and stopping at Lake Village (with a picnic area, general store, and Yellowstone Lake views), the West Thumb Geyser Basin (the largest geyser basin on the shore of Yellowstone Lake), Kepler Cascades (viewable from a pullout), and the world-famous Old Faithful Geyser, which erupts about every 90 minutes. From there, stretch your legs on the paths and boardwalks of the three-mile round-trip Upper Geyser Basin Trail for its many geysers and spur trails. Head up the western side of the loop to find Gibbon Falls, the short trail to Artists Paintpots (a hydrothermal area of colorful hot springs), and the Norris Geyser Basin Museum, a national historic landmark. If you continue along the full loop, check out the views of Roaring Mountain, Obsidian Cliff, the geysers around the Mammoth and Albright Visitor Centers, Undine and Wraith Falls, Tower Fall, and LeHardys Rapids, a steplike cascade marking the end of the Yellowstone River.

A few other routes are also worth taking:

→ *Take the short detour off the western portion of Grand Loop toward the* **Firehole River**, *with its falls and canyon. Or take the* **North Rim Drive** *detour on the west side to see Grandview and Lookout Points—get out of the car for the short trail to Lower Falls, which tumbles 308 feet and is the park's largest cascade.*
→ *Drive the highest road in the park,* **Dunraven Pass**, *an offshoot of the Grand Loop Road between Tower Roosevelt and Canyon Junctions. Get out of the car at the Dunraven Pass parking lot to tackle the difficult, switchback-filled* **Mount Washburn Trail**, *which offers spectacular views amid wildflowers and possible grizzly sightings (bring bear spray).*
→ *Drive into the park on East Entrance Road and don't miss the one-mile* **Lake Butte Scenic Drive**, *which ends at an overlook of the lake.*

DRIVE

Castle Geyser steams near the Firehole River.

Great Fountain Geyser at Lower Geyser Basin

A hot spring in Norris Geyser Basin

Mammoth Hot Springs

Lamar Buffalo Ranch

→ EXPLORE

 Yellowstone is a park like no other, and that brings with it opportunities to participate in activities and excursions you won't find anywhere else.

→ A trip to Yellowstone wouldn't be complete without seeing some of the **500-plus active geysers** in the park. Before you head out, it's a good idea to check the geyser activity online, on the National Park System app, or at a visitors center. Nearly everyone sees Old Faithful on their trip, and you should too. Also stop at Norris Geyser Basin, the oldest and hottest in the park. Stop by Midway Geyser Basin to see the colorful thermophiles around the bright blue water. Steamboat Geyser is the tallest in the park. Learn about the connection between hot springs and geysers at the Lion Geyser Complex.

→ Visit the trailside **Norris Geyser Basin Museum**, which focuses on the natural history of Yellowstone, and the **Museum of the National Park Ranger**, which celebrates the history of the men and women who have spent their lives protecting these special places.

→ Along with geysers, the park is home to more than 10,000 geothermal features. Walk the boardwalks around **Mammoth Hot Springs**, a network of fractures and fissures that change throughout the day. Visit **New Blue Spring** and its travertine terraces, and **Canary Spring**, which runs down orange terraces given color by sulfur-dependent bacteria.

→ At Mammoth Hot Springs, take the time to tour historic **Fort Yellowstone**. Between the 1890s and early 1900s, the U.S. Army managed and protected the park, and the buildings from that time are still standing.

→ Visit **Lamar Buffalo Ranch**, a site of major conservation success in the park. As the bison population dwindled down to only 25 in 1901, the government added to the herd and managed them in Lamar Valley. Once the animals grew, they were released into the park. Today the population numbers in the thousands.

→ Bring your **bike** to see the park's sights on two wheels. Try the challenging 10-mile Bunsen Peak Road around the peak, or follow the Firehole River on the Lone Star Geyser Trail to the geyser. Hop on the Natural Bridge Bike Trail for a shorter route on an old, paved road.

→ Head to Yellowstone in the winter to travel the miles of trails open to **skiers** and **snowshoers**. Try the **Canyon Rim Ski Trail** to go through a forest or **Cascade Lake Ski Trail** to see the frozen lake and meadows.

→ Park visitors have been **fishing** in Yellowstone for more than a century, and the park supports the practice as a way to preserve native species. Regulations allow for catching brook, brown, lake, and rainbow trout.

Must-Do Activity

RANGER RECOMMENDATION

Visit **West Thumb Geyser Basin**, where historic expeditions took place and visitors often arrived via stagecoach. This area of Yellowstone Lake was formed by a volcanic explosion 150,000 years ago and is about the same size as Crater Lake in Oregon (page 548). Walk the boardwalk that weaves around the basin and see all its pools and hydrothermal features to learn about the underwater geysers that create slick spots in the summer or melt holes in the lake's icy surface in the winter.

→ PACIFIC SOUTHWEST

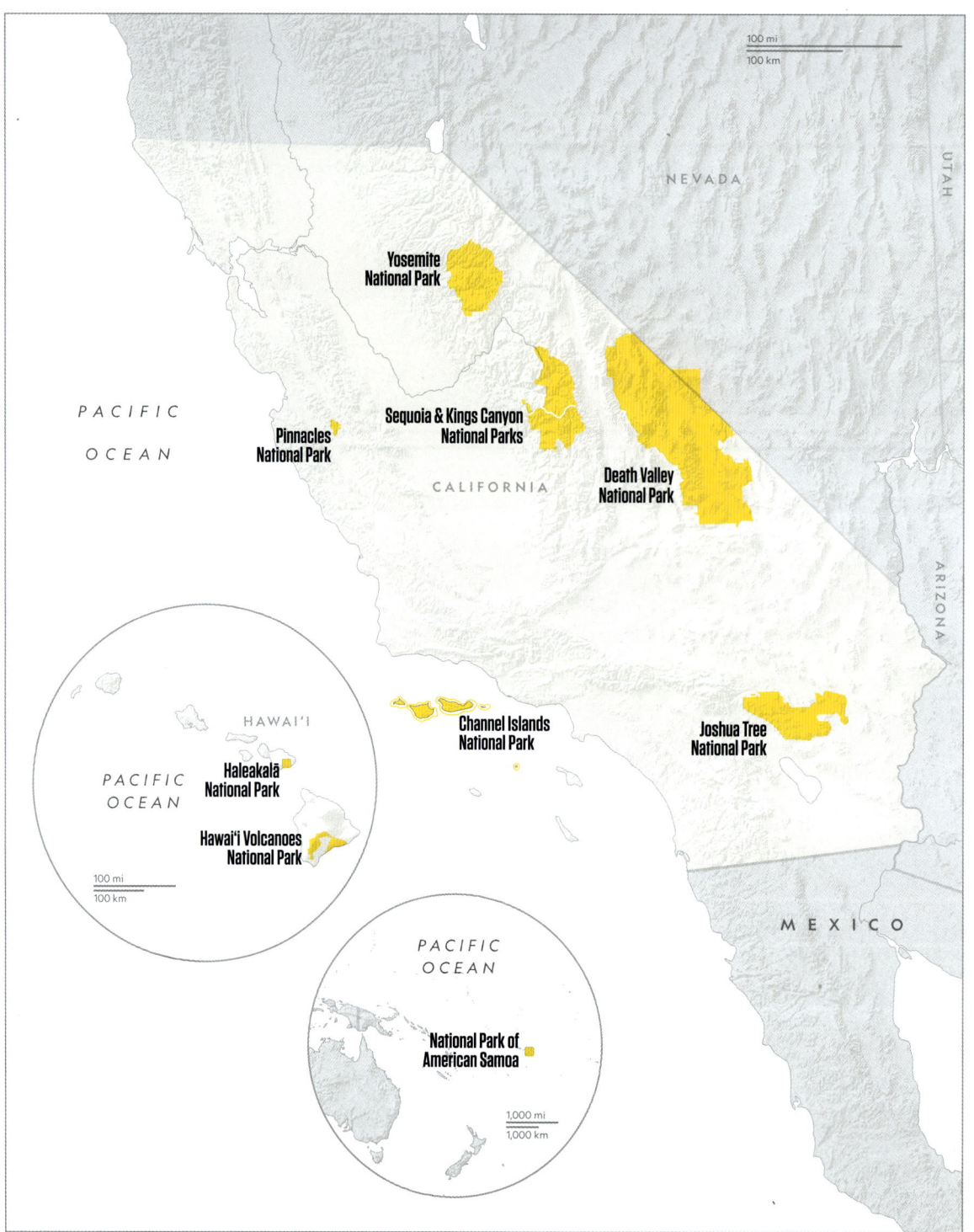

100 mi
100 km

NEVADA

UTAH

Yosemite
National Park

PACIFIC

OCEAN

Pinnacles
National Park

Sequoia & Kings Canyon
National Parks

CALIFORNIA

Death Valley
National Park

ARIZONA

HAWAI'I

Channel Islands
National Park

Joshua Tree
National Park

PACIFIC
OCEAN

Haleakalā
National Park

Hawai'i Volcanoes
National Park

100 mi
100 km

MEXICO

PACIFIC
OCEAN

National Park of
American Samoa

1,000 mi
1,000 km

These nine national parks range from tropical idylls to snow-capped peaks. Haleakalā (page 478) and Hawai'i Volcanoes (page 490) protect endemic plants and geological history. Nearly 3,000 miles away, American Samoa (page 452) shelters reefs and rainforests, while off the coast of California, Channel Islands (page 460) safeguards seals, sea lions, and sea birds. Sequoia & Kings Canyon (page 520) and Yosemite (page 530) protect the Sierra Nevada range, while Pinnacles (page 512) provides a successful conservation example in the California condors that soar the skies. To the south, Joshua Tree (page 502) and Death Valley (page 468) offer two desert perspectives.

LEFT: Echo-Titus Circuit in Death Valley National Park (page 468) **PREVIOUS PAGES:** Yosemite Falls, Yosemite National Park (page 530)

NATIONAL PARK OF **AMERICAN SAMOA**

AMERICAN SAMOA

ESTABLISHED: October 31, 1988

SIZE: 13,500 acres

VISITORS CENTER: The visitors center in Pago Pago on Tutuila is open year-round and has educational exhibits and resources for your trip.

TRANSPORTATION: No in-park transportation

DOGS ALLOWED: No

WHEN TO GO: June–September is dry season and best for hiking, snorkeling, and swimming. October–May is rainy with the chance of tropical storms.

CONTACT: 684-633-7082 ext. 22; nps.gov/npsa
MHJ Building, Second Floor
Pago Pago, AS 96799

The captuline of American Samoa at dawn
The coastline of American Samoa at dawn

T The National Park of American Samoa is a tale of celebration and exploration. It's lush, green, and gorgeous. The three volcanic islands that make up the park are covered almost entirely in tropical rainforests, from the peaks to the shorelines. And then there's more to discover beneath the waves in the protected, colorful coral reefs. The park celebrates the traditions and beliefs of the Samoan people, who have called this space sacred for more than 3,000 years.

Respect the local culture while you're there: Always ask before taking a photograph of someone; note that swimming and other activities are not permitted on Sundays, which are considered sacred; and dress modestly.

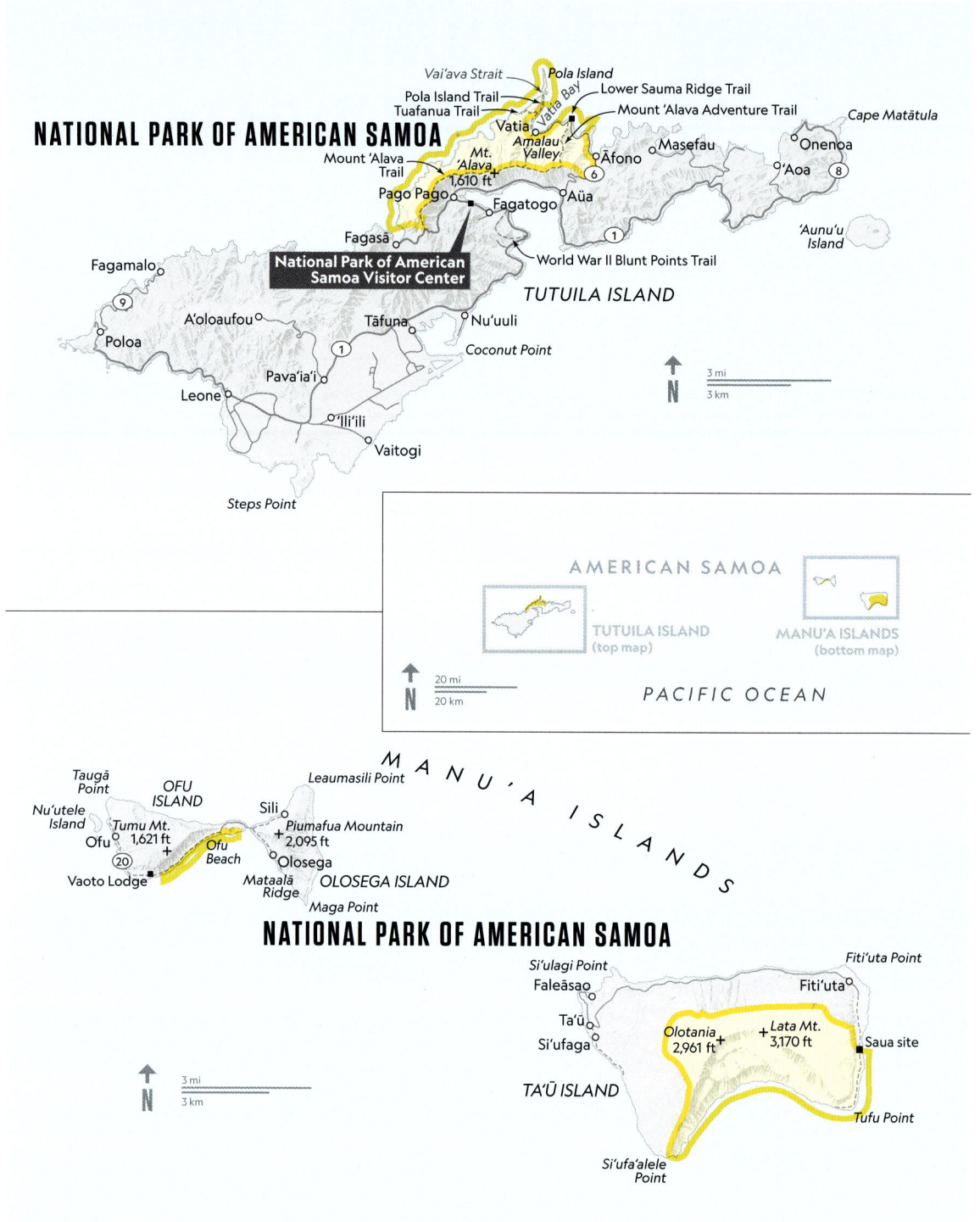

NATIONAL PARK OF AMERICAN SAMOA

Vai'ava Strait

Pola Island

Pola Island Trail

Lower Sauma Ridge Trail

Tuafanua Trail

Mount 'Alava Adventure Trail

Vatia

Vatia Bay

Amalau Valley

Cape Matātula

Mount 'Alava Trail

Mt. 'Alava 1,610 ft

Āfono

Masefau

Onenoa

'Aoa

Pago Pago

Aūa

6

Fagatogo

8

Fagasā

National Park of American Samoa Visitor Center

World War II Blunt Points Trail

'Aunu'u Island

TUTUILA ISLAND

Fagamalo

1

9

A'oloaufou

Tāfuna

Nu'uuli

Coconut Point

Poloa

1

Pava'ia'i

N

3 mi

3 km

Leone

'Ili'ili

Vaitogi

Steps Point

AMERICAN SAMOA

TUTUILA ISLAND (top map)

MANU'A ISLANDS (bottom map)

N

20 mi

20 km

PACIFIC OCEAN

M A N U ' A   I S L A N D S

Taugā Point

OFU ISLAND

Leaumasili Point

Nu'utele Island

Sili

Ofu

Tumu Mt. 1,621 ft

Piumafua Mountain 2,095 ft

20

Ofu Beach

Olosega

Vaoto Lodge

Mataalā Ridge

OLOSEGA ISLAND

Maga Point

NATIONAL PARK OF AMERICAN SAMOA

N

3 mi

3 km

Si'ulagi Point

Fiti'uta Point

Faleāsao

Fiti'uta

Ta'ū

Si'ufaga

Olotania 2,961 ft

Lata Mt. 3,170 ft

Saua site

TA'Ū ISLAND

Tufu Point

Si'ufa'alele Point

Tutuila's picturesque coastline

SLEEP

 Your best bet for lodging is to book a resort or hotel on the southern side of Tutuila Island, the main island of American Samoa. On Ofu, there's one option: **Vaoto Lodge**; ask for a room that catches the wind and doesn't run hot. Camping is prohibited in the park. On Taʻū, there are only homestay options.

Island houses in Pago Pago on Tutuila Island

Explore Taʻū Island.

HIKE

(T) There are 10 official day hikes on Tutuila and three on the Manuʻa Islands (Taʻū, Ofu, and Olosega). Each one merges the history of the land and its communities, from the impacts of war to the vegetation of the rainforest.

→ The very short **Pola Island Trail** on Tutuila is the only hike in the park ranked as easy by the Park Service. It's a 0.6-mile out-and-back route that's relatively flat and leads to a rocky beach with views of the coastline.

→ Reach the park's volcanic summit on Tutuila after hiking through a rainforest filled with bats and birds on the **Mount ʻAlava Trail**. Heighten the challenge even more by traversing the **Mount ʻAlava Adventure Trail**, which will take you along the ridgelines and up and down 783 rope-assisted steps.

→ Begin at the northern edge of the Amalau Valley on Tutuila and hike the short **Lower Sauma Ridge Trail** to the archaeological site of an early settlement, including house foundations and stone tools. Learn more about the region and its people through the exhibits along the way.

→ On the island of Taʻū, considered the birthplace of Polynesia, is the ancient village of **Saua**, one of the most sacred sites in the park. Reach its wells, mounds, and early architectural features from the main road in Fitiʻuta. Once the road gives way to a dirt path, follow it through the coastal fort to the southeastern tip of the island. The village of Saua sits along the way.

Must-Do Hike

Family Friendly

(Y) You won't find much in the way of wildlife on land in the park, but you'll have good luck if you look to the skies and the seas. Keep an ear out for birds as you trek, and reserve a guided boat trip to find aquatic creatures while snorkeling or scuba diving.

→ Follow the shoulder between Mataalā Ridge and Maga Point on the Manuʻa Islands to spot **boobies** and **frigate birds**. Look for **petrels** and **shearwaters** as they fly along the sea.

→ Listen to tropical birds as you walk the historical World War II Blunt Points Trail. Spot **honeyeaters**, **tropical doves** and **pigeons**, **cardinals**, and **Samoan starlings** along your hike.

→ Head to the waters around the islands in September and October to see **migrating humpback whales**. The migrating and breeding whales are strongly protected by both local and federal governments. Book a boat trip and keep your distance.

→ On land, you might be able to spot one of three species of **bats** that live on the island—the only land mammals native to the islands. You also might see **geckos**, **skinks**, and **toads** as you hike.

A bristle-thighed curlew

SPOT

Pink cauliflower coral and damselfish

FLOAT

I In American Samoa, it's less about getting on a boat and more about getting in the water. Get out to the coral reefs if you can.

➜ Head to the park's smaller islands, **Ofu** and **Olosega**, for the best snorkeling and scuba diving. Fly to the island of Ta'ū and then hire a local fisher to take you across to the islands in their boat. Bring your own gear and jump in to see more than **950 species of fish** (including atule, damselfish, parrotfish, surgeonfish, and wrasse) and **250 species of coral**.

➜ Swim at **Ofu Beach**—its soft sand and blue waters have earned it the accolade "best beach in the park" by many. You might even get lucky and spot a whale from your beach blanket.

Y You can dig more deeply into the park by discovering its history, both human and natural. Just remember, it can be hard to know exactly where the park ends and the rest of the island begins, so take care to be respectful of village and private lands.

➜ Spend some time at the park's **visitors center** to learn about its tropical rainforests, coral reefs, and endemic fruit bats as well as Samoan life past and present.

➜ **Fishing** in American Samoa is a protected activity that is allowed only for customary and traditional uses. Staff at the park can help you connect with a permissible experience and facilitate the permission you need from a local village.

➜ Jump into the water at **Vatia Bay**, where a small community lives along a sandy beach. The park surrounds the bay and village, and you can reach it by Route 6. While there, take the time to explore the concrete bunkers from World War II that remain on the beach.

Western Tutuila offers a view into American Samoa's history, including defensive fortifications in Poloa.

EXPLORE

Sunset Cliffs on Anacapa Island

CHANNEL ISLANDS NATIONAL PARK

CALIFORNIA

ESTABLISHED: March 5, 1980

SIZE: 249,500 acres

VISITORS CENTERS: The Robert J. Lagomarsino Visitor Center in Ventura provides the most comprehensive park info as well as a marine life display and park exhibits. The Outdoors Santa Barbara Visitor Center has great views and park information. There are also small inland visitors centers on Santa Barbara and Anacapa Islands, along with Scorpion Ranch on Santa Cruz Island. All are open year-round.

TRANSPORTATION: Island Packers Cruises is the park's official boat concessionaire.

DOGS ALLOWED: No

WHEN TO GO: Summer for getting in the water and whale-watching; fall for bird migrations; winter for gray whales and elephant seals; spring for wildflowers

---

CONTACT: 805-658-5730; nps.gov/chis
1901 Spinnaker Drive
Ventura, CA 93001

W While the Channel Islands are right off the coast of California, they're far removed from the bustling cities along the shoreline. These remote, protected spaces are home to remarkable wildlife populations, immense biological diversity, and unique archaeological sites. The five islands are fragile and rugged, and some of the least visited national park locations in the country. If you're willing to make the effort to explore these islands, you'll share waters with humpback whales and camp amid the sound of crashing waves.

SANTA BARBARA CHANNEL

CHANNEL ISLANDS
NATIONAL MARINE
SANCTUARY

CHANNEL ISLANDS NATIONAL PARK

West Point

Harris Point

Cuyler Harbor

San Miguel Island
Campground

Lester Ranch site
Caliche Forest

Point
Bennett

Tyler
Bight

San Miguel Hill
831 ft

Crook Pt.

SAN MIGUEL
ISLAND

San Miguel Passage

Sandy
Point

Lobo Canyon Trail

Carrington
Point

Santa Cruz Channel

Mt. Diablo
2,450 ft

Pelican Bay

Prisoners Harbor

Del Norte campground

NPS
property

Water
Canyon
Beach

Bechers
Bay

Vail & Vickers Cattle Ranch
Water Canyon Campground

Black Mt.
1,298 ft

Telephone Rd.

Torrey
Pines

Skunk Pt.

The Nature Conservancy property

SANTA ROSA
ISLAND

Soledad Pk.
1,574 ft

East Point

Morse
Point

SANTA CRUZ
ISLAND

Johnsons
Lee

South
Point

CHANNEL ISLANDS NATIONAL MARINE SANCTUARY

PACIFIC OCEAN

N

10 mi

10 km

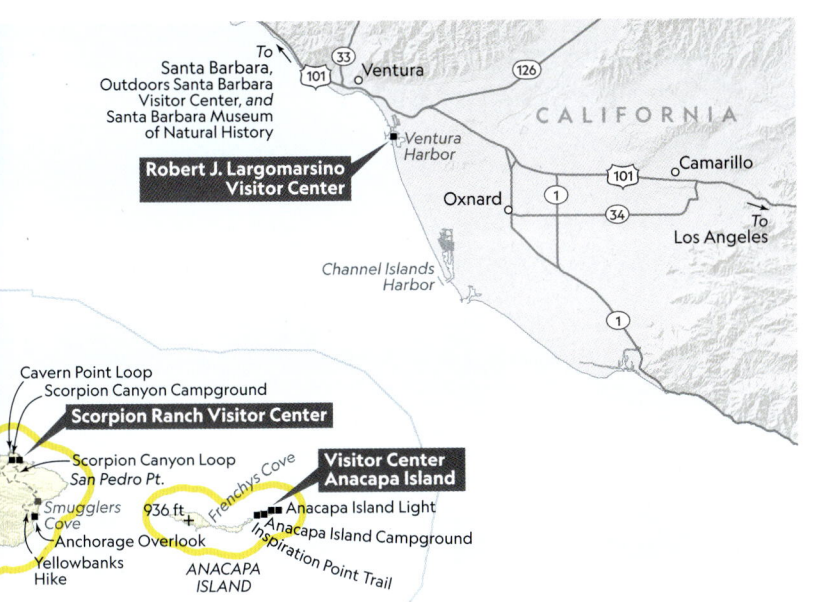

Campsites on the islands come with picnic tables.

SLEEP

(E) Each of the five islands has one established campground (open year-round, tent only) and reservations are required at all: **Anacapa** (7 sites), **eastern Santa Cruz** (31 sites, potable water), **Santa Rosa** (15 sites, potable water), **San Miguel** (9 sites), and **Santa Barbara** (10 sites). No camping is allowed on the western side of Santa Cruz, which is property of the Nature Conservancy. There are no services at the campgrounds, so pack everything you need and be able to carry it from the landing to the campground.

Find backcountry camping on Santa Cruz at the **Del Norte backcountry campground** (near Prisoner's Harbor) or **beach camping** on Santa Rosa. Advanced reservations for permits are required and can be made by phone or online. For help with coordination, book the **Santa Rosa Basecamp Adventure** from Nomadic by Nature, which will handle coordinating boat trips, hiking, camping, and sightseeing.

 # HIKE

Ranger Required

Ⓣ The only way around the islands is by foot. Organize your itinerary by island and then pick your hikes.

On Anacapa:

→ Follow the 1.5-mile round-trip **Inspiration Point Trail** to one of the park's best views. Stop along the hike at Pinniped Point for its historic lighthouse, Eastern Terrace Overlook (where the park's first lighthouse was constructed in 1912), and Cathedral Cove, where you might spot harbor seals and sea lions.

On Santa Rosa:

→ The two-mile walk along white-sand **Water Canyon Beach** is perfect for bird-watching and seashell-spotting. If you head out from the Becher's Bay Pier, it's a three-mile walk round-trip.

→ Wind along the challenging 9.6-mile round-trip **Lobo Canyon Trail** to see the honeycomb-like tafoni (geological formations created by erosion).

On Santa Barbara:

→ The **Arch Point Hike** (1 mile) is best for springtime wildflowers, the difficult **Elephant Seal Cove Trail** (2.5 miles) is great for spotting creatures, and the **Sea Lion Rookery Overlook Hike** (2 miles) has a wildlife-focused viewpoint.

On San Miguel:

→ Discover the park's sheep ranching history at the now destroyed **Lester Ranch**, a short walk from the visitors center. The ranch, constructed in 1906, was the largest ranch house on the island. It burned down in 1967.

→ **Point Bennett** is accessible only with the guidance of a ranger, since unexploded ordnance still remain from the island's days as a former bombing range. Make a point to stop by the Caliche Forest for its otherworldly calcified ancient vegetation.

On Santa Cruz:

→ Whale-watching and coastal vistas have made the moderate **Cavern Point Loop** one of the park's most popular hikes. Start at the campground and work your way clockwise to avoid a steep climb. In total the hike is two miles round-trip.

→ Book with Island Packers Cruises for a guided four-mile hike in **Pelican Bay** with sweeping Pacific views and great bird-watching.

Ⓣ The substantial and steady protection of the Channel Islands and the waters around them have provided a space for wildlife to thrive.

→ The park's protected areas are a breeding ground for **California sea lions**, **northern fur seals**, **harbor seals**, and **northern elephant seals**. San Miguel is your best bet for seeing the most variety, and Point Bennett is a great starting point—just prepare for the 15-mile hike. Visit in June to see babies.

→ Channel Islands is renowned for its bird-watching. Split your trip into two for the best experience: First, stay on your boat to view **seabirds** and **shorebirds**, then head inland to find some of the 40 species of land birds, including the endemic **island scrub jay**.

→ Look for **western gulls** in the rocks along the coast of the islands, particularly on Anacapa, where the largest protected breeding colony lives. Try a May or June visit to see recently hatched chicks.

→ Anacapa and Santa Barbara are the only places in the western U.S. where **California brown pelicans** breed, though they also roost in Santa Cruz. See them by boat.

→ The Elephant Seal Cove Overlook, a 2.5-mile sojourn along the Santa Barbara shoreline, puts hikers in view of **elephant seal** feeding grounds. The island's kelp forests are in jeopardy but still provide protection for the loud marine creatures.

→ **Twenty-seven whale species** have been spotted in the waters around the islands. Find them frequently in the Santa Barbara Channel feeding area, designated a national marine sanctuary.

→ Peer into the well-protected tide pools along Frenchys Cove on Anacapa, Smugglers Cove on Santa Cruz, East Point on Santa Rosa, and eastern Cuyler Harbor on San Miguel to see **anemones**, **sea stars**, **urchins**, **barnacles**, and more.

Family Friendly

SPOT

A dive vessel floats over a kelp forest near Anacapa Island.

FLOAT

W Water is queen in Channel Islands, which makes boating and paddling adventures royalty.

→ Join a tour on a luxury 85-foot catamaran with the **Santa Barbara Sailing Center**. Group offerings include sunset cruises, whale-watching sails, and even New Year's Eve and Valentine's Day itineraries. Private charters are also available, where you are guided to coves and sea caves and can kayak, paddleboard, and more.

→ **National Geographic Expeditions** offers a Wild California Escape itinerary. From your ship, Zodiac boats take you to explore the national park, kayak its waters, and hike its pristine beaches. Trips are five days, departing from Los Angeles. Or opt for the 12-day voyage from the Channel Islands to Baja California.

→ Bring your own **kayak** to paddle-friendly Santa Barbara, where you can self-explore the wildlife-filled waters. Or book a guided trip with an outfitter that can take you to its popular Scorpion beach area, known for its sea caves, beach access, and camping spots.

T There's more excitement to be had on the islands if you expand beyond hiking and paddling. Try one of these:

→ Learn more about the archaeology of **Santa Rosa**, where paleontologists discovered a pygmy mammoth in 1994 and archaeologists excavated the site of the Arlington Springs Man, who lived around 13,000 years ago. Exhibits of both are displayed inland at the **Santa Barbara Museum of Natural History**.

→ If you're more into flora than fauna, head to Santa Barbara, Anacapa, and San Miguel from the end of winter through spring to see the islands' **peak wildflower blooms**. Together, the islands are home to more than 800 plant species.

→ Visit Santa Rosa's **Vail & Vickers Cattle Ranch**, where cattle were raised from the early 1900s through 1998, when the Park Service facilitated a final roundup. Today, the site has a historic bunkhouse, barn, and schoolhouse.

→ Book a private boat and **surf the waters** of Santa Cruz, Santa Rosa, and San Miguel Islands. Ride the waves on the north shore in winter and spring and the south shore in the summer and fall.

→ Get closer to marine wildlife by going underwater. Book a **snorkeling** or **diving** trip with an outfitter and explore the kelp forests, sea caves, and coves. Stick to Santa Barbara, Anacapa, and eastern Santa Cruz unless you're a serious expert.

The Channel Island tree poppy, discovered on Anacapa Island

EXPLORE

Experts Only

RANGER RECOMMENDATION

Hike to Santa Rosa Island's **Lobo Canyon**, *where light dances through the rock wall's contours, until you eventually end up at the Pacific Ocean. This strenuous 9.6-mile hike is truly a one-of-a-kind experience. The remote island is the site of wild paleontological resources and a rich web of marine life.*

Salt pan polygons at Badwater Basin

DEATH VALLEY NATIONAL PARK

CALIFORNIA

ESTABLISHED: October 31, 1994

SIZE: 3,422,024 acres

VISITORS CENTERS: The year-round Furnace Creek Visitor Center offers museum exhibits, a bookstore with food for purchase, and knowledgeable rangers.

TRANSPORTATION: No in-park transportation

DOGS ALLOWED: Only in developed areas; dogs are not allowed on trails.

WHEN TO GO: Visit November–May for the easiest weather and most open amenities.

CONTACT: 760-786-3200; nps.gov/deva
PO Box 579
Death Valley, CA 92328

D Death Valley is as extreme as its name. Its basin is the lowest spot in North America, there's a consistent drought (the park receives less than two inches of rain a year), and the summer heat is literally deadly—the park holds the world record high temperature of 134°F. Still, some of its peaks are topped with snow, and rare rainstorms sometimes arrive, bringing fields of wildflowers. For a place with such a morose name, there's plenty of life to find if you know where to look.

Enjoy the pool area at the Inn at Death Valley.

Top-Notch
Stay

SLEEP

Nine developed and five primitive campgrounds are in Death Valley. Most are first come, first served, but plan in advance during busy season (October–April).

→ The only campground that accepts reservations, **Furnace Creek** (open year-round) is packed with amenities, including flush toilets, potable water, and a store. It has 136 sites, including ADA sites and 18 sites with electric hookups.

→ **Mesquite Spring** (open year-round) sits at 1,800 feet in elevation and offers access to the northern parts of the park. There are 40 sites but few amenities.

→ **Emigrant** (open year-round) has

10 tent-only sites sitting at 2,100 feet in elevation. The campground looks out over the Panamint Range.

→ **Stovepipe Wells** (open early November–May 15) has the most amenities of all Death Valley campgrounds. There are 190 sites (28 tent-only) here along with those at an adjacent privately operated RV park. You'll have views of Death Valley and the Mesquite Flat Sand Dunes and be near a general store and a ranger station.

→ **Wildrose** has no fee for its 23 sites (open year-round, no hookups available). It's nestled in the Panamint Range at 4,100 feet elevation. Prepare for high winds and few amenities. The trade-off: sunrise views of the surrounding rolling hills.

→ Head to the primitive **Saline Valley** only if you're comfortable with nudity, because this hot spring area and campground is clothing optional. You'll also need a high-clearance vehicle with all-terrain tires to get there. You'll find 15 sites, available year-round.

→ **Backpacking**, **roadside**, and **four-by-four roadside camping** are options in

Death Valley, but all require permits. Most can be secured six months in advance.

If camping isn't your thing, there are plenty of nearby hotels, inns, and ranches.

→ The historic **Inn at Death Valley** has been hosting visitors since 1927. It has a spring-fed swimming pool, a spa, and an old-timey soda fountain and ice cream parlor.

→ **Panamint Springs Resort**, with its western-style motel rooms, cabins, and on-site campground and RV park, has been in business since 1937. It now has a restaurant and bar, gas station, and general store.

→ **The Ranch at Death Valley** was transformed from a working ranch to a family-friendly oasis in 1933. Find a golf course, spring-fed pool, playground, stables, and communal fire pits.

→ The basic **Stovepipe Wells village** has been providing modern comforts for more than 100 years. Accommodations range from a rustic motel to a campground and RV park.

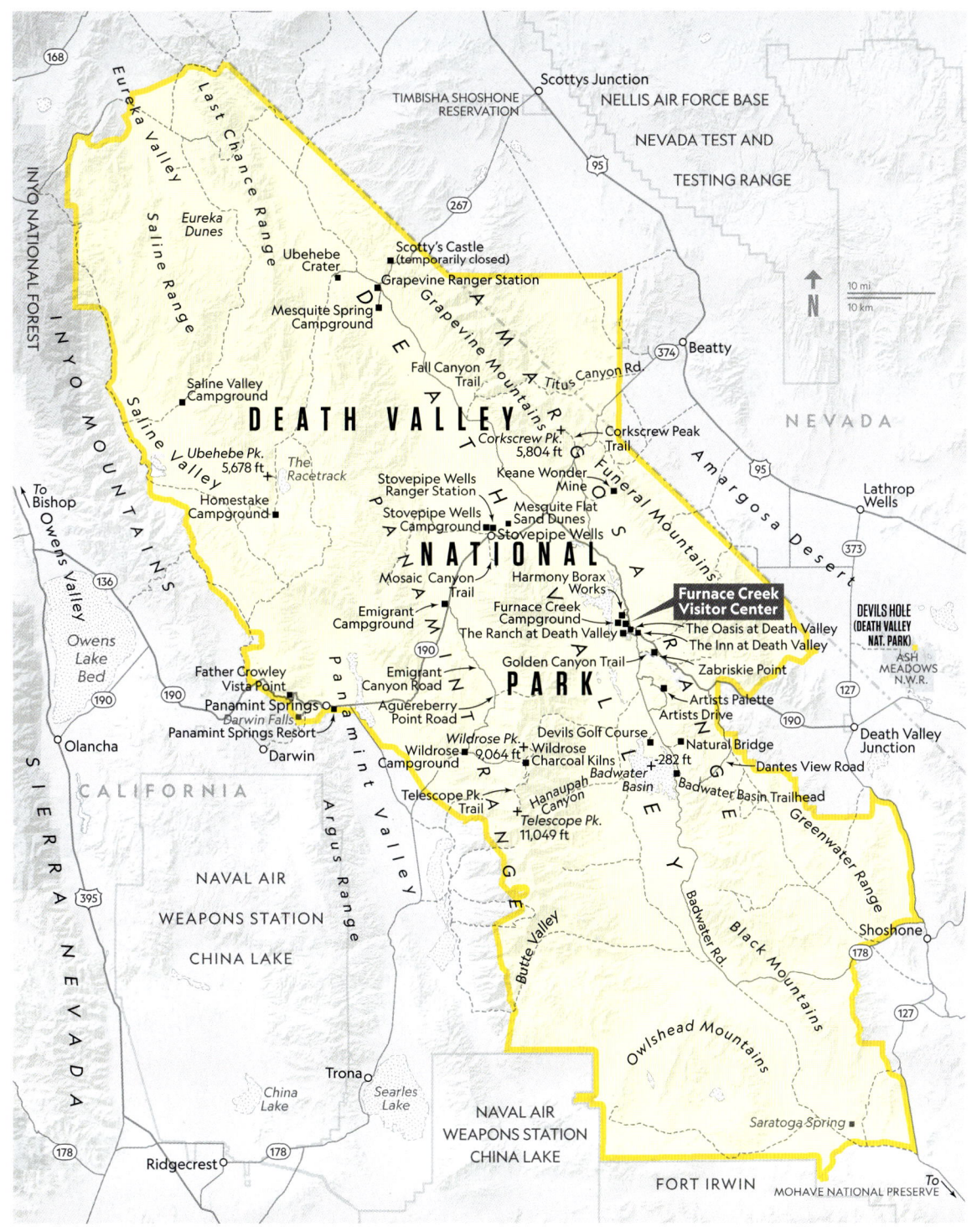

168

Eureka Valley

Last Chance Range

INYO NATIONAL FOREST

Saline Range

Eureka Dunes

Ubehebe Crater

Mesquite Spring Campground

Scotty's Castle (temporarily closed)

Grapevine Ranger Station

TIMBISHA SHOSHONE RESERVATION

Scottys Junction

NELLIS AIR FORCE BASE

NEVADA TEST AND TESTING RANGE

95

267

Beatty

374

Grapevine Mountains

Fall Canyon Trail

Titus Canyon Rd.

Saline Valley Campground

INYO MOUNTAINS

Saline Valley

DEATH VALLEY

Ubehebe Pk. 5,678 ft

The Racetrack

Homestake Campground

To Bishop

Owens Valley

136

Owens Lake Bed

190

190

Olancha

Panamint Springs

Darwin Falls

Panamint Springs Resort

Darwin

CALIFORNIA

395

Corkscrew Pk. 5,804 ft

Corkscrew Peak Trail

Keane Wonder Mine

Stovepipe Wells Ranger Station

Stovepipe Wells Campground

Mosaic Canyon Trail

Emigrant Campground

Mesquite Flat Sand Dunes

Stovepipe Wells

NATIONAL

Harmony Borax Works

Furnace Creek Campground

The Ranch at Death Valley

Golden Canyon Trail

Furnace Creek Visitor Center

The Oasis at Death Valley

The Inn at Death Valley

Zabriskie Point

Funeral Mountains

Amargosa Desert

95

373

Lathrop Wells

DEVILS HOLE (DEATH VALLEY NAT. PARK)

ASH MEADOWS N.W.R.

NEVADA

PANAMINT VALLEY

Argus Range

Emigrant Canyon Road

Aguereberry Point Road

PARK

Artists Palette

Artists Drive

127

190

Death Valley Junction

Father Crowley Vista Point

PANAMINT RANGE

Wildrose Pk. 9,064 ft

Wildrose Campground

Devils Golf Course

Wildrose Charcoal Kilns

Natural Bridge

-282 ft

Dantes View Road

Telescope Pk. Trail

Hanaupah Canyon

Badwater Basin

Badwater Basin Trailhead

Telescope Pk. 11,049 ft

SIERRA NEVADA

NAVAL AIR WEAPONS STATION CHINA LAKE

Butte Valley

Badwater Rd.

Greenwater Range

Shoshone

178

Olancha

China Lake

Trona

Searles Lake

NAVAL AIR WEAPONS STATION CHINA LAKE

Black Mountains

127

178

Ridgecrest

178

Owlshead Mountains

Saratoga Spring

FORT IRWIN

MOHAVE NATIONAL PRESERVE

To

10 mi
10 km

N

Zabriskie Point, a top spot for catching a sunrise

An aerial view of the Sierras

→ DRIVE

D Death Valley—the largest park in the lower 48 states—can feel inaccessible. Luckily, many of its wonders are easy to see and experience along its roads. **Badwater Road**, just south of the Furnace Creek Visitor Center, connects some of the park's most otherworldly spots. Take the route to see the famous, fragile salt flats and stop at these spots:

→ *Artists Drive is the most popular route in the park. See the park's iconic beauty without much walking, from rainbow hills formed by volcanic deposits to Artists Palette, a filming destination for* Star Wars: A New Hope (Episode IV). *The drive is nine miles long and one-way only. Cyclists share the road, which has many dips and sharp turns.*

→ *Take the side road to* **Devils Golf Course**, *where you won't find a spot to tee off. Rather, this is a landscape of eroded rock salt that's so jagged "only the devil could play golf on such rough links."*

→ *Drive toward* **Natural Bridge** *and take a one-mile unmarked trail to the 35-foot-tall arch made of rock, gravel, and sediment.*

→ *Get out of the car again to hike the one-mile* **Badwater Basin Trail** *to the lowest spot in North America. A wooden boardwalk runs through the salty basin.*

State Route 190 also provides access to some of the park's best overlooks. Stop by the Father Crowley Vista Point overlooking Rainbow Canyon, take a short hike to Darwin Falls (an 18-foot-tall cascade that flows year-round), the Mesquite Flat Sand Dunes, and Zabriskie Point, an amazing sunrise and sunset spot. Pull down **Dantes View Road** for a panorama of the white salt flats below and the Panamints in the distance.

→ HIKE

(S) Summer temperatures in Death Valley are dangerous, so it's safest to hike from November through March. Bring more water than you think you need—at least a gallon per person for longer warm-season hikes—and plenty of sun protection. Be honest about your abilities, then add the appropriate hikes to your list.

→ The complete circuit around the **Golden Canyon** is 7.8 miles, starting at either Zabriskie Point or the Golden Canyon parking lot. Travel past rocky corridors, an ancient lake bed, and the walls of Red Cathedral. (A shorter two-mile round-trip jaunt runs from the parking area to Red Cathedral and back but involves a rock scramble.)

→ The partly paved 0.4-mile **Harmony Borax Works** interpretive trail takes you back in time with placards about borax and 20-mule teams, one of the region's first successful mining ventures.

→ Scramble your way through **Mosaic Canyon**. The four-mile out-and-back trail moves through multiple canyons, though many visitors turn back after the first gorgeous set.

→ Gain 2,200 feet when you hike **Wildrose Peak** from the historic Wildrose Charcoal Kilns, beehive-like structures built in 1877 to supply the mines. Follow the path through the forest, across switchbacks, and up to the peak to look down at Badwater Basin.

→ Striking narrow walkways and waterfall chutes call hikers to the six-mile **Fall Canyon**. Look for chuckwallas and bighorn sheep as you walk.

→ The challenging, unmaintained 7.1-mile, out-and-back **Corkscrew Peak Trail** leads to 360-degree views of the surrounding peaks. Get a map at the visitor center before you start.

→ Trekking to the bottom of the volcanic **Ubehebe Crater** isn't too challenging, but getting back out of the 600-foot crater is. If you want to avoid the ascent, walk the 1.5-mile rim loop to see it all, but beware of loose footings.

→ The 14-mile **Telescope Peak Trail** climbs along the Panamint Range through piñon pine and mahogany forests. Get unobstructed views of the valley, Hanaupah Canyon, Badwater Basin, and, eventually, the Sierra Nevada and Mount Whitney.

Zabriskie Point

Sunlight highlights the rippling Mesquite Flat Sand Dunes.

Keep a respectful distance if you spy coyotes in the park.

D Death Valley is home to abundant wildlife, from **desert shrews** to **collared lizards**. Keep a careful eye on the ground for small, resilient desert creatures and to the sky for feathered foragers.

→ Nearly **400 species of birds** have been spotted in Death Valley, including many migratory groups. Bird-watchers will have good luck at Furnace Creek Ranch, Scotty's Castle, Wildrose, the high Panamints, and Saratoga Spring.

→ You might be happy to see **burros** (often called donkeys) on your visit, but the ecosystem isn't so grateful, as they compete with the native animals, like bighorn sheep, for vegetation and vital water sources. Miners brought them, and the invasive creatures now wander through the Saline Valley and Butte Valleys and along Emigrant Canyon Road.

→ **Desert bighorn sheep** are a testament to survival, with their complex digestive systems and excellent climbing skills. Look for them in Titus Canyon.

SPOT

EXPLORE

T There's more than one way to see the wonders of Death Valley, so amp up your visit with a twist.

→ You'll have to off-road to reach **The Racetrack**, a dry lake bed at the bottom of Ubehebe Peak, famous for its mysterious "moving" rocks. Scientists believe an unusual combination of wet ground and wind cause the rocks to move—and leave their tracks—along the desert floor.

→ **Mountain bike** along Titus Canyon Road to see the towering Red Pass, the ghost town Leadfield, and the bighorn sheep at Klare Spring. Book a shuttle back to your starting point so your whole trip is downhill.

→ **Horseback ride** with a guide from Furnace Creek Stables on a family-friendly, one-hour sunrise, sunset, or moonlight tour.

→ Walk the **Mesquite Flat Sand Dunes** near Stovepipe Wells village. There are no marked trails, so be mindful of the fragile ecosystem, home to nocturnal kangaroo rats and sidewinder rattlesnakes. Time the hike to watch the sun rise or set.

→ Death Valley has been named a Gold-Tier Dark Sky Park, the highest designation, by DarkSky International. Rangers recommend **stargazing** at the Mesquite Flat Sand Dunes, Harmony Borax Works, Badwater Basin, and Ubehebe Crater. At the annual **Dark Sky Festival**, you can attend expert talks, meet with astrophotographers, and participate in family-friendly activities.

→ Visit the **Keane Wonder Mine**, which thrived in the early 1900s. Hike the steep one-mile trail into the Funeral Mountains to step back into mining history.

Family Friendly

→ RANGER RECOMMENDATION ←

*Drive the precarious and unpaved, but beautiful, six-mile **Aguereberry Point Road**. Talk to rangers first, and have a full-size spare tire with you. You'll be rewarded with a breathtaking view of the Pana-mint Range overlooking Death Valley Basin.*

Sunlight breaks over the rocky terrain of Haleakalā.

HALEAKALĀ
NATIONAL PARK

HAWAII

ESTABLISHED: August 1, 1916

SIZE: 33,265 acres

VISITORS CENTERS: The Headquarters Visitor Center is one mile inside the Summit District entrance gate; the Haleakalā Visitor Center is at the edge of the volcanic valley; and the Kīpahulu Visitor Center is in the coastal district. All are open year-round; center hours vary but bathrooms at each are available 24 hours a day.

TRANSPORTATION: No in-park transportation

DOGS ALLOWED: Only in parking lots, on roadways, and on paved pathways. Dogs are not allowed on trails or in campsites.

WHEN TO GO: Summer is the most crowded, and winter weather can close the park. Visit in shoulder seasons and between sunrise and sunset to avoid crowds. Reservations are required for access to the Summit District from 3 a.m. to 7 a.m.

CONTACT: 808-572-4400; nps.gov/hale
PO Box 369
Makawao, HI 96768

T There's a deep connection between culture and environment in the sacred space of Haleakalā National Park. Since people first arrived on Maui, the volcano Haleakalā has provided cultural, religious, scientific, and community interest. To Native Hawaiians, the summit is a *wahi pana*, or legendary place, and a *wao akua*, or realm of the gods. Today, astronomers have built modern observatories for viewing the cosmos.

But the park isn't only about its peak. The Haleakalā ecosystem protects some of the most endangered species on Earth. Explore the volcanic landscape from both the high-elevation Summit District and the coastal Kīpahulu District to appreciate its marvels.

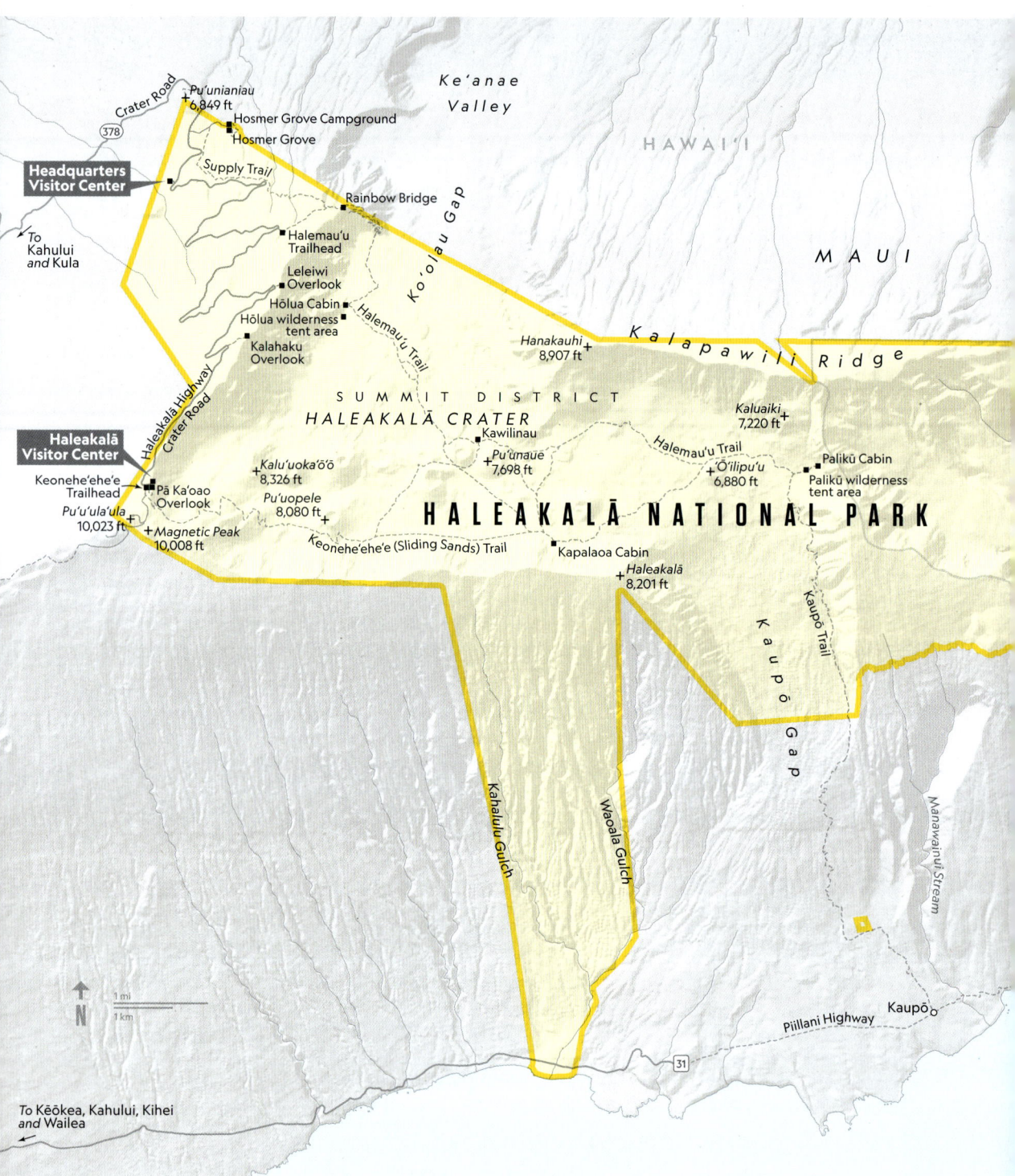

Ke'anae Valley

HAWAI'I

Crater Road
378

Pu'unianiau
6,849 ft

Hosmer Grove Campground
Hosmer Grove

Headquarters Visitor Center

Supply Trail

Rainbow Bridge

To Kahului and Kula

Halemau'u Trailhead

Leleiwi Overlook

Hōlua Cabin
Hōlua wilderness tent area
Kalahaku Overlook

Ko'olau Gap

MAUI

Kalapawili Ridge

Hanakauhi
8,907 ft

SUMMIT DISTRICT
HALEAKALĀ CRATER

Kawilinau

Haleakalā Highway

Crater Road

Haleakalā Visitor Center

Keonehe'ehe'e Trailhead

Pu'u'ula'ula
10,023 ft

Pā Ka'oao Overlook

Magnetic Peak
10,008 ft

Kalu'uoka'ō'ō
8,326 ft

Pu'uopele
8,080 ft

Pu'unaue
7,698 ft

Halemau'u Trail

Kaluaiki
7,220 ft

'Ō'ilipu'u
6,880 ft

Palikū Cabin
Palikū wilderness tent area

Halemau'u Trail

HALEAKALĀ NATIONAL PARK

Keonehe'ehe'e (Sliding Sands) Trail

Kapalaoa Cabin

Haleakalā
8,201 ft

Kaupō Trail

Kaupō Gap

Kahului Gulch

Waoala Gulch

Manawainui Stream

N
1 mi
1 km

Piilani Highway

Kaupō

31

To Kēōkea, Kahului, Kihei and Wailea

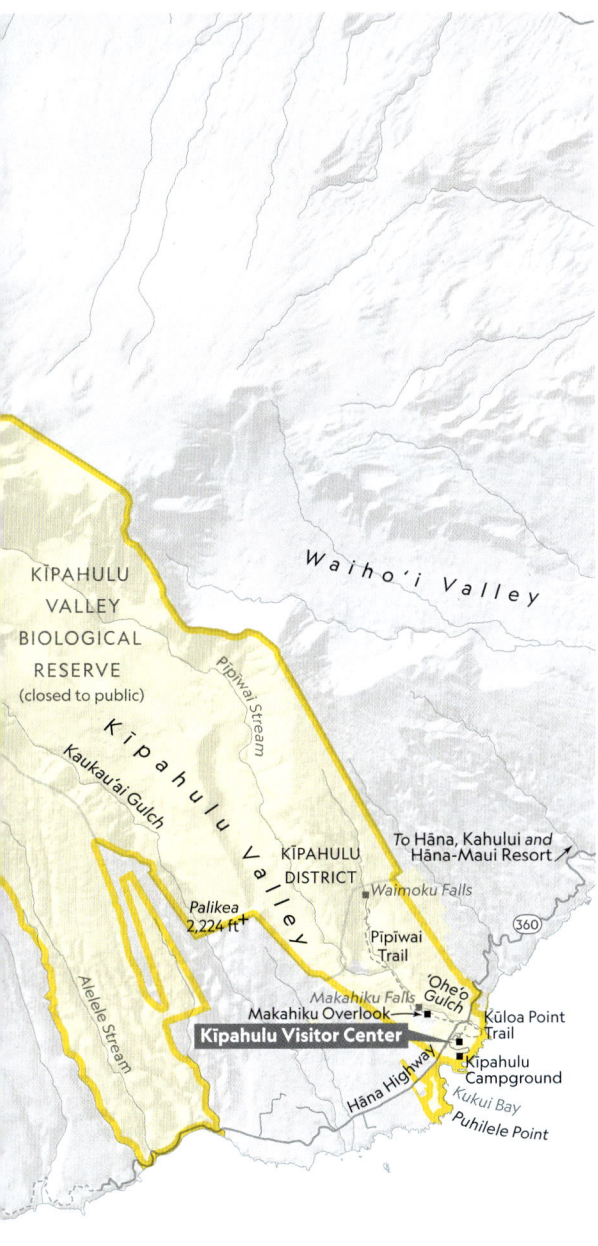

KĪPAHULU
VALLEY
BIOLOGICAL
RESERVE
(closed to public)

Waihoʻi Valley

Pipiwai Stream

Kaukauʻai Gulch

Kīpahulu Valley

KĪPAHULU
DISTRICT

To Hāna, Kahului and
Hāna-Maui Resort

Waimoku Falls

Palikea
2,224 ft

360

Pīpīwai
Trail

Alelele Stream

Makahiku Falls

ʻOheʻo Gulch

Makahiku Overlook

Kīpahulu Visitor Center

Kūloa Point
Trail

Kīpahulu
Campground

Hāna Highway

Kukui Bay

Puhilele Point

PACIFIC OCEAN

Hāna-Maui Resort, 10 miles from the southern end of the park

SLEEP

H Hotels and resorts are all over the towns outside the park's bounds, including in Kula, Wailea, Kihei, and Hāna. To stay inside the park, book a campsite or cabin in advance.

→ There are three 12-person historic wilderness cabins at elevation in Haleakalā, but you'll have to hike between 3.7 and 9.3 miles from either the Halemauʻu or Keoneheʻeheʻe Trailheads to get to them. **Hōlua Cabin** sits at the base of the crater wall. **Palikū Cabin** is on the east end of the valley near the base of a rainforest cliff (be ready for rain at all times). **Kapalaoa Cabin** is at a grassy site at the southern end of the valley. Reservations must be made online (reserve up to six months in advance), and there is a three-night maximum. Pit toilets and water are available near the cabins, which have padded bunks and both wood-burning and propane stoves.

→ **Hosmer Grove Campground**, at 7,000 feet elevation, has six grassy sites, each with a picnic table and grill. It also has pit toilets and access to potable water and a nature trail. Reservations are required and available on a rolling, monthly basis.

→ The nine sites at **Kīpahulu Campground** look out over ocean cliffs, though there isn't any beach access. There are picnic tables, grills, and pit toilets. The campground is surrounded by historic rock walls and archaeological sites—look but don't touch.

→ The park also offers two primitive wilderness campsites: **Hōlua** and **Palikū**. Both require advanced reservations, are accessible only by trail, and offer pit toilets and non-potable water.

HIKE

The park's trails provide views and insights to Haleakalā's history that you can't find anywhere else. These park ecosystems are fragile and culturally significant, so stay on marked trails at all times. Keep in mind that hiking groups are restricted to 12 people.

→ The **Hosmer Grove trail**, just over half a mile long, passes through an old research forest and is a great representation of how native and non-native species have merged in the park.

→ Walk the four-mile round-trip **Pīpīwai Trail** in the Kīpahulu District. It weaves past a winding stream; the Makahiku Overlook, where you can see the majestic falls; a unique bamboo forest with boardwalks and bridges; and the towering 200-foot-tall Waimoku Falls.

→ The rocky path of the **Halemau'u Trail** travels across the "Rainbow Bridge" (a narrow, natural land bridge). To reach the crater floor at the Ko'olau Gap, the hike is just over two miles one-way.

→ The **Keonehe'ehe'e (Sliding Sands) Trail** is a challenging 11-mile route that traverses the valley floor and ends at the Halema'u Trailhead.

→ Take the **Kūloa Point Trail** from the Kīpahulu Visitor Center to learn more about the region's archaeology and community history. See the pools of 'Ohe'o Gulch to balance history with nature.

→ More than a dozen outfitters will take you through the park on **various tours**. Try a sunrise trip with Haleakalā Ecotours or Valley Isle Excursions. Focus on astronomy when you visit with Kaze Enterprises or Maui Stargazing. Or focus on hiking with Explore Maui Nature, Hawaii by Storm, or Hike Maui.

Prepare for your hike: Don't be fooled by the weather on the coast. You need gear for the sun and the cold if you plan to hike to the summit of Haleakalā. Temperatures can drop to below freezing at any time when the winds rise, and hypothermia is a real possibility. The high elevation can cause altitude sickness, so watch out for nausea, headaches, dizziness, or shortness of breath. Pack sun protection and for wet weather, and wear sturdy shoes. Be sure to bring plenty of snacks and water.

The Pīpīwai Trail winds through a bamboo forest.

SPOT

Unique Bird-watching

| If you're looking to spot endemic species, pull out your binoculars and look to the skies.

→ The **native songbirds** of Maui have lived in what's now Haleakalā for millions of years, but their home and survival are now being threatened by disease, habitat loss, and invasive plants, among other issues. Walk through any of the forest trails and listen for the 17 species of **honeycreepers** left in the park, as well as the native **kiwikiu** (Maui parrotbill). Hosmer Grove is a good spot for sightings.

→ Try to spot the **nene**, the Hawaiian goose and state bird of Hawaii. They've been reintroduced to multiple islands. In the park, find them between 5,500 and 8,000 feet of elevation.

The nene (Hawaiian goose) is endemic to the Hawaiian Islands.

Sunset from the summit of Maui's Haleakalā Crater

Observatories on the summit of Haleakalā Crater

The Keoneheʻeheʻe (Sliding Sands) Trail and Haleakalā Crater

A A portion of the famous **Hāna Highway** (better known as the Road to Hāna) runs through 12 miles of the coastal portion of the Kīpahulu District. Most travelers stop at ʻOheʻo Gulch on the way to Hāna. If you do, don't try to swim in the pools, as the waters contain harmful parasites.

The other driving route is between the Headquarters Visitor Center and **Puʻuʻulaʻula**, the highest point in the park, at 10,023 feet. On your way up the road, you'll get crater views at the Leleiwi Overlook, the Kalahaku Overlook (with expansive crater views from the edge of a cliff), the Haleakalā Visitor Center, the Pā Kaʻoao Overlook, and ultimately the Puʻuʻulaʻula observation deck. Reservations are required to take the route between 3 a.m. and 7 a.m.

DRIVE

A freshwater stream in 'Ohe'o Gulch

B Beyond its trails, there are plenty of ways to make your time at Haleakalā more interesting.

→ *Get personal with the Milky Way.* The high elevation and low light pollution at the park mean clear skies that are perfect for **stargazing**. Just be sure to dress in layers, since temperatures drop drastically after sunset.

→ *Get a permit to* **watch the sunrise** *from the summit at Haleakalā (available six months in advance). Spend the morning above the clouds soaking in the remarkable colors.*

→ *On the flip side, you don't need a permit to experience* **sunset at the summit**. *Pack warm clothes and all the food and drink you'll need, as there are no services on the summit. Arrive at the peak early, because parking fills quickly.*

→ *Check the park calendar to plan a* **ranger-led activity**, *such as a full-moon night at the peak, a forest bird hike to spot Maui's honeycreepers and learn about their behaviors, or a Hosmer Grove hike to listen for forest birds and learn about endemic plants. There are also Junior Ranger activities at the park.*

→ *Grab your* **bicycle** *and try to make it to the summit via Haleakalā Highway (Crater Road). Even experienced cyclists struggle with the high altitude, elevation gains, and unpredictable weather, but it's a struggle with a big reward. Many bikers catch a ride to the top, then cycle down, instead of up, if that fits your abilities better.*

→ *Learn about the botany of the region, conservation in the valley, the area's early archaeology, and Hawaiian spirituality and its connection to the park at the* **visitors centers**.

Family Friendly

EXPLORE

→ **RANGER RECOMMENDATION** ←

Stop at the often-skipped **Kalahaku Overlook**. Most visitors continue past it to reach the summit, but this overlook provides a fantastic view of the crater any time of day—especially at sunrise or for stargazing. The structure at the overlook is in the same spot as a house built by architect Charles W. Dickey and is a nesting ground for the native seabird, the ʻuaʻu, and the Hawaiian dark-rumped petrel.

Lava races into the sea at the coastline of the park.

HAWAI'I VOLCANOES NATIONAL PARK

HAWAII

ESTABLISHED: August 1, 1916

SIZE: 335,259 acres

VISITORS CENTER: The Kīlauea Visitor Center (reopening in 2027) is staffed with rangers who provide information on current conditions and hiking recommendations.

TRANSPORTATION: No in-park transportation

DOGS ALLOWED: Only in parking lots, on limited roads, and in some campgrounds

----

WHEN TO GO: Spring and fall for better temperatures. Always check updates on volcanic activity and park and road closures.

CONTACT: 808-985-6011; nps.gov/havo
1 Crater Rim Drive
Hawaii National Park, HI 96718

(S) Stretching from the Pacific shoreline to the 13,677-foot summit of Mauna Loa on the Big Island of Hawaii, Hawai'i Volcanoes National Park is home to two of the world's most active volcanoes. The ongoing activity of Kīlauea and Mauna Loa results in an extraordinary, one-of-a-kind environment that's home to specially adapted plants and animals, an ever changing series of paths, and a landscape of lava tubes, rainforest, and lava fields that looks different each decade. The park is a real-world course in geology, Hawaiian culture, rare species of flora and fauna, and Polynesian mythology.

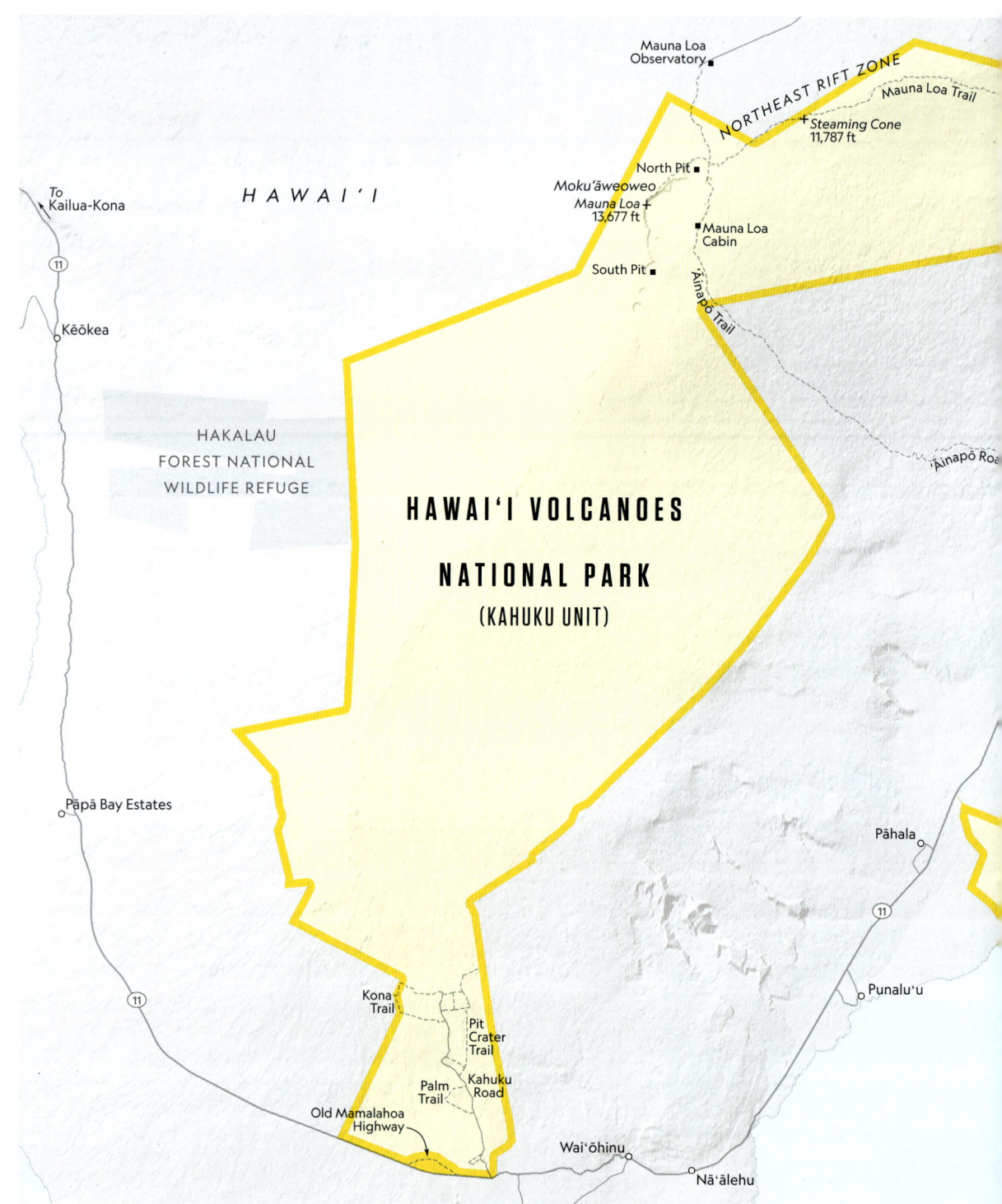

HAWAI'I

To Kailua-Kona

11

Kēōkea

HAKALAU
FOREST NATIONAL
WILDLIFE REFUGE

Pāpā Bay Estates

11

Mauna Loa
Observatory

NORTHEAST RIFT ZONE

Mauna Loa Trail

Steaming Cone
11,787 ft

North Pit

Moku'āweoweo
Mauna Loa
13,677 ft

Mauna Loa
Cabin

South Pit

'Ainapō Trail

'Ainapō Road

HAWAI'I VOLCANOES

NATIONAL PARK
(KAHUKU UNIT)

Pāhala

11

Punalu'u

Kona
Trail

Pit
Crater
Trail

Kahuku
Road

Palm
Trail

Old Mamalahoa
Highway

Wai'ōhinu

Nā'ālehu

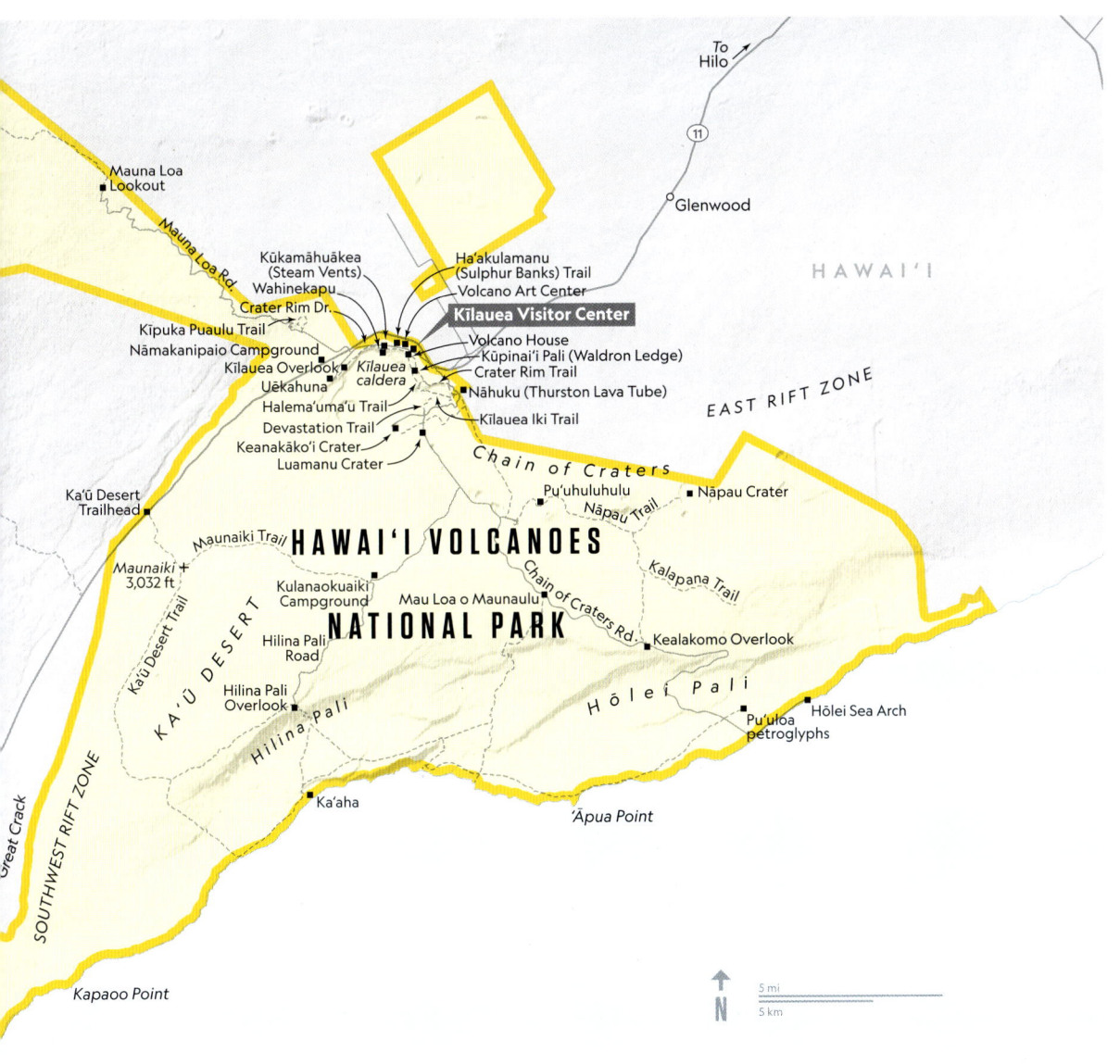

To Hilo

Glenwood

HAWAI'I

Mauna Loa Lookout

Mauna Loa Rd

Kūkamāhuākea (Steam Vents)
Wahinekapu
Crater Rim Dr.
Kīpuka Puaulu Trail
Nāmakanipaio Campground
Kīlauea Overlook
Uēkahuna
Halema'uma'u Trail
Devastation Trail
Keanakāko'i Crater
Luamanu Crater

Ha'akulamanu (Sulphur Banks) Trail
Volcano Art Center
Kīlauea Visitor Center
Volcano House
Kūpinai'i Pali (Waldron Ledge)
Crater Rim Trail
Nāhuku (Thurston Lava Tube)
Kīlauea Iki Trail

Kīlauea caldera

EAST RIFT ZONE

Chain of Craters

Pu'uhuluhulu
Nāpau Trail
Nāpau Crater

Ka'ū Desert Trailhead

Maunaiki Trail

Kalapana Trail

HAWAI'I VOLCANOES

Maunaiki + 3,032 ft

Kulanaokuaiki Campground

Mau Loa o Maunaulu

Chain of Craters Rd.

NATIONAL PARK

KA'Ū DESERT

Hilina Pali Road

Kealakomo Overlook

Hilina Pali Overlook

Hilina Pali

Hōlei Pali

Pu'uloa petroglyphs
Hōlei Sea Arch

Great Crack

SOUTHWEST RIFT ZONE

Ka'ū Desert Trail

Ka'aha

'Āpua Point

Kapaoo Point

N

5 mi
5 km

PACIFIC OCEAN

Volcano House

→ SLEEP

Kulanaokuaiki Campground

M Modern hotels, rustic cabins, maintained campsites, and backcountry offerings are available throughout the park.

→ The historic **Volcano House** is next to the Kīlauea Visitor Center. Guests at the hotel will arrive to welcome mimosas and wake up to views of the caldera. Originally built in 1846 as a one-room shelter for visitors, the hotel now boasts 33 guest rooms, a bike loan service, daily guided tours, Wi-Fi, and a restaurant.

→ **Nāmakanipaio Campground** sits just a few miles from the hotel and is run by the same operator. Stay in one of 10 one-room cabins or a tent (there are 16 sites), which the resort will set up if you don't have your own. All have access to toilets, showers, picnic tables, and barbecue pits. Either way, you'll sleep in a grove of eucalyptus trees 4,000 feet above the sea.

→ As long as there isn't a high fire risk, you can stay at **Kulanaokuaiki Campground**. There are nine first-come-first-serve tent-only sites available, with vault toilets but no water. One rule of note: no campfires.

→ **Backcountry camp** in the park as long as you are a mile from a road or camp area and get a permit. You can obtain a permit up to 90 days in advance online (though a small number of walk-ins are permitted). Pick it up at the Backcountry Office up to seven days before your trip, which is when you'll also get a safety briefing. Eight backcountry sites, some with cabins, are available to hikers.

Explore the galleries at the Volcano Art Center in the park.

DRIVE

M Most visitors will drive along Crater Rim Drive and Chain of Craters Road. Many of the park's must-do activities are accessible from these routes.

→ Start your trip on **Crater Rim Drive** at the Kīlauea Visitor Center, where you can get updated on trails and closures. On the drive, stop at Uēkahuna, a significant site for Native Hawaiian rituals with views of the Kīlauea caldera. Make a point to see the steaming volcanic vents at Wahinekapu, and look to the skies at the bird-watcher's paradise of Haʻakulamanu (Sulphur Banks). The striking Kīlauea Iki Overlook offers a view of what was once a lava lake and Puʻupuaʻi, a cinder cone. The short hike into Nāhuku (Thurston Lava Tube) is worth stretching your legs for. Other worthwhile stops include the crater and cinder cone at the Puʻupuaʻi Overlook and the pit crater at Keanakākoʻi Crater.

→ The 18.8-mile **Chain of Craters Road** is filled from start to finish with striking views and overlooks. Be sure to stop at Luamanu Crater to see birds, take in the astonishing drops at Puhimau Crater, and park at the trailhead for a short hike to the Puʻuhuluhulu cinder cone. You'll also see the lava flows at Mau Loa o Maunaulu, Pacific views from the Kealakomo Overlook, the sacred Puʻuloa petroglyphs, and the lava rock Hōlei Sea Arch stretching into the Pacific.

Chain of Craters Road

H Hike a few trails to get a deeper understanding of the park's geology and cultural history. These trails will give you a broad experience:

→ The easy **Crater Rim Trail** gives a great perspective of this active volcano. Access it from Crater Rim Drive, the Uēkahuna, the Kīlauea Overlook, Kūkamāhuākea (Steam Vents), or the Volcano House hotel. The Kūpinai'i Pali, or Waldron Ledge, portion of the trail was once part of Crater Rim Drive, but an earthquake made it impossible for cars to pass, so now it's pedestrian only.

→ The **Halema'uma'u Trail** is a gorgeous, green walk through the rainforest. The 1.8-mile round-trip trek leaves from behind Volcano House and drops down from the Crater Rim Trail to the floor of Kaluapele, the Kīlauea caldera. Look for lava while you're there.

→ Get down into the crater on the **Kīlauea Iki Trail**. The steep, rocky descent is a challenge and takes anywhere from 3.3 to six miles depending on your entrance point. Be careful of deep cracks and sharp terrain—and remember you have to climb back up.

→ The **Devastation Trail** is a stroll through a recovering landscape once buried by cinder from 1959 lava foundations. Access the one-mile round-trip walk from the Pu'upua'i or Devastation Trail parking lots—and don't feed the geese that roam nearby.

→ Take one of the many hikes in the Kahuku Unit, once a huge cattle ranch that produced beef and hides for 150 years. Follow the **Palm Trail** to see panoramic views, and cross the main lava channel or challenge yourself with the **Pit Crater Trail**, which travels to the edge of a massive crater.

→ The 2.5-mile round-trip **Pu'uhuluhulu Trail** is a great place to see the impacts of volcanic eruptions. Look for lava tree molds and different types of lava rocks as you hike up to the forested cinder cone. There's one really strict rule: Leave the lava rocks alone; absolutely no stacking or stealing.

→ Move through the different environments of the park when you trek the **Nāpau Trail**, accessed from the Maunaulu parking area or the Nāulu Trailhead on Chain of Craters Road. See recent lava flows, rainforests covered in ferns, and pit craters.

→ Hiking the **Kīpuka Puaulu Trail** is a great way to see the native plants and animals that have called the park home since it is well protected from volcanic eruptions. Listen for the sounds of native birds and look for native butterflies as you walk.

Lava flows from Kilauea, an active volcano.

A volcanic sea arch

A nene (Hawaiian goose)

The Puʻuloa petroglyphs on the eastern side of the park

Nāhuku (Thurston Lava Tube)

SPOT

T The treacherous and evolving landscape of Hawaiʻi Volcanoes National Park isn't an easy place for wildlife to live, but certain species thrive amid the challenges. Look and listen carefully for the ones that do.

→ *Try to find some of the many native birds that call the park home—but keep your distance.* **Nene** *(Hawaiian geese) live throughout the park, as do* **Hawaiian honeycreepers***, which can be found in high-elevation forests.*

→ *A walk along the Haʻakulamanu Trail is a good choice for* **bird-watchers***—the name literally means "gathering place for birds." The sulfur smell from the volcanic gases that seep from the ground isn't pleasant, but pretend you don't mind and you'll get time with plenty of winged friends.*

→ *While* **Hawaiian hawksbill turtles***, or honuʻea, nest on the protected beaches in the park from late May until December, they'll be difficult to spot. They come ashore only at night, and their spaces are heavily protected.*

→ *Tackle serious switchbacks from the Hilina Pali Overlook to get down to Kaʻaha on the southern coastline of the park. The mostly grassy trail leads to a protected cove that's perfect for snorkeling, seeing* **green sea turtles***, and looking for other marine wildlife.*

EXPLORE

Ⓣ Take the time for one or more of these extra adventures to discover more of this land and its people.

→ Explore **Nāhuku**, or the Thurston Lava Tube, to follow the path of molten lava. The cave that was carved out by a river of lava was discovered in 1913 and used to be covered in lava drippings. They're gone now, thanks to less-than-thoughtful visitors, but you can still travel through the massive cavity. Go in the morning or late afternoon to avoid crowds.

→ Check out the 23,000 petroglyphs at **Pu'uloa**. Access a protective boardwalk from a pullout off Chain of Craters Road. The boardwalk extends across a lava field where early Hawaiian settlers left rock art that dates back more than 500 years.

→ The two main roads, Crater Rim Drive and Chain of Craters Road, are popular routes for **cyclists**, who can pedal them for the same overlooks and trailheads as drivers.

→ Join a **ranger-led program** at the park, like a guided hike, living history presentation, or demonstration of the arts and culture of Hawaii. Check with the rangers or the online calendar of events for offerings.

→ Connect with the history of the land in the **Ka'ū Desert**, a harsh, moonlike environment heavily impacted by volcanic eruption. A 1790 explosion pushed Native Hawaiians across the land, leaving behind fossilized footprints in the ash. Check out the exhibit at the shelter near the Ka'ū Desert Trailhead.

A fern- and ohia-filled forest

One-day-old, ropy pahoehoe lava

Plants grow from a lava flow on
Kilauea caldera.

*Hike the **Kūpina'i Pali** portion of the Crater Rim Trail. It's an easy route, and one that many locals take to see the caldera and crater. It's also wheelchair and stroller accessible, since it's paved, though there are some steep sections.*

An iconic Joshua tree curls over a Mojave yucca plant.

JOSHUA TREE
NATIONAL PARK

CALIFORNIA

ESTABLISHED: October 31, 1994

SIZE: 795,156 acres

VISITORS CENTERS: The Joshua Tree National Park Visitor Center and Cottonwood Visitor Center are open year-round; the Black Rock Nature Center is closed during weekdays in the summer. The Joshua Tree Visitor Center is five miles outside the west entrance in downtown Joshua Tree.

TRANSPORTATION: No in-park transportation

DOGS ALLOWED: Only on dirt roads and the paved Oasis of Mara Trail

WHEN TO GO: Spring and fall for the best weather

CONTACT: 760-367-5500; nps.gov/jotr
74485 National Park Drive
Twentynine Palms, CA 92277

J Joshua Tree is as beautiful as it is dangerous—and both its beauty and dangers can sneak up on you. Covering where the Mojave and the Colorado Deserts meet, the park is made up of massive rockscapes sculpted by wind and rain. The park offers clear night skies, striking and wild geology, and resilient desert wildlife—but no water, food, electricity, or cell service. It is at once accessible and remote: It's open 24 hours, 7 days a week, 365 days a year, but you may or may not find someone at an entrance booth. Explore this wild, protected space with awe, respect, and preparation.

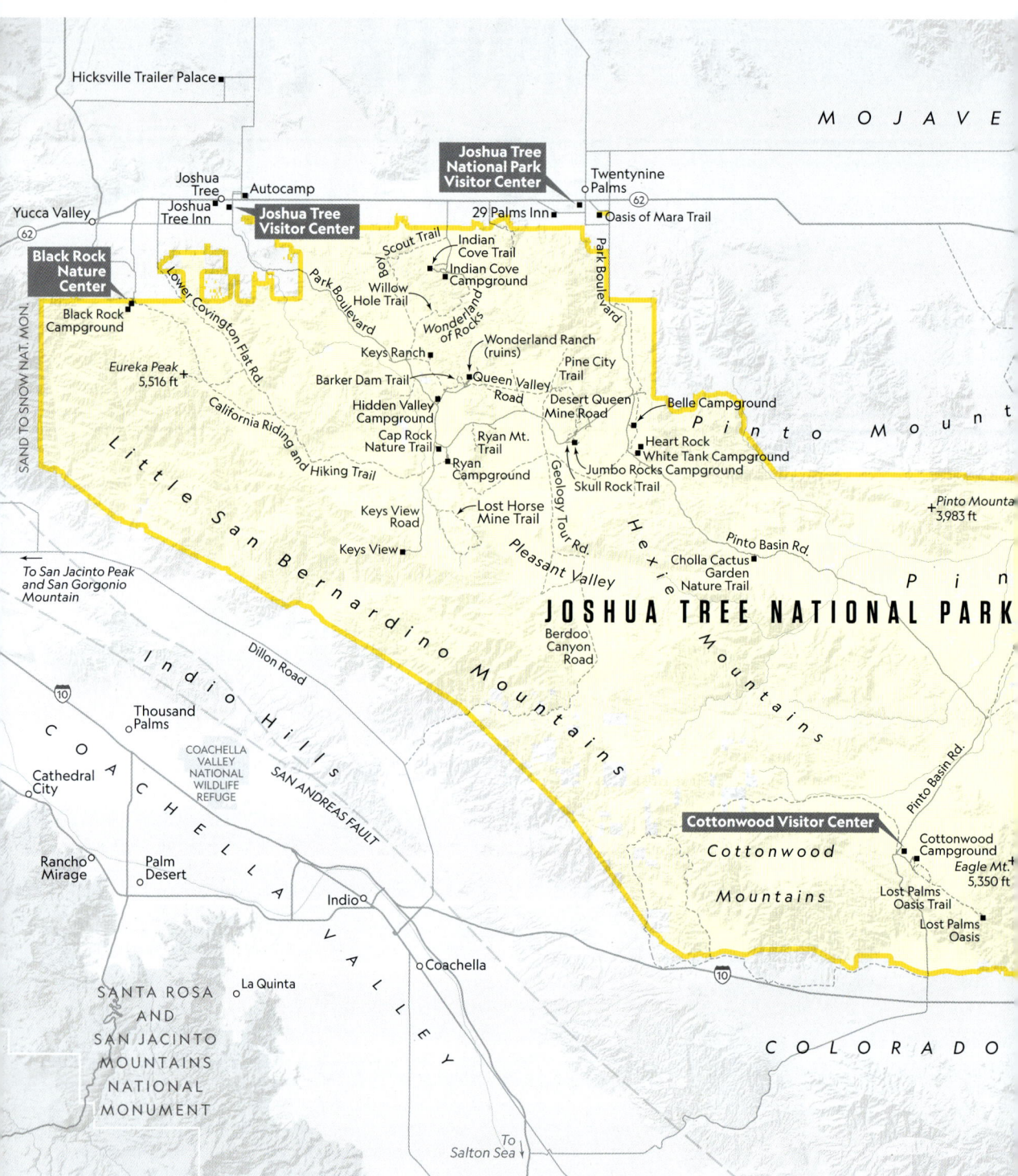

Hicksville Trailer Palace

MOJAVE

Joshua Tree National Park Visitor Center

Joshua Tree
Joshua Tree Inn
Autocamp
Joshua Tree Visitor Center

Yucca Valley
62

Twentynine Palms
29 Palms Inn
62
Oasis of Mara Trail

Black Rock Nature Center

Black Rock Campground

SAND TO SNOW NAT. MON.

Boy Scout Trail
Indian Cove Trail
Indian Cove Campground

Willow Hole Trail
Wonderland of Rocks

Park Boulevard

Lower Covington Flat Rd.

Eureka Peak 5,516 ft

California Riding and Hiking Trail

Keys Ranch
Barker Dam Trail
Hidden Valley Campground
Cap Rock Nature Trail

Wonderland Ranch (ruins)
Queen Valley Road

Pine City Trail
Desert Queen Mine Road

Belle Campground

Pinto Mount

Ryan Mt. Trail
Ryan Campground

Heart Rock
White Tank Campground
Jumbo Rocks Campground
Skull Rock Trail

Pinto Mounta 3,983 ft

Keys View Road

Lost Horse Mine Trail

Geology Tour Rd.

Pleasant Valley

Hexie Mountains

Pin

Keys View

JOSHUA TREE NATIONAL PARK

Little San Bernardino Mountains

To San Jacinto Peak and San Gorgonio Mountain

Cholla Cactus Garden Nature Trail

Pinto Basin Rd.

Berdoo Canyon Road

Dillon Road

Indio Hills

10

Thousand Palms

COACHELLA VALLEY NATIONAL WILDLIFE REFUGE

SAN ANDREAS FAULT

Cathedral City

Rancho Mirage

Palm Desert

Indio

COACHELLA VALLEY

Cottonwood Visitor Center

Cottonwood Mountains

Pinto Basin Rd.

Cottonwood Campground
Eagle Mt. 5,350 ft

Lost Palms Oasis Trail

Lost Palms Oasis

La Quinta

Coachella

10

SANTA ROSA AND SAN JACINTO MOUNTAINS NATIONAL MONUMENT

COLORADO

To Salton Sea

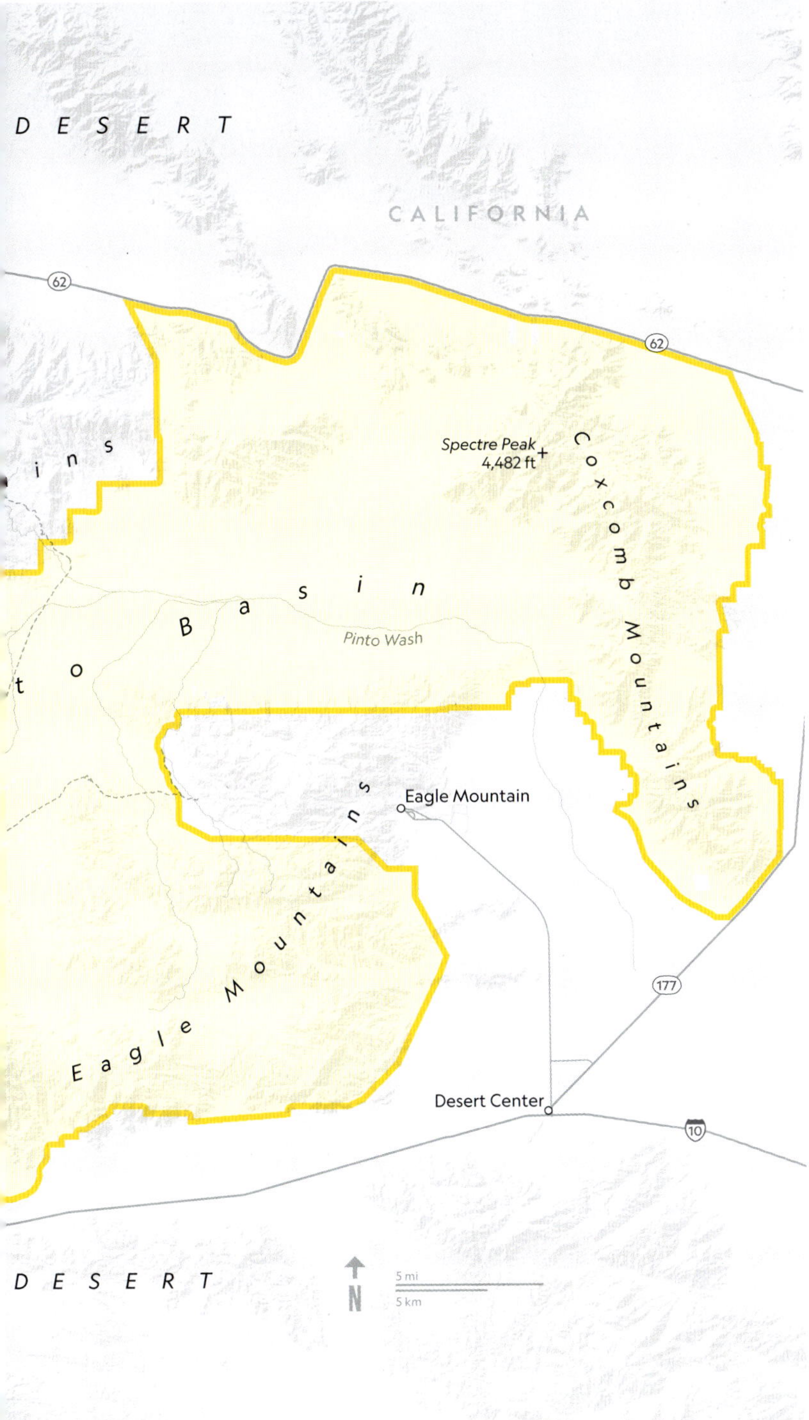

SLEEP

(T) The campgrounds in Joshua Tree are low on amenities and high on beauty.

→ **Jumbo Rocks** *is the park's most popular campground, with 124 sites within view of awe-inspiring rock formations. Reservations are required (up to six months in advance).*
→ **Indian Cove** *provides easy access to hikes. Its 101 sites require reservations, which are available six months in advance.*
→ *Centrally located* **Ryan** *(32 reservation-only sites) has four equestrian sites and is near the California Riding and Hiking Trail. Cyclists can also book the three bike sites.*
→ **Cottonwood**'s *62 reservation-only campsites have water and flush toilets.*
→ **Black Rock** *has 99 sites to accommodate tent and RV camping, plus an equestrian camping area. Reservations are required.*
→ *Photographers and stargazers love the 15 first-come-first-serve sites at* **White Tank**, *which gets busy in the evenings.*
→ *Nearby, the quiet, first-come-first-serve* **Belle** *also has fantastic night views and fewer crowds. There are 18 sites, pit toilets, and fire grates, but no water.*
→ *Climbers prefer* **Hidden Valley**, *which sits at an elevation of 4,200 feet. Its 44 sites are open year-round on a first-come-first-serve basis.*
→ **Backcountry camp** *with a low-cost permit—available online, by phone, or at the park's headquarters in Twentynine Palms. Permits can be booked up to six months in advance or picked up same-day until 4 p.m. at park headquarters.*

DESERT

CALIFORNIA

62

Spectre Peak
4,482 ft

Coxcomb Mountains

Basin

Pinto Wash

Eagle Mountain

Eagle Mountains

177

Desert Center

10

DESERT

5 mi
5 km

N

→ HIKE

During a nighttime hike, the park is illuminated in a whole new way.

J Joshua Tree has 300 miles of trails, and each one serves striking geological formations, resilient flora and fauna, and otherworldly experiences. These hikes are beautiful and dangerous. Protect yourself by packing enough water, staying on trails, and telling someone your plan.

→ Mining history is strong along the **Lost Horse Mine Trail**, which travels four miles through one of the most successful gold mines in the park. Stay within the bounds of the fences to protect the site.

→ Get deep into the **Wonderland of Rocks**. Your options to explore this area of the park are the half-mile Indian Cove Trail, the one-mile Barker Dam Trail, or the more difficult seven-mile Willow Hole Trail and eight-mile Boy Scout Trail. The area is a labyrinth of rock formations and vegetation. Keep an eye out for the worn-down pink buildings (the ruins of the Wonderland Ranch), massive formations, rock climbers, and desert plants.

→ At three miles one-way, the **Ryan Mountain Trail** is one of the most popular hikes in the park, and for good reason. The 5,461-foot summit provides 360-degree views of Eagle Mountain and the Salton Sea.

→ The mostly flat, four-mile **Pine City Trail** starts at the end of Desert Queen Mine Road and moves through dense juniper and piñon trees before ending up at an old mining site.

→ Get ready for a climb when you hike the **Lost Palms Oasis**. The 7.5-mile out-and-back trail treks through sandy washes and rolling terrain until you eventually reach the remote fan palm oasis at the bottom of the canyon. Be ready for a difficult scramble back out of the canyon.

→ Follow the easy 1.7-mile **Skull Rock Trail** through boulder piles and desert washes to its namesake rock formation.

→ The half-mile **Cap Rock Nature Trail** loops by views of striking boulder piles, thriving Joshua trees, and other desert plants.

→ The paved **Keys View loop** provides one of the best overlooks in the park via a short, though steep, quarter-mile walk. At the top, find views of the San Andreas Fault, San Jacinto Peak, San Gorgonio Mountain, and the Salton Sea.

→ Explore the quarter-mile **Cholla Cactus Garden Nature Trail**, which runs through 10 acres of unusual teddy-bear cholla and hedgehog cacti.

Wildflowers like these poppies grow at lower elevations.

A phainopepla balances on the tip of a plant.

S Somehow animals have found a way to thrive in the harsh environment of Joshua Tree. Look for these creatures while you're there:

→ *Reptiles are synonymous with the desert, and that's true in Joshua Tree. Look for threatened* **Mojave Desert tortoises**, **southern desert horned lizards**, *and* **California lyre snakes**.

→ *More than* **250 bird species** *call Joshua Tree home, either permanently or for a season. Look for* **roadrunners**, **mockingbirds**, *and* **prairie falcons** *all year. In the winter, spot* **sage sparrows** *and* **American robins**, *while spring and summer bring* **ash-throated flycatchers** *and* **western bluebirds**.

→ *Up to 200* **desert bighorn sheep** *live in Joshua Tree, frequenting the steep, rocky terrain as they graze for vegetation, including cacti. In the evenings, you might see signs of their only park predator:* **mountain lions**.

SPOT

Book Ahead

The landscape provides inspiration to a painter.

→ EXPLORE

The unique landscape of Joshua Tree makes for unique opportunities. Expand your experience in the park with these adventures:

→ **Rock climbers** and **boulderers** come from around the globe to test their skills in Joshua Tree. With more than 8,000 climbing routes, 2,000 boulder problems, and hundreds of natural gaps, the park is truly a world-class location. Take a guided course from Cliffhanger Guides, Stone Adventures, or Mojave Guides. Or, if you're an experienced climber, head out independently.

→ Ride through the 253 miles of **equestrian trails** on horseback with your own horse or on a tour with an outfitter like Knob Hill Ranch or Desert Wonder Tours.

→ See stars, planets, and meteors at this Dark Sky Park. Check the ranger calendar for a stargazing event or attend the annual **Night Sky Festival** for unparalleled views of the Milky Way.

→ **Bike** along the park's vehicle roads—just stay off the trails. Try the 18-mile Geology Tour Road to take in some of the most stunning landscapes in the park.

→ **Desert Institute**, the educational branch of the Joshua Tree National Park Association, offers field classes, social events, and recreational adventures. Learn about the park's wildlife, try out dark-sky photography, bring the kids for a painting class, and so much more.

→ Take a ranger-led tour of **Keys Ranch** to learn about Native American culture and mining, ranching, and homesteading history in the park. A tour is the only way to visit the protected site, so book tickets early.

January to mid-April is peak blooming season.

Give your eyes 30 minutes to adjust for optimal stargazing.

Rock formations dot the landscape on either side of the road.

An unpaved road curves through a group of Joshua trees.

DRIVE

Y You can see many of Joshua Tree's most popular sights along its main roads.

→ Get on **Park Boulevard** at either the north or west entrance, then keep an eye out for popular rock formations and Joshua trees. Hop on and off for short hikes along the way. Combine the drive with **Pinto Basin Road** to extend the trip.

→ Travel south from the north entrance and pull off at Keys View Road toward the **Keys View lookout**, where you'll take in the Santa Rosa Mountains, the snow-covered peak of San Gorgonio Mountain, Coachella Valley, and, sometimes, Mexico's Mount Signal.

→ The 13.4-mile network of backcountry roads, called the **Queen Valley Roads**, can be driven in most two-wheel-drive vehicles. You'll see Joshua trees, rock piles, and Queen Mountain—be mindful of the cyclists sharing the roads.

→ RANGER RECOMMENDATION ←

*Get a one-of-a-kind sunrise view all to yourself at **Heart Rock**. Though the spot is close to the popular Jumbo Rocks Campground, it's rarely visited in the early morning. There's no path up to the unique formation, so you'll need to scramble over class 3 and 4 rocks before the break of dawn (consider a headlamp). It's worth it for the special moment you'll get at the top.*

Jagged rock formations cast shadows deep into the canyon.

PINNACLES NATIONAL PARK

CALIFORNIA

ESTABLISHED: January 10, 2013

SIZE: 27,214 acres

VISITORS CENTERS: The Pinnacles Park Store has exhibits, and there is a small bookstore in the Pinnacles campground. Rangers at the Bear Gulch Nature Center can answer all your wildlife questions. The West Pinnacles Visitor Contact Station may close seasonally.

TRANSPORTATION: No in-park transportation

DOGS ALLOWED: Only in developed areas (campgrounds, parking lots, picnic areas, and paved roads)

WHEN TO GO: Spring for flowers. Weekends are busy. Cave flooding can cause closures.

CONTACT: 831-389-4486l; nps.gov/pinn
5000 East Entrance Road
Paicines, CA 95043

The wild spires and deep canyons of Pinnacles National Park were born 23 million years ago through volcanic eruptions, when tectonic plates shifted, lava flowed, and boulders slid. Once the landscape settled, it became home to Native American communities, including the Chalon Indians. Eventually, Spanish missionaries and early homesteaders settled the area. It finally took shape as a park after the Pinnacles Boys and the Civilian Conservation Corps took charge of its protection and development. Today, you'll find quiet talus caves, towering rock pillars, oak woodlands, and green fields. A space that was once full of chaos is now a beacon of calm.

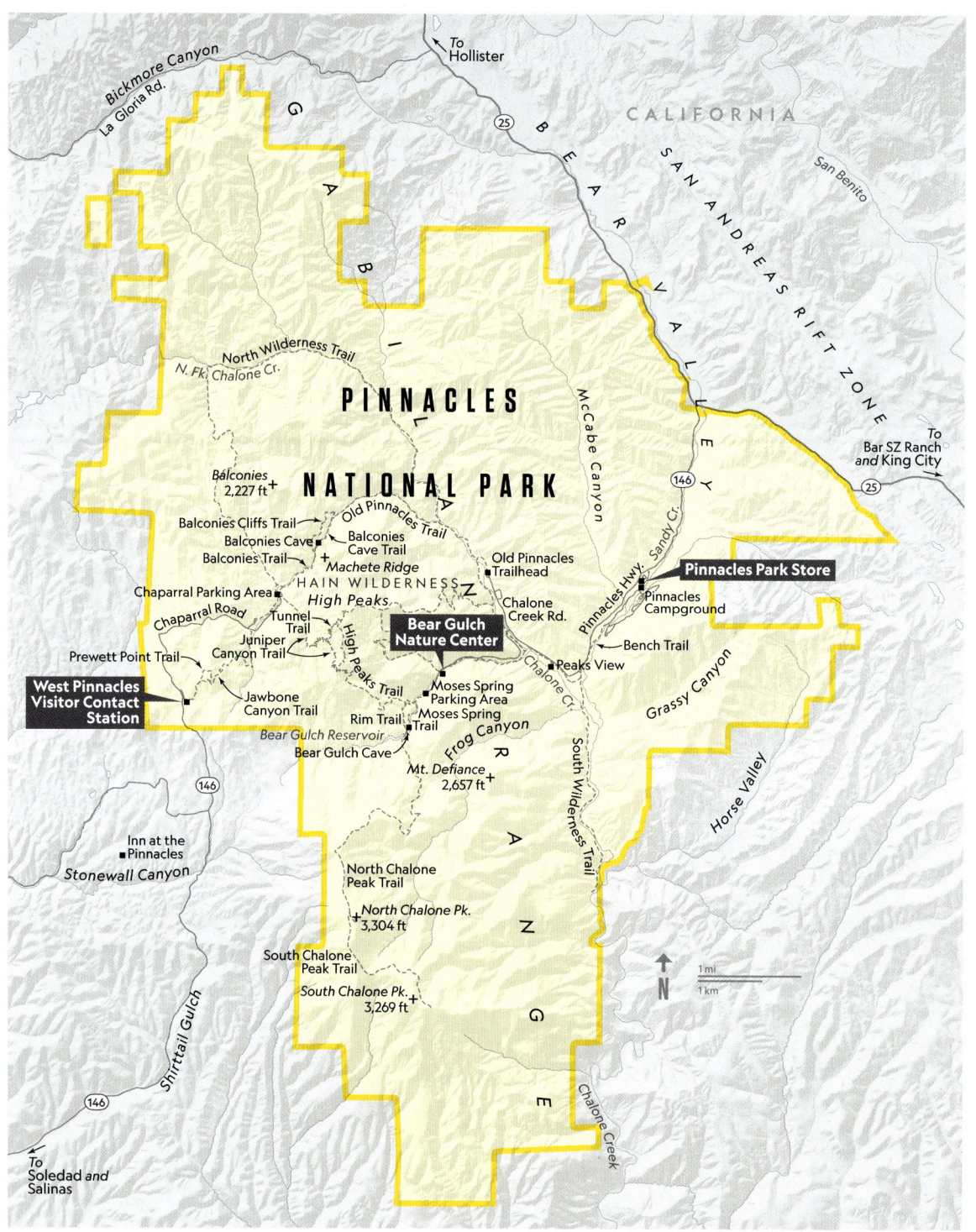

To Hollister

BICKMORE CANYON
La Gloria Rd.

GABILAN

CALIFORNIA

San Benito

BEAR VALLEY

SAN ANDREAS RIFT ZONE

North Wilderness Trail

N. Fk. Chalone Cr.

PINNACLES

NATIONAL PARK

Balconies
2,227 ft

Balconies Cliffs Trail
Balconies Cave
Balconies Trail
Balconies Cave Trail
Machete Ridge
HAIN WILDERNESS
High Peaks

Old Pinnacles Trail
Old Pinnacles Trailhead

McCabe Canyon

Pinnacles Park Store

Pinnacles Campground

Chaparral Parking Area
Chaparral Road
Tunnel Trail
Juniper Canyon Trail
High Peaks Trail
Bear Gulch Nature Center
Chalone Creek Rd.
Bench Trail

Peaks View

West Pinnacles Visitor Contact Station
Jawbone Canyon Trail
Moses Spring Parking Area
Moses Spring Trail
Rim Trail
Bear Gulch Reservoir
Bear Gulch Cave
Mt. Defiance 2,657 ft
Frog Canyon
Grassy Canyon

Prewett Point Trail

Chalone Cr.

RANGE

146

Inn at the Pinnacles
Stonewall Canyon

South Wilderness Trail

Horse Valley

North Chalone Peak Trail
North Chalone Pk. 3,304 ft

South Chalone Peak Trail
South Chalone Pk. 3,269 ft

Shirttail Gulch

146

Chalone Creek

146

To Soledad and Salinas

To Bar SZ Ranch and King City

Pinnacles Hwy.
Sandy Cr.

146

25

25

1 mi
1 km
N

Inside the Bar SZ Ranch's log cabin

SLEEP

Ⓣ Tent or RV camp at **Pinnacles Campground,** open all year. The campground has one of the only pools at a national park (open April–September), along with showers, toilets, and a camp store. Get to the shady sites from the east entrance. Most RV sites have electrical hookups. Tent and RV sites can be booked up to six months in advance; group sites can be reserved a year in advance.

If camping isn't for you, find lodging in Soledad, Hollister, or Salinas. Try the homey **Inn at the Pinnacles** or the luxurious and private **Bar SZ Ranch.**

Pinnacles Campground

HIKE

The trails at Pinnacles may not cover as many miles as bigger parks, but they encompass plenty of ecosystems and bring plenty of thrills.

Try these east-side treks:

→ Hike the 5.3-mile round-trip **Old Pinnacles Trail** to Balconies Cave, then pass Machete Ridge and the Balconies Cliffs along the flat route. Don't forget a flashlight to explore the cave (subject to seasonal closures).

→ Wander along the 6.5-mile round-trip **South Wilderness Trail**, accessible from the Bench Trail at the campground. Bring binoculars to bird-watch as you weave through the huge grove of valley oaks.

→ Get to the relatively easy 2.2-mile round-trip **Moses Spring Trail to the Rim Trail** loop by heading south from the Moses Spring Parking Area on the High Peaks Trail. The winding hike takes you toward Bear Gulch Cave and to iconic views of the Bear Gulch Reservoir along the Rim Trail.

Consider these west-side hikes:

→ The challenging 4.3-mile round-trip **Juniper Canyon Trail** is full of steep switchbacks through the High Peaks. At the top, wind between rock formations on the High Peaks Trail, then head down on the Tunnel Trail.

→ Follow the Balconies Trail to the 2.4-mile **Balconies Cliffs– Cave loop**. Cross up and over the cave and then come back through it, scrambling along the talus passages. Be prepared to wade through water.

→ Give yourself an entire day to hike the 9.3-mile unmaintained **North Wilderness Trail** loop. Climb along the park's ridgetops and then descend into the Chalone Creek bed. Come back via the Old Pinnacles and Balconies Trails.

→ The gentle one-mile round-trip **Prewett Point Trail** offers some of the best lookouts over High Peaks and the Hain Wilderness. This sunny trail connects to the Jawbone Canyon Trail, a mile-long trek across Chaparral Road to the Chaparral Parking Area.

The most striking wildlife in Pinnacles is up in the air. Look for birds and winged creatures as you hike, spelunk, and climb your way through the park, especially these:

→ Fourteen species of **bats** call the park's talus caves home, including the colony of **Townsend's big-eared bats** in Bear Gulch Cave and the colony of **western mastiff bats** in the Balconies Caves. Protect these carnivorous creatures by cleaning your gear before entering the caves.

→ Bird-watchers will be in bliss. Look for **California quail** and **northern flickers** around the Pinnacles Visitor Center and Campground. Spot **American kestrels** and other raptors at the Bear Gulch Nature Center. **White-throated swifts** and **golden eagles** soar along the Balconies Trail, while the High Peaks welcome both **California condors** and **turkey vultures**.

→ The smallest wildlife in the park are mighty in numbers. Look for some of the 500 species of **moths**, 400 species of **bees**, 70 species of **butterflies**, and 24 species of **dragonflies**.

A California condor takes flight.

SPOT

Buckwheat in the High Peaks area of the park

G Getting into the nooks and crannies of a place as unique as Pinnacles takes more than a stroll. Add these activities to your itinerary for a meaningful experience:

→ *Discover the mystery inside the park's **talus caves**, created when earthquakes from the area's volcanic rock caused the steep canyons to fill with massive boulders. Walk the paths built in the 1930s by the Civilian Conservation Corps, but check beforehand for closures due to flooding or hibernating Townsend's big-eared bats.*

→ *Experienced **rock climbers** can test their skill on the spires, crags, walls, and cliffs across the park—all made of volcanic breccia. Try Tourist Trap and Discovery Wall from the east side or Passion Play and Game Show from the west side. Guided expeditions, like those by Adventure Out and Outdoor Adventure Club, are offered. Safety note: Many of the bolts at Pinnacles are old or damaged, so inspect them carefully before using. The park maintains a list of restricted areas to protect breeding raptors.*

→ *Photograph Pinnacle's **wildflowers**—colorful manzanita, shooting stars, California poppies, milkmaids, baby blue eyes, orchids, and more—from March to May.*

EXPLORE

The park offers challenges for expert rock climbers.

DRIVE

P Pinnacles isn't really a park you can experience by car. Its only road turns into a trail at its middle. On the west side, **Chaparral Road** goes from the West Pinnacles Visitor Contact Station to the Chaparral Parking Area. On the east side, take **Pinnacles Highway** down to the park store and campground. Stop by Peaks View for vistas and access to the easy Bench Trail, then stop at the Bear Gulch Nature Center and Moses Spring Parking Area for trail access. You can also take the split up Chalone Creek Road to the Old Pinnacles Trailhead.

Experts Only

→ RANGER RECOMMENDATION ←

Continue south from Bear Gulch Reservoir and hike the strenuous **North Chalone Peak Trail** to the highest point in the park. The eight-mile out-and-back offers breathtaking views, a chance to spot California condors, and an unmarked trail for an optional extended hike to South Chalone Peak.

Among the trees in Sequoia National Park

SEQUOIA & KINGS CANYON NATIONAL PARKS

CALIFORNIA

ESTABLISHED: Sequoia on September 25, 1890;
Kings Canyon on March 4, 1940

SIZE: 865,964 acres (total)

VISITORS CENTERS: Sequoia has the Foothills Visitor Center, one mile past the Ash Mountain Entrance, and the Lodgepole Visitor Center, in the conifer zone, both open year-round. There's also the Giant Forest Museum in the Giant Forest sequoia grove, open year-round. The Mineral King Ranger Station, at 7,600 feet, is open in summer only, and wilderness permits are available here. Kings Canyon has the Kings Canyon Visitor Center in Grant Grove Village, open year-round, and the Cedar Grove Visitor Center, next to the South Fork of the Kings River, open in summer only.

TRANSPORTATION: The free Sequoia Shuttle runs in the summers and during some winter holidays.

DOGS ALLOWED: Only in developed areas (campgrounds, parking lots, picnic areas, and paved roads)

WHEN TO GO: Summer is busiest, and winter has road closures, so consider the shoulder seasons.

CONTACT: 559-565-3341; nps.gov/seki
47050 Generals Highway
Three Rivers, CA 93271

E Everything about Sequoia & Kings Canyon is unique. For starters, the two parks are administered jointly, meaning one entry fee gets you into both. Then add the giant sequoias that tower over everything else in the region, the largest trees by volume on Earth; the vastness of the canyons (including one of the deepest in North America); and caves that match the enormity of the parks' trees. There's no place quite like these two parks, and there will be no trip like the one you take in them.

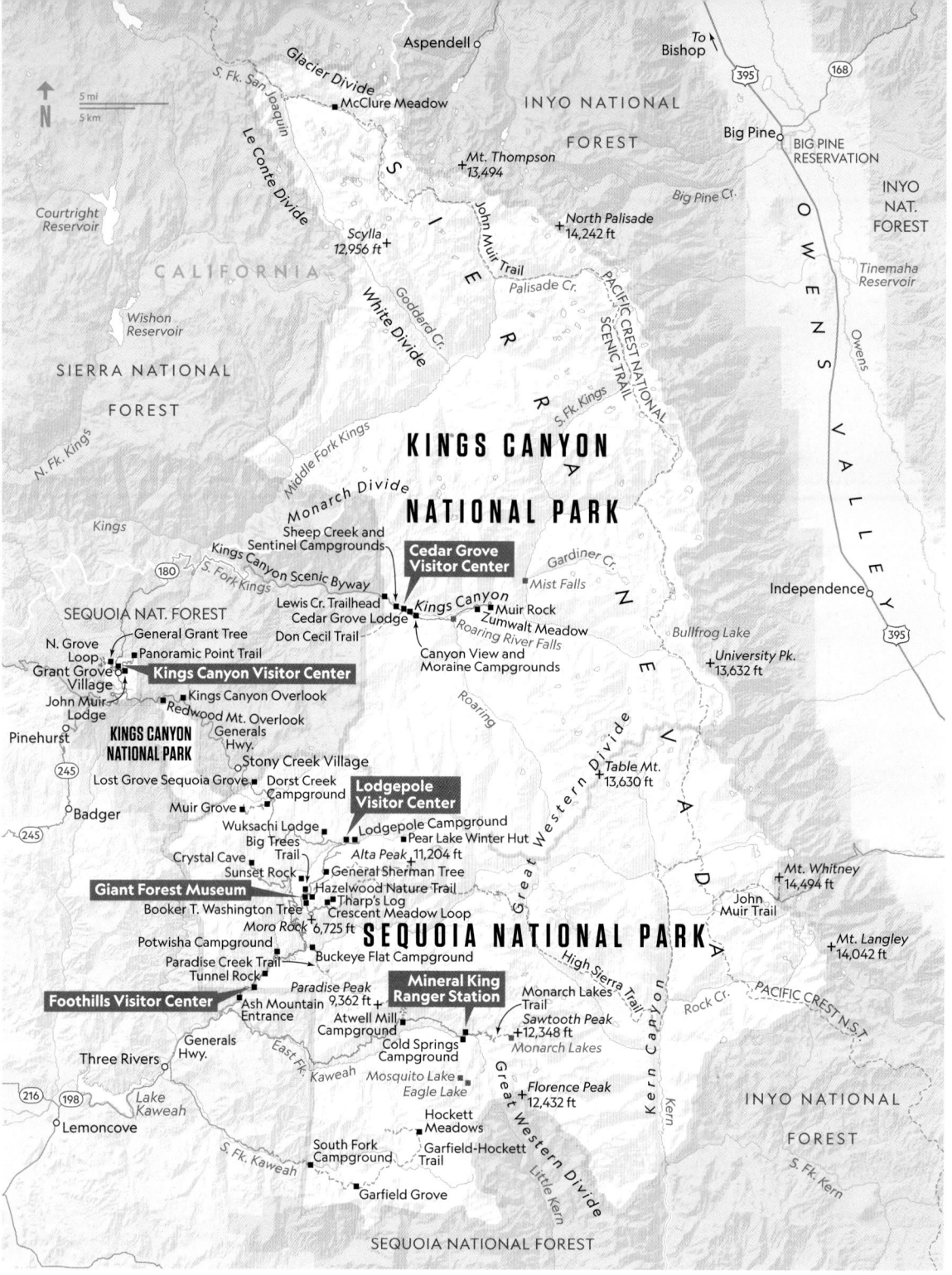

N 5 mi / 5 km

Aspendell

To Bishop

Glacier Divide

S. Fk. San Joaquin

McClure Meadow

INYO NATIONAL FOREST

395

168

Le Conte Divide

Mt. Thompson 13,494

Big Pine

BIG PINE RESERVATION

Big Pine Cr.

INYO NAT. FOREST

Courtright Reservoir

SIERRA

Scylla 12,956 ft

North Palisade 14,242 ft

CALIFORNIA

John Muir Trail

Palisade Cr.

PACIFIC CREST NATIONAL SCENIC TRAIL

OWENS VALLEY

Tinemaha Reservoir

Wishon Reservoir

White Divide

Goddard Cr.

Owens

SIERRA NATIONAL

FOREST

S. Fk. Kings

Owens

N. Fk. Kings

Middle Fork Kings

KINGS CANYON

Monarch Divide

NATIONAL PARK

Kings

Gardiner Cr.

Mist Falls

Independence

Sheep Creek and Sentinel Campgrounds

Kings Canyon Scenic Byway

180

S. Fork Kings

Cedar Grove Visitor Center

Kings Canyon

Muir Rock

Zumwalt Meadow

Roaring River Falls

Bullfrog Lake

Lewis Cr. Trailhead

Cedar Grove Lodge

SEQUOIA NAT. FOREST

General Grant Tree

Panoramic Point Trail

Don Cecil Trail

Canyon View and Moraine Campgrounds

Roaring

University Pk. 13,632 ft

395

N. Grove Loop

Kings Canyon Visitor Center

Grant Grove Village

John Muir Lodge

Kings Canyon Overlook

Redwood Mt. Overlook

Pinehurst

KINGS CANYON NATIONAL PARK

Generals Hwy.

Stony Creek Village

Table Mt. 13,630 ft

Great Western Divide

245

Lost Grove Sequoia Grove

Dorst Creek Campground

Lodgepole Visitor Center

Badger

Muir Grove

245

Wuksachi Lodge

Lodgepole Campground

Pear Lake Winter Hut

Big Trees Trail

Alta Peak 11,204 ft

Mt. Whitney 14,494 ft

Crystal Cave

General Sherman Tree

John Muir Trail

Sunset Rock

Hazelwood Nature Trail

Giant Forest Museum

Tharp's Log

Booker T. Washington Tree

Crescent Meadow Loop

Moro Rock 6,725 ft

SEQUOIA NATIONAL PARK

Mt. Langley 14,042 ft

Potwisha Campground

Buckeye Flat Campground

High Sierra Trail

PACIFIC CREST N.S.T.

Paradise Creek Trail

Tunnel Rock

Rock Cr.

Foothills Visitor Center

Paradise Peak 9,362 ft

Mineral King Ranger Station

Monarch Lakes Trail

Ash Mountain Entrance

Atwell Mill Campground

Sawtooth Peak 12,348 ft

Kern Canyon

Kern

Generals Hwy.

Cold Springs Campground

Monarch Lakes

INYO NATIONAL

Three Rivers

East Fk. Kaweah

Mosquito Lake

Eagle Lake

Florence Peak 12,432 ft

FOREST

216

198

Lake Kaweah

Great Western Divide

Lemoncove

Hockett Meadows

S. Fk. Kaweah

South Fork Campground

Garfield-Hockett Trail

Little Kern

S. Fk. Kern

Garfield Grove

SEQUOIA NATIONAL FOREST

The exterior of John Muir Lodge

SLEEP

Ⓣ There are 14 campgrounds across Sequoia and Kings Canyon, two of which are open all year. Though the sites are plentiful, they fill up quickly.

→ The trailhead for the famous Muir Grove of giant sequoias is at **Dorst Creek Campground**. Its central location also makes the campground a great base for a trip to both parks. Reservations are required for all 222 sites. The campground is usually open mid-June through Labor Day weekend.

→ **Lodgepole Campground** typically opens before Memorial Day and closes in phases through December. All 214 sites are reservation only, made on a four-month rolling basis. Nearby Lodgepole Village is packed with amenities. In the summer, the free Sequoia Shuttle makes pickups and drop-offs here.

→ Cedar Grove is a relatively remote area in Kings Canyon with four reservation-only campgrounds: **Sentinel** (82 sites; open April–October), next to the visitors center; **Canyon View Group Campground** (16 sites; open May–January), a quarter mile from Cedar Grove Village; **Moraine** (121 sites; open May–early September); and **Sheep Creek** (111 sites; open May–September), on the floor of the canyon.

→ Grant Grove Village is the entry point to Kings Canyon, and three evergreen-packed campgrounds are in the area: **Azalea** (110 sites) is open year-round and requires reservations, except from November to Memorial Day. Both **Crystal Springs** (35 sites) and **Sunset** (158 sites) are open May to September and require reservations.

→ In the Mineral King area, **Cold Springs** and **Atwell Mill** are accessible only by unpaved roads off Highway 198. Open in the summer, these tent-only, reservation-only sites are the highest in the park, at 7,500 feet.

→ There are three campgrounds in the foothills of Sequoia: **Potwisha** (42 sites; open year-round), **Buckeye Flat** (27 tent-only sites; open March–September), and **South Fork** (10 tent-only sites, year-round). All three require advanced reservations.

There are also fantastic lodges and cabins within park bounds.

→ The centrally located and modern **Wuksachi Lodge** boasts spectacular mountain views. It's close to Lodgepole Village, the Giant Forest Museum, and trails to Cahoon Meadow and Twin Lakes.

→ The classic **John Muir Lodge** sits in Grant Grove Village, close to a sequoia grove, visitors center, market, restaurants, and a post office. You'll also be near trails to the iconic General Grant Tree.

→ Nearby **Grant Grove Cabins** have the same access with a more rustic overnight experience. Choose from a timber or tent-style cabin. The "Honeymoon Cabin," or Cabin 9, built in 1910, is the oldest structure still standing in Grant Grove Village.

→ The remote **Cedar Grove Lodge** inside Kings Canyon is reachable via a scenic 35-mile drive from Grant Grove Village. You'll be close to North Dome, Grand Sentinel, Zumwalt Meadow, Roaring River Falls, and Muir Rock.

Easy Access

Accessible Option

S Sequoia and Kings Canyon are filled with the most awesome, massive trees in the world. That might make you think that you need to take awesome, massive hikes to see them, but you'd be wrong. While the parks have outstanding multiday treks and towering peaks to summit, there are also accessible, doable sojourns that take you right into their hearts.

→ Have a picnic at Crescent Meadow in Sequoia, then take the 1.3-mile **Crescent Meadow Loop** around the blooming flora.

→ Two trails lead to the must-see **General Sherman Tree**: The main trail is a half mile to the tree from Wolverton Road. A short (500-foot) wheelchair-accessible trail is off Generals Highway. While the 2,200-year-old tree, named after William Tecumseh Sherman (a general in the Union Army), isn't the tallest or widest, it does have the most wood in volume in its trunk of any tree on Earth. Don't forget to take that *photograph*.

→ Though most people summit Mount Whitney from the Inyo National Forest side, apply for a wilderness permit to reach the peak from the west. The

HIKE

60-mile one-way hike along the **High Sierra Trail** to the John Muir Trail takes at least 10 days.

→ **Alta Peak** is a challenging climb. It's steep and requires high-altitude preparation. Keep a careful eye on the trail conditions before you begin, since snow can stay on the mountain though the summer. If you can manage the trek, you'll be rewarded with gorgeous panoramic views, including of Mount Whitney.

→ The paved **General Grant Tree Trail** is a 0.3-mile walk from the parking area. You'll get to see one of the largest living trees in the world, named the Nation's Christmas Tree in 1926 by President Calvin Coolidge.

→ The eight-mile round-trip walk to **Mist Falls** in Kings Canyon is relatively flat until the last forested mile. As one of the largest cascades in the park, this is a popular hike, so be prepared for crowds. Once you arrive at the falls, which drop 100 feet, watch out for wet and slippery rocks.

→ The same challenging trail leads to **Eagle Lake** if you take the split to the left after two miles. The glacially carved, emerald-colored tarn is a popular destination, so expect company.

→ The hike up to **Paradise Peak** isn't a long one, but you'll trek high enough to find fantastic views. As the trees part, look out over the parks' valleys and peaks.

→ If you'd like a sequoia grove all to yourself, hike five miles to the Garfield Grove along the **Garfield-Hockett Trail**. The steep route levels out as it nears the Hockett Meadows, and there's a backcountry campsite after four miles.

→ The **Panoramic Point Trail** provides one of the best views in the park in an easy-to-reach way. Pull off the main road near the Kings Canyon Visitor Center toward the picnic area and trailhead, then travel the half-mile paved path to a striking overlook of the Sierra Nevada.

→ Get an early start on the hike to the **Upper and Lower Monarch Lakes** in Mineral King. The 4.2-mile one-way trek passes through meadows, red fir forest, and the avalanche-impacted Chihuahua Bowl. Before reaching the foot of Sawtooth Peak, you'll see Timber Gap and the Great Western Divide. Continue past them to Sawtooth Pass to get expansive views of the southern Sierras.

→ The **North Grove Loop** is not as popular as other big-tree walks, which is a surprise. It's an easy and quiet trek in close view of the sequoias. Find the trailhead at the Grant Tree parking area. Combined with the **Dead Giant Loop**, the route is about 2.5 miles.

→ The accessible **Big Trees Trail** is flat, paved, and full of educational displays. It's also a great spot to look for wildlife like yellow-bellied marmots and bears. If you have the time, hop across the road to walk the **Hazelwood Nature Trail**. The trails cover two different sections of the same sequoia grove.

→ Take the short **Beetle Rock Vista Trail** from the Giant Forest Museum. You'll find views of the western edge of the park and the San Joaquin Valley. Take a moment to appreciate the trees and plants that thrive in the rocky crevasses. You can climb on the rock once you arrive, but there are no paths or maintenance.

Mist Falls in Paradise Valley

A fun (and humbling) size comparison at the base of a giant sequoia

Plan your hike for beautiful sunrises
or sunsets amid the trees.

A pale swallowtail perches on a western wallflower.

SPOT

T The varied ecosystems of Sequoia and Kings Canyon are home to equally varied wildlife. As you hike from low to high elevations, you'll see a change in the types of animals you spot.

→ *If you're looking for mammals, it's best to split your expectations by elevation.* **Gray foxes**, **bobcats**, **black bears**, **woodrats**, *and* **white-footed mice** *flock to the oak woodlands and riverside vegetation of the park's low-elevation foothills. Meanwhile, the montane forests and meadows welcome* **mule deer**, **black bears**, **mountain lions**, *and* **gray squirrels**. *The high country of the subalpine and alpine regions is home to* **marmots**, **pika**, *and* **white-tailed jack rabbits**.

→ *Reptile fans will have the best luck sticking to the foothills, where* **gopher snakes**, **California kingsnakes**, **western whiptail lizards**, *and* **California newts** *meander.*

→ *More than* **200 species of birds** *venture through or stay in Sequoia and Kings Canyon, both designated as Globally Important Bird Areas. Look for* **California quail**, **band-tailed pigeons**, *and* **acorn woodpeckers** *in the foothills; trek higher to find* **Clark's nutcrackers**, **golden eagles**, *and* **peregrine falcons**.

T There's one main route through the parks' most popular and quintessential sights. **Generals Highway** will take you from just south of the Kings Canyon Visitor Center down to the Foothills Visitor Center. Stop at the Redwood Mountain and Kings Canyon Overlooks for their panoramic vistas before exiting official park grounds and entering Sequoia. Your next stop should be the Lost Grove Sequoia Grove, where giant sequoias abut the roadway. From there, find the Muir Grove Trailhead at the back of the Dorst Creek Campground for a short, gentle hike through the trees, then stop at Little Baldy to look over the Great Western Divide mountain ranges.

As you continue south, you'll pass the Lodgepole Visitor Center, the famous General Sherman Tree, the Giant Forest Museum (a great spot to learn the history of the park and its natural wonders), the Eleven Range Overlook (with an outdoor exhibit and views of Kaweah Canyon and the San Joaquin Valley), Amphitheater Point (an overlook to Moro Rock), the Hospital Rock pictographs (sacred to the Mono, Yokut, and Tübatulabal peoples), Tunnel Rock (a granite boulder pass-through), and the Foothills Visitor Center.

If you pull off on Crescent Meadow Road, stop at the Booker T. Washington Tree (now more than 120 years old). Take the Moro Rock Loop and hike up the 350 steps to the top of its namesake for unmatched views above the tree canopy. Steep drop-offs are blocked by handrails, but it's still dangerous for small children.

The other route worth driving is **Kings Canyon Scenic Byway**, which closes in the winter. Starting just before the Lewis Creek Trailhead, travel east past a series of campgrounds to the Canyon View Overlook, historic Knapp's Cabin (built in 1928 as a fishing and camping getaway), and short hikes to the Roaring River Falls, Zumwalt Meadow, and Muir Rock.

DRIVE

The Rae Lakes area is a great spot to camp, swim, or hike.

Hikers can join ranger-led night hikes of Moro Rock for stargazing.

Fog hovers among the trees at golden hour.

→ EXPLORE

G Get a different perspective on the parks by dipping into the waters, climbing up the cliffs, and going underground.

→ Book a ticket ahead of time to tour **Crystal Cave**. You'll get to walk a half-mile loop through the marble cavern, hearing the water that flows through it and wandering past its ancient geological formations.

→ Find a **cool swimming hole** as you hike the Paradise Creek Trail in Sequoia or at Muir Rock in Kings Canyon. Just be careful of the risks when swimming in a river. There are also small "beach-like" spots just upstream from Muir Rock to lay out a blanket and picnic.

→ The rock in Sequoia and Kings Canyon is similar to that in Yosemite, making it a great spot for **rock climbers**. In Sequoia, try climbing Moro Rock or the remote Angel Wings off the High Sierra Trail.

→ Experience the park on **horseback** in the summer. Book a trip for an afternoon or a multiday adventure with an outfitter like Grant Grove Stables or Cedar Grove Pack Station.

→ Check the park's website for available winter programs, such as a **ranger-led snowshoe trek** or a **cross-country ski** through Giant Forest and Giant Grove. If you want to turn your excursion into an overnight, book the **Pear Lake Winter Hut**, a historic and cozy 10-person cabin nestled in the mountains.

→ Get an introduction to the region's forests, meadows, and human history at the **Giant Forest Museum**, converted from the historic Giant Forest market building. The museum is meant to serve as a jumping-off point to better experience the giant sequoias.

→ Catch a sunset at, you guessed it, **Sunset Rock**. Time your 1.4-mile round-trip hike from the Giant Forest Museum correctly to watch the colors change over the canyon.

Winter Wonderland

→ RANGER RECOMMENDATION ←

In Kings Canyon, take the **Don Cecil Trail** to Sheep Creek Cascade. In just a mile and a half, you'll get lovely views of the landscape and see a little waterfall roll under a bridge. The easy-access route leaves right from the visitors center.

In Sequoia, head to **Tharp's Log**, located in the Giant Forest—also home to the General Sherman Tree. While the region is popular, there are miles of trails that get little foot traffic. This fallen sequoia was fashioned into a rustic cabin by cattle rancher Hale Tharp before the national park was established. It's a striking sight on the edge of a sequoia-lined meadow often frequented by black bears.

Yosemite Falls and Half Dome

YOSEMITE NATIONAL PARK

CALIFORNIA

ESTABLISHED: October 1, 1890

SIZE: 747,956 acres

VISITORS CENTERS: Yosemite Valley Welcome Center, Tuolumne Meadows Visitor Center (seasonal), Happy Isles Art and Nature Center, Big Oak Flat Information Station, Wawona Visitor Center

----

TRANSPORTATION: The free Yosemite Valley shuttle, Mariposa Grove Shuttle (April–November), and a free shuttle between Yosemite and the Badger Pass Ski Area (December–March). Glacier Point Bus Tours can be booked, and hikers can utilize the Yosemite Valley–Tuolumne Meadows Hiker's Bus (mid-June–early September).

DOGS ALLOWED: Only on paved roads, sidewalks, and bicycle paths and in campgrounds

----

WHEN TO GO: The park is open all year, but some roads (Glacier Point, Tioga) close mid-November to late May. Expect crowds in late spring, summer, and early fall. Winter brings snow.

CONTACT: 209-372-0200; nps.gov/yose
9039 Village Drive
Yosemite National Park, CA 95389

Y Yosemite National Park is at once intimate and expansive, towering and deep, historic and enduring. It might seem like the wonders of the park are obvious, but there's more to this vast landscape than its sheer rock walls and green canyons. Geologically, the landscape has been shaped by glacial erosion, water, and ice. From a human perspective, it's been shaped by exploration, settlement, conflict, conservation, and tourism. Bring your story to Yosemite and see where it fits in.

SLEEP

Y Yosemite's popularity impacts every part of the park experience, including where you stay. If you want to sleep within park bounds, you need to plan ahead and book early. Decide which of the park's 13 campgrounds is your best fit by figuring out where you'd like to set your home base. These are your options:

→ Four campgrounds are in the popular Yosemite Valley, where the park's most iconic sights tower above and visitors have access to the services and amenities of nearby Yosemite Village. **Upper Pines** (235 sites, 32 RV only, 5 tent only; open year-round), **Lower Pines** (73 sites, 9 RV only; open mid-April–mid-October), and **North Pines** (80 sites, 13 RV only; open mid-April–October) all book five months in advance—and there's an early-access lottery for North Pines. **Camp 4** (61 tent-only sites; open year-round), which sits close to Yosemite Falls, books out one week in

advance from May to September and is first come, first served from October to May.

→ North of Yosemite Valley, **Tuolumne Meadows** (open July–September) has 304 sites, including seven ADA-compliant sites and four equestrian sites. The campground can accommodate RVs up to 35 feet.

→ The quieter, smaller **Tamarack Flat** (52 tent-only sites) is just east of Crane Flat and available June through mid-October by reservation only.

→ **Crane Flat** (151 sites, 35 tent-only; open July–October), **White Wolf** (74 sites; open July–September), **Yosemite Creek** (75 tent-only sites; open July–September), and **Porcupine Flat** (52 sites, 48 tent only; open July–October) all book out two weeks in advance during the summer and are easily accessible off the main Tioga Road. **Hodgdon Meadow** (105 sites; open year-round) books out five months ahead.

→ Stay south of Yosemite Valley at **Wawona** (99 sites; open year-round, reservations required April–October) to get close to the distinguished Mariposa Grove of Giant Sequoias and the Yosemite History Center. The nearby historic town of the same name is home to a visitors center, hotel, and market.

→ Between Wawona and Yosemite Valley is **Bridalveil Creek** (115 sites, 41 tent-only; open mid-July–early September), where you can sleep surrounded by a canopy of red fir and lodgepole pine. The sites are available by reservation only.

→ Get a permit to experience the park's **backcountry camping**. You can get one in

advance online or in person no more than two days before your trip. The park maintains 293 of these sites. Enter the early-access lottery for better luck.

Roughing it isn't the only way to spend an evening in the park. There are four lodges in Yosemite Valley and three outside of it:

→ **The Ahwahnee**, previously known as the Majestic Yosemite Hotel, is a luxury lodge built in the 1920s. Listed on the National Register of Historic Places, it boasts floor-to-ceiling windows, world-class dining, a candy shop, and a cozy lounge.

→ The natural design of the family-friendly **Yosemite Valley Lodge** fits perfectly into its surroundings. Kids will love the outdoor swimming pool, and adults will appreciate the unmatched views.

→ **Curry Village** and **Housekeeping Camp** provide the perfect balance of comfort and adventure. Fall asleep on real beds and wake up to the great outdoors in these canvas cabins.

→ Outside the valley, stay at the historic **Wawona Hotel**, one of the state's first mountain resorts. Established in 1856, the Victorian-era lodge brings its guests together for barbecues, music, swimming, and horseback riding.

→ Find canvas tents outside the valley at **White Wolf Lodge**, **Tuolumne Meadows Lodge**, and **High Sierra Camps**. The first two were built as a peaceful community respite, while the third is a remote experience up in the mountains, accessible only by foot or mule.

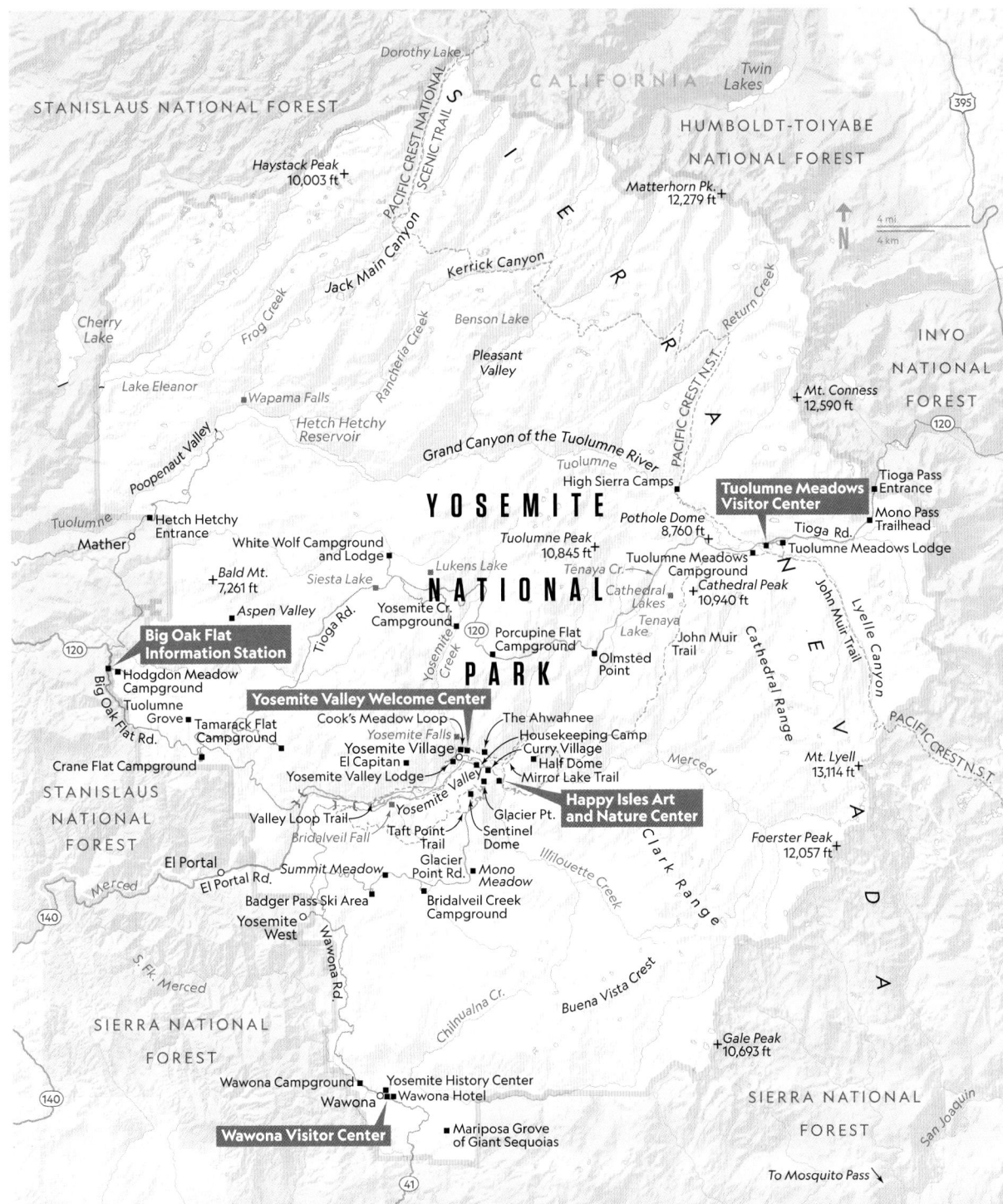

STANISLAUS NATIONAL FOREST

Haystack Peak
10,003 ft

Dorothy Lake

CALIFORNIA

Twin Lakes

HUMBOLDT-TOIYABE NATIONAL FOREST

Matterhorn Pk.
12,279 ft

Kerrick Canyon

Jack Main Canyon

PACIFIC CREST NATIONAL SCENIC TRAIL

SIERRA

Frog Creek

Rancheria Creek

Benson Lake

Pleasant Valley

Return Creek

PACIFIC CREST N.S.T.

Cherry Lake

Lake Eleanor

Wapama Falls

Hetch Hetchy Reservoir

Grand Canyon of the Tuolumne River

Tuolumne

High Sierra Camps

Mt. Conness
12,590 ft

INYO NATIONAL FOREST

Poopenaut Valley

Tuolumne

Mather

Hetch Hetchy Entrance

YOSEMITE

Tioga Pass Entrance

Mono Pass Trailhead

Tuolumne Meadows Visitor Center

Pothole Dome
8,760 ft

Tioga Rd.

Tuolumne Meadows Lodge

White Wolf Campground and Lodge

Bald Mt.
7,261 ft

Siesta Lake

Aspen Valley

Lukens Lake

Tuolumne Peak
10,845 ft

NATIONAL

Tenaya Cr.

Tuolumne Meadows Campground

Cathedral Peak
10,940 ft

Cathedral Lakes

John Muir Trail

Cathedral Range

John Muir Trail

Lyell Canyon

Yosemite Cr. Campground

Tioga Rd.

Yosemite Creek

Tenaya Lake

Big Oak Flat Information Station

Porcupine Flat Campground

Olmsted Point

PARK

Hodgdon Meadow Campground

Tuolumne Grove

Big Oak Flat Rd.

Tamarack Flat Campground

Yosemite Valley Welcome Center

Cook's Meadow Loop

The Ahwahnee

Housekeeping Camp

Mt. Lyell
13,114 ft

Crane Flat Campground

Yosemite Falls

Yosemite Village

Curry Village

Half Dome

Merced

STANISLAUS NATIONAL FOREST

El Capitan

Yosemite Valley Lodge

Mirror Lake Trail

Happy Isles Art and Nature Center

Valley Loop Trail

Yosemite Valley

Glacier Pt.

Sentinel Dome

Foerster Peak
12,057 ft

El Portal

Bridalveil Fall

Taft Point Trail

Mono Meadow

Clark Range

N

E

V

A

D

A

El Portal Rd.

Summit Meadow

Glacier Point Rd.

Illilouette Creek

Badger Pass Ski Area

Bridalveil Creek Campground

Yosemite West

SIERRA NATIONAL FOREST

Wawona Rd.

S. Fk. Merced

Buena Vista Crest

Chinquapin Cr.

Gale Peak
10,693 ft

Wawona Campground

Wawona

Yosemite History Center

Wawona Hotel

SIERRA NATIONAL FOREST

San Joaquin

Wawona Visitor Center

Mariposa Grove of Giant Sequoias

To Mosquito Pass

Cathedral Peak and Upper Cathedral Lake

It's nearly impossible to narrow down the list of worthwhile hikes in a park as tremendous as Yosemite, but these few are at the top of the list for many visitors.

→ One hike gets first billing for most Yosemite visitors: **Half Dome**. The formation is a true national park icon, and fit hikers can climb to its top. (Before you get there, however, stop to see Vernal and Nevada Falls.) Thousands of people reach the summit each year, but hundreds also need help from rangers. Get a permit during the March lottery and prepare for a 14- to 16-mile round-trip hike with 4,800 feet of elevation gain. Pull yourself up two metal cables for the last 400 feet. Safety tip: Take your time and stay within the cable's bounds.

→ The moderate 11.5-mile **Valley Loop Trail** is relatively flat and relatively solitary. There are multiple touchpoints for the trail, and you can hop on and off as you need. See the Three Brothers rock formation,

Merced River, El Capitan Bridge, and so much more.

→ Walk the easy one-mile **Cook's Meadow Loop** from the Yosemite Valley Welcome Center. Look up toward Yosemite Falls, Half Dome, Glacier Point, and Sentinel Rock as you stroll. Use the bike path to return.

→ Find the **Mirror Lake Trail** at shuttle stop 17, and start your hike with a mile-long walk down a paved service road. Get on the top at its end and trek along Tenaya Creek, crossing two bridges, and returning past Mirror Lake itself. Do this hike in spring and early summer to see the lake at its fullest.

→ Take in an unmatched view of the park after scrambling up the granite slope of **Sentinel Dome**. Get there by hiking the moderate 1.8-mile trail of the same name and make it a loop by adding the 2.2-mile **Taft Point Trail**. Watch out for fractures in the granite that can drop up to 2,000 feet.

→ Trek the five-mile round-trip trail to **Wapama Falls** from the Hetch Hetchy Entrance. This lesser-visited section sits at a lower elevation and is home to a massive reservoir. The trail follows its shoreline.

→ Hike to the Cathedral Lakes at the foot of Cathedral Peak on the popular **John Muir Trail**. Look for rock climbers ascending its 800 feet of granite as you move toward Upper Cathedral Lake. Take the spur down to the lower lake, then turn back the way you came. Hop on the shuttle bus to this trailhead to avoid crowded parking lots.

HIKE

Iconic Hike

A diverse array of reptiles call the park home.

→ SPOT

(F) From small insects to large mammals, creatures reside in every corner of the park. It's truly impossible to travel through Yosemite without seeing one of its non-human residents.

→ **Alpine butterflies** are a unique breed. These 60 species need alpine plants to survive, so they will brave the cold that comes with higher elevations. Slow down your stroll and look for many of them, like the Sierra Nevada parnassian butterfly, along Tioga Road.

→ Mono Meadow off Glacier Point Road is a special place for bird-watchers. Look for **Steller's jays**, **common ravens**, **mountain chickadees**, and **western bluebirds**—just some of the 262 species in the park—as you wait in the meadow. Look higher to see **prairie falcons**, **sharp-skinned hawks**, and **American kestrels**.

→ Bring your binoculars to Lukens Lake to spot **northern flickers**, **brown creepers**, **golden-crowned sparrows**, and **orange-crowned warblers**. The 1.6-mile round-trip route starts off Tioga Road.

→ It's not wise to get close to **American black bears**, but many visitors hope to spot one of the 300 to 500 in the park. If that's you, head to a meadow at dusk and be patient. When you see one, keep your distance.

→ After being gone from Yosemite for more than 100 years, **Sierra Nevada bighorn sheep** are back. John Muir called them the "bravest of all Sierra Mountaineers," and you can see them climb the rocky slopes that other animals avoid.

→ Only two native populations of the carnivorous, tree-dwelling **fishers** remain in California, and one is in the Sierra Nevada. Look for them near the Merced River.

A purple-headed hummingbird pauses mid-flight.

A baby deer ducks into a tallgrass meadow.

A mischievous black bear cub ventures upward.

Sights of a lifetime appear around
every curve in Yosemite.

DRIVE

Y Yosemite is massive, so most visitors rely on its roads to get from site to site. Take your car or rely on its free shuttles—the Valleywide and East Valley ones are popular and excellent avenues for seeing Yosemite's grandeur. Either way, consider these routes through the park:

→ **Tioga Road** is the main west-east route through the park, open seasonally. Hop on it near Tuolumne Grove, then continue on to the Tamarack Flat Trailhead, Siesta Lake, Lukens Lake Trailhead, Yosemite Creek Picnic Area, Porcupine Flat Campground, Olmsted Point, Tenaya Lake, Pothole Dome, Lembert Dome, and Mono Pass Trailhead.

→ Turn on **Glacier Point Road** off Wawona Road and take the route to El Portal View, Badger Pass Ski Area, Summit Meadow, Bridalveil Creek Amphitheater, Sentinel Dome, Taft Point Trailhead, Washburn Point, and Glacier Point.

→ Follow **Northside and Southside Drives**, which eventually turn into El Portal and Wawona Roads, respectively, in and out of Yosemite Village. Stop at Tunnel View, Bridalveil Fall, Sentinel Meadow, Cook's Meadow Loop Trailhead, Lower and Upper Yosemite Fall Trailheads, El Capitan Meadow, and Valley View.

→ Book the ranger-led **Yosemite Valley Floor Tour** on an open-air tram between mid-April and mid-October. It departs from Yosemite Valley Lodge and passes views of Yosemite Falls, Half Dome, El Capitan, Tunnel View, and Bridalveil Fall.

A climber at Mosquito Pass

EXPLORE

A A lot of parks claim to have an activity for every kind of visitor, but that's truly the case in Yosemite. Lovers of art, history, water, and wildlife will all discover something to love.

→ Join an art program at the family-friendly **Happy Isles Art and Nature Center**. Participate in an art retreat, bring the kids for a class, or head to Yosemite Valley Lodge for a paint-and-sip date.

→ Book a two-hour or all-day **horseback ride** at the Wawona Stable. Follow the Meadow Loop Trail and imagine how early pioneers rode their way through the park on the same route.

→ Visit the **Yosemite History Center** (formerly the Pioneer History Center) to head back in time. Ride a horse-drawn wagon under a covered bridge, see the park's historic buildings, and watch blacksmiths forge iron tools.

→ Kayak the peaceful waters of **Tenaya Lake** after renting a vessel from an outfitter like the Padyak Shack. Take a break on the lakeshore for a quiet picnic.

→ Rest your feet after hiking and spend some time in **Yosemite Village**. Visit the Yosemite Museum (the first museum built in the National Park System) and its Native American cultural exhibits, the Ansel Adams Gallery, and the Wilderness Center, where you can learn about the wildlife in the park, rent gear, pick up permits, and plan.

→ Wander through 500 massive, mature trees at the **Mariposa Grove of Giant Sequoias**, which inspired President Lincoln to first protect this land in 1864.

→ **Climbers** have long honored Yosemite as one of the greatest climbing spots on the planet, and there are truly an endless number of challenges to tackle. Contact the Yosemite Mountaineering School and Guide Service to get started. Make sure to secure a permit for an overnight climbing trip.

→ Raft along the **Merced River** in the summer. Rent a raft at Curry Village and drop in at the Stoneman Bridge, then paddle out to the Sentinel Beach Picnic Area.

→ Don't shy away from Yosemite in the winter. **Badger Pass Ski Area**, the oldest downhill ski resort in California, is a great place to start, with its tubing track, terrain park, equipment rentals, lessons, guided tours, groomed cross-country trails, and ski lifts. A free shuttle runs between Yosemite Village and the ski area.

Family Friendly

→ **RANGER RECOMMENDATION** ←

*Get away from the crowds in one of the most popular areas of the park by hiking the **Valley Loop Trail**. Pop in and out of this route easily, since it follows the base of the granite cliffs, meadows, and rivers inside the valley on its east-west trails and wagon roads.*

→ PACIFIC NORTHWEST

North Cascades
National Park

Olympic
National Park

Mt. Rainier
National Park

Crater Lake
National Park

Redwood National
and State Parks

Lassen Volcanic
National Park

CANADA

MONTANA

WASHINGTON

IDAHO

PACIFIC

OCEAN

OREGON

NEVADA

CALIFORNIA

100 mi

100 km

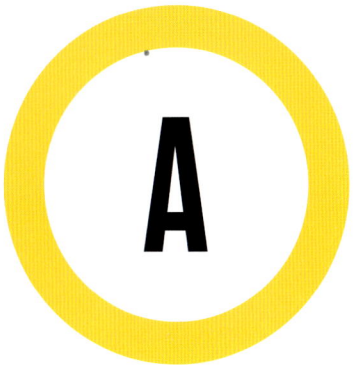

Almost all the large ancient forests left in the lower 48 grow in the Pacific Northwest's six rugged national parks. Visitors can hike the cathedral-like glades of Douglas fir and western red cedar in Mount Rainier (page 566), Olympic (page 586), and North Cascades (page 576). Redwood (page 600) has trees in their second millennium. Then there are the volcanoes: Lassen (page 558) is evidence of the planet's violence in broken mountains and boiling mud pots, while Crater Lake (page 548) showcases forces that collapsed a mountaintop and formed a six-mile-wide lake, the nation's deepest. These are lands of extremes—in geological forces, depths and heights, and beauty.

LEFT: Crater Lake via the Cleetwood Cove Trail, Crater Lake National Park (page 548) **PREVIOUS PAGES:** Mount Rainier National Park (page 566)

CRATER LAKE ← NATIONAL PARK

OREGON

ESTABLISHED: May 22, 1902

SIZE: 183,224 acres

VISITORS CENTERS: The Rim Visitor Center (open in summer) offers educational exhibits and ranger assistance. The Steel Information Center is open year-round.

TRANSPORTATION: Boat tours and summer trolleys

DOGS ALLOWED: Only in restricted areas and on select trails. Check the park's pet page online to plan accordingly.

WHEN TO GO: Rim Drive usually closes by November 1, but Rim Village remains open year-round. Winter lasts long and offers many snow activities. Summer brings good weather—and crowds.

CONTACT: 541-594-3000; nps.gov/crla
1 Sager Building
Crater Lake, OR 97604

C Crater Lake was formed 7,700 years ago when a volcanic eruption collapsed a massive mountain peak and the giant hole filled with rain and snow, eventually creating the deepest lake in the United States, at 1,943 feet. The sapphire-colored, pristine water (more than five trillion gallons of it) has nowhere to drain, so it stays cradled in what remains of Mount Mazama, the ecosystem thriving around it.

A wintry view of the park's namesake

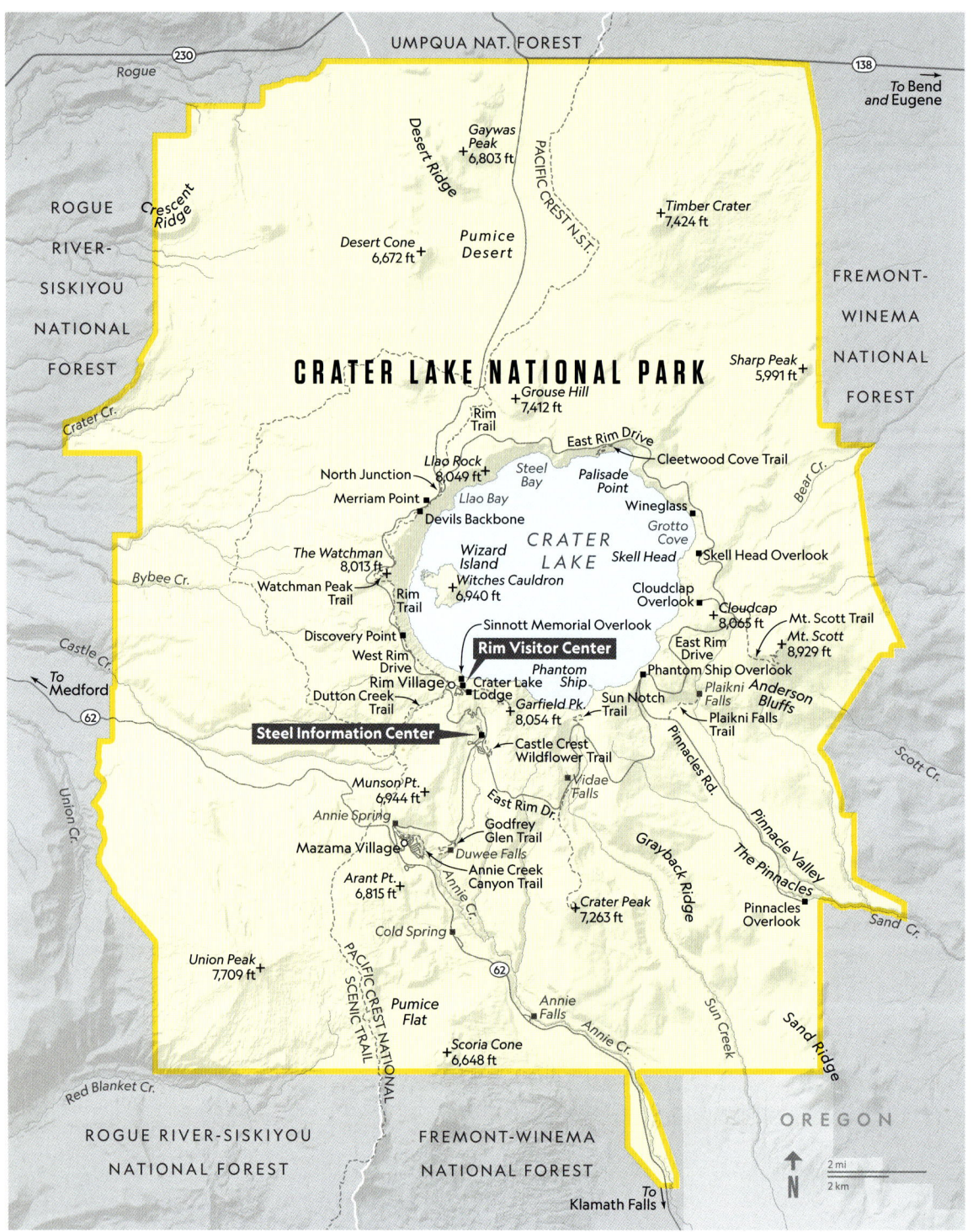

CRATER LAKE NATIONAL PARK

UMPQUA NAT. FOREST

Rogue

To Bend
and Eugene

ROGUE
RIVER-
SISKIYOU
NATIONAL
FOREST

Crescent
Ridge

Crater Cr.

FREMONT-
WINEMA
NATIONAL
FOREST

Desert Ridge

Gaywas
Peak
6,803 ft

Desert Cone
6,672 ft

Pumice
Desert

PACIFIC CREST N.S.T.

Timber Crater
7,424 ft

Sharp Peak
5,991 ft

Grouse Hill
7,412 ft

Rim
Trail

East Rim Drive

Cleetwood Cove Trail

Bear Cr.

North Junction

Llao Rock
8,049 ft

Merriam Point

Steel
Bay

Palisade
Point

Devils Backbone

Llao Bay

Wineglass

CRATER
LAKE

Grotto
Cove

Bybee Cr.

The Watchman
8,013 ft

Wizard
Island

Skell Head

Skell Head Overlook

Watchman Peak
Trail

Witches Cauldron
6,940 ft

Rim
Trail

Cloudclap
Overlook

Cloudcap
8,065 ft

Mt. Scott Trail

Discovery Point

Sinnott Memorial Overlook

Rim Visitor Center

East Rim
Drive

Mt. Scott
8,929 ft

Castle Cr.

To
Medford

62

West Rim
Drive

Rim Village

Dutton Creek
Trail

Crater Lake
Lodge

Phantom
Ship

Garfield Pk.
8,054 ft

Sun Notch
Trail

Phantom Ship Overlook

Plaikni
Falls

Plaikni Falls
Trail

Anderson
Bluffs

Union Cr.

Steel Information Center

Castle Crest
Wildflower Trail

Pinnacles Rd.

Scott Cr.

Munson Pt.
6,944 ft

East Rim Dr.

Vidae
Falls

Annie Spring

Godfrey
Glen Trail

Mazama Village

Duwee Falls

Arant Pt.
6,815 ft

Annie Creek
Canyon Trail

Grayback Ridge

Pinnacle Valley

The Pinnacles

Cold Spring

Crater Peak
7,263 ft

Pinnacles
Overlook

Sand Cr.

Union Peak
7,709 ft

PACIFIC CREST NATIONAL SCENIC TRAIL

Pumice
Flat

Annie
Falls

62

Annie Cr.

Sun Creek

Sand Ridge

Scoria Cone
6,648 ft

Red Blanket Cr.

ROGUE RIVER-SISKIYOU
NATIONAL FOREST

FREMONT-WINEMA
NATIONAL FOREST

To
Klamath Falls

OREGON

N

2 mi
2 km

SLEEP

M Match your overnight stays to your desire for luxury, whether that draws you to an all-inclusive lodge with gorgeous views or a backcountry site amid all the park's wonders. Here are your options:

→ Book a room at the historic **Crater Lake Lodge**, which first opened in 1915 and was reconstructed in 1995. Ask for a lake view and use the lodge as a base for your hiking, swimming, and touring adventures. There's also a restaurant and a nearby café.

→ Stay in a cabin or campsite in **Mazama Village**, surrounded by pine trees and seven miles south of Rim Village. The cabins are modern and well stocked, while the campground has 214 spots with water and electric hookups. Campground reservations are required from July through August; many sites close in October when snow arrives. A store and restaurant are nearby.

→ Take your stay into your own hands by planning a **backcountry camping trip**. You'll need a permit, which must be obtained in person from the ranger station at park headquarters, near the Steel Information Center, no more than a day in advance of your trip. And visitors do, in fact, camp during every season in the park. Be warned: In the summer, no campsites have views of the lake.

Find cabins and picnic areas at Mazama Village.

→ HIKE

Accessible Option

A cliff overlooking Wizard Island

M Most people are focused on trails that provide glimpses of the lake, and the park has plenty of those, but there are also treks to explore other geological wonders. Consider these for your itinerary:

→ The **Pacific Crest National Scenic Trail** takes hikers from the borders of Mexico and Canada along a 2,650-mile route through the United States. Thirty-three miles of that route run through Crater Lake National Park, and trekking that portion offers beautiful views of the lake. Hikers take the **Dutton Creek Trail** up to the rim, follow it for six miles, and then head out to Grouse Hill.

→ Get stunning summit views at the top of the 3.5-mile out-and-back **Garfield Peak Trail**, with its trailhead near Crater Lake Lodge. Travel along the southern rim of Crater Lake before reaching the 8,054-foot peak.

→ Take the 1.6-mile **Watchman Peak Trail** from West Rim Drive to The Watchman, an observation station that was originally designed as a fire lookout in the 1900s. The station sits at 8,013 feet above sea level, so be prepared for the elevation.

→ Hike the steep **Cleetwood Cove Trail** (2.2 miles round-trip), the only route with legal access to the shore of Crater Lake. The switchback-filled, slippery hike is usually open from early summer to mid-fall. Once you're at the lake, it's perfectly OK for you to swim, wade, and fish in the water. Pro tip: Don't rush this challenging hike. Use the benches.

→ Travel along the **Godfrey Glen Trail** to find views of Annie Creek Canyon. The trail is pet friendly and accessible for all-terrain wheelchairs. Pass through an old-growth forest before the view opens up for striking pinnacles of the canyon.

→ Reach the park's highest—and oldest—peak on the 4.4-mile round-trip **Mount Scott Trail**. This 8,929-foot summit provides the only unobstructed views of the entire lake.

→ The 0.8-mile uphill walk on the **Sun Notch Trail** leads you through a grass meadow in view of Crater Lake. Look closely to see the lake and the Phantom Ship, a small island in the lake whose rock formations led to its name.

→ The half-mile **Castle Crest Wildflower Trail** loop is covered in greenery and wildflowers every summer. Grab a brochure that helps identify the native flora at the trailhead off East Rim Drive.

Signage guides hikers to the trails.

U Unsurprisingly, this vast, clear lake breathes life into the ecosystem. Keep an eye out wherever you go, and you're bound to encounter animals who call the park home, like **black bears**, **pine martens**, **red foxes**, **yellow-bellied marmots**, **snowshoe hares**, and **Roosevelt elk**.

The birds at Crater Lake are nearly everywhere. Still, patience will pay off if you're looking for less common species. Try to spot **great gray owls**, **three-toed and black-backed woodpeckers**, **mountain chickadees**, and **ruby-crowned kinglets**. Some summer days, the park partners with the Klamath Bird Observatory for a bird-banding demonstration and a talk about the observatory's birds.

SPOT

A Sierra red fox pauses in the snow.

FLOAT

T There's one chance to explore the waters of Crater Lake: a ranger-guided **boat tour** with the park's official concessionaire. Get to the bottom of the challenging Cleetwood Cove Trail to hop on board. Do yourself a favor and use the bathroom before you get on the two-hour ride.

Rim Drive doesn't have shoulders, so travel with care.

DRIVE

T The main road around the park is **Rim Drive**, the highest road in Oregon. The 33-mile loop connects 30 overlooks, parking lots, trailheads, five picnic areas, and several waterfalls and rock formations. Take the same route by bicycle, or hop on a ranger-led trolley tour in the summer. Don't miss the Sinnott Memorial Overlook, Discovery Point, Cloudcap Overlook, Phantom Ship Overlook, and Skell Head Overlook.

You might think the only option for exploring this landscape is a hike around the caldera, but there's plenty more to do in the park.

→ Take a **boat tour to Wizard Island**, a cinder cone created when the lake filled with water after the volcanic collapse. Circle the lake, then spend three hours on the island hiking a mile up to its highest point.

→ **Fish** in Crater Lake or any of its streams (except Sun and Lost Creeks). Efforts are being made to restore a sustainable population of bull trout, the only fish native to the region's streams. Find kokanee and rainbow salmon, two species that were stocked between 1888 and 1941. Follow licensing and catch-and-release regulations.

→ There are more than 3,000 acres of dry meadow in Crater Lake, known as the **Pumice Desert**, named after the huge amount of pumice the valley was buried under after multiple eruptions of Mount Mazama roughly 7,700 years ago. Explore this expansive and harsh environment to see what can and can't thrive.

→ Discover the area's history on the **Rim Village Walking Tour**. Start at the Rim Visitor Center and then check out the Sinnott Memorial Overlook, 1924 Community House, and Mather Observation Bay.

→ Join a free **ranger-led snowshoe walk** on winter weekends. These one- to two-mile-long treks don't follow a specific trail but usually weave through the forests and meadows. Borrow snowshoes from the ranger if needed.

→ Bold **skiers** and **snowboarders** sometimes tackle the up-and-down routes of the park, though not in the caldera. There aren't any chairlifts, but there's plenty of snow. If you're willing to hike, you can ride down the snowy slopes. The same goes for **sledders**, though it's a less extreme experience.

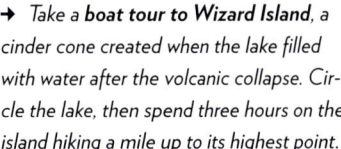
A stream slips through a meadow in the park.

E
X
P
L
O
R
E

→ **RANGER RECOMMENDATION** ←

Head to **The Watchman** during sunrise or sunset to get a 360-degree view of the landscape. You'll likely be alone up at the top, but you can join a ranger-led sunset tour if you prefer the company and guidance.

Brokeoff Mountain and Lake Helen

LASSEN VOLCANIC NATIONAL PARK

CALIFORNIA

ESTABLISHED: August 9, 1916

SIZE: 106,000 acres

VISITORS CENTERS: The Kohm Yah-mah-nee Visitor Center has an exhibit hall, store, and dining options. The historic Loomis Museum is open only in summer and offers exhibits and ranger-led programs.

TRANSPORTATION: No in-park transportation

DOGS ALLOWED: Only in developed areas (paved roads, campgrounds, picnic areas, and parking lots)

WHEN TO GO: Open year-round but facilities close mid-October– late May

CONTACT: 530-595-6100; nps.gov/lavo
38050 Highway 36 East
Mineral, CA 96063

D Don't be fooled by Lassen Volcanic's name: It's more than just volcanoes and dust. The park is packed with mountain lakes, alpine meadows, hydrothermal waters, deep craters, and tall peaks—all created as the result of thousands of years of eruptions. The last ones happened between 1914 and 1917, with the most explosive in 1915. Eventually, all that turmoil turned to beauty, and the park now stands as an example of that powerful shift.

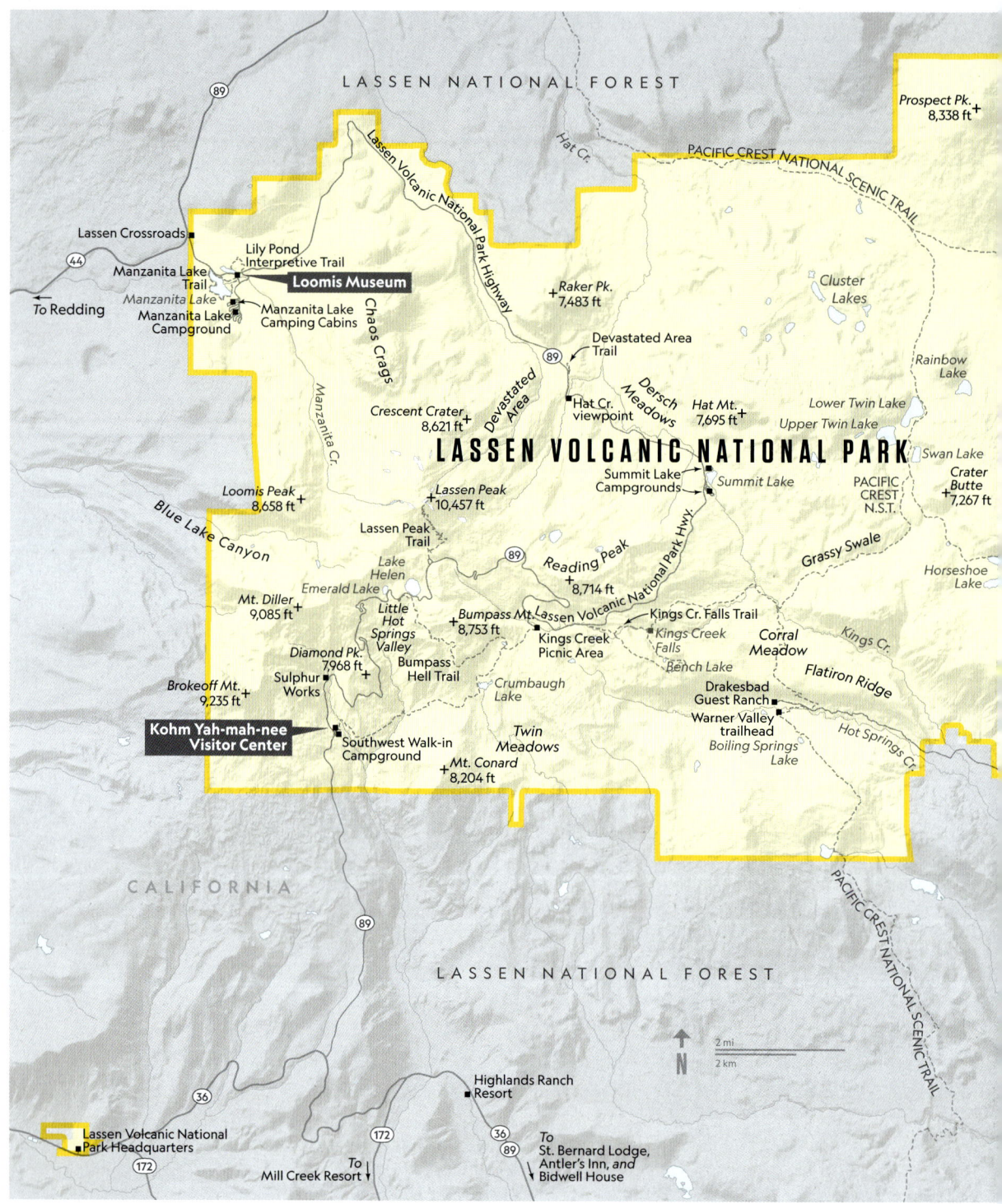

LASSEN NATIONAL FOREST

Prospect Pk.
8,338 ft

PACIFIC CREST NATIONAL SCENIC TRAIL

Hat Cr.

Cluster
Lakes

Lassen Crossroads

Lily Pond
Interpretive Trail

Loomis Museum

Manzanita Lake
Trail

To Redding

Manzanita Lake

Manzanita Lake
Camping Cabins

Manzanita Lake
Campground

Chaos Crags

Manzanita Cr.

Lassen Volcanic National Park Highway

Raker Pk.
7,483 ft

Devastated Area
Trail

89

Hat Cr.
viewpoint

Devastated
Area

Crescent Crater
8,621 ft

Dersch
Meadows

Hat Mt.
7,695 ft

Rainbow
Lake

Lower Twin Lake

Upper Twin Lake

Swan Lake

Crater
Butte
7,267 ft

LASSEN VOLCANIC NATIONAL PARK

Summit Lake
Campgrounds

Summit Lake

PACIFIC
CREST
N.S.T.

Loomis Peak
8,658 ft

Lassen Peak
10,457 ft

Lassen Peak
Trail

Blue Lake Canyon

Lake
Helen

Emerald Lake

Reading Peak
8,714 ft

Lassen Volcanic National Park Hwy.

Grassy Swale

Horseshoe
Lake

Mt. Diller
9,085 ft

Little
Hot
Springs
Valley

Bumpass Mt.
8,753 ft

Kings Cr. Falls Trail

Kings Creek
Picnic Area

Kings Creek
Falls

Corral
Meadow

Kings Cr.

Flatiron Ridge

Diamond Pk.
7,968 ft

Sulphur
Works

Bumpass
Hell Trail

Crumbaugh
Lake

Bench Lake

Drakesbad
Guest Ranch

Brokeoff Mt.
9,235 ft

Kohm Yah-mah-nee
Visitor Center

Southwest Walk-in
Campground

Twin
Meadows

Warner Valley
trailhead

Boiling Springs
Lake

Hot Springs Cr.

Mt. Conard
8,204 ft

CALIFORNIA

89

PACIFIC CREST NATIONAL SCENIC TRAIL

LASSEN NATIONAL FOREST

N

2 mi
2 km

36

172

Highlands Ranch
Resort

Lassen Volcanic National
Park Headquarters

172

89

36

172

To
Mill Creek Resort

To
St. Bernard Lodge,
Antler's Inn, and
Bidwell House

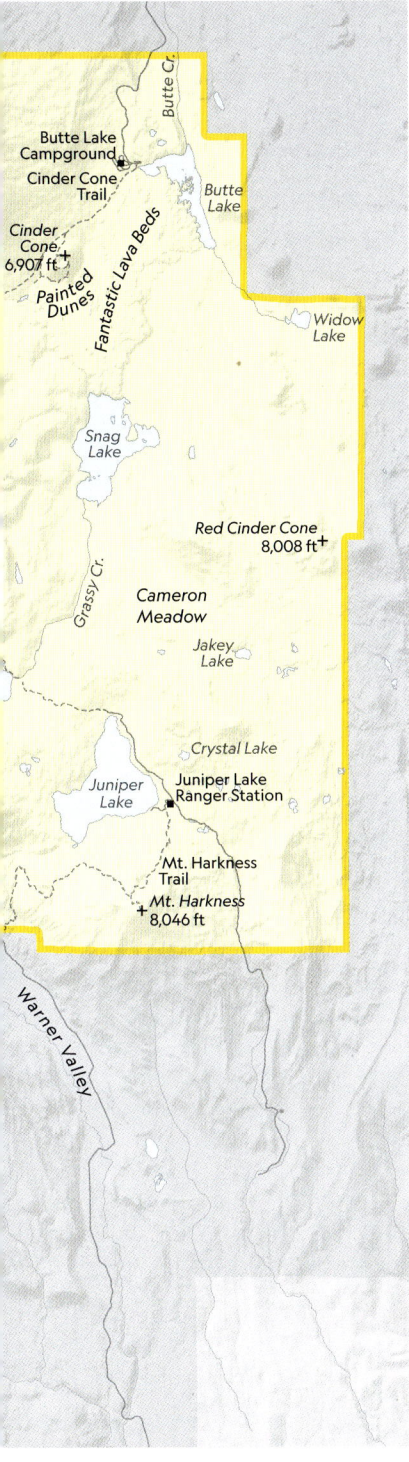

SLEEP

T The lodges, cabins, and camp-grounds inside Lassen make for great base camps from which to explore—and it's easy to find a community of adventurers or some quiet solitude.

→ *Drakesbad Guest Ranch* offers lodge rooms and bungalows, a swimming pool, and guided trips. Kids will love the camp-fire s'mores, archery, and table tennis—and parents will love the children's discounts.

→ The newly built **Manzanita Lake Camping Cabins** come with propane heaters, bear-proof storage, and showers. Bring your own bedding.

→ Stay at one of the seven developed campgrounds, most of which are available by reservation only between June and Sep-tember. Remote northeastern **Butte Lake** (101 sites) offers peaceful paddles along the lake's lava-rock shores. Family-friendly **Manzanita Lake** (170 sites) is large and close to the most amenities, like the nearby camp store. The north and south sections of **Summit Lake Campground** (46 sites) are connected by a short trail, which also leads to the lake. Swim on the north shore, but sleep at quieter sites on the south shore. **Juniper Lake**, **Warner Valley**, and **Southwest Walk-in Campgrounds** are first come, first served only.

→ **Backcountry camp** in the park's wilder spaces. Get a permit (available online only, up to 90 days prior to your trip) and look out for signs designating protected regrowth areas in the Dixie Footprint.

E Explore everything from hydro-thermal areas to volcanic peaks on 150 miles of trails.

→ The challenging **Lassen Peak Trail** reaches its summit during a 4.9-mile round-trip trek. Stay on the switchbacks to the first summit, where the maintained trail ends, then head into the crater or hike up to the final summit.

→ From the trailhead off Lassen Volcanic National Park Highway, take the **Kings Creek Falls Trail** past Lower Kings Creek Meadow to visit a 30-foot waterfall.

→ The gravel **Devastated Area Trail** loop takes 15 minutes and showcases the impact of the 1915–16 Lassen Peak eruption.

→ Trek a portion of the **Pacific Crest National Scenic Trail**, accessible from the Warner Valley trailhead. Head south toward Boiling Springs Lake or north toward Corral Meadow.

→ Find the largest hydrothermal area at the bottom of the **Bumpass Hell Trail**, open in the summer and fall. The 2.8-mile round-trip hike starts with a gentle climb, followed by a steep descent.

→ It's 2.4 miles round-trip on the **Cinder Cone Trail** to the base of the volcano and four miles round-trip to the summit.

→ Visit the **Mount Harkness fire tower**, actively used since 1930, from the trail at the Juniper Lake Ranger Station. The switchbacks lead through a thick forest, across a mountain meadow, and up a cinder cone volcano.

HIKE

SPOT

Y You might think Lassen's tumultuous landscape makes it a difficult place for wildlife, but mammals, birds, insects, fish, amphibians, and reptiles all thrive in the varied ecosystems of the park. Keep an eye out for these creatures:

→ *While grizzly bears no longer live in the park,* **black bears** *still wander through it.* **Bobcats***,* **mountain lions***,* **coyotes***, spotted skunks, and* **American badgers** *also roam the meadows and mountains to hunt the park's smaller mammals:* **mule deer***,* **marmots***, and* **snowshoe hares***.*

→ *Look up in the evenings to see the park's eight species of bats, including* **California myotis***,* **hoary bats***, and* **silver-haired bats***.*

→ *Most of the* **216 bird species** *known in Lassen are neotropical migrants that summer in the park, but 96 of them have bred within its bounds. Bird-watchers should look for* **Steller's jays***,* **mountain chickadees***,* **pileated woodpeckers***, and* **ruffed grouse***.*

A wild osprey at Manzanita Lake

O One main drive cuts through the park: **Lassen Volcanic National Park Highway**. Begin at the southern entrance at the Kohm Yah-mah-nee Visitor Center. From there, you'll find dozens of viewpoints and trailheads. Stop at the Sulphur Works area to observe the hydrothermal waters, marvel at Lassen Peak at the Diamond Peak pullout, and take in the tranquility over Little Hot Springs Valley.

Continue on to see Emerald Lake's wildflowers and the often icy Lake Helen. Then take a short hike to the Kings Creek Picnic Area and meadows, or photograph the fall colors at Hat Creek viewpoint. Imagine the volcanic journey of the rocks at Chaos Crags before finally reaching the Loomis Museum and Manzanita Lake.

The colorful Bumpass Hell Basin

DRIVE

Manzanita Lake with Mount Lassen in the distance

FLOAT

The mountain lakes and streams of Lassen are bright and blue, and they offer a welcome respite from the park's strenuous hikes. Try one of these water activities:

→ **Fish** for rainbow, brown, and brook trout at Horseshoe Lake or Manzanita Lake. Avoid the brush in the water by throwing your line from a non-motorized boat. Book a guided trip with Confluence Outfitters or Lance Gray & Company.

→ **Rent kayaks**, grab snacks at the Manzanita Lake Camper Store, and get out on the clear waters of Manzanita, Butte, Juniper, and Summit Lakes.

→ **Swim** in the cool waters of those same lakes. Just stick to designated swim areas and avoid the park's hydrothermal waters, such as Boiling Springs Lake.

Lassen's volcanoes have fostered a wilderness packed with high peaks and green meadows, and there are so many ways to discover it. Give your hiking boots a break and try one of these other adventures:

→ *See the impact of the volcanic eruption through photographs at the **Loomis Museum**, built from native stone.*

→ ***Horseback ride** 100 miles of trails in the park. Get a permit from the self-registration kiosk and stay at the corrals at Butte, Juniper, or Summit Lakes, or book a trip with an outfitter like Drakesbad Guest Ranch or St. Bernard Lodge.*

→ ***Stargaze** during a ranger-led evening walk or from roadside lookouts at Lake Helen or Kings Creek Meadow, join the annual **Dark Sky Festival**, or take a **full-moon hike**.*

→ ***Sled, snowshoe, cross-county ski, backcountry ski,** or **snowboard** if you're experienced and can do it without any lifts, grooming, or help. If not, join a **ranger-led snowshoe walk**.*

→ *Book a class with the Lassen Association's **Field Seminar Program**. Check the schedule of photography, hiking, and history sessions.*

The Milky Way rises above Lake Manzanita.

EXPLORE

A wildflower-dotted trail leads to the mountains.

MOUNT RAINIER NATIONAL PARK

WASHINGTON STATE

ESTABLISHED: March 2, 1899

SIZE: 236,381 acres

VISITORS CENTERS: Sunrise Visitor Center (open July–mid-September), Ohanapecosh Visitor Center (open late June–September), Longmire Museum (open year-round, hours change seasonally), Henry M. Jackson Memorial Visitor Center (open year-round, but weekends only November–March)

TRANSPORTATION: Crystal Mountain Resort shuttle; Talking Rocks Outdoor Company offers trailhead shuttles.

DOGS ALLOWED: Only in developed areas (campgrounds, public roads, picnic areas)

WHEN TO GO: Wildflowers peak in early August (so do the crowds). Mid-September offers ideal weather and fewer people. Most roads open in late June or July and close in early December.

CONTACT: 360-569-2211; nps.gov/mora
55210 238th Avenue East
Ashford, WA 98304

M Mount Rainier is an active volcano—and the most glaciated peak in the contiguous United States. Its fiery exterior has been replaced by glaciers that feed five major rivers, and its wildflower meadows provide striking contrast to the starkness of its peak. It appears desolate at the summit, while marmots sun on the rocks at the base and wildflowers bloom in summer. As a visitor, you'll feel the extremes as you move from one adventure to another, witnessing firsthand how it all coexists.

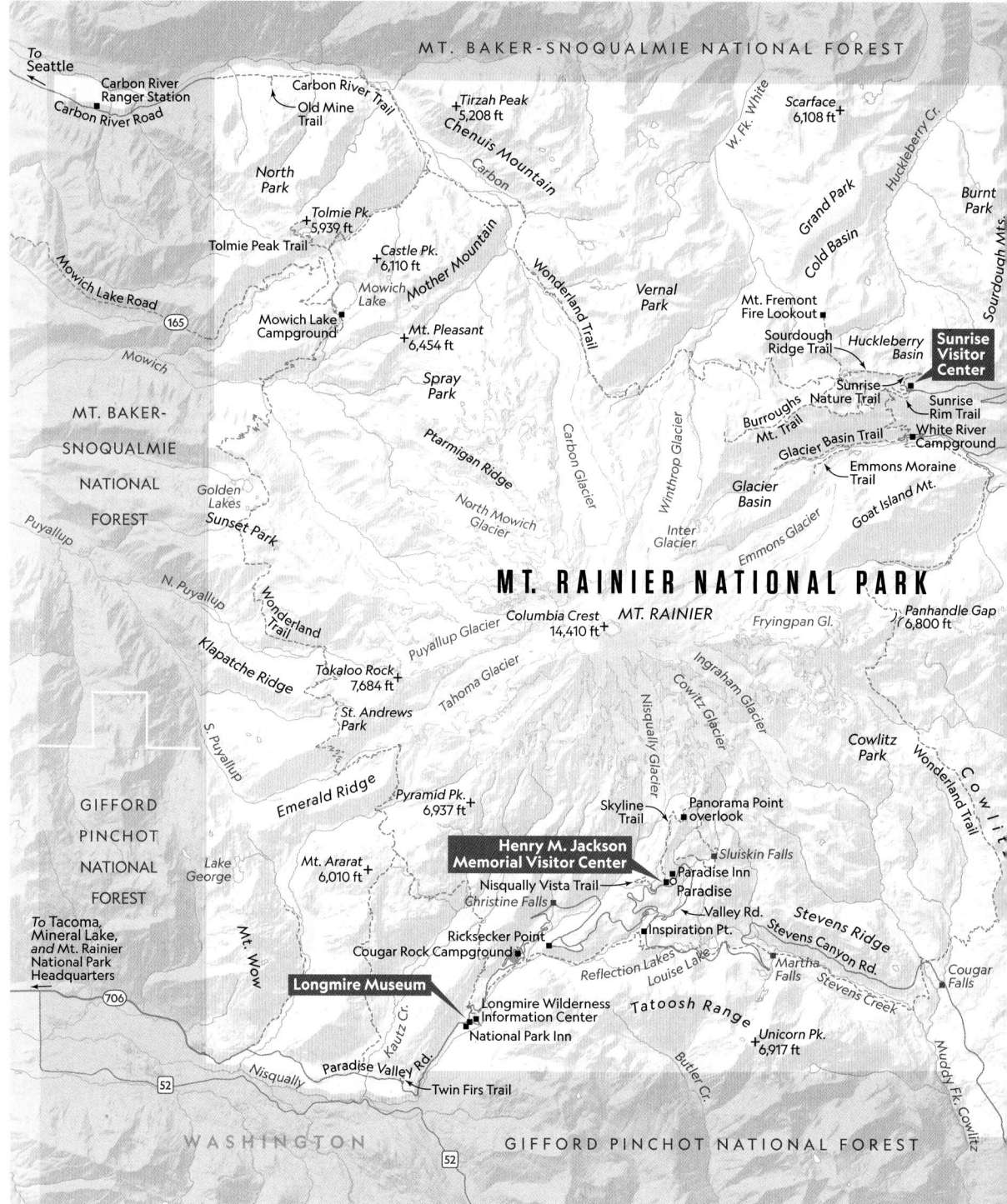

MT. BAKER-SNOQUALMIE NATIONAL FOREST

To Seattle

Carbon River Ranger Station

Carbon River Road

Carbon River Trail
Old Mine Trail

Tirzah Peak
5,208 ft

Chenuis Mountain

Carbon

North Park

Scarface
6,108 ft

W. Fk. White

Huckleberry Cr.

Sourdough Mts.

Grand Park

Cold Basin

Burnt Park

Tolmie Pk.
5,939 ft

Tolmie Peak Trail

Castle Pk.
6,110 ft

Mowich Lake

Mother Mountain

Wonderland Trail

Vernal Park

Mt. Fremont Fire Lookout

Mowich Lake Road

165

Mowich Lake Campground

Mt. Pleasant
6,454 ft

Sourdough Ridge Trail

Huckleberry Basin

Sunrise Visitor Center

Mowich

Spray Park

Sunrise Nature Trail

Sunrise Rim Trail

MT. BAKER-

Ptarmigan Ridge

Carbon Glacier

Burroughs Mt. Trail

Glacier Basin Trail

White River Campground

SNOQUALMIE

Golden Lakes

Winthrop Glacier

Emmons Moraine Trail

NATIONAL

Sunset Park

North Mowich Glacier

Glacier Basin

Goat Island Mt.

Puyallup

FOREST

Inter Glacier

Emmons Glacier

N. Puyallup

Wonderland Trail

MT. RAINIER NATIONAL PARK

Panhandle Gap
6,800 ft

Klapatche Ridge

Columbia Crest
14,410 ft

MT. RAINIER

Fryingpan Gl.

Ingraham Glacier

S. Puyallup

Puyallup Glacier

Takaloo Rock
7,684 ft

Tahoma Glacier

Nisqually Glacier

Cowlitz Glacier

Cowlitz Park

Wonderland Trail

St. Andrews Park

Cowlitz

GIFFORD

Emerald Ridge

Pyramid Pk.
6,937 ft

Skyline Trail

Panorama Point overlook

PINCHOT

Lake George

Mt. Ararat
6,010 ft

Henry M. Jackson Memorial Visitor Center

Sluiskin Falls

NATIONAL

Nisqually Vista Trail

Paradise Inn

Paradise

Stevens Ridge

FOREST

Christine Falls

Valley Rd.

Stevens Canyon Rd.

Cougar Falls

To Tacoma, Mineral Lake, and Mt. Rainier National Park Headquarters

Mt. Wow

Ricksecker Point

Inspiration Pt.

Cougar Rock Campground

Reflection Lakes

Louise Lake

Martha Falls

Stevens Creek

706

Longmire Museum

Kautz Cr.

Longmire Wilderness Information Center

National Park Inn

Tatoosh Range

Butler Cr.

Unicorn Pk.
6,917 ft

52

Nisqually

Paradise Valley Rd.

Twin Firs Trail

Muddy Fk. Cowlitz

WASHINGTON

52

GIFFORD PINCHOT NATIONAL FOREST

National Park Inn

→ SLEEP

(T) There's no lack of overnight options at Mount Rainier, with its two inns, three maintained campgrounds, one primitive campground, and plenty of backcountry sites. Nearby Mineral Lake and Lewis County also host plenty of lodging. Here are some in-park choices:

→ The **National Park Inn** in the Longmire Historic District is open year-round. It has 25 guest rooms, a restaurant, and a store.

→ Built in 1916, the historic **Paradise Inn** is larger but open only spring through early fall. Along with its 125 guest rooms, the inn has a shop, post office, café, and restaurant.

→ The three established campsites in the park are open from spring until early fall: **Cougar Rock Campground** (179 sites, reservations required), **Ohanapecosh Campground** (179 sites, reservations required), and **White River Campground** (88 sites, first come, first served). All have water, flush toilets, and fire grates.

→ The primitive **Mowich Lake Campground** (13 tent sites) requires a permit and has no potable water. In the park's northwest corner, it is accessible from Mowich Lake Road and is a good base for the Wonderland Trail. Permits can be reserved in advance at least two days ahead of your trip; about one-third of permits are issued on a first-come-first-serve basis at the park wilderness information centers.

Iconic
Hike

→ HIKE

T The queen of the park is Mount Rainier, and plenty of hikes focus on its peak. But there are also other wonderful treks through the park.

→ The **Wonderland Trail** is the quintessential route for experienced and determined hikers. It's 93 miles long and circles the volcano through lowland forests and valleys and up across high alpine regions. You'll need a permit (which you should try to get through the early-access lottery) as well as experience in completing long, strenuous backcountry hikes.

→ Hike up the **Skyline Trail** (5.5 miles round-trip) from the Paradise Meadows and Skyline Trailhead to the Glacier Vista and Panorama Point for views of Nisqually Glacier. Then travel back down the slope to Sluiskin and Myrtle Falls, where you'll weave through the colorful meadows.

→ The seven-mile round-trip **Glacier Basin Trail** was once an old mining road. The endeavor failed, but the route makes for a great trek along the White River and into Glacier Basin. Explore the wetland plants that grow in the basin before reaching the base of Inter Glacier.

→ Hike 1.2-miles of **Carbon River Road** to the steep **Old Mine Trail** quarter-mile spur, which leads to the gated entrance of an old mine.

→ The easy 1.5-mile **Sunrise Nature Trail** starts at a picnic area trailhead and loops around the region with views of Mount Rainier and the Cascades.

→ Gain 900 feet of elevation over 4.8 miles when you hike the First Burroughs portion of the **Burroughs Mountain Trail**; then gain 1,200 feet of elevation over six miles when you hike the second. Start this challenging route from the **Sourdough Ridge Trail**; return on the **Sunrise Rim Trail**.

→ Follow the **Glacier Basin Trail** for one mile before turning off to catch the three-mile **Emmons Moraine Trail** to traverse the moraine, rock, and sediment that was deposited by the glacier.

→ Take the **Ohanapecosh Walking Tour** through peaceful forests and under sky-high firs and hemlocks until you reach the Ohanapecosh Hot Springs. Find the trailhead for this half-mile loop at the Ohanapecosh Visitor Center.

A footbridge takes hikers over a waterfall.

Mount Fremont Fire Lookout

A Palos Verdes blue butterfly on a flowering pearly everlasting

I Interested in **white-river elk** or **black bears**? Try taking the Mount Fremont Trail to the lookout over Huckleberry Basin for a chance to spot them. Go above Carbon River to look for **mountain goats**. Luckily, **marmots** aren't difficult to spot; they roam across most of the meadows, especially when the weather is good. Try Sourdough Ridge or the Emmons Moraine Trail.

Bird-watchers can see some of the 182 species that fly above and live within the park. Look for **Steller's jays**, **commons ravens**, **bluebirds**, **hummingbirds**, **flycatchers**, **woodpeckers**, and **finches**.

SPOT

FLOAT

T There are boating restrictions in Mount Rainier, even for nonmotorized vessels. Paddlers are allowed on **Mowich Lake**, however, and there's road access for canoes and kayak drop-ins. The surrounding wildflower meadows and towering peak make for a powerful experience while you're on the water. Combine the trip with a hike up to the Tolmie Peak lookout to see the park from top and bottom.

Crystal clear Mowich Lake

DRIVE

O Only a few drives around the park prioritize views and trail access. Here are some:

→ Take **Paradise Valley Road** from the southwest corner of the park up to the Henry M. Jackson Memorial Visitor Center, stopping at Kautz Creek, the short Twin Firs Trail, the Longmire Museum, the Cougar Rock Picnic Area, the Christine Falls Overlook, Ricksecker Point, and the Paradise region.

→ Drive Paradise Valley Road to **Valley Road**, which eventually turns into **Stevens Canyon Road**. Don't miss Inspiration Point, Reflection Lakes, the Louise Lake Trailhead, the Martha Falls exhibit panel, the Box Canyon lookout and tunnel, and Cougar Falls.

→ The short and winding **Mather Memorial Parkway** heads to the Tipsoo Lake lookout. Turn on **Sunrise Road** to find the Sunrise Road pullout, rock formation, and road exhibit panel, as well as the Sunrise Visitor Center. From there, hike up to the Mount Fremont Fire Lookout.

Catch sunrise while exploring the park from your car.

A peaceful morning beckons fishing enthusiasts at a pond.

A subalpine meadow bursting with lupines

→ EXPLORE

(M) Make the most of a Mount Rainier experience by slowing down. Try a peaceful fishing trip, an afternoon with the wildflowers, or an educational program with a ranger.

→ **Climb Mount Rainier**—*if you have a permit and the ability. The trek to the peak gains more than 9,000 feet and requires experience with glacier-travel rope skills. Tackle the trip independently or with a guide from one of the four trailheads.*

→ **Search for wildflowers** *like you would search for wildlife. Pack a park guide to identify what you find as you hike along the basins and meadows.*

→ *Familiarize yourself with the very particular guidelines about native versus non-native species, lakes versus streams, and retaining versus catch-and-release rules before* **fishing** *the streams and lakes of Mount Rainier. One species you can keep without concern: the non-native brook trout.*

→ *Join a ranger-led program, like a* **night-sky telescope evening** *or an* **educational program**, *at the Cougar Rock Campground Amphitheater. Check the calendar before your visit.*

→ RANGER RECOMMENDATION ←

*Exploring the snowiest place (where extreme weather is regularly recorded) on Earth is a true thrill. **Snowshoe** in the park to experience the quiet and wonder of the wilderness during this season. Unlike in summer, when you're restricted by trails and fragile terrain, snowshoers can move through sensitive spaces like the meadows of Paradise and Sunrise. This provides much more freedom to explore. Bring a GPS and winter navigation skills, or join a free ranger-guided snowshoe tour (even the snowshoes are provided) on the Nisqually Vista Trail at Paradise.*

Shockingly vibrant trees encircle a lake at the park.

NORTH CASCADES ◀
NATIONAL PARK
WASHINGTON STATE

ESTABLISHED: October 2, 1968

SIZE: 501,199 acres

VISITORS CENTERS: The North Cascades Visitor Center and Skagit Information Center are near Newhalem; the Forest Information Center and park headquarters are in Sedro-Woolley; there's also a Wilderness Information Center in Marblemount, the Golden West Visitor Center in Stehekin, and the Glacier Public Service Center in Glacier. All are generally open May–October.

TRANSPORTATION: The *Lady of the Lake* ferry between Chelan and Stehekin makes stops at Fields Point and Lucerne, with reduced service in winter.

DOGS ALLOWED: Only on the Pacific Crest National Scenic Trail and in paved areas, as well as in national recreation areas and national forest lands

----

WHEN TO GO: Winter offers snow activities, but the main highway is closed (use the ferry); mid-June–mid-September offers the best temperatures and is when most trails and facilities are open.

CONTACT: 360-854-7200; nps.gov/noca
810 State Route 20
Sedro-Woolley, WA 98284

F For nearly all visitors to North Cascades National Park, their trips will inevitably include Ross Lake National Recreation Area and Lake Chelan National Recreation Area, as all three make up the North Cascades National Park complex. There are borders on a map, but as North Cascades teaches, human-made borders don't bind the natural world. The waters, wildlife, and mountains spread across drawn boundaries, expanding arbitrary limits set by governments. Adventurers in the North Cascades are just as unbridled.

BRITISH COLUMBIA

Chilliwack Lake

Silver Lake

Hozomeem

CANADA
UNITED STATES

ROSS LAKE NATIONAL RECREATION AREA

+ *Mt. Spickard* 8,979 ft

Little Beaver Cr.

To Glacier Public Service Center ←

Baker

+ *Mt. Shuksan* 9,131 ft

Picket Range

+ *Mt. Fury* 8,303 ft

Big Beaver Cr.

PACIFIC NORTHWEST N.S.T.

PACIFIC NORTHWEST NATIONAL SCENIC TRAIL

WASHINGTON

Ross Lake

East Bank Trail

Baker River Trail

+ *Mt. Blum* 7,680 ft

North Cascades Environmental Learning Center
Sourdough Mountain Trail

Baker Lake To Mt. Baker

Gorge Lake Campground
Gorge Creek Falls
Gorge Overlook
Diablo
Pyramid Lake Trail

Skagit Information Center

Goodell Creek Campground

North Cascades Visitor Center

Ross Lake Resort
Ross Lake Overlook
Happy Creek Forest Walk
Diablo Lake Overlook
Diablo Lake
Colonial Creek North and South Campgrounds

Newhalem
Newhalem Creek Campground

Skagit

PACIFIC CREST N.S.T.

NORTH CASCADES NATIONAL PARK

Wilderness Information Center

20

Marblemount

Skagit

Rockport

To Forest Information Center and North Cascades Institute

Monogram Lake Trail

Easy Pass Trail

20

To Winthrop →

Liberty Bell Mountain 7,750 ft +

Washington Pass Overlook

Cascade

Forbidden Peak 8,844 ft +

Cascade River Road

Cascade Pass Trail

Thunder Creek Trail

Park Creek Pass

Goode Ridge Trail

Bridge Creek Trail

530

Cascade Pass

Stehekin

Upper Stehekin Valley Trail

Bridge Creek Camp

LAKE CHELAN NATIONAL RECREATION AREA

GLACIER PEAK

WILDERNESS

Agnes Mountain 8,131 ft +

Chickamin Glacier

Agnes Gorge Trail

Stehekin Valley Ranch

Rainbow Falls

Buckner Homestead Historic District

Silver Bay Inn
Stehekin

North Cascades Lodge

PACIFIC CREST NATIONAL SCENIC TRAIL

Golden West Visitor Center

530

Darrington

N

5 mi
5 km

Holden Village

Lake Chelan

Lucerne

SLEEP

(C) Camping choices abound in and near North Cascades. Choose from drive-in campgrounds, boat-in campsites, and backcountry sites.

The drive-in ones sit between the park's northern and southern units along the Skagit River. **Newhalem Creek** (107 sites; open May–September, reservations required) and **Goodell Creek** (19 sites; open year-round, reservations required in peak season) are close to the North Cascades Visitor Center and the town of Newhalem. **Gorge Lake** (8 sites; open year-round, reservations accepted May–September) sits beside a clear body of water and is a great starting point for the Sourdough Mountain climb or the Pyramid Lake Trail. **Colonial Creek North** (38 sites; open May–September, reservations required) and **Colonial Creek South** (93 sites; some sites available year-round, reservations required May–September) are separated by the main road, but both have good access to the water and forest hikes.

Alternatively, stay at one of the 25 **backcountry boat-in sites** along the shores of Lake Chelan, Ross Lake, and Diablo Lake or the 140 **hike-in sites** with a permit. Permits are limited and can be reserved in advance for peak season; winter permits can be self-issued outside the Wilderness Information Center in Marblemount.

If you'd prefer a hotel, check out **Ross Lake Resort**, **North Cascades Lodge**, **Silver Bay Inn**, or **Stehekin Valley Ranch**.

Tent camping near Mount Baker

A waterfall along the East Bank Trail

D Don't be intimidated by the enormous peaks that tower over the park. Not every hike in North Cascades is an epic trek—though there are plenty of those. Find the hike that's right for you.

→ The long but easy **Bridge Creek Trail** is a portion of the Pacific Crest National Scenic Trail. Eighteen miles of the trail pass through the park, but this popular bit is 12.8 miles long. Hike down 2,500 feet of elevation from State Route 20 to Bridge Creek Camp.

→ The five-mile one-way **Goode Ridge Trail** is a challenge. Hike 4,400 feet to the end of the **Upper Stehekin Valley Trail** for views of the Stehekin River and glaciated peaks.

→ Take the **Thunder Creek Trail** into the heart of the park. Start in ancient forests and follow the cloudy blue creek to its origins at Park Creek Pass. The entire hike covers just under 28 miles.

→ Hike the 0.3-mile **Happy Creek Forest Walk** as it loops along an accessible boardwalk through old-growth forest. The creek below eventually leads into Ross Lake and Skagit River.

→ The 2.5-mile **Agnes Gorge Trail** is home to colorful wildflowers, fluttering butterflies, and singing birds. Cross over into the U.S. Forest Service's Glacier Peak Wilderness to reveal gorgeous views of Agnes Mountain and Chickamin Glacier.

HIKE

A trail zigzags up the hillside.

A mountain goat pauses its ascent.

SPOT

N North Cascades is a refuge for threatened and endangered animals that need vast wild spaces to survive. Find many of them as you hike through their rugged lands. Look for **gray wolves**, **grizzly bears**, and **Canada lynx**—all protected under the Endangered Species Act. Keep an eye out for elusive **black bears**, **wolverines**, **river otters**, and **cougars**; **mule deer** and **hoary marmots** are more common.

Bird-watchers might get lucky and spot three threatened species: **marbled murrelets**, **spotted owls**, and **bald eagles**, especially since the park is home to the largest group of wintering bald eagles in the continental U.S.

W With much of North Cascades inaccessible by road, its waters have become its pathways. Get out on the rivers and lakes for thrills, beauty, and connection.

→ *Traverse the sparkling **Diablo Lake** and **Ross Lake** by boat, either on your own or through an outfitter like the North Cascades Institute.*
→ ***Whitewater rafting** the Skagit River is an intense adventure. The upper half is packed with Class II S-curve rapids, while the lower half rolls more gently through the iconic scenery of the park. Book a trip with an outfitter like Alpine Adventures or Triad River Tours.*
→ ***Ride the** Lady of the Lake schooner from Lake Chelan to the remote town of Stehekin. Sign up for a special trip, like a haunted boat ride for Halloween or a fireworks dinner cruise.*

Ross Lake National Recreation Area

FLOAT

(T) There aren't many drives in North Cascades, but the ones available have major payoffs.

→ Drive the 30-mile portion of **State Route 20** through the park. From west to east, stop at the North Cascades National Park Visitor Center, the Gorge Dam and Powerhouse at Newhalem, the short Gorge Creek Falls walk, the Diablo Lake Overlook, the Happy Creek Forest Walk, and the Ross Lake Overlook.

→ Travel **Cascade River Road** from the west side of the park for 23 miles along the valley of the Cascade River. Get views of the mountains until you finally reach the trailhead for the popular Cascade Pass Trail.

→ Join a famous "heritage style" **Red Bus tour** from North Cascades Lodge to the mountain's sights, including the 312-foot Rainbow Falls, named for the light refractions that shine on sunny days.

DRIVE

A view of the park via Washington Pass Overlook on Highway 20

Washington Pass Overlook

Children learn about nature from rangers and graduate students.

A mountain biker hoists his cycle over an obstacle.

→ EXPLORE

The best visit to North Cascades includes more than hiking and paddling. Try adding one of these activities to your trip:

→ **Climbing** in North Cascades is a rugged, beautiful experience. Technical rock climbers love the challenge of the Liberty Bell massif's northern summit, including Concord Tower and the Early Winter Spires. The Skagit Gorge offers excellent opportunities for **bouldering**, while the West and North Ridges of Forbidden Peak are top picks for **mountaineers**. Attempt a trip on your own with a permit or book one with an outfitter.

→ Visit the small Old West town of **Winthrop** to walk the boardwalk, buy souvenirs at local boutiques, peruse its art galleries, and grab a bite at pizza shops, bakeries, ice cream parlors, and taverns. Don't miss the weekend farmers market.

→ Explore **Stehekin**, an old gold-prospecting town open for bike tours, horseback riding trips, hikes, fishing, and paddling, with options for overnight stays in its multiple cabins. From there, wander the 160-acre **Buckner Homestead Historic District**, which includes a home, working buildings, orchards, and pastures.

→ Hike up the peaks and make your way down on a **downhill skiing tour** with an outfitter like North Cascades Mountain Guides. For a tamer experience, **cross-country ski** or **snowshoe** the miles of trails around Stehekin.

→ Book an educational tour or course with the **North Cascades Institute** and **North Cascades Environmental Learning Center**. Hear from scientists, paint with artists, and paddle with environmentalists.

→ **Horseback ride** through the mountains either with your own steed or with an outfitter. The routes along Bridge Creek are popular, as are the East Bank, Big Beaver, and Thunder Creek Trails.

→ **Cast a fishing line** in the Skagit River, home to salmon, steelhead, cutthroat trout, freshwater trout, and char. Get your license before you begin.

Experts Only

There are only a few roads that enter the park, so most people end up at Cascade Pass and Diablo Lake. However, a deeper hike will provide great views from the **Baker River**, **Easy Pass**, and **Monogram Lake Trails**. They all start on U.S. Forest Service land but eventually enter the park. Easy Pass and Monogram Lake are strenuous and have a long winter season.

The haunting coastline of the park meets the Pacific.

OLYMPIC NATIONAL PARK

WASHINGTON STATE

ESTABLISHED: June 29, 1938

SIZE: 922,651 acres

VISITORS CENTERS: The Olympic National Park Visitor Center, Hoh Rain Forest Visitor Center, and Wilderness Information Center are open year-round. The Kalaloch Ranger Station is open seasonally.

TRANSPORTATION: No in-park transportation

DOGS ALLOWED: Only in developed areas (campgrounds, parking lots, picnic areas, and paved roads) and on limited trails

---

WHEN TO GO: Summer is the busiest time, but has the most open roads and facilities and full programming; spring is full of wildlife and waterfalls; winter brings cold-weather activities; fall brings rain.

CONTACT: 360-565-3130; nps.gov/olym
3002 Mount Angeles Road
Port Angeles, WA 98362

N No single experience can encapsulate Olympic National Park. Each corner is so vastly distinct. Over a week in the park, you can traverse glacier-topped peaks and ocean coastlines, old-growth temperate rainforests and resilient alpine forests. Every ecosystem is diverse—and they're all thriving, fostering spaces that feel enchanted and mystical. Hiking, paddling, swimming, and driving through Olympic will make you feel like you've been transported to another world again and again and again.

MAKAH
RESERVATION

Sekiu

Clallam Bay

112

Pysht

LOWER ELWHA
RESERVATION

Hoko-Ozette Rd.

OZETTE
RESERVATION

Ozette Ranger
Station

Ozette Campground

Hoko

113

Dickey
Lake

Storm King
Ranger Station

Log Cabin
Resort

Fairholme
Campground

Pyramid
Peak Trail

Ozette
Lake

Sappho

Olympic Discovery Trail

101

Lake Crescent

Lake
Crescent
Lodge

Beaver

Sol Duc

La Poel

Norwegian
Memorial

Aurora Creek Trail

Marymere
Falls Trail

OLYMPIC

NATIONAL

FOREST

PACIFIC NORTHWEST N.ST.

Sol Duc Hot
Springs Resort

Sol Duc
Falls Trail

Chilean Memorial

Sol Duc

South Fork Calawah

Sol Duc

Mora
Campground

110

Forks

Mora's Hole
in the Wall

Rialto Beach

Mora Rd.

Slough Trail

QUILEUTE
RESERVATION

La Push

Bogachiel

Hoh Rain Forest
Visitor Center

Hoh River Trail

Hoh

Undie Road

Hoh Rain Forest
Campground

OLYMPIC

NATIONAL

PARK

101

One Mile Pullout
Nature Trail

Big Spruce Tree
Nature Trail

Upper Hoh Rd.

Hoh

South Fork Hoh

Oil City

WASHINGTON

Pelton Peak
5,301 ft

HOH
RESERVATION

101

Ruby Beach

Kalaloch Big Cedar
Nature Trail

Hoh Mainline

Clearwater

Queets

PACIFIC

OCEAN

Big Douglas-fir tree

Kalaloch Beach

Kalaloch Campground

Kalaloch Ranger Station

OLYMPIC

Kalaloch Lodge

NATIONAL

South Beach

Queets

FOREST

Quinault Valley

QUINAULT
RESERVATION

101

Quinault Rain Forest
Ranger Station

Lake
Quinault

5 mi

5 km

N

Amanda Park

Lake Quinault
Lodge

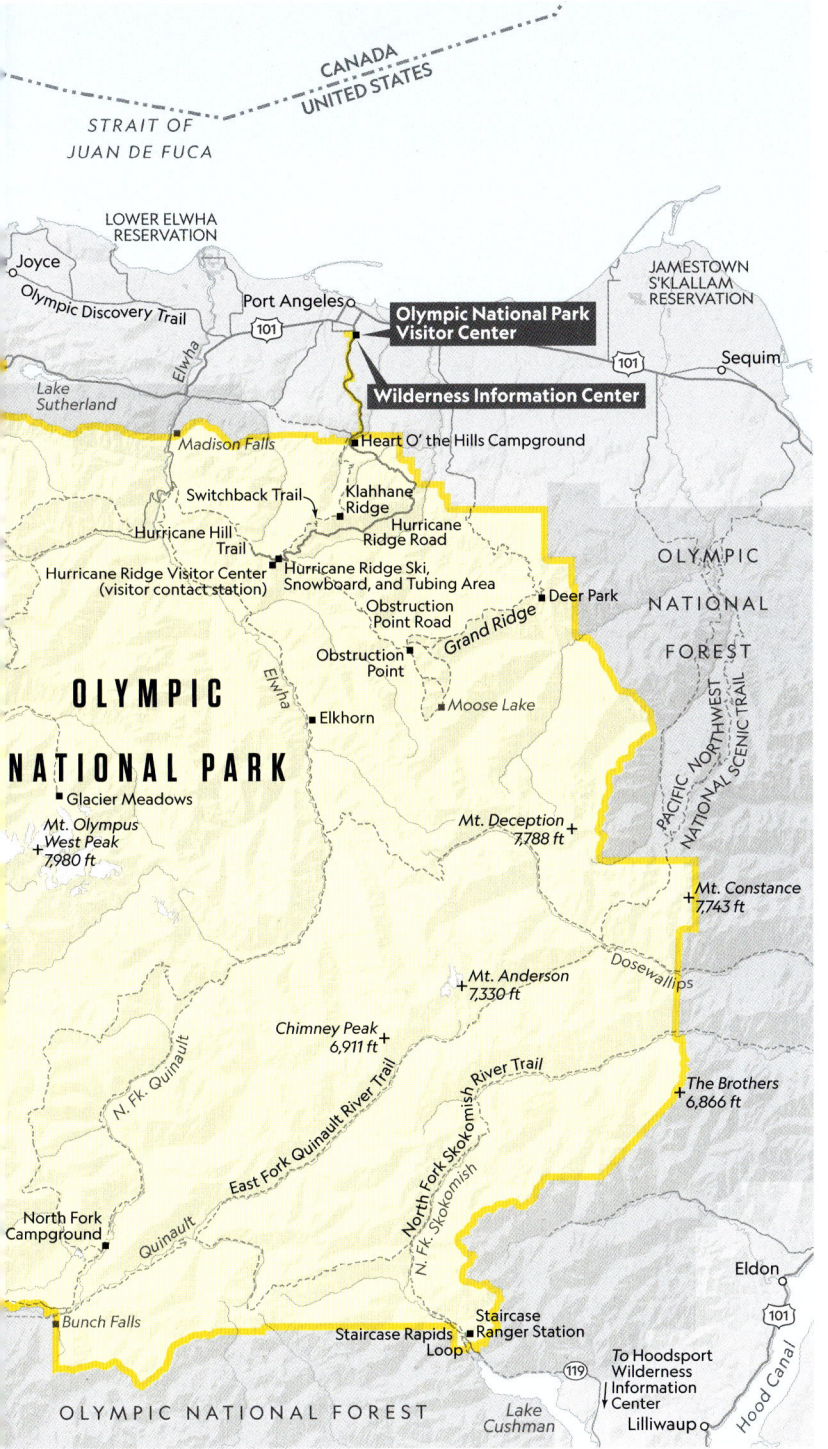

SLEEP

T Thirteen drive-in campgrounds are in the park, and some accept reservations during the busiest summer months.

→ Book ahead at **Hoh Rain Forest** (77 sites; open year-round, reservations available May–September), **Kalaloch** (170 sites; open year-round, reservations available May–September), **Mora** (94 sites; open year-round, reservations available May–September), and **Sol Duc Hot Springs Resort** (82 sites with electric hookups; open March–November, reservations required). **Heart O' the Hills** (97 sites; open year-round) and **North Fork Campground** (9 sites; open year-round) are first come, first served. Kalaloch and Sol Duc have group sites. The only campground with showers and laundry is **Log Cabin Resort** (38 sites; open May–September, reservations required by phone), run by a concessionaire.

Those who prefer lodges and cabins have five choices in the park:

→ The historic **Lake Crescent Lodge** offers boat rentals, while the nearby **Log Cabin Resort** boasts stunning lake views.
→ Guests at **Sol Duc Hot Springs Resort** can soak in the warm waters of its mineral and freshwater pools.
→ From **Kalaloch Lodge**, watch the waves of the Pacific Ocean roll, set out on miles of hiking trails, and spot wildlife in the marine sanctuary.
→ Built in 1926, **Lake Quinault Lodge** has a historic dining room and lakeside views.

The Hoh Rain Forest near Mineral Creek on the Hoh River Trail

![The park's lush forests make for plentiful hiking opportunities.](image)

The park's lush forests make for plentiful hiking opportunities.

S Since roads are minimal in the region, walking is the best way to get to the park's top views and popular sights.

→ Head out on the **Hoh River Trail** from the Hoh Rain Forest Visitor Center. Though you can easily hike just a portion of the trail, a 17.4-mile trek through the temperate rainforest will take you to Glacier Meadows. Tackle the whole route and find campsites along the way to make for easy overnights. Be prepared for some water crossings.

→ Get up into the mountains on the wide, maintained 3-mile round-trip **Hurricane Hill Trail**, which gains 700 feet in elevation. The start of the trail is paved; the rest is smoothed gravel. Travel the switchbacks up to a windy summit view from atop exposed Hurricane Hill.

→ If you don't mind some crowds, do the most popular hike at Lake Crescent. The **Marymere Falls Trail**, from either the Storm King Ranger Station or Lake Crescent Lodge, takes just under a mile to get to the lush 90-foot waterfall.

→ Hike the **Pyramid Peak Trail**, which starts in an old-growth forest and eventually leads through a rock slide, up tight switchbacks, and across a plateau to the top of the ridge. Check out the view from a cabin built during World War II. Over the trail's 3.5 miles (one-way), you will climb 2,600 feet.

→ Catch the trailhead for the **Sol Duc Falls Trail** near the Sol Duc Hot Springs Resort. After just under a mile, you'll reach the often photographed, multichannel falls. Get a permit to stay overnight in the backcountry.

→ The southern edge of the park is less visited, and the 2.1-mile loop to Staircase Rapids is both stunning and quiet. Take the **Staircase Rapids Loop** across a suspension bridge to see the river and rapids, then follow the **North Fork Skokomish River Trail** back to the parking area.

→ Catch the **Switchback Trail** from Hurricane Ridge Road up to Klahhane Ridge. There are a few routes up to the ridge, but the switchbacks are the quickest. Wildflowers bloom around the trail in the summer, and wildlife often wanders this region.

→ DRIVE

T   There aren't a lot of roads in Olympic, and that's part of what protects this magical space. Most visitors travel along U.S. Highway 101 and then hop into the park through a series of cyclist-friendly roads. Here are a few worth traveling:

→ *One of the two sections of **U.S. Highway 101** that go through the park runs along the south side of Lake Crescent. On the route, take in views of the lake, stop at Lake Crescent Lodge, head out on the popular Marymere Falls Trail and the Aurora Creek Trail, pause for a picnic at La Poel, and go for a swim in Lake Crescent.*

→ *Continue down U.S. Highway 101 toward the coast and drive the **Kalaloch sections** for access to Ruby Beach, the short Kalaloch Big Cedar Nature Trail, many easy treks to different beaches, Kalaloch Campground and Lodge, and South Beach trails.*

→ ***Hurricane Ridge Road** is open, but access is limited. Get there early and drive up the road to the now closed visitors center (a contact station is staffed during the summer). The views are still excellent, and trails to Cirque Rim and the High Ridge meadows are nearby.*

→ *Take the **Mora Road** offshoot to the ranger station, boat launch, and campground, along with the Slough Trail, a portion of the Pacific Northwest National Scenic Trail, and Rialto Beach.*

→ *Drive the gravel **Obstruction Point Road** from the Hurricane Ridge Visitor Center. The eight-mile trip, which closes for snow, travels winding turns up to the striking view at Obstruction Point and the starting point for backpacking trips to Deer Park, Grand Ridge, and Moose Lake.*

→ *Take **Upper Hoh Road** to the One Mile Pullout Nature Trail, Big Spruce Tree Nature Trail, and Hoh Rain Forest Visitor Center and Campground. There are also multiple pullouts along the way that go deeper into the park.*

A view of a winding road through the park

A yellow-headed blackbird clings to prairie grass.

An ochre sea star in a tide pool

Ruby Beach at dusk

An Olympic marmot, endemic to the park

SPOT

If you're set on spotting a certain animal, plan your trip around its habitat. No matter where you travel, you'll see creatures you won't find in your backyard.

→ Head to the lower valleys and rainforest at dawn or dusk to see **Roosevelt elk**, but keep your distance. They can be particularly aggressive in the spring and fall.

→ Walk along the beach to look for **Pacific harbor seals** all year long. They're usually close to shore to feed or resting on offshore rocks.

→ Explore the tide pools with the care and caution required by the pools' fragile creatures. The most popular spots are Kalaloch Beach 4 and Mora's Hole in the Wall, though Ruby Beach is also a great spot. See **sea stars**, **rock crabs**, **barnacles**, **sea snails**, and more. Remember: Timing is everything. Check the daily schedule for tides under one foot.

→ Follow the Whale Trail to Rialto Beach. The trail maps more than 100 sites where you're likely to spot sea mammals. Look for **orcas**, **gray whales**, and **Steller sea lions** at Rialto Beach.

→ Spot **Olympic marmots** traveling near the alpine trails. They're especially visible in the summer when they roam the region enjoying the sunshine. No matter how cute they look or how friendly they seem, don't feed them.

→ Look for birds wherever you go in Olympic, as more than 250 species rely on the park's varied habitats. **Blue grouse**, **woodpeckers**, and **gray jays** fly through the meadows, while **bald eagles**, **rhinoceros auklets**, and **western gulls** soar above the coastlines.

G Getting out on the water in Olympic is at once a calming and thrilling experience. The sparkling lakes are the best option for most visitors, though experienced paddlers can set out on the park's rivers.

→ Rent a canoe or kayak from Lake Crescent Lodge, Fairholme General Store, Log Cabin Resort, or a nearby outfitter, and set out on **Lake Crescent**. Paddle through the glacially carved lake and watch the reflections of the mountains along its edges.

→ Unlike the lakes, the rivers of Olympic aren't for the inexperienced or weak paddler. The **Elwha River** is open most of the year, but it contains multiple sections that have turned deadly—some of which are now closed. The **Hoh** and **Queets Rivers** are often filled with logjams and debris that make them difficult to maneuver, while the **Quinault** and **Sol Duc** both require hikes into the backcountry. Any of these rivers will provide an absolutely unique perspective on the park.

→ Launch from Ozette Ranger Station or Ozette Campground to paddle **Ozette Lake**, which is filled with water lilies in the summer. Kayaking or canoeing through the secluded spot also provides access to a few backcountry camping sites.

FLOAT

Peaceful waters offer memorable sunset kayaking.

Raft the Elwha River with a knowledgeable guide.

Cycling on Upper Hoh Road

→ EXPLORE

B Beyond hiking, camping, wildlife spotting, and paddling, there are plenty of extra excursions and adventures that will boost your experience in Olympic.

→ The **beaches at Kalaloch and Ruby** are less about swimming and more about discovery. Walk a trail along the coast, stop at low tide to observe protected marine life, and look for birds in the rocky spires. Spend more time on the coast by staying at one of the ocean-side campgrounds.

→ **Snowshoe** and **cross-country ski** the miles of ungroomed trails along Hurricane Ridge. Beginners should stick to the meadow above the visitors center—also the spot to catch a ranger-led snowshoe trip. For more thrills, head to the **Hurricane Ridge Ski, Snowboard, and Tubing Area** for two rope tows, a Poma lift, and a tubing park.

→ Summers are the perfect time to catch impressive night views at Olympic, where nearly the entire sky is absent of human-created light. Join a **night-sky program** with a ranger or look through telescopes with a master observer at a **Hurricane Ridge astronomy program**. Dress warmly, because the temperatures will drop.

→ **Bike the 130-mile Olympic Discovery Trail**, which travels along the north side of the state and the northern edge of the park. Stop at the Fairholme Campground along the way to see the north side of Lake Crescent.

→ **Mountaineers** and **alpine climbers** can choose from three major peaks in Olympic, but only experienced climbers should attempt this dangerous feat. Mount Olympus is the highest peak, at 7,980 feet, followed by Mount Deception and Mount Constance.

Star-gazing Paradise

RANGER RECOMMENDATION

Explore the **Quinault Valley** as a less trafficked alternative to the Hoh Rain Forest. Drive the scenic loop and hop on shorter trails that lead into the heart of the rainforest environment—and away from the crowds. Use the road as a starting point to hike up to alpine meadows and sparkling lakes, getting out for long hikes on the north or east forks of the East Fork Quinault River Trail. Wildlife is equally drawn to the region, so watch for bears and elk.

A hiker pauses to marvel at the grandeur of the redwood trees.

REDWOOD NATIONAL AND STATE PARKS

CALIFORNIA

ESTABLISHED: October 2, 1968

SIZE: 131,983 acres

VISITORS CENTERS: The Thomas H. Kuchel Visitor Center on Redwood Creek Beach has exhibits and a store; the Hiouchi Visitor Center, with cultural and art exhibits, is the northernmost visitor center; the Crescent City Information Center is in the park's headquarters; and the Prairie Creek Visitor Center, in Prairie Creek Redwoods State Park, with a Civilians Conservation Corps exhibit, are all open year-round. The Jedediah Smith Visitor Center in the Jedediah Smith Redwoods State Park campground is only open in the summer.

TRANSPORTATION: Redwood Coast Transit; Redwood Park Conservancy for people with disabilities; and Redwood Adventures shuttle services

---

DOGS ALLOWED: Only in developed areas (campgrounds, parking lots, picnic areas, and paved roads); not allowed on trails

---

WHEN TO GO: Summer is incredibly busy; spring is good for flowers, and fall for leaves; winter is cold and rainy but less crowded.

CONTACT: 707-464-6101; nps.gov/redw
1111 Second Street
Crescent City, CA 95531

R Redwood National Park—administered alongside several state parks—is famous for its towering trees. These giants started growing around 2,000 years ago and are now the tallest trees on the planet. While they once covered two million acres in California, the gold rush of 1848 and urban growth took out most of them. Today, just 4 percent of that land remains home to these magnificent trees. Even with the smaller footprint, the landscape of the park, which also includes coastal regions, still feels enormous and dramatic.

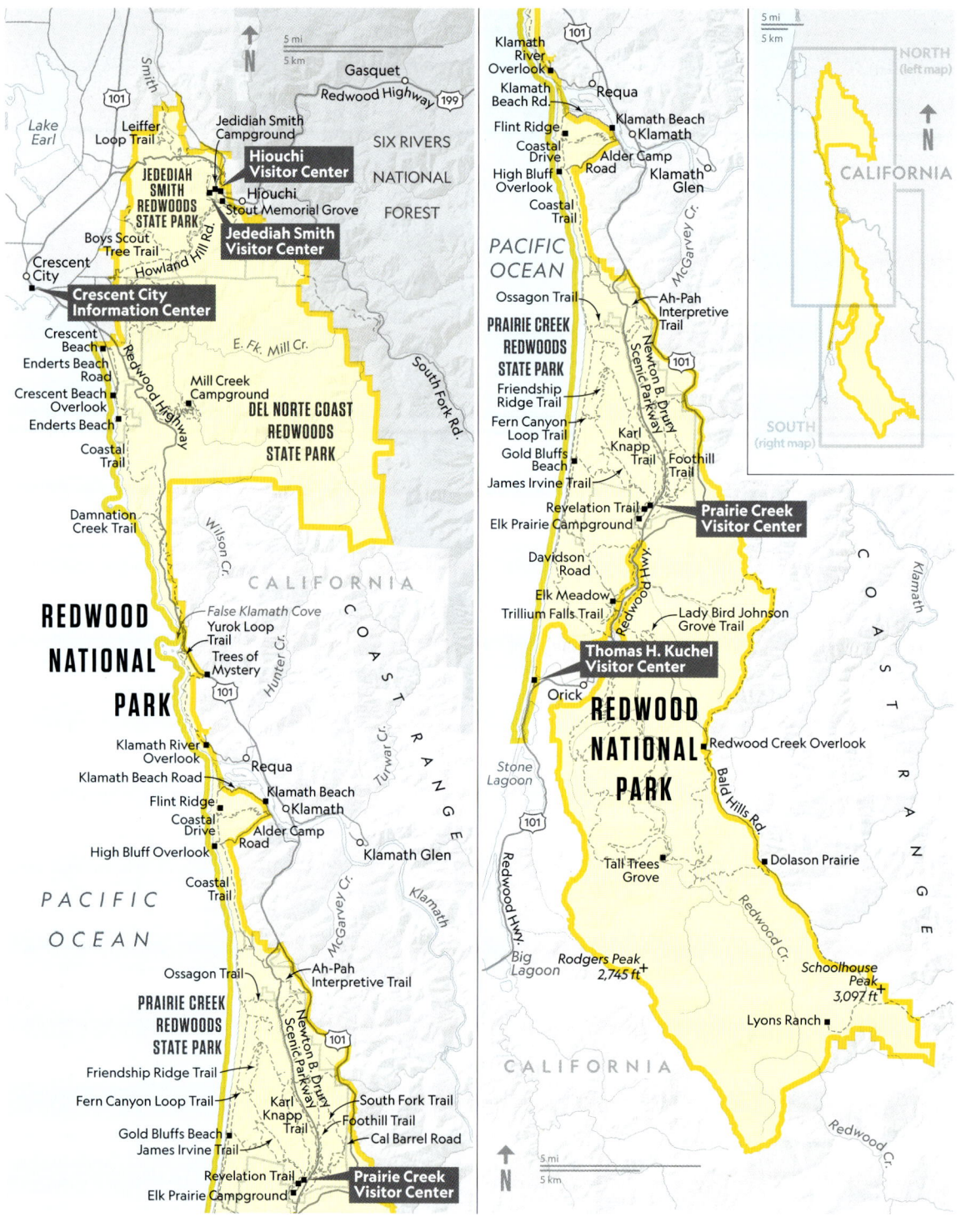

Gold Bluffs Beach Campground

SLEEP

C Camping is the only way to stay within park bounds (although those bounds are a bit of a loose concept, with the way protected lands weave through unprotected areas).

→ A site or cabin at **Jedidiah Smith Campground** (86 sites; open year-round, reservations recommended) will have you sleeping under the canopy of an old-growth redwood grove and listening to the sounds of the rolling Smith River. Meanwhile, the redwoods at **Mill Creek Campground** (145 sites; open May–October, reservations recommended) are younger, but the sites are close to the water and trails.

→ Stay on the Pacific coastline at **Gold Bluffs Beach Campground** (26 sites; open year-round)—though access, via a small dirt road, may be limited due to winter conditions. Watch for Roosevelt elk and enjoy an evening stroll on a secluded bit of nearby beach.

→ Camp among black-tailed deer and maybe an elk or two in the ancient coastal redwoods at **Elk Prairie Campground** (75 sites; open year-round, reservations required May–October), which also offers four cabins. It's a good starting point for hiking, biking, and ranger programs.

→ Get a backcountry permit ahead of time to stay at one of the seven designated **backcountry sites** or anywhere along the backcountry trails. Permits can be booked online the same day (by 1 p.m.) or up to 180 days in advance.

Ranger-Led Hike

R Redwood rangers insist there's truly no "best" trail in the park. With hundreds of miles across various ecosystems, each step has something special to offer.

→ The short, peaceful **Trillium Falls Trail** passes through old-growth redwoods, maples, ferns, huge firs, and trillium flowers. These tiny white blooms brighten the half-mile walk to the small cascades. Turn back at the falls or continue along the 2.7-mile loop.

→ Secure one of the 50 free daily reservations online before you arrive to explore **Tall Trees Grove**. The 4.5-mile round-trip trek climbs 1,600 feet through an area once featured in a 1963 *National Geographic* issue highlighting what used to be the tallest tree in the world. (The Libby Tree, or "Tall Tree," lost the title in 1994 when the top died back.)

→ If you can't get a reservation for Tall Trees Grove, set out on the **Karl Knapp Trail** and the **Foothill Trail**. The flat 2.5-mile path weaves along a creek shore and under some of the tallest redwoods in the world.

→ Walk through a historic redwood grove along the 1.5-mile **Lady Bird Johnson Grove Trail** loop. Learn about the park's development—including its name—on a ranger-led summer stroll.

HIKE

→ Take all day to hike the **James Irvine Trail** to Fern Canyon, a popular stop for photo-loving visitors. The first section moves through an old-growth redwood forest and then connects with the **Friendship Ridge Trail** and, eventually, the **Fern Canyon Loop Trail**. Take it to Gold Bluffs Beach, then turn back the way you came.

→ Hike two miles from Bald Hills Road to the historic **Lyons Ranch**. The 19th-century sheep farm, high above the forests, is home to pioneer barns, a bunkhouse, and a cemetery. Come for the history and stay for the night skies.

→ See beautiful and accessible old-growth redwoods on the quarter-mile **Revelation Trail**. Follow the interpretive signs to deepen your experience of the forest.

→ Not every hike in Redwood is about the trees. Pull off U.S. Highway 101 to walk the short **Yurok Loop Trail**. Watch the waves crash onto the shore and look for marine wildlife in the park's protected waters. Set your gaze north to find False Klamath Cove and west to spot millions of shorebirds.

→ The popular **Damnation Creek Trail** drops 1,000 feet to the shore from its Highway 101 trailhead. Start under massive redwoods that get younger and smaller as you make your way to the small, rocky beach at its end.

→ Redwood contains 70 miles of the **Coastal Trail**, which you can hike to find fragile tide pools, sandy beaches, and jagged coastlines. Walk the Crescent Beach Section for a family-friendly option.

→ Bring your pup to the quiet 3.5-mile **Cal Barrel Road**, once an old logging road, now one of the only routes in the park you can walk with your dog.

Find up-close views of the trees along the Leiffer Loop Trail.

A male elk in Fern Canyon

A seal near Klamath Beach

A Steller's jay

→ SPOT

(R) Redwood's distinct ecosystems, from rocky coastlines to redwood forests, have been designated a UNESCO World Heritage site—and the wildlife in the park is equally diverse and impressive.

→ Get up high on Coastal Drive to see migrating **California gray whales** that visit Redwood in the summer. These massive marine creatures travel 9,000 to 12,000 miles during this coastal migration. Look for **sea lions** and **harbor seals** while you're there.

→ Bird-watchers should organize their trip by region. Look for **flycatchers**, **warblers**, **swifts**, **jays**, and **woodpeckers** in the conifer forests. Try to spot **red-tailed hawks**, **western scrub jays**, **white-tailed kits**, and **California quail** in the oak woodlands and grasslands. **American dippers** and **yellow warblers** prefer the streams, while **egrets**, **bald eagles**, and **ospreys** move through the estuaries.

→ Seabirds love this protected coastline. In California, 40 percent of seabirds breed along 40 miles of this safeguarded region. Visit the beaches to see **whimbrels**, **sanderlings**, and **sandpipers**, and look toward coastline cliffs to see **sea ducks**, **loons**, and **grebes**.

→ Seven herds of **Roosevelt elk** call Redwood home. Look for them in the Crescent Beach area, Prairie Creek Redwoods State Park, Elk Meadow, and Lower Redwood Creek. Find the largest herd, at 250 animals, in Bald Hills. You might also see **black-tailed deer**, **black bears**, and **mountain lions**.

→ The North California Condor Restoration Program has brought the **Prey-go-neesh**, the Yurok name for the condor, back to its home in Redwood. The small group has been thriving in its new (but old) habitat.

DRIVE

Thanks to the joint efforts of the national and state park systems, along with the Redwood parks' own gains toward increased accessibility, there are plenty of roads running through these protected lands.

→ Pull onto **Davidson Road** from U.S. Highway 101, stopping at the Trillium Falls Trail, Gold Bluffs Beach, and Fern Canyon. Look over the Coastal Trail as you drive for ocean views.

→ Drive the **Newton B. Drury Scenic Parkway** through 10 miles of the ancient redwoods, stopping at the Prairie Creek Visitor Center, the South Fork and Ossagon Trailheads, and the Ah-Pah Interpretive Trail.

→ Take the loop created by **Alder Camp Road**, **Coastal Drive**, and **Klamath Beach Road** to circle Flint Ridge, stop at the High Bluff Overlook, and enjoy the beach at Klamath River.

→ Meander **Howland Hill Road** at the north end of the park. Stop at Stout Memorial Grove and the Boy Scout Tree Trail, and enjoy a view of Howland Summit.

→ Take **Enderts Beach Road** along the coastline, pulling over for Crescent Beach access and trailhead, along with the lookout at the end of the road.

→ Turn onto the long **Bald Hills Road** from Redwood Highway. Stop at the Lady Bird Johnson Grove Trail, then continue along the eastern side of the park. Stop at the Redwood Creek Overlook, the Dolason Prairie and Lyons Ranch Trailheads, and the pullout to Schoolhouse Peak.

Coastal Drive

Find waterfalls along the Boy Scout Tree Trail.

Clovers at Redwood Creek

R Redwood offers a bevy of landscapes, wildlife, and activities to explore. Consider these activities for a more rounded trip.

→ Discover the wildlife in the **Enderts Beach tide pools**: ochre sea stars, black turban snails, limpets, isopods, purple shore crabs, hermit crabs, and white sea cucumbers. Don't try to swim on the coast; tides can easily pull you out into the ocean.

→ Visit **Gold Bluffs Beach** to enjoy a picnic by the water and listen to the shorebirds sing above the waves.

→ Explore the **Klamath River Valley**, the homeland of the Yurok people, to better understand the human history of this protected space. See why the valley's eponymous river has long been a source of food, trade, and tradition for this community.

→ Stop at the **Trees of Mystery**, a historic roadside attraction with a canopy trail, gondola ride, collection of curios, forest café, and "vintage" roadside motel. The unique stop has been family-run since 1946.

→ Book a **guided horseback riding trip** through the park with an outfitter. Try Redwood Creek Buckarettes, Crescent Trail Rides, or Redwood Trails Horse Rides to plan a day-long or multiday excursion.

→ Paddle the nearby **Big Lagoon** with an outfitter like Bigfoot Adventure Academy. Glide through the calm wetland habitat during this easy float as you watch for waterfowl and Roosevelt elk.

→ RANGER RECOMMENDATION ←

*Hike the half mile down to **Enderts Beach**, where you'll find tide pools full of marine life. From there, continue to a hidden beach, then go through a tunnel of rocks to find an even more deserted one. There are no redwoods on this hike, so it's ignored by many visitors, to everyone else's gain.*

→ ALASKA

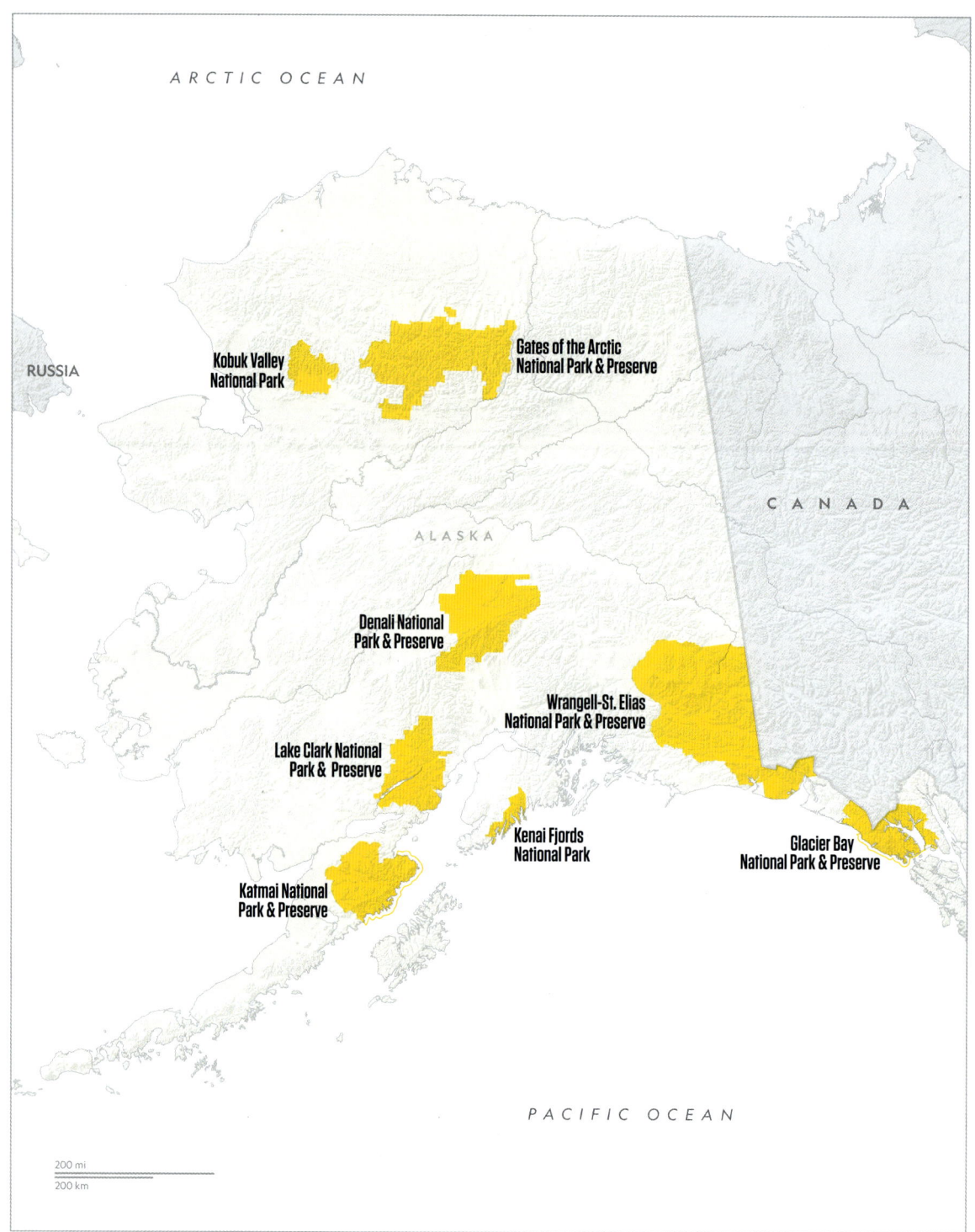

ARCTIC OCEAN

RUSSIA

CANADA

Kobuk Valley
National Park

Gates of the Arctic
National Park & Preserve

ALASKA

Denali National
Park & Preserve

Wrangell-St. Elias
National Park & Preserve

Lake Clark National
Park & Preserve

Kenai Fjords
National Park

Glacier Bay
National Park & Preserve

Katmai National
Park & Preserve

PACIFIC OCEAN

200 mi
200 km

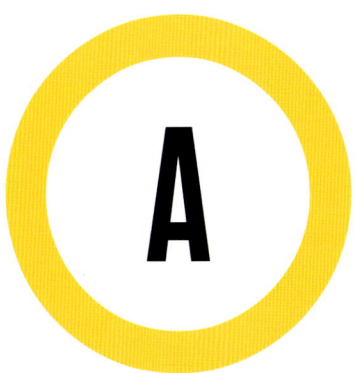

A

Alaska's eight national parks and preserves protect more than 41 million acres of natural treasures. Katmai (page 652) and Lake Clark (page 678) lie along the Pacific Ring of Fire— a region of active volcanoes and giant brown bears. Whales, sea lions, and seabirds seek the cold, food-laden waters of Glacier Bay (page 640) and Kenai Fjords (page 662), while Wrangell-St. Elias (page 686) is a jumble of rugged mountains and glaciers. Above the Arctic Circle, Gates of the Arctic (page 630) and Kobuk Valley (page 670) protect tundra and migrant herds of caribou. By comparison, Denali (page 616) seems tame, with its railroad and hotels—yet wildlife is so abundant here it's nicknamed the "subarctic Serengeti."

LEFT: Brooks Range, Gates of the Arctic National Park & Preserve (page 630) **PREVIOUS PAGES:** Takahula Lake, Gates of the Arctic National Park & Preserve (page 630)

A pond near Mt. McKinley (Denali)

DENALI NATIONAL PARK & PRESERVE

ALASKA

ESTABLISHED: February 26, 1917, as Mount McKinley National Park; renamed December 2, 1980

- -

SIZE: 6,075,030 acres

- -

VISITORS CENTERS: The Denali Visitor Center and the Walter Harper Talkeetna Ranger Station are both open in the summer; the latter has some limited availability throughout the year. The Murie Science and Learning Center and the Eielson Visitor Center are open year-round.

- -

TRANSPORTATION: Three free shuttle bus lines operate throughout the park during the summer: Savage River, Riley Creek Loop, and Sled Dog Demonstration.

- -

DOGS ALLOWED: Only on paved roads, parking lots, and campground roads. Dogs are not allowed on most trails or on buses.

- -

WHEN TO GO: Summer offers the best weather and open facilities (most close mid-September–May), but the park is open year-round. Fall colors peak in late August or early September.

- -

CONTACT: 907-683-9532; nps.gov/dena
Mile 3 on Denali Park Road
Denali Park, AK 99755

D Denali National Park & Preserve is a space that remains mostly unchanged from its wild, tranquil past. The park has only one road and one entrance, so direct human impact is minimal. Rather, shifts in the park come from climate change, which has brought shrinking glaciers, thawing permafrost, and rising tree lines.

Still, the park shines as a beacon of conservation, both human and natural. Denali protects the legacy of the people who have called this area home for at least 12,000 years and the wonder of its untamed ecosystems.

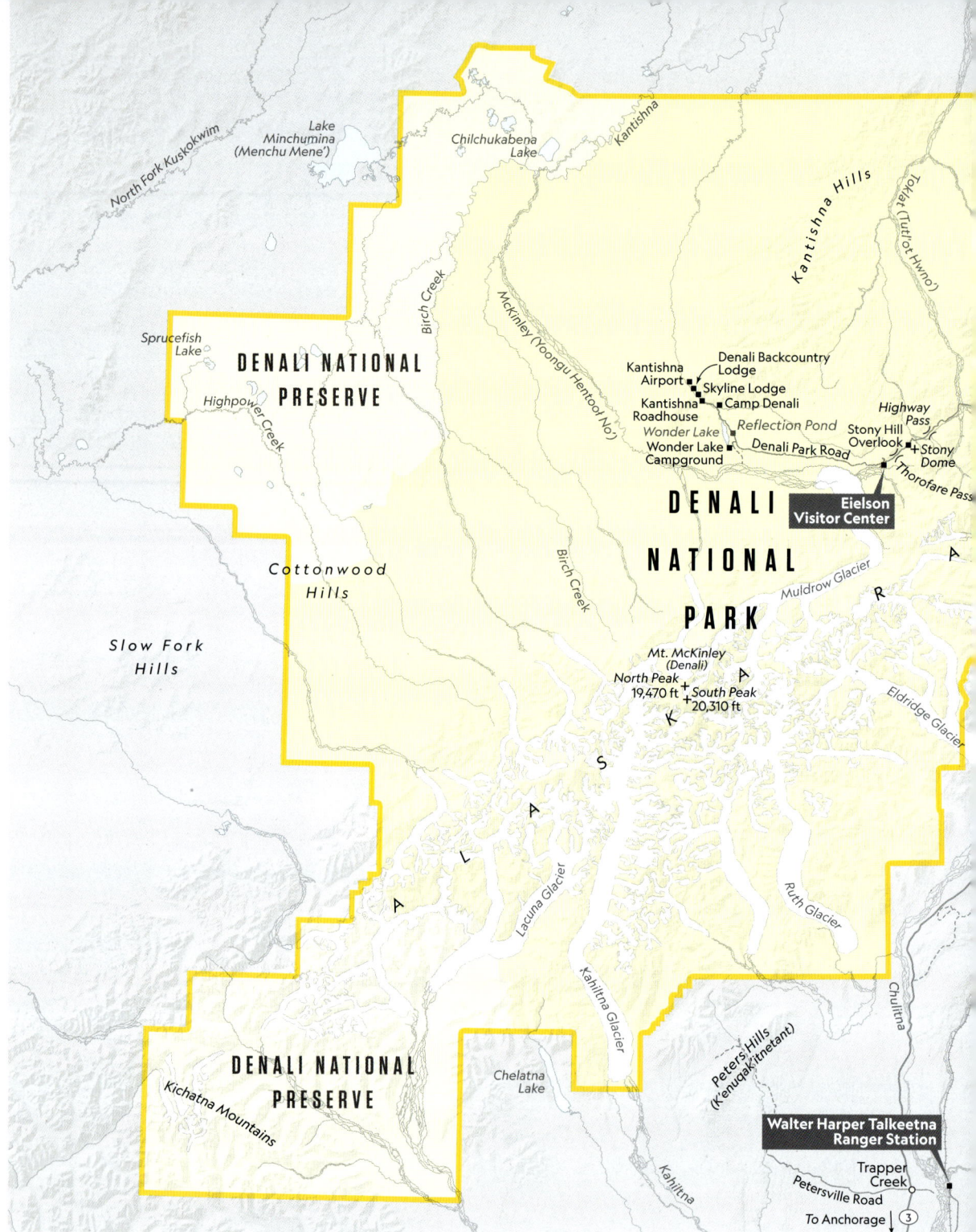

North Fork Kuskokwim

Lake Minchumina (Menchu Mene')

Chilchukabena Lake

Kantishna

Kantishna Hills

Tokiat (Tut'ot Hwno')

Sprucefish Lake

DENALI NATIONAL PRESERVE

Birch Creek

Highpower Creek

McKinley (Yoongu Hentool No')

Kantishna Airport
Denali Backcountry Lodge
Skyline Lodge
Kantishna Roadhouse
Camp Denali
Wonder Lake
Reflection Pond
Wonder Lake Campground
Denali Park Road

Highway Pass
Stony Hill Overlook
Stony Dome
Thorofare Pass

Eielson Visitor Center

Cottonwood Hills

Birch Creek

DENALI

Muldrow Glacier

NATIONAL

Slow Fork Hills

PARK

Mt. McKinley (Denali)
North Peak
19,470 ft
South Peak
20,310 ft

Eldridge Glacier

A L A S K A R A

Lacuna Glacier

Ruth Glacier

Kahiltna Glacier

Chulitna

DENALI NATIONAL PRESERVE

Kichatna Mountains

Chelatna Lake

Peters Hills (K'enuqak'itnetant)

Walter Harper Talkeetna Ranger Station

Kahiltna

Trapper Creek

Petersville Road

To Anchorage ↓ ③

Map labels

To Fairbanks

Teklanika

Nenana

3

Healy

Savage River Loop Trail

Mt. Healy Trail

Mt. Healy 5,700 ft

Murie Science and Learning Center

Primrose Ridge

Savage Alpine Trail

Sled Dog Kennels

Horseshoe Lake Trail

Riley Creek Campground and McKinley Station Trail

Sanctuary River Campground and Bridge

Denali Visitor Center

Teklanika River Campground

Savage River Campground and Mountain Vista Loop Trail

Igloo Creek Campground

Sable Pass

Polychrome Overlook

N   G   E

Cantwell

8

Denali Highway

Summit

3

Alaska Railroad

ALASKA

George Parks Highway

Devils Canyon

Susitna

Talkeetna

N

15 mi
15 km

→ **SLEEP**

Ⓓ Denali has six campgrounds, all on Denali Park Road. From closest to farthest from the park's one and only entrance, you'll find these:

→ *Campers willing to sacrifice some quiet for a few modern conveniences should choose* **Riley Creek**. *You'll have cell reception, a nearby camp store, laundry, restrooms, and access to a bus depot. There's a fee for the 142 tent and RV sites in the summer. Reservations are strongly recommended between May and September.*
→ *The heavily wooded* **Savage River** *(32 sites) and* **Sanctuary River** *(7 tent-only sites) offer a bit more privacy between sites and chances for sunrise and sunset mountain views. Both campgrounds are open May to September; reservations are recommended.*
→ **Teklanika River** *is open to RVs staying at least three nights, though there are no hookups, and car-free tent campers staying of any length of time. There are 53 sites in total, and reservations are recommended. The campground is open May to September.*
→ *The more remote* **Igloo Creek**, *open May to September, is accessible only by camper bus and offers just vault toilets for its seven first-come-first-serve tent sites. At* **Wonder Lake**, *the closest camp to Mt. McKinley (Denali), wake up to once-in-a-lifetime views. It offers 28 tent-only sites, and reservations can be made online.*

Four lodges are inside the park: **Camp Denali**, **Kantishna Roadhouse**, **Denali Backcountry Lodge**, and **Skyline Lodge**. These lodges are located at the end of Denali Park Road, so road closures make them difficult to reach by vehicle. Book a flight into Kantishna Airport for your arrival. You'll need to book a room far in advance.

Backcountry camping is welcome throughout the park. Submit your plans the day before or day of your trip to the Backcountry Information Center for a free permit.

The north and south peaks of Mt. McKinley
(Denali) as seen from Stony Dome

DRIVE

To protect the park's landscape and prevent overcrowding, private vehicles are prohibited on **Denali Park Road** after 15 miles in the summer and three in the winter. That won't keep you from the experience, however. Just hop on a bus—either a shuttle or tour—in the summer.

Get trip guidance from an expert on a **tan narrated tour bus**, or direct your own trip on a **green non-narrated transit bus**. Both trips are run by an outside company and can be booked online at *reservedenali.com*.

Stop all along the road, but don't miss these biggies:

→ *The 900-foot-long **Alaska Railroad Trestle** was completed in 1922. A train between Anchorage and Fairbanks still runs across it daily.*

→ *Stretching from miles 37 to 42, **Sable Pass** is a favorite for landscape and wildlife photographers.*

→ ***Polychrome Overlook** at mile 45 is a major stop for park buses. Get the camera ready for a stunning breadth of rivers, ponds, and peaks.*

→ *The **Stony Hill Overlook** at mile 62 offers the first base-to-summit view of Mt. McKinley (Denali) from the road.*

→ *Make it to mile 86 for **Reflection Pond** and **Wonder Lake**. On the calmest days of the year, you'll be rewarded with an unobstructed reflection of Mt. McKinley (Denali) on the still waters.*

HIKE

W While the park has 20 established and maintained trails, most of its land is open for adventure. If that's not something you're used to doing, don't stress. Denali makes it easy. Hop on one of the park's transit buses and hop off when you see a place you'd like to explore. When you're done, head back to the main road and get on the bus again. Talk with a ranger before you head off-trail. Also, pack enough food and water, bring a first aid kit and a way to treat water, wear appropriate clothing, and plan for bad weather. Try some of these trail-free hikes:

→ Experience the alpine tundra along **Primrose Ridge** at mile 16. Access the region along the west side of the Savage River Canyon or from Denali Park Road west of the river. The 1,500-foot ridge is great for birding, wildflower views, and alpine camping.

→ Hike into the gravel bar on the eastern side of the **Toklat River** at mile 53. Camp in a protected area to stay out of the high southern winds and actively avoid grizzly bears. If you manage that, you'll be rewarded with spontaneous and surprising wildlife spottings.

→ Get great views of grizzly bears and Dall sheep when you jump off the bus at the **Sanctuary River Bridge**. South of the road, the landscape is thick with vegetation—and many of the well-trodden routes are used by large animals. Set aside

at least three days to explore these headwaters, which start about 14 miles from Sanctuary River Campground.

If you want to stick to the beaten path, opt for one of these marked, yet still wild, hikes:

→ The **Mount Healy Trail** starts near the Denali Visitor Center, off the Taiga Trail. It's one of the park's steepest hikes, with switchbacks that gain 1,700 feet in elevation, ending at a photo-perfect overlook of more southern peaks. This 2.7-mile one-way trek doesn't get you to the peak—and it's best not to try to summit Mount Healy unless you're an experienced mountaineer.

→ The **Savage River Loop Trail**, a flat two-mile river loop that includes a bridge crossing, is one of the park's few round-trip hikes. The four-mile **Savage Alpine Trail** is a steeper, more challenging walk that connects the river and Savage River Campground. Get to both by car

or on the free Savage River Shuttle, and dress for wind.

→ The **Horseshoe Lake Trail** starts with a short, steep hike to a lake overlook, then drops down to water level. From there, take the two-mile round-trip trail in either direction. On the west side of the lake, try to spot a moose or beaver in the water.

→ Get a history lesson on the **McKinley Station Trail**. This 1.6-mile one-way hike starts at the visitors center and takes you past the site of Mount McKinley Park Hotel (the 1937 building, which often hosted elegant galas, burned down in 1972), the original park headquarters, a looming steel bridge built in 1922, and an old fox-farming ranch.

→ Travel the **Mountain Vista Loop Trail** for panoramic views of the Savage River Valley, Mount Healy, and Mount McKinley (Denali). Sandwiched between the boreal forest and tundra, the ADA-compliant trail is flat, six feet wide, and covers 0.6 mile round-trip.

Accessible Option

A glacial pool on lower Ruth Glacier

A bus pauses for a glimpse of wildlife.

A grizzly bear ambles through the brush.

D Denali was created to safeguard wildlife, and it continues to do exactly that. It's now home to 39 mammal species, 169 bird species, and one amphibian species: the resilient wood frog.

→ *Denali was first designated as a national park to protect the **Dall sheep**, and it worked. It's hard for rangers to get good numbers on wildlife in the massive park, but estimates of the population range from 1,000 to 2,000. Spot them at Igloo Canyon, along the road at Polychrome, or at the Eielson Visitor Center.*

→ ***Grizzly bears** usually hang out at the Savage River, Teklanika River, and Toklat River to hunt for salmon. See them at Sable Pass, Highway Pass, and Thorofare Pass.*

→ ***Caribou** usually gather in small groups in the summer, but you might catch a crew of more than 100 if you're lucky. Look for them where the grizzlies are.*

→ *Look for **coyotes** and **foxes** at Stony Dome. Stop by Horseshoe Lake or Wonder Lake to find **beavers**.*

→ *Head to the park's wetter regions, usually between miles 70 and 85, to search for **waterfowl** among the many ponds.*

→ *Hike into the forest to see **owls**, and keep an eye on the ridgelines to catch a glimpse of soaring **golden eagles**.*

SPOT

Hiking lower Ruth Glacier

Mount McKinley (Denali)

*Family
Friendly*

G Getting out onto the snow, into the air, or on two wheels are great ways to have a different look at the land.

→ *Denali is the only national park with a **sled dog kennel** (the dogs are used to help park rangers patrol the area). Watch a daily demonstration of this traditional Alaskan transportation in the summer. Get there by hiking Rock Creek Trail from the Denali Visitor Center or taking the free shuttle.*

→ *Trails around the Murie Science and Learning Center are open and beautiful year-round. Come winter, strap on a pair of **cross-country skis** or **snowshoes**. The learning center also serves as the park's winter visitor center. You can borrow a set*

of snowshoes here if you don't have your own.

→ *Tour Denali by air with one of the myriad outfitters that leave from nearby towns. Sheldon Air Service, Fly Denali, K2 Aviation, and Talkeetna Air Taxi all give **aerial tours** of the park and have permission to land on the glaciers for passengers to hike along the ice formations.*

→ ***Bike** Denali Park Road, but do so with caution—avoiding buses and bears. Rack your bike on a bus when you're ready to turn back or need a break.*

→ ***Raft** the eastern boundary of the park with outfitters like Denali Raft Adventures or New Wave Adventures to paddle down the rapids of the Nenana River Canyon. Extend the trip with an overnight pack-raft adventure.*

E
X
P
L
O
R
E

A bird's-eye view of upper Ruth Glacier

SUMMIT

R Reaching the top of **Mount McKinley** (Denali)—the tallest peak in North America—is a monumental feat. The first recorded ascent of the 20,310-foot-tall mountain was in 1913; only about half of the nearly 51,000 climbers who have attempted to reach the summit since have succeeded. The mountain is called Denali by the local Athabaskan people, meaning "the great one" in the Koyukon language, which is spoken on the northern side of the park.

Summiting requires careful planning and preparation. Mountaineers must review park documents and apply for a special-use permit. Unless you are an extremely experienced climber, make plans through an expedition outfitter, like Alpine Ascents International, RMI Expeditions, or Alaska Mountaineering School.

Before any attempt of this multiweek endeavor, complete numerous ascents in other glaciated peaks, and prepare for the cold, the altitude, and heavy-pack climbing. Train to carry a 40- to 50-pound backpack while pulling a 60- to 80-pound sled on moderate terrain for six to eight hours at a time.

→ **RANGER RECOMMENDATION** ←

*Join a ranger on the park's ever changing **Discovery Hike**, which shifts daily, depending on the weather and the whims of your guide. Outlying factors aside, expect uneven terrain, stream crossings, and deep wilderness. You'll get expert insights on the land, a carefully curated trek, and the chance to talk with a ranger about your interests. Sign up at a visitors center.*

The North Fork of the Koyukuk River

GATES OF THE ARCTIC NATIONAL PARK & PRESERVE

ALASKA

ESTABLISHED: December 2, 1980

SIZE: 8,472,505 acres

VISITORS CENTERS: In the park, the Anaktuvuk Pass Ranger Station is staffed during the summer. Outside the park are the Bettles Ranger Station and Visitor Center, Arctic Interagency Visitor Center, and Fairbanks Alaska Public Lands Information Center.

TRANSPORTATION: Most people arrive by plane, though rafting is an exciting option. Dalton Highway, the nearest road, gets you five miles from the eastern boundary.

DOGS ALLOWED: Yes, in all areas. Consider the remote wilderness and wildlife before bringing your pup.

WHEN TO GO: July and August are nearly perfect, and autumn offers brilliant colors. The park is open in winter, but visits are challenging.

CONTACT: 907-459-3730; nps.gov/gaar
101 Dunkel Street
Fairbanks, AK 99701

G Gates of the Arctic is set in the Brooks Range, which humans have traversed for as many as 13,000 years. Twelve communities—the Alatna, Allakaket, Ambler, Anaktuvuk Pass, Bettles, Evansville, Hughes, Huslia, Kobuk, Nuiqsut, Shungnak, and Wiseman—call this remote land home and serve as its caretakers. Preserving the park's landscapes and history are at the root of its designation, and visitors will feel this goal with every step.

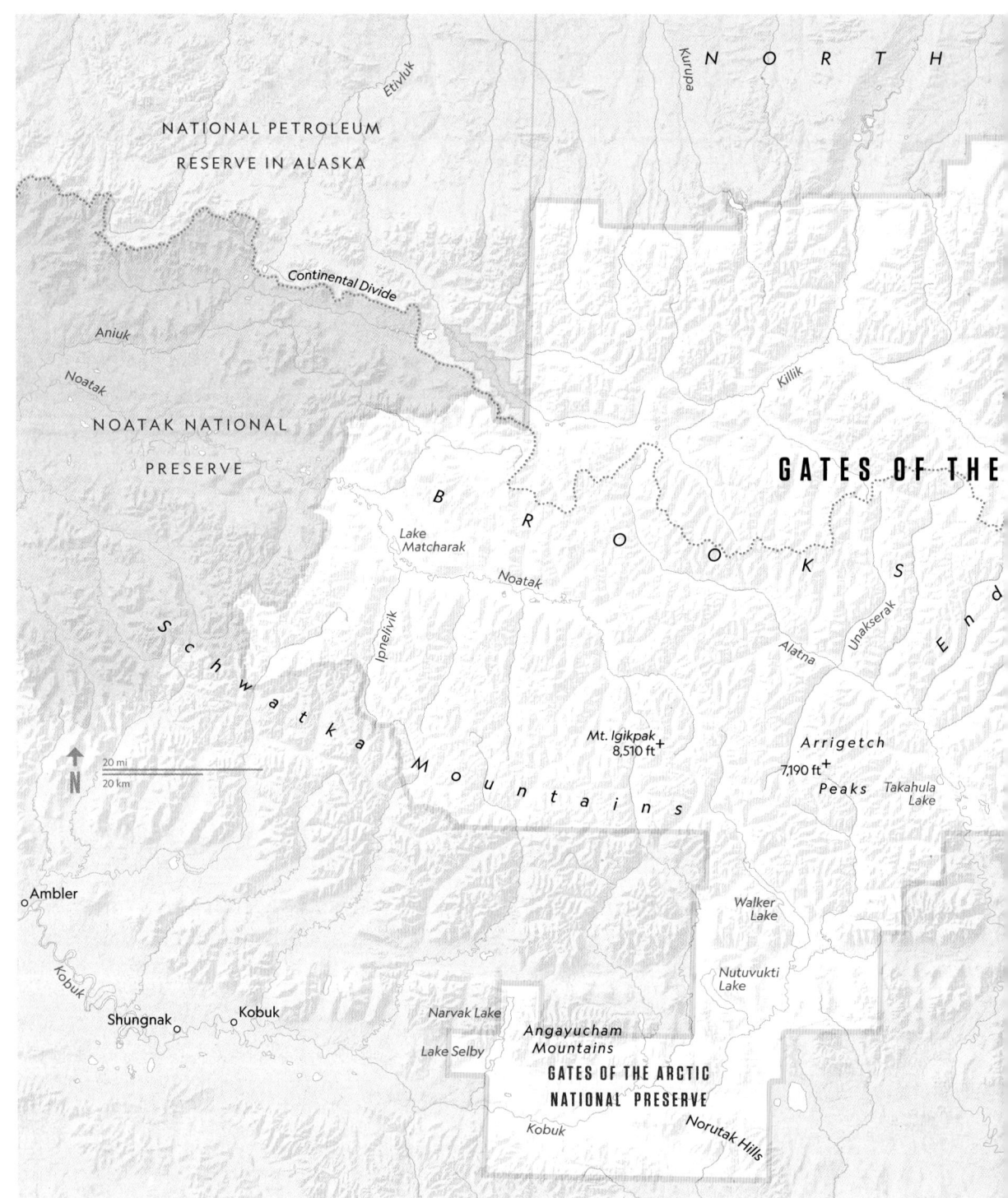

NORTH

Etivluk

Kurupa

NATIONAL PETROLEUM
RESERVE IN ALASKA

Continental Divide

Aniuk

Killik

Noatak

NOATAK NATIONAL

PRESERVE

GATES OF THE

B R O O K S

Lake
Matcharak

Noatak

Alatna

Unakserak

End

S c h w a t k a

Ipnelivik

Mt. Igikpak +
8,510 ft

Arrigetch

7,190 ft +

M o u n t a i n s

Peaks

Takahula
Lake

20 mi
20 km

N

Walker
Lake

Ambler

Nutuvukti
Lake

Kobuk

Kobuk

Narvak Lake

Shungnak

Lake Selby

Angayucham
Mountains

GATES OF THE ARCTIC

NATIONAL PRESERVE

Kobuk

Norutak Hills

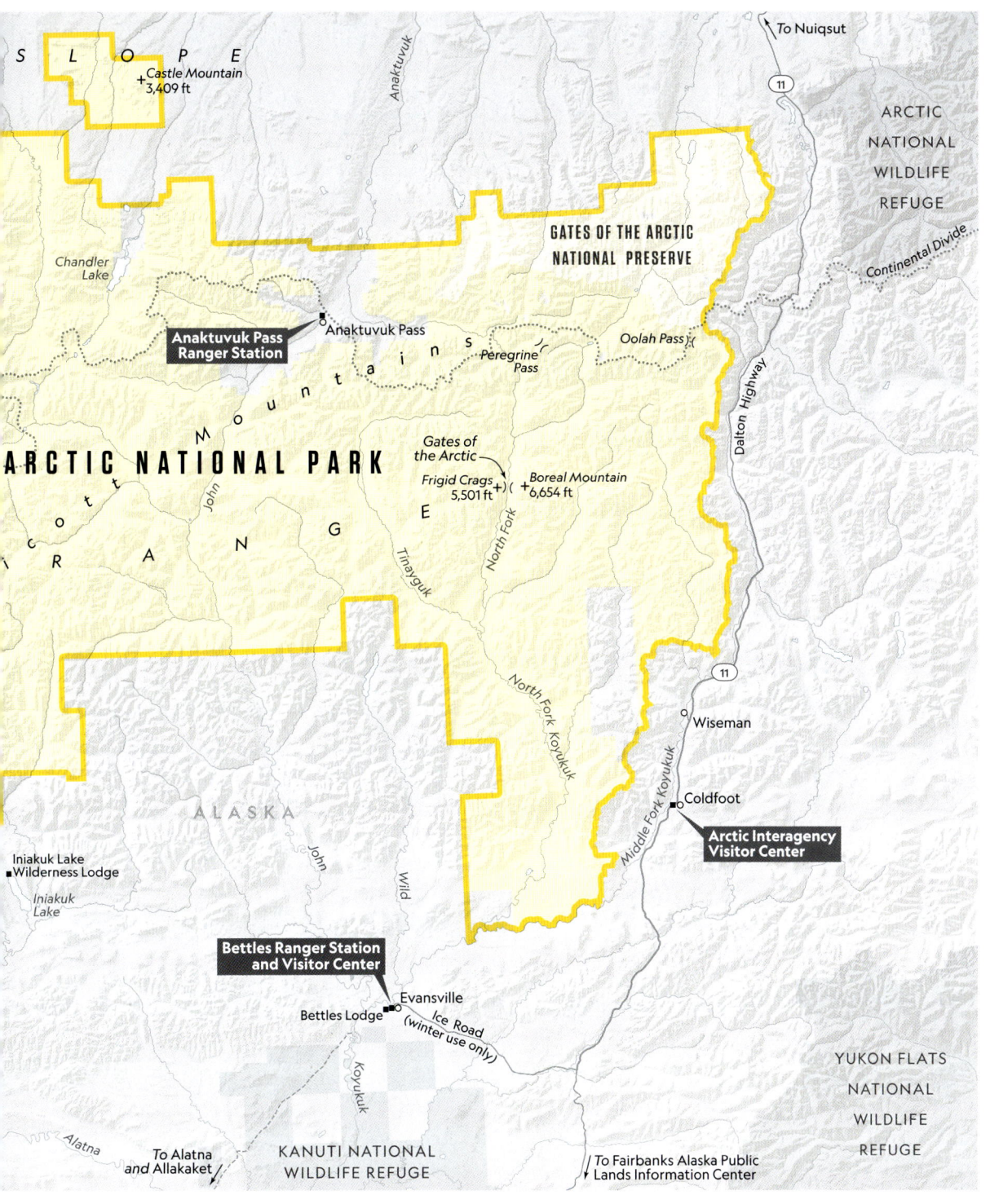

S L O P E

Castle Mountain
3,409 ft

Chandler
Lake

Anaktuvuk

**Anaktuvuk Pass
Ranger Station**
Anaktuvuk Pass

Mountains

GATES OF THE ARCTIC
NATIONAL PRESERVE

Peregrine
Pass

Oolah Pass

ARCTIC

NATIONAL

WILDLIFE

REFUGE

Continental Divide

ARCTIC NATIONAL PARK

Gates of
the Arctic

Frigid Crags
5,501 ft

Boreal Mountain
6,654 ft

John

Tinayguk

North Fork

icott

R A N G E

Dalton Highway

North Fork Koyukuk

Wiseman

A L A S K A

Iniakuk Lake
■ Wilderness Lodge

*Iniakuk
Lake*

John

Wild

Middle Fork Koyukuk

Coldfoot

**Arctic Interagency
Visitor Center**

**Bettles Ranger Station
and Visitor Center**

Evansville
Bettles Lodge   Ice Road
(winter use only)

Koyukuk

Alatna

To Alatna
and Allakaket

KANUTI NATIONAL
WILDLIFE REFUGE

To Fairbanks Alaska Public
Lands Information Center

YUKON FLATS

NATIONAL

WILDLIFE

REFUGE

To Nuiqsut

11

11

S L E E P

(T) There aren't any official campgrounds, campsites, or lodges, but you can **backcountry camp** anywhere in the park that's safe for you and the environment. The park doesn't issue permits, but it does ask visitors to attend a backcountry orientation with information about current conditions, wildfire alerts, backcountry safety, and leave-no-trace practices.

Be conscious of your impact on the land. Make **camp on durable surfaces**, like gravel bars above current water levels, to protect the landscape from any permanent damage—and to protect yourself from mosquitoes. If a vegetated site is your only option, choose one covered in grass or sedge, not lichen or moss. Wherever you are, **don't cut any branches or dig any trenches** for your campsite. Always keep your food and cooking items at least 100 yards from where you sleep, unless you want a bear to wake you up.

If you'd rather not camp, try one of these lodges outside the park:

→ *Bettles Lodge has served as an all-inclusive base camp for summer and winter visitors to the Brooks Range for three decades. While you're there, explore the history of the town, which was founded during the gold rush era.*
→ *Just south of the Brooks Range, **Iniakuk Lake Wilderness Lodge** was built by hand by its owners. The luxury space is solar-powered, accessible only by plane, and offers summer and winter trips into the park.*

Backcountry camping during the long daylight hours

HIKE ←

Alatna River

G Gates of the Arctic is a remote and wild park—emphasis on the wild. There are **no established hiking trails**; the entire landscape is open for exploration. Rangers encourage personalized routes to protect the fragile ground cover and promote self-assessment of trekking skills. They also ask that visitors account for condition fluctuations.

Heed some advice for a better hike: Walk along the riverbeds or above the tree lines for easier navigation. Download a detailed map on a GPS device that you can use without internet or cell service. Bring a bear canister: You don't want any unwelcome guests at your campsite.

A few regions and routes in the park are particularly popular:

→ Trek through several phases of alpine glacier activity around the granite pinnacles of the **Arrigetch Peaks**. The peaks cover 38,313 acres and rise 4,000 feet from the valley.
→ Hike the difficult 65-mile **Oolah Pass** from the village of Anaktuvuk Pass, home to mostly Nunamiut people, to Dalton Highway. Over all those miles, you'll wander across the flowing Grizzly Creek, down to the headwaters of the North Fork of the Koyukuk River, and into Peregrine Pass.
→ Explore **Walker Lake**, which sits on the southern slope of the Brooks Range, to experience the resilience and beauty of a glacial lake, from its crystal clear waters to its green spruce shoreline.

Challenging Hike

W Wildlife far outnumber people here, especially since the park neighbors the 19-million-acre Arctic National Wildlife Refuge.

→ The best way to see the park's animals is by water. Transition from plane to paddle when you land in Lake Matcharak and make your way down the Noatak River. Look for **raptors**, **caribou**, **musk oxen**, **Dall sheep**, and **grizzly bears**.
→ Float the John River, with its low valley and nearby slopes, in the fall and spring for a chance at spotting one of the three **caribou** herds that frequent the narrow corridor. Contact rangers before your trip to be sure, since environmental changes are impacting migration patterns.
→ The 24 hours of daylight in the summer make this a popular, established spot for **migratory birds**. About 145 species of birds have been spotted at the park, including **long-tailed jaegers** and **short-eared owls**.

Bear tracks

SPOT

A bull caribou watches rafters on the Etivluk River.

An aerial view of the Arrigetch Peaks

A A park this massive can be a beast to explore—outfitters can help. Figure out which activity would give you the most joy, then book the adventure of a lifetime.

→ Reach out to Arctic Treks, Wilderness Alaska, Arctic Wild, Alaska Alpine Adventures, or Expeditions Alaska for **rafting excursions** that take you along the Alatna River from its Continental Divide headwaters through the Brooks Range. You'll see the diversity of the park, from tundra to forest, along the trip, which can be up to a week long.

→ Book a **flightseeing trip** with Golden Eagle Outfitters, Brooks Range Aviation, Wright Air Service, Coyote Air, or Arctic Backcountry Flying Service. From the air, you'll see towering snowcapped peaks, grizzly and black bears wandering the shores, and birds of prey flying above.

→ **Fishing** is allowed in both the park and preserve, and it's best to start when the snow begins to melt in late June. Find arctic grayling, lake trout, arctic char, northern pike, and sheefish. Practice catch-and-release fishing or keep only what you will immediately eat, given their low growth rates and productivity.

Float along a route that has been used for thousands of years by Native communities. The **Noatak River** is a designated National Scenic and Wild River and moves through alpine tundra, crosses plains, and ends in a coastal delta leading to Kotzebue Sound. A week-long paddle with an outfitter like Arctic Wild is manageable for those with some canoeing experience. Camp on the gravel bars along its banks—be sure to avoid nearby vegetation, which is being destroyed by visitors.

Tarr Inlet with Margerie Glacier in the distance

GLACIER BAY NATIONAL PARK & PRESERVE

ALASKA

ESTABLISHED: December 2, 1980

SIZE: 3,284,500 acres

VISITORS CENTERS: The Glacier Bay Visitor Center in Glacier Bay Lodge is staffed in the summer. You'll find trip planning resources and advice, along with interpretive programs. Rangers at the Visitor Information Station in Bartlett Cove are available in the summer for permits and advice.

TRANSPORTATION: Most visitors see Glacier Bay from the deck of a cruise ship. You can also get to the park by shuttle, plane, ferry, or boat.

DOGS ALLOWED: Only on Bartlett Cove Public Use Dock and the beach between the dock and the National Park Service Administration Dock

---

WHEN TO GO: While the park is open year-round, most services close mid-September–mid-May. Visit in the summer.

CONTACT: 907-697-2230; nps.gov/glba
1 Park Road
Gustavus, AK 99826

N Nature is ever changing, and that's certainly the case at Glacier Bay National Park & Preserve. About 250 years ago, the landscape was covered in ice that has since retreated 60 miles. Each day, the tides come and go. Each season, the wildlife patterns shift. Visitors to Glacier Bay must balance the need for careful and critical planning with a mindset of flexibility and freedom. If you can do that, you'll be rewarded with unencumbered shorelines, towering icy peaks, and roaming wildlife.

A tent pitched beside the Tatshenshini River

→ SLEEP

I If you're on one of the cruise ships, most will have a Park Service ranger board the ship to provide information about the landmarks and sights. For passengers who disembark, tours last a full day. But if you'd like to see the park from land, you have a few options for places to sleep:

→ Get a room at **Glacier Bay Lodge** (open summer only) in Bartlett Cove, just inside the mouth of the bay. There, you'll also find the official visitors center, a restaurant, bookable excursions, and stunning views.

→ Pitch your tent at the **Bartlett Cove Campground**. At the free, walk-in-only sites, you'll find bear-proof storage, composting toilets, a beach fire pit, and a small warming shelter.

→ Stay at a hotel, bed-and-breakfast, or RV park in **Gustavus**, just eight miles from the Glacier Bay Visitor Center and often called the "gateway to Glacier Bay National Park." From there, you can take a shuttle, ferry, or plane into the park. Get supplies here as well, but prepare for a high price tag.

→ Pick up a **backcountry camping permit** and a bear-proof canister from the Visitor Information Station in Bartlett Cove, where you'll also take a required in-person orientation class (available May–September) and get advice about your trip from rangers.

→ While **kayak camping trips** can be done independently, it's a good idea for many visitors to go through an outfitter, of which there are many. Try Alaska Mountain Guides or Spirit Walker Expeditions.

Camp With a Guide

To Shawshe
(Dalton Post)

3

Tatshenshini

BRITISH COLUMBIA

Alsek Ranges

Klehini

CANADA
U.S.

Chilkat

Klukwan

Skagway

ALASKA

7

Haines

Chilkoot Inlet

Grand Pacific Glacier

Carroll Glacier

TAKHINSHA MOUNTAINS

Mt. Krause
6,978 ft

CANADA
U.S.

Tarr Inlet

Margerie Glacier

Mt. Rice
6,658 ft

Sullivan
Island

Mt. Fairweather
15,300 ft

Mt. Merriam
5,083 ft

WEST ARM

Gloomy Knob

EAST ARM

Muir Inlet

Beartrack Mts.

TONGASS
NATIONAL
FOREST

F A I R W E A T H E R   R A N G E

GLACIER BAY

NATIONAL PARK

GLACIER
BAY

South Marble
Island

Chilkat Range

Lituya
Bay

Brady
Icefield

Crillon
Lake

Beardslee
Islands

Bartlett

Bartlett
Lake

Excursion Ridge

Bartlett River Trail
(Huna Tribal House) Xunaa Shuká Hít

Glacier Bay Lodge and Visitor Center

Visitor Information Station

Bartlett
Lake Trail

Brady Glacier

Bartlett Cove

Forest and Beach Trails

Bartlett Cove
Campground

Glacier Bay Sea Kayaks

Gustavus

I C Y   S T R A I T

Point
Adolphus

Cape
Spencer

Cross Sound

Elfin Cove

TONGASS NATIONAL
FOREST

Hoonah

Cape
Bingham

CHICHAGOF ISLAND

The iceberg-strewn waters of the bay

An old-growth forest near Grand Plateau Glacier

HIKE

This wild and remote park is open for hiking anywhere that's safe for you and the environment. On-site rangers give tips on finding your way through the landscape, such as these:

→ **Get advice on current conditions** from a ranger; weather can vary greatly day to day.
→ **Beware of slippery spaces.** Glacier Bay is very moist and wet. Wet wooden walkways, docks, locks, and rocks can all be hazards.
→ Hiking along beaches and through alpine meadows can be a great option, but be ready to tangle with the **widespread, toothy Sitka alder** plants that grow over much of the land.
→ It might be summer, but your body can still experience hypothermia in the rainy and cold weather. **Bring the right gear.**
→ **Get out of the way of moose.** They are not your friends.

While there are plenty of untamed areas to explore, the established trails from Bartlett Cove are a good start:

→ The 10-mile out-and-back **Bartlett Lake Trail** from Bartlett Cove to tranquil Bartlett Lake is a full-day trip. Pack everything you'll need, from food to rain gear.

→ At the same trailhead, you can take a shorter hike along the **Bartlett River Trail**. This walk is four miles out-and-back and will take you through a dense rainforest toward the mouth of the Bartlett River. In the summer, you'll see otters, eagles, seals, and bears—all attracted to the water's spawning salmon.

→ Combine the **Forest Trail** and the **Beach Trail** for a short round-trip hike that will take you through a forest, near a few quiet ponds with viewing decks, and back along the shore. There are daily guided hikes on this route with park rangers.

→ At the end of the boardwalk at Bartlett Cove, right by Xunaa Shuká Hít (Huna Tribal House), the **Tlingit Trail** begins. On this easy one-mile out-and-back walk, you'll see a traditional Tlingit canoe, a complete whale skeleton, many native plants, and striking views of the bay.

Must-Do Activity

SPOT

D Despite the harsh environment, wildlife is abundant in Glacier Bay. The water is filled with **sea otters**, **humpback whales**, **harbor porpoises**, and **sea lions**. **Grizzly bears**, **Dall sheep**, **mountain goats**, and **moose** also call the park home. More than **280 species of birds** have been recorded in the park. No matter the excursion, you're bound to see something wild.

→ *The park has noted 15 locations for excellent bird-watching, from the very accessible Bartlett Cove to the paddlers-only Beardslee Islands. Keep an eye out for **eagles**, **migrant warblers**, **thrushes**, **diving ducks**, and more.*

→ *At South Marble Island, watch boisterous **Steller sea lions**—mostly bachelors who can't challenge males at the nearby breeding islands—play and flip in the sun, along with colonies of nesting birds, including **tufted puffins**, **black-legged kittiwakes**, and **pigeon guillemots**.*

→ *Boat or kayak the Icy Strait, a section of water that flows just outside the bay, to search for the whales who visit in the summer to dine on fish. **Humpbacks** are protected in the park, and the population is growing each year.*

Steller sea lions sunning themselves

A horned puffin floats in the waters off South Marble Island.

A small ship anchors in Bartlett Cove.

If you're going to paddle or boat Glacier Bay, you need to understand when and how much its tides change—up to 25 feet every six hours. Once you get a feel for the tide tables and get comfortable on the water, you'll be able to see sights not available from land.

→ **Rent a kayak** from Glacier Bay Sea Kayaks for a day trip around Bartlett Cove or up the Bartlett River to one of the two dozen Beardslee Islands, where you'll see lots of marine wildlife, including humpback whales, sea otters, and harbor seals. It's also a great spot for beach camping. Just don't get stranded in a mudflat by timing the tides wrong.

→ Rent those same kayaks for longer **camping trips** around the bay. An overnight paddling trip to the West Arm will take a minimum of four days, while a trip up through the East Arm and Muir Inlet (where motorized boats are not allowed in the summer) will take a minimum of seven.

With the help of Glacier Bay Sea Kayaks, you can paddle in one direction and take the tour boat back the other.

→ **Kayak over to Point Adolphus** to watch for majestic humpbacks.

→ Catch a ride on the **Glacier Bay Tour Boat** that leaves from Bartlett Cove for a seven-hour trip through the bay, floating past South Marble Island to see the wildlife, moving along the coastal mountainside, and eventually reaching the icy glacier on the northern end—viewable from your boat's deck.

→ Get a thrill on a **white-water rafting trip** on the Tatshenshini and Alsek Rivers, which have rapids rated between Class II and IV. Alsek River Adventures, Canadian Outback Rafting, and Nahanni River Adventures all offer tours that start at Shäwshe (Dalton Post).

→ **Take your own boat** inside Glacier Bay with a permit from the park. Plan ahead: Only 25 permits are available each day, some in advance and some by short notice.

E X P L O R E

(**G**) Get a deeper cultural perspective of Glacier Bay with one of these experiences:

→ Gather at **Xunaa Shuká Hít** (Huna Tribal House) of the Tlingit community—the Native people who have traditionally occupied Southeast Alaska and the region of Glacier Bay. This space, created in partnership with the Hoonah Indian Association, is the first permanent clan house in Glacier Bay since the Native villages were destroyed by a glacier hundreds of years ago.

→ Three lodges in Glacier Bay National Preserve cater mostly to visitors who'd like to **fish and hunt**. Johnny's East River Lodge, Northern Lights Haven Lodge, and Alsek River Lodge all offer cozy accommodations, remote wilderness experiences, and guided excursions.

→ Outfitters like Fly Drake, Ward Air, and Alkan Air take you on **flightseeing trips** past the tallest peaks and lowest valleys of the park's winding glaciers. On clear days, see icy waters flowing, rugged slopes with wildlife, and remote mountain lakes.

Twenty-one-mile-long Margerie Glacier

Must-See

Boat or paddle to **Gloomy Knob**, a mostly barren tract of limestone where mountain goats wander at unusually low elevations. In the summer, kids (the goat kind, not human) climb along the protected cliff ledges, where they're safe from predators. Geologists have found clues about the formation of this carbonate rock. Look for the wavy, layered lines that show how it came from deep underwater in the tropical equator. Its gouges and grooves highlight how it was carved by glacial waters after being pushed north by tectonic plate action.

The northern coastline of the park near Mount Douglas

KATMAI
NATIONAL PARK & PRESERVE

ALASKA

KATMAI
EST 1980

ESTABLISHED: December 2, 1980

SIZE: 4,093,077 acres

VISITORS CENTERS: Visitors centers are open in the summer. The most popular is the Brooks Camp Visitor Center, with its educational programming, resources, and bear orientation. Nearby, and accessible by bus tour or road, is the Robert F. Griggs Visitor Center. The King Salmon Visitor Center is next to the airport, making it an easy and informational stop on the way to the park.

TRANSPORTATION: No in-park transportation; accessed exclusively by boat or plane

----

DOGS ALLOWED: Only in restricted areas. Remember the high concentration of brown bears and the remote location.

WHEN TO GO: June–mid-September for hiking, fishing, and boating. July, September, and October are peak bear-viewing months.

CONTACT: 907-246-3305; nps.gov/katm
1000 Silver Street
Building 603
King Salmon, AK 99613

C   Come for the bears and stay for the volcanic landscapes. Most visitors head to Katmai National Park & Preserve to watch its famous brown bears feed on the salmon that fill the waters at Brooks Camp. Others go to fish for that abundant salmon themselves. The park will absolutely fulfill both of those promises—and so much more. Take the time to explore the volcano-altered environment and learn about the people who once called this place home.

→ SLEEP

(K) Katmai is home to a range of overnight options, from forest-filled campgrounds to luxury lodges.

→ The campground at **Brooks Camp** doesn't have any designated sites, but it does have a capacity limit. Reservations open in January online or by phone. Get reservations early for peak times; they often book within hours of opening. It has cooking shelters, potable water, vault toilets, and an electric fence to deter the bears.

→ Reserve **Fure's Cabin** on Naknek Lake's Bay of Islands. Built in 1926 for a local trapper and miner, the one-room space is now available to paddlers and hikers year-round. The combination of history and nature makes for an epic adventure.

→ Enter the lottery for a campsite at the **McNeil River State Game Sanctuary and Refuge**. While not part of Katmai, the adjacent land serves as a protective region for brown bears and other wildlife and is accessible only by air taxi.

→ **Backcountry camping** at Katmai is always an option, but you should camp out in the open to avoid surprising the bears and choose spots that look like they've already been impacted by other visitors. Try Valley of Ten Thousand Smokes, American Creek, or Hallo Bay.

→ Two lodges are authorized by the park and sit on park land: Walk from **Brooks Lodge** to Brooks Falls to watch the bears fish—and book excursions to go fishing yourself. The exclusive, camp-like **Grosvenor Lodge** opens its cabins and main lodge to no more than six guests at a time, who all must arrive by air.

→ Lodges on private lands surrounding the boundaries of the park also offer all-inclusive excursions, fishing expeditions, and remote wilderness experiences. Check out **Enchanted Lake Lodge**, **Katmai Wilderness Lodge**, **Kulik Lodge**, and **Royal Wolf Lodge**.

Augustine
Island

ALASKA

*Gibraltar
Lake*

Funnel Cr.

COOK

Kamishak Bay

INLET

Moraine Cr.

McNEIL RIVER
STATE GAME
SANCTUARY
AND REFUGE

Kukaklek Lake

KATMAI NATIONAL
PRESERVE

■ Battle River
Wilderness Retreat

Kamishak Special
Use Area

Nonvianuk Lake

■ Kulik Lodge

McNeil

■ Enchanted
Lake Lodge

*Kulik
Lake*

American Creek

Douglas

Mt. Douglas +
7,063 ft

Cape
Douglas

*Hammersly
Lake*

KATMAI

Grosvenor
Lodge

*Swikshak
Lagoon*

Fure's
Cabin

Savonoski Loop
Portage
Trail

*Lake
Grosvenor*

NATIONAL PARK

Kaguyak Crater +

■ Swikshak Patrol Cabin

Swikshak Bay

Bay of Islands

Savonoski

Iliuk Arm

○ Savonoski
(abandoned village)

**Robert F. Griggs
Visitor Center**

*Hallo
Bay*

S
H
E
L
I
K
O
F

S
T
R
A
I
T

Three Forks
Overlook

Mt. Denison
7,606 ft

+ Mt. Steller
7,300 ft

+ Mt. Griggs
7,600 ft

■ Katmai Wilderness
Lodge

+ Snowy Mountain
7,090 ft

AFOGNAK
ISLAND

Mt. Katmai
6,716 ft

*Geographic
Harbor*

Amalik Bay
■ Patrol Cabin

Amalik Bay
Archeological District

Takli Island

KODIAK NATIONAL
WILDLIFE REFUGE

*Alinchak
Bay*

↑
N

20 mi
20 km

KODIAK ISLAND

HIKE ←

 Much of Katmai is unmaintained, which means backcountry hiking and camping. Trade trail support for untamed freedom in places along the Pacific coast, Moraine Creek, and Naknek for the chance to walk hundreds of miles in rugged, wild space. You don't need a permit, but you should send your itinerary to the Katmai dispatch office.

If you want a more established experience, try one of these maintained trails:

→ *The **Brooks Camp Cultural Site Trail** is right across from the visitors center and presents the archaeological record of the communities who once lived in the region. Just a quarter mile each way, the walk takes you to the home site of three different Indigenous groups and highlights their traditions.*

→ *The **Brooks Falls Trail** is one nearly every Katmai visitor walks—and for good reason. Though the distance is short (0.6 mile each way) and the unpaved route is mostly flat, you might be startled by the bears walking and sleeping on the path. The trail runs through boreal forest and ends at two raised platforms with views of the Brooks River and the bears fishing within.*

→ *Hike up the **Dumpling Mountain Trail** from Brooks Camp to get a better view of Naknek Lake. This eight-mile out-and-back trail climbs 800 feet in the first 1.5 miles, so be prepared for a vertical journey.*

→ *Take **Lake Brooks Road** for an easy one-mile walk to the lake to see salmon spawning in the late summer. Enjoy a lunch at the covered picnic area.*

A trail leading to a bear-viewing platform at Brooks Falls

A brown bear fishing for sockeye salmon at Brooks Falls

SPOT

T There's really only one animal that brings visitors here: bears. They're everywhere in Katmai, but here are a few tried-and-true places for watching bears live, eat, and play:

➜ *Observe the brown bears at the famous* **Brooks Camp overlooks**, *including the coveted spot at Brooks Falls. Get a different view of the bears from each of the three viewing platforms in the camp.*

➜ *Venture farther out from Brooks Camp to get a quieter experience—or find more bears outside of peak season. In June, try* **Hallo Bay** *or* **Swikshak Lagoon**. *In August, head to* **Geographic Harbor** *or* **Moraine** *and* **Funnel Creeks**.

➜ *Outside the park,* **McNeil River State Game Sanctuary and Refuge** *provides close-up looks at more bears than you can count. Fly into the campground and hike through an aquatic environment to the viewing falls.*

➜ *To see wildlife from above, book a* **flightseeing tour** *with one of the many outfitters operating in Katmai. You'll get views of the Pacific coast, the lowland tundra, and roaming animals.*

A red fox nestles in the grass.

Kayaks float at the edge of the Savonoski Loop.

A cluster of bog blueberry blossoms

W Water is in every corner of Katmai. It's what brings the wildlife—and, thus, the visitors. Freely explore the hundreds of miles of rivers, massive lakes, and many small ponds to feel the life-blood of the region.

→ *Paddle the 80-mile* **Savonoski Loop**. *Besides a short portage trail near Fure's Cabin, spend four to 10 days, depending on pace and plans, floating through the gorgeous backcountry of the park.*

→ *Paddle an out-and-back route to the* **Savonoski River** *from Brooks Camp. You'll earn your views on this one, with its por-tages, bugs, and wind.*

→ *Go with a guide to the* **Bay of Islands** *in North Arm Naknek Lake for a shorter trip with equally gorgeous views.*

→ *Take a salmon, arctic char, or rainbow trout* **fishing trip** *along American Creek. A journey along this scenic, 40-mile river usually starts at Hammersly Lake and takes up to 10 days.*

Experts Only

F
L
O
A
T

→ RANGER RECOMMENDATION ←

There isn't much driving to be done in Katmai, but you can visit the site that led to its designation. Take the **bus tour to Valley of Ten Thousand Smokes** from Brooks Lodge to the Robert F. Griggs Visitor Center and the Three Forks Overlook. From there, hike 3.4 miles round-trip to the valley floor to see the enduring results of a 60-hour volcanic explosion in 1912. For a longer experience, forgo the bus trip and walk the entire route on a multiday hike from Brooks Camp.

Dwarf fireweed lines a lake in Bear Glacier Lagoon.

KENAI FJORDS
NATIONAL PARK

ALASKA

ESTABLISHED: December 2, 1980

SIZE: 699,983 acres

VISITORS CENTERS: The Kenai Fjords National Park Visitor Center is in Seward, a nearby harbor town. The Exit Glacier Nature Center serves as the educational, informational, and meeting point for anyone exploring Exit Glacier or the Harding Icefield. Both spots are only open in summer.

TRANSPORTATION: Just one road goes into the park, and it's only open from spring through fall.

DOGS ALLOWED: Only on the road to Exit Glacier and in the parking lot of its nature center

----

WHEN TO GO: Explore in the summer when boat trips are offered. Flightseeing companies offer tours year-round out of Seward. In winter, the road opens to snowshoers, cross-country skiers, and dogsledders once there's enough snow. Hikers and bicyclists are allowed on the road year-round.

CONTACT: 907-422-0500; nps.gov/kefj
PO Box 1727
Seward, AK 99664

K Kenai Fjords National Park was once covered entirely by ice, and 51 percent of it still is. Despite the harsh environment, resiliency shines through in the plants, animals, and people who continue to thrive in its breathtaking spaces. A visit to the park is like opening up a portal to days gone by. See how this story is unfolding for yourself.

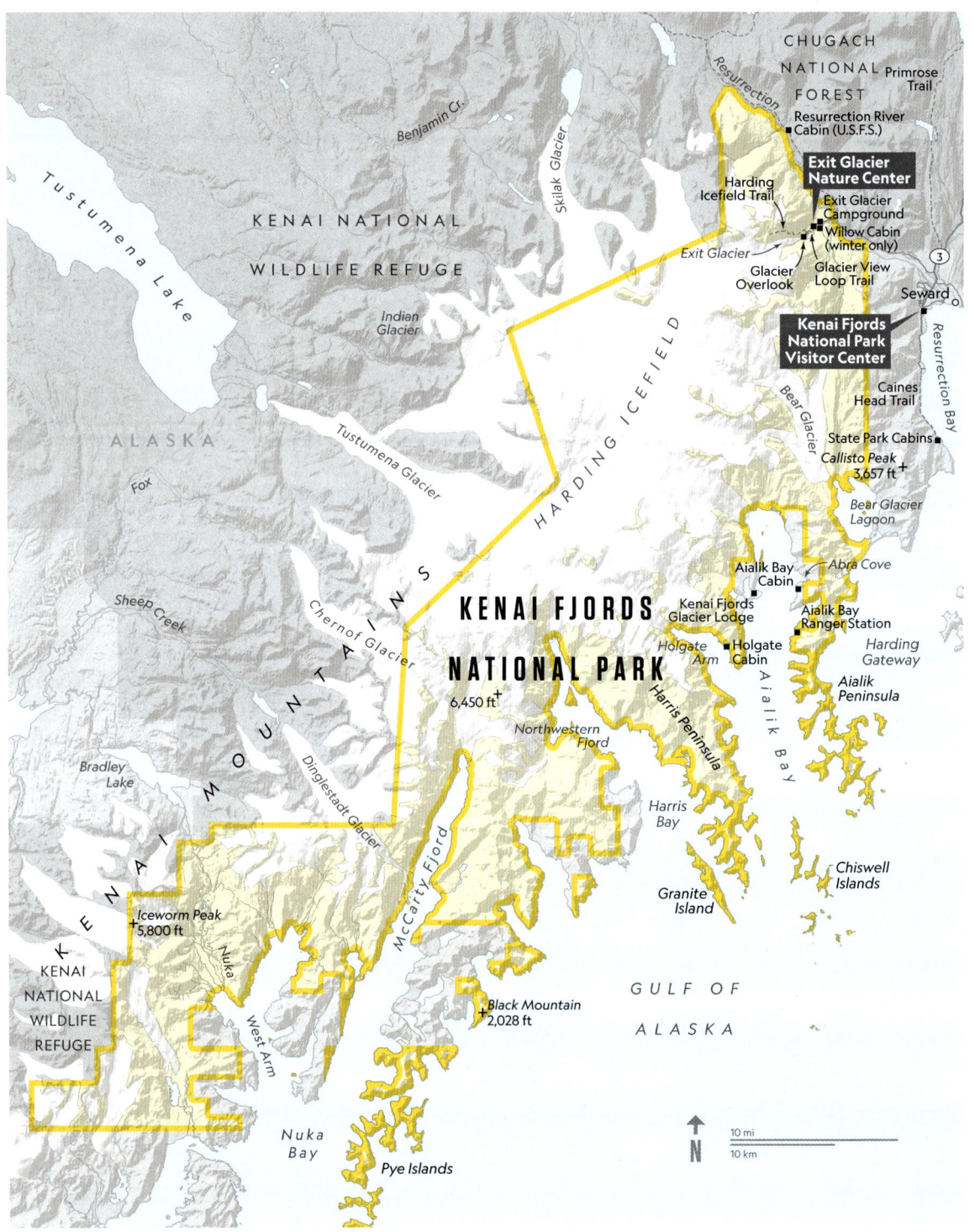

CHUGACH

NATIONAL FOREST

Primrose Trail

Resurrection River Cabin (U.S.F.S.)

Exit Glacier Nature Center

Harding Icefield Trail

Exit Glacier Campground

Willow Cabin (winter only)

Exit Glacier

Glacier Overlook

Glacier View Loop Trail

Seward

3

Kenai Fjords National Park Visitor Center

Caines Head Trail

State Park Cabins

Callisto Peak 3,657 ft

Bear Glacier

Bear Glacier Lagoon

Abra Cove

Aialik Bay Cabin

Aialik Bay Ranger Station

Harding Gateway

Kenai Fjords Glacier Lodge

Holgate Arm

Holgate Cabin

Aialik Peninsula

Aialik Bay

Benjamin Cr.

Skilak Glacier

KENAI NATIONAL

WILDLIFE REFUGE

Indian Glacier

Tustumena Lake

Tustumena Glacier

ALASKA

Fox

Sheep Creek

HARDING ICEFIELD

KENAI FJORDS NATIONAL PARK

6,450 ft

Northwestern Fjord

Harris Peninsula

Harris Bay

Granite Island

Chiswell Islands

Chernof Glacier

Dinglestadt Glacier

KENAI MOUNTAINS

McCarty Fjord

Bradley Lake

Iceworm Peak 5,800 ft

Nuka

West Arm

KENAI NATIONAL WILDLIFE REFUGE

Nuka Bay

Pye Islands

Black Mountain 2,028 ft

GULF OF ALASKA

Resurrection Bay

10 mi

10 km

N

A tent on the terminal moraine of Bear Glacier

SLEEP

Ⓨ Your overnight options in Kenai Fjords National Park mostly consist of campsites and cabins, but there is one lodge in the park.

→ Pitch a tent or park your RV at **Exit Glacier Campground**. The 12 sites are first come, first served and fill fast in July and August. The campground has drinking water, pit toilets, and a cooking shelter with storage.

→ **Backcountry camp** in the many coves along the shore, where you'll find peaceful mornings and calm evenings. You don't need a permit, but you should check with rangers for closures and advice.

→ Two cabins are available to visitors during the summer, both on the coast of Aialik Bay: **Aialik Bay Cabin** is a great starting point for a hike to Abra Cove (a permit for deeper exploration is required, since the land is owned by the Port Graham Corporation), while guests at **Holgate Cabin** can hear its namesake glacier calving at night.

→ For more modern luxuries, book a stay at **Kenai Fjords Glacier Lodge**. Built within an Indigenous-owned wildlife sanctuary, it offers 16 cabins, a dining room with panoramic views, beach access, and excursions into the water and mountains.

Family-Friendly Stay

Accessible Option

HIKE

U Unlike in many other Alaskan national parks, rangers don't recommend any off-trail hiking in Kenai, where steep and rugged terrain creates difficult scrambles. Here are your maintained-trail options:

→ *Join a ranger-led walk from the Exit Glacier Nature Center to the **Glacier Overlook**. The program takes about 90 minutes, and you'll get insider details on the stunning landscape, with views of Exit Glacier and the Harding Icefield, the 700 square miles of glaciers central to the park experience.*

→ *Take the one-mile, wheelchair-accessible **Glacier View Loop Trail** to see where Exit Glacier falls from the Harding Icefield. You'll find the start of the half-paved, half-gravel path at the Exit Glacier Nature Center.*

→ *Get to the strenuous 8.2-mile round-trip **Harding Icefield Trail** from the Exit Glacier area. Pack warm clothes, rain gear, and sunscreen. After gaining about 1,000 feet every mile, find views of what the icy landscape once was—miles of ice and snow as far as the eye can see.*

Give sea kayaking a try in Bear Glacier Lagoon.

O Outside of the established hikes, the water is the best way for you to see everything the park has to offer, from towering icy peaks to free-roaming wildlife.

→ *Book a **boat tour on Resurrection Bay** with one of the outfitters there. Try Alaska Shore Excursions, Major Marine Tours, or Kenai Fjord Tours. All trips leave from Seward Harbor but vary by interest, including day trips on basic vessels all about the views to luxury multiday trips on boats with heated cabins and dining options. Look for humpback whales, orcas, harbor seals, Steller sea lions, Dall's porpoises, and sea otters during your cruise.*

→ *Experienced paddlers can take on these waters themselves. A **sea kayak** will get you closer views of the cliffs and glaciers, but it is a risky endeavor—especially as you move south. Be prepared for wind, rain, summer storms, ocean swells, landings with strong surfs, and few protected coves.*

→ *Less experienced but determined paddlers can **float through Aialik Bay on a guided tour**. See a tidewater glacier or head to a less crowded northwestern fjord, where you will find an array of glacier types. Contact Liquid Adventures or Kayak Adventures Worldwide.*

The Harding Icefield Trail

FLOAT

G Get into the air, onto the rivers, or out to the coast with one of these excursions:

→ *You won't be able to land in the park, but a* **flightseeing trip** *with one of the many outfitters in the region is worth the airtime. Outfitters can be easy to find in Seward, and trips usually entail taking off from a glacially fed lake and landing on a glacier for a hike.*

→ *Take a* **fishing trip** *in the region, where you can find both fresh- and saltwater fish, including salmon and halibut, with an outfitter like Saltwater Safari Company or Alaska River Adventures. Get a license before you throw your line.*

→ *Kenai Fjords is the perfect park to* **look for coastal Alaskan birds***. Board a boat and keep an eye out for bald eagles, black-billed magpies, puffins, peregrine falcons, and more.*

→ **Mountaineers** *who want to explore the Harding Icefield more intimately can take the route from Tustumena or Chernof Glaciers to Exit Glacier, but they should be confident in their glacial and crevasse abilities. The tough terrain is truly only for tested experts.*

→ *Book a winter tour with one of the nearby outfitters. You can* **dogsled, snowmobile, boat, snowshoe,** *and* **ice climb***. If you're lucky, you'll spot some moose on your adventures.*

A bald eagle ready to take flight

An orca spotting near Seward

E X P L O R E

→ RANGER RECOMMENDATION ←

Experience the **Exit Glacier region during the colder months** to truly enjoy the solitude and challenges of an Alaskan winter. Book a stay at the rustic, winter-only Willow Cabin. It's seven miles to the cabin by snowshoe, snowmobile, or cross-country skis, but it's worth the effort for silence and beauty. Watch for wolves, moose, wolverines, and bald eagles as you look out the window from the cozy, propane-heated space.

KOBUK VALLEY
NATIONAL PARK

ALASKA

Ahnewetut Creek meanders through
the Great Kobuk Sand Dunes.

ESTABLISHED: December 2, 1980

SIZE: 1,750,716 acres

VISITORS CENTER: The Northwest Arctic Heritage Center is open year-round. It's in Kotzebue, 80 miles southwest of the park, and offers advice for your trip, kid-friendly programming, and a museum on the ecosystem and Inupiat culture. Get your bear-proof container here.

TRANSPORTATION: No in-park transportation. Access the park by plane, snowmobile, dogsled, foot, or watercraft.

DOGS ALLOWED: Yes, but be mindful of bears.

WHEN TO GO: Only experienced wilderness adventurers should visit in the winter. If that's not you, head here in the summer months.

CONTACT: 907-442-3890; nps.gov/kova
171 Third Avenue
Kotzebue, AK 99752

It's easy to go miles without seeing another person at Kobuk Valley National Park. There are no roads, trails, or campsites. There are no public tours, entrance gates, or visitors centers inside the park. There are, however, acres and acres of wild land and water—accessible only by foot, plane, or paddle. What the park lacks in infrastructure, it makes up for in wildlife, tradition, and wonder. Take your time in this rugged landscape to watch wildlife move totally unconcerned by onlooking humans, and test your own survival skills.

Okoklik Lake

Lake Kangilipak

Noatak

Uluksian Creek

Aklumayuak Creek

NOATAK NATIONAL PRESERVE

Noatak

Sapun Creek

Nanielik Creek

Kunyanak Creek

Imelyak

Kaluich Creek

Cutler

Kanatok Mt.
3,320 ft

ALASKA

B A I R D

Anaktok Creek

Salmon

Sheep Cr.

Mt. Angayukaqsraq
4,670 ft

Natmotirak Creek

Hunt

M O U N T A I N S

Akiak Creek

Akiak Mountains

Nelik

Nikok

Tutuksuk

Nekakte Creek

Akillik

KOBUK VALLEY

Kirlik

NATIONAL PARK

Hunt

Kaliguricheark

Salmon
(Qalugruaq)

Kallarichuk

Kaliguricheark

Jade Mountains

Kallarichuk Hills

Kallarichuk

Kobuk

Jade Creek

Miluet Creek

Onion Portage
Archaeological District
(Paatitaaq)

Ambler

Kobuk

Kallarichuk Ranger Station
(seasonal)

Kavet Creek

Great Kobuk
Sand Dunes

Ahnewetut Cr.

Onion Portage
Ranger Station
(seasonal)

To Walker
Lake

To Northwest Arctic
Heritage Center
and Kotzebue

Kobuk

Little Kobuk
Sand Dunes

SELAWIK NATIONAL WILDLIFE REFUGE

10 mi

10 km

N

You can camp along Ahnewetut Creek.

SLEEP

Register for a **backcountry camping** permit to stay inside Kobuk Valley, where there are no maintained campsites. Most campers either book an organized trip, hike into the backcountry from the river, or fly to the Great Kobuk Sand Dunes—200,000 acres of dunes created by the retreat of the glaciers 14,000 years ago. Otherwise, the nearest town with lodges is **Kotzebue**, 80 miles away, also home to the park's visitors center.

Set camp in a forested area of the park.

HIKE ←

Creek waters curl through the Great Kobuk Sand Dunes.

W Without maintained trails, Kobuk Valley is prime for personal adventure. Get into the dunes or the forest for a truly wild hiking experience on one of these treks:

→ *Hike two to three miles from the river at Kavet Creek toward the 100-foot-high* **Great Kobuk Sand Dunes***. You'll need strong orienteering skills to get there and back.*
→ *It's easier to hike in the mountains than along the soft riverbank or challenging dunes. Get your pilot to drop you near the* **Baird Mountains***, but not on its peaks, which isn't allowed. Plan to hike along the ridgelines, looking down at the park's vast green fields and up to spot soaring golden eagles.*
→ *If you aren't confident in your orienteering or backcountry skills, book a trip with an outfitter for a day-long or multiday* **guided hike***. Try Arctic Wild or Golden Eagle Outfitters.*

Challenging Hike

K Kobuk Valley is vast and remote, so there aren't many tried-and-true wildlife sites. Explore, be patient, and hope for a bit of luck. Still, there are a few experiences that might show you the creatures of the park:

→ *For more than 8,000 years, the Inupiat have met at Paatitaaq, or Onion Portage, to hunt* **migrating caribou***. Find the same migration there every fall, along with people from around the region who still participate in the hunts.*
→ *Migratory birds from all seven continents nest in Kobuk Valley each summer. Bring your binoculars and camera to capture the phenomenon and see* **harlequin ducks***,* **tundra swans***, and* **four species of gulls***.*
→ *Backcountry camp for the solitude and calm, as well as the best chance of seeing* **grizzly bears***,* **caribou***,* **moose***, and* **bald eagles***. Wake up early and watch for the animals that move around at dawn.*

A male northern pintail

SPOT

Kayakers on the Kobuk River

See the park from the sky to appreciate its scope.

S Stepping foot in Kobuk Valley is an adventure, no matter what you do. Get off the land and into the water or air for a new perspective on the space.

➜ *Float down the Kobuk River for one of the best ways to see the valley. The water is mostly slow-moving and shallow, as long as you avoid the eight miles below Walker Lake. Fly in with your gear or reserve a trip with an outfitter, like Northwest Alaska Back Country Outfitters.*

➜ *This is a remote fishing spot. Explore on your own to find sheefish, salmon, grayling, pike, or Dolly Varden. Be sure to stay out of the way of subsistence fishers.*

➜ *See the park by plane if you'd rather not backcountry hike. Charter a flightseeing trip with one of the many authorized outfitters in the region and get above the park for an hour or a day.*

Must-Do Trip

RANGER RECOMMENDATION

There are myriad ways to enjoy the majesty of the **Salmon River**, a National Wild and Scenic River. It is a great place to fish for northern pike, grayling, chum salmon, and trout. Watch the fantastic landscape go by, and if you're lucky, see bears, wolves, and moose in their natural habitat. Or take to the air in a small bush plane to the headwaters in the Baird Mountains and then paddle down to the confluence with the Kobuk River.

Turquoise Hickerson Lake, tucked among the mountains of the park

LAKE CLARK
NATIONAL PARK & PRESERVE

ALASKA

ESTABLISHED: December 2, 1980

SIZE: 4,030,006 acres

VISITORS CENTER: You can get to the year-round Port Alsworth Visitor Center only by plane or boat, but you'll find educational exhibits and trip-planning resources once you arrive.

TRANSPORTATION: The park is primarily accessed by small aircraft.

DOGS ALLOWED: Yes, but the Park Service recommends leaving pets at home due to the rugged terrain and wildlife.

WHEN TO GO: Peak season is June–mid-September, when you'll find warm temperatures—and mosquitoes. Wildflowers are best in late June. August and September are wet; fall colors peak in mid-September. Year-round, be prepared for everything from sunshine to snow.

CONTACT: 907-644-3626; nps.gov/lacl
1 Park Place
Port Alsworth, AK 99653

People have lived on the land in what's now Lake Clark National Park & Preserve for thousands of years, hunting for caribou, fishing for salmon, and foraging for berries. Despite this human presence, the area has flourished—undisturbed and wild. A trip to Lake Clark highlights the long and deeply rooted give-and-take relationship between the land and human communities there. It's also one that you'll mostly have to do on your own or with a hired guide.

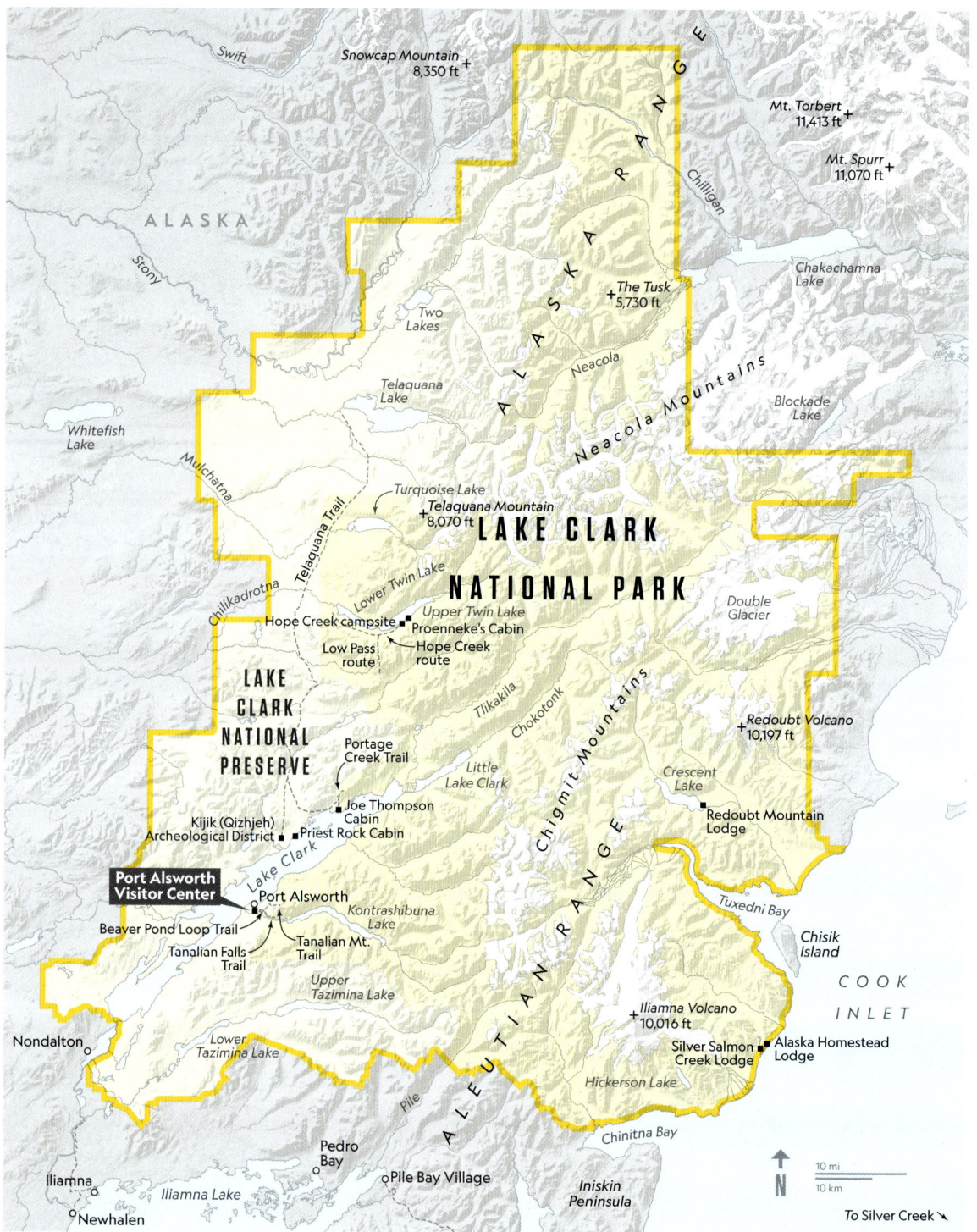

Swift

Snowcap Mountain
8,350 ft +

Mt. Torbert
11,413 ft +

Mt. Spurr
11,070 ft +

ALASKA

Stony

ALASKA

Two
Lakes

Telaquana
Lake

Chakachamna
Lake

Neacola

The Tusk
5,730 ft +

NEACOLA MOUNTAINS

Blockade
Lake

Whitefish
Lake

Mulchatna

Telaquana Trail

Turquoise Lake

Telaquana Mountain
8,070 ft +

LAKE CLARK

NATIONAL PARK

Double
Glacier

Chilikadrotna

Lower Twin Lake
Upper Twin Lake

Hope Creek campsite
Proenneke's Cabin
Hope Creek
route

Low Pass
route

Tlikakila

Chokotonk

CHIGMIT MOUNTAINS

Redoubt Volcano
10,197 ft +

LAKE
CLARK
NATIONAL
PRESERVE

Portage
Creek Trail

Little
Lake Clark

Crescent
Lake

Redoubt Mountain
Lodge

Kijik (Qizhjeh)
Archeological District

Joe Thompson
Cabin
Priest Rock Cabin

Lake Clark

Tuxedni Bay

**Port Alsworth
Visitor Center**

Port Alsworth

Kontrashibuna
Lake

Chisik
Island

Beaver Pond Loop Trail

Tanalian Mt.
Trail

COOK

Tanalian Falls
Trail

Upper
Tazimina Lake

INLET

ALEUTIAN RANGE

Iliamna Volcano
10,016 ft +

Nondalton

Lower
Tazimina Lake

Silver Salmon
Creek Lodge

Alaska Homestead
Lodge

Pile

Hickerson Lake

Iliamna

Pedro
Bay

Pile Bay Village

Chinitna Bay

Iniskin
Peninsula

Newhalen

Iliamna Lake

N

10 mi
10 km

To Silver Creek

Pitch your tent on a beach in the Twin Lakes area of the park.

SLEEP

(B) Backcountry camping is welcomed and encouraged at Lake Clark, where most of the land is free for exploration. Leave your itinerary and emergency contact information with rangers at the Port Alsworth Visitor Center along with a voluntary registration form. Don't forget an extra battery, weather-resistant gear, and bear-proof containers.

If you're looking for more established spots to stay, you have a few options:

→ *The primitive* **Hope Creek campsite** *at the Upper Twin Lake is a first-come-first-serve site that gets crowded with guided groups, so try to arrive early.*

→ *Book one of the two public-use cabins in the park: The six-person* **Priest Rock Cabin** *has a woodstove and an outhouse. The rustic* **Joe Thompson Cabin** *sleeps three people in its wooden bunks—just bring your own pads and bedding. Arrive by boat or plane to both spots, and be prepared to treat your water.*

→ *Make Port Alsworth your home base and reserve a room at an accommodation there. Both the* **Wilder B&B** *and the* **Farm Lodge** *can help book excursions into the park and offer a respite on your return.*

→ *Reserve a spot at one of the private lodges within the park's boundaries, such as* **Redoubt Mountain Lodge**, **Silver Salmon Creek Lodge**, *or* **Alaska Homestead Lodge**, *which serve as good starting points to search for puffins by boat, fish at Silver Salmon Creek, or photograph the park's bears.*

Unique Stay

Trek between peaks and beside the water throughout the park.

HIKE

(T) The terrain in Lake Clark is challenging, and there are very few maintained trails. Still, a few well-loved regions are worth a focus:

→ Take the **Beaver Pond Loop Trail** or the **Falls and Lake Trail** until you reach the **Tanalian Mountain Trail**. The trail is maintained almost until the peak, but a wilder route takes you to the top.
→ Follow the unmaintained **Tanalian Falls Trail** to the cascade and Kontrashibuna Lake. There, your only company will be bears, fish, and sunshine.
→ The **Portage Creek Trail** navigates three miles one-way along the Lake Clark shoreline through forest and alpine tundra.
→ Trek the **Hope Creek route** around Upper Twin Lake for gorgeous views of the blue waters and decent treks (with some bushwhacking) through the alpine terrain.
→ Steep hills west of Proenneke's Cabin follow the lakeshore and lead down to the **Low Pass route**. Once you get there, the journey is calm and the meadow views are sweeping.
→ Walk along the **Telaquana Trail**, an ancestral Dena'ina Athabaskan route from Telaquana Lake to the Kijik (Qizhjeh) Archeological District. This historic trek takes about a week and requires some bushwhacking.

(L) Lake Clark is packed with fish and bears, and the region provides a chance to see them both—and more—if you're patient. Head to one of these places:

→ Hop on a plane or a boat to spot **bears** at Chinitna Bay on Lake Clark's Cook Inlet. Stay at one of the private lodges in the inlet for an even better chance of a photo-worthy opportunity. Silver Creek and Crescent Lake are also good bear-viewing regions.
→ More than **185 bird species** have been spotted in Lake Clark, from raptors to waterfowl, seabirds to songbirds. Though they are nearly everywhere, a field guide and a set of binoculars will give you the best experience.
→ Search for **moose** just below the tree line in the transitions from forest to tundra or water to land. If you spot one, keep your distance.

A puffin midair

SPOT

FLOAT ←

Kayakers paddle one of the park's many waterways.

U Unsurprisingly, paddling is a popular way to get around Lake Clark. If that's your style, try out one of these aquatic adventures:

→ Get your Alaska **fishing license** and search for salmon, rainbow trout, grayling, and arctic char out on the park's lakes and rivers. Try Crescent Lake in the Chigmit Mountains or fish along with the bears at Silver Salmon Creek.
→ Take your pick of any of the fantastic **kayaking**, **rafting**, and **pack rafting** lakes in the park. Telaquana, Turquoise, Twin, Kontrashibuna, and Tazimina Lakes, as well as Lake Clark, all offer fantastic, but different, wildlife and views.
→ Go **white-water rafting** on the Tlikakila River, where you'll find Class II and III rapids. The waters are fed by the glaciers above, and they run quickly through the center of the park.

H Human and geological history are woven into every thread of Lake Clark.

→ Visit amateur naturalist **Richard Proenneke's cabin**, now a national historic site, to see how he lived alone in the wild for three decades, beginning in 1967. Get there by floatplane, sit at his desk, and read his telling journals.
→ See the two towering active volcanoes in the park, **Redoubt** and **Iliamna**, from afar and learn how they've shaped the land and the communities who live on it.

The inside of Proenneke's Cabin

EXPLORE

→ RANGER RECOMMENDATION ←

*The best way to explore Lake Clark is by boat, especially on **Crescent Lake**, a gorgeous body of water nestled in the Chigmit Mountains. There, you'll be able to spot two of the main draws of the park: brown and black bears, and the fish they both love: sockeye and salmon. The lake is one of the park's most visited locations, but it still feels remote and isolated.*

A bush plane flies over a glacier.

WRANGELL-ST. ELIAS NATIONAL PARK & PRESERVE

ALASKA

ESTABLISHED: December 2, 1980

SIZE: 13,188,000 acres

VISITORS CENTERS: The Copper Center Visitor Center Complex is home to the Wrangell-St. Elias Visitor Center and the Ahtna Cultural Center. The Slana and Chitina Ranger Stations are open mid-May–mid-September. The Kennecott Visitor Center is accessible by foot from McCarthy, and the Yakutat District Office is accessible by plane or boat.

TRANSPORTATION: No in-park transportation

DOGS ALLOWED: Yes, but keep them leashed at all times.

WHEN TO GO: The park is open year-round, but most visitors should stick to summer months. Only experienced winter campers should brave the colder months.

CONTACT: 907-822-5234; nps.gov/wrst
PO Box 439
Mile 106.8 Richardson Highway
Copper Center, AK 99573

W Wrangell-St. Elias is the largest national park in the United States. Four towering mountain ranges meet within its bounds. One of the largest active volcanoes in North America still lets off steam. The largest subpolar icefield in the continent spurs massive, record-breaking glaciers, which have carved deep valleys and rivers into the sprawling landscape. Everything about Wrangell-St. Elias is tremendous—except the crowds. The park's massive space will make you feel small in the very best way.

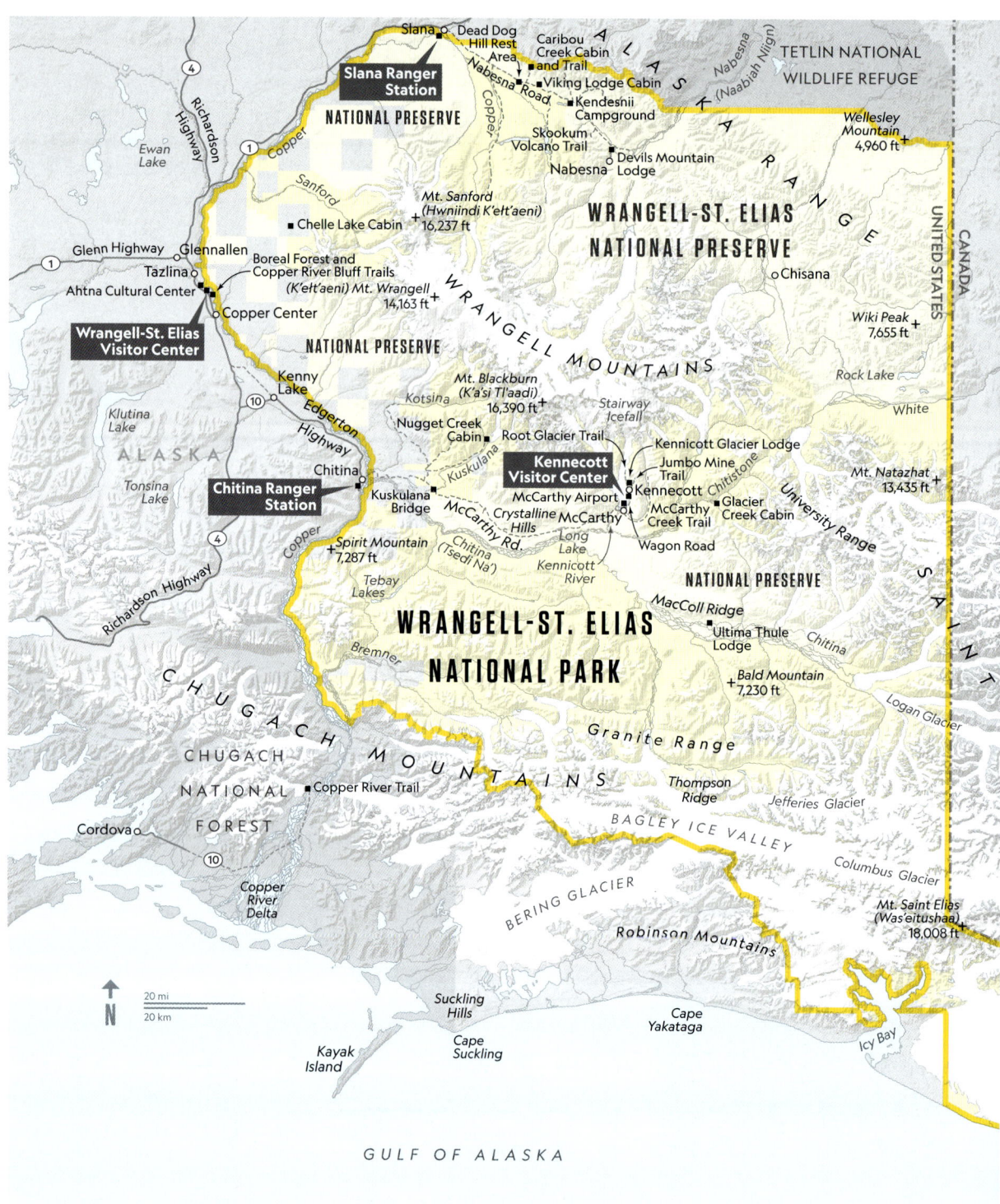

Slana
Dead Dog Hill Rest Area
Caribou Creek Cabin and Trail
Nabesna Road
Viking Lodge Cabin
Copper
ALASKA
Nabesna (Naabiah Niign)
TETLIN NATIONAL
WILDLIFE REFUGE

Slana Ranger Station

NATIONAL PRESERVE

Kendeshii Campground
Skookum Volcano Trail
Devils Mountain Lodge
Nabesna

Richardson Highway

Copper

1

Ewan Lake

Sanford

Chelle Lake Cabin
Mt. Sanford (Hwniindi K'elt'aeni) 16,237 ft

RANGE

Wellesley Mountain 4,960 ft

WRANGELL-ST. ELIAS
NATIONAL PRESERVE

W R A N G E L L   M O U N T A I N S

Chisana

Glenn Highway   Glennallen
Tazlina
Ahtna Cultural Center
Boreal Forest and Copper River Bluff Trails (K'elt'aeni)
Mt. Wrangell 14,163 ft
Copper Center

UNITED STATES
CANADA

Wiki Peak 7,655 ft

1

Wrangell-St. Elias Visitor Center

NATIONAL PRESERVE

Kenny Lake

10

Edgerton Highway

Klutina Lake

Kotsina

Mt. Blackburn (K'a'si Tl'aadi) 16,390 ft
Nugget Creek Cabin
Root Glacier Trail

Stairway Icefall
Kennicott Glacier Lodge
Jumbo Mine Trail

Rock Lake

White

ALASKA

Kuskulana

Kennecott Visitor Center
Kennecott

Chititstone

Mt. Natazhat 13,435 ft

Tonsina Lake

Chitina Ranger Station

Chitina
Kuskulana Bridge

McCarthy Airport
Crystalline Hills
McCarthy Rd.
Long Lake
McCarthy
Crystalline Hills
McCarthy Creek Trail
Glacier Creek Cabin
Wagon Road

University Range

4

Copper

Spirit Mountain 7,287 ft

Chitina (Tsedi Na')
Kennicott River

NATIONAL PRESERVE

Richardson Highway

Tebay Lakes

MacColl Ridge
Ultima Thule Lodge
Chitina

SAINT

Bremner

**WRANGELL-ST. ELIAS
NATIONAL PARK**

Bald Mountain 7,230 ft

Logan Glacier

CHUGACH

G r a n i t e   R a n g e

Thompson Ridge

Jefferies Glacier

CHUGACH NATIONAL FOREST

M O U N T A I N S

Copper River Trail

BAGLEY ICE VALLEY

Columbus Glacier

Cordova

10

BERING GLACIER

Robinson Mountains

Mt. Saint Elias (Was'eitushaa) 18,008 ft

Copper River Delta

Suckling Hills

Cape Yakataga

Icy Bay

Kayak Island

Cape Suckling

N
20 mi
20 km

GULF OF ALASKA

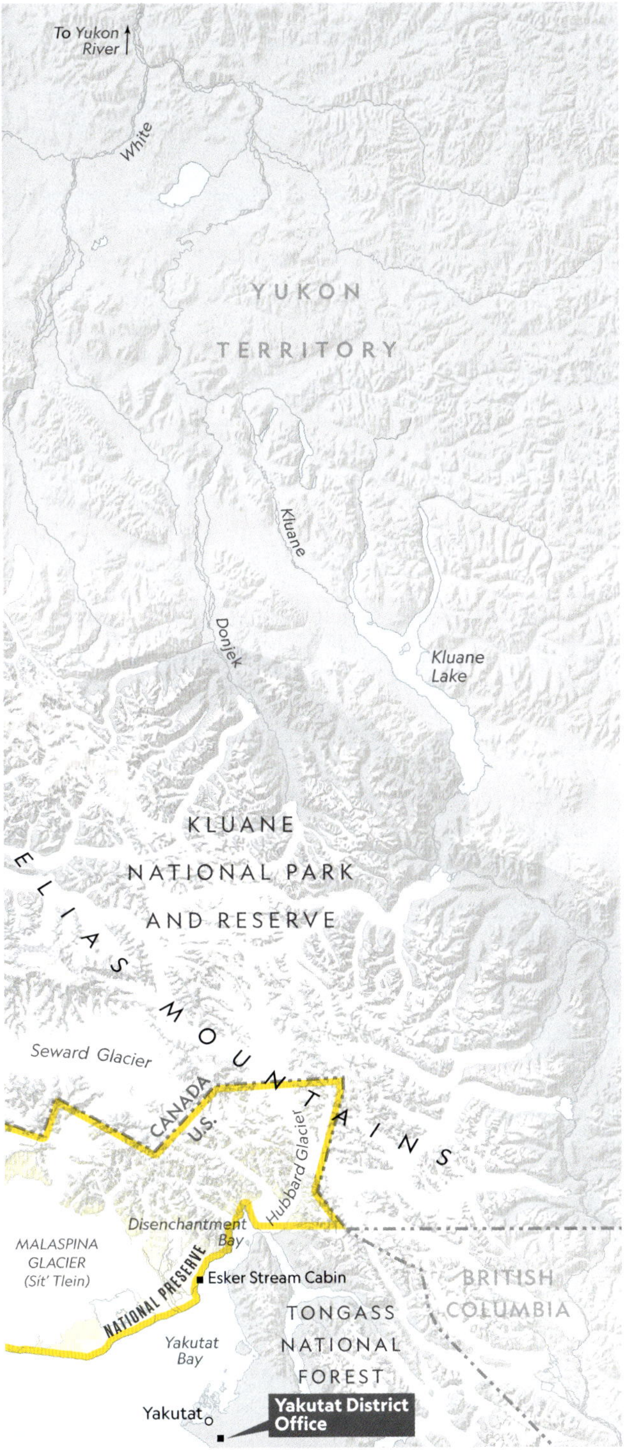

An old cabin in the park

→ SLEEP

Find everything from remote backcountry camping sites to luxurious waterside lodges.

→ Pitch a tent or park your RV in one of the first-come-first-serve sites along **Nabesna Road** or at the primitive 10-spot **Kendesnii Campground**, with picnic tables, fire rings, and vault toilets.

→ **Backcountry camp** without a permit wherever it's safe for you and the land. Even if you don't need a permit, it's still a good idea to share your itinerary with the rangers at a visitors center.

→ Book one of the few backcountry cabins that offer reservations. **Nugget Creek Cabin** is at the end of a trail by the same name, off McCarthy Road. **Viking Lodge Cabin** is a quarter-mile walk from the Rock Lake Turnout off Nabesna Road, while **Caribou Creek Cabin** is at the end of its three-mile trail off the same road. **Esker Stream Cabin** near Yakutat is accessible only by plane and a quarter-mile hike across a stream. Most of the cabins have bunks, woodstoves, and pit toilets; only Esker has an oil stove.

→ The rest of the backcountry cabins in the park are first come, first served and require a plane for access. Check out the forested **Chelle Lake Cabin** or the rustic and isolated **Glacier Creek Cabin** near the Chitistone River.

→ Get to **Devils Mountain Lodge** in Nabesna by road, or fly to **Ultima Thule Lodge** on the Chitina River. Stay at **Kennicott Glacier Lodge** for unique access to the glacier or **Ma Johnson's Historical Hotel** in McCarthy for the chance to truly step back in time.

HIKE ←

Must-Do Hike

W While there are millions of acres of unmaintained land in the park available to explore, there are also plenty of marked and maintained trails. No matter which path you choose, keep your wits about you. Watch out for all-terrain vehicles, wildlife, and mine tailings of the past. If you plan to go off-trail, travel along the ridgelines, since lower trails will likely require river crossings.

Follow some of these maintained hikes:

→ Head off on one of the short trails near the Wrangell-St. Elias Visitor Center. Both the **Boreal Forest** and the **Copper River Bluff Trails** are half-mile loops, with the first being much easier than the second.

→ Leave downtown McCarthy and hike the 10-mile round-trip **McCarthy Creek Trail** for some solitude and peace. Move through the creek bed and end at the river. If you're brave and the conditions are right, cross and go through a mining-era tunnel before turning back.

→ Experience an extinct, eroded volcanic system and resilient alpine plants on the challenging **Skookum Volcano Trail**. Find the trailhead just past mile 36 on Nabesna Road. Trek 2.5 miles to a high pass, then continue over the pass and loop back to the road through a steep, rocky streambed.

→ Walk—or bike—from the McCarthy Museum to the Kennecott mill and mining town on the **Wagon Road**. The easy route passes the historic Kennecott cemetery, runs nine miles round-trip, and provides access to the toe of the Kennicott Glacier.

→ Leave Kennecott and take the **Root Glacier Trail** on a four-mile round-trip walk to the glacier, with views of Mount Blackburn and mining artifacts along the way. Be mindful of bears and swift water.

→ Take the 10-mile round-trip hike along the **Jumbo Mine Trail** from Kennecott. The trail splits off the Root Glacier Trail after about a half mile. It offers striking mountain views as a payoff for the steep, rocky hike to the old mining site.

→ It's possible to trek to the **Stairway Icefall** on your own, but it's best to book a guided trip. Follow the Root Glacier Trail, continue past the rockslide to a campsite, and then eventually head north off-trail toward the 7,000-foot vertical ice wall.

Descending the Skookum Volcano Trail

Wrangell-St. Elias is huge, and it's nearly all wild. To protect its dynamic environment, only two unpaved roads enter the park. **McCarthy Road** begins at the town of Chitina and takes you to McCarthy, an old mining town that now offers visitor amenities, including restaurants, lodging, tour guides, and shops. Along the way, stop to see the Kotsina and Chitina Rivers, the Kuskulana Bridge and canyon, and salmon-filled Long Lake.

Nabesna Road begins on the Tok Cutoff on Glenn Highway—about mile 60. Start at the Slana Ranger Station and continue past views of the Wrangell Mountains and the Dead Dog Hill Rest Area, a great spot to look for moose, caribou, and birds.

Edgerton Highway (Route 10) offers breathtaking views on the way to McCarthy Road.

DRIVE

A rock ptarmigan, a hardy species of grouse

W Wildlife is relatively undisturbed in the park, so animals venture nearly every place you will. However, it's still important to be cautious and make good choices, including where you eat and store your food. Here are a few spots for good sightings:

→ Bring your camera on the six-mile round-trip Caribou Creek Trail, where you'll find **wolves**, **bears**, and **moose** among the many wildflowers, including gorgeous bluebells and prickly rose.

→ With or without binoculars, you'll see plenty of birds in the park. **Willow and rock ptarmigans**, **spruce grouse**, **hawk owls**, **woodpeckers**, **gray jays**, **ravens**, and **magpies** all call the region home. In the winter, only 34 tough species stay in the park, including **chickadees**, **redpolls**, and **pine grosbeaks**.

→ Stop at around mile 34 on McCarthy Road to check out the **Dall sheep** along the Crystalline Hills. Look carefully, as they might blend with the snow.

SPOT

A fireweed flower in bloom

The *St. Theodosius* tour boat near Hubbard Glacier in Disenchantment Bay

A kayaker crosses Icy Bay with Mount St. Elias in the distance.

FLOAT

O One of the best ways to experience this tremendous park is by water, though the routes aren't all simple to explore. Book a guide to show you the way, or stick to one of the calmer regions.

➔ Paddle **Icy Bay** to explore bright blue waters surrounded by glacial peaks. Most kayakers use collapsible vessels, since you can access the bay only by plane. You can easily find an outfitter in Yakutat for the trip.

➔ The 290-mile long **Copper River** begins at the glacier and empties into the Gulf of Alaska. You can raft this wild ride and explore the many deltas it supports, but it's a difficult route. Book a guided trip unless you've already led your own white-water Alaskan raft trip.

➔ Fish for arctic grayling, Dolly Varden trout, whitefish, salmon, and northern pike in one of the two major watersheds in the park: the **Copper and Yukon Rivers**. Don't forget your fishing license.

Experts Only

The expansive view from McCarthy Airport

Though maintained access is limited, offseason in the park brings its own wonders. Or add an off-the-beaten-path activity to your itinerary during peak season to truly shape your own adventure.

➔ *Turn off Nabesna Road at mile 4 and explore the* **Slana settlement**, *10,000 acres that were opened for homesteading. While 800 claims to the land were filed, most were abandoned because of the harsh Alaskan winters. About 50 hardy homesteaders remain.*

➔ *Get a guided tour of the historic mill in* **Kennecott** *in the summer. The mining town processed nearly $200 million worth of copper from 1911 to 1938 and once had a hospital, general store, school, skating rink, tennis court, recreation hall, and dairy.*

➔ *Visit the park in the winter for a totally different experience.* **Snowmobile**, **cross-country ski**, *or* **snowshoe** *anywhere there's enough snow to safely traverse, but keep an eye out for traplines. The trails around the Wrangell-St. Elias Visitor Center are a good place to start.*

➔ *See the park from the air on a* **flight-seeing excursion** *from one of the many regional outfitters. Book a plane to get a tour of the peaks, glaciers, and rivers, or ask to land on one of the airstrips in the park to kick off a backcountry adventure.*

E
X
P
L
O
R
E

*Climb the steel catwalk under the **Kuskulana Bridge**. The precarious route isn't for the faint of heart. If you're brave enough, however, you can stare down into the 238-foot gorge as you walk beneath the bridge and listen to the rolling water roar through the gorge under your feet.*

Mount Rainier National Park (page 566)

Everglades National Park (page 70)

Rocky Mountain National Park (page 422)

Katmai National Park & Preserve (page 652)

Zabriskie Point, Death Valley National Park (page 468)

Bridalveil Fall and Cathedral Rock, Yosemite National Park (page 530)

ACKNOWLEDGMENTS & ABOUT THE AUTHOR

ACKNOWLEDGMENTS

A At National Geographic, thank you to executive editor Allyson Johnson and editorial project manager Ashley Leath. To art director Sanáa Akkach and designer TJ Tucker, thank you for reimagining our guidebooks. Thank you to cartographers Debbie Gibbons, Mike McNey, and Greg Ugiansky. Thank you as well to senior production editor Michael O'Connor and copy editor M. P. Klier. And a big shout out to the photo editing team who spent hours working with photographers and vetting photos from our Image Collection: director of photography Adrian Coakley, senior photo editor Meredith Wilcox, and photo editor Katie Dance. To the photographers who hiked, snowmobiled, paddled, and climbed to get these images, thank you for making this book so inspiring.

ABOUT THE AUTHOR

L Lindsay Smith is a travel and culture writer whose work has appeared in *National Geographic* magazine, *Metro Parent*, and *Chicago Parent*. She was a contributing writer for National Geographic's *Great Outdoors U.S.A.* and works with nonprofits and businesses to craft their editorial content. Outside the world of words, she can't say no to a waterfall hike, lake jump, or doughnut break. Find her at *lindsaynicolesmith.com* or @lindsayn_smith.

Arches National Park (page 262)

CREDITS

Maps

General sources: Bureau of Land Management; National Park Service; National Elevation Dataset (NED), Earth Resources Observation and Science (EROS) Center; Natural Resources Canada; OpenStreetMap, openstreetmap.org/copyright; U.S. Forest Service; U.S. Geological Survey; U.S. Fish & Wildlife Service.

Photographs

Front cover and spine: Chris Burkard; back cover: Sofía Jaramillo; 2–3, Louise Johns; 5, Chris Burkard; 6–7, Sofía Jaramillo; 8–9, Tara Kerzhner; 12, NPS/Yellowstone Photo Collection; 13, NPS/Yellowstone Photo Collection/William H. Jackson; 14–5, Chris Burkard; 16–7, Chris Burkard/Verb Photo; 18–9, Sofía Jaramillo; 20–1, Tara Kerzhner; 22–3, Elliot Hawkey; 24–5, Raul Touzon/National Geographic Image Collection; 26–7, Michael Nichols/National Geographic Image Collection; 28–9, Elliot Hawkey Photography; 30–1, Mac Stone/National Geographic Image Collection; 33, Nick Palastro/Alamy Stock Photo; 34–5, Adam Woodworth/Cavan Images; 37 (UP), Tim Laman/National Geographic Image Collection; 37 (LO), Sunpix Travel/Alamy Stock Photo; 38, Darlyne Murawski/National Geographic Image Collection; 39, Robbie George/National Geographic Image Collection; 40, Michael Hanson/Cavan Images; 41, Warren Marr/Panoramic Images; 42, Brian G. Green/National Geographic Image Collection; 43 (UP LE), Jonathan Irish/National Geographic Image Collection; 43 (UP RT), Mauricio Handler/National Geographic Image Collection; 43 (LO LE), Darlyne Murawski/National Geographic Image Collection; 43 (LO RT), Robbie George/National Geographic Image Collection; 44–5, Jack Fusco; 46–7, Patryce Bak/Stone/Getty Images; 48–9, Constance Mier/Alamy Stock Photo; 50, Douglas R. Clifford, Times/ZUMA/Alamy Stock Photo; 51, Stefanie Payne; 52 (LE), Tom Uhlman/Alamy Stock Photo; 52 (RT), Michael Melford/National Geographic Image Collection; 53 (UP), Sandra Foyt/Alamy Stock Photo; 53 (LO), Destination Scenics/Alamy Stock Photo; 54–5, NPS/Alamy Stock Photo; 56–9, Mac Stone; 60, Cliford Mervil; 61, Mac Stone; 62–5, Lee Rentz/Alamy Stock Photo; 66, Sandra Foyt/Alamy Stock Photo; 67, Chris Ross/Cavan Images; 68 (LE), Katy Danca Galli/Alamy Stock Photo; 68 (RT), Sandra Foyt/Alamy Stock Photo; 69, Michael Runkel/imageBROKER/Alamy Stock Photo; 70–3, Mac Stone; 74, Jeffrey Isaac Greenberg/Alamy Stock Photo; 75–76 (UP), Mac Stone; 76 (LO), Andy Mann/National Geographic Image Collection; 77 (UP), Ian Dagnall/Alamy Stock Photo; 77 (LO), Mark Andrew Thomas/Alamy Stock Photo; 78–9, Mac Stone; 80–1, Bonnie Jo Mount/The Washington Post via Getty Images; 82–9, Cliford Mervil; 89, Michael Melford/National Geographic Image Collection; 90–1, Cliford Mervil; 92–3, Chris Murray/Cavan Images; 93, Pat & Chuck Blackley/Alamy Stock Photo; 94–5, Images By T.O.K./Alamy Stock Photo; 96–100, Jonathan Irish/National Geographic Image Collection; 101 (LE), Zachary Frank/Alamy Stock Photo; 101 (RT), Raymond Gehman; 102 (UP), Pat & Chuck Blackley/Alamy Stock Photo; 102 (LO), Joe Tabb/Alamy Stock Photo; 103, Tom Uhlman/Alamy Stock Photo; 104–5, Stephen Alvarez/National Geographic Image Collection; 106–9, Becky Hale/National Geographic; 110 (LE), Zach Zimet/iStock/Getty Images; 110 (RT), Cameron Lawson; 111, D Guest Smith/Alamy Stock Photo; 112–3, diversbelow/Alamy Stock Photo; 114–5, Cavan Images; 117, Jeff Mauritzen/National Geographic Image Collection; 118–9, Hannele Lahti; 119, Nick Palastro/Alamy Stock Photo; 120 (UP), John Cancalosi/National Geographic Image Collection; 120 (LO), Phil Schermeister/National Geographic Image Collection; 121, Jonathan Irish/National Geographic Image Collection; 122, Harrison Shull/Cavan Images; 122–3, Jeffrey Isaac Greenberg/Alamy Stock Photo; 124–5, Nick Palastro/Alamy Stock Photo; 126–7, Dennis Frates/Alamy Stock Photo; 129, cdwheatley/iStock/Getty Images; 130 (UP), Kerrick James/Alamy Stock Photo; 130 (LO), Bkamprath/iStock/Getty Images; 131, Stephen Frink; 132, George Oze/Alamy Stock Photo; 132–3, Tom Bol/Cavan Images; 134–5, Marc Muench/Alamy Stock Photo; 136–141, Sofía Jaramillo; 144 (LE), Aramark Destinations; 144 (RT), Giovanni Saini/Alamy Stock Photo; 145 (UP), Dennis Frates/Alamy Stock Photo; 145 (LO), Louise Heusinkveld/Alamy Stock Photo; 146–7 (UP), Sofía Jaramillo; 147 (LO), NPS Photo/Alamy Stock Photo; 148–9, Sofía Jaramillo; 150–1, Melissa Farlow/National Geographic Image Collection; 154 (LE), Peter Essick/Cavan Images; 154 (RT), Sara Guren; 155, Jonathan Irish; 156–7, Jeffrey Gibson; 158–9, Joel Sartore/National Geographic Image Collection; 161 (UP), Hyatt Regency St. Louis at The Arch; 161 (LO), Lori Epstein/Alamy Stock Photo; 162 (UP), AP Photo/Jeff Roberson; 162 (LO), Kit Leong/Shutterstock; 163 (BOTH), QT Luong/Terra Galleria; 164–5, Jonathan Irish; 166–7, Keith Ladzinski; 169, Stefanie Payne; 170, Michael Burke/Alamy Stock Photo; 171 (UP), Wildnerdpix/Shutterstock; 171 (LO), Jonathan Irish; 172 (ALL), Rafi Wilkinson; 173, NPS/Katrina George; 174–5, Daniel/Adobe Stock; 176–7, Jonathan Irish; 180 (UP), Alex Messenger/TandemStock; 180 (LO), Jonathan Irish; 181, NPS/Ruth Harker; 182 (LE), Phil Schermeister/National Geographic Image Collection; 182 (RT), Jim Brandenburg/Minden Pictures; 183 (UP), Natural History Collection/Alamy Stock Photo; 183 (LO LE), NPS/Brett Seymour, Submerged Resources Center; 183

CREDITS

(LO RT), QT Luong/Terra Galleria; 184–5, Aaron Peterson; 186–7, Sofía Jaramillo; 189, NPS/Jeff Van Hooser; 190–2, Sofía Jaramillo; 193 (UP), Sébastien Mamy/hemis.fr/Alamy Stock Photo; 193 (LO), Chuck Haney; 194–5, Sofía Jaramillo; 196–7, Kevin Palmer; 198–9, Richard Olsenius/National Geographic Image Collection; 202, David Guttenfelder; 203 (UP), Phil Schermeister/National Geographic Image Collection; 203 (LO), Richard Olsenius/National Geographic Image Collection; 204 (UP), Jonathan Irish; 204 (LO), NPS Photo; 205, The Pattiz Bros—More Than Just Parks; 206–7, Brandon Kline Wilderness & Nature Photographs; 208–9, Sofía Jaramillo; 211, Ryan Goebel; 212–3, Sofía Jaramillo; 214–5, Virginia W. Mason; 216–7, Phil Schermeister; 219, Stephen L. Alvarez/National Geographic Image Collection; 220–1, Bryan Schutmaat/National Geographic Image Collection; 224, Dawn Kish/National Geographic Image Collection; 225 (LE), Grant Ordelheide/TandemStock; 225 (RT), Andrew Coleman/National Geographic Image Collection; 226, Bryan Schutmaat/National Geographic Image Collection; 227, Phil Schermeister/National Geographic Image Collection; 228–9, Witold Skrypczak/Alamy Stock Photo; 230–1, Phil Schermeister/National Geographic Image Collection; 233, courtesy Fiddler's Inn; 234–5, Lee Rentz/Alamy Stock Photo; 236–7, Phil Schermeister; 239, Christian/Adobe Stock; 240, QT Luong/Terra Galleria; 241 (LE), Rich Leighton; 241 (RT), Phil Schermeister; 242–3, Inge Johnsson/Alamy Stock Photo; 244–5, Jonathan Irish; 247 (LE), EWY Media/Shutterstock; 247 (RT), Jonathan Irish; 249, NPS/Calvin Smith; 250–1, Mike Theiss/National Geographic Image Collection; 253, Aidong Ning/iStock/Getty Images; 254, Laura San Fillipo/Cavan Images; 255 (UP), Adam Woolfitt/robertharding; 255 (LO), Mike Theiss/National Geographic Image Collection; 256–7,

LOOK-foto/Image Professionals GmbH/Alamy Stock Photo; 258–9, Tara Kerzhner; 261, Phil Schermeister/National Geographic Image Collection; 262–8, Tara Kerzhner; 269 (UP), Raul Touzon/National Geographic Image Collection; 269 (LO), John P Kelly/Stone/Getty Images; 270–1, Tara Kerzhner; 272–3, Morey Milbradt/Alamy Stock Photo; 274–5, Phil Schermeister/National Geographic Image Collection; 278, Jeff Diener/Cavan Images; 279, Jonathan Irish; 280–1, Efrain Padro/Alamy Stock Photo; 282–3, Jonathan Irish; 286, John Elk III/The Image Bank/Getty Images; 287, Jonathan Irish; 288 (UP), Raymond Gehman/National Geographic Image Collection; 288 (LO), Daniela Duncan/Moment/Getty Images; 289, @TimLaman; 290–1, Colin D. Young/Alamy Stock Photo; 292–3, Tara Kerzhner; 295, Lynn Wegener/robertharding; 296–7, Tara Kerzhner; 298 (UP), Thomas Kitchin & Victoria Hurst/Design Pics/Alamy Stock Photo; 298 (LO), Jon G. Fuller/VWPics/Alamy Stock Photo; 299 (BOTH), Tara Kerzhner; 300–1, Babak Tafreshi/National Geographic Image Collection; 302–3, Tara Kerzhner; 304–5, Tim Fitzharris/Minden Pictures; 307, James Kay/SCPhotos/Alamy Stock Photo; 308, Whit Richardson/Cavan Images; 309 (UP), Ed Reschke/Stone/Getty Images; 309 (LO), Gerald Corsi/iStock/Getty Images; 310 (UP), Michael DeFreitas/robertharding; 310 (LO), Joey Hayes/Travel RM/Design Pics/Alamy Stock Photo; 311, Greg Winston/National Geographic Image Collection; 312–3, John Elk III/The Image Bank/Getty Images; 314–5, Derek von Briesen/National Geographic Image Collection; 319–320, Pete McBride/National Geographic Image Collection; 322, Deep Desert Photography & Digital Art/Cavan Images; 323 (UP), Dugald Bremner; 323 (LO), Michael Nolan/robertharding; 324 (BOTH), Aaron Huey/National Geographic Image Collection;

325, Pete McBride/National Geographic Image Collection; 326–7, Michael Nichols/National Geographic Image Collection; 328–332, Mylo Fowler; 333 (UP), StevenSchremp/iStock/Getty Images; 333 (LO), Mylo Fowler; 334 (UP), Jim West/Alamy Stock Photo; 334 (LO) and 335 (UP), Mylo Fowler; 335 (LO), Blake Gordon/Cavan Images; 336–7, Mylo Fowler; 338–9, Ira Block/National Geographic Image Collection; 341 (UP), Markus Haberkern/Alamy Stock Photo; 341 (LO), Matt Claiborne/Alamy Stock Photo; 342, Mark Andrews/Alamy Stock Photo; 343, Michael Szönyi/imageBROKER/Alamy Stock Photo; 344 (UP), Terry Sohl/Alamy Stock Photo; 344 (LO), John Sirlin/Alamy Stock Photo; 345 (UP), Phil Schermeister/National Geographic Image Collection; 345 (CTR), Jeremy Wade Shockley/Cavan Images; 345 (LO), Phil Schermeister/National Geographic Image Collection; 346–7, kellyvandellen/iStock/Getty Images; 348–9, Jonathan Irish/National Geographic Image Collection; 351, Mark Goodreau/Alamy Stock Photo; 352, Daniel Borzynski/Alamy Stock Photo; 353 (LE), Chuck Place/Alamy Stock Photo; 353 (RT), DeepDesertPhoto/RooM the Agency/Alamy Stock Photo; 354–5, DeepDesertPhoto/RooM the Agency/Alamy Stock Photo; 356–7, Larry Geddis/Alamy Stock Photo; 359 (UP), Ron Niebrugge/Alamy Stock Photo; 359 (LO), Stefanie Payne; 360, Raquel Mogado/Alamy Stock Photo; 361, Manuela Durson/Alamy Stock Photo; 362, Nick Fox/Alamy Stock Photo; 363 (ALL), Kike Calvo/National Geographic Image Collection; 364–5, Marc Dozier/hemis/Alamy Stock Photo; 366–7, Eric Foltz/E+/Getty Images; 368–373, Keith Ladzinski; 374–5, Alex Treadway/National Geographic Image Collection; 376–7, Barrett Hedges/National Geographic Image Collection; 378, Leon Werdinger/Alamy Stock Photo; 378–381, Keith Ladzinski; 382–3, Keith Ladzinski/National Geographic Image Collection;

CREDITS ←

385, Louise Johns; 386–7, Keith Ladzinski/ National Geographic Image Collection; 389–393, Louise Johns; 394 (UP), NPS/Jacob W. Frank; 394 (LO) and 395 (UP), Louise Johns; 395 (LO), NPS/Tim Rains; 396–7, © Tom Dempsey/PhotoSeek; 398–9, Keith Ladzinski/ National Geographic Image Collection; 402–3, Jimmy Chin/National Geographic Image Collection; 404, Aaron Huey/National Geographic Image Collection; 405, NPS/D. Lehle; 406 (ALL), Charlie Hamilton James/National Geographic Image Collection; 407 (LE), QT Luong/Terra Galleria; 407 (RT), Greg Winston/National Geographic Image Collection; 408–9, Bill Hatcher/National Geographic Image Collection; 410–1, NPS/Mattson; 412–3, Chris Burkard/Verb Photo; 415, NPS/Kris Illenberger; 416, Taylor Kennedy; 417 (UP), NPS/ Patrick Myers; 417 (LO), NPS/Kris Illenberger; 418, NPS/Patrick Myers; 418–9, Chris Burkard/ Verb Photo; 420–1, NPS/Patrick Myers; 422–3, Cagan Sekercioglu/National Geographic Image Collection; 424 (UP), Keith Ladzinski/ National Geographic Image Collection; 424 (LO), Rich Reid/National Geographic Image Collection; 426, Phil Schermeister; 427, Paul Damien/National Geographic Image Collection; 428–9, Richard Seeley/National Geographic Image Collection; 429, Cagan Sekercioglu/National Geographic Image Collection; 430 (UP), Phil Schermeister/National Geographic Image Collection; 430 (LO), Paul Damien/National Geographic Image Collection; 431, Richard Olsenius/National Geographic Image Collection; 432–3, ImagesofRMNP; 434–5, Drew Rush/National Geographic Image Collection; 437–9, NPS/ Neal Herbert; 440 (UP), Michael Nichols/ National Geographic Image Collection; 440 (CTR), Barrett Hedges/National Geographic Image Collection; 440 (LO), Ronan Donovan/ National Geographic Image Collection; 441

(LE), NPS/Neal Herbert; 441 (RT), NPS/ Diane Renkin; 442–3, Tom Murphy/National Geographic Image Collection; 444 (UP LE), Michael Melford/National Geographic Image Collection; 444 (UP RT), Erika Larsen/National Geographic Image Collection; 444 (LO), Babak Tafreshi/National Geographic Image Collection; 445, NPS/Al Nash; 446–7, Babak Tafreshi/ National Geographic Image Collection; 448–9, Andrew Coleman/National Geographic Image Collection; 451, Emily Bei Cheng; 452–3, Peter Laurence; 455 (LE), Irina/Adobe Stock; 455 (RT), Patrick/Adobe Stock; 456 (BOTH), NPS Photo; 457 (LE), Seaphotoart/Alamy Stock Photo; 457 (RT), courtesy American Samoa Historic Preservation Office; 458–9, Philip Game/Alamy Stock Photo; 460–1, NPS/Yash Trikannad; 463, Josiah Roe/Visit Ventura; 465 (UP), Mauricio Handler/National Geographic Image Collection; 465 (LO), Macduff Everton/ National Geographic Image Collection; 466–7, Russ Bishop/Alamy Stock Photo; 468–9, Neale Clarke/robertharding; 470, Earth Pixel LLC/ Alamy Stock Photo; 472–4, Chris Burkard; 475, Melvin Sandelin/Shutterstock; 476–7, Tim Fitzharris/Minden Pictures; 478–9, Robert Bush/Alamy Stock Photo; 481, courtesy Hāna-Maui Resort; 482–3, Andrew Coleman/ National Geographic Image Collection; 484, Christian Kober/Alamy Stock Photo; 484–6 (UP), Babak Tafreshi/National Geographic Image Collection; 486 (LO), David Fleetham/ Alamy Stock Photo; 487, Susan Seubert/ National Geographic Image Collection; 488–9, Ben Horton/National Geographic Image Collection; 490–1, Patrick Kelley/National Geographic Image Collection; 494 (UP LE), Christian Kober/Alamy Stock Photo; 494 (UP RT), Shaun Astor; 494 (LO), Franco Salmoiraghi/Photo Resource Hawaii/Alamy Stock Photo; 495, Niels van Kampenhout/Alamy Stock Photo; 496 (UP), Maridav/Adobe Stock;

496 (LO), Todd Gipstein/National Geographic Image Collection; 497 (UP), Fotofeeling/Westend61/Alamy Stock Photo; 497 (CTR), Karen Kasmauski/National Geographic Image Collection; 497 (LO), Douglas Peebles/Alamy Stock Photo; 498, Franco Salmoiraghi/Photo Resource Hawaii/Alamy Stock Photo; 498–9, Macduff Everton/National Geographic Image Collection; 499, Donna O'Meara/National Geographic Image Collection; 500–1, fnendzig/ Adobe Stock; 502–3, Keith Ladzinski/National Geographic Image Collection; 506–8, Keith Ladzinski; 509 (UP), Melody Coarsey/Cavan Images; 509 (LO), Ben Horton/National Geographic Image Collection; 510–1, Natural History Library/Alamy Stock Photo; 512–3, Matt Propert; 515 (LE), Erin Feinblatt; 515 (RT), Bar SZ Ranch and Creatiful; 516, NPS/Kurt Moses; 517 (UP), Michael Macor/The San Francisco Chronicle via AP; 517 (LO), Ryan Tuttle/Cavan Images; 518–9, Sundry Photography/Shutterstock; 520–1, Keith Ladzinski; 523, Delaware North; 525 (UP LE), Joe Eldridge/Alamy Stock Photo; 525 (UP RT), Stacy Gold/National Geographic Image Collection; 525 (LO), Chris Burkard; 526, Rich Reid/TandemStock; 527 (UP and CTR), Chris Burkard; 527 (LO), Keith Ladzinski/National Geographic Image Collection; 528–9, Chris Burkard; 530–1, Joshua Cripps Photography, The Mt Whitney Gallery, Lone Pine, California; 534–5, Tomas Tichy/ Shutterstock; 536 (UP), Keith Ladzinski; 536 (CTR), Michael F. Miller/Shutterstock; 536 (LO), Richard T. Nowitz; 537, Andreas Müller/ Alamy Stock Photo; 538–9, Chris Burkard/Verb Photo; 540–1, Keith Ladzinski; 542–3, Ray Wise/Moment/Getty Images; 544–5, Bill Hatcher/National Geographic Image Collection; 547, D Currin/Shutterstock; 548–9, Elliot Hawkey Photography; 551, Claudio Beduschi/ Reda&Co/Alamy Stock Photo; 552 (UP), Bryan Jolley/TandemStock; 552 (LO), Kelly

CREDITS ←

INDEX ⬅

INDEX

INDEX

INDEX ⬅

INDEX

INDEX

INDEX ←

INDEX

INDEX ⬅

INDEX

INDEX ←

INDEX

INDEX

INDEX

INDEX ⬅

INDEX ←

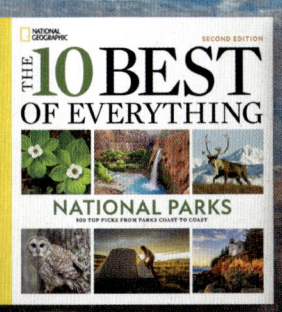
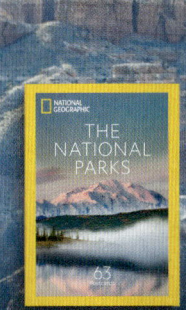
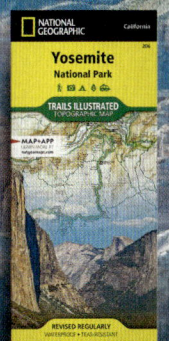
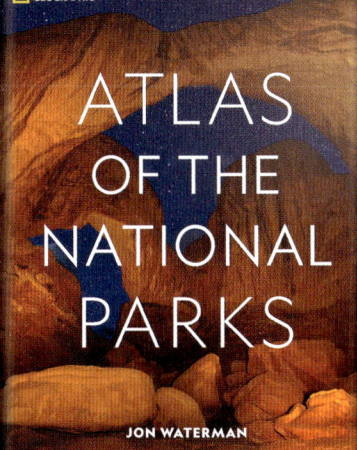
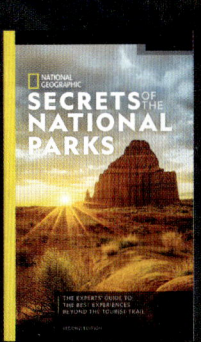
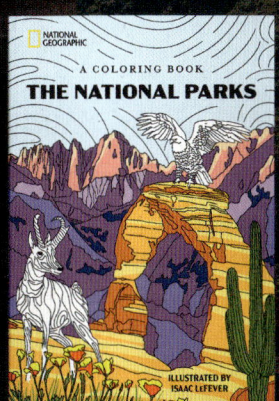
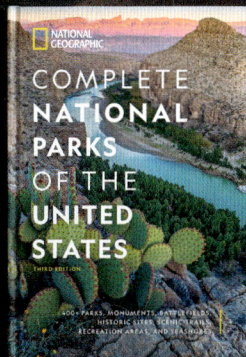

Since 1888, the National Geographic Society has funded more than 15,000 research, conservation, education, technology, and storytelling projects around the world. National Geographic Partners distributes a portion of the funds it receives from your purchase to National Geographic Society to support their mission to illuminate and protect the wonder of our world.

National Geographic Partners, LLC
1145 17th Street NW
Washington, DC 20036-4688 USA

Get closer to National Geographic Explorers and photographers, and connect with our global community. Join us today at nationalgeographic.org/joinus

For rights or permissions inquiries, please contact National Geographic Books Subsidiary Rights: bookrights@natgeo.com

ISBN: 978-1-4262-2338-9

The authorized representative in the EU for product safety and compliance is Disney Trading B.V., Asterweg 15S, 1031 HL, Amsterdam, The Netherlands email: DCP.DL-EU.bookscontact@disney.com

Printed in China

26/LPC/1

The information in this book has been carefully checked and to the best of our knowledge is accurate. However, details are subject to change, and the publisher cannot be responsible for such changes, or for errors or omissions. Assessments of sites, hotels, and restaurants are based on the author's subjective opinions, which do not necessarily reflect the publisher's opinion.